3276
KANAB

"Amazingly easy to use. Very portable, very complete."

—*Booklist*

♦

"Complete, concise, and filled with useful information."

—*New York Daily News*

♦

"Hotel information is close to encyclopedic."

—*Des Moines Sunday Register*

♦

"The only mainstream guide to list specific prices. The Walter Cronkite of guidebooks—with all that implies."

—*Travel & Leisure*

Frommer's®

2nd
Edition

Utah

by Don & Barbara Laine

Macmillan • USA

ABOUT THE AUTHORS

Residents of northern New Mexico, **Don and Barbara Laine** have written about and traveled extensively throughout the Rocky Mountains and the Southwest for more than 25 years. In addition to *Frommer's Utah,* they author *Frommer's Colorado; Frommer's Denver, Boulder & Colorado Springs; Frommer's Portable Zion & Bryce Canyon National Parks;* and have contributed to *Frommer's USA* and *Frommer's National Parks of the American West.* They have also written *New Mexico & Arizona State Parks* (The Mountaineers Books).

MACMILLAN TRAVEL

A Simon & Schuster Macmillan Company
1633 Broadway
New York, NY 10019

Find us online at **www.frommers.com**

ISBN 0-02-862047-X
ISSN 1087-3546

Editor: Leslie Shen
Production Editor: Mark Enochs
Design by Michele Laseau
Digital Cartography by Peter Bogaty and Ken Rizzo

SPECIAL SALES

Bulk purchases (10+ copies) of Frommer's and selected Macmillan travel guides are available to corporations, organizations, mail-order catalogs, institutions, and charities at special discounts, and can be customized to suit individual needs. For more information write to Special Sales, Macmillan General Reference, 1633 Broadway, New York, NY 10019.

Manufactured in the United States of America

Contents

1 The Best of Utah 1

1 The Best Travel Experiences 1

2 The Best Views 2

3 The Best Family Vacations 2

4 The Best Scenic Drives 3

5 The Best Hiking Trails 3

6 The Best Places to Go Mountain Biking 4

7 The Best Destinations for Fishing & Water Sports 4

8 The Best Wildlife Watching 5

9 The Best Downhill Skiing 6

10 The Best Cross-Country Skiing 6

11 The Best Four-Wheeling 7

12 The Best Places to Experience Native American Culture 7

13 The Best Mormon History Sites 8

14 The Best Luxury Hotels & Inns 8

15 The Best Bed-&-Breakfasts 9

16 The Best Lodges 9

17 The Best Places to Eat 10

18 The Best of the Performing Arts 10

2 Land of Natural Wonders & Pioneers: Introducing Utah 11

1 The Regions in Brief 11

★ *Did You Know?* 12

2 Utah Today 16

3 History 101 17

★ *Dateline* 17

4 A Brief Look at Modern Mormonism— or Yes, You Can Get a Cup of Coffee in Utah 21

5 Recommended Books, Films & Recordings 23

3 Planning a Trip to Utah 24

1 Visitor Information & Money 24

2 When to Go 25

★ *Utah Calendar of Events* 26

3 Health & Insurance   29

4 Tips for Travelers with Special Needs   30

5 Getting There   31

6 Getting Around   32

★ *Fast Facts: Utah*   35

4   For Foreign Visitors   37

1 Preparing for Your Trip   37

2 Getting to the U.S.   39

3 Getting Around the U.S.   40

★ *Fast Facts: For the Foreign Traveler*   41

5   The Active Vacation Planner   45

1 Preparing for Your Active Vacation   45

2 Visiting Utah's National Parks   47

3 Outdoor Activities A to Z   48

★ *Life on the Open Road: Planning an RV or Tenting Vacation to Utah*   50

6   Introducing the Salt Lake Valley & the Wasatch Front   54

★ *Planning for the Year 2002: The Winter Olympic Games Come to Utah*   56

1 How We've Covered This Area   57

2 Getting Outside Along the Wasatch Front   57

7   Salt Lake City   59

1 Orientation   59

★ *Neighborhoods in Brief*   61

2 Getting Around   61

★ *Fast Facts: Salt Lake City*   62

3 Accommodations   63

★ *Family-Friendly Hotels*   68

4 Dining   70

★ *Family-Friendly Restaurants*   75

5 Exploring Temple Square   75

6 More to See & Do   76

7 Organized Tours   85

8 Outdoor Activities & Spectator Sports   85

9 Shopping   87

10 Salt Lake City After Dark   88

11 Rolling the Dice on the Nevada State Line:
    An Easy Side Trip to Wendover   90

**8   The Northern Wasatch Front:
     The Great Salt Lake & Utah's Old West   91**

1 The Great Salt Lake & Antelope Island State Park   91

2 Ogden: Utah's West at Its Wildest   94

★ *Walking Tour—Historic Downtown Ogden*   98

3 Where East Met West: Golden Spike National
   Historic Site   108

4 Skiing Ogden Valley & the Northern Wasatch
   Front   109

5 Logan   113

★ *Nineteenth-Century Logan Comes to Life—
   Walking Tour of Historic Main Street*   116

**9   The Southern Wasatch Front:
     World-Class Skiing & More   123**

1 The Cottonwood Canyon Resorts: Brighton, Solitude,
   Alta & Snowbird   123

2 Park City, Utah's Premier Resort Town   130

3 Side Trips from Park City: Heber City, Strawberry
   Reservoir & Some Great State Parks   146

4 Sundance Resort & Institute   154

★ *So You Wanna Be in Pictures . . .*   156

5 Provo & Environs   158

★ *Walking Tour—Historic Downtown Provo*   160

6 Timpanogos Cave National Monument   169

**10   Dinosaurs & Natural Wonders in
      Utah's Northeast Corner   171**

1 The Mirror Lake Highway & the Uinta Mountains   171

2 Vernal: Gateway to the Region's Top Recreational
   Areas   172

3 Dinosaur National Monument   177

4 Flaming Gorge National Recreation Area   180

**11   Utah's Dixie & the Colorful Southwest
      Corner   187**

1 Getting Outside in Utah's Color Country   188

2 St. George, Gateway to Southern Utah's
   Natural Wonders   190

3 Enjoying the Outdoors Around Cedar City:
Cedar Breaks National Monument &
the Southern Ski Resorts   203

★ *Renaissance Pleasures on the Colorado Plateau:
The Utah Shakespearean Festival*   205

4 Kanab: Movies, Sand Dunes & Gateway to
the Grand Canyon   211

12   Zion National Park   221

★ *How Nature Painted Zion's Landscape*   224

1 Just the Facts   224

2 Seeing the Highlights   227

3 Exploring Zion by Car   228

4 Sports & Activities   229

5 Camping   231

6 Accommodations   232

7 Dining   234

8 Virtual Nature at Two Nearby Theaters   235

13   Bryce Canyon National Park   237

1 Just the Facts   238

2 Seeing the Highlights   241

3 Exploring Bryce Canyon by Car   241

4 Sports & Activities   242

5 Camping   245

6 Accommodations   246

7 Dining   248

8 Activities & More Beautiful Scenery Just Outside
Bryce Canyon   249

9 A Nearby State Park: Kodachrome Basin State Park   250

10 From Bryce Canyon to Capitol Reef:
Grand Staircase-Escalante National Monument &
the Highway 12 Scenic Drive   251

★ *A National Monument Is Born in Controversy*   256

★ *Rock or Wood—What Is This Stuff?*   259

14   Capitol Reef National Park   261

1 Just the Facts   262

2 Exploring the Highlights by Car   264

★ *Butch Cassidy, Utah's Most Infamous Son*   265

3 From Petroglyphs to a Pioneer Schoolhouse:
   Capitol Reef's Historic Sites   265

4 Sports & Activities   266

5 Camping   268

6 Accommodations   270

7 Dining   272

15 Lake Powell & Glen Canyon National Recreation Area   273

1 Just the Facts   273

2 Exploring Lake Powell by Boat   276

3 Seeing the Sights   277

★ *Lake Powell: Natural Wonder or Man-Made Curse?*   279

4 Sports & Activities   279

5 Camping   281

6 Accommodations & Dining   281

7 In Memory of John Wesley Powell:
   A Nearby Museum   282

16 From Moab to Arches & Canyonlands National Parks   283

1 Moab: Gateway to the National Parks   283

2 Arches National Park   299

3 Canyonlands National Park   305

★ *Canyonlands' Creatures Great & Small*   310

4 North & West of the Parks   314

17 The Four Corners Area   318

1 A Base Camp in Bluff   318

2 Monument Valley Navajo Tribal Park   320

3 Natural Bridges National Monument   323

4 Edge of the Cedars State Historical Monument   326

5 Hovenweep National Monument   326

★ *Kokopelli: Casanova or Traveling Salesman?*   327

6 Four Corners Monument   328

7 Farther Afield in Colorado: Mesa Verde National
   Park   328

Index   331

List of Maps

Utah 14

Utah Driving Distances & Times 33

The Wasatch Front 55

Salt Lake City Accommodations 67

Salt Lake City Dining 73

Downtown Salt Lake City Attractions 77

Greater Salt Lake Valley Attractions 80

The Park City Area 133

Walking Tour—Historic Downtown Provo 161

The Northeast Corner 173

The Southwest Corner 189

St. George & Environs 191

Zion National Park 222

Bryce Canyon National Park 239

Grand Staircase-Escalante National Monument 255

Capitol Reef National Park 263

Glen Canyon National Recreation Area 275

Southeast Utah 285

Arches National Park 301

Canyonlands National Park 307

AN INVITATION TO THE READER

In researching this book, we discovered many wonderful places—hotels, restaurants, shops, and more. We're sure you'll find others. Please tell us about them, so we can share the information with your fellow travelers in upcoming editions. If you were disappointed with a recommendation, we'd love to know that, too. Please write to:

Frommer's Utah, 2nd Edition
Macmillan Travel
1633 Broadway
New York, NY 10019

AN ADDITIONAL NOTE

Please be advised that travel information is subject to change at any time—and this is especially true of prices. We therefore suggest that you write or call ahead for confirmation when making your travel plans. The authors, editors, and publisher cannot be held responsible for the experiences of readers while traveling. Your safety is important to us, however, so we encourage you to stay alert and be aware of your surroundings. Keep a close eye on cameras, purses, and wallets, all favorite targets of thieves and pickpockets.

WHAT THE SYMBOLS MEAN

✪ Frommer's Favorites

Hotels, restaurants, attractions, and entertainment you should not miss.

The following abbreviations are used for credit cards:

AE	American Express	EURO	Eurocard
CB	Carte Blanche	JCB	Japan Credit Bank
DC	Diners Club	MC	MasterCard
DISC	Discover	V	Visa
ER	enRoute		

FIND FROMMER'S ONLINE

Arthur Frommer's Outspoken Encyclopedia of Travel (www.frommers.com) offers more than 6,000 pages of up-to-the-minute travel information—including the latest bargains and candid, personal articles updated daily by Arthur Frommer himself. No other website offers such comprehensive and timely coverage of the world of travel.

The Best of Utah

1

From its desolate red rock canyons to its soaring pine-covered peaks, Utah is spectacular. There aren't many places in the world where the forces of nature have come together with such dramatic results, creating a magnificent outdoor playground. It's also a land of cultural discovery; all the peoples who have settled here, from the ancient Anasazi to Brigham Young's Mormons, have left their distinctive mark, contributing to a wild, colorful history.

With so much to see and do, how to choose? It can be bewildering to plan your trip with so many options vying for your attention. We've made this task easier for you by scouring the entire state from top to bottom and choosing the very best that Utah has to offer—the places and experiences you won't want to miss.

1 The Best Travel Experiences

Of all the wonderful vacations you can have in Utah, several stand out for their uniqueness, tremendous natural beauty, and just plain fun.

- **Boating at Flaming Gorge National Recreation Area:** Flaming Gorge is a man-made creation, the result of the damming of the Green River for flood control, water storage, and electricity generation. But all that's not really important; what truly matters (in our view, at least) is the by-product of the project—a huge, gorgeous, many-fingered lake. This little-known gem is a boater's paradise—floating out here, you'll feel like you're all alone in the world. It also happens to offer some of the best fishing in the West. See chapter 10.
- **Exploring Bryce Canyon National Park:** One of Utah's—maybe the nation's—most scenic parks, Bryce Canyon is also one of the most accessible. Several trails lead down into the canyon—really walks rather than hikes—so just about everyone can get to know this beautiful jewel up close and in person; part of the Rim Trail is even wheelchair accessible. The colorful rock formations are impressive when viewed en masse from the rim, but they become enchanting and fanciful works of art as you walk among them along the trails. See chapter 13.
- **Enjoying Capitol Reef National Park:** This tranquil park isn't as popular as Bryce or Zion, but it has a subtle beauty all its own. And it's not too demanding, either: Wander around the orchards

of Fruita, hike to Cassidy Arch, stroll up the Grand Wash, or just sit under the stars roasting marshmallows over your campfire. See chapter 14.

- **Houseboating on Lake Powell:** Kick back and relax while floating on the deep blue waters of Lake Powell, with towering red rocks all around and an azure sky above. This is the life—no telephone to answer, no meetings to attend, no deadlines to meet. Feeling warm? Slip over the side for a dip in the cool water. Want a little exercise? Anchor yourself at one of the canyons and hike a bit. See chapter 15.

2 The Best Views

- **Boulder Mountain Viewpoints** (between Escalante and Torrey): The panoramas from the roadside along the crest of Boulder Mountain are extraordinary. You can see majestic Capitol Reef, miles to the east, and any number of valleys and lakes nestled in between. It's like a tiny fairyland; we almost expected to see a little steam train chugging along or a horse-drawn carriage passing through. See chapter 13.
- **The Narrows, Zion National Park:** The sheer 1,000-foot-high walls are awe-inspiring, almost frightening, as they enclose you in a 20-foot-wide world of hanging gardens, waterfalls, and sculpted sandstone arches, with the Virgin River running beneath your feet. The Narrows are so narrow that you can't walk beside the river, but have to wade right through it—but the views are worth getting your feet wet. See chapter 12.
- **The Queen's Garden, Bryce Canyon National Park:** Presided over by majestic Queen Victoria herself, carved in stone by Mother Nature, these thousands of colorfully striped spires present a magnificent display when viewed from the rim. From the trail below, they dazzle as the early morning sun throws them into stark relief. See chapter 13.
- **Monument Valley Buttes at Sunset:** These stark sentinels of the desert are impressive at any time, but they take on a particularly dignified aura when the setting sun casts its deep colors over them, etching their profiles against a darkening sky. Although the park generally closes before sunset, you can arrange a sunset tour, and it's well worth it. See chapter 17.

3 The Best Family Vacations

- **Cherry Hill Family Campground** (Ogden): This fun-packed park offers something for everybody: a water park with slides, pools, even a pirate ship, plus miniature golf, batting cages, and aeroball (it's kind of like basketball). It's like staying in a theme park—practically a kid's dream come true. And you're not likely to find a more immaculately groomed and well-run campground. See chapter 8.
- **Heber Valley Historic Railroad:** Take a railroad trip back in time on the "Heber Creeper," so called because of the way this historic steam train inched its way up the canyon from Provo. This once-proud passenger and freight branch line will let you experience travel the way it was in your grandparents' day. Kids of all ages, from 6 to 60, will love it. See chapter 9.
- **Northeast Utah's Dinosaurland:** This is the real *Jurassic Park*—no special effects here. Stop first at Vernal's Utah Field House of Natural History State Park, where you can stroll around the Dinosaur Garden and admire the 17 life-size dinosaurs and other prehistoric creatures in a delightful garden that simulates the dinosaurs'

actual habitat. Then head for Dinosaur National Monument to see and touch—yes, touch—real fossilized dinosaur bones. See chapter 10.

- **Zion National Park:** The Junior Ranger Program, available at most national parks, is really extensive here, with both morning and afternoon activities all summer geared toward teaching kids what makes this natural wonder so special. They'll have so much fun, they won't even notice they're learning something. See chapter 12.

4 The Best Scenic Drives

- **The Golden Spike Tour:** Heading out of Ogden on Old U.S. 89, you'll first pass through some fine fruit country (be sure to stop at a roadside stand). At the small town of Willard, turn west toward I-15; head north on I-15 to exit 368, and turn west on Utah 83. This will take you along the north side of the Great Salt Lake through picturesque farming communities, until you reach the turnoff to the spot where, in 1869, the last spike was driven for the transcontinental railroad, connecting East and West for the first time. If you love trains as we do, you'll thrill to both the sound of the whistle and the sight of the puffing steam as the engine chugs away and back again. See chapter 8.

- **The National Park Tour:** From the canyons of Zion, head north along U.S. 89 through majestic forests to Red Canyon, with its walls of brilliant red rock, and then east on Utah 12 to Bryce Canyon, with its fascinating amphitheaters of multi-colored stone. The route from Bryce Canyon to Capitol Reef along Utah highways 12 and 24 takes in some of the most spectacular scenery in a state of unsurpassed landscapes. See chapters 12, 13, and 14.

- **Moab to Monument Valley:** This may be red rock country at its finest. From Moab, U.S. 191 south takes you past huge slabs of rock—outposts of Canyonlands National Park—through one-horse towns with few services, but enough character to make up for it. At Bluff, turn southwest on U.S. 163 and drive through more ruddy desert, past the sombrero-shaped rock for which Medicine Hat was named, and finally to the solemnity of Monument Valley. See chapters 16 and 17.

5 The Best Hiking Trails

You don't have to be able to scale Mt. Everest in order to enjoy these trails:

- **Indian Trail** (Ogden): Easily accessible from downtown Ogden, this 5-mile trail gets you out of town quickly, into a thick forest of spruce and fir and onto a mountainside that offers spectacular views of Ogden Canyon, including a beautiful waterfall. See chapter 8.

- **Hidden Piñon Trail, Snow Canyon State Park** (St. George): This fairly easy, self-guided nature trail will reward you with breathtaking panoramic views. You'll wander among lava rock, into canyons, and over rocky flatland, along a trail lined with Mormon tea, cliffrose, prickly pear cactus, banana yucca, and other wild desert plants. See chapter 11.

- **Lower Emerald Pools Trail, Zion National Park:** If green is your color, you'll love this trail—algae keeps the three pools glowing a deep, rich shade of emerald. The first part of the trail, navigable by wheelchairs with assistance, leads through a forest to the Lower Emerald Pool, with its lovely waterfall and hanging garden. The small pool just above it is so still and calm that the reflections of the towering cliffs in the water seem like a photograph lying on the ground. See chapter 12.

- **Navajo Loop/Queen's Garden Trail, Bryce Canyon National Park:** To truly experience magical Bryce Canyon, you should climb down into it; this not-too-difficult trail is a good way to go. Start at Sunset Point and get the hardest part out of the way first. You'll pass Thor's Hammer and wonder why it hasn't fallen, ponder the towering skyscrapers of Wall Street, and visit with some of the park's most fanciful formations, including majestic Queen Victoria herself. See chapter 13.

- **Petrified Forest Trail, Escalante State Park** (Escalante): Along this steep nature trail, you'll find yourself walking in a stunted forest of junipers and piñons before reaching a field strewn with colorful chunks of petrified wood. As you progress, you'll have panoramic views of the town of Escalante and the surrounding stair-step plateaus. See chapter 13.

6 The Best Places to Go Mountain Biking

Mountain bikes aren't just for the mountains, and Utah offers spectacular trails not only through beautiful forests high in the mountains, but also over slippery slickrock and across wide-open deserts. These rides and destinations will offer a challenge—if that's what you're after—and provide a means to see spectacular scenery as well.

- **Moab Slickrock Bike Trail:** A rite of passage for serious mountain bikers, this challenging but rewarding trail takes 4 or 5 hours to complete. Between your huffing and puffing, you'll enjoy breathtaking views of the Colorado River far below, the La Sal Mountains towering above, and the red arches of Arches National Park in the distance. See chapter 16.

- **Brian Head Resort:** At 9,600 feet, there may not be a lot of oxygen, but the air is pure and clear, and the biking is great—especially when you can ride a chairlift up the mountain and bicycle down. There are trails everywhere, each with more magnificent scenery than the last. See chapter 11.

- **Dave's Hollow Trail:** Situated just outside the entrance to Bryce Canyon National Park, this trail heads off into the national forest. The double track takes you through sun-dappled glades surrounded by tall Ponderosa pines and spruce trees, all the way to fishing and camping at Tropic Reservoir if you so desire. See chapter 13.

7 The Best Destinations for Fishing & Water Sports

- **Strawberry Reservoir:** The number-one trout fishery in Utah for both cutthroat and rainbow, this gem of a lake is magnificently set among tall pines. You're really out in the woods here: The nearest town of any size is 30 miles away. So pick your spot, out in the middle of the reservoir or tucked away in a quiet nook, and cast your line for dinner—you can't beat fresh-caught trout cooked over an open fire. See chapter 9.

- **Jordanelle State Park** (near Park City): This boomerang-shaped reservoir has been divided into three distinctly different recreational areas. The middle and widest part is designated for speedboats, and is perfect for waterskiing; above that, cut off by an arm of land, lies the wakeless area, great for sailboating and quiet fishing; at the other end of the boomerang, low-speed motorboats are allowed. Whichever area you choose, you'll have the beautiful Wasatch Mountains on all sides. See chapter 9.

- **The Green River through Dinosaur National Monument:** The best way to see this spectacularly desolate country is from the river, the way explorer John Wesley Powell did in 1869. Do you crave excitement? Run the foaming rapids. Is peace and quiet your thing? Float mindlessly in the placid waters, leaving your troubles behind. See chapter 10.
- **Flaming Gorge National Recreation Area:** Smaller and more intimate than Lake Powell and located in a gloriously colorful setting, Lake Flaming Gorge is one of Utah's real hidden treasures. You can skim the water on skis or just doze off on the deck of a houseboat. As for the fishing, if you feel like the big ones always get away, this is the place for you—they're all big here. See chapter 10.
- **Quail Creek State Park** (near St. George): Quail Creek has the warmest water in the state, so if you prefer being in the water to boating on top of it, this is the place to be. It's also a premier fishing spot for largemouth bass, and you can angle for rainbow trout, blue gill, and crappie as well. A fish-cleaning station and barbecue grills in the picnic area allow you to enjoy your catch immediately. See chapter 11.
- **Lake Powell:** This sprawling lake has what seems like zillions of finger canyons reaching off the main watercourse of the Colorado River. You could spend weeks—maybe even months—waterskiing, swimming, fishing, exploring the myriad side canyons, and just loafing about in the sun. See chapter 15.
- **The Colorado River near Moab:** Tackle the placid stretches on your own in a canoe or kayak, or sign up with one of the many outfitters and shoot the rapids. Whatever you choose, a trip down the spectacular, scenic Colorado River is an adventure. See chapter 16.

8 The Best Wildlife Watching

- **Rock Cliff, Jordanelle State Park** (near Park City): More than 160 species of birds either live here or pass through; this is an especially good place to spot eagles and other raptors who nest in the area. Boardwalks and trails throughout the riparian wetlands reduce the environmental impact of your visit, and give you a great chance to watch wetland life do their thing. See chapter 9.
- **Flaming Gorge National Recreation Area:** Take a boat trip to see bighorn sheep—the imposing beasts are sometimes seen on Kingfisher Island and near Hideout Canyon on the north side of the reservoir in spring and early summer. And keep your eyes peeled for the lovely osprey and rare peregrine falcon, occasionally spotted near their nests on the high rocky spires above the lake. See chapter 10.
- **Coral Pink Sand Dunes State Park:** If you climb the dunes early in the morning, you're sure to see the footprints of jackrabbits, kangaroo rats, even an occasional mule deer or coyote. But the real fun comes after dark, with the late-night scorpion hunt: You can follow a park ranger out onto the dunes and, using a black light, spot the luminescent creatures as they scurry across the sand. See chapter 11.
- **Escalante State Park** (Escalante): Willows and cottonwoods line the banks of the reservoir, one of the few wetland bird-watching sites in southern Utah. It's home to a wide variety of ducks, plus coots, grebes, herons, and swallows. You might also see eagles, osprey, American kestrels, and other raptors. Small creatures of the furry variety, including cottontail and blacktail jackrabbits, ground squirrels, and even beaver, inhabit the area as well. See chapter 13.

- **Boulder Mountain** (between Escalante and Torrey): As you drive through the beautiful conifers and aspens atop Boulder Mountain, you're likely to see mule deer, smaller mammals—squirrels, chipmunks, snowshoe hares, cottontails—and any number of songbirds. If you're lucky, you might even spot a wild turkey. Get out of your car and onto a hiking trail, and your chances are even better. See chapter 13.

9 The Best Downhill Skiing

- **Beaver Mountain** (The Northern Wasatch Front): Visiting this small, family-oriented ski area is like going home to see the folks—it's just plain comfortable. There's no glitz, no fancy anything, just lots of personal attention, plenty of snow, and great terrain with beautifully maintained trails. See chapter 8.
- **Snowbasin** (Ogden Valley): Families really love Snowbasin because there's something for everyone here, no matter what their ability. It's particularly popular with intermediates, who love the long, easy, well-groomed cruising runs, but experts have plenty to keep them happy, too, including an abundance of untracked powder and the state's third-highest vertical drop. See chapter 8.
- **Alta** (Little Cottonwood Canyon): All serious skiers make a pilgrimage to Alta at one time or another. It offers the best skiing in the state—and some of the lightest powder in the world—especially for advanced skiers willing to hike a bit for perfect conditions. But if you're not up to black-diamond level yet, don't worry: Beginners and intermediates will find plenty of cruising ground, too. And at $28 for an all-day adult lift ticket, Alta also happens to be one of the best skiing bargains around. See chapter 9.
- **Park City and Deer Valley:** These resorts offer not only excellent powder skiing on a wide variety of terrain, but also the best shopping, nightlife, accommodations, and dining of all Utah's ski areas—for that matter, in all of Utah. Park City is the party town; Deer Valley is its more grown-up, sophisticated sibling. They're less than 5 minutes apart, so you can take advantage of the best of both. Who says you can't have everything? See chapter 9.

10 The Best Cross-Country Skiing

- **Solitude Nordic Center** (Big Cottonwood Canyon): Close to Salt Lake City, Solitude is the perfect destination for a half- or full-day cross-country excursion. At 8,700 feet, the 20 kilometers of groomed trails pass through Alpine forests and meadows and around picturesque Silver Lake. There's also a children's trail. See chapter 9.
- **Sundance Nordic Center:** These expertly groomed trails are in a perfect forest and meadow setting at the base of Mt. Timpanogos. Part of the Sundance Resort complex, Sundance Nordic Center is easily accessible from downtown Provo but light years away from civilization. See chapter 9.
- **Bryce Canyon National Park:** Once the summer crowds go home and a blanket of snow adorns the multicolored hoodoos with a sparkling white mantle, it's time to take out the cross-country skis. Just follow the warm-weather hiking trails around the rim. Outside the park, at Ruby's Inn, you'll find groomed trails and rental equipment. See chapter 13.

11 The Best Four-Wheeling

Four-wheeling isn't for everyone, but for those who enjoy it, it's an exhilarating mix of muscle and machine that takes you where you could never go under the power of your own two feet.

- **Coral Pink Sand Dunes State Park** (near Kanab): Skim across the swells of smooth rose-colored sand, uphill and down, over the ever-shifting dunes. With the sun and sand and wind in your face, it's an unending challenge—and a real thrill. See chapter 11.
- **White Rim Road, Canyonlands National Park:** A hundred miles of winding, rocky road meanders around Canyonlands' Island in the Sky, offering ever-changing views. Sometimes the scene is a grand panorama of monumental stone as far as the eye can see; at other points, you'll enjoy a close-up view of a stately tower of red rock or a colorful canyon wall. A high-clearance 4X4 is necessary for this one. See chapter 16.
- **Klondike Bluffs to Willow Flats Road, Arches National Park:** This 19-mile excursion takes you into high desert terrain, to the tops of tall hills, and past spectacular rock formations such as stately Eye of the Needle arch, towering Elephant Butte, and the solemn Courthouse Towers. You'll have sweeping views of forested mountains, drifting sand dunes, and, at every turn, more red rock. See chapter 16.
- **Poison Spider Mesa Trail** (near Moab). This is another of southwestern Utah's serious 4X4 roads; you'll need a short wheelbase vehicle to negotiate some of these steep hairpin turns. Before you reach the top, you'll pass through a sandy canyon and some rocky areas that really stretch the meaning of the word *road*. Below—and growing ever more distant as you climb—lies the Colorado River, winding its way through the Moab Valley. See chapter 16.

12 The Best Places to Experience Native American Culture

- **The Great Gallery in Horseshoe Canyon, Canyonlands National Park:** In a remote and hard-to-reach section of Canyonlands National Park is the Great Gallery, an 80-foot-long panel of rock art that dates back several thousand years. It's one of the biggest and best prehistoric murals you'll find anywhere. See chapter 16.
- **Hovenweep National Monument:** This deserted valley contains some of the most striking and most isolated archaeological sites in the Four Corners area—the remains of curious sandstone towers built more than 700 years ago by the ancestral Puebloans (also known as Anasazi). These mysterious structures are still keeping archaeologists guessing. See chapter 17.
- **Mesa Verde National Park:** The largest archaeological preserve in the country is also home to the most impressive cliff dwellings in the Southwest. The sites run the gamut from simple pit houses to complex cliff dwellings, and they're all fascinating to explore. See chapter 17.
- **Monument Valley Navajo Tribal Park:** For most of us, Monument Valley *is* the Old West. We've seen it dozens of times in movie theaters, on TV, and in magazine and billboard advertisements. The Old West may be gone, but many

Navajos still call this home. A Navajo guide will give you the Navajo perspective on this majestic land and take you into areas not otherwise open to visitors. See chapter 17.

13 The Best Mormon History Sites

- **Temple Square** (Salt Lake City): This is a centerpiece of the Latter-day Saints headquarters, and its significance is apparent in the magnificent structures and beautiful statuary set among vibrant gardens. The egg-shaped Tabernacle may look a little peculiar, but its interior acoustics make up for it. You can take a guided tour to learn more about the Latter-day Saints (LDS) and the square itself, stroll around on your own, or just sit and meditate; Temple Square is a lovely haven in the center of a bustling city. See chapter 7.
- **Beehive House** (Salt Lake City): Brigham Young built this house in 1854 as his family home. Restored to resemble as closely as possible the way it looked when Young lived here, Beehive House serves as a looking glass into the lifestyle of the Mormon leader. Originally from New England, Young designed his home in that region's architectural style; he even included a widow's walk for keeping an eye on the surrounding desert. See chapter 7.
- **Jacob Hamblin Home** (St. George): This simple home, built of pine and stone, looks as if the family just stepped out for a stroll and are expected back for dinner soon. It's cozy and comfortable, with furnishings you'd expect to find in any pioneer home. Then you notice the two identical bedrooms—one for each of Jacob's wives—and you realize that these weren't just any pioneers. See chapter 11.
- **St. George Tabernacle** (St. George): A magnificent example of old-world craftsmanship, from the hand-quarried red stone walls to the pine detailing finished to look like fine hardwoods and marble—a painstaking craft that clearly illustrates the strength and depth of the pioneers' religious beliefs. See chapter 11.

14 The Best Luxury Hotels & Inns

Luxury is not a word we generally associate with Utah, but there are a few uniquely exquisite places to stay, where comfort is synonymous with elegance, and grandeur has a certain coziness to it.

- **Inn at Temple Square** (Salt Lake City; ☎ **800/843-4668** or 801/531-1000): The finest accommodations downtown, this quietly elegant hotel offers beautifully appointed rooms, a lovely dining room, and an all-around aura of old-world graciousness. Although it may look formal, it's really relaxed and homey—come on in and set a spell. See chapter 7.
- **Brigham Street Inn** (Salt Lake City; ☎ **800/417-4461** or 801/364-4461): A showcase of understated elegance, the Brigham Street Inn is a delight to the eye. It also happens to be a great place to relax and put your feet up—there are comfortable chairs in every room and fireplaces in most. See chapter 7.
- **Goldener Hirsch Inn** (Deer Valley; ☎ **800/252-3373** or 435/649-7770). This place feels like a Bavarian Alps lodge, with roaring fireplaces, hand-painted furniture, windows looking out onto the ski slopes, feather-light down comforters, and the kind of personalized service you'd expect to find in a fine European hotel. See chapter 9.
- **Stein Eriksen Lodge** (Deer Valley; ☎ **800/453-1302** or 435/649-3700). The Stein Eriksen is grandly elegant yet warm and welcoming, with cozy niches in the

dignified lobby and lavishly comfortable suites. Attendants in the whirlpool, sauna, and fitness room are always on hand to pamper you and see to your every need, but they're so unobtrusive that you'll feel right at home—contentedly, luxuriously at home. See chapter 9.

15 The Best Bed-&-Breakfasts

- **Center Street Bed & Breakfast Inn** (Logan; ☎ 435/752-3443): Welcome to fantasyland. This highly imaginative B&B is a delight for those adults who don't mind letting their inner child out now and then. The Arabian Nights Suite has sand-colored carpet, a huge round bed with a sultan's tent and stars above, and a camel and elephant surrounding the heart-shaped whirlpool tub. In the Ice Fantasy, you'll find polar bears and penguins, snow drifts on the mirrored walls, and icicles hanging from the ceiling of a snow cave. Need we say more? See chapter 8.
- **Snowberry Inn Bed & Breakfast** (near Ogden; ☎ 801/745-2634): This new log B&B is lovingly decorated with antiques and collectibles, and each bedroom has its own personality. Although it's a wide-open design with a broad front porch, it still manages to have a cozy, homelike atmosphere; guests gather in the kitchen to sip coffee and watch, or help, as breakfast is being prepared. See chapter 8.
- **Seven Wives Inn Bed & Breakfast** (St. George; ☎ 800/600-3737 or 435/ 628-3737): This was the first B&B in Utah, and it's one of the loveliest. There are no polygamists hiding in the attic anymore, but you'll still feel like you've stepped back in time when you stay here. The B&B is housed in two historic 19th-century homes outfitted with antiques, mostly Victorian and Eastlake. We loved the several decks, porches, and balconies. The innkeepers are friendly, but not intrusive. See chapter 11.
- **Sunflower Hill Bed & Breakfast Inn** (Moab; ☎ 435/259-2974). Loaded with country charm, this delightful B&B makes you feel like you've gone back to Grandma's, where family relics surround you during the day and handmade quilts keep you warm at night. What's more, this may be the quietest lodging in Moab, and the grassy, shady grounds are very inviting on a hot day. See chapter 16.

16 The Best Lodges

This is the West, a rugged land of rugged pioneers who literally carved out a place for themselves in the forests and red rock canyons. At these lodges, you can feel a part of that past without having to sacrifice any of today's modern comforts.

- **Red Canyon Lodge** (Flaming Gorge National Recreation Area; ☎ 435/ 889-3759): This is not really a lodge at all, but rather a group of delightful cabins dating from the 1930s, and remodeled in the 1990s. They offer a range of accommodations from rustic to luxurious, and all have freestanding wood stoves. See chapter 10.
- **Bryce Canyon Lodge** (☎ 435/834-5361). This handsome sandstone and ponderosa-pine lodge is the perfect place to stay while you're visiting the national park. The several suites are outfitted with white wicker furniture, ceiling fans, and separate sitting rooms. But our choice would be one of the snug cabins—they're fairly small, but the high ceilings provide a feeling of spaciousness, and the gas-burning stone fireplaces, pine-board walls, and log beams make them appropriately cozy. See chapter 13.

17 The Best Places to Eat

Generally, food in Utah is good, not great. Perhaps harkening back to the Scandinavian roots of many of the Mormon pioneers who settled Utah, much of the food here is basic, nourishing, and tasty without being overly exciting. Following are several noteworthy exceptions.

- **The New Yorker** (Salt Lake City; ☎ **801/363-0166**): Our favorite in Salt Lake City, The New Yorker offers superb service, a comfortable but upscale decor, and a wide choice of excellently prepared food. Desserts are magnificent. See chapter 7.
- **Lamb's Restaurant** (Salt Lake City; ☎ **801/364-7166**): A delightful and sometimes innovative restaurant with reasonable prices—how can you beat that? So sit back in one of the cozy booths, relax, and enjoy a good meal while watching the who's who of Utah parade through. See chapter 7.
- **Glitretind Restaurant** in the Stein Eriksen Lodge (Deer Valley; ☎ **435/649-3700**): Possibly the most elegant restaurant in Utah, the Glitretind serves inventive, exquisitely prepared dishes. See chapter 9.
- **Cafe Basila's—Mediterranean** (St. George; ☎ **435/673-7671**): This Greek and Mediterranean restaurant in Utah's Dixie is something special. The crusty homemade bread is worth a visit in itself, but don't eat too much—you'll want to save room for one of Basila's splendid entrees, not to mention the Greek custard bread pudding for dessert. See chapter 11.

18 The Best of the Performing Arts

- **Mormon Tabernacle Choir** (Salt Lake City): You can hear the glorious sounds of this world-renowned all-volunteer choir in its home on Temple Square. When not on tour, the choir rehearses Thursday evenings and performs its weekly radio and television broadcasts Sunday mornings; both events are open to the public, free of charge. See chapter 7.
- **Utah Symphony** (Salt Lake City, Park City): Who'd expect to find one of the country's top symphony orchestras in Utah? Well, here it is: an excellent ensemble that not only tours worldwide and has produced numerous recordings, but also performs each year in schools across the state. Our favorite time to enjoy this world-class orchestra is during the symphony's summer series, when outdoor performances of Tchaikovsky's *1812 Overture* in Park City are accompanied by the booming of genuine cannons. See chapters 7 and 9.
- **Mountain Man Rendezvous at Fort Buenaventura** (Ogden): Trappers gathered in the early 1800s to trade their furs for supplies here, instead of having to travel east to established markets. This twice-yearly tribute honors the mountain men who chose the site for their rendezvous. These festival-like events are fun for everyone, participants and onlookers alike. You'll enjoy the music, Dutch-oven food, and contests that usually include a tomahawk throw, canoe race, shooting competition, and foot races, with all competitors in pre-1840s dress. See chapter 8.
- **Utah Shakespearean Festival** (Cedar City): To go or not to go, that is the question. If theater's your thing, go. Four of the Bard's plays, plus two by other playwrights, are presented each summer, and they're grand entertainment. See chapter 11.

Land of Natural Wonders & Pioneers: Introducing Utah

2

Barren wasteland and scenic wonderland, an adventurer's paradise and picture-perfect Middle America—this is Utah, a land of extremes, where mountain peaks receive more than 500 inches of snow each winter and desert lowlands bake at well over 115°F in the summer. Utah is an extraordinarily beautiful place. It has a rugged beauty, with stark stone monoliths alternating with deep red canyons, tall forested mountains standing guard over a huge inland salt sea.

This relatively quiet, relatively unknown corner of America is beginning to draw nationwide, even worldwide, attention. More and more people are coming—to visit its majestic national parks, explore its pristine wilderness, bike its slickrock trails, ski the best powder in the world, and discover the all-around charm of its cities and towns. To some, this is America as it should be—a wide-open country with plenty of room to roam, and some of the friendliest people on earth. Of course, it isn't quite that simple, but it comes close. But don't just take it from us; find out for yourself. Come to Utah, discover, and enjoy.

1 The Regions in Brief

Take a big knife and it's easy to cut Utah into three distinct regions: the Colorado Plateau, in the southern half of the state where all those fantastic rock formations are; Rocky Mountain Utah, with rugged peaks, stately pines, deep blue lakes, and most of the state's residents; and the Great Basin Desert, the big middle-of-nowhere where you've always wanted to send that distant cousin of yours you never really liked.

Since the state is so big, we've concentrated our coverage on those areas visitors tend to be most interested in, rather than trying to catalog each of the three regions from A to Z. Truth be told, certain sections of Utah just have a whole lot of nothing. So we've organized this book by destination, based on where you'll probably want to go or where you'll base yourself while exploring outlying areas.

We start out in the **Wasatch Front.** Eighty percent of Utah's population lives in this Rocky Mountain region, the 175-mile-long north-central section of the state from Logan to Provo. **Salt Lake City** is Utah's most populous city by far, as well as its most cosmopolitan. It's also the international headquarters of the Church of

❷ Did You Know?

- Utah's population is the youngest in the nation.
- Utah boasts one of the world's largest dinosaur graveyards at Dinosaur National Monument.
- The Mormon Tabernacle in Salt Lake City is so acoustically sensitive that a pin dropped at one end can be clearly heard at the other, 170 feet away.
- 94% of residents age 20 and over can read and write, and 80% have graduated from high school—more than in 49 other states.
- Utah is among the fastest-growing states in the nation—while the country's population increased 1.11% from 1992 to 1993, Utah's population swelled 2.71% in the same period.
- The waters of the Great Salt Lake cover 2,500 square miles and contain eight times more salt than any ocean.
- Utah's state bird is the California seagull, chosen because the gull saved the Mormons' first crops from a plague of crickets in 1848.
- Robbers Roost, an outlaw hideout for years even before Butch Cassidy found it in 1884, is located southwest of the confluence of the Green and Colorado rivers, partly within the boundaries of Canyonlands National Park.
- Four Corners Monument, at the southeast corner of Utah, is the only place in America where you can stand—or sit, if you prefer—in four states at once: Utah, Colorado, New Mexico, and Arizona.
- Hundreds of movies, TV shows, and commercials have been filmed in the magnificent red rock country of southern Utah—Monument Valley will look mighty familiar when you get there.

Jesus Christ of Latter-day Saints, more commonly known as the Mormons; Temple Square is Utah's most-visited attraction. Keep in mind, though, that Salt Lake City is still a relatively small city, and not as sophisticated or glitzy as New York or Los Angeles. Maybe that's what we like best about it. One advantage Salt Lake has over all other Rocky Mountain cities its size is, as any real estate agent will tell you, its location; within an hour you can be skiing some of the best downhill slopes in the West.

That brings us to the rest of the Wasatch Front. We've designated that section of the Wasatch Front that's roughly north of Salt Lake the **Northern Wasatch Front.** Here you'll find that mystery of nature, the **Great Salt Lake,** eight times saltier than any of the world's oceans; the city of **Ogden;** and **Logan,** Utah's northernmost town of any size. Historic Ogden and Logan are both worthy of visits unto themselves; they also make good bases for exploring the nearby mountains. The Great Salt Lake is really part of the Great Basin Desert (see below), but we've covered it here because of its proximity to Salt Lake City, and because it's really the only thing going on in that flat, salty desert.

Those areas basically east and south of Salt Lake City we've called the **Southern Wasatch Front.** This region contains beautiful **Big and Little Cottonwood Canyons,** with some of the state's best skiing, as well as great hiking and biking in the summer; **Park City,** Utah's premier ski resort town—and a great destination all year round—with a historic Main Street dominated by a variety of shops and restaurants; some fun spots just outside of Park City, including Heber City, Strawberry

Reservoir (a real gem of a lake), and several terrific state parks; Robert Redford's Sundance Institute; and **Provo,** a small, conservative city whose main claim to fame is Brigham Young University.

The western side of Utah, beginning just west of Salt Lake City, is dominated by the vast, salty nothingness of the Great Basin Desert, which includes the pristinely white Bonneville Salt Flats, so flat that you can actually *see* the curvature of the earth, and famous for the land speed records held there. This is not the sort of place you want to go for a picnic—it's hot, the water's undrinkable, and there's really nothing there except for **Wendover,** a little gambling town straddling the Utah/Nevada state line, which we've covered as an excursion from Salt Lake City.

Next we head to **Northeastern Utah,** with two terrific recreational areas that creep into the adjoining states: **Flaming Gorge National Recreation Area,** which wanders into Wyoming; and nearby **Dinosaur National Monument,** which extends from northeastern Utah into Colorado. Both are what we consider Undiscovered Utah, because they're really off the beaten path and not what most people imagine when they think of Utah. But, as you'll notice as you peruse this book, we love this region, and consider it well worth a visit.

The **Colorado Plateau,** which extends along the state's entire southern border and halfway up the east side, is where all five of Utah's national parks are located, and with good cause—it's undeniably beautiful. Ancient geologic forces, erosion, oxidation, and other unfathomable natural forces have carved spectacular rock sculptures—delicate and intricate, bold and stately—and painted them in a riot of color. This is quite likely why you came to Utah in the first place, and these chapters should help you spend your time wisely and enjoyably. Check out our chapter on **Zion National Park** for hints on how to avoid the crowds at the state's most popular national park; see if you agree that **Bryce Canyon National Park,** with its marvelous stone sculptures (called hoodoos), is the West's best. The chapter on **Capitol Reef National Park** explains why this little-known national park is one of Utah's hidden treasures; and we'll direct you to some of the best ways to explore eastern Utah's beautiful red rock country in the chapter on **Moab** and **Arches and Canyonlands national parks.**

But the Colorado Plateau isn't just national parks—it's got even more to offer. Its biggest population and cultural center is in and around St. George, which you'll find in the chapter called **"Utah's Dixie & the Colorful Southwest Corner."** This area offers great museums, historic Mormon sites, live theater, dance, and music, as well as skiing (believe it or not) and the state's best golf. If you're heading into Utah from Las Vegas, Nevada, this is also the first Utah town you'll see.

Utah's best destination for water sports—maybe the best in the West—is explored in our chapter on **Lake Powell and Glen Canyon National Recreation Area.** A boating vacation here is the stuff that stressed-out big-city dreams are made of.

In **"The Four Corners Area,"** we cover the state's southeast corner, with a few jaunts into adjacent states. Spectacular Native American sites, such as Monument Valley, make a visit here truly worthwhile. But keep in mind that you'll be driving a long way through the West's vast, empty spaces to get there.

Impressions

TV you can make on the back lot, but for the big screen, for the real outdoor dramas, you have to do it where God put the West . . . and there is no better example of this than around Moab.

—John Wayne, while filming *The Comancheros* in 1961

Utah

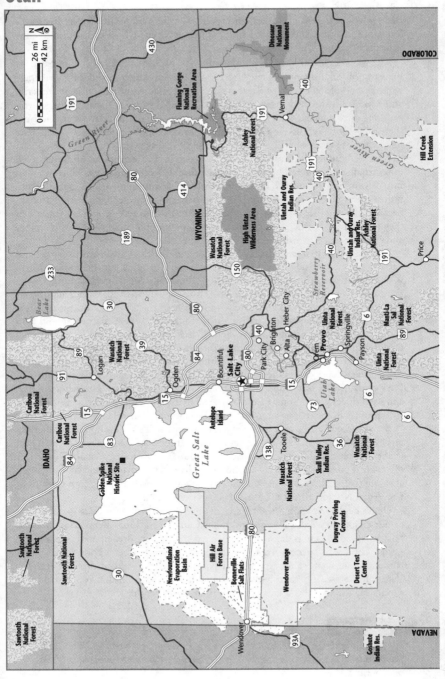

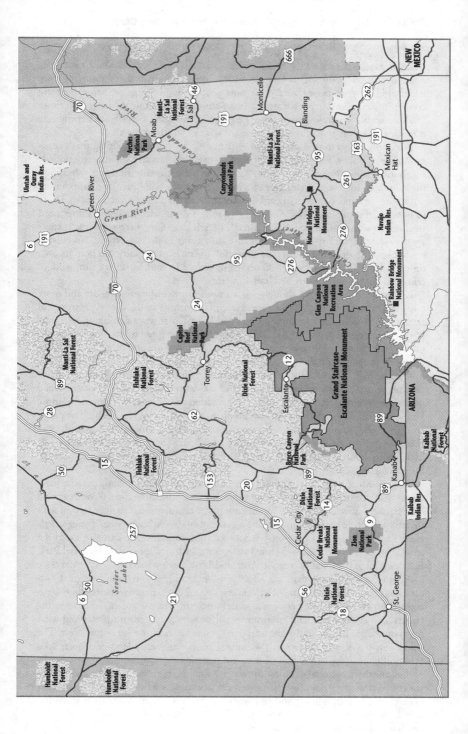

15

2 Utah Today

Some people really think that Utah is stuck in the '50s—quaintly or annoyingly so, depending on your perspective. This time warp is due in large part to the strong church influence and the corollary Mormon emphasis on family values, which make Utah a notably family-oriented state. People here are quite friendly, the crime rate is low, and Utah is generally a very pleasant state in which to travel.

But don't expect to find the level of restaurants, nightlife, and lodging that's commonplace in Dallas, San Francisco, or even Denver and Santa Fe. With a few notable exceptions, it just doesn't exist here. And while we personally find this refreshing, those looking for five-star elegance or a happening scene will likely be disappointed.

Liquor laws and attitudes toward alcohol in Utah are, simply put, archaic. Those of us who enjoy a glass of wine or beer or a mixed drink with lunch or dinner need to choose our restaurants carefully. Outside of Salt Lake City, even some night spots are dry, like the country-and-western dance club in Provo that advertises "No cussin', no smokin', no drinkin'!" This isn't universal, of course; Park City can hold its own on nightlife with any of the top ski resorts in Colorado, and Moab is a fun, wild 'n' crazy kind of place—at least by Utah standards.

Changes are in the wind, though—along with some conflicts—as more and more outsiders move to Utah. Many escapees from California's smog, crime, crowds, and taxes have brought their mountain bikes and West Coast way of thinking to southern Utah's national park country, while others have been lured to the Wasatch Front, particularly between Salt Lake City and Provo, by computer and other high-tech industries setting up shop there. These newcomers—some 40,000 from California alone in the first half of the decade—have brought demands for more services, better restaurants, upscale shops, and a greater range of activities; in many cases, they've opened businesses themselves that they felt were needed. They're also accused by some Utahns of bringing with them the very problems they sought to leave behind. A police chief in a small southern-Utah town was criticized when he announced in mid-1995 that many of the crimes in his community were being committed by newcomers. It may not be politically correct to say so, he admitted, but statistics seem to back up his statement.

The growth of tourism is causing traffic congestion problems, mainly because there are so many of us, and because we all want to visit at the same time. Zion National Park has been affected the most. By the turn of the century, in an attempt to deal with the problem, the park hopes to institute a mandatory shuttle bus service. If your schedule is at all flexible, avoid the busy school vacation months. You can also avoid the crowds by seeking out the lesser-visited attractions, such as Capitol Reef National Park, Flaming Gorge National Recreation Area, and Utah's many spectacular state parks.

Another current issue that will affect you—especially if you enjoy the great outdoors—is the wilderness-versus-development debate. As in many western states, Utah endures an ongoing battle between business interests, who see federal lands as prime targets for development, and environmentalists, who are intent on preserving what they consider to be one of the last unspoiled wildernesses of the American West. The wilderness-preservation side sees the businesspeople as greedy land-destroyers who care nothing for the future and understand America only as a commodity to be exploited for their personal gain; on the other hand, the ranchers, loggers, and miners see the environmentalists as selfish, well-off newcomers who don't care that other people need to earn a living and just want the government to designate vast wilderness areas for their personal playgrounds. To some extent, they're both right. We'll just have to wait and see what happens.

Even though its feet may be planted in the 1950s, Utah is really looking toward the next century. It's trying to tackle such problems as population growth and air pollution, for instance, head-on. But the future's not all grim: The Beehive State is looking forward to—and, in true fashion, working hard preparing for—the formidable but thrilling task of hosting the 2002 Winter Olympic Games.

3 History 101

A walk through Utah is a walk through the American West. You can ponder the meaning of petroglyphs etched into canyon walls more than a thousand years ago; follow paths tread by Spanish padres hundreds of years ago; seek out the hiding places of famed outlaw Butch Cassidy; raft the same rapids explorer John Wesley Powell did in 1869; and see railroads, homes, ranches, and spectacular houses of worship built by the mountain men, miners, missionaries, and all the other pioneers who created the Utah we see today.

THE FIRST PEOPLES   The first known inhabitants were the Desert Gatherers, who, from about 9000 B.C., wandered about the Great Basin and Colorado Plateau searching for food. Unfortunately, being nomadic, they left little evidence of their time here. The Anasazi (also known as ancestral Puebloans) appeared in the Four Corners region at about the time of Christ; by A.D. 1200, their villages were scattered throughout present-day Utah. For some reason—possibly drought—by 1250 the villages had been abandoned, leaving the ruins we see standing today in Hovenweep National Monument and at other sites. The descendants of these early people—Shoshone, Ute, Goshute, and Paiute—were among the Native Americans inhabiting the area when the first Europeans came.

Another prehistoric Native American group, the Fremont peoples, settled in central Utah, establishing small villages of pit houses. They arrived about A.D. 1200, but had disappeared by the time the first Europeans reached Utah.

Spanish explorer Juan Maria Antonio Rivera and his European expedition arrived at the Colorado River near present-day Moab in 1765. Eleven years later, two Spanish Franciscan friars reached Utah Lake and mapped it, hoping to return to establish a Spanish colony. Spain did not pursue the idea, however, and the next Europeans to explore the area were fur traders in the early 1800s. Then, in July of 1847, Brigham Young led the first Mormons (a nickname for members of the Church of Jesus Christ of Latter-day Saints) into the Salt Lake

Dateline

- **9000 B.C.** Desert Gatherers wander the region now called Utah.
- **50 B.C.–A.D. 1300** The Anasazi establish thriving communities in the Four Corners Area.
- **1776** Spanish friars lead an expedition to explore the region now called Utah.
- **1801** Brigham Young is born in New England.
- **1824** Scout Jim Bridger becomes the first white man to see the Great Salt Lake.
- **1847** Brigham Young leads Mormon pioneers into the Salt Lake Valley.
- **1848** United States wins the Utah region from Mexico.
- **1849** Mormons establish the provisional state of Deseret and adopt a constitution, but their request for statehood is denied.
- **1850** U.S. Congress creates the Utah territory.
- **1860–61** Pony Express riders cross Utah on their 2,000-mile, 10-day route between St. Joseph, Missouri, and Sacramento, California.
- **1861** Telegraph lines are joined at Salt Lake City, creating transcontinental telegraph service and putting an end to the need for the Pony Express.
- **1869** Railroad tracks laid from the East and the West Coasts are joined at Promontory, Utah, creating the first transcontinental railroad and connecting

continues

East and West for the first time.

- **1877** Brigham Young dies at home after a brief illness.
- **1890** Church president Wilford Woodruff issues a manifesto advising Mormons that the practice of polygamy is no longer acceptable.
- **1893** Mormon Temple is dedicated in Salt Lake City.
- **1896** Utah becomes the 45th state in the Union.
- **1896** Utahn Martha Hughes Cannon becomes the first female U.S. Senator.
- **1904** Polygamy is formally prohibited by the church.
- **1913** Strawberry River Reservoir, the state's first large reclamation project, is completed by the U.S. Bureau of Reclamation.
- **1919** Zion National Park is created.
- **1926** Commercial airlines start operating in Utah.
- **1928** Utah National Park, established in 1924, is renamed Bryce Canyon National Park.
- **1934** Utah ratifies prohibition repeal amendment and passes stringent state liquor laws.
- **1940** Wendover Air Force Base is established.
- **1950** Mabel Young Sanborn, 87, the last of Brigham Young's 56 children, dies of natural causes. She was his 54th child.
- **1952** Uranium is discovered near Moab.
- **1964** Glen Canyon Dam and the Flaming Gorge Dam are completed, ensuring water supply and creating scenic recreation areas. Canyonlands National Park is established.
- **1971** Capitol Reef, a national monument since 1937, becomes a national park. Arches, a national monument

continues

Valley, and the flood of Mormon immigrants began; these were the people who established Utah as we know it today.

MEET THE MORMONS   The Church of Jesus Christ of Latter-day Saints is a relatively young faith. It was born in the 1820s when Joseph Smith had a revelation: After much prayer asking which of the many Christian churches he should join, Smith was told by God and Jesus that he would be the one to restore the church that Christ established when he walked the earth. An angel named Moroni then gave Smith some ancient gold tablets that, under divine inspiration, he was able to translate into the Book of Mormon. In 1830, Smith and his followers published the Book of Mormon and founded the Church of Jesus Christ of Latter-day Saints (LDS) in upstate New York. Smith's revelations and the fervor with which his followers believed and tried to spread the word bred hostility in their more skeptical neighbors; the early Mormons were soon forced to leave New York.

Smith and his followers settled in Ohio and Missouri in the early 1830s. A few years of prosperity were succeeded by strife, and the growing Mormon community was once again forced to flee. Gathering along the Mississippi River, they established their church headquarters at Nauvoo, Illinois, reclaiming a swampy area along the river. Within a few years, Nauvoo was the second-largest city in Illinois, and the Mormons continued to grow and flourish, planning a university and laying the foundation for a temple. Also during these years, the practice of polygamy began slowly and quietly among church leaders. Both their nonconformism and their success bred fear and anger in their opponents, who considered Smith and his followers to be a real political, economic, and religious threat. In 1844, a mob stormed the jail in Carthage, Illinois, where Joseph Smith and his brother Hyrum were being held on treason charges, and murdered them. Brigham Young and other church leaders soon decided that the Mormons had to move west, beyond the reach of the fearful communities and angry mobs.

Young, a confidant of Smith, became the second leader of the church, displaying a genius for organization in the evacuation of Nauvoo and the subsequent migration westward in search of a new Zion. In 1846 the Mormons headed west from Illinois, establishing winter quarters on the far side of the Missouri River, near present-day Omaha, Nebraska. Young studied maps and journals of explorers, looking for a place that nobody else wanted, where Mormons could build their own community and practice their religion without interference.

FOUNDING ZION   In the spring of 1847, Brigham Young started out with the first group of emigrants—two children, three women, and 143 men, handpicked for the journey based on their abilities. Future groups were similarly organized, making this the safest and most successful migration across the American West. When the first group reached the mouth of Emigration Canyon and looked out upon the empty wasteland of Salt Lake Valley, Young reportedly said, "This is the right place." Within hours of their arrival, the pioneers had begun building an irrigation system and establishing fields for growing food. In the next few days, Young chose the site of the temple and laid out the new city in a grid system beginning at the southeast corner of Temple Square. Having established their new Zion, most of the company headed back to Winter Quarters to bring their families west.

That first year almost ended the settlement before it had properly begun. The flat sod roofs leaked under heavy spring snow and rain; provisions ran low, forcing the pioneers to eat whatever they could find, including the sego lily bulb (now the state flower); a late frost damaged the wheat and vegetables; and drought damaged more. Then a plague of crickets descended on the crops, consuming the little that was left. The people tried everything they could think of to battle the crickets—beating them, drowning them, setting them on fire—but nothing worked. Suddenly, seagulls appeared from the Great Salt Lake, devouring the insects by the thousands, disgorging them, and eating more. After 2 weeks, the crickets were effectively eliminated, and enough of the crops were saved to feed the pioneers. The seagull is now Utah's state bird, and a monument stands in Temple Square commemorating the Mormons' deliverance from famine.

By the end of 1848, almost 3,000 Mormons had arrived in the Salt Lake Valley. It was now a part of the United States, ceded to the Union by Mexico along with California, Nevada, most of New Mexico and Arizona, and parts of Wyoming and Colorado. In 1849, the Mormons petitioned to have their territory declared the State of Deseret, a name that comes from the Book of Mormon and means honeybee. Denied statehood, the territory of Utah—named after the Ute tribe—was created in 1850, with Brigham Young as territorial governor. Although no longer run by the church, the territory was assured of its continued influence, since the vast majority of voters were Mormons who elected church leaders to positions of authority in the civic domain as well.

since 1938, is expanded and made a national park.

- **1977** Gary Gilmore, convicted of the murders of two Utahns, is executed by firing squad following a media circus that garnered international attention. It's the first execution in the United States in 10 years, following the Supreme Court's reinstatement of the death penalty.

- **1978** LDS Church announces a revelation saying priesthood is now open to worthy men of any race, reversing a policy that had excluded blacks from leadership roles in the church.

- **1982** Worldwide membership in the Church of Jesus Christ of Latter-day Saints exceeds five million.

- **1995** Utah is chosen to host the 2002 Winter Olympic Games.

- **1995** More than 600 inches—that's 50 feet—of snow during the season keeps the lifts running at Snowbird, in Little Cottonwood Canyon east of Salt Lake City, through the Fourth of July—the latest lift-served skiing ever in Utah.

- **1996** By executive order, U.S. President Bill Clinton creates the 1.7-million-acre Grand Staircase-Escalante National Monument, which is hailed by environmentalists but condemned by Utah Senator Orrin Hatch and other opponents as "the mother of all land-grabs."

In these years, non-Mormons—or "Gentiles," as the Mormons call them—began traveling through the valley, many on their way to the gold fields of California. Salt Lake City was an ideal spot for resting and re-supplying before setting out again. Some came through on their eastbound return trip after giving up on the West. The Mormons often bought horses, livestock, and supplies, in turn reselling what they didn't need to other travelers. The travelers who passed through to rest and trade took with them a collection of sometimes-confused ideas about the Mormons, including their fascinating practice of polygamy. The journals of these travelers gave the nation its first real knowledge—however incomplete—of Mormon faith and customs.

THE UTAH WAR   In 1857, a new governor was sent from Washington to supplant Young. Fearing he would be rejected, President Buchanan sent federal troops to escort him. The Mormons harassed the troops by driving off livestock and attacking their supply trains, forcing them to winter in western Wyoming. Although the Mormons were prepared to fight to keep the army out, neither Brigham Young nor President Buchanan wanted bloodshed. As the new governor entered Salt Lake City, Mormon families packed their belongings and awaited the order to move.

An estimated 30,000 Mormons left their homes in Salt Lake City and the northern settlements, moving south over a period of 2 months, leaving the capital virtually deserted by mid-May. The exodus drew national and international attention and placed the U.S. government in quite an unfavorable light—the government had persecuted innocent people, steamrolling over the fundamental right to religious freedom. An uneasy peace was finally established, the Mormons returned to their homes, and the two groups lived side by side until the outbreak of the Civil War, when the army was called back East.

BECOMING THE BEEHIVE STATE   After the close of the Civil War, attention was again directed toward the enforcement of antipolygamy laws, and many Mormons were imprisoned. Finally, in 1890, the church leaders issued a statement: Based on a revelation from God, the church was no longer teaching plural marriage and no person would be permitted to enter into it. With this major bar to statehood removed, Utah became the 45th state on January 4, 1896.

The Depression hit Utah hard; the unemployment rate reached 35% and per capita income was cut in half. Not until World War II was industry brought back to life in Utah. Several military bases established during the war became permanent installations, and missile plants were built along the Wasatch Front. After the war, steel companies reopened, the mining industry boomed, and high-tech businesses moved in. By the mid-1960s, the economy base had shifted from agricultural to industrial.

Dams were built—Glen Canyon Dam, creating Lake Powell; Flaming Gorge Dam, creating Lake Flaming Gorge; plus several smaller ones—to further the cause of industry and to ensure water and energy supplies, but they also had an additional

Impressions

When I was a boy on the farm in Illinois there was a great deal of timber on the farms which we had to clear away. Occasionally we would come to a log which had fallen down. It was too hard to split, too wet to burn, and too heavy to move, so we plowed around it. That's what I intend to do with the Mormons. You go back and tell Brigham Young that if he will let me alone, I will let him alone.

—President Abraham Lincoln, 1862, when asked what his plans were for the Mormons benefit: They provided recreational opportunities for a modern society with an increasing amount of discretionary income and more and more free time. Ski resorts began opening in the Wasatch Mountains. In the early 1980s, once outsiders started showing interest in the new playground of Utah, Salt Lake City International Airport and the city's cultural center, the Salt Palace complex, expanded. As the mining industries began winding down, tourism and service industries grew; today, they account for more of the state's economy than any other industry. The Mormons, who spent their first decades fleeing from outsiders, are now welcoming them with open arms, and they're coming in droves.

4 A Brief Look at Modern Mormonism—or Yes, You Can Get a Cup of Coffee in Utah

Utah is a Mormon state. Not officially, of course—strict state and federal laws keep church doctrine out of government—and not as much as in the past, when practically all Utahns (and definitely all the decision makers) were LDS church members. But when about three-quarters of the state's population belong to the Church of Jesus Christ of Latter-day Saints, and given that most of them take their religion very seriously, it's inevitable that the teachings and values of the church would have a strong influence in the voting booth and echo throughout the halls of government.

While some conflict is inevitable as government and community leaders try to adapt to Utah's growing cultural diversity, this discord means little to most visitors, who come to Utah to experience its scenery, recreation, and history. What you'll discover is that Utah is much like the rest of the United States, although generally not as hip as California or as multicultural as New York. The state is inhabited in large part by actively religious people who believe it's detrimental to one's health to use tobacco or addictive drugs, or to drink alcoholic beverages, coffee, or tea. In accordance with church teachings, Mormons generally strive to be hardworking and honest, with high moral standards.

WHAT MORMONS BELIEVE

Mormons are Christians, believing in Jesus Christ as the Son of God and the Bible as the Word of God, as do all the many offshoots of Christianity. But a significant difference is the role played by another book they believe to be God's Word as well— the Book of Mormon, as revealed to and translated by church founder Joseph Smith.

This book tells of two tribes of people who left Israel in Biblical times and made their way to the western hemisphere. Mormons believe that these people were the ancestors of today's American Indians. The Book of Mormon teaches that after his resurrection, Christ spent about 40 days among these people, preaching, healing, and establishing his church. The Mormons believe that Joseph Smith was commanded to restore the church as organized by Christ during his ministry on earth.

The first four principles of the faith are belief in Jesus Christ, repentance, baptism by immersion, and the laying on of hands to receive "the Gift of the Holy Ghost" (in which a priest places his hands on a church member for the transference of spirituality). Another important tenet of the church is respect for the supreme authority of church leaders and the belief in the revelations from God to these leaders.

The family unit is of paramount importance to Mormons, and they believe that marriage lasts literally forever, transcending death. They believe that sex outside of marriage, including homosexual behavior—two ideas that run contrary to the sanctity of the traditional family—is a sin. The church encourages the family to work, play, and study together, and young adults—most men and some women—generally spend 1 or 2 years as missionaries. Mormons also believe in the baptism and redemption of those already dead—hence their strong interest in genealogy.

It's practically impossible to discuss the church without discussing polygamy, the practice of men having more than one wife, which caused so much antagonism toward church members in the 19th century. But that's really a shame, because polygamy—or plural marriage, as the church dubbed it—has little to do with what the church was and is about. Polygamy came about as a "revelation" to church founder Joseph Smith in the 1840s, was practiced by a relatively small percentage of church members, and was outlawed by church officials in 1890. Today, polygamy is prohibited both by church doctrine and state law. It reportedly continues among a small number of rebels, who have left the church to practice their own brand of religion, but they're few and far—very far—between.

WHAT MORMONISM MEANS FOR YOU, THE VISITOR TO UTAH

This strong religious influence has brought about some strange laws regarding alcoholic beverages, although it's definitely not true that you can't get a drink here. Cigarettes and other tobacco products are also readily available, but smoking is prohibited by state law in all restaurants—legislation that is becoming more and more common across America these days. Although cola drinks contain caffeine, a stimulant that is generally considered to be mildly addictive, the church doesn't specifically prohibit their consumption. Some Mormons drink Coke or Pepsi, while others refrain. You'll generally have no trouble at all purchasing whatever type of soft drink you want, with or without caffeine. Interestingly, there are exceptions: Although there are plenty of soda machines on the campus of church-owned Brigham Young University in Provo, they stock only noncaffeinated products, and this is also true of church offices.

What we found pleasantly surprising is that although the Mormons of Utah can be pretty tough on themselves regarding the above-mentioned "sins," virtually every Utahn we encountered in researching this book—and a great many were Mormons— were extremely tolerant of others' beliefs and lifestyles. We can't guarantee that you won't run across some holier-than-thou busybody who insists on lecturing you on the evils of Demon Rum, tobacco, promiscuity, or homosexuality, but our experience has been that they generally respect each individual's right to make his or her own moral choices.

Be forewarned, though—Mormons are practically missionaries by definition, and will, with only the slightest encouragement, want to enthusiastically help you see the wisdom of their ways.

Because the church emphasizes the importance of family, you'll see lots of kids— Utah is noted for having the highest fertility rate in the nation. This makes Utah a very kid-friendly state, with lots of family-oriented activities and many attractions that are designed specifically with kids in mind. Overall, prices for kids and families are often very reasonable. And since most Mormon families observe Monday evening as a time to spend together, sports facilities, amusement parks, and similar venues often offer family discounts on Mondays; if you're traveling with your family, watch for them.

Although about 75% of Utah's population are LDS church members, you'll find that church membership varies greatly from community to community, so the number of Mormons you'll encounter will vary considerably. Although it's the world headquarters of the church, Salt Lake City is just under half Mormon, while some of the smaller towns approach 100%. Of major cities, Provo has the strongest church influence; although St. George was historically a major stronghold for church members, recent immigration from other parts of the United States is gradually diluting that influence. You'll probably find the least church influence in Park City and Moab, which in recent years have attracted large numbers of outsiders.

5 Recommended Books, Films & Recordings

To catch the mood of southern Utah, we recommend Edward Abbey's *Desert Solitaire* (New York: McGraw-Hill, 1968), a nonfiction work based on time Abbey spent in Arches National Monument, before it gained national-park status. Those who like a good Western story will want to grab a copy of Zane Grey's *Riders of the Purple Sage* (New York: Pocket Books, 1974).

An excellent source for additional information about Mormonism is *Church History in the Fulness of Times* (Salt Lake City: Church of Jesus Christ of Latter-day Saints, 1989), a detailed history of the church. A short, easy-to-read book with simple, concise explanations of Mormon beliefs is *What Do Mormons Believe?* (Salt Lake City: Deseret Book Company, 1992) by Rex E. Lee. And, of course, the Book of Mormon is available from the church. For an insightful look at Mormon life and Salt Lake City in the mid-19th century, you might enjoy reading *The City of the Saints and Across the Rocky Mountains to California* (New York: Alfred A. Knopf, 1963, first pub. in London, 1861) by Richard Burton.

Outdoor enthusiasts might want *The Mountain Biker's Guide to Utah* (Helena, Mont.: Falcon Press, 1994) by Greg Bromka, with detailed descriptions and maps of 80 rides; or *The Hiker's Guide to Utah* (Falcon Press, 1991) by Dave Hall and Ann Seifert. Jim Cole's *Utah Wildlife Viewing Guide* (Falcon Press, 1990) describes 92 of the best wildlife viewing sites in Utah.

If you're a budding or amateur geologist, or would just like a little more background on the rocks you're going to see, you should investigate *Pages of Stone, Geology of Western National Parks & Monuments, 4: Grand Canyon and the Plateau Country* (Seattle: The Mountaineers, 1988) by Jalka Chronic. It includes discussions of Grand Canyon, Arches, Bryce Canyon, Canyonlands, Capitol Reef, and Zion national parks, and Cedar Breaks, Natural Bridges, and Rainbow Bridge national monuments.

Western-movie buffs will want a copy of *"Where God Put the West": Movie Making in the Desert* (Moab: Four Corners Publications, Inc., 1994) by Bette L. Stanton, which includes fascinating stories and photos from the numerous Hollywood productions shot in southern Utah. Anyone who's seen the 1969 film *Butch Cassidy and the Sundance Kid* will enjoy *The Wild Bunch at Robbers Roost* (Lincoln: University of Nebraska Press, 1989) by Pearl Baker, which tells the real story of these famous outlaws.

Speaking of movies, of the hundreds filmed in Utah, the two that say the most about the state are *Stagecoach* and *Wagon Master,* black-and-white classics by famed director John Ford that can be found in most decently stocked video-rental outlets. *Stagecoach,* released in 1939, offers spectacular scenes of Monument Valley, and stars a young John Wayne on his road to stardom. Released 11 years later, *Wagon Master,* starring Ben Johnson, Joanne Dru, and Ward Bond, was filmed in the Moab area, and tells a fictionalized but highly entertaining story of a Utah-bound Mormon wagon train.

Several travel videos that let you see Utah before your trip are *Utah: Nature's Wonderland,* a splendid hour of Utah's scenic beauty; *The Iron Road,* about the completion of the first transcontinental railroad at Promontory, Utah; and *Grand Circle Tour,* a 1,400-mile tour of Grand Canyon, Zion, Bryce Canyon, Capitol Reef, Canyonlands, Arches, and Mesa Verde national parks. You can get these and other videos, many in both VHS and PAL formats, from **INTERpark**, P.O. Box 3590, Farmington, NM 87499 (☎ **800/687-5967** or 505/325-6136).

3

Planning a Trip to Utah

Utah is an easy state to visit—you can usually expect to pay less for food and lodging than you would in other parts of the country, roads are good and generally uncrowded, and it would be hard to find friendlier people. But once you leave the Wasatch Front—the area around Salt Lake City, Ogden, and Provo—to explore the natural wonders of Utah, distances between towns are long with few services along the way. So you'll want to plan your trip carefully and make reservations in particularly popular areas, such as the national parks, or for especially popular times, like ski season, as far in advance as possible. The pages that follow will help you do that and more—we've compiled everything you need to know to handle the practical details of planning your trip in advance.

1 Visitor Information & Money

VISITOR INFORMATION

For advance information on the state as a whole, as well as an official state map, contact the **Utah Travel Council,** Council Hall, Salt Lake City, UT 84114 (☎ **800/200-1160** or 801/538-1030; fax 801/538-1399). The travel council also provides information **on-line** at www.utah.com.

Numerous agencies can provide information on a variety of activities and destinations in Utah. For information on Utah's national forests, contact the **U.S. Forest Service,** Federal Building, Room 8301, 125 S. State St., Salt Lake City, UT 84138 (☎ 801/524-5030); for forest and wilderness maps, contact the **U.S. Forest Service Intermountain Region,** 2501 Wall Ave., Ogden, UT 84401 (☎ 801/625-5306); for topographic maps, contact the **U.S. Geological Survey,** 2300 S. 2222 West, West Valley City, UT 84117 (☎ 801/975-3742). The Utah State Office of the **U.S. Bureau of Land Management** is at 324 S. State St., Suite 301 (P.O. Box 45155), Salt Lake City, UT 84145-0155 (☎ 801/539-4001). For information on Utah's state parks, contact **Utah Parks and Recreation,** 1594 W. North Temple, Suite 116 (P.O. Box 146001), Salt Lake City, UT 84116-6001 (☎ 801/538-7220; 800/322-3770 for campground reservations); and for information on guides and outfitters throughout the state, contact **Utah Guides & Outfitters,** 153 E. 7200 South, Midvale, UT 84047 (☎ 801/566-2662). You'll find additional information sources for planning your outdoor recreation vacation in Utah in chapter 5, "The Active Vacation Planner."

MONEY

ATMs (automatic teller machines) are practically everywhere, including many supermarkets. For the location of the nearest ATM, dial ☎ **800/424-7787** for the Cirrus network or ☎ **800/843-7587** for the Plus system. Most ATMs will make cash advances against MasterCard and Visa, but make sure you have your personal identification number (PIN) with you.

American Express cardholders can write a personal check, guaranteed against the card, for up to $1,000, getting $200 in cash and the balance in traveler's checks, at any American Express office. The Utah office is in Salt Lake City at 175 S. West Temple (☎ **801/328-9733**). It's open Monday through Friday from 9am to 5pm.

U.S. dollar **traveler's checks** are accepted practically everywhere in Utah, including small towns, and can be exchanged for cash at banks and most check-issuing offices. However, be aware that smaller businesses may not be able to cash traveler's checks or even American currency in large denominations (over $50).

2 When to Go

Deciding when to visit Utah will depend on what you want to do and which sections of the state you plan to see. Generally, those traveling without children will want to avoid visiting during school vacations. In particular, stay away from ski resorts during the Christmas–New Year's holidays and from the national parks during July and August if you want to avoid the crowds. The best times to visit the parks and almost everything else in southern Utah are in spring and fall, anyway; summers are too hot, particularly in the St. George area.

Utah has four seasons, but because of the vast range in elevations—from 2,200 feet to 13,528 feet—conditions vary considerably across the state. Generally, as in the other desert states, summer days are hot but nights are cool. Winters are cold and snowy, except in southwest Utah's "Dixie" (where St. George is located)—it seldom gets very cold and snow is rare. Mountain temperatures are always pleasantly cool and can be very cold at night, even in the summer.

Average Monthly High/Low Temperatures (°F) & Precipitation (inches)

		Jan	Feb	Mar	Apr	May	June	July	Aug	Sept	Oct	Nov	Dec
Moab	Temp. (°F)	42/19	51/25	61/33	71/42	82/50	93/58	99/65	96/63	88/53	75/41	57/30	45/21
	Precip. "	0.6	0.5	0.7	0.9	0.7	0.4	0.5	0.8	0.7	0.9	0.7	0.7
Elev. 3,965'													
Park City	Temp. (°F)	27/6	31/10	36/15	48/24	60/33	71/39	79/47	76/45	67/36	54/28	39/17	31/11
Mountains	Precip. "	3.1	2.6	2.9	2.4	1.3	1.3	1.1	1.4	1.0	2.5	2.4	3.2
Elev. 8,085'													
St. George	Temp. (°F)	54/27	61/32	67/37	76/44	86/52	96/61	102/68	99/66	93/57	81/45	65/34	55/27
	Precip. "	1.0	0.9	1.0	0.5	0.5	0.2	0.6	0.7	0.5	0.6	0.8	0.7
Elev. 2,760'													
Salt Lake	Temp. (°F)	37/20	44/27	52/30	61/37	72/45	83/53	93/62	90/60	80/50	67/39	50/29	39/22
City	Precip. "	1.4	1.3	1.7	2.2	1.5	1.0	0.7	0.9	0.9	1.1	1.2	1.4
Elev. 4,222'													

UTAH CALENDAR OF EVENTS

January

- **Utah Winter Games,** Salt Lake City, Park City, and other locations. Amateur athletes compete in downhill and Nordic skiing, figure skating, and hockey. Call ☎ **800/959-8824** or 801/975-4515. Ongoing through most of the month.
- **Sundance Film Festival,** Park City. Sponsored by Robert Redford's Sundance Resort, this festival honors the best of independent films with screenings and seminars. For more information, see p. 156–157 or call ☎ **801/328-3456.** Last half of January.

February

- **Bryce Canyon Winter Festival,** Bryce. A winter celebration amid the colorful rock formations of the Bryce Canyon National Park area. Call ☎ **800/468-8660.** Mid-February.

March

- **Hostler Model Railroad Festival,** Ogden. Fans of model trains gather at historic Union Station, where trains of all shapes and sizes are on display, and model-train collectors can locate those hard-to-find items. Call ☎ **801/629-8446.** First week in March.
- **SnowShine Festival,** Park City. Family ski races, snow softball, and other fun-in-the-snow events. Call ☎ **435/649-8111.** Late March to early April.

April

- **World Conference of the LDS Church,** Salt Lake City. The church president, believed to be a prophet, speaks to Mormons from throughout the world at church headquarters on Temple Square. Those who are not members of the LDS Church are also welcome. Call ☎ **801/240-2531.**
- **Spring Salon,** Springville. A varied media art exhibit with an emphasis on Utah artists. Call ☎ **801/489-2727.** Ongoing all month.
- ✪ **Mountain Man Rendezvous,** Ogden. A gathering of mountain men at Fort Buenaventura State Park, with black-powder shooting contests and other early-19th-century activities. Call ☎ **801/621-4808.** Early to mid-April.

May

- **Golden Spike Anniversary,** Golden Spike National Historic Site. Commemorates the moment in 1869 when rail lines from the East and West Coasts were joined, linking the nation. A must for historic-railroad buffs. Call ☎ **435/471-2209.** May 10.
- **Living Traditions Festival,** Salt Lake City. A celebration of Utah's ethnic diversity, including food, music, and traditional activities. Call ☎ **801/533-5760.** Mid-May.
- **Scandinavian Festival,** Ephraim. Utahns celebrate their Scandinavian roots in one of the state's most authentic and enthusiastic folklife festivals. Call ☎ **435/283-6890** or 435/283-4535. Late May.

June

- **America's Freedom Festival,** Provo. This celebration includes fun runs and other sporting events, patriotic-music concerts, art festivals, parades, and fireworks. Call ☎ **801/345-2008.** Mid-June through Independence Day.
- **Utah!,** St. George. A highly acclaimed live outdoor drama brings Utah's early Mormon history to life, with music, comedy, drama, and spectacular special

effects, including fireworks and a flood. Call ☎ **800/746-9882.** Mid-June through mid-October.

❂ **Utah Shakespearean Festival,** Cedar City. A highly respected professional theater production of several plays by William Shakespeare, plus a few contemporary offerings. Call ☎ **435/586-7878.** Late June through August.

- **Utah Arts Festival,** Salt Lake City. Exhibits by artists and craftsmen, plus music and dance performances. Call ☎ **801/322-2428.** Late June.
- **Music in the Mountains,** Park City. A spectacular series of concerts, including appearances by the Utah Symphony, in an equally spectacular setting. Call ☎ **435/649-6100.** June through September.

July

- **Land Speed Opener, Bonneville Salt Flats,** Wendover. Jet-cars and other super-fast mechanical wonders try to break speed records on the incredibly smooth salt flats—so flat that you can see the curvature of the earth. Call ☎ **800/426-6862** or 801/977-4300. Mid-summer through early fall.
- **Dinosaur Roundup Rodeo,** Vernal. A Wild West rodeo, with bull riding, calf roping, barrel racing, steer racing, a Western dance, and parade. Call ☎ **800/421-9635.** Mid-July.
- **World Folkfest,** Springville. A community celebration that includes dance and music from around the world. Call ☎ **801/489-2700.** Third week in July.
- **Pioneer Day,** statewide. Everything comes to a halt in Utah while residents commemorate, with parades and other activities, the day in 1847 on which Brigham Young led the first group of Mormon pioneers to the spot that would become Salt Lake City. July 24.
- **Utah Jazz and Blues Festival,** Snowbird. Big-name musicians make this one of Utah's premier music events. Call ☎ **801/521-6040.** Late July.
- **Festival of the American West,** Logan. A multimedia historical pageant is presented nightly; there's also a fair with traditional Old West food, music, craft demonstrations, and live entertainment, including medicine-man shows and square dancing. Call ☎ **800/225-FEST.** Late July to early August.

August

- **Brian Head Bash**, Brian Head. A weekend of bicycling tours, catered luncheons on trails, prizes, and chairlift rides for bikers who then ride down the mountain. Call ☎ **435/677-2035.** Early August.
- **Railroader's Festival,** Golden Spike National Historic Site. Re-enactments of the Golden Spike ceremony, uniting the nation by rail; plus a spike-driving contest, railroad-handcar races and rides, and a buffalo-chip-throwing contest. Call ☎ **435/471-2209.** Mid-August.
- **Utah Belly Dance Festival,** Salt Lake City. Middle Eastern dancers do their thing in Liberty Park. Call ☎ **801/486-7780.** Third week in August.

September

- **Oktoberfest,** Snowbird. A traditional Oktoberfest celebration with German music, food, and, of course, beer. Call ☎ **801/521-6040.** September and October weekends.
- **Southern Utah Folklife Festival,** Springdale. Pioneer life is highlighted with craft demonstrations, music, and food. Call ☎ **435/772-3757.** First week in September.
- **Utah State Fair,** Salt Lake City. Live entertainment, a horse show, a rodeo, livestock judging, arts and crafts exhibits, and typical state-fair fun. Call ☎ **801/538-FAIR.** Early September.

- **Mountain Man Rendezvous,** Ogden. A gathering of mountain men at Fort Buenaventura State Park, with black-powder shooting contests and other early-19th-century activities. Call ☎ **801/621-4808.** Early September.

- **Greek Festival,** Salt Lake City. The music, dance, and food of Greece are featured, along with tours of the historic Holy Trinity Greek Orthodox Cathedral. Call ☎ **801/328-9681.** Early September.

- **Hole-in-the-Rock Jeep Jamboree,** Blanding. A variety of events for four-wheel-drive vehicles, including a day on the Hole-in-the-Rock Road, a trail used by pioneers in 1879. Call ☎ **800/574-4386.** Early September.

- **Moab Music Festival,** Moab. Live classical, jazz, bluegrass, and other types of music, presented in a beautiful red rock amphitheater and other locations. Call ☎ **435/259-8431.** Mid-September.

- **Fall Colors Fat Tire Festival**, Brian Head. A weekend of bicycling tours, chairlift rides for bikers who can then ride down the mountain, catered luncheons on trails, and prizes. Call ☎ **435/677-2029.** Late September.

October

- **Ogden Oktoberfest,** Ogden. A true Oktoberfest celebration honoring Ogden's sister city of Hof, Germany, with authentic German beer, music, and food. Call ☎ **800/255-8824** or 801/627-8288. Mid-October.

- **World Senior Games,** St. George. An extremely popular Olympics-style competition for seniors, with a variety of athletic events. Call ☎ **435/674-0550.** Mid-October.

- **Red Rock Gem and Mineral Show,** Moab. Rockhounders show off exotic rocks, gems, and minerals. Call ☎ **435/259-5904.** Mid-October.

- **Canyonlands Fat Tire Festival,** Moab. Mountain-bike guided tours, hill climbs, and related events. Call ☎ **435/259-8825.** Late October to early November.

- **Buffalo Roundup,** Antelope Island State Park. Stop by the park and watch the annual buffalo roundup, conducted on horseback and by helicopter. Take binoculars and get a close-up view of the buffalo as they receive their annual medical exams. The event also includes a dance. Call ☎ **801/773-2941.** Late October to early November.

November

- **Christmas Parade and Lighting of the Dinosaur Gardens,** Vernal. Life-size replicas of dinosaurs are illuminated for Christmas. Call ☎ **435/789-6932.** Late November.

- **America's Cup Ski Races,** Park City. Sanctioned World Cup ski races and demonstrations. Call ☎ **435/649-8111.** Late November.

- **Parade of Lights,** Bullfrog Marina, Lake Powell. A limited number of boats are available to rent and decorate; a number of privately owned boats are entered. The parade is led by the ferry, and prizes are awarded for boat decorations. Spectators throng the area to see lights from about 50 boats reflected in the waters of Lake Powell. Call ☎ **435/684-3046.** Saturday after Thanksgiving.

- **Ogden Christmas Parade and Christmas Village,** Ogden. A parade begins the Christmas season, when the municipal park is transformed into a Christmas village, with thousands of lights, music, and animated decorations. Call ☎ **801/629-8214.** Late November through December.

- **Temple Square Christmas Lights,** Salt Lake City. A huge, spectacular display of Christmas lights decorates Temple Square. Call ☎ **801/240-1000.** From the Friday after Thanksgiving to January 1.

December

- **Festival of Lights,** Wahweap Marina, Lake Powell. The *Canyon King* paddle wheeler leads a parade of illuminated boats that seem larger than life with all their lights reflected in the waters of Lake Powell. Both spectators and participants are welcome, and prizes are awarded. Call ☎ **800/528-6154** or 520/645-2433. Early December.
- **Railroader's Film Festival and Winter Steam Demonstration,** Golden Spike National Historic Site. Showings of classic Hollywood railroad films, plus a steam-engine demonstration. Call ☎ **435/471-2209.** Late December.
- **First Night Celebration,** Ogden. This family party rings in the New Year with bands, storytelling, and arts and crafts, ending with a spectacular fireworks display. Call ☎ **800/255-8824** or 801/627-8288. December 31.
- **First Night New Year's Eve Celebration,** Salt Lake City. This New Year's Eve family party brings downtown Salt Lake City alive with arts and crafts, live entertainment, storytelling, and numerous other family-oriented activities, culminating in a midnight fireworks display. Call ☎ **801/359-5118.** December 31.

3 Health & Insurance

STAYING HEALTHY IN UTAH

Utah's extremes of climate—from burning desert to snow-covered mountains—can produce health problems if you're not prepared. If you haven't been to the desert before, the heat, dryness, and intensity of the sun can be difficult to comprehend. If you're prone to dry skin, moisturizing lotion is a must; even if you're not, you may end up using it. Everyone needs to use a good-quality sunblock and wear a hat and sunglasses with full ultraviolet protection. Hikers and others planning to be outdoors will also need to carry water—at least a gallon per person, per day is recommended.

The other potential problem is elevation. Utah's mountains rise to over 13,500 feet—there's less oxygen and lower humidity when you're up that high. This creates a unique set of problems for short-term visitors. If you have heart or respiratory problems, consult your doctor before planning a trip to the mountains. If you're in generally good health, you don't need to take any special precautions, but it's advisable to ease into high elevations by changing altitude gradually. Don't fly in from sea level in the morning and plan to be hiking at 10,000-foot Cedar Breaks National Monument that afternoon. Spend a day or two at 4,000- or 5,000-feet elevation to let your body adjust. Also, get lots of rest, avoid large meals, and drink plenty of nonalcoholic fluids, especially water.

State health officials have lately been warning outdoor enthusiasts to take precautions against the Hantavirus, a rare but often fatal respiratory disease first recognized in 1993. About half of the country's confirmed cases have been reported in the Four Corners states of Colorado, New Mexico, Arizona, and Utah. The disease is usually spread by the urine and droppings of deer mice and other rodents, and health officials recommend that campers avoid areas with signs of rodent droppings. Symptoms of Hantavirus are similar to flu, and lead to breathing difficulties and shock.

INSURANCE

Before starting out, check your medical insurance policy to make certain you're covered while away from home. If you're not, you can purchase a special traveler's policy from your travel agent, insurance agent, or travel club. Traveler's policies are relatively inexpensive and can usually be purchased for the exact duration of your trip. Be sure to carry a medical-insurance identification card or other proof of insurance with you at all times while traveling.

Travel insurance can also be purchased to cover accidents, lost luggage, and trip cancellation (an especially handy thing if you've prepaid a large chunk of your vacation expenses). Again, check with your travel agent, insurance agent, or travel club. Before you buy, though, check your homeowners' or renters' policy—off-premises theft and loss of your personal property may already be covered. And most credit and charge cards offer automatic flight insurance when you purchase your airline ticket with their card.

If you're planning to drive in Utah, be sure to carry proof of automobile-liability insurance, and be certain that your policy includes protection from uninsured motorists. If you're renting a car, check your credit cards to see if any of them pick up the collision-damage waiver (CDW) when you rent with their card. Also check your personal auto policy to see if it covers the CDW before you rent. The CDW can run as much as $12 per day in addition to the basic rental charge.

4 Tips for Travelers with Special Needs

FOR TRAVELERS WITH DISABILITIES

Travelers with disabilities should find Utah a generally easy place to get around. Many parks have at least one wheelchair-accessible trail. Some historic buildings, however, are not wheelchair accessible; check before going.

If you're planning to visit Utah's national parks and monuments, you can get the National Park Service's **Golden Access Passport**, available at all the parks for free. This lifetime pass is issued to any U.S. citizen or permanent resident who is medically certified as disabled or blind. The pass permits free entry and gives a 50% discount on park-service campgrounds and activities (but not on those offered by private concessionaires).

The **Utah information and referral line for people with disabilities** is ☎ **800/ 333-8824.** Mobility International USA, P.O. Box 10767, Eugene, OR 97440 (☎ and TDD **541/343-1284;** fax 503/343-6812), is a national nonprofit member organization that provides travel information, referrals, and other services for travelers with disabilities.

Amtrak will, with 24 hours' notice, provide porter service, special seating, and a discount (☎ **800/USA-RAIL**). If you're traveling with a companion, **Greyhound** will carry you both for a single fare (☎ **800/231-2222**).

FOR GAY & LESBIAN TRAVELERS

The **Utah Stonewall Center,** a community center for gays and lesbians, is located at 770 S. 300 West in Salt Lake City (☎ **801/539-8800**).

FOR SENIORS

Many Utah hotels and motels offer a senior-citizen's discount, and more and more restaurants, attractions, and public transportation systems are now offering special rates as well.

You can save sightseeing dollars if you are 62 or over by picking up a **Golden Age Passport** from any national park, recreation area, or monument. This lifetime pass has a one-time fee of $10 and provides free admission to parks, plus a 50% savings on camping and recreation fees.

Membership in the **American Association of Retired Persons (AARP),** 601 E St. NW, Washington, DC 20049 (☎ **800/424-3410** or 202/434-2277), entitles you to discounts at numerous places, and they can also help with specifics on motels, cruise lines, and car rentals.

FOR TRAVELERS WITH PETS

Many of us wouldn't dream of going on vacation without our pets. Under the right circumstances, it can be a wonderful experience for both you and your animals. Dogs and cats are accepted at many motels around the state, but not as universally in resorts and at the more expensive hotels. Throughout this book, we've tried to consistently note those lodgings that take pets. Some properties require you to pay a fee or damage deposit in advance, and most insist they be notified at check-in that you have a pet.

Be aware, however, that national parks and monuments and other federal lands administered by the National Park Service are not pet-friendly. Dogs are prohibited on all hiking trails, must always be leashed, and in some cases cannot be taken more than 100 feet from established roads. On the other hand, U.S. Forest Service and Bureau of Land Management areas, as well as practically all of Utah's state parks, are pro-pet, allowing dogs on trails and just about everywhere except inside buildings. State parks require that dogs be leashed; regulations in national forests and BLM lands are generally looser.

Aside from regulations, though, you need to be attentive to your pet's well-being. Just as people need extra water in Utah's hot, dry climate, so do pets. And keep in mind that, particularly in southern Utah's red rock country, trails are rough, and jagged rocks can cut the pads on your dog's feet. It's a good idea to check your pet's feet frequently and to carry tweezers to remove cactus spines. Remember, too, that dogs, who usually spend most of their time sleeping, aren't used to 10-hour hikes up mountainsides, and more than one exhausted pooch has had to be carried back to camp by its owner.

One final note on pets: There is no punishment too severe for the human who leaves a dog or cat inside a closed car parked in the sun. The car heats up faster than you'd suspect, so don't do it, even for a minute.

FOR STUDENTS

Be sure you have your student ID in your pocket, and ask about student discounts wherever you go. Joining **Hostelling International-American Youth Hostels,** Box 37613, Washington, DC 20013-7613 (☎ **202/783-6161**), will give you access to economical accommodations almost anywhere you travel; it's also a great way to meet other traveling students. They'll send you a directory of all hostels in the United States and Canada for $3 to cover postage and handling; the directory is free with HI-AYH membership. A 12-month membership costs $25 for those ages 18 to 54 and $10 for those 17 and under.

5 Getting There

BY PLANE

Utah's only major airport is **Salt Lake City International** (☎ 801/575-2400); you can fly directly to Salt Lake City from many cities in the United States and Canada. Airlines serving the airport include **America West** (☎ 800/235-9292), **American** (☎ 800/433-7300), **Continental** (☎ 800/525-0280), **Delta** (☎ 800/221-1212),

Northwest (☎ 800/225-2525), **Skywest/Delta** (☎ 800/453-9417), **TWA** (☎ 800/221-2000), and **United** (☎ 800/241-6522). In-state flights connect Salt Lake City to several other Utah cities, including Cedar City, Moab, St. George, and Vernal. See the relevant sections in this book for additional information.

An alternative for visitors planning to go to southern Utah is to fly into **McCarran International Airport** (☎ **702/261-5743**) in Las Vegas, Nevada, which is only 120 miles southwest of St. George, Utah. Budget-conscious travelers should check airline and vehicle-rental prices at both airports to see which will provide the better deal for their particular circumstances.

BY CAR

Utah is easy to reach by car, via I-80 from the west or east, I-70 from the east, I-15 and I-84 from the north, and I-15 from the southwest. Salt Lake City is 600 miles from Albuquerque, 500 miles from Denver, 430 miles from Las Vegas, and 650 miles from Phoenix. Keep in mind that there will be long distances between services approaching Utah from any direction, as well as within the state.

Before you set out on a road trip, you might want to join the **American Automobile Association (AAA)** (☎ **800/222-4357**), which has hundreds of offices nationwide. Members receive excellent maps and emergency road service; they'll even help you plan an exact itinerary.

BY TRAIN

Amtrak offers several routes through Utah. The *Desert Wind* runs from Chicago to Los Angeles, with stops in Salt Lake City and a few other Utah towns; the *California Zephyr* stops in several Utah towns, including Salt Lake City, on its run from Chicago to San Francisco. You can get a copy of Amtrak's national timetable from any Amtrak station or your travel agent, or by contacting Amtrak, 400 N. Capitol St. NW, Washington, DC 20001 (☎ **800/USA-RAIL**). Also request a brochure outlining prices, and be sure to ask about special family plans, tours, and other money-saving promotions Amtrak might be offering.

6 Getting Around

BY CAR

Driving yourself is the best way to get around Utah; in fact, it's the only way to get to many destinations. However, visitors who plan to drive their own cars to and around Utah will find that steep mountain roads can put a severe strain on their vehicles, particularly on the cooling and braking systems. Tires rated for mud and snow are needed in most regions in winter, and are required on roads leading to several major ski areas from November through March. Also keep in mind that Utah is a big state; it's a 5-hour drive from Salt Lake City to St. George, and it can easily take 6 or 7 hours to get from St. George to Moab.

CAR RENTALS   Car rentals are available in every sizable town and city in the state, and almost always at local airports. Widely represented agencies include **Avis** (☎ 800/331-1212), **Budget** (☎ 800/527-0700), **Dollar** (☎ 800/800-4000), **Hertz** (☎ 800/654-3131), **National** (☎ 800/227-7368), **Payless** (☎ 800/729-5377), and **Thrifty** (☎ 800/367-2277).

DRIVING RULES   Utah law requires all drivers to carry proof of insurance as well as a valid driver's license. Safety belts are required for drivers and all front-seat

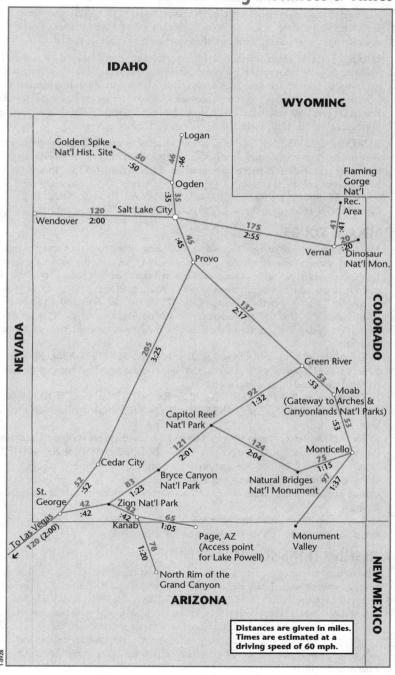

IDAHO

WYOMING

Logan

Golden Spike
Nat'l Hist. Site
50
:50
:46
:46
Ogden

Flaming
Gorge
Nat'l
Rec.
Area

120
2:00
Wendover

Salt Lake City
35
:35
:35

175
2:55

41
:41

NEVADA

:45
45
Provo

Vernal
20
:20
Dinosaur
Nat'l Mon.

137
2:17

205
3:25

Green River

COLORADO

53
:53
Moab
(Gateway to Arches &
Canyonlands Nat'l Parks)

92
1:32

Capitol Reef
Nat'l Park

124
2:04

53
:53

Cedar City

121
2:01

Monticello
75
1:15

St.
George
52
:52

83
1:23
Bryce Canyon
Nat'l Park

Natural Bridges
Nat'l Monument

97
1:37

42
:42
:42
42
Zion Nat'l Park
Kanab

65
1:05

Page, AZ
(Access point
for Lake Powell)

Monument
Valley

To Las Vegas
120 (2:00)

78
1:20

North Rim of the
Grand Canyon

ARIZONA

NEW MEXICO

**Distances are given in miles.
Times are estimated at a
driving speed of 60 mph.**

1-0928

33

passengers; restraints are required for all children under 8, regardless of where they are sitting. Radar detectors are permitted. Utah law allows drivers to make a right turn at a red signal after coming to a complete stop, unless otherwise posted.

MAPS You can get an official state highway map at State Welcome Centers or by mail (see "Visitor Information," above). Otherwise, maps are available at bookstores, gas stations, or from the American Automobile Association if you're a member (see "Getting There," above). **State Welcome Centers** are located along I-15 near Brigham City, I-80 near Echo Junction, I-15 near St. George, I-70 near Thompson Springs, and at the Utah Field House of Natural History in Vernal.

ROADSIDE ASSISTANCE In case of an accident or road emergency, contact the state police. American Automobile Association members can get free emergency road service by calling **AAA's emergency number** (☎ 800/AAA-HELP). In Utah, AAA headquarters is located at 560 E. 500 South (P.O. Box 1079), Salt Lake City, UT 84110 (☎ **800/541-9902** or 801/364-5615). AAA also has offices in Ogden (☎ **801/476-1666**) and Orem (☎ **801/225-4801**).

PACKAGE TOURS

Most visitors to Utah design their own tours, using either their own cars or rentals. However, those who prefer looking at the scenery rather than the road have several tour companies from which to choose. **Western Leisure of Salt Lake City** offers numerous tours, which you can book through your travel agent. **Gray Line Motor Tours,** 553 W. 100 South, Salt Lake City, UT 84101 (☎ **800/309-2352** or 801/521-7060; fax 801/521-7086), offers several national-park packages in the summer, including a 3-day, 2-night trip to Zion and Bryce Canyon national parks and Grand Canyon.

   Maupintour, 1515 St. Andrews Dr., Lawrence, KS 66047 (☎ **800/255-4266** or 913/843-1211), one of the world's largest tour companies, offers trips to the state's national parks and other destinations.

   Tauck Tours, 276 Post Road West, P.O. Box 5027, Westport, CT 06881-5027 (☎ **800/468-2825;** fax 203/221-6828), offers several tours that include parts of Utah.

   For those who enjoy train travel, **American Orient Express Railway Company**, 2025 First Ave., Suite 830, Seattle, WA 98121 (☎ **888/759-3944** or 206/441-2725; fax 206/727-7309), offers vintage carriages outfitted in polished mahogany and brass, and dining cars decked out with china, silver, crystal, and linen, and a cuisine to match. They offer a variety of tours, several of which include jaunts through Utah.

   A number of companies also offer specialized tours for outdoor-recreation enthusiasts. See chapter 5, "The Active Vacation Planner."

A RESERVATIONS SERVICE

An excellent compromise between doing your own thing and joining an organized tour is to work with **Utah Reservation Service,** 2812 E. Bijou St., Suite 103, Colorado Springs, CO 80909 (☎ **800/557-8824;** fax 719/473-7508). Tell the destination counselors where you want to go, how long you want to stay, and how much you want to spend, and they will make lodging reservations for you r entire trip. They can also take care of airline reservations and car rentals and offer other trip-planning assistance. The company can make either immediate or advance reservations.

FAST FACTS: Utah

Area Code   The area code is **801** in the Wasatch Valley, which includes Salt Lake City, Provo, and Ogden; most of the rest of the state has a **435** area code.

Business Hours   Banks are typically open Monday through Thursday from 9am to 3pm, and on Friday from 9am to 6pm. Drive-up windows may be open later. In general, business hours are Monday through Friday from 9am to 5pm. Many stores are also open on Friday evening and Saturday; those in major shopping malls have Sunday afternoon hours as well, and discount stores and supermarkets are often open later. Some supermarkets are open 24 hours a day.

Embassies/Consulates   See chapter 4, "For Foreign Visitors."

Emergencies   In almost all parts of Utah, the number to dial for any emergency is ☎ **911**; money is not required for emergency calls at pay phones. In a few rural areas, it will be necessary to dial "0" (zero) for an operator.

Holidays   In addition to the standard holidays, Pioneer Day, July 24, is a big holiday for many Utahns; many business and government offices close to celebrate the arrival of Brigham Young and the first wagon train of Mormon pioneers in the Salt Lake Valley.

Liquor Laws   The legal drinking age is 21. Utah's drinking laws are a bit odd, but you can buy alcoholic beverages almost everywhere in the state. Regarding package goods, you can buy 3.2% beer (see below if you're not sure what that means) and wine or malt coolers in supermarkets and convenience stores 7 days a week; stronger beer, wine, and hard liquor is available only at state-owned liquor stores and package agencies, which are closed Sundays and state holidays.

Buying liquor, beer, or wine by the drink is a bit more complicated. Most of the better restaurants can serve alcoholic beverages with meals starting at noon. In most cases, you'll have to ask for a drink; they won't offer to serve you one. Some establishments are licensed as taverns, and can sell 3.2% beer only. There are also private clubs, which aren't really private: They're essentially bars, and may or may not be attached to restaurants. You have to be a member to enter, but you can go in as a guest of a member or buy a 2-week membership, usually for $5. Private clubs can serve beginning at 10am Monday through Saturday and at noon on Sunday. Liquor by the drink cannot be sold after 1am Monday through Saturday or after midnight on Sunday. Compared to beer available elsewhere, 3.2% beer, which is only sold in Utah, Oklahoma, Colorado, and Kansas, does have less alcohol. According to the Budweiser people, 3.2% beer has about 4% alcohol by volume (which is equivalent to 3.2% alcohol by weight), while full-strength American beers have about 5% alcohol by volume.

Newspapers/Magazines   The state's two largest daily newspapers, both published in Salt Lake City, are the *Salt Lake City Tribune* and the *Deseret News.* Several other towns and regions have daily newspapers, and many smaller towns publish weeklies. You can get national newspapers such as *USA Today* and the *Wall Street Journal* on the streets of Salt Lake City and at major hotels, and you can find newspapers from other major U.S. cities at **Jeanie's Smoke Shop,** 156 S. State St., Salt Lake City (☎ **801/322-2817**), and **Hyatts Magazines,** 1350 E. State St., Salt Lake City (☎ **801/486-9925**), which also stocks a number of international periodicals and maps of Salt Lake City and other areas of the state. The above shops also carry a wide selection of magazines, and many major bookstores and convenience stores also stock current magazines.

Police   Dial ☎ **911** almost everywhere, except in a few rural areas where you should dial "0" (zero) for an operator.

Smoking   Utah is "smoke-free." The Utah Indoor Clean Air Act prohibits smoking in any public building or office and in all enclosed places of public access. This includes restaurants but not private clubs, lounges, or taverns.

Taxes   A combination of state and local sales taxes, from 6% to 7%, is added to your bill in all areas of Utah except Indian reservations. Local lodging taxes usually add an additional 3% or 4%.

Time Zone   Utah is on mountain time, 1 hour ahead of the West Coast and 2 hours behind the East Coast. The state recognizes daylight saving time, which is usually in effect from the first Sunday in April to the last Sunday in October.

Useful Telephone Numbers   For **road conditions** in Salt Lake City, call ☎ **801/ 964-6000;** for the rest of the state, call ☎ **800/492-2400.** The **poison control hotline** is ☎ **800/456-7707.**

Weather   For current statewide weather information, call ☎ **801/975-4499** or 801/524-5133.

For Foreign Visitors   4

American fads and fashions have spread across other parts of the world to such a degree that the United States may seem like familiar territory before your arrival. But there are still many peculiarities and uniquely American situations that any foreign visitor may find confusing or perplexing. This chapter will provide some specifics about getting to the United States as economically and effortlessly as possible, plus some helpful information about how things are done in Utah—from receiving mail to making a local or long-distance telephone call.

1 Preparing for Your Trip

ENTRY REQUIREMENTS

DOCUMENT REGULATIONS   Canadian nationals need only proof of Canadian residence to visit the United States. Citizens of the United Kingdom and Japan need only a current passport. Citizens of other countries, including Australia and New Zealand, usually need two documents: a valid passport with an expiration date at least 6 months later than the scheduled end of their visit to the United States and a tourist visa, available at no charge from a U.S. embassy or consulate.

To get a tourist or business visa to enter the United States, contact the nearest American embassy or consulate in your country; if there is none, you will have to apply in person in a country where there is a U.S. embassy or consulate. Present your passport, a passport-size photo of yourself, and a completed application, which is available through the embassy or consulate. You may be asked to provide information about how you plan to finance your trip or show a letter of invitation from a friend with whom you plan to stay. Those applying for a business visa may be asked to show evidence that they will not receive a salary in the United States. Be sure to check the length of stay on your visa; usually it is 6 months. If you want to stay longer, you may file for an extension with the Immigration and Naturalization Service once you are in the country. If permission to stay is granted, a new visa is not required unless you leave the United States and want to re-enter.

MEDICAL REQUIREMENTS   No inoculations are needed to enter the United States unless you are coming from, or have stopped over in, areas known to be suffering from epidemics, particularly cholera or yellow fever.

If you have a disease requiring treatment with medications containing narcotics or drugs requiring a syringe, carry a valid, signed generic prescription from your physician to allay any suspicions that you are smuggling drugs. The prescription brands you are accustomed to buying in your country may not be available in the United States.

CUSTOMS REQUIREMENTS   Every adult visitor may bring into the United States, for their own personal use, free of duty: 1 liter of wine or hard liquor; 200 cigarettes or 100 cigars (but no cigars from Cuba) or 1 pound of smoking tobacco; and $100 worth of gifts. These exemptions are offered to travelers who spend at least 72 hours in the United States and who have not claimed them within the preceding 6 months. It is altogether forbidden to bring into the country foodstuffs (particularly cheese, fruit, cooked meats, and canned goods) and plants (vegetables, seeds, tropical plants, and so on). Foreign tourists may bring in or take out up to $10,000 in U.S. or foreign currency with no formalities; larger sums must be declared to Customs on entering or leaving.

INSURANCE

Unlike most other countries, the United States does not have a national health-care system. Because the cost of medical care is extremely high, we strongly advise all travelers to secure health coverage before setting out on their trip.

You may want to take out a comprehensive travel policy that covers (for a relatively low premium) sickness or injury costs (medical, surgical, and hospital); loss or theft of your baggage; trip-cancellation costs; guarantee of bail in case you are arrested; costs of accident, repatriation, or death. Such packages (for example, "Europ Assistance" in Europe) are sold by automobile clubs at attractive rates, as well as by insurance companies and travel agencies and at some airports.

MONEY

The U.S. monetary system has a decimal base: One American **dollar** ($1) = 100 **cents** (100¢). Dollar bills commonly come in $1 (a "buck"), $5, $10, $20, $50, and $100 denominations (the last two are not welcome when paying for small purchases and are usually not accepted in taxis or at subway ticket booths). There are six coin denominations: 1¢ (one cent or a "penny"); 5¢ (five cents or a "nickel"); 10¢ (ten cents or a "dime"); 25¢ (twenty-five cents or a "quarter"); 50¢ (fifty cents or a "half dollar"); and the $1 pieces (both the older, large silver dollar and the newer, small Susan B. Anthony coin).

Traveler's checks in U.S. dollars are accepted at most hotels, motels, restaurants, and large stores. Sometimes picture identification is required. American Express, Thomas Cook, and Barclay's Bank traveler's checks are readily accepted in the United States.

Credit cards are the method of payment most widely used: Visa (BarclayCard in Britain), MasterCard (EuroCard in Europe, Access in Britain, Diamond in Japan), American Express, Discover, Diners Club, enRoute, JCB, and Carte Blanche, in descending order of acceptance. You can save yourself trouble by using "plastic" rather than cash or traveler's checks in 95% of all hotels, motels, restaurants, and retail stores. A credit card can also serve as a deposit for renting a car, as proof of identity, or as a "cash card," enabling you to draw money from automatic-teller machines (ATMs) that accept them.

If you plan to travel for several weeks or more in the United States, you may want to deposit enough money into your credit-card account to cover anticipated expenses and avoid finance charges in your absence. This also reduces the likelihood of your receiving an unwelcome big bill on your return.

You can telegraph money, or have it telegraphed to you very quickly, using the **Western Union** system (☎ **800/325-6000**).

SAFETY

While tourist areas are generally safe, crime is on the increase everywhere, and urban areas in the United States tend to be less safe than those in Europe or Japan. Visitors should always stay alert. This is particularly true of large U.S. cities. It's wise to ask the city's or area's tourist office if you're in doubt about which neighborhoods are unsafe.

Remember also that hotels are open to the public, and in a large hotel, security may not be able to screen everyone entering. Always lock your room door—don't assume that once inside your hotel you are automatically safe and no longer need be aware of your surroundings.

DRIVING   Safety while driving is particularly important. Question your rental agency about personal safety, or ask for a brochure of traveler safety tips when you pick up your car. Obtain written directions, or a map with the route marked in red, from the agency showing how to get to your destination. And, if possible, arrive and depart during daylight hours.

Recently more and more crime has involved cars and drivers. If you drive off a highway into a doubtful neighborhood, leave the area as quickly as possible. If you are involved in an accident, even on the highway, stay in your car with the doors locked until you assess the situation or until the police arrive. If you are bumped from behind on the street or are involved in a minor accident with no injuries and the situation appears to be suspicious, motion to the other driver to follow you. Never get out of your car in such situations, but drive to the nearest police station, service station, or all-night store.

If you see someone on the road who indicates a need for help, do not stop. Take note of the location, drive on to a well-lighted area, and telephone the police by dialing 911.

Park in well-lighted, well-traveled areas if possible. Always keep your car doors locked, whether attended or unattended. Never leave any packages or valuables in sight. If someone attempts to rob you or steal your car, do not try to resist the thief or carjacker, and report the incident to the police department immediately.

You may wish to contact the **Utah Travel Council** (☎ **800/200-1160**) to discuss your plans and ask their advice.

2 Getting to the U.S.

Travelers from overseas can take advantage of the APEX (Advance Purchase Excursion) fares offered by all the major U.S. and European carriers. Aside from these, attractive values are offered by Virgin Atlantic Airways from London to New York/Newark.

Airlines offering international flights into Salt Lake City include **American** (☎ 800/433-7300; 0181/572-5555 in London), **Continental** (☎ 801/359-9800; 4412/9377-6464 in the United Kingdom), **Delta** (☎ 800/221-1212 or 801/532-7123; 0800/414-767 in London), **Northwest** (☎ 800/225-2525 or 801/447-4747),

TWA (☎ 800/221-2000 or 801/539-1111; 0181/814-0707 in London), and **United** (☎ 800/241-6522; 0181/990-9900 in London). International travelers can also take flights to O'Hare International Airport in Chicago, DIA in Denver, LAX in Los Angeles, and JFK International Airport in New York, and catch connecting flights to Salt Lake City from there.

Visitors arriving by air, no matter what the port of entry, should cultivate patience and resignation before setting foot on U.S. soil. Getting through Immigration control may take as long as 2 hours on some days, especially summer weekends, so have your guidebook or other reading material handy. Add the time it takes to clear Customs and you'll see that you should allow extra time for delays when planning connections between international and domestic flights—an average of 2 to 3 hours at least.

In contrast, travelers arriving by car or by rail from Canada will find border-crossing formalities streamlined to the vanishing point. And air travelers from Canada, Bermuda, and some places in the Caribbean can sometimes go through Customs and Immigration at the point of departure, which is much quicker.

3 Getting Around the U.S.

BY PLANE Some large U.S. airlines offer travelers on their trans-Atlantic or trans-Pacific flights special discount tickets for any of their U.S. destinations (American Airlines' Visit USA program and Delta's Discover America program, for example). These tickets are not for sale in the United States, and must therefore be purchased before you leave your foreign point of departure. These programs are the best, easiest, and fastest ways to see the United States at low cost. You should obtain information well in advance from your travel agent or the office of the airline concerned, since the conditions attached to these discount tickets can be changed without advance notice.

BY RAIL Amtrak (☎ 800/USA-RAIL) connects Salt Lake City to both the East and West Coasts. International visitors can buy a **USA Railpass,** good for 15 or 30 days of unlimited travel on Amtrak, available through many foreign travel agents. Prices in 1998 for a 15-day pass are $260 off-peak, $375 peak; a 30-day pass costs $350 off-peak, $480 peak (off-peak is from August 21 to June 16). With a foreign passport, you can also buy passes at some Amtrak offices in the United States, including those in San Francisco, Los Angeles, Chicago, New York, Miami, Boston, and Washington, D.C.

Amtrak also offers low-cost passes available to anyone, covering certain regions of the country. Reservations are generally required for train travel and should be made for each part of your trip as early as possible.

Visitors should also be aware of the limitations of long-distance rail travel in the United States. With a few notable exceptions, service is rarely up to European standards: Delays are common, routes are limited and often infrequently served, and fares are rarely significantly lower than discount airfares. Thus, cross-country train travel should be approached with caution.

BY BUS The cheapest way to travel the United States is by bus. **Greyhound/ Trailways** (☎ 800/231-2222), the sole nationwide bus line, offers an **Ameripass** (☎ 888/454-7277) for unlimited nationwide travel for 7 days (for $199), 15 days (for $299), 30 days (for $409), and 60 days (for $599). Be aware that bus travel in the United States can be both slow and uncomfortable, so this option isn't for everyone. In addition, bus stations are often located in undesirable neighborhoods.

BY CAR Because much of Utah is rural, with limited or nonexistent public transportation, the best way to explore the state is by car. Many car-rental companies (see city listings) offer unlimited-mileage weekly specials that can be quite affordable.

FAST FACTS: For the Foreign Traveler

Automobile Organizations Auto clubs will supply maps, suggested routes, guidebooks, accident and bail-bond insurance, and emergency road service. The major auto club in the United States is the **American Automobile Association (AAA),** with close to 1,000 offices nationwide, including offices in Salt Lake City, Ogden, and Orem. Members of some foreign auto clubs have reciprocal arrangements with the AAA and enjoy its services at no charge. If you belong to an auto club, inquire about AAA reciprocity before you leave home. The AAA can also provide you with an **International Driving Permit** validating your foreign license. You may be able to join AAA even if you are not a member of a reciprocal club. For AAA emergency road service, call ☎ **800/222-4357.** In addition, some automobile-rental agencies now provide these services; ask about their availability when you rent your car.

Automobile Rentals To rent a car, you need a major credit card and a valid driver's license. You usually need to be at least 25 years old. Some companies do rent to younger people, but add a daily surcharge. Be sure to return your car with the same amount of gas you started out with; rental companies charge excessive prices for gasoline. See "Getting Around" in chapter 3.

Business Hours Banks are usually open weekdays from 9am to 3 or 4pm, often until 6pm on Friday, and sometimes on Saturday. There's 24-hour access to the automatic-teller machines (ATMs) at most banks, plus in many shopping centers and other outlets.

Generally, business offices are open weekdays from 9am to 5pm. Stores are open 6 days a week, with some open on Sunday, too; department stores usually stay open until 9pm at least 1 day a week. Discount stores and supermarkets are often open later than other stores, and some supermarkets are open 24 hours a day.

Climate See "When to Go" in chapter 3.

Currency See "Money" in "Preparing for Your Trip," above.

Currency Exchange The "foreign-exchange bureaus" so common in Europe are rare in the United States. They're at major international airports, and there are a few in most major cities, but they're nonexistent in medium-size cities and small towns. Try to avoid having to change foreign money, or traveler's checks denominated in anything other than U.S. dollars, at small-town banks, or even at branches in a big city. In fact, leave any currency other than U.S. dollars at home (except the cash you need for the taxi or bus ride home when you return to your own country); otherwise, your own currency may prove more nuisance to you than it's worth.

Electricity The United States uses 110-120 volts, 60 cycles, compared to 220-240 volts, 50 cycles, as in most of Europe. In addition to a 100-volt converter, small appliances of non-American manufacture, such as hair dryers or shavers, will require a plug adapter, with two flat, parallel pins.

Embassies/Consulates All embassies are located in the nation's capital, Washington, D.C.; some consulates are located in major cities, and most nations have a mission to the United Nations in New York City. Foreign visitors can obtain telephone numbers for their embassies and consulates by calling "Information" in

Washington, D.C. (☎ **202/555-1212**). The following countries have consulates in the Salt Lake City area: **Finland,** 79 S. Main St. (☎ 801/246-5259); **France,** 175 E. 400 South (☎ 801/524-1000); **Italy,** 1784 W. 9580 South, South Jordan (☎ 801/254-7500); **Mexico,** 458 E. 200 South (☎ 801/521-8502); **New Zealand,** 1379 N. Brookhurst Circle, Centerville (☎ 801/296-2494); **Norway,** 958 W. 3265 South (☎ 801/978-9325); and **Switzerland,** 1455 S. 1100 East (☎ 801/487-0450).

Emergencies   Call ☎ **911** for fire, police, and ambulance. If you encounter such traveler's problems as sickness, accident, or lost or stolen baggage, call Traveler's Aid, an organization that specializes in helping distressed travelers. (Check local directories for the location nearest you.) U.S. hospitals have emergency rooms, with a special entrance where you will be admitted for quick attention.

Gasoline (Petrol)   One U.S. gallon equals 3.75 liters, while 1.2 U.S. gallons equals 1 Imperial gallon. You'll notice there are several grades (and price levels) of gasoline available at most gas stations, and that their names change from company to company. Unleaded gasoline with the highest octane is the most expensive, but most rental cars will run fine with the least expensive "regular" unleaded.

Holidays   On the following legal national holidays, banks, government offices, post offices, and some government-run attractions are closed: January 1 (New Year's Day), third Monday in January (Martin Luther King, Jr. Day), third Monday in February (Presidents' Day), last Monday in May (Memorial Day), July 4 (Independence Day), first Monday in September (Labor Day), second Monday in October (Columbus Day), November 11 (Veterans' Day/Armistice Day), fourth Thursday in November (Thanksgiving Day), and December 25 (Christmas). The Tuesday following the first Monday in November is Election Day and is a legal holiday in presidential-election years.

Stores and some restaurants often close only for New Year's Day, Easter, and Christmas.

Legal Aid   The foreign tourist, unless positively identified as a member of organized crime or a drug ring, will probably never become involved with the American legal system. If you are stopped for a minor infraction, such as speeding or some other traffic violation, never attempt to pay the fine directly to a police officer; you may be arrested on the much more serious charge of attempted bribery. Pay fines by mail or directly to the clerk of the court. If you are accused of a more serious offense, it's wise to say and do nothing before consulting a lawyer. Under U.S. law, an arrested person is allowed one telephone call to a party of his or her choice; call your embassy or consulate.

Liquor Laws   See "Liquor Laws" under "Fast Facts: Utah," in chapter 3.

Mail   If you want your mail to follow you on your vacation and you aren't sure of your address, your mail can be sent to you, in your name, c/o General Delivery at the main post office of the city or region where you expect to be. The addressee must pick it up in person and produce proof of identity (driver's license, passport, etc.).

Mailboxes are blue with a blue-and-white eagle logo, and carry the inscription UNITED STATES POSTAL SERVICE. Within the United States, it costs 20¢ to mail a standard-size postcard and 32¢ to send an oversize postcard (larger than 4 1/4 by 6 inches, or 10.8 by 15.4 centimeters). Letters that weigh up to 1 ounce (that's about five pages, 8 by 11-inches or 20.5 by 28.2 centimeters) cost 32¢, plus 23¢ for each additional ounce. A postcard to Mexico costs 35¢, a half-ounce letter 66¢;

a postcard to Canada costs 40¢, a 1-ounce letter 52¢. A postcard to Europe, Australia, New Zealand, the Far East, South America, and elsewhere costs 40¢, while a letter is 60¢ for each half ounce.

If your mail is addressed to a U.S. destination, don't forget to add the five-digit postal code, or ZIP (zone improvement plan) code, after the two-letter abbreviation of the state to which the mail is addressed (UT for Utah, CA for California, NY for New York, and so on).

Newspapers/Magazines   National newspapers generally available in Utah include the *New York Times, USA Today,* and the *Wall Street Journal.* National news magazines include *Newsweek, Time,* and *U.S. News & World Report.* The state's major daily newspapers are the *Salt Lake City Tribune* and the *Deseret News,* which is owned by the LDS Church.

Post   See "Mail," above.

Radio & Television   Six coast-to-coast networks—ABC, CBS, NBC, PBS (Public Broadcasting Service), Fox, and CNN (Cable Network News)—play a major part in American life. In Utah, television viewers usually have a choice of at least a dozen channels via cable or satellite, although some of the major Salt Lake City hotels offer only five or six. PBS and the cable channel Arts and Entertainment (A&E) broadcast a number of British programs. You'll also find a wide choice of local radio stations, each broadcasting particular kinds of talk shows and/or music—classical, country, jazz, pop—punctuated by news broadcasts and frequent commercials.

Safety   See "Safety" in "Preparing for Your Trip," above.

Taxes   In the United States, there is no VAT (value-added tax) or other indirect tax at a national level. Every state, as well as each city and county, has the right to levy its own local tax on all purchases, including hotel and restaurant checks, airline tickets, and so on. Sales taxes in Utah vary, but usually total about 6%. An exception is the tax on lodging, which often runs to 10%. Sales tax is not included in the price tags you'll see on merchandise. These taxes are not refundable.

There is a $10 Customs tax, payable on entry to the United States, and a $6 departure tax.

Telephone, Fax & Telegraph   The telephone system in the United States is run by private corporations, so rates, especially for long-distance service, can vary widely even on calls made from public telephones. Local calls in the United States usually cost 25¢ from pay telephones, but some of the more expensive hotels charge 50¢ to 75¢.

In the past few years, many American companies have installed voice-mail systems, so be prepared to deal with a machine instead of a receptionist if calling a business number.

For long-distance or international calls, it's most economical to charge the call to a telephone charge card or a credit card. If using change, the pay phone will instruct you on how much to deposit and when to deposit it into the slot at the top of the telephone box.

For long-distance calls in the United States, dial 1 followed by the area code and number you want. For direct overseas calls, first dial 011, followed by the country code (Australia, 61; Republic of Ireland, 353; New Zealand, 64; United Kingdom, 44; and so on), and then by the city code (for example, 171 or 181 for London, 21 for Birmingham) and the number of the person you wish to call.

Before calling from a hotel room, always ask the hotel phone operator if there are any telephone surcharges. There almost always are—often as much as 75¢ or $1, even for a local call. These charges are best avoided by using a public phone, calling collect, or using a telephone charge card.

For reversed-charge or collect calls and for person-to-person calls, dial 0 (zero, not the letter "O") followed by the area code and number you want; an operator will then come on the line, and you should specify that you are calling collect, or person-to-person, or both. If your operator-assisted call is international, immediately ask to speak with an overseas operator.

For local **directory assistance** ("information"), dial ☎ **1-411;** for **long-distance information,** dial 1, then the appropriate area code and 555-1212.

Fax facilities are readily available in hotels, and 24-hour service is available at numerous copy centers.

Like the telephone system, **telegraph** services are provided by private corporations such as ITT, MCI, and, above all, **Western Union.** You can bring your telegram in to the nearest Western Union office (there are hundreds across the country), or dictate it over the phone (☎ **800/325-6000**). You can also telegraph money, or have it telegraphed to you, very quickly over the Western Union system.

Time   The United States is divided into four **time zones** (six, including Alaska and Hawaii). From east to west, these are: eastern standard time (EST); central standard time (CST); mountain standard time (MST), which includes Utah; Pacific standard time (PST); Alaska standard time (AST); and Hawaii standard time (HST). Always keep time zones in mind if you are traveling (or even telephoning) long distances in the United States. For example, noon in New York City (EST) is 11am in Chicago (CST), 10am in Salt Lake City (MST), 9am in Los Angeles (PST), 8am in Anchorage (AST), and 7am in Honolulu (HST).

Daylight saving time (DST) is in effect in Utah and most of the country from the first Sunday in April through the last Saturday in October (actually, the change is made at 2am on Sunday). Daylight saving time moves the clock 1 hour ahead of standard time. Note that Arizona (except for the Navajo nation), Hawaii, part of Indiana, and Puerto Rico do not observe DST.

Tipping   Some rules of thumb: bartenders, 10–15%; bellhops, at least 50¢ per bag, or $2–$3 for a lot of luggage; cab drivers, 10% of the fare; cafeterias and fast-food restaurants, no tip; chambermaids, $1 per day; checkroom attendants, $1 per garment; theater ushers, no tip; gas-station attendants, no tip; hairdressers and barbers, 15–20%; waiters and waitresses, 15–20% of the check; valet-parking attendants, $1.

Toilets   Foreign visitors often complain that public toilets are hard to find in most U.S. cities. There are few on the streets, but you can usually find a clean one in a visitor information center, shopping mall, restaurant, hotel, museum, department or discount store, or service station (although service-station facilities often leave much to be desired). Note, however, a growing practice in some restaurants of displaying a sign: REST ROOMS ARE FOR PATRONS ONLY. You can just ignore this sign or, better yet, avoid arguments by paying for a cup of coffee or soft drink, which will qualify you as a patron.

The Active Vacation Planner

U tah is one big outdoor adventure, with millions of acres of public lands where you can cast for trout or herd cattle, go rock climbing or four-wheeling, sail or ski—whatever your pleasure. Here you'll find five spectacular national parks, seven national monuments, two national recreation areas, one national historic site, seven national forests, some 22 million acres administered by the federal Bureau of Land Management, and 45 state parks. But who's counting? It's enough to say that almost 80% of Utah's 85,000 square miles are yours to enjoy.

If you're a seasoned active traveler, you might want to skip section 1; it should be a good primer, though, for those who are new to this kind of travel or who haven't been to Utah before. The next section provides some up-to-date information on visiting Utah's national parks. Following that are lists of activities you can pursue in Utah, from A to Z. Find your favorite activity, and we'll point you to the best places in the state to pursue your interest, or give you the general information you need to get started. You'll find more details in the appropriate regional chapters. Have fun!

1 Preparing for Your Active Vacation

WHAT TO PACK—AND WHAT TO RENT

Planning for a trip into the great outdoors immediately brings to mind those cartoons of vacationers loaded down with equipment, surrounded by golf clubs, skis, cameras, tents, canoes, bikes, and those wonderful Coleman lanterns and coolers that are fixtures of garages and basements across America. If a car or light truck is your mode of travel, try to keep the heaviest items between the axles and as close to the floor of your vehicle as possible; this helps improve handling, especially in today's lighter cars. If you have a bike rack on the rear bumper, make sure the bike tires are far from the exhaust pipe; an owner of one bike shop told us he does a good business replacing exhaust-cooked mountain-bike tires. Those with roof racks will want to measure the total height of their packed cars before leaving home. Underground parking garages often have less than 7 feet of clearance.

One alternative to carrying all that stuff is to rent it. Many sporting-goods shops in Utah rent camping equipment; virtually all ski areas and popular mountain-bike areas offer rentals; and major boating centers such as Lake Powell and Lake Flaming Gorge rent boats. You'll find many rental sources listed throughout this book. There's also a complete rental department at **Recreational Equipment, Inc.,** better known as REI, 3285 E. 3300 South in Salt Lake City (☎ **801/486-2100**).

In packing for your trip, you'll want to be prepared for all your favorite activities, of course, but also keep in mind that this is a land of extremes, with an often unforgiving climate and terrain. Those planning to hike and bike should take more drinking-water containers than they think they'll need—experts recommend at least 1 gallon of water per person per day on the trail—as well as good-quality sunblock with a high SPF, hats and other protective clothing, and sunglasses with ultraviolet protection. Summer visitors will want to carry rain gear for the typical afternoon thunderstorms, and jackets or sweaters for cool evenings. Winter visitors will need not only warm parkas and hats, but also lighter clothing—the bright sun at midday, even in the mountains, can make it feel like June.

DOING IT YOURSELF VS. USING AN OUTFITTER

Except for those instances in which safety or skill is a factor, we prefer the do-it-yourself vacation route, especially in Utah, which is really a do-it-yourself kind of state. You'll have no trouble finding detailed topographic maps—essential for wilderness trips—and whatever equipment and supplies you need will likely be readily available. In addition, we found that—despite the well-publicized cuts in budgets and work forces in national parks, recreation areas, and forests—every single ranger we encountered was more than willing to take the time to help visitors plan their backcountry trips. And many sporting-goods shops are staffed by area residents who know their locales and activities well, and are happy to help the would-be adventurer. In almost all cases, if you ask, there will be someone willing and able to help you make the most of your trip.

However, some activities, such as cattle driving, require an outfitter or adventure-travel operator. Other activities, such as rafting or four-wheeling, require equipment you'd have to buy or rent if you were to go on your own; besides, an outfitter might be able to take you somewhere or help you do something you couldn't do yourself. Some travelers just like the camaraderie of a group of like-minded adventurers; others don't want to deal with making all the arrangements on their own. And a professional is a must if you're attempting a dangerous sport, such as rock climbing, or trying something new; then it's best to go with someone who knows the ropes.

For those who want to go with an outfitter or adventure-travel operator, we've listed below some of the most respected and reliable companies operating in Utah. Most specialize in small groups and have trips for various levels of ability and physical condition. They also offer trips in a range of price categories, from basic to luxurious, and of varying length.

American Wilderness Experience, 2820-A Wilderness Place, P.O. Box 1486, Boulder, CO 80306 (☎ **800/444-0099** or 303/444-2622; fax 303/444-3999), offers mountain biking, hiking, horseback riding, cattle-driving, and rafting excursions throughout the West, including numerous multiday trips in Utah. AWE's website is www.gorp.com/awe.

Backcountry Tours, P.O. Box 4029, Bozeman, MT 59772 (☎ **800/575-1540** or 406/586-3556; fax 406/586-4288), provides guided multiday mountain biking, hiking, and combination tours in the Bryce Canyon and Zion national parks areas, and biking and off-road tours in the Moab area. The company's website is www.backcountrytours.com.

Backroads, 801 Cedar St., Berkeley, CA 94710-1800 (☎ **800/GO-ACTIVE** or 510/527-1555; fax 510/527-1444), offers a variety of multiday guided biking and hiking tours to the national parks in southern Utah. There's a hiking tour of Arches, Canyonlands, and Capitol Reef; a road-bike tour of Zion, Bryce, and the Grand Canyon; a mountain-bike tour of Arches, Canyonlands, and the Moab area; and a hiking-only plus a combination hiking-and-biking tour of Zion and Bryce. You can either bring your own bicycle or rent one from them. Their website is www.backroads.com.

Go West, 305 S. Congress Ave., Austin, TX 78704 (☎ **512/912-2500;** fax 512/912-2552), can put together almost any kind of vacation trip you want—skiing in winter, backpacking or biking in summer. It's a one-stop shop. Their website is www.GoWest.com.

Moguls Ski & Snowboard Tours, 5589 Arapahoe Ave., #208, Boulder, CO 80303 (☎ **800/666-4857** or 303/440-7921; fax 303/440-4160; 800/929-7300 for reservations), will put together a customized ski package from start to finish. The company's website is www.skimoguls.com.

Roads Less Traveled, 2840 Wilderness Place, #F, Boulder, CO 80301 (☎ **800/488-8483** or 303/413-0938; fax 303/413-0926), offers quality backcountry hiking and biking tours throughout the Southwest, including Bryce and Zion national parks. Their website is www.roadslesstraveled.com.

STAYING SAFE & HEALTHY IN THE OUTDOORS

The wide-open spaces and rugged landscape that make Utah such a beautiful place to explore can also be hazardous to your health, especially if you're not used to the extreme climate; see "Health & Insurance" in chapter 3 for details on dealing with desert climes and high altitudes. Since the isolation of many of the areas you'll seek out means there may be no one around to help in an emergency, the answer is to be prepared, like any good Boy Scout. See "What to Pack—and What to Rent," above, for tips on what to bring to protect yourself from Utah's blazing sun. Also, be sure to carry a basic first-aid kit. Most important of all, check with park offices, park rangers, and other local outdoor specialists about current conditions before heading out.

OUTDOOR ETIQUETTE

Many of the wonderful outdoor areas you'll be exploring in Utah are quite isolated; although you're probably not the first human being to set foot there, you may feel like you are. Not too long ago, the rule of thumb was to "leave only footprints"; these days, we're trying not to do even that. It's relatively easy to be a good outdoor citizen—it's mostly common sense. Pack out all trash, stay on established trails, be especially careful not to pollute water, and, in general, do your best to have as little impact on the environment as possible. Some hikers go even further, carrying a small trash bag to pick up what others may have left behind.

2 Visiting Utah's National Parks

For many people, including us, the best part of a Utah vacation is exploring the state's five national parks. Unfortunately, these beautiful national treasures have become too popular; they're being overrun with visitors at a time when the federal government is cutting budgets, making it difficult for the parks to cope with their own success.

To get the most from your national-park visit, try to go in the off-season. The parks are busiest in the summer, when most children are out of school, so try to visit at almost any other time. Fall is usually the best season. Spring is okay, but it can be windy and there may be snow at higher elevations. Winter can be delightful if you don't mind snow and cold. If you have to travel in summer, be patient. Allow extra time for traffic jams and standing in lines, and try to hike some of the longer and lesser-used trails. Rangers will be able to tell you which trails are best for getting away from the crowds.

One way to save money if you'll be visiting a number of national parks and monuments within a year is to buy a **Golden Eagle Pass,** $50 at press time, which allows the bearer, plus everyone in his or her vehicle, free admission. Camping fees are not included. The **Golden Age Passport,** for those 62 and older, has a one-time fee of $10 and provides free admission to parks plus a 50% savings on camping fees. And the **Golden Access Passport,** free for U.S. citizens who are permanently disabled according to federal law, allows free access to parks and 50% off camping fees. Passes are available at the parks.

3 Outdoor Activities A to Z

For a state that's largely desert, Utah certainly has a lot of lakes and reservoirs, from huge Lake Powell in the south to Flaming Gorge Lake in the north, and numerous reservoirs in between. We highly recommend both lakes, which are administered as national recreation areas and have complete marinas with boat rentals. Also, don't forget the lesser-known state parks, such as Jordanelle near Park City or Quail Creek—with the state's warmest water—near St. George. One of our favorite lakes is picturesque but chilly Strawberry Reservoir, southeast of Park City in the Uinta National Forest. For brochures on boating opportunities in Utah's state parks as well as information on state boating laws, contact **Utah Parks and Recreation** (☎ 801/538-7220).

CAMPING

Utah is a perfect place to camp; in fact, at some destinations, such as Canyonlands National Park, it's practically mandatory. Just about every community of any size in the state has at least one commercial campground, and several have more campgrounds than motels. Campsites are available at all the national parks and national recreation areas, but they're often crowded in the summer. However, those who can stand being without hot showers for a day or so can often find free or very reasonable campsites just outside the national parks, in national forests or on Bureau of Land Management lands. Another good bet are Utah's state parks; among those with the best campgrounds are Kodachrome, just outside Bryce National Park; Coral Pink Sand Dunes, just west of Kanab; and Snow Canyon, near St. George.

CATTLE DRIVES

Opportunities abound in the western states for you to play cowboy on cattle drives that last from a day to a week or longer. You can actually take part in the riding and roping, just like Billy Crystal in *City Slickers.* You'll certainly get a feel for what it was like to be on a cattle drive 100 years ago, but the conditions are generally a lot more comfortable than what "real" cowboys experienced. The food will be a lot better, that's for sure. Each cattle drive is different, though, so you'll want to ask very specific questions about food, sleeping arrangements, and other conditions before plunking down your money. It's also a good idea to book your trip as early as possible. **American Wilderness Experience,** 2820-A Wilderness Place, P.O. Box 1486, Boulder, CO 80306 (☎ 800/444-0099 or 303/444-2622; fax 303/444-3999) can help you plan your Utah cattle-drive adventure.

FISHING

Utah has over 1,000 lakes and countless streams and rivers, with species that include rainbow, cutthroat, Mackinaw, and brown trout, plus striped bass, crappie, bluegill, walleye, and whitefish. Lake Flaming Gorge and Lake Powell are both great fishing lakes, but Strawberry Reservoir is Utah's premier trout fishery—in fact, it's one of the best in the West. Fly-fishing is especially popular in the Park City area and in the streams of the Wasatch-Cache National Forest above Ogden. Contact the **Utah Division of Wildlife Resources,** 1596 W. North Temple, Salt Lake City, UT 84116 (☎ **801/538-4700**), for a copy of the current *Utah Fishing Proclamation.*

Fishing licenses are available from state wildlife offices and sporting-goods stores. Keep in mind that several fishing locations, such as Lake Powell and Lake Flaming Gorge, cross state boundaries, and you'll need licenses from the adjoining state to fish those waters.

FOUR-WHEELING

The Moab area and Canyonlands National Park in particular are probably the best-known four-wheeling destinations in Utah, but there are also plenty of old mining and logging roads throughout the national forests and on BLM land. Those with dune buggies like to head for Coral Pink Sand Dunes State Park, west of Kanab. Throughout this book, we've tried to include information on where four-wheeling is and is not allowed; still, you should always make sure before you start out. Brochures and other information on four-wheel driving in Utah can be obtained from the **Utah Division of Parks and Recreation** (☎ **801/538-7220**), the **U.S. Forest Service** (☎ **801/524-5030**), and the **Bureau of Land Management** ☎ **801/ 539-4001**).

GOLF

Utah golf courses are known for their beautiful scenery and variety of challenging terrain. They range from mountain courses set among the beautiful forests of the Wasatch to desert courses with scenic views of Utah's spectacular red rock country. The warm climate of St. George, in Utah's southwest corner, makes it a perfect location for year-round golf, and it has become the premier destination for visiting golfers. *Golf Digest* recently chose St. George's Sunbrook Golf Course as Utah's best course. In the northern part of the state, the course at the Homestead Resort near Park City is well worth the trip. A free directory of the state's more than 80 courses is available from the **Utah Travel Council** (☎ **800/200-1160** or 801/538-1030).

HIKING

Hiking is the best—and sometimes the only—way to see many of Utah's most beautiful and exciting areas, and the state is interlaced with hiking trails. Particularly recommended destinations for hikers are all five of Utah's national parks. You'll find splendid forest trails and more of a wilderness experience at Flaming Gorge National Recreation Area and in the Wasatch Mountains around Ogden and Logan. Those looking for spectacular panoramic views won't do better than the trails on the BLM land around Moab. In America's newest national monument, Grand Staircase-Escalante, east of Bryce Canyon, you'll discover few developed trails but numerous undeveloped hiking routes that explore some of the nation's most rugged country. State parks with especially good trails include Kodachrome, near Bryce Canyon National Park; Jordanelle, near Park City; Dead Horse Point, just outside the Island in the Sky District of Canyonlands National Park; and Escalante, in the town of Escalante.

Life on the Open Road: Planning an RV or Tenting Vacation to Utah

One of the best ways to explore Utah, especially in the warm months, is in an RV—a motor home, truck camper, or camper trailer—or a tent, if you don't mind roughing it a bit more. If you own an RV, we advise you to have the mechanical systems checked out thoroughly, keeping in mind that there are some extremely steep grades in Utah; once that's done, pack up and go. If you don't have an RV or a tent, we suggest that you consider renting one for your Utah trip.

Why Camp?   One advantage to this type of travel is that many of the places you'll want to go, such as Canyonlands National Park, don't offer any lodging. If you can't accommodate yourself, you'll end up sleeping 30 or 40 miles away and missing those spectacular sunrises and sunsets, and that inexplicable feeling of contentment that comes from living the experience rather than just visiting it. If you have special dietary requirements, you won't have to worry about trying to find a restaurant that can meet your needs; you'll be able to cook for yourself, either in your motor home or trailer or on a camp stove.

There are disadvantages, of course. Tents, small trailers, and campers can be cramped, and even the most luxurious motor homes and trailers provide somewhat close quarters. Facilities in most commercial campgrounds are less than what you'd expect in moderately-priced motels; and if you cook your own meals, you miss the opportunity to experience the local cuisine. But, all this aside, camping is just plain fun—especially in a setting as spectacular as this one.

Renting an RV   Camping to save money is possible if you limit your equipment to a tent, a pop-up tent trailer, or a small pickup-truck camper, but renting a motor home will probably end up costing almost as much as driving a compact car, staying in moderately-priced motels, and eating in family-style restaurants and cafes. That's because the motor home will go only one-third as far on a gallon of gas as your compact car will, and they're expensive to rent—generally between $1,000 and $1,100 per week in mid-summer, when rates are highest.

If you're flying into the area and renting an RV when you arrive, choose your starting point carefully; rates vary depending on the city in which you pick up your

When you prepare for a hike, keep in mind weather conditions, such as the brutal summer heat around St. George and the likelihood of ice and snow on high mountain trails from fall through spring. Because of loose rock and gravel on trails in the southern part of the state, good hiking boots with aggressive soles and firm ankle support are needed.

HORSEBACK RIDING

It's fun to see the Old West the way the pioneers of 100 years ago did—from the back of a horse. Although you won't find many dude ranches in Utah, there are plenty of stables and outfitters who lead rides lasting from 1 hour to several days. We particularly recommend the rides at Bryce and Zion national parks, although you're likely to be surrounded by a lot of other riders and hikers. If you'd like a bit more solitude, head north to the mountains around Logan in the Wasatch Front or Flaming Gorge National Recreation Area. See the relevant regional chapters for outfitters and stables in those areas.

RV. Cruise America, one of the country's largest RV rental companies, quoted us a weekly rate of $1,093 for a 23-foot motor home for July 1998, if we started out in Salt Lake City; the rate was $1,032 for the same motor home if we rented it in Las Vegas, Nevada. Both rates included 1,000 free miles. Since most of Utah's national parks are closer to Las Vegas than Salt Lake City anyway, you could save by starting and ending your trip in Las Vegas. Cruise America also rents truck campers, complete with truck. For information, contact **Cruise America** (☎ **800/327-7799** or fax 602/464-7321). Their website is www.cruiseamerica.com.

Choosing a Campground   Once you've got a rig or tent, you'll need a place to put it, of course. Camping in the national parks, other federal lands, state parks, and many communities is discussed in the following sections of the book. For a brochure on the excellent campgrounds in Utah's state parks, contact the **Utah Division of Parks and Recreation** (☎ **801/538-7220;** 800/322-3770 for campground reservations). To find out about U.S. Forest Service facilities throughout the state, call ☎ **801/524-5030.** Most of Utah's national park campgrounds are assigned on a first-come, first-served basis only. You should contact each park individually for details on camping there; see the appropriate destination chapters.

A nationwide directory of KOA franchise campgrounds (there are 15 in Utah) is available free at any KOA campground, or by mail for $3 from **Kampgrounds of America (KOA), Inc.,** Executive Offices, Billings, MT 59114-0558.

Members of the **American Automobile Association (AAA)** can request the club's free *Southwestern CampBook* (☎ **800/222-4357**), which includes campgrounds and RV parks in Utah, Arizona, Colorado, and New Mexico. And several massive campground directories can be purchased in major bookstores, including our favorite, *Trailer Life Campground RV Park & Services Directory,* published annually by TL Enterprises, Inc., 2575 Vista Del Mar Drive, Ventura, CA 93001-2575 (☎ **800/234-3450**), which sells for about $20.

HOUSEBOATING

Among the best ways to experience either Lake Powell or Flaming Gorge Lake is from the comfort of a houseboat. Marinas at each of these national recreation areas have them for rent, although you'll find the best selection at Lake Powell. Essentially floating RVs, houseboats provide all the comforts of home—toilets, showers, sleeping quarters, and full kitchens—but in somewhat tighter quarters. Some of the larger ones have facilities for up to a dozen people. And you don't have to be an accomplished boater to drive one of these things: Houseboats are easy to maneuver, and can't go very fast. No boating license is required, but you'll need to reserve your houseboat well in advance, especially for summer use, and send in a sizable deposit.

MOUNTAIN BIKING

Although there are a few areas where road biking is popular, Utah really belongs to mountain bikers. With some of the grades you'll find, be sure you have plenty of gears. Moab claims to be Utah's mountain-biking capital, but there's no dearth of opportunities in other parts of the state, either. Be aware that mountain bikes must remain on designated motor-vehicle roads in most national parks, but are welcome almost everywhere in areas administered by the U.S. Forest Service and Bureau of Land Management. In addition to the exciting and often challenging slickrock trails of Moab, you'll find excellent trail systems just outside Zion and Bryce Canyon national parks; we also like the 30-mile Historic Union Pacific Rail Trail bike path at Park City and the warm-weather biking at Brian Head Ski Resort near St. George. For a free copy of the annual *Bicycle Utah Vacation Guide,* contact **Bicycle Utah,** P.O. Box 738, Park City, UT 74060 (☎ **435/649-5806**). The website is www.bicycleutah.com.

RIVER TRIPS

The Green and Colorado Rivers are considered to be among America's top destinations for both serious white-water as well as flat-water rafting; they're also popular with kayakers and canoeists. A favorite river trip, with plenty of white water, is down the Green River through Dinosaur National Monument. Trips on the Green also start in the town of Green River, north of Moab.

The Colorado River sees more boaters than the Green, though, and has a greater range of conditions, from flat, glassy waters—you just float along—to rapids so rough they can't be run at all. Most Colorado River trips originate in Moab. Several companies there will rent you a raft, canoe, or kayak, give you some instruction, and then wish you luck. They'll also help you decide which stretches of river are suitable for your abilities and thrill-seeking level, and can arrange for a pick-up at the take-out point. See the appropriate chapter for details on contacting these outfitters.

Although river trips through the Grand Canyon, which we discuss in the chapter on Utah's Dixie, are very popular, they're actually too popular for us, especially in mid-summer when rafts are bumper-to-bumper. A worthwhile and lesser-known river trip, in the Four Corners area, is along the San Juan River in Bluff. This relaxing excursion will take you to relatively unknown Native American archaeological sites and striking rock formations.

A recorded report on statewide river flows and reservoir information is available from the **Colorado Basin River Forecast Center** (☎ 801/539-1311). You can obtain information on river rafting from the **Bureau of Land Management** (☎ 801/ 539-4001), and be sure to request a copy of *Raft Utah* from the **Utah Travel Council** (☎ **800/200-1160** or 801/538-1030).

ROCK CLIMBING

This dizzying sport is growing in popularity in Utah. It's growing so much, in fact, that several popular areas have imposed moratoriums on bolting, and allow climbers to use existing bolt holes only. Among the more dramatic rock-climbing spots is Zion National Park, where it's as much a spectator sport as participatory activity. You'll also find some inviting walls of stone in Snow Canyon State Park near St. George, in Logan Canyon, and throughout the Wasatch Mountains in the Salt Lake City area.

For details on where you're allowed to climb and other information on climbing in Utah, contact the **Utah Travel Council** (☎ **800/220-1160** or 801/538-1030) or the government agency that controls the land you're interested in (see "Visitor Information" in chapter 3).

SKIING & OTHER WINTER SPORTS

Utah residents like to brag that the state has "the greatest snow on earth"—and one winter trip will make it clear that they just might be right. Utah's ski resorts are characterized by absolutely splendid powder, runs as scary or as mellow as you'd like, and a next-door-neighbor friendliness many of us had come to believe was extinct. With a few notable exceptions—particularly Park City and Deer Valley—you won't find the poshness and amenities that dominate many of the ski resorts next door in Colorado, but you won't find the high prices either. What you will discover are top-notch ski areas that are surprisingly easy to reach—half are within an hour's drive of Salt Lake City Airport. And they're relatively uncrowded, too: Utah generally receives about one-quarter to one-third of the skiers that Colorado gets—so you'll see fewer lift lines and plenty of wide-open spaces.

Cross-country skiers who enjoy doing their own thing can break trail to their heart's content in plenty of national forest areas. Particularly good are the mountains above Ogden, the Homestead Cross Country Ski Center near Heber City, and the old logging and mining roads southeast of Moab. Several downhill ski areas, including Brian Head, Sundance, and Solitude, offer groomed cross-country trails; and some of the hiking trails at Bryce Canyon National Park are open to cross-country skiers in winter. Bryce Canyon is also attracting a growing number of snowshoers. Snowmobilers can generally use the same national-forest roads as cross-country skiers, and both cross-country skiers and snowmobilers head to Cedar Breaks National Monument in the winter, when those are the only ways to get into the monument.

Contact **Ski Utah,** 150 W. 500 South, Salt Lake City, UT 84101 (☎ **801/534-1779** or fax 801/521-3722; on-line at www.skiutah.com), for a free copy of the *Ski Utah Vacation Planner,* which contains information on downhill and cross-country ski areas, as well as other winter recreation possibilities. The **Utah Travel Council** (☎ **800/200-1160** or 801/538-1030) and **Utah Parks and Recreation** (☎ **801/538-7220**) offer maps and information on safe snowmobiling and riding areas. Call ☎ **801/521-8102** for the daily ski report, ☎ **801/364-1581** for the daily avalanche and mountain weather report, ☎ **801/964-6000** for highway conditions and a road construction update, and ☎ **801/975-4499** for a statewide weather forecast.

WILDLIFE WATCHING & BIRDING

The great expanses of undeveloped land in Utah make it an ideal habitat for wildlife. In most cases, it isn't even necessary to hike very far into the backcountry to find it. There's plenty for you to see—waterbirds at many of the lakes and reservoirs, elk and antelope in the Wasatch Mountains, lizards and snakes in the red rock country of the south, and deer and small mammals practically everywhere. All the national parks have excellent wildlife-viewing possibilities, as do many state parks. Coral Pink Sand Dunes near Kanab is known for its luminescent scorpions; Escalante State Park boasts the best wetland bird habitat in southern Utah. Hikers on Boulder Mountain, near Escalante, are likely to see deer, elk, and wild turkey, and birders will enjoy the wide variety of songbirds to be found there.

The mountains above Ogden and Logan are especially good places to spot elk, deer, and even moose. The relatively remote Flaming Gorge National Recreation Area is one of the best areas of the state to find wildlife, so don't be surprised if a pronghorn antelope joins you at your campsite. Birders have a good chance of seeing osprey, peregrine falcons, swifts, and swallows along the cliffs; and hikers on the Little Hole National Recreation Trail just below Flaming Gorge Dam should watch for a variety of birds, including bald eagles in winter. Antelope Island State Park in the Great Salt Lake is another excellent destination for bird-watchers.

6 Introducing the Salt Lake Valley & the Wasatch Front

Seeking an escape from religious persecution, Brigham Young led a group of 148 Mormon pioneers from Illinois to the Salt Lake Valley in the mid-1800s. Arriving on July 24, 1847, Young declared, "This is the place." Soon a city was born, then a state, and, as the saying goes, the rest is history.

Today, from Logan in the north to Provo in the south, the strip known as the Wasatch Front—the Wasatch Mountains and Salt Lake Valley, including Salt Lake City—holds some 80% of Utah's population and practically all its industry. But this isn't your typical urban center; in fact, one of the things we find particularly attractive about this area is its casual atmosphere. There's no urban feel here, no high-energy tension, and residents don't see themselves as city dwellers. These Wasatch Front communities, even Salt Lake City, Ogden, and Provo—the state's largest cities—are just overgrown, relatively unsophisticated towns. We like that.

Although this certainly feels like small-town America, calling these cities unsophisticated is probably unfair. Attending a performance by the Utah Symphony or Mormon Tabernacle Choir, both world-class performing-arts organizations, will silence any big-city naysayer. But what really matters, the big draw for many who come to work and live here as well as those who come to play, is what lies beyond the cities' boundaries. This isn't the barren rock and desert that often come to mind when you think of Utah; this is mountain Utah, with lush canyons, rushing streams, and stately pines.

Opportunities to enjoy the spectacular outdoors abound. The region's canyons all offer magnificent views from the highways that traverse them and even more incredible experiences once you get out of the car. The lakes and reservoirs dotting the region offer abundant opportunities for boating, fishing, and swimming; the best-known are the Great Salt and Utah lakes, but we'll also tell you about our favorites, two undiscovered jewels. The forests are terrific for hiking, mountain biking, and horseback riding. And then there's the spectacular skiing: Tucked away in delightful little canyons, these resorts offer awesome scenery year-round at a reasonable price. They usually get more than 500 inches of powder snow each year, and they're probably the easiest ski areas to reach in the West.

This is a great place to relive frontier history, too. You can visit the spot where the final spike was driven to complete the first transcontinental railroad, the oldest continuously operating saloon in

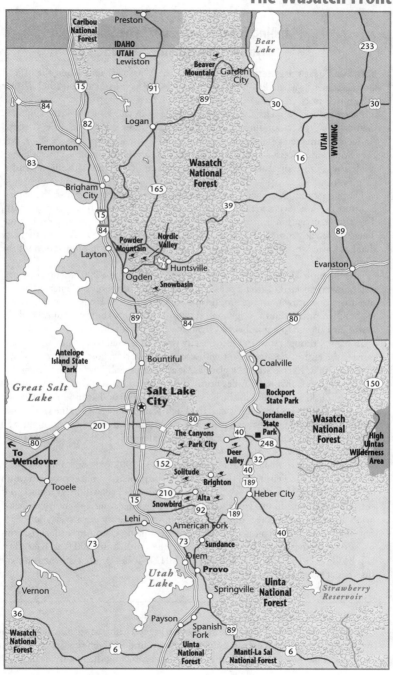

Planning for the Year 2002: The Winter Olympic Games Come to Utah

You could hear the cheering up and down the Wasatch Front when the official announcement was made—Utah had been selected as the site for the 2002 Winter Olympic Games.

Never before has a city the size of Salt Lake been chosen to host the Olympic Games. But its surrounding mountains, reliable snow conditions (the Wasatch Range gets an average of about 530 inches of light, fluffy powder a year), and easy worldwide access—combined with years of serious lobbying for the honor—made the Utah capital the overwhelming choice of the International Olympic Committee.

Despite its size, Salt Lake City is remarkably well-prepared to host the games. Eight of the nine event venues are either already in place or under construction. The city's convention center, the Salt Palace, will serve as the Main Press Center. There are already more hotel rooms in and around Salt Lake than in any other city that has hosted the Winter Games, and more are being built in preparation for the Games.

The Olympic Village—slated to accommodate all of the 4,000 athletes, coaches, and trainers expected to attend the Games—couldn't be more convenient: 10 minutes from downtown, on the grounds of the University of Utah campus adjacent to the Olympic Stadium. A light-rail system will link the southern suburbs of the metro area (home to a number of Olympic venues) with downtown.

In reality, though, it wasn't just the city that was chosen by the Olympic Committee; the entire Wasatch Front will serve as the world's host for those 2 winter weeks in 2002. Events will take place as far away from Salt Lake as Snowbasin Ski Area in Ogden Canyon, 55 miles north of downtown. As you'd expect, a number of downhill ski and other Nordic events will be held in and around Park City, at Park City Ski Area, Deer Valley, and the Utah Winter Sports Park, the world-class training facility that is the area's pride and joy. At the end of the day, though, it all comes back to the city: The daily medal ceremonies will be held at Olympic Plaza, in the heart of downtown.

If you're ready to make plans to see the action in 2002 (scheduled to take place from February 9 to February 24), you'll have to be patient—a ticket program won't be in place until 1999. However, about 1.7 million tickets will be available, so if you stay on top of things, you should be able to garner some for yourself. Ticket prices are expected to range from $25 to $300, with the average price at about $55. For more information contact the Salt Lake Organizing Committee for the Olympic Winter Games of 2002 (SLOC), 257 E. 200 South, Suite 600, Salt Lake City, UT 84111 USA (☎ **801/322-2002;** fax 801/364-7644). Or visit them on the Internet at **www.slc2002.org**.

—Cheryl Farr

Utah, and the fort where 19th-century mountain men gathered to exchange news and swap furs for supplies. You can even go underground in a genuine silver mine, and you'll also find a terrific collection of airplanes chronicling the history of flight.

1 How We've Covered This Area

Since this is such a large region—175 miles from top to bottom—you probably won't be touring the entire Wasatch Front; you're more likely to set your sights on specific destinations and explore those particular areas. To make our coverage of the region more manageable, we've divided it into three chapters.

Chapter 7 covers Salt Lake City, Utah's capital and major population center, and world headquarters of the Church of Jesus Christ of Latter-day Saints, otherwise known as the Mormon Church.

Chapter 8 explores the northern section of the Wasatch Front: the Great Salt Lake, one of the country's most remarkable natural wonders, and Antelope Island State Park; Ogden, an excellent starting point for discovering Utah's Old West; the pretty town of Logan; and Golden Spike National Historic Site, a must-see for railroad buffs. This area is also a great base for outdoor recreation, with three ski resorts as well as lush, rugged mountains that provide numerous outdoor recreation opportunities year-round.

Chapter 9 covers the southern half of the Wasatch Front, from Park City, home of several of the state's best ski resorts, to Provo, site of Brigham Young University. This area also includes the splendid cave formations of Timpanogos Cave National Monument, and a handful of lakes and state parks—real hidden gems that make this a terrific warm-weather playground as well. Provo makes a good base for skiing, hiking, or horseback riding at Sundance Resort and Institute in Provo Canyon.

2 Getting Outside Along the Wasatch Front

The Wasatch Front is mountain Utah, with lofty pines, rushing streams, and, in winter, an abundance of light, powdery snow. The rugged mountains and steep canyons that surround the Great Salt Lake Valley are home to lush forests, cool lakes and reservoirs, and plenty of sunshine—just right for an hour-long nature walk, an early-morning birding excursion, an exciting day of downhill skiing or mountain biking, a relaxing weekend fishing trip, or any one of a number of other adventures. There's an activity for everyone, every day of the year.

WINTER ACTIVITIES

Nowhere else in the American West will you find so many excellent ski resorts in one place. Just fly into Salt Lake City in the morning, rent a car or hop a shuttle, and you can be on the slopes of your choice by early afternoon. It doesn't get any easier. Solitude and Brighton—which welcome snowboarders as well as downhill skiers—are in Big Cottonwood Canyon. At the top of Little Cottonwood Canyon is graceful, sylvan Alta, with clouds of light snow; down the canyon is the more developed Snowbird. If you crave the lap of luxury, head for the Park City resorts—Park City, The Canyons, and elegant Deer Valley—where you'll find "champagne" snow and European-style lodges. Nordic Valley, Powder Mountain, and Snowbasin, near Ogden, plus Beaver Mountain, near the Idaho border, are all at the other end of the scale, simply offering good skiing on long, uncrowded runs—no pretensions here. Rustic, comfortably posh Sundance is nestled in the pines on the eastern slope of Mt. Timpanogos, north of Provo.

Those who prefer other forms of winter recreation have plenty of options. The old logging and mining roads throughout the national forests are great for cross-country skiing. Sundance Nordic Center, near Provo, offers groomed trails and lots of spectacular mountain scenery. Park City also has a Nordic center, White Pine, that offers splendid cross-country skiing for everyone from beginner to expert. Solitude Nordic Center, Utah's oldest cross-country ski center, even has a children's trail. Snowmobilers will want to head to beautiful Strawberry Reservoir, a pristine lake near Park City that's also great for ice fishing.

WARM-WEATHER ACTIVITIES

Once the winter snows melt into fields of wildflowers, hiking boots, mountain bikes, and horses replace snowboards, skis, and snowmobiles. Hikers and mountain bikers share most of the trails here, including the well-maintained downtown riverside trails in both Provo (chapter 9) and Ogden (chapter 8). Other favorites of ours are the 30-mile Historic Union Pacific Rail Trail from Park City to Echo Reservoir, and the 5-mile Indian Trail that leads through a dense forest in Ogden Canyon (chapter 8). The national forests are popular for horseback riding; some of the best opportunities are in the rugged country outside Logan (chapter 8) and at Park City.

There's boating at Utah Lake State Park (chapter 9), but it gets crowded, especially on weekends. The Great Salt Lake is popular with both powerboaters and sailboaters, but no rentals are available. For our money, it's well worth the drive to Strawberry Reservoir, a beautiful lake set in a quiet national forest; it's ideal for trout fishing, boating, and hiking along its shores. Or head to the lake at Jordanelle State Park, one of Utah's newest parks. Both lakes are close to Park City and provide launching ramps and boat rentals. Ogden's Fort Buenaventura State Park (chapter 8) is essentially a historical park, so finding several delightful ponds there, with canoe rentals, was a nice surprise.

Strawberry Reservoir also offers some of the best fishing in the state. The lakes and streams in the Wasatch-Cache National Forest (chapter 8) above Ogden are good trout habitat. The streams above Park City are also a good bet for fly-fishing.

The Wasatch Front is dotted with golf courses, but our favorites, for both the challenge and scenic beauty they offer, are in the Park City area: Park Meadows Golf Club, in Park City, and the courses at Wasatch Mountain State Park and The Homestead Resort, near Heber City.

WILDLIFE VIEWING & BIRD WATCHING

Because the Wasatch Front (like most of Utah) is largely undeveloped, you'll find plenty of opportunities for wildlife viewing and birding. Practically anywhere in the mountains, you have a chance of spotting deer, elk, maybe even a moose, plus smaller animals such as badgers, chipmunks, and rabbits. Willard Bay State Park near Ogden (chapter 8) is a good place to see deer, smaller creatures, and waterbirds; and the Great Salt Lake is home to a variety of saltwater birds. At Antelope Island State Park, you'll have an easy time seeing not antelope, but buffalo—relatively domesticated ones, not actual "wildlife," per se.

Salt Lake City 7

In a valley in north-central Utah, nestled between the Wasatch Mountains on the east and the Great Salt Lake on the west, lies Salt Lake City. Utah's capital and major population center is small as modern American cities go, with a population of only 171,000. But travelers come from around the world to visit magnificent Temple Square, world headquarters of the Church of Jesus Christ of Latter-day Saints (LDS) and to hear the inspired voices of the unequaled Mormon Tabernacle Choir. Salt Lake City is to Mormonism what Rome is to Catholicism—it's the center of the Mormon universe.

Although Salt Lake City may be best known for its religious prominence—and an undeserved reputation as a stodgy, uptight town where you can't get a drink—it's growing in popularity as a home base for skiers and other outdoor enthusiasts. Exhilarating outdoor recreation possibilities are only about an hour's drive from the city, and include some of the country's best ski resorts plus miles of terrific mountain trails for hiking, mountain biking, and horseback riding. With its rising prominence as an outdoor recreation center as well as its preparations to host the 2002 Winter Olympic Games—which include the addition of many new hotels, restaurants, and attractions—Salt Lake City is beginning to shed its image as "that boring Mormon town with the choir."

Incidentally, one of the first things visitors notice upon arrival is how sensibly organized and pleasantly wide the streets are. Early church leader Brigham Young laid out the city streets in a grid pattern with the Temple at the center, and decreed that the streets should be 132 feet wide so that a team of four oxen and a wagon could make a U-turn. A more tantalizing tale has it that the streets were made wide enough for polygamist Young and all his wives to walk comfortably down the street arm-in-arm, with no one forced into the gutter.

1 Orientation

ARRIVING

BY PLANE   Direct flights connect Salt Lake City to more than 65 cities in the United States and Canada. **Salt Lake City International Airport** (☎ 801/575-2400) is located just north of I-80 at exit 115, on the west side of the city. Airlines serving the airport include

American (☎ 800/433-7300), **America West** (☎ 800/247-5692), **Continental** (☎ 800/525-0280 or 801/359-9800), **Delta** (☎ 800/221-1212 or 801/532-7123), **Northwest** (☎ 800/225-2525), **Skywest** (☎ 800/453-9417), **Southwest** (☎ 800/435-9792), **TWA** (☎ 800/221-2000 or 801/539-1111), and **United** (☎ 800/241-6522).

BY CAR   Salt Lake City is 303 miles north of St. George, 238 miles northwest of Moab, 45 miles north of Provo, and 35 miles south of Ogden. You can reach it from the east or west via I-80 and from the north or south via I-15.

BY TRAIN   **Amtrak** has several trains arriving daily from both coasts. The passenger station is located at 320 S. Rio Grande Ave., just west of Temple Square (☎ **800/872-7245** or 801/364-8562).

VISITOR INFORMATION

The **Salt Lake Convention and Visitors Bureau** has an information center downtown in the Salt Palace at 90 S. West Temple (☎ **800/541-4955** or 801/521-2868; e-mail slcvb@saltlake.org; www.saltlake.org). It's open Monday through Friday, 8am to 5pm, and Saturday from 9am to 4pm, with extended hours in the summer. Another information center, at Salt Lake City International Airport Terminal II (☎ **801/575-2800** or 801/575-2660), is open Sunday through Friday from 9am to 9pm.

The **Utah Tourism and Recreation Information Center,** in Council Hall on Capitol Hill at 300 N. State Street (☎ **801/538-1030**), is staffed by members of the Utah Travel Council, Utah Division of State Parks and Recreation, National Park Service, U.S. Forest Service, Bureau of Land Management, and the Zion Natural History Association. Hours are Monday through Friday, 8am to 5pm, and Saturday, Sunday, and federal holidays, 10am to 5pm.

A great place to buy outdoor guides and detailed topographic maps is the bookstore at the **Department of Natural Resources Utah Geological Survey,** 1594 W. North Temple, Suite 3110 (Box 146100), Salt Lake City, UT 84114-6100 (☎ **801/537-3320;** fax 801/537-3395). The bookstore is open from 7:30am to 6pm Monday through Friday and from 9am to 1pm on Saturday.

CITY LAYOUT

Salt Lake City is laid out in a simple grid system centered on Temple Square. The roads bounding the Square are North Temple, South Temple, West Temple, and Main Street, with ground zero at the southeast corner (the intersection of Main and South Temple), the site of the Brigham Young Monument. The road numbers increase from there by 100s in the four cardinal directions, with West Temple taking the place of 100 West, 100 North called North Temple, and 100 East known as State Street.

Addresses may seem confusing at first, but are really quite clear once you get used to them. For instance, 1292 S. 400 West Street lies almost 13 blocks south of Temple Square and 4 blocks west, and 243 N. 600 East Street lies about 2 blocks north and 6 blocks east.

Impressions

Salt Lake City was healthy—an extremely healthy city. They declared there was only one physician in the place and he was arrested every week regularly and held to answer under the vagrant act for having "no visible means of support."

—Mark Twain, 1872

A good, detailed city map is produced by Gousha, and can be purchased at most bookstores. The *Salt Lake City Visitor's Guide,* available free at the visitor center, includes maps showing the approximate location of many restaurants, motels, and attractions.

NEIGHBORHOODS IN BRIEF

Downtown   The downtown area, centered on Temple Square, is both a business district and the administrative center for the LDS Church. Church offices, the Family History Library, the Museum of Church History and Art, and other church buildings surround the Square. This is most likely where you'll spend the bulk of your time. Within a few blocks south, west, and east are hotels, restaurants, stores, businesses, and two major shopping centers. Not far away are the Salt Palace Convention Center; Maurice Abravanel Concert Hall, home of the Utah Symphony; and the Capitol Theatre, the home of several performing companies.

Capitol Hill   The Capitol Hill district lies north of the Square and encompasses the 40 acres around the Utah State Capitol Building and Council Hall. Some lovely old homes are located in the blocks surrounding the Capitol.

Marmalade District   The blocks lying west of the Capitol to Quince Street are known as the Marmalade District. The streets in this small area were named for the nut and fruit trees brought in by early settlers—hence its cognomen. The houses represent a variety of the city's early architectural styles; many of these old homes are now being renovated.

Avenues District   The Avenues District lies east of the Capitol and north of South Temple. Most of the larger homes here date from the silver boom in Little Cottonwood Canyon, when they were built by successful miners and merchants. Today, the tenants are mostly college students and young professionals.

2 Getting Around

BY CAR   This is the best way to get around the city. There is a public bus system (see below), but it's geared to locals rather than visitors. The following national car-rental companies have offices in Salt Lake City: **Avis** (☎ 800/831-2847 or 801/575-2847), **Budget** (☎ 800/527-0700 nationwide or 801/575-2830; 800/237-7251 in Park City), **Dollar** (☎ 800/800-4000 or 801/575-2580 at the airport), **Hertz** (☎ 800/654-3131 or 801/575-2683 at the airport), **National** (☎ 800/227-7368 or 801/575-2277 at the airport), **Payless** (☎ 800/729-5377 or 801/596-2596), and **Thrifty** (☎ 800/367-2277 or 801/595-6677 at the airport).

You'll find many public parking lots in the downtown area, costing from $1 to $4 per day. Some lots are free with validation from a particular merchant or restaurant. Parking on streets downtown is metered, costing 25¢ per half hour, and usually limited to 1 or 2 hours. For larger RVs and motor homes, parking is limited; there's one large lot—the entire block between North and South Temple and 200 and 300 West—where you can park for $2 to $6 per hour. You might also try the lot behind the Capitol, where there are some designated large-vehicle spaces; East Capitol Street is a possibility as well (and it's not metered).

PUBLIC TRANSPORTATION   The **Utah Transit Authority** (☎ **801/287-4636** or TDD 801/287-4657) provides bus service around the city, with a "free fare zone" in the downtown area, roughly from 400 South to North Temple, continuing up Main Street to 500 North to include the State Capitol, and between 200 East and West Temple. You can ride the bus free within this zone, getting on and off as many times as you like. You should be aware that a number of bus routes traverse Main and State Streets and North and South Temple, so if you're not sure that the bus stopping for you is the one you need, ask the driver before getting on. Route schedules and maps are available at malls, libraries, visitor centers, and other places around the valley. Large-print and Braille schedules are available upon request. To find the nearest bus stop or to determine the best route to your destination, ask at the front desk of your hotel or call ☎ **801/287-4636.** Some buses are wheelchair accessible, and others have bicycle carriers.

The **Centennial Discovery Trolley** offers alternative transportation to historic sites and other attractions around the city. It travels from Trolley Square to Tracy Aviary (in Liberty Park), around to Temple Square and out to the museums at the university, and to the zoo and This is the Place State Park at the mouth of Emigration Canyon. Tickets can be purchased aboard the trolley or at the ZCMI Center Mall information desk (36 S. State St.; ☎ **801/359-4540**). Call ☎ **801/287-4636** for more information.

BY TAXI   The three main companies are the **City Cab Co. (**☎ **801/363-5550), Yellow Cab (**☎ **801/521-2100)**, and **Ute Cab (**☎ **801/359-7788)**, all of which are available 24 hours a day. **Handi-Van, Inc.,** provides wheelchair transportation "door through door" (☎ **801/486-8416**).

FAST FACTS: Salt Lake City

American Express   The American Express Office is located at 175 S. West Temple (☎ **801/328-9733**), and is a full-service travel agency. It's open Monday through Friday from 9am to 5pm.

Business Hours   Banks are usually open weekdays from 9am to 4pm or 5pm, often until 6pm on Friday; some have hours on Saturday. There's 24-hour access to the automatic-teller machines (ATMs) at most banks, as well as in shopping centers and other outlets. Generally, business offices are open weekdays from 9am to 5pm. Stores are usually open 6 days a week, with some also open on Sunday afternoon. Department stores usually stay open until 9pm at least 1 day a week. Discount stores and supermarkets are often open later than other stores, and some supermarkets are open 24 hours a day.

Camera Repair   Several camera stores offer repair services. Among the larger ones is **Forster's Camera Service, Inc.,** 40 W. 2950 South, South Salt Lake (☎ **801/ 487-1288**), which has been in business since 1971.

Dentist   For dental referrals, contact the **Utah Dental Association,** 1151 E. 3900 South (☎ **801/261-5315**), during normal business hours.

Doctor   For medical referrals, contact the **Utah Medical Association,** 1151 E. 3900 South (☎ **801/355-7477**), during normal business hours. At other times, contact the nearest hospital; in an emergency, dial ☎ 911.

Emergencies   Dial ☎ **911** for police, fire, or ambulance.

Hospitals   **LDS Hospital** is the closest to downtown, at 8th Avenue and C Street (☎ **801/321-1100**). Other city hospitals include **Salt Lake Regional Medical Center,** 1050 E. South Temple (☎ **801/350-4111**); **Primary Children's Medical Center,** 100 N. Medical Dr. (☎ **801/588-2000**); and **University Hospital and Clinics,** 50 N. Medical Dr. (☎ **801/581-2897**).

Hotlines   The **Utah Poison Control Center** number is ☎ 800/456-7707 or 801/581-2151. The **Rape Crisis Center** is at 2035 S. 1300 East (☎ 801/467-7273). Call the **Crisis/Suicide Prevention Hotline** at ☎ 801/483-5444 in North Salt Lake County; at ☎ 801/566-2455 in South Salt Lake County; and at ☎ 801/773-7051 in Davis County, north of Salt Lake City.

Liquor Laws   See "Liquor Laws" in chapter 3.

Newspapers/Magazines   The two major daily newspapers are the *Salt Lake City Tribune* and the church-owned *Deseret News.* Also of interest is *Salt Lake City Magazine,* a slick publication with a section on current events.

Police   For emergencies call ☎ 911. For nonemergency police assistance, call ☎ 801/799-3000.

Post Office   The main post office is located at 1760 W. 2100 South (☎ 801/978-3005). The one closest to downtown is at 230 W. 200 South (☎ 801/978-3001).

Radio   Among AM stations, KISN (570 AM) is all sports; KFAM (700 AM) offers easy listening; KSVN (730 AM) plays Latin music; KSOS (800 AM) plays oldies; KAPN (860 AM) is all news; KANN (1120 AM) is a Christian station; KSOP (1370 AM) plays modern country music; and KCPZ (1600 AM) plays adult contemporary music.

Of the FM stations, KCPW (simulcast on 88.3 and 105.1 FM) broadcasts National Public Radio; KUER (90.1 FM) plays classical, jazz, and news broadcasts; KLZX (simulcast on 92.1, 96.7, and 106.9 FM) plays classic rock; KXRK (96.1 FM) offers modern music; KKAT (101.9 FM) plays young country; and KUMT (105.7 FM) plays eclectic rock.

Smoking   The Utah Indoor Clean Air Act prohibits smoking in any publicly owned building or office and in all enclosed indoor places of public access. This includes restaurants but not private clubs, lounges, and taverns.

Taxes   Utah's state sales tax is about 6%, but Salt Lake and Davis counties add a mass-transit tax, bringing the usual sales tax to over 6%. Lodging taxes total about 10%, and restaurant taxes total just over 7%.

Television   Local stations include KUTV on channel 2 (CBS), KTVX on channel 4 (ABC), KSL on channel 5 (NBC), KUED on channel 7 (PBS), KBYU on channel 11, KJZZ on channel 3, and KSTU on channel 13 (FOX).

Transit Info   Call ☎ 801/287-4636 (TDD 801/287-4657) for **Utah Transit Authority** bus information.

Useful Telephone Numbers   For local road conditions, call ☎ 801/964-6000; for statewide conditions, call ☎ 800/492-2400. The latter also includes information on major road construction statewide. For major construction on on- and off-ramps and the interstates within Salt Lake City, call ☎ 800/I15-INFO (415-4636).

Weather   Call ☎ 801/575-7669 for a weather report, or ☎ 801/975-1212 for the temperature and time.

3   Accommodations

You'll have no trouble finding comfortable lodgings in Salt Lake City, usually in convenient locations and priced at relatively reasonable rates compared to other western cities. One disappointment for us is the scarcity of grand old hotels of the late 19th and early 20th centuries that you find all over Colorado and other parts of the West. What would have been Salt Lake City's grandest historic lodging, the majestic 1911 Hotel Utah, has been converted from a hotel to LDS church offices. There are, however, a number of fine hotels here, including some with at least a bit of history, as well as several bed-and-breakfasts that offer a glimpse into Salt Lake City's past.

Among major chain and franchise lodging properties, we recommend the following: the **Best Western Olympus Hotel Conference Center,** 161 W. 600 South, Salt Lake City, UT 84101 (☎ 800/426-0722 or 801/521-7373; fax 801/524-0354), has 393 units, with rates ranging from $99 to $129 for two people, $275 for a suite; the **Salt Lake City Days Inn Airport,** 1900 W. North Temple, Salt Lake City, UT 84116 (☎ 800/DAYS-INN or 801/539-8538; fax 801/539-8538), offers rates of $57 to $64 for two people; **Econo Lodge,** 715 W. North Temple, Salt Lake City, UT 84116 (☎ 800/424-4777 or 801/363-0062; fax 801/359-3926), charges $58 to $68 for two people; the **Hampton Inn Downtown,** 425 S. 300 West, Salt Lake City, UT 84101 (☎ 800/426-7866 or 801/741-1110; fax 801/741-1171), has rates for two persons of $89 to $99; the **Travelodge,** 144 W. North Temple, Salt Lake City, UT 84103 (☎ 800/578-7878 or 801/533-8200; fax 801/596-0332), offers doubles at rates from $49 to $85; and **Super 8 Motel,** 616 S. 200 West, Salt Lake City, UT 84101 (☎ 800/800-8000 or 801/534-0808; fax 801/355-7735), charges from $60.88 to $71.88 for two people. All of these are perfectly good standard properties where you'll get exactly the kind of comfort and service you would expect from reliable chains.

Rates listed here are the rack rates; make a point of asking for any possible discounts. They're often given to senior citizens, members of the military, business travelers, and members of travel clubs or other organizations. The major downtown hotels that cater to businesspeople often offer particularly good discounts on weekends. Because the chain hotels' national reservation services may not be able to offer discounts, it's often best to call individual hotels directly to get the lowest rate.

Hotels are organized under the following price categories, based on the nightly rates for the majority of rooms: **expensive,** over $125; **moderate,** $50 to $125; **inexpensive,** less than $50. Tax added to lodging bills in Salt Lake City totals about 10%. Parking is free unless otherwise noted. Pets are not accepted unless otherwise noted.

EXPENSIVE

The Armstrong Mansion Bed & Breakfast

667 E. 100 South, Salt Lake City, UT 84102. ☎ **800/708-1333** or 801/531-1333. Fax 801/531-0282. 14 rms. A/C TV TEL. $89–$229 double. Rates include full breakfast. AE, DC, DISC, MC, V.

This stately red brick mansion, an opulent Queen Anne–style Victorian home decorated with antiques and reproductions, exudes an overall feeling of splendor and luxury, from its stained-glass windows to its intricately carved oak staircase. The four-story mansion, built in 1893 and listed on the National Register of Historic Places, was renovated in 1981 and again in 1994, and has an elevator. The ornate stencils on the walls are reproductions of the mansion's original decorative patterns, discovered during renovation. A variety of rooms are available, some with double beds, many with queens, and a few with kings; most have whirlpool tubs. With your room, you'll enjoy a full breakfast consisting of a hot dish, muffins, and fruit.

✪ Brigham Street Inn

1135 E. South Temple, Salt Lake City, UT 84102. ☎ **800/417-4461** or 801/364-4461. Fax 801/521-3201. 8 rms, 1 suite. A/C TV TEL. $125–$140 double; $185 suite. Rates include continental breakfast. AE, MC, V.

Located in a handsome three-story historic mansion, the elegant but relaxed Brigham Street Inn is a comfortable alternative to a luxury hotel. The inn is filled with antiques, reproductions, and original art from various periods, as well as some modern touches. Most of the individually decorated guest rooms contain queen-size beds, and more than half have fireplaces. Common rooms on the main floor include the dining room, living room, and a parlor. Guests also have access to a fax and copy machine. The continental breakfast is a scrumptious offering of homemade pastries or croissants, fresh fruit, juice, coffee, and tea.

✪ Inn at Temple Square

71 W. South Temple, Salt Lake City, UT 84101. ☎ **800/843-4668** or 801/531-1000. Fax 801/536-7272. 95 units, including 10 suites. A/C TV TEL. $125–$145 double; $165–$240 suite. Rates include full breakfast. AE, DC, DISC, MC, V.

A beautiful hotel brimming with 18th-century European elegance and style, the Inn at Temple Square is an exquisite little gem, offering wonderful service, food, and facilities. Actually built in 1930, the inn has been restored and then some—it offers an experience reminiscent of the grand hotels of old, but with a warm, homey touch. The lobby is like a living room, with fine artwork, couches, and chairs you can sink into. On the mezzanine level, you'll find a baby grand piano, a library with inviting reading areas, and a fireplace. Rooms are spacious, with a comfortable, old-world feel, and all have at least one upholstered chair.

The Inn's Carriage Court Restaurant serves three meals daily in a quietly elegant setting. Guest services include a free pass to a nearby health club, valet parking, airport shuttle, room service, and same-day valet service.

The inn is centrally located, just across from Temple Square and within easy walking distance of downtown theaters, restaurants, spectator sports, historic sites, and shopping. The entire facility is smoke-free.

Radisson Hotel Salt Lake City Airport

2177 W. North Temple, Salt Lake City, UT 84116. ☎ **800/333-3333** or 801/364-5800. Fax 801/364-5823. 127 units, including 29 suites. A/C TV TEL. $129–$139 double; suites $139 and up; weekend rates $84–$114. AE, CB, DC, DISC, MC, V.

You might think you've just arrived in the Swiss Alps when you first see this rugged gray stone building. It could be a Swiss chalet or hunting lodge; actually, it's a well-appointed contemporary hotel. The spacious and elegant lobby features a gracefully curving stairway to the second floor, with richly stained carved-and-turned woodwork and a pastoral mural. The "signature," or basic, rooms all contain a gas fireplace and handsome country French decor, and top-floor rooms have cathedral ceilings. Loft suites have an upstairs sleeping area and a kitchen with a balcony overlooking the living room. The French provincial furnishings are simultaneously homey and plush.

The gracious services include concierge, room service, airport transportation, dry cleaning, laundry service, and morning coffee and newspaper. Also available are a whirlpool, large outdoor pool, sundeck, conference rooms, and an executive exercise room.

Salt Lake City Marriott

75 S. West Temple, Salt Lake City, UT 84101. ☎ **800/228-9290** or 801/531-0800. Fax 801/532-4127. 515 units, 6 suites. A/C TV TEL. $159–$169 double; $275–$600 suite; weekend rates $119 double. AE, CB, DC, DISC, MC, V. Parking $5 per day or $1 per hour up to 8 hours; vehicle height limit is 6'2".

Just a block south of Temple Square and adjoining the Crossroads Plaza, this Marriott is a good choice for those visiting downtown Salt Lake. Geared to business travelers, the standard rooms are attractively decorated, with solid cherry furniture, plush chairs, large work desks, and two telephones with a computer data port. The spacious, skylit lobby contains a cozy fireplace and lots of plants. Several restaurants, a bar, and an espresso kiosk are also on the premises.

Services include a concierge, room service, dry cleaning and laundry service, newspaper delivery, massage, express checkout, airport shuttle, courtesy car, and valet parking. Facilities include a large indoor/outdoor heated pool, health club, whirlpool, sauna, sundeck, business center, conference rooms for up to 1,500 people, self-serve laundry, car-rental desk, and gift shop.

Salt Lake Hilton

150 W. 500 South, Salt Lake City, UT 84101. ☎ **800/HILTONS** or 801/532-3344. Fax 801/531-0705. 351 units, including 33 suites. A/C TV TEL. $120–$175 double; $150–$350 suite. AE, CB, DC, DISC, MC, V.

Many of the rooms in this modern hotel offer incredible views of the surrounding city and mountains. All are spacious, comfortably designed and decorated, and perfect for relaxing in after a busy day of sightseeing, skiing, or whatever. Some of the more sumptuous suites have large sunken baths, and the attractive courtyard king rooms, overlooking lawn and trees, provide an especially quiet and peaceful atmosphere. The concierge level offers on-floor check-in and -out, a private lounge, and other exclusive amenities.

Restaurants on the premises serve three meals a day, and the hotel has its own bar. Services include a concierge, dry cleaning, baby-sitting, and valet parking. Guests can use the on-site fitness center, whirlpool, sauna, beauty salon, and video game room. The business center offers laptop computer rental and complete conference facilities. Pets are accepted, with a deposit.

Wyndham Hotel

215 W. South Temple, Salt Lake City, UT 84101. ☎ **800/553-0075** or 801/531-7500. Fax 801/328-1289. 381 units, including 7 suites. A/C TV TEL. Rms $79–$159; suites $200 and up. AE, CB, DC, DISC, MC, V. Parking $6; vehicle height limit is 6'2", but there's an outside lot for taller vehicles.

This modern high-rise hotel is an excellent choice for both the business traveler and vacationer; it's just a block from Temple Square and very close to convention and spectator-sports facilities. Rooms are spacious, with either one king or two double beds and a large working desk. Some king rooms have a sofa sleeper or an easy chair and ottoman. All rooms include hair dryers, coffeemakers with supplies, full-size ironing boards, and irons. The upper floors have terrific views of the mountains, Temple Square, and the Capitol. On-site, you'll find a restaurant and private club (bar), a full-service business center, a small indoor heated pool, an exercise room (plus access to two nearby health clubs), and all the other amenities and services you'd expect at a top-notch hotel. In late 1997, the lobby, all rooms, and meeting space underwent a major $5.5-million renovation.

MODERATE

Anton Boxrud Bed & Breakfast Inn

57 S. 600 East, Salt Lake City, UT 84102. ☎ **800/524-5511** or 801/363-8035. Fax 801/596-1316. 7 rms (2 with shared bath). A/C. $79–$139 double. Rates include full breakfast. AE, DC, DISC, MC, V.

This beautiful three-story red brick structure, built in 1901, is listed on the Salt Lake City Historical Register as "Victorian Eclectic." A boardinghouse between 1938 and

Salt Lake City Accommodations

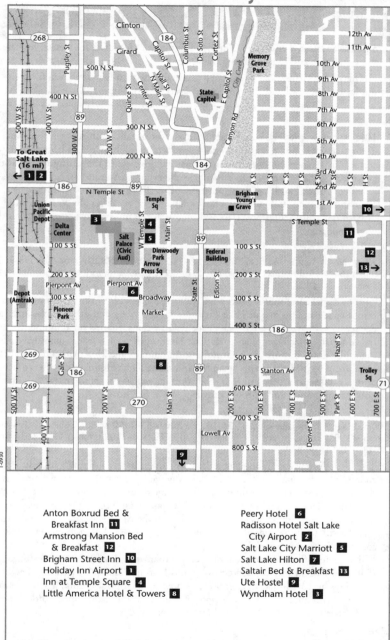

Anton Boxrud Bed &
    Breakfast Inn **11**
Armstrong Mansion Bed
    & Breakfast **12**
Brigham Street Inn **10**
Holiday Inn Airport **1**
Inn at Temple Square **4**
Little America Hotel & Towers **8**

Peery Hotel **6**
Radisson Hotel Salt Lake
    City Airport **2**
Salt Lake City Marriott **5**
Salt Lake Hilton **7**
Saltair Bed & Breakfast **13**
Ute Hostel **9**
Wyndham Hotel **3**

🏢 Family-Friendly Hotels

Salt Lake Hilton *(see p. 66)*   The video game room is perfect for teens, everyone loves the pool, and kids can bring their pets.

Holiday Inn Airport *(see p. 68)*   The central courtyard is a safe haven from city traffic, and the pool and volleyball court keep everyone in shape.

1968, it's now a lovely, comfortable bed-and-breakfast. Each room is individually decorated with a mix of antiques and reproductions; all have queen beds with down comforters. Pocket doors and stained-glass windows grace the sitting room, where guests can gather to enjoy refreshments in the evening. An outdoor hot tub is available year-round, and a private business office for guest use is furnished with a fax, copier, phone, and modem. The homemade full breakfast always includes a hot dish, and a continental breakfast is available for early risers. Special diets can be accommodated.

Holiday Inn Airport
1659 W. North Temple, Salt Lake City, UT 84116. ☎ **800/HOLIDAY** or 801/533-9000. Fax 801/364-0614. 191 units. A/C TV TEL. $77–$79 double. Rates include continental breakfast. AE, CB, DC, DISC, JCB, MC, V.

This modern, comfortable hotel adjacent to the airport isn't too far from the many things to see and do in Salt Lake City; in fact, the lobby and other public areas are decorated with art showing the city's many attractions. Rooms surrounding the central courtyard offer views of an attractively landscaped pool; outside rooms have parking at the door, but may be a bit noisier. All contain one king or two double beds, a comfortable easy chair with ottoman, and a desk. The Holiday Inn offers a fitness center, outdoor hot tub, and volleyball court, as well as complimentary 24-hour airport transportation and in-room movies.

Little America Hotel & Towers
500 S. Main St., Salt Lake City, UT 84101. ☎ **800/453-9450** or 801/363-6781. Fax 801/596-5911. 850 units, including 17 suites. A/C TV TEL. $65–$109 double; $124–$134 suite. AE, CB, DC, DISC, MC, V.

The Little America is among Salt Lake City's finest hotels, offering a wide variety of rooms, all individually decorated. Choices range from standard courtside rooms in the two-story motel-like buildings to extra-large deluxe tower suites in the 17-story high-rise. All are gracefully yet comfortably appointed in French provincial style, and come complete with 31-inch color televisions and pay-per-view movies. The locally popular coffee shop opens at 5am; there's also an elegant dining room and a lounge for afternoons and evenings.

The hotel offers concierge, room service (6am to midnight), in-room massage, twice-daily maid service, dry cleaning and laundry, and valet parking. Facilities include a health club with exercise equipment, whirlpool, sauna, a second-floor sundeck with an indoor/outdoor pool plus a beautifully landscaped outdoor pool, conference rooms, a beauty salon, boutiques, and shops.

Peery Hotel
110 W. 300 South (Broadway), Salt Lake City, UT 84101. ☎ **800/331-0073** or 801/521-4300. Fax 801/575-5014. 77 rms. A/C TV TEL. $69–$179 double. Rates include continental breakfast. AE, CB, DC, DISC, MC, V. Parking $9 per day.

The Peery is one of the few truly historic hotels left in Salt Lake City. Built in 1910, it has been restored to its former understated elegance, offering comfortable, tastefully decorated accommodations. The lobby is delightful, with old-style pigeon-holes for letters, room keys behind the front desk, and a broad central staircase to the upper floors. Each unique room is a bit small, but most contain a large closet, double bed, vanity outside the bath, and a desk and chair. Facilities include a whirlpool, sauna, exercise room, conference rooms, business center, boutiques, full bar, and restaurant serving three meals daily. Among the services offered are daily newspapers, airport shuttle, dry cleaning and laundry, room service, in-room massage, concierge, and secretarial services.

Saltair Bed & Breakfast

164 S. 900 East, Salt Lake City, UT 84102. ☎ **800/733-8184** or 801/533-8184. Fax 801/595-0332. 8 units (3 with shared bath), including 3 suites. A/C. $55–$149 double. Rates include full breakfast. AE, DC, DISC, MC, V.

Established in 1980, the Saltair is one of the oldest continuously operating B&Bs in Utah, although the building itself is quite a bit older. Now listed on the National Historic Register, it was constructed in 1903 and housed Salt Lake City's Italian Consulate in the early part of the century. Named for the resort built on the Great Salt Lake in the late 1800s (see "Great Salt Lake State Park" in chapter 8), this inn boasts an enormous collection of Saltair memorabilia, from humorous postcards to knickknacks of all kinds. Rooms vary in size and specifics, but all are comfortably furnished with an eclectic variety of antiques, and goose-down comforters grace each bed. Bathrooms have showers only except in the suites, which have whirlpool tubs for two. There's also an outdoor hot tub. Although no covered parking is available, the staff will happily brush snow off your vehicle when needed. The Saltair recently acquired a second Victorian home, where conference and workshop space and meeting rooms are available. Call for details.

INEXPENSIVE

The Ute Hostel

21 E. Kelsey Ave., Salt Lake City, UT 84111. ☎ **801/595-1645.** Fax 801/539-0291. 14 beds in 3 dorm rms, 2 private rms. A/C. $13–$15 dorm bed; $30–$35 private rm. No credit cards.

Located in a safe residential neighborhood, this hostel offers bunk beds in three dorm rooms, plus two private rooms—each with one queen bed. As you would expect, everyone shares bathrooms and showers. There's a fully equipped kitchen with free beverages, both smoking and nonsmoking lounges with cable TV and video games, and a public telephone. Particularly popular with international students, the hostel is unusually clean and provides free linen. Complimentary pick-up and drop-off at the airport, train and bus depots, and information center are available, as is free off-street parking. Inexpensive bike, ski, skate, and golf rentals can be arranged. Small pets are accepted.

CAMPGROUNDS

Camp VIP

1400 W. North Temple, Salt Lake City, UT 84116. ☎ **800/226-7752** or 801/328-0224. 490 sites. $20–$27; camping cabins $30–$34. MC, V.

This huge campground is the closest camping and RV facility to downtown Salt Lake City. Facilities include two pools, a hot tub, two playgrounds, a video arcade, two coin-operated laundries, several bathhouses, a convenience store with RV supplies, propane sales, an RV and car wash, well-maintained grassy areas for tents, and large shade trees. It offers six instant phone hookups, 80 sites with 50 amps, and a jogging/pet-walk/bicycle trail behind the campground. Bus route 50 heads east on North Temple to downtown, providing easy access to the sites there. Advance reservations are recommended from May through September. Those with RVs who plan to hook up to the campground's water supply should take or plan to buy regulators to control the erratic water pressure. Pets are accepted.

4 Dining

Salt Lake City restaurants are more casual than those in most major American cities, but the service is generally excellent and very friendly. Alcoholic drinks are not offered when diners are seated; except in private clubs, you'll have to ask for a drink. Diners should also be aware that since many Utahns do not drink coffee or tea, you may have to request your morning beverage—servers do not typically wander the dining room carrying a coffeepot.

Restaurants have been organized into the following price categories: **expensive,** most main courses at dinner priced over $18; **moderate,** most main courses at dinner priced between $10 and $18; and **inexpensive,** most main courses at dinner priced under $10.

EXPENSIVE

Market Street Broiler

260 S. 1300 East. ☎ **801/583-8808.** Reservations not accepted. Main courses $6.99–$29.99 dinner, $4.99–$15.99 lunch. AE, DISC, MC, V. Mon–Thurs 11am–10pm; Fri 11am–10:30pm; Sat 4–10:30pm; Sun 4–9:30pm. Bus: 8, 11, 52, or 54; on 1300 East between 200 and 300 South. SEAFOOD.

Market Street Broiler combines the atmosphere of the San Francisco wharf with the Southwest's famed mesquite wood to produce—drum roll, please—mesquite-grilled fresh seafood. The Broiler's lobby is actually a fresh-fish market (open daily 9am to 9:30pm); you could take some fish home to prepare yourself, but it's a lot more fun to sit at the counter around the glass-enclosed kitchen and watch the chef-artisans do their thing with some mesquite, a match, and fish that's flown in fresh daily. Those not interested in a show can eat in the upstairs dining room or on the patio in summer.

Favorites from the mesquite broiler include the scallops, shrimp, and halibut plate, prepared on a skewer with bell peppers and onion, and the fresh Pacific red snapper. If you're not in the mood for mesquite, there's always the fryer—try the halibut fish-and-chips or the fresh catfish. Those not interested in seafood at all still won't leave hungry—other entrees include hickory-smoked barbecued baby-back ribs, several varieties of barbecued chicken, and steaks. Full liquor service is available.

Market Street Grill

48 Market St. ☎ **801/322-4668.** Reservations not accepted. Main courses $13.99–$44.99 dinner, $5.99–$14.99 lunch, $2.69–$9.99 breakfast. AE, DISC, MC, V. Mon–Thurs 6:30am–11pm; Fri 6:30am–midnight; Sat 7am–midnight; Sun 10am–10:30pm. Bus: 19, 20, or 23 along Main St.; at the east end of Market St. SEAFOOD/STEAK.

A fancier version of Market Street Broiler (it's owned by the same company), the Market Street Grill is quite possibly Utah's best seafood restaurant. Expect a wait before you're led into the noisy, somewhat cramped dining room. There's a good reason the place is packed—fresh fish is flown in daily from around the world, and the Grill knows how to do it up right.

Favorites include the Pacific red snapper Monterey, served with fresh tomato sauce, sliced mushrooms, garlic, parsley, white wine, and gulf shrimp; and the cioppino, a seafood stew of lobster, shrimp, crab, clams, snapper, and mussels; or choose one of almost two dozen other seafood offerings. You'll also find a good choice of dinner salads, pastas, and steaks, including an excellent slow-roasted prime rib if you arrive early enough. Look for all the standard choices during the day, plus a seafood omelet, of course, at breakfast. Full liquor service is available.

✪ The New Yorker

60 Market St. ☎ **801/363-0166.** Reservations recommended. Dining-room main courses $12.95–$49.95 dinner, $6.95–$15.95 lunch; cafe main courses $8.95–$22.95. AE, DISC, MC, V. Mon–Thurs 11:30am–2pm and 5:30–10pm; Fri 11:30am–2pm and 5:30–11pm; Sat 5:30–11pm. Bus: 19, 20, or 23 along Main St.; at the east end of Market St. AMERICAN.

This is Salt Lake's finest restaurant. With rich woods, understated elegance, quiet sophistication, excellent food, and impeccable service, The New Yorker feels more like a London club than a Utah one. Technically a private club, you'll have to buy a membership to enter ($5 for 2 weeks), but trust us—it's worth it. Sit either in the dining room or in the less formal cafe, where you'll dine under the original stained-glass ceiling from the old Hotel Utah.

From the dining-room dinner menu, you might choose the sautéed sweetbreads and fresh foie gras with port wine and orange sauce; Dungeness crab cakes, which aficionados say are as good as—or better than—those you'll find anywhere else; or the rack of lamb with rosemary cream sauce. The lunch menu offers dishes such as sautéed chicken breast with tomato, artichokes, olives, thyme, and garlic; an excellent tenderloin of beef with cabernet sauce; and sandwiches and salads as well. The cafe menu, served from 11:30am weekdays and 5:30pm Saturdays, offers somewhat lighter choices with such favorites as pizza, pasta, fresh fish, and salads. As a private club, The New Yorker offers complete liquor service. Unlike many restaurants, you can buy a drink here without ordering any food.

MODERATE

Baci Trattoria

134 W. Pierpont Ave. ☎ **801/328-1500.** Reservations accepted. Main courses $6.99–$18.99. AE, DISC, MC, V. Mon–Thurs 11:30am–3pm and 5–10pm; Fri 11:30am–3pm and 5–11pm; Sat 5–11pm; Sun 5–10pm. Bus: 81 along 200 South, about 1 1/2 blocks north of Pierpont Ave.; or 19, 20, or 23 along Main St., about 2 blocks east. NORTHERN ITALIAN.

This handsome and popular restaurant serves excellent Italian cuisine, and plenty of it. The long bar features three large, art deco–style glass panels; behind them is a long, narrow dining room. You can also eat outside under the roof, beside the parking lot. The traditional northern Italian menu includes a wide selection of pizzas and pastas, plus chicken, lamb, veal, and seafood dishes. Try the lasagna, prepared with spicy Italian sausage and baked in a wood-burning oven; or the *Pappardelle con Pollo,* wide pasta ribbons with grilled chicken, sun-dried tomatoes, snow peas, and a roasted garlic cream sauce. Service is well-timed, friendly, and efficient. Full liquor service is available.

Ferrantelli

Trolley Sq. ☎ **801/531-8228.** Reservations required for 6 or more. Main courses $5.95–$8.50 lunch, $7.95–$16.95 dinner; pizza $6.95–$7.95. AE, DC, DISC, MC, V. Mon–Thurs 11:30am–10pm; Fri–Sat 11am–11pm; Sun 1–10pm. Bus: 33 or 45. NORTHERN ITALIAN.

A busy shopping-mall restaurant with an atrium greenhouse setting, Ferrantelli is known for its reliable northern Italian dishes—made fresh from scratch—as well as for being a super late-evening dessert stop. For dinner, we suggest either of the lasagna choices: The vegetarian lasagna has roasted eggplant, grilled zucchini, caramelized onions, spinach, and a light sauce; meat eaters will love the beef and sausage version, with ricotta and grilled mushrooms. If seafood's your thing, try the *Pescatore*—shrimp, mussels, and clams lightly sautéed with garlic, shallots, and fresh herbs, and served with a tomato sauce and angel-hair pasta. The Italian-style desserts are baked fresh daily. Full liquor service is available.

☉ Lamb's Restaurant

169 S. Main St. ☎ **801/364-7166.** Main courses $3.65–$17.95. AE, DC, DISC, MC, V. Mon–Fri 7am–9pm; Sat 8am–9pm. Bus: 19, 20, or 32. AMERICAN/CONTINENTAL.

Opened in 1919 in the northern Utah town of Logan by Greek immigrant George Lamb, the restaurant moved to Salt Lake City's Herald Building in 1939 and has been serving the Who's Who of Utah in this location ever since. But this isn't one of those fancy places you go to just to be seen; Lamb's is successful simply because it consistently serves very good food at reasonable prices, with friendly, efficient service.

Decorated with antiques and many furnishings from the 1920s and '30s, Lamb's is comfortable and unpretentious, from the long counter and softly padded booths in front to the more formal dining rooms with white-linen tablecloths in back. The extensive menu offers mostly basic American and continental fare, although the restaurant's Greek origins are also evident. In a tip of the hat to the restaurant's moniker, several lamb dishes appear on the menu, including broiled French-style lamb chops and barbecued lamb shank.

Other popular dinner selections—all available after 11:30am and cooked to order, of course—are broiled New York steak with sautéed mushrooms, grilled calf's liver with sautéed onions, steamed finnan haddie, Greek-style broiled half chicken with oregano, and grilled fresh rainbow trout. You'll also find a good selection of sandwiches and salads, daily pasta and salad specials, and a variety of desserts, including an extra-special rice pudding and a Burgundy wine Jell-O(!). Full liquor service is available.

Pierpont Cantina

122 W. Pierpont Ave. ☎ **801/364-1222.** Reservations not accepted. Main courses $6.99–$13.99. AE, DISC, MC, V. Mon–Thurs 11:30am–10pm; Fri 11:30am–11pm; Sat 4–11pm; Sun 10am–2:30pm and 3–10pm. Bus: 81 along 200 South, walk south about 1 1/2 blocks to Pierpont Ave.; or 19, 20, or 23 along Main St., walk about 2 blocks west. MEXICAN.

A lively Americanized version of a Mexican cantina, the Pierpont is decorated with red, green, and white streamers (the colors of the Mexican flag) and other festive touches that give the restaurant an every-day-is-a-fiesta atmosphere. Portions are generous, to say the least, and the quality is excellent, although those used to the fiery chile of New Mexico may find some of the dishes here a bit tame. All of the standard combination plates are available, as well as a variety of tacos, enchiladas, burritos, and chile rellenos. But the fajitas are the real attraction—choose from mesquite-grilled chicken, steak, or shrimp, delivered to your table sizzling hot along with onions, guacamole, black beans, and hot tortillas. Also highly recommended is the crunchy almond shrimp, an appetizer of Mexican gulf shrimp dipped in almonds and coconut, deep-fried, and served with jalapeño jelly. For dessert, try the flan, a traditional Mexican custard covered with caramel sauce. Complete liquor service is available.

Piña Restaurant

327 W. 200 South. ☎ **801/355-PINA.** Reservations recommended for dinner. Main courses $8.95–$18.95 dinner, $5.95–$12.95 lunch. AE, DISC, MC, V. Mon–Thurs 11am–10pm; Fri 11am–11pm; Sat 4:30–11pm; Sun 10:30am–2:30pm and 4:30–9pm. Bus: 81. AMERICAN.

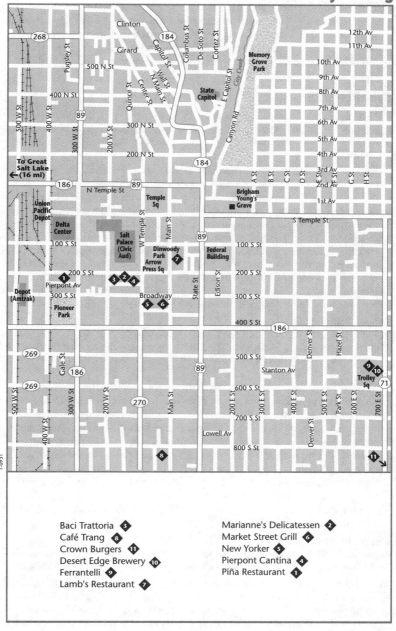

Baci Trattoria **3**
Café Trang **8**
Crown Burgers **11**
Desert Edge Brewery **10**
Ferrantelli **9**
Lamb's Restaurant **7**

Marianne's Delicatessen **2**
Market Street Grill **6**
New Yorker **5**
Pierpont Cantina **4**
Piña Restaurant **1**

1-0931

This open dining room, with its high ceilings, light plaster walls, and rich wood contrast, provides a welcoming environment for a relaxing meal. Offerings include sandwiches and salads, pizza and pasta, and dinner entrees such as curry-coconut-crusted mahimahi, Cajun fried chicken, paella for two, grilled steak, and smoked baby-back ribs. The menu runs the gamut from the familiar to unusual and exotic dishes. Full liquor service is available.

INEXPENSIVE

Café Trang
818 S. Main St. ☎ **801/539-1638.** Reservations recommended in the winter. Main courses $5–$16.95. AE, MC, V. Sun–Thurs 11:30am–9:30pm; Fri–Sat 11:30am–10pm. Bus: 47. VIETNAMESE/CHINESE.

Known for having the best Vietnamese food in the state practically since it opened in 1987, this family-owned and -operated restaurant now also serves Chinese dishes, mostly Cantonese with some Vietnamese influences. The dining room is unpretentious—plain would probably be a better word—but the consistently good food makes up for the lack of ambiance. Menu items are listed by number—from 1 to 197—with brief English descriptions of each one; little hearts indicate dishes that are completely vegetarian, and stars indicate spiciness. Among popular vegetarian specialties is the fried bean curd with grilled onions and crushed peanuts, served with rice papers, a vegetable platter, and peanut sauce. Meat eaters will likely enjoy the spicy *Bun Ga Xao,* rice vermicelli noodles with sautéed chicken and lemongrass, served with grilled onions and peanuts. Beer is available with meals.

Crown Burgers
3190 S. Highland Dr. ☎ **801/467-6633.** Main courses 99¢–$6. DISC, MC, V. Mon–Sat 10am–10pm. From downtown, follow State St. south to 2100 South and turn left (east); go about $1^1/_2$ miles and turn right (south) onto Highland Dr.; Crown is about 2 miles down on your right. FAST FOOD.

In-the-know locals say this place serves the best fast-food burger in Salt Lake City. Drive into the parking lot and you'll see this isn't your average hamburger joint. Decorated like a European hunting lodge, with wall sconces, chandeliers, and a stone fireplace, Crown is something of an upscale fast foodery—but you still order at the counter, wait for your number to be called, and pick up your paper-wrapped food yourself. The mini-chain's signature burger is a cheeseburger covered with pastrami; the menu also offers plain old burgers, beef burritos, hot pastrami sandwiches, steak sandwiches, gyros, fishburgers, fries, onion rings, and more. The food is good, hot, and fast—just like you want it. No alcohol is served.

Additional Salt Lake City locations include 377 E. 200 South (☎ **801/532-1155**) and 118 N. 300 West (☎ **801/532-5300**).

Desert Edge Brewery
Trolley Sq. ☎ **801/521-8917.** Main courses $8.95–$10.95 dinner, $5.50–$7.50 lunch. Mon–Wed 11am–midnight; Thurs–Sat 11am–1am; Sun noon–10pm. Bus 33 or 45. AMERICAN.

This is your usual busy brewpub, with cafe-style tables and chairs. Offerings include hot and cold pub sandwiches—and you can try two by getting half of one and half of another—as well as burgers, soups, and salads. After 5pm you can order grilled marinated flank steak, vegetable lasagna, herb-seared salmon, or barbecue chicken. Some half-dozen, Utah-brewed ales and lagers are available, plus domestic beer on tap—any of which you can order by the glass, pint, pitcher, or growler to go.

Marianne's Delicatessen
149 W. 200 South. ☎ **801/364-0513.** Main courses $3.50–$7.95. AE, MC, V. Restaurant Mon–Sat 11am–3pm. Delicatessen Mon–Fri 9am–6pm; Sat 9am–4pm. Bus: 81. GERMAN.

🤸 Family-Friendly Restaurants

Market Street Broiler *(see p. 70)*   The kitchen-view counter here provides a show that's almost as good as your kids' favorite TV show.

Pierpont Cantina *(see p. 72)*   Kids love the fiesta-like atmosphere and the yummy Mexican finger foods served up at this noisy cantina.

Crown Burgers *(see p. 74)*   All kids like fast-food joints; this is one even parents will like. The burgers are fresh and good, and the hunting lodge–like setting is much more pleasant than your average Burger King.

At this cafe-style combination delicatessen-restaurant, you can peruse a German newspaper or magazine over a bratwurst or liverwurst sandwich, a variety of sausage platters, or a bowl of the goulash soup that locals love (it's served Tuesdays and Fridays only). As you would expect in a German restaurant, portions are generous, and all the sausage is homemade in Marianne's own kitchen. Try the sausage sampler platter, with a small bratwurst, knackwurst, and weisswurst, served with buttered rye bread and your choice of potato salad, sauerkraut, fried potatoes, or red cabbage. The sausages and other menu items are available to go from the deli. Domestic and imported beer is served.

5 Exploring Temple Square

This is Mecca for the members of the Church of Jesus Christ of Latter-day Saints, also known as Mormons. The 10-acre square is enclosed by 15-foot walls, with a gate in the center of each. In addition to the church buildings, the square is home to the North and South Visitor Centers as well as lovely gardens and statuary. Even if you start at the South Visitor Center, you may want to stop into the North Visitor Center for a look at its murals and 11-foot replica of Thorvaldsen's *Christus*.

The ✪ **Temple** is used only for the Mormons' most sacred ordinances and is not open to the public. Brigham Young chose the site within 4 days of entering the valley, and work was begun on the six-spired granite structure in 1853. It took 40 years to complete.

The oval **Tabernacle** seats 6,500 people and has one of the West's largest unsupported domed roofs. The Tabernacle, which has unbelievable acoustics, has served as the city's cultural center for over a century. The Utah Symphony performed here for years before moving to the new Symphony Hall in 1979.

On Thursday evenings, you can listen to the ✪ **Mormon Tabernacle Choir** rehearse (except when they're on tour; call ☎ **801/240-3221** to check), and on Sunday mornings you can attend their broadcast from 9:30 to 10am (you must be seated by 9:15am). The choir, composed entirely of volunteers, was formed shortly after the first pioneers arrived; many husband-and-wife members and families participate, sometimes over several generations. The Tabernacle organ has been rebuilt several times over the years, and has grown from the original 1,600 pipes and two manuals to 10,857 pipes and five manuals. The organ is said to have an instantly recognizable signature sound and individual character. Half-hour organ recitals take place Monday through Saturday at noon, and on Sunday at 2pm. Admission to all these performances at the Tabernacle is free.

The Gothic-style **Assembly Hall** was constructed in 1880 from leftover granite from the Temple, and is often the site of concerts and lectures. Inquire at one of the visitor centers for schedules. Two monuments stand in front of the Assembly Hall: One depicts a pioneer family arriving with a handcart filled with their belongings, while the second commemorates the salvaging of the first crops from a plague of crickets (seagulls swooped down and ate the insects).

Guided tours of the Square, lasting approximately 45 minutes, leave every 10 or 15 minutes from in front of the Tabernacle; personnel in the visitor center can direct you. Tour guides provide a general history of the church (touching upon the church's doctrine), and take you around the Square, briefly explaining what you are seeing. Our favorite part of the tour is in the Tabernacle: To demonstrate the incredible acoustics, the group is ushered to the back of the seats while someone stands at the podium and drops three pins—the sound is as clear as a bell! The tour ends at the North Visitor Center with a short film on Mormon beliefs. You are then asked to fill out a card with your name and address, indicating whether you would like to receive a visit from Mormon missionaries.

The square is bounded by Main Street on the east and North, South, and West Temple Streets. The enclosed square is open daily from 6:30am to 10:30pm. Tours are given continuously from 8am to 9pm. Hours are shorter on Christmas Day. Call ☎ **801/240-2534** for more information. Buses 3, 4, 5, 23, and 50 will get you there.

6 More to See & Do

Family History Library

35 N. West Temple. ☎ **801/240-2331**. Free admission. Mon 7:30am–6pm; Tues–Sat 7:30am–10pm. Closed major holidays and July 24. Bus: 3, 4, 5, 23, or 50 to Temple Sq.

This incredible facility contains what is probably the world's largest collection of genealogical records under one roof. Most of the records date from about 1550 to 1910, and are from governments, many different church denominations, other organizations, and individuals. The collection is composed of a substantial number of records from around the United States, fairly comprehensive data from Scotland and England, and information from many other countries; it's growing all the time.

Why did the Mormons create such a huge genealogical library? They believe that families may be united for eternity through marriage and other sacred ordinances in the temples. These ordinances can be done on behalf of ancestors—hence the interest in tracing all deceased family members.

When you enter the library, you'll find people ready and willing to assist with your research. They'll offer forms you can fill out with any and all data you already know (so come prepared with copies of whatever you have), and can direct you from there. Other helpful orientation tools include a 15-minute video that explains procedures, a 25¢ booklet that will help you focus your search, and a map of the library. Volunteers are also stationed in various areas to help should the volumes become overwhelming.

Many of the records are in books, while many have been converted to microfilm, microfiche, and computer files. Don't let the technology scare you; the volunteers will show you how to use any unfamiliar machines. One of the easiest ways to begin is with the place where your ancestor lived, since records are organized first by the geographical origin of the data. From there, you can spend hours immersed in discovering the whos, whats, wheres, and whys of your family history—we know, we did it!

Downtown Salt Lake City Attractions

Beehive House **8**

Capitol Building **1**

Council Hall **2**

Family History Library **6**

Governor's Mansion **10**

Hansen Planetarium **9**

John W. Gallivan Utah Center **12**

Joseph Smith Memorial Building **7**

Museum of Church History and Art **5**

Pioneer Memorial Museum **3**

Salt Lake Art Center **11**

Temple Square **4**

Utah State Historical Society Museum **13**

HISTORIC BUILDINGS & MONUMENTS

✪ Beehive House
67 E. S. Temple. ☎ **801/240-2672.** Free admission. Mon–Sat 9:30am–4:30pm; Sun 10am–1pm; closes at 1pm on all holidays. Bus: 3, 4, 5, 23, or 50 to Temple Sq., and walk a half block east.

Brigham Young built this house in 1854 as his family home, but he also kept an office and entertained church and government leaders here. Young, who loved New England architecture, utilized much of that style, even including a widow's walk for keeping an eye on the surrounding desert. The house, which gives visitors a glimpse into the lifestyle of this famous Mormon leader, has been restored and decorated with period furniture to resemble as closely as possible the way it appeared when Young lived here, as described in a journal by his daughter Clarissa. Many pieces are original to the home. Young's bedroom is to the left of the inviting entrance hall (handy when late callers arrived to confer with him). The Long Hall, where formal entertaining took place, is on the second floor; when necessary, it was used as a dormitory to house visitors. The sewing room was a gathering place for the children, where they helped with chores, bathed by the cozy stove, and studied Christian principles. Of Brigham Young's 27 wives, only one lived in the Beehive House at a time; the rest, with some of the children, lived next door in the **Lion House** (not open for tours), or in other houses. Built of stuccoed adobe in 1855–56, the Lion House was named for the stone lion guarding its entrance.

Before you leave, be sure to catch a glimpse of **Eagle Gate,** a 76-foot gateway that marked the entrance to the Brigham Young 1859 homestead, located at the corner of State Street and South Temple. It's been altered several times over the years, and the original wooden eagle has been replaced by a 6,000-pound metal version with a 20-foot wingspan.

Brigham Young Monument and Meridian Marker
At Main and S. Temple sts.

The marker, at the southeast corner of Temple Square, serves as the starting point for the city's numbering system. The monument was placed here to honor Young, the 148 other pioneers who accompanied him here in 1847, and the Native Americans and fur trappers who preceded them.

✪ Capitol Building
Capitol Hill, at the north end of State St. ☎ **801/538-3000.** Free admission. Memorial Day–Labor Day Mon–Sat 6am–8pm; Labor Day–Memorial Day Mon–Sat 6am–6pm. Closed major holidays. Bus: 23 up Main St.

Built between 1912 and 1915 of unpolished Utah granite and Georgia marble, the capitol rests on a hill in a beautifully landscaped 40-acre park. The state symbol, the beehive (representing industry and cooperation), is a recurring motif both inside and out. You can take a guided tour of the building (call Council Hall at ☎ **801/538-1030** for schedules), or walk through on your own.

The **Rotunda,** which stretches upward 165 feet, is decorated with murals painted during the WPA years (the four largest depict important scenes in the state's early history) and houses several busts of prominent historical figures, including Brigham Young and Philo T. Farnsworth, the man whom we can all thank for bringing us television. The chandelier is astounding—it weighs 6,000 pounds and hangs from a 7,000-pound chain.

Other rooms worth seeing are the State Reception Room, known as the Gold Room because the walls are made from locally mined gold-traverse marble; the offices of the governor and lieutenant governor at the west end; the Hall of Governors, a portrait gallery that honors all those who have served as governor of Utah since statehood in 1896; and at the east end, the offices of Utah's attorney general. Downstairs, you'll find a small souvenir shop and some exhibits, including a large topographical map of Utah.

The third floor houses the Senate, House of Representatives, and Supreme Court of Utah. You can either climb one of the two marble staircases or take the elevator. The state legislature meets for 45 days in January and February; visitors are welcome to sit in the galleries on the fourth floor, which overlook the chambers. In front of the House of Representatives you'll see a replica of the Liberty Bell, one of 53 bronzed and cast in France in 1950.

Council Hall

Capitol Hill, 300 N. State St. ☎ **801/538-1467.** Free admission. Mon–Fri 8am–5pm; Sat–Sun and federal holidays 10am–5pm. Bus: 23 to the Capitol.

Completed in 1866, the Hall is a fine example of Federal–Greek Revival architecture. Originally located downtown, it first served as City Hall and the meeting place for the Territorial Legislature; it was later dismantled, coded, and reassembled in its present location. Today it houses the Utah Travel Council upstairs, and the Utah Tourism and Recreation Information Center and a gift shop on the ground floor.

Governor's Mansion

603 E. South Temple. ☎ **801/538-1005.** Tours by reservation, May–early Dec, Tues and Thurs 2–4pm. Bus: 4.

Silver magnate Thomas Kearns built this palatial home around the turn of the century, sparing no expense to make it as lavish as possible; African and Italian marble and exotic woods from around the world were used extensively throughout. Kearns' widow deeded it to the state in 1937, and the 36-room mansion is now the governor's residence.

Joseph Smith Memorial Building

15 E. South Temple. ☎ **801/536-7277.** Free admission. Mon–Sat 9am–10pm. Bus: 3, 4, 5, or 50 to Temple Square.

Formerly the historic Hotel Utah, this magnificent building has been renovated and converted into offices, meeting space, restaurants, and reception areas (it's very popular for wedding receptions). Between 1911 and 1987, this was a world-renowned hotel; the lobby retains its art-glass ceiling and massive marble pillars, and the architectural details have been lovingly restored throughout. It's worth a stop for a peek inside.

A big-screen theater offers free showings of "Legacy," the story of the early days of the Church of Jesus Christ of Latter-day Saints in Nauvoo, Illinois, and the trek west. It's just under an hour long, with about 10 showings a day. Although it's free, you do need to reserve a seat and get a ticket; call ☎ **801/240-4383.**

MUSEUMS

Hansen Planetarium

15 S. State St. ☎ **801/538-3383.** Free admission to museum, $3.50–$7.50 for shows. Mon–Thurs 9:30am–9pm; Fri–Sat 9:30am–midnight; Sun noon–5:30pm. Bus: 1, 2, or 49.

Housed in the former city library, this planetarium presents star shows (☎ **801/538-2104** for information) and laser music concerts (☎ **801/363-0559** for information), plus three floors of interactive exhibits ranging from the naming of the planets to a Foucault pendulum. The planetarium's original Spitz star projector is also on display.

Greater Salt Lake Valley Attractions

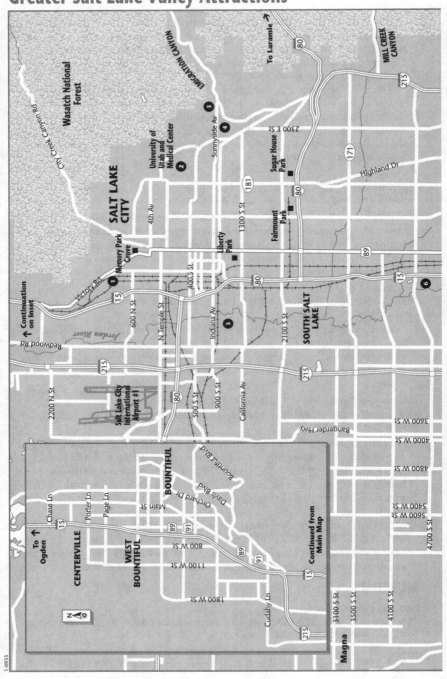

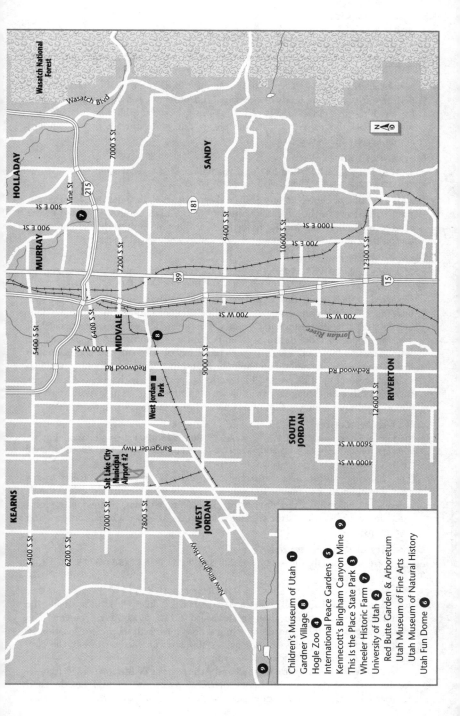

Children's Museum of Utah **1**
Gardner Village **8**
Hogle Zoo **4**
International Peace Gardens **5**
Kennecott's Bingham Canyon Mine **9**
This Is the Place State Park **3**
Wheeler Historic Farm **7**
University of Utah **2**
Red Butte Garden & Arboretum
Utah Museum of Fine Arts
Utah Museum of Natural History
Utah Fun Dome **6**

The John W. Gallivan Utah Center

36 E. 200 South (the entire block between Main and State sts., and 200 and 300 South). ☎ **801/532-0459.** Free admission. Daily 7am–10pm. Bus: 23 along Main St.

Some call this Salt Lake City's outdoor living room. You'll find intimate spaces, performances, food, all kinds of characters and activities, and good vantage points for watching the goings-on. Wander through the large art exhibit and the gigantic outdoor chess board with waist-high pieces, and enjoy the ice rink and pond, amphitheater, and aviary.

Museum of Church History and Art

45 N. West Temple. ☎ **801/240-3310.** Free admission. Mon–Fri 9am–9pm; Sat–Sun 10am–7pm; closed major holidays. Bus: 3, 4, 5, or 50 to Temple Sq.

This collection of church art and artifacts, begun in 1869, includes the plow that cut the first furrows in the valley. The history of the LDS Church is related in the exhibits on each of the church presidents, from Joseph Smith to the present, and a theater presentation describes the museum's work and related topics.

Pioneer Memorial Museum

300 N. Main St. ☎ **801/538-1050.** Free admission, but contributions are welcome. Mon–Sat 9am–5pm year-round; June–Aug Sun 1–5pm; closed major holidays. Bus: 23.

Operated by the Daughters of Utah Pioneers, this museum, housed in a Grecian-style building, contains an immense collection of pioneer portraits and memorabilia. Built in 1950, it's a replica of the old Salt Lake Theatre, which was torn down in 1928. The main floor includes theatrical exhibits, paintings, photos, and the personal effects of church leaders Brigham Young and Heber C. Kimball. The collection also includes a manuscript room, household displays, and exhibits on spinning, weaving, railroading, mining, and guns. All four stories are crammed with relics of Utah's history. You can walk through on your own or with the aid of a guide sheet; tours are also available. A 12-minute film is shown at 30-minute intervals, or on request.

Salt Lake Art Center

In the Salt Palace complex, 20 S. West Temple. ☎ **801/328-4201.** Free admission, but donations are welcome. Tues–Thurs and Sat 10am–5pm; Fri 10am–9pm. Bus: 23 along South Temple.

The changing exhibits here, featuring local, regional, and national artists, aren't exactly world-class, but they're still worth a visit. There are generally several simultaneous exhibitions in a variety of media, including paintings, photographs, sculptures, and ceramics. Check the schedule for lectures, poetry readings, concerts, and workshops.

University of Utah Museums

At the University of Utah, University and 200 South sts. ☎ **801/581-6773.** Bus: 1, 2, 5, 7, or 29.

The Mormons opened the University of Deseret in 1850, just $2^1/_2$ years after they arrived in the Salt Lake Valley. It closed 2 years later, due to lack of funds and the greater need for primary education, but reopened in 1867 as a business academy. The name changed in 1892, and the growing school moved to its present location in 1900. The University now sprawls over 1,500 acres on the east side of the city, almost at the mouth of Emigration Canyon.

The university's **Red Butte Garden and Arboretum** (☎ 801/581-4747 for a recording, 801/585-5322 for the visitor center) features 25 acres of display gardens and another 200 acres in their natural state, with 4 miles of nature trails. Located in the foothills of the Wasatch Mountains, this is a terrific spot to take a break from hectic city sightseeing. The gardens are open daily from 9am to dusk (about 8pm), May through September; Tuesday through Sunday from 10am to 5pm, October through April. Admission is $3 for adults, $2 for children ages 4 to 15 and seniors over 60, and free for children under 4. The first Monday of every month in summer is free. From downtown, drive east on 400 South, past the university entrance, continuing until 400 South becomes Foothill Drive; turn east on Wakara Way and continue to the entry drive for the gardens. Via bus, take no. 4 and ask for the Red Butte Garden stop.

The **Utah Museum of Fine Arts,** 1530 E. South Campus Dr. (☎ **801/ 581-7332**), is probably the best art museum in the state, with small, select exhibits of the museum's permanent collection, plus changing exhibits. The displays cover 4,000 years of human artistic endeavors, from ancient Egypt to the Italian Renaissance, European and American art from the 17th century to the present, and art objects from Southeast Asia, China, Japan, and African and pre-Columbian cultures. Admission is free. The museum is open Monday through Friday from 10am to 5pm and weekends from noon to 5pm.

Utah Museum of Natural History, 215 S. 1350 East, University Street at President's Circle (☎ **801/581-4303**), located in the old university library building, covers over 200 million years. Some 200 exhibits take you on a journey through time, describing the geologic and natural creation of Utah right up to the present. The museum is open Monday through Saturday from 9:30am to 5:30pm and on Sundays and holidays from noon to 5pm. Admission is $3 for adults, $1.50 for seniors and children ages 3 to 14, and free for children under 3.

Utah State Historical Society Museum

300 S. Rio Grande St. ☎ **801/533-3500.** Free admission. Mon–Fri 10am–5pm; Sat 10am– 2pm. Bus: 81 along 200 South; walk a block south on Rio Grande.

This museum, housed in the waiting room of the 1910 Denver and Rio Grande Depot, exhibits pioneer regalia and historic photos and paintings. You'll see full-size replicas of a Conestoga wagon and a Mormon handcart, as well as one of the artificial hearts developed in 1976 by the University of Utah's Dr. Robert Jarvik. The large gift shop offers a variety of early Americana gifts and toys, plus one of the state's widest selections of books on Utah—travel and otherwise.

PARKS & GARDENS

International Peace Gardens

Jordan Park, 1000 S. 900 West. Free admission. May–Sept dawn to dusk. Bus: 16 or 17.

Begun in 1939 by the Salt Lake Council of Women, the Peace Gardens have grown and expanded over the years, and now belong to the city. Take a soothing stroll along the Jordan River, through the many gardens and past statuary and displays representing different countries; benches are scattered about for moments of rest and contemplation.

This Is the Place State Park

2601 Sunnyside Ave. ☎ **801/584-8391.** Admission $5 adults, $2 children 3–11 and seniors 62 and over. Apr–Oct 1 Tues–Sat 11am–5pm, plus Thurs until 8pm Memorial Day–Labor Day. Deseret Village daily 8am–5pm. Bus: 4.

Brigham Young and the first group of pioneers got their first glimpse of the Salt Lake Valley at the site of this historic park. A tall granite and bronze sculpture was erected in 1947 to commemorate the centennial of their arrival. **Old Deseret** is a pioneer village made up of many original pioneer buildings from across the state. In the summer, it becomes a living history museum of the period from 1847 to 1869, featuring people in period garb living and working the way their forefathers did. Pioneer events and demonstrations are offered throughout the year.

The visitor center contains exhibits depicting the Mormon pioneers' trek from Illinois to the Great Salt Lake Valley in 1847. The park, which covers over 1,600 acres, also offers hiking along part of the trail used by the pioneers, with opportunities for cross-country skiing in winter. It's also a good place for wildlife viewing and birding in winter and spring, with additional songbirds and raptors present in summer and fall. There's a picnic area, but no camping.

ESPECIALLY FOR KIDS

In addition to what's listed below, the **Hansen Planetarium** and **Utah Museum of Natural History** (see pp. 78 and 83) offer shows and exhibits kids will love. And once they tire of the more educational diversions, you might want to head for the **Utah Fun Dome,** an entertainment mall with bowling alleys, rollerskating, bungee jumping, miniature golf, arcades, and more. It's located at 4998 S. 360 West in the Salt Lake City suburb of Murray (☎ **801/263-8769**). To get there, take I-15 exit 303 for 5300 South, head west to the traffic light at 700 West, and turn north.

The Children's Museum of Utah

840 N. 300 West. ☎ **801/328-3383.** Admission $3, free for children under 2. Mon–Thurs and Sat 9:30am–5pm; Fri 9:30am–8pm. Bus: 70.

Activities and hands-on exhibits are the attraction here. Kids can try face painting and folk dancing, operate a telephone switchboard, uncover an animal skeleton on an archaeological dig, or pilot a jet. Target ages are 2 through 12, and children must be accompanied by an adult.

Hogle Zoo

2600 E. Sunnyside Ave. ☎ **801/582-1631.** Admission $5 adults, $3 children 4–14 and seniors over 65, free for children under 4. Nov–Feb daily 9am–4:30pm; Mar–May and Sept–Oct daily 9am–5pm; June–Aug 9am–6pm. Closed Christmas and New Year's Day. Bus: 4.

This small but modern zoo near the entrance to Emigration Canyon offers a good selection of creatures for kids of all ages to ogle. There's a petting zoo for the little ones, as well as a small replica of an 1869 steam train that gives rides in the summer for the bargain-basement price of 70¢. You'll also find a solarium with exotic plants and birds, a recently-completed primate forest, and a giraffe house with a balcony so you can see eye-to-eye with the tall-necked creatures. Emigration Creek meanders through the tree-shaded grounds. As with any zoo, it's best to visit in one of the cooler seasons, or at least the coolest part of the day, when more animals are out and about.

Wheeler Historic Farm

In the Cottonwood Regional Park, 6351 S. 900 East (just north of I-215 exit 9). ☎ **801/264-2241.** Admission $3 adults, $2 children 3–11 and seniors 65 and older. Spring and fall daily 9:30am–5pm; summer daily 9:30am–8pm; winter daily 1–5pm. Bus: 9 or 27.

Kids particularly enjoy visiting this working farm during the summer ice-cream social in late June. Other special events occur throughout the year, including a brass-band festival in August, a teddy-bear Victorian tea party in September, and breakfast with Santa in December. You can take a hay ride in the summer or a sleigh ride in the winter; historic farming demonstrations take place during the summer season. Call for a schedule of events. And be sure to check out the facilities while you're there: The restored Victorian farmhouse boasts the first indoor bathroom in the county.

NEARBY ATTRACTIONS

Gardner Village

1100 W. 7800 South, West Jordan. ☎ **801/566-8903.** Free admission. Shops open Mon–Thurs 10am–6pm; Fri–Sat 10am–8pm; Sun noon–5pm. Please call for easy directions from I-15.

This quaint village is a cluster of historic homes restored and converted into stores and dining places. The village museum tells the story of pioneer and polygamist Archibald Gardner, who first built a sawmill, then replaced it with a larger flour mill. As the area grew, he added a woolen mill and mattress, broom, and button factories. Be sure to check out the furniture store in the restored 1877 mill.

Kennecott's Bingham Canyon Mine

Utah 48 (7200 South), about 25 miles southwest of Salt Lake City outside of Copperton. ☎ **801/252-3234.** Admission $3 per car, $2 per motorcycle. Apr–Oct daily 8am–8pm. Closed Nov–Mar. Take I-15 south to exit 301 for Midvale, and head west on Utah 48 to the mine.

The world's largest open-pit copper mine is a sight to see. The visitor center is inside the mine, with exhibits and a video presentation that show the history and geology and describe the operations of the mine. No guided tours are offered, but you'll get a spectacular view of the open-pit mine from an observation area; you might even see an explosion, as rock is blasted away to expose additional copper ore.

7 Organized Tours

Gray Line Tours, 553 W. 100 South (☎ **800/309-2352** or 801/521-7060), offers several tours of the city and surrounding areas, including the Bingham Copper Mine and Great Salt Lake beaches. A 2 1/2-hour tour of the city and Mormon Trail costs $16 for adults and $9 for children ages 5 through 12; kids 4 and under are free. A 4-hour tour to the mine and lake is $26 for adults and $13 for children. You can get an all-day combination tour for $40 and $20, respectively. The line also offers several national-park package tours.

Innsbrook Tours, 57 W. South Temple, No. 400 (☎ **801/534-1001**), offers city tours, with pickups at several locations around town, including some campgrounds and motels. Cost is $15, and you can add a side trip to the Great Salt Lake for $5. Pickups are between 10 and 11am, and the city tour ends at 3pm (the one including the lake ends at 4pm). Call before 10am to reserve a seat.

Old Salty, a replica trolley, gives 1 1/2-hour historical tours of the city from Memorial Day weekend through the first week in October. Departures are from Temple Square South Gate at 11am, 1pm, and 3pm, and from the Trolley Square Water Tower at 12:15pm and 2:15pm daily. Cost for the tour is $7.50 adults, $6.50 seniors, $3.25 children ages 5 to 12, free for children 4 and under. A family pass, for parents and up to eight children under age 18, runs $24. Tickets can be purchased at Rainbows at Trolley Square and from the conductor, or you can make reservations by calling ☎ **801/359-8677** and using a credit card.

8 Outdoor Activities & Spectator Sports

OUTDOOR ACTIVITIES

Gart Sports outlets, open Monday through Friday from 9am to 9pm, Saturday from 9am to 7pm, and Sunday from 10am to 6pm, can meet most of your recreational-equipment needs. There are several locations in the Salt Lake City area, including 1176 E. 2100 South (☎ 801/487-7726); 5550 S. 900 East, Murray (☎ 801/

263-3633); and 10200 S. State St., Sandy (☎ 801/566-7404). **Recreational Equipment, Inc. (REI),** offers a wide range of sporting goods, both sales and rentals. They're located at 3285 E. 3300 South (☎ 801/486-2100) and in Orem at 322 W. 1300 South (☎ 801/222-9500).

BIKING You'll find a number of bikeways along city streets, some separate from but running parallel to the road, some a defined part of the road with a line designating the bike lane, and others sharing the driving lane with motor vehicles. From mid-May through September, City Creek Canyon, east of Capitol Hill, is open only to bicyclists on odd-numbered days; on even-numbered days it is open only to cars. Bicycle rentals and repairs are available from **Bike Board Blade,** downtown at 703 E. 1700 South (☎ 801/467-0992) and in Sandy at 8801 S. 700 East (☎ 801/561-2626); and **Guthrie Bicycle,** downtown at 156 E. 200 South (☎ 801/363-3727) and at the University of Utah at 1330 E. 200 South (☎ 801/581-9977).

BOATING The Great Salt Lake, at the city's front door, has marinas on the south shore and on Antelope Island. See chapter 8, "The Northern Wasatch Front: The Great Salt Lake & Utah's Old West," for details.

FISHING Trout can be found in the rivers feeding into the Great Salt Lake, although no fish can live in the lake itself. Popular fishing spots include Big and Little Cottonwood creeks and Mill Creek. Fishing licenses are required; you can get one, along with maps and suggestions, at most sporting-goods stores. A good source for supplies is **Anglers Inn,** 2292 S. Highland Dr. (☎ 801/466-3921), which also offers guided fishing trips.

GOLF There are seven city courses with one central telephone number for general information and reservations (☎ 801/972-7888). All require 7 days' notice for reservations: the 18-hole, par-72 **Bonneville,** at 954 Connor St. (☎ 801/583-9513), with hills, a large ravine, and creek; the 9-hole, par-36 **Forest Dale,** 2375 S. 900 East (☎ 801/483-5420), a re-designed historic course with huge trees; the 18-hole, par-72 **Glendale,** 1630 W. 2100 South (☎ 801/974-2403), one of the most popular of Salt Lake City's courses; the 36-hole, par-72 **Mountain Dell** in Parley's Canyon east on I-80 (☎ 801/582-3812), a challenging mountain course; the 9-hole, par-34 **Nibley Park,** 2780 S. 700 East (☎ 801/483-5418), a good beginner course; the flat but challenging 18-hole, par-72 **Rose Park,** 1386 N. Redwood Rd. (☎ 801/596-5030); and the city's top course, the 18-hole, par-72 **Wingpointe,** 3602 W. 100 North, near the airport (☎ 801/575-2345), a links-style course designed by Arthur Hills.

From Monday through Thursday, greens fees for city courses are $7 to $9 for 9 holes and $14 to $17 for 18 holes. Add $1 to $2 on weekends and holidays.

HIKING The Salt Lake Valley offers innumerable hiking opportunities. City Creek Canyon, located east of Capitol Hill, is a great spot for hikers. Another prime hiking area in the city is Red Butte Garden and Arboretum (see "Museums," above), with its 4 miles of trails. For maps and detailed information on trails in the mountains south and east of the city, contact the **Wasatch-Cache National Forest,** 6914 S. Grant Blvd. (☎ 801/943-2667).

Those of you traveling with pets should note that they're not welcome on trails in watershed areas.

ICE-SKATING The **John W. Gallivan Utah Center** has an ice rink; see p. 82 for details.

IN-LINE SKATING Stop at **Classic Skating,** 9151 S. 255 West, Sandy (☎ 801/561-1791), for rentals.

JOGGING   Memory Grove Park and City Creek Canyon are both terrific places for walking and jogging. The park is on the east side of the Capitol, and the canyon follows City Creek to the northeast. In town, stop at one of the city parks, such as Liberty Park (entrance at 600 E. 900 South, between 900 and 1300 South streets and 500 and 700 East streets; ☎ 801/596-5036).

ROCK CLIMBING   The Wasatch Mountains are a climber's paradise. Contact **Exum Mountain Adventures,** 7350 S. Wasatch Blvd. (☎ 801/944-5493), for courses and guided tours in rock, ice, and Alpine climbing. **Extreme Sports Center,** 8700 S. Sandy Pkwy., Sandy (☎ 801/562-1400), has a three-story climbing wall and offers instruction for all levels, beginner through advanced.

SKIING   For all the details on the nearby ski resorts, see chapters 8 and 9, "The Northern Wasatch Front: The Great Salt Lake & Utah's Old West" and "The Southern Wasatch Front: World-Class Skiing & More."

TENNIS   There are numerous public courts in the city if your hotel doesn't have one. Check with the front desk for the one closest to you, or call the city parks department at ☎ 801/972-7800. A pro shop is located at Liberty Park, entrance at 600 E. 900 South, between 900 and 1300 South streets and 500 and 700 East streets (☎ 801/596-5036).

SPECTATOR SPORTS

COLLEGIATE SPORTS   The **University of Utah's Runnin' Utes** and **Lady Utes** compete in the NCAA and Western Athletic Conference. The football team plays at Rice Stadium (☎ 801/581-8314 for information, 801/581-6641 for tickets), and the gymnastics and highly-rated basketball teams compete at Jon M. Huntsman Center (☎ 801/581-8314 for information, 801/581-6641 for tickets). The women's gymnastics team is phenomenal. Tickets are usually available on fairly short notice, although it's best to call as far in advance as possible for football games.

MINOR LEAGUE BASEBALL   The city's newest sports team, the Triple-A **Salt Lake Buzz** (☎ 801/485-3800) of the Pacific Coast League, plays at Franklin Quest Field, at the intersection of 1300 South and West Temple. Tickets are usually available on short notice.

PRO BASKETBALL   The NBA's **Utah Jazz** (☎ 801/355-3865) plays basketball—not music—at Delta Center, 301 W. South Temple. Star players John Stockton and Karl Malone are both veterans of the U.S. Olympic "Dream Team." This winning team usually packs the house, so get your tickets early.

PRO HOCKEY   The **Utah Grizzlies** (☎ 801/988-7825) of the International Hockey League currently play in the new 10,000-plus-seat "E" Center, 3200 S. Decker Lake Blvd. in West Valley City (off I-215 exit 20). As the team's popularity is growing, it's best to call early for tickets.

VOLLEYBALL   The **Utah Predators** (☎ 801/485-9799) are members of the National Volleyball Association, created in 1996 by the existing women's professional volleyball teams. Call for game locations and other details.

9 Shopping

Salt Lake City is not a major shopping destination. You'll certainly find plenty of stores, but with a few exceptions they're the same as the ones you have at home.

Many stores are closed Sundays—the influence of the LDS Church—and typical store hours are Monday through Saturday from 9am to 6pm. Shopping malls are the exception; they're often open Sunday afternoons from noon to 5 or 6pm, and also stay open a few hours later on weeknights.

THE TEMPLE SQUARE AREA   This is the city's top shopping destination. The best place to start is **Crossroads Plaza,** 50 S. Main St. (☎ 801/531-1799), right across the street from the Square. This enclosed mall houses more than 140 stores, and can satisfy almost all of your wants and needs, from books and clothing to music boxes and original art.

Nearby, **ZCMI Center Mall,** 36 S. State St. (☎ 801/321-8745), is the home of the original **Zion's Cooperative Mercantile Institution,** which claims to be America's first department store, opened by the LDS Church in 1868. Also here is **Deseret Books,** where you'll find an abundance of books on the LDS Church and recordings of the Mormon Tabernacle Choir; plus Gart Sports, a branch post office, and several dozen food and specialty shops. **Mormon Handicraft,** begun during the Depression to encourage home industry and preserve pioneer arts, is also in the mall. The shop carries a large inventory of quilting fabrics and supplies, as well as handmade quilts, a wide variety of other crafts, and religious books and videos. The mall is closed on Sundays.

TROLLEY SQUARE   Another popular shopping spot for visitors is **Trolley Square,** 600 South at 700 East (☎ 801/521-9877), where you'll find modern shops, galleries, and restaurants in an old-fashioned setting. You'll also see two of the city's original trolley cars on their original tracks, a historic water tower, and two of the city's first street lamps.

WESTERN WEAR   If you can't go home without a genuine Stetson hat or your very own pair of Tony Lama cowboy boots, head to **Sheplers,** 5584 S. Redwood Rd. (☎ 801/966-4200), a chain and catalog store that claims to be the largest western-wear retailer in the world.

OUTLET SHOPPING   Shoppers looking for bargains should head to the **Factory Stores of America,** 12101 S. Factory Outlet Dr., in Draper (☎ 801/571-2933). Located just south of Salt Lake City, off I-15 at exit 294, this complex houses almost three dozen outlets, including VF Factory Outlet, Carter's Childrenswear, Danskin, Welcome Home, Van Heusen, Bugle Boy, and Bass Shoes.

10 Salt Lake City After Dark

PERFORMING ARTS

The theater season in Salt Lake City runs primarily from September through May, but many companies stage presentations year-round, and music festivals help fill up the summer months. Get the Friday morning issue of the *Salt Lake Tribune* and Friday evening's *Deseret News* for listings of upcoming events. For additional entertainment news and event listings, you can pick up one or both of the free papers: *The Event* and *Private Eye,* which also offers alternative news articles. What's more, the Salt Lake City Convention and Visitors Bureau publishes an annual calendar of events, along with monthly updates; inquire at the visitor center.

At the historic **Capitol Theatre,** 50 W. 200 South (☎ **801/355-2787** box office), home to several local performing-arts companies, you can attend dance, theater, and musical productions (see below), including Broadway musicals. Call to see what's scheduled during your visit.

CLASSICAL MUSIC

The highly acclaimed ✪ **Utah Symphony,** considered one of the country's top symphony orchestras, performs year-round in Abravanel Hall, 123 W. South Temple

(☎ 801/533-6683), an elegant 2,800-seat venue known for its excellent acoustics. Favorite annual performing-arts events include the November "Messiah Sing-in," with the Utah Chorus and soloists, and "New Year's Eve at Symphony Hall." But the summer series in July is probably the best time to see the orchestra, when it performs Tchaikovsky's *1812 Overture,* using real cannons at outdoor concerts at Snowbird and Park City.

The **Utah Music Festival** offers fine chamber music during July and most of August in Salt Lake City, Snowbird, Logan, and Deer Valley. In Salt Lake, performances take place at the Utah Museum of Fine Arts at the University, and at Temple Square. Contact the Festival at P.O. Box 3381, Logan, UT 84323-3381 (☎ 800/816-UTAH).

DANCE

The nationally acclaimed **Ballet West** performs at Capitol Theatre (see above). There are usually four productions between September and March, ranging from classical to contemporary.

Modern-dance lovers should check out two companies, both also at Capitol Theatre. The **Repertory Dance Theatre** produces mostly American works, both classical and contemporary; and the **Ririe-Woodbury Dance Company,** one of the ten most active national touring companies, performs locally several times each year.

For information and tickets, call the Capitol Theatre (☎ 801/355-2787 box office).

OPERA

Also at the Capitol Theatre (see above) is the **Utah Opera Company,** featuring international artists. Operas are sung in their original language, with super-titles providing English translations. For information and tickets, call the Capitol Theatre (☎ 801/355-2787 box office).

THEATER

The **Pioneer Theatre Company,** 300 S. 1340 East (☎ 801/581-6961), is Utah's resident professional theater. Located on the University campus, its repertoire ranges from classical to contemporary plays and musicals. Call for a current schedule.

THE CLUB SCENE
LIVE MUSIC

COUNTRY   The **Dead Goat Saloon,** 156 S. West Temple, in Arrow Press Square (☎ 801/328-4628), is a fun, funky beer bar with live acoustic and blues bands every night, plus satellite TV, darts, pool, and grill food. **Sandy's Station,** 8925 S. 255 West, Sandy (☎ 801/255-2078), is a popular country-western swing bar.

JAZZ, BLUES & FOLK   For jazz and blues, try the **Zephyr Club,** 301 S. West Temple (☎ 801/355-2582). **D.B. Coopers,** 19 E. 200 South (☎ 801/532-2948), has been around for 25 years, featuring folk and rhythm and blues, including occasional big-name entertainers.

AFTER-THEATER

Club Baci, 140 W. Pierpont Ave. (☎ 801/328-1333), is a fun place to stop after a show, since the Capitol Theatre is only about a half block northeast. Two other great before- or after-theater choices are **The New Yorker,** 60 Market St. (☎ 801/363-0166), and the **Oyster Bar** (☎ 801/531-6044), located above The New Yorker. They're just 1¹/₂ blocks south of the Capitol Theatre, close to several parking areas.

11 Rolling the Dice on the Nevada State Line: An Easy Side Trip to Wendover

The little community of Wendover sits along I-80 at the edge of the Bonneville Salt Flats, half in Utah and half in Nevada. It isn't really close to anything. One of Wendover's claims to fame is that the terrain here is so flat, you can actually see the curvature of the earth. Remarkable geography aside, Wendover is a popular gambling destination for Salt Lake City residents, who park their cars at the casinos on the Nevada side of town.

Wendover is also the site of a World War II Air Force Base, where a bomber crew was trained before taking off to drop atomic bombs on Hiroshima and Nagasaki, Japan. A small museum is located in the hangar once occupied by the B-29 bomber Enola Gay, which carried the bomb to Hiroshima. Stop at the Wendover Welcome Center (see below) for information and directions.

ESSENTIALS

GETTING THERE   Wendover is 120 miles west of Salt Lake City on I-80, at the Utah/Nevada border.

VISITOR INFORMATION   The **Wendover Welcome Center** is on Wendover Boulevard, just off I-80 at exit 1 in Nevada. They'll provide exact directions to the best vantage point—about a mile west on Wendover Boulevard—to see the earth's curvature. Outside the visitor center sits a 20-foot-tall stone Peace Monument, displaying a metal sculpture of the Enola Gay bomber. For additional information on Wendover, contact the **Wendover USA Visitor and Convention Bureau,** P.O. Box 2468, Wendover, NV 89883 (☎ **800/426-6862** or 702/664-3414).

THE CASINOS

Casinos offering lodging, food, live big-name entertainment, seemingly endless rows of slot machines and gambling tables, and all the other Vegas-style trappings include **The State Line,** straddling said state line at 295 E. Wendover Blvd. (☎ **800/ 848-7300** or 435/665-2226); **The Red Garter Hotel and Casino,** west of the Welcome Center at the corner of Wendover Boulevard and Camper Drive (☎ **800/ 982-2111** or 702/664-2111); and **Peppermill Inn and Casino,** just across Wendover Boulevard from the Welcome Center (☎ **800/648-9660** or 702/ 664-2255).

THE NEARBY SALT FLATS

Even those without the urge to roll the dice or wrestle one-armed bandits enjoy watching the famous land speed trials at the salt flats, about 10 miles east of Wendover off I-80, or just staring out across this unbelievable white expanse. The adventurous might even want to do a few time trials of their own, although it's unlikely that many Sunday drivers would want to even approach the 622.4-mph speed—a world record at the time—reached by Gary Gabolich in his rocket car, "Blue Flame," in 1970. There are displays and information on the salt flats at viewpoints along I-80, and a short access road leads out onto them. For information, contact the Bureau of Land Management, Salt Lake District, 2370 S. 2300 West, Salt Lake City, UT 84119 (☎ **801/977-4300**).

The Northern Wasatch Front: The Great Salt Lake & Utah's Old West

Just northwest of Salt Lake City is the Great Salt Lake, one of the most extraordinary natural features in North America and one of the city's favorite playgrounds. The lake's largest island, Antelope Island, is also Utah's largest state park. North of Salt Lake City on I-84 is Ogden, which owes its prosperity to the transcontinental railroad; it's a good starting point for discovering northern Utah's Old West. It's also a great home base for outdoor recreation; there's skiing at three nearby resorts in the winter, and hiking and horseback riding in the rugged mountains in the summer. Considered mandatory for all railroad buffs is a visit to Golden Spike National Historic Site, the point at which the East and West coasts of the United States were joined by rail in 1869. I-84 also leads to U.S. 89/91 and the pretty little town of Logan, which offers good hiking, horseback-riding, and biking opportunities.

1 The Great Salt Lake & Antelope Island State Park

You wouldn't expect to come across what is essentially a small ocean in the middle of the desert, but here it is: the Great Salt Lake. The lake is all that's left of ancient Lake Bonneville, which once covered most of western Utah and parts of Idaho and Nevada. Unlike its mother lake, though, the Great Salt Lake has no outlet, so everything that flows into it—some 2 million tons of minerals annually—stays there until someone or something—usually brine flies, brine shrimp, birds, and man—removes it. So when you see swarms of flies, don't wonder why the powers that be haven't eliminated them. Besides, they don't bite, and rarely even light on people. Minerals, including salt, potassium, and magnesium, are mined here; don't be surprised to see front-end loaders moving huge piles of salt to the Morton Company along I-80, on the lake's south shore.

This natural wonder might be worth checking out, but don't expect much. Although Salt Lake City residents enjoy spending weekends at the lake, it really isn't a major tourist destination, and facilities are limited. Boaters should bring their own boats, as no rentals are available. Despite its salinity, it's a relatively flat lake—kind of like a big puddle—so don't pack your surfboard. Campers will find an acceptable but uninspiring campground at Great Salt

Lake State Park, and some pleasant primitive camping—plus the lake's best beaches, with the cleanest sand—at Antelope Island State Park.

ANTELOPE ISLAND STATE PARK

The largest of 10 islands in the Great Salt Lake, measuring about 5 miles wide and 15 miles long, Antelope Island was named by Kit Carson and John Frémont in 1843 for the many pronghorns they found here. Hunting wiped out the herd by the 1870s, but buffalo were introduced in 1893, and have been joined by elk, deer, and other wildlife.

The beaches of Antelope Island don't have the fine-grained sand and shells of an ocean beach; rather, they're a mixture of dirt and gravel. But the water is a great place to relax; because of its high salinity, you don't have to work very hard to stay afloat—the water buoys you up effortlessly.

ESSENTIALS

GETTING THERE   Antelope Island is about 30 miles northwest of downtown Salt Lake City and about 16 miles southeast of downtown Ogden. Take I-15 to exit 335, go 6$^1/_2$ miles west to the park entrance, and cross the 7-mile causeway to the island.

INFORMATION   For information, contact **Antelope Island State Park,** 4528 W. 1700 South, Syracuse, UT 84075-6868. The visitor center (☎ **801/773-2941**), open daily in summer from 10am to 5pm and in winter from 10am to 3pm, has exhibits and information on the Great Salt Lake and the island's wildlife and migratory birds.

FEES   Day-use fees are $6 per vehicle and $2.50 for walk-ins and those on bicycles or in-line skates. The marina offers dock rental overnight.

PETS   Pets are welcome in the park, but should be leashed at all times.

SPORTS & OUTDOOR ACTIVITIES

BIKING, HIKING & HORSEBACK RIDING   Most of the island is closed to vehicular traffic, but there are over 30 miles of hiking trails and bike and horse paths. Although generally unmarked, trails follow old ranch roads. Check at the visitor center or talk with a ranger before heading out; they can fill you in on current conditions and tell you where you're most likely to spot wildlife.

At this writing, there are no concessions for rentals on the island, so you'll have to bring your own bikes (and horses, if you'd like to ride). For information on bike-rental shops in Salt Lake City, see p. 86.

The 3-mile **Lake Side Trail** leaves the Bridger Bay Campground and follows the beach around the northwestern tip of the island to the group camping area on White Rock Bay. The walk is magnificent at sunset. Other trails take you away from the crowds, where you might catch a glimpse of buffalo or some of the other wildlife that make the island their home.

SWIMMING   The largest beach is at Bridger Bay, where you'll find picnic tables and modern rest rooms with outdoor showers to wash off the salt.

WILDLIFE WATCHING   You can drive to the buffalo corral and see these great shaggy creatures fairly close up. If you head into the less-traveled areas, you might see deer, buffalo, bobcats, elk, coyote, or bighorn sheep.

The annual bison roundup takes place in late November and early December. You can usually see wranglers herding the bison into corrals on the last weekend of November (binoculars might be helpful), and get a close-up view the next weekend as the bison receive their annual checkups. Call to find out exactly when the roundup will be.

CAMPING

There are two camping areas in the park: **Bridger Bay Campground** offers primitive camping at $9 per night; you can also use the parking area at **Bridger Bay Beach** for $11 per night (extra vehicles are $7). Although there are no hookups at either area, there are modern rest rooms with showers, and picnic tables at Bridger Bay Beach. Camping reservations can be made with a major credit card by calling ☎ **801/773-2941.**

MORE TO SEE & DO

Ten miles south of the visitor center, down a washboard-like gravel road, is the **Fielding Garr Ranch House.** The original three-room adobe house, built in 1848, was inhabited until the state acquired it in 1981. In addition to the ranch house, there's a small building that was a schoolroom by day and sleeping quarters for the farmhands at night, plus a spring house, the only freshwater source.

There's a small food concession at the ranch (open only when the ranch is open), as well as a large shady picnic area. Half-hour wagon rides are available at a cost of $5 for adults, $4 for children ages 6 to 12, and $20 for a family of up to six. Check with the visitor center for schedule information.

GREAT SALT LAKE STATE PARK

A less-than-exciting stretch of muddy-sandy beach greets you as you step out of your car at the beach end of this park. But the expanse of water and distant islands can be lovely, especially at dusk or early in the morning. Prickly pear cactus blooms along the shore of the Great Salt Lake in the late spring. And for those susceptible to the lure of the sea, this huge inland ocean is mysteriously irresistible any time of year.

One thing you need to be prepared for: The air can be heavy with the stench of rotting algae at times, making even a brief stroll on the beach here quite unpleasant. At other times, when the wind is right or the lake high enough, trekking out to the water's edge is downright enjoyable. If you brought a boat, this is a perfect spot for getting out into the Great Salt Lake.

ESSENTIALS

GETTING THERE   Great Salt Lake State Park is 16 miles west of Salt Lake City. Take I-80 west out of Salt Lake City to exit 104; head east on the frontage road about 2 miles to the park entrance.

INFORMATION   For information, contact **Great Salt Lake State Park,** P.O. Box 323, Magna, UT 84044-0323 (☎ **801/250-1898**). Park headquarters are located at the marina, 2 miles west of the I-80 exit 104 interchange.

FEES & REGULATIONS   Day use from 8am to sunset is free. Alcoholic beverages are forbidden.

PETS   Pets are not allowed in this park, although they are permitted at most of Utah's state parks.

OUTDOOR ACTIVITIES

Sailing and water sports are the main attractions here, plus lazing on the beach. You'll find picnic tables, open showers for washing off salt and sand after a float in the lake, and modern rest rooms. The marina, 2 miles west of the I-80 exit 104 interchange, is open year-round. Boat slips and a launching ramp are available, but no boat rentals.

CAMPING

Camping is allowed along the beach, where there are a few picnic shelters, flush toilets, and outdoor showers for washing off sand and salt. Camping fees, collected by a ranger, are $7 Sunday through Thursday, and $8 on Fridays, Saturdays, and holidays.

MORE TO SEE & DO

Set on the south side of the Great Salt Lake, the Moorish **Saltair Resort & Pavilion** (☎ **801/250-4400**) is a striking sight. The original resort, even more lavishly Moorish, was built in 1893 on 2,500 10-inch wooden pillars and extended out over the water. The resort, burned to the pilings in 1925, was rebuilt, abandoned in the late 1950s after the receding lake left it high and dry, and finally burned again in 1970. After several revival attempts, all of which succumbed to flooding and fire, the present building was built south of the original site, back on the sand.

Dances and concerts take place in the huge domed ballroom, and a variety of food concessions operate here. It's open daily from 10am to 8pm in the summer and until 5pm in the winter, with extended hours on concert nights. Admission fees vary depending on the event; inquire at the information desk or check the daily newspaper entertainment section for schedules and prices.

2 Ogden: Utah's West at Its Wildest

Located in the deltas of the Ogden and Weber rivers, Ogden has always been a bit different, a city apart from the rest of Utah. Although founded by Mormon pioneers, laid out by church leader Brigham Young, and called home by a sizable Mormon population, Ogden really began life as a popular rendezvous site for mountain men and fur trappers in the 1820s, and became—much to the chagrin of the church—a seriously rowdy railroad town in the 1870s. It retains some of that devil-may-care attitude today.

But Ogden's current popularity has little to do with such sinful beginnings. Like other Wasatch Front communities, the bustling city of more than 60,000 has fine little museums and historic sites, as well as good restaurants and hotels. More important, though, is its location: Ogden serves as a great base for enjoying the surrounding mountains, whatever your preference—skiing, snowmobiling, hiking, mountain biking, horseback riding, or boating. Mt. Ben Lomond Peak, which lies to the east of the city, may look familiar—it inspired the famous Paramount Pictures logo.

ESSENTIALS

GETTING THERE

BY CAR   Ogden is 35 miles north of Salt Lake City. It's easily accessible from the north and south via I-15, and from the east and northwest from I-84.

BY AIRPORT SHUTTLE   Shuttle service is available to and from Salt Lake International Airport from **Prime Time Shuttle** (☎ **800/397-0773**). The one-way, per-person cost is $22 to $24. For best service, call at least 24 hours in advance. **Classic Limousine** (☎ **801/774-6027**) offers private vehicle service for up to 10 persons; cost is $70 per hour plus 20% gratuity, with a 2-hour minimum; 1 hour or less costs $100 flat rate, plus 20% gratuity.

INFORMATION

The **Ogden/Weber Convention and Visitor's Bureau** maintains an information center in Union Station, 2501 Wall Ave., Ogden, UT 84401 (☎ **800/255-8824** or

801/627-8288). From I-15 north/I-84 west, take exit 344A and head east to Wall Avenue; turn north (left) to the station.

For information regarding the national forests in the area, contact the **Ogden Ranger District,** Wasatch-Cache National Forest, 507 25th St., Suite 103, Ogden, UT 84401 (☎ **801/625-5112**). Information on national forests is also available at the visitor center at Union Station.

GETTING AROUND

As in most of Utah, driving is the easiest way to get around Ogden. The streets are laid out in typically neat Mormon-pioneer fashion, but with a slightly different nomenclature. Those running east to west are numbered from 1st Street in the north to 47th in the south, and north–south streets are named for U.S. presidents and other historical figures. The city center is usually considered to be at the intersection of historic 25th Street and Washington Boulevard.

Car-rental agencies with offices in Ogden include **Avis** (☎ 800/831-2847 or 801/394-5984), **Budget** (☎ 800/237-7251 or 800/527-0700), **Hertz** (☎ 800/654-3131 or 801/621-6500), **National** (☎ 800/227-7368 or 801/393-8800), **Sears** (☎ 800/237-7251), and **Thrifty** (☎ 800/367-2277 or 801/627-3069).

The **Utah Transit Authority,** 135 W. 17th St. (☎ **801/627-3500**), provides regular bus transportation throughout the greater Ogden area, Monday through Saturday. Schedules are available at the information center in Union Station.

For taxi service, call **Yellow Cab Co.** (☎ **801/394-9411**). Limousine service is available from **Classic Limo** (☎ **801/774-6027**) and **Legend Limousine** (☎ **801/393-6707**).

FAST FACTS: OGDEN

There are two fairly large hospitals in Ogden: the **McKay-Dee Hospital Center,** 3939 Harrison Blvd. (☎ **801/627-2800;** in emergencies 801/625-2020), and the **Columbia Medical Center,** 5475 S. 500 East (☎ **801/479-2111;** in emergencies 801/479-2376). The **main post office** is at 3680 Pacific Ave. (☎ **801/627-4184**). The local **newspaper** is the *Standard Examiner* (☎ **801/625-4200**). **Sales tax** in Ogden is just over 6%.

WHAT TO SEE & DO

Eccles Community Art Center

2580 Jefferson Ave. ☎ **801/392-6935**. Free admission. Mon–Fri 9am–5pm; Sat 10am–4pm. From I-15, take exit 345 and head east on 24th St. to Jefferson Ave.; turn right (south); the Art Center is 2 blocks ahead.

This 2¹/₂-story turreted, castlelike mansion was built in 1893 and purchased 3 years later by David and Bertha Eccles. Throughout her life, Bertha welcomed community groups into her home and made it known to her family that she wished the house to always be used for education and cultural enrichment. Since 1948 her wish has been fulfilled; in 1959, the Ogden Community Arts Council moved in.

Changing art exhibits are displayed in the Main House, with works by local, regional, and national artists in a variety of media. The Carriage House sales gallery features local arts and crafts, including paintings, pottery, fabric art, and jewelry.

Classes in the visual arts and dance are offered, as well as occasional piano recitals; call for schedules and details.

✪ Fort Buenaventura State Park

2450 South "A" Ave. ☎ **801/392-5581**. Admission $1.50 adults, $1 children ages 6–15, $6 maximum per family. Daily 8am–dark. Take 24th St. west across the railroad tracks and turn south onto "A" Ave. to the park.

With a replica of an 1846 fort and trading post and exhibits depicting the mountain men and fur trade of the area back to the 1820s, this historical park shows what life was like in this rugged land before "civilization" arrived. Built in 1846 by fur trapper and horse trader Miles Goodyear, Fort Buenaventura was the first permanent Anglo settlement in the Great Basin. The Mormons bought the fort when they arrived in 1849, and the city of Ogden grew up around it.

Today, the reconstructed fort represents the area's transition from the territory of nomadic Native American tribes and trappers to permanent settlements in the American West. The ranger who guides your tour will be able to answer any questions you have about the mountain-man era. A visitor center has exhibits of Native American artifacts typical of the area; there's also a huge buffalo head on the wall.

Fort Buenaventura hosts several traditional mountain-man rendezvous each year, with music, Dutch-oven food, and a variety of contests that usually include a tomahawk throw, canoe race, shooting competition, and foot races, with all competitors in pre-1840s dress. The rendezvous are usually scheduled on Easter (with a nondenominational sunrise service and Easter-egg hunt) and Labor Day weekends. A Pioneer Skills Festival takes place on July 24th.

Mountain-man supplies are available in a shop in the fort every Saturday year-round. The park also has ponds, canoes for rent ($5 per hour, $10 for 3 hours), and a picnic area. A 2-mile hiking trail meanders around the park, and fishing is permitted with a current license. There is group camping only (be sure to make a reservation) at all times except rendezvous weekends.

George S. Eccles Dinosaur Park

1544 E. Park Blvd., Ogden River Pkwy. ☎ **801/393-3466.** Admission $3.50 adults, $1.50 children ages 3–17, $2.50 seniors. Apr–May and Sept–Oct Mon–Sat 10am–6pm, Sun noon–6pm; June–Aug Mon–Sat 10am–8pm, Sun noon–6pm. Take 12th St. east 5 miles to the mouth of Ogden Canyon and follow the signs.

Wander among life-size reproductions of more than 100 prehistoric creatures from the Cretaceous, Jurassic, and Triassic periods. You'll encounter interactive displays and activities and a youth learning center open daily from noon to 4pm.

Hill Aerospace Museum

7961 Wardleigh Rd., Hill Air Force Base. ☎ **801/777-6818.** Free admission. Mon–Fri 9am–4:30pm; Sat–Sun 9am–5:30pm. From I-15, take exit 341 to the museum.

You'll get a close-up view of more than 50 planes, plus missiles and bombs, on your self-guided walking tour through this museum. Among the most prized displays are the SR-71 "Blackbird" spy plane and the B-17 "Flying Fortress." You'll also see a World War II chapel, a fire truck, a Gatling gun, and a Norden bombsight. Displays show visitors the history of the Air Force, how aircraft fly, and what the Air Force does today.

Ogden Nature Center

966 W. 12th St. ☎ **801/621-7595.** Admission $1 ages 4 and older, free for children under 4. Mon–Sat 10am–4pm. From I-15, take exit 347 and head east on 12th St.

An escape from the hustle and bustle of the city, this wildlife sanctuary is also a rehabilitation center where injured birds are treated and released back into the wild. There are trails for warm-weather strolling or, when snow blankets the ground, snowshoeing and cross-country skiing. A Learning and Visitors Center houses hawks, ravens, and other birds; exhibits; a library; and a museum shop. The center also sponsors various educational programs.

Treehouse Children's Museum

Ogden City Mall. ☎ **801/394-9663**. Admission $1.50 adults, $3 children ages 2–12. Mon 10am–noon (10am–9pm in summer and on Mon holidays); Tues–Thurs 10am–6pm; Fri 10am–9pm; Sat 10am–6pm. Take exit 246 off I-15 and head east on 21st St. to Washington Blvd.; turn right for 1 block, then right at 22nd St., and enter the north mall parking lot.

Both kids and grown-ups will find this an entertaining, hands-on learning experience, where you can climb into the giant tree house or walk around the state of Utah in a matter of minutes. In the Pen and Ink Studio, you can make books, bookmarks, cards, or stationery. A planned expansion will focus on classic literature including the tales of King Arthur and Robin Hood. Scheduled events include a theater program and group craft activities based on children's books; call for information. And, just like the kids it attracts, Treehouse keeps growing and changing—so who knows what you might find on your visit?

Union Station

2501 Wall Ave. ☎ **801/629-8535**. Admission to museums $3 adults, $1.50 seniors 65 and over, $1 children under 12. Mon–Sat 10am–5pm; Sun in summer 11am–3pm. Take exit 344 off I-15 and follow 31st St. east to Wall Ave.; go north 6 blocks to the station.

This stately depot faces historic 25th Street, with lovely flowers and a fountain gracing the cobbled courtyard in front. Built in 1924 to replace the original depot (which was destroyed by fire), the station now houses several museums, an art gallery, a gift shop, a theater, the Union Grill (see "Where to Dine," below), a visitor information center, and the Ogden/Weber Convention and Visitors Bureau.

The station's restored **lobby,** now stripped of the long wooden benches of yesteryear, houses an information center. The immense room boasts a mural at either end commemorating the building of the railroad and the linking of east and west (which you can learn more about on a visit to Golden Spike National Historic Site; see p. 108). Both 12-by-50–foot murals were done in the late 1970s by Edward Laning, and are based on murals he painted in 1935 for New York's Ellis Island Immigration Building.

The **Utah State Railroad Museum** displays gas turbine locomotive designs and has an extensive HO-gauge layout that depicts the construction and geography of the 1,776-mile transcontinental route. You can either wander around on your own or be guided through by a railroad buff who can describe the whys and wherefores of what you'll be seeing.

The **Browning Firearms Museum** displays Browning guns from 1878 to modern times. There's also a replica of an 1880s gun shop and a film describing the Browning legacy.

The **Browning-Kimball Car Collection** displays beautiful examples of classic cars, mostly luxury models. You can see about a dozen vehicles from the early 1900s, including a 1901 curved-dash Oldsmobile, Pierce-Arrows from 1909 and 1931, a 1910 Simplex Runabout, a 1931 Lincoln, and a 1932 Lincoln 12-cylinder Berline. There's also a display of historical license plates and early gas pumps.

The **Myra Powell Gallery** exhibits a variety of art through invitational and competitive shows.

The **Eccles Rail Center** pays tribute to the Goliaths of the rails—locomotives designed to pull long trains through the steep mountains of the west. On display are the Big Blow, a gas turbine rated at over twice the horsepower of typical modern locomotives, and the largest diesel locomotive, the Centennial.

WALKING TOUR
Historic Downtown Ogden

A walk through Ogden's past is a walk through the history of the American West. Allow between 1 and 2 hours, and begin your tour at the:

1. **Miles Goodyear Cabin and The Weber Stake Relief Society Building,** 2148 Grant Ave., on Tabernacle Square. The cabin was built in 1845 of cottonwood logs on the Weber River at Fort Buenaventura, now a state park (see above), and is believed to be the first permanent pioneer home in Utah. The 1902 Gothic-style brick Relief Society Building now houses the Daughters of Utah Pioneers Museum (☎ 801/393-4460), containing pioneer photographs, artifacts, and memorabilia, and is open Monday through Saturday in the summer.

Now head south on Grant Avenue for 3 blocks to:

2. **Ogden Post Office,** 298 24th St. This is one of two fine examples of Classical Revival Federal architecture in Utah (the other is the Salt Lake City Post Office). This building, constructed between 1905 and 1909, held a post office, a courthouse, and offices until 1974. The lobby, elevator, second-floor courtroom, and much of the beautiful woodwork have been lovingly renovated; the building now houses a reception center and other offices.

Next turn east on 24th Street; a block down the street, you'll reach the:

3. **Eccles Building,** 385 24th St. This steel-framed, brick-faced, boxlike 1913 building with "Chicago-style" windows combines elements of the Prairie style with classical details, evident in the terra-cotta figurines and geometric motifs along the second- and eighth-floor cornices.

Turn south onto Washington Boulevard, and continue to the:

4. **Peery's Egyptian Theater,** 439 Washington Blvd. Built as a movie theater in the Egyptian Revival style in 1924, it reopened in 1997 after extensive renovation. The facade has four fluted columns, with two sculpted Pharaohs between each, and two sculptures of deities perched on the roof. The exotic interior is equally unusual for this area, with the proscenium decorated with paintings of Egyptian figures and colorful columns. Adjoining the theater is the David Eccles Conference Center, a new two-story building designed to complement the theater and meet a wide variety of conference needs.

Cross the street now to the:

5. **Historic Radisson Suite Hotel,** 2510 Washington Blvd., located in the Italian Renaissance Revival Bigelow Hotel, built in 1927 around the remains of the 1890 Reed Hotel. Check out the fascinating lobby, with its rococo trim, elaborate ceilings, and crystal chandeliers.

Finally, cross again to the:

6. **Municipal Building,** 2539 Washington Blvd. One of the finest representations of the art deco style of architecture in Ogden, and probably all of Utah. It's also an excellent example of a WPA project from the 1930s. Built in 1939, the Municipal Building is composed of a series of rectangular brick blocks with glazed terra-cotta trim, symmetrically tapered to the tall central mass—grand and awe-inspiring.

WINDING DOWN Take a few minutes to walk along **Historic 25th Street.** This collection of early–20th-century buildings has been undergoing a much-needed renovation over the last few years. Many of the old businesses have moved to suburban shopping centers, but antiques shops, restaurants, and pubs are taking over. A few empty lots, though, serve as silent reminders that some of the past has been lost forever.

NEARBY SIGHTS & ATTRACTIONS
HUNTSVILLE: "THE SIN & SALVATION TOUR"

Locals jokingly refer to visiting Huntsville as taking the "Sin and Salvation Tour." The town is about 15 miles east of Ogden on Utah 39; it'll take you 20 to 25 minutes to get there, but it's well worth the drive.

First, stop at the **Shooting Star Saloon,** 7350 E. 200 South (☎ **801/ 745-2002**), for a draft beer and one of the best hamburgers in the state. Established in 1879, it's said to be the oldest continuously operating saloon in Utah. The decor is eclectic, to say the least—dollar bills are pinned to the ceiling, and the walls are decorated with animal trophies, steer skulls, and cowboy art; a pool table and a juke-box round out the fun. Don't forget to pat the St. Bernard's head that's hanging above one of the booths. The Shooting Star is open Monday through Saturday from noon and Sunday from 2pm; closing is usually around midnight, give or take an hour.

Now that you've done a bit of sinning, head to the **Abbey of Our Lady of the Holy Trinity Trappist Monastery,** 1250 S. 9500 East (☎ **801/745-3784**), for a bit of saving. To get there, take Utah 39, turn southeast (right) at the Huntsville American Legion Hall, and follow the signs to the monastery. This community of about two dozen monks established themselves here in 1947 to live "an austere and simple life of prayer and manual labor." They farm, raise Herefords, tend colonies of bees, and make and sell flavored and straight honeys in liquid and cream form, whole-grain cereals, and baked goods (their whole-wheat and raisin breads are a real treat). The reception room and chapel are open to the public, and visitors are wel-come to attend any of the scheduled services. Hours for the reception room are Mon-day through Saturday, from 8am to noon and 1:15 to 5pm.

A HISTORIC FAMILY-FUN CENTER IN FARMINGTON

Lagoon, 375 N. Lagoon Lane, Farmington (☎ **800/748-5246** or 801/451-8000), is a delightful combination of an amusement park, water park, and entertaining his-torical park. In the beginning, swimming was the attraction; then, in 1906, an early version of a roller coaster opened. Next came a carousel of 45 hand-carved animals (still in operation today), and so on; now there are more than 125 rides, games, shops, and food courts, plus all sorts of family entertainment, from stage shows to march-ing bands.

Lagoon's Pioneer Village represents Utah as it was a hundred years ago. Here you'll see one of America's finest collections of horse-drawn carriages, a gun collec-tion, and exhibits of pioneer and Indian artifacts. But it's not just a museum: You can browse through the 19th-century shops, ride the stagecoach and train, and en-joy both the musical entertainment and the gunslingers, outlaws, and desperadoes throwing their weight around.

If it's water you delight in, visit the **Lagoon A Beach,** with a 65-foot twisting, turning enclosed tube ride, three serpentine slides, white-water rapids you shoot in a river tube, and more. For the less intrepid, there's a lazy river with crystal-clear wa-terfalls, exotic tunnels, steamy hot tubs, and sultry lagoons.

Basic park admission costs $15 and is free for senior citizens. All-day passes, which include use of the water park and all rides and entertainment, cost $26.95 for adults up to age 60 and all those over 50 inches tall, $20.95 for children over 4 but under 51 inches tall, and $13 for seniors over 60 and toddlers under 4. The park is open from Memorial Day to Labor Day, Sunday and Monday from 11am to 10:30pm, Tuesday to Thursday till 11pm, and Friday and Saturday till midnight; from mid-April to May and the month of September, Saturday and Sunday from 11am to 8pm.

It's closed all winter, but opens for a special Halloween event in October. Hours are subject to change, so it's a good idea to call before going. To get there, take exit 326 from I-15.

There's also an RV park and campground with over 200 shady sites, both pull-through with hookups and grassy tent sites. The campground has a mini-store, and campers receive discounts on Lagoon All-Day Passports. Call ☎ **800/748-5246,** ext. 3100, for current rates and reservations.

SPORTS & OUTDOOR ACTIVITIES

There are plenty of opportunities for outdoor recreation in the nearby Wasatch National Forest. For all your sporting-goods needs, visit **Gart Sports** (☎ **801/399-2310**) in the Ogden City Mall, 24th Street and Washington Boulevard.

BIKING   The ✪ **Ogden River Parkway** is a 3-mile handicapped-accessible paved path along the Ogden River, extending from the mouth of Ogden Canyon west to Washington Boulevard. It's excellent for walking, jogging, and bicycling; it also leads to Big D Sports Park, Lorin Farr Park (see "Parks & Recreation Centers," below), and George S. Eccles Dinosaur Park (see "What to See & Do," above).

There are two strenuous road rides east of Ogden. The **Trappers Loop Road** winds 9 miles along Utah 167 from Mountain Green (exit 92 off I-84) north to Huntsville. This route alternates between wide-open meadows backed by high mountain peaks and tall evergreens and aspens that seem to envelop you.

The second, along **Snowbasin Road,** climbs over 2,000 feet from Pineview Reservoir to the base of Snowbasin Ski Resort. Your effort will be rewarded at the end with stunning views of the ski runs and towering peaks all around.

You can get additional trail information at the visitor information center in Union Station—ask for the Ogden Trails Network brochure. For bicycle repairs and accessories, stop at **Bingham Cyclery,** 3259 Washington Blvd. (☎ **801/399-4981**), or **Canyon Sports Outlet,** 705 W. Riverdale Rd. (☎ **801/621-4662**).

FISHING   Brown, rainbow, cutthroat, brook, and lake trout are abundant in the lakes, reservoirs, and streams of the Wasatch-Cache National Forest around Ogden. You might also find perch, bass, catfish, whitefish, and crappie. For your fishing needs, try **Anglers' Inn,** 4510 S. 900 West (☎ **801/621-6481**), or **Wild Country Outfitters and Fly Shop,** 4305-5 S. Harrison Blvd. (☎ **801/479-1194**).

GOLF   There are several public courses in the Ogden area. The challenging **Mount Ogden Golf Course,** 3000 Taylor Ave. (☎ **801/629-8700**), is an 18-hole, par-71 championship course located on the east side of the city against the mountains. Another 18-hole, par-71 course is **Schneiter's Riverside Golf Course,** 5460 S. Weber Dr., Riverdale, near exit 81 off I-84 (☎ **801/399-4636**), with a clubhouse and driving range. The **Ben Lomond Golf Course,** 1600 N. 500 West, Harrisville, north of Ogden off U.S. 89 (☎ **801/782-7754**), is an 18-hole, par-72 course.

El Monte Golf Course, 1300 Valley Dr. (☎ **801/629-8333**), is a scenic 9-hole, par-35 course of rolling hills and old-style greens. The **Golf City Golf Course,** 1400 E. 5600 South (☎ **801/479-3410**), offers something for the entire family. There's a night-lighted driving range, a baseball and softball batting cage, miniature golf, and a 9-hole, par-27 course. For one of the finest practice areas around, try **Mulligan's Golf and Games,** 1690 W. 400 North, at exit 349 off I-15 (☎ **801/392-4653**), which features a 9-hole, par-27 course, two 18-hole miniature golf courses, and a night-lighted driving range.

HIKING   In addition to the **Ogden River Parkway** (see "Biking," above), several hiking trails are accessible from the east side of downtown Ogden. ✪ **Indian Trail**

takes off from the parking area at 22nd Street and Buchanan Avenue and winds 5 miles along a narrow path through thick stands of oak, spruce, and fir trees. The trail offers some of the finest views of the canyon from above—particularly of the waterfall at the mouth of Ogden Canyon—before dropping down to the parking area on Utah 39. The trail is moderately difficult, and takes about 4 hours one-way.

A little over a half mile along Indian Trail, **Hidden Valley** trail cuts off sharply to the south. The route is difficult, climbing steadily through the old Lake Bonneville terraces, with dense stands of oak, maple, and aspen. After 2 miles, you'll reach a turn-around; from here, enjoy the clear view of the rugged face of Mt. Ogden to the southeast. The hike takes about 2 hours one-way.

An easy 1½-hour hike is the **Mt. Ogden Exercise Trail,** linking the parking lots at 29th and 36th streets. It's mostly flat, surfaced with bark chips, and follows the east edge of a golf course much of the way, encountering splashing streams and even the occasional small wildlife. The views are inspiring at sunrise and sunset.

For additional trail information, ask for the Ogden Trails Network brochure at the visitor information center in Union Station. It describes a number of hiking trails, some of which are also open for biking and horseback riding.

HORSEBACK RIDING   There are numerous opportunities for horseback riding in the national forest around Ogden. For guided trail rides, contact **Red Rock Outfitters,** 13554 E. Utah 39, Huntsville, UT 84401 (☎ **801/745-6393**). They offer children's rides ranging from 30 minutes to 8 hours ($10 to $84) and adult rides from 1 to 8 hours ($15 to $95), plus a 2-hour Dutch-oven-dinner ride ($42 adult, $37 child). Pack trips are also available (limited space; call for dates), as well as sunset, sunrise, covered-wagon, and moonlight sleigh rides.

The Ogden Trails Network brochure—available at the visitor information center in Union Station—describes three trails open to horseback riding.

ICE-SKATING   **The Ice Sheet,** 4390 Harrison Blvd., in the southeast part of the city (☎ **801/399-8750**), offers ice-skating year-round and will host curling events during the 2002 Olympic Games.

IN-LINE SKATING   The **Classic Skating Center,** 4181 Riverdale Rd., at exit 342 off I-15 or exit 81 off I-84 (☎ **801/394-0822**), is open for afternoon skating Monday, Wednesday, and Friday from 3 to 6pm for $3.50, and Saturday from 11am to 5pm for $4. Skate on Monday evening from 6 to 9pm for $3.50; Tuesday (Dollar Night) from 6 to 8pm or 8 to 10pm for just $1; and Friday and Saturday nights from 7pm to midnight for $4.

WATER SPORTS   Willard Bay State Park (see "Parks & Recreation Centers," below) is your destination for boating, waterskiing, and swimming. Also see the discussion on Lagoon, above, under "Nearby Sights & Attractions."

PARKS & RECREATION CENTERS

Big D Sports Park
1250 Park Blvd., Ogden River Pkwy. ☎ **801/629-8284.** Free admission.

You'll find a playground at this day-use-only park, along with soccer, baseball, and volleyball fields; a basketball court; and pavilions, shelters, and picnic grounds.

Lorin Farr Park
700 Canyon Rd., Ogden River Pkwy. ☎ **801/629-8691.**

This is a great place to come to cool off. Facilities include water slides and a swimming pool, plus a playground and a picnic area with grills. Admission to the park is free, but there are charges for swimming ($2.75 for an all-day pass for everyone 4 and older; children under 4 free). The park is open year-round, but the swimming pool is open Memorial Day through Labor Day only (call for hours).

Swenson Gymnasium

Weber State University, south end of the campus. ☎ **801/626-6466.**

Swenson Gym has swimming, racquetball, tennis, basketball, indoor-track, and weight-room facilities open to the public. Hours and availability of the various facilities vary according to school and class schedules; call ahead. Call for fees (there's a whole mess of different fees; it all depends on what you want to do).

Willard Bay State Park

650 N. 900 West A, Willard, UT 87340-9999. ☎ **801/734-9494.** Take I-15 exit 354 to South Marina, or exit 360 for North Marina.

For boating and waterskiing, head 10 miles north to Willard Bay State Park. Popular with locals and tourists alike, Willard Reservoir offers birding, wildlife viewing, and wetland plant observation in addition to water recreation. **South Marina,** open April through October, has a 30-site campground and modern rest rooms. Larger **North Marina,** open year-round, has 62 campsites, modern rest rooms with showers, and a sewage disposal station. A trail leads from the Willow Creek Campground at North Marina (between sites 45 and 48) to a wide sandy beach for swimming and sunbathing. Other footpaths branch off toward the ponds to the east where ducks and geese often paddle. The Willow Creek Campground has some open waterfront sites, but most are along a meandering access road among the cottonwoods and willows that grow profusely along Willard Creek. Day-use fee is $4; camping costs $10.

SPECTATOR SPORTS

Weber State University, southeast of downtown, belongs to the Big Sky Athletic Conference for men's sports and the Mountain West Athletic Conference for women's. Basketball and football games take place in **Dee Events Center,** 4450 Harrison Blvd.; call ☎ **801/626-8500** to find out what's on.

WHERE TO STAY

In addition to the lodging choices described below, there are several chain and franchise motels in the Ogden area, including the **Sleep Inn,** 1155 S. 1700 West, Ogden, UT 84404 (☎ 800/221-2222 or 801/731-6500), with rates of $44 to $99 double; **Days Inn,** 3306 Washington Blvd., Ogden, UT 84401 (☎ 800/999-6841 or 801/399-5671; fax 801/621-0321), with rates of $74 to $82 double; **Travelodge,** 2110 Washington Blvd., Ogden, UT 84401 (☎ 800/578-7878 or 801/394-4563; fax 801/394-4568), with rates of $45 to $55 double; **Super 8 Motel,** 1508 W. 2100 South, Ogden, UT 84401 (☎ 800/800-8000 or 801/731-7100; fax 801/731-2627), with rates of $44 to $50 double; and **Motel 6,** 1455 Washington Blvd., Ogden, UT 84404 (☎ 801/627-4560; fax 801/392-1878), with rates of about $37 double.

Room tax added to lodging bills totals just over 9%. Pets are not allowed unless otherwise noted.

Best Western High Country Inn

1335 W. 12th St., Ogden, UT 84404. ☎ **800/594-8979** or 801/394-9474. Fax 801/392-6589. 111 units. A/C TV TEL. $55–$75 double. AE, CB, DC, DISC, MC, V. Just off I-15 exit 347.

This handsome hotel offers comfortable, attractively furnished rooms characterized by a bright, airy feel. Guests have a choice of one or two queen-size beds or one king. Facilities include an outdoor heated swimming pool, whirlpool tub, exercise room, ski lockers, laundry, and a restaurant serving three meals daily. You'll have easy access to the Golden Spike Arena Events Center, Weber County Fairgrounds, and George S. Eccles Dinosaur Park. Pets are accepted with a deposit.

Best Western Ogden Park Hotel

247 24th St., Ogden, UT 84401. ☎ **800/421-7599** or 801/627-1190. Fax 801/394-6312. 287 units, including 18 suites. A/C TV TEL. $89–$109 double; suites $115 and up. Rates include full buffet breakfast. AE, CB, DC, MC, V. From northbound I-15, take exit 345; from southbound I-15, take exit 346.

This modern, full-service hotel and convention center is located in downtown Ogden, just a block north of historic 25th Street and a few blocks from Union Station. The recently renovated public areas are casually decorated, with comfortable seating, a gift shop, a liquor store, and a restaurant for family-style dining. Rooms are spacious and traditionally decorated; suites include wet bars, and many have large sunken tubs.

The hotel van provides transportation around town with advance notice. Services include room service, dry cleaning, laundry, secretarial service, and express checkout; facilities include a large indoor pool, fitness center, whirlpool tub, sundeck, game room, business center, conference rooms, beauty salon, boutiques, private club and sports bar, and access to a nearby health club. Pets are accepted with a damage deposit.

Big Z Motel

1123 W. 2100 South, Ogden, UT 84401. ☎ **801/394-6632.** 32 units, including 4 family units. A/C TV TEL. $35–$45 double; family units $45–$50. AE, DISC, MC, V.

The Big Z is a good motel, basic yet homey. Rudy and Edith Zuech built the place in 1978 on part of their family farm and have been running it ever since. Rooms are generally furnished with either two double beds or one queen; four family units sleep up to six comfortably, with a separate bedroom and complete kitchen. The restaurant serves three meals daily. Small pets are accepted with prior approval.

Comfort Suites of Ogden

1150 W. 2150 South, Ogden, UT 84401. ☎ **800/462-9925** or 801/621-2545. Fax 801/627-4782. 142 suites. A/C TV TEL. $65–$95 double, regular suite; $130–$180 presidential suite. Rates include full buffet breakfast. AE, DC, DISC, JCB, MC, V. Take exit 346 off I-15, head east on Utah 24 about a block, turn south.

This modern property is comfortable and reasonably priced. Standard suites have two queen-size beds or one king, a sleeper sofa, a large closet, a big-screen TV, a small refrigerator, and a microwave. There are two presidential suites, each with king bed and three rooms; one has a view of the indoor pool, and the other, on the top floor, has a vaulted ceiling and a beautiful view of the Wasatch Mountains to the east.

Services include room service, laundry, dry cleaning, secretarial service, express checkout, and free refreshments in the lobby. Facilities include kitchenettes, movie channel, indoor heated pool, exercise room, whirlpool tub, sundeck, lighted tennis court, business center, conference rooms that accommodate 450, and coin-operated laundry. Cactus Red's Restaurant serves three meals daily (see "Where to Dine," below). Pets are allowed with a deposit.

Historic Radisson Suite Hotel

2510 Washington Blvd., Ogden, UT 84401. ☎ **800/333-3333** or 801/627-1900. Fax 801/394-5342. 144 units. A/C TV TEL. $79–$199 double. Rates include full buffet breakfast. AE, CB, DC, DISC, MC, V.

This may be Utah's only hotel listed in the National Register of Historic Places. Located on the corner of historic 25th Street and Washington Boulevard, the Radisson is a stately building, with hand-painted ceilings and graceful chandeliers. Each of the luxury suites is attractively outfitted with reproductions in solid wood, a large bath, a cozy sitting area, two TVs, a wet bar, refrigerator, and microwave. Standard suites are somewhat simpler, but still come with wet bars and refrigerators. There are also about 20 standard motel rooms available.

IN HUNTSVILLE

Jackson Fork Inn

7345 E. 900 South (Utah Hwy. 39), Huntsville, UT 84317. ☎ **800/255-0672** or 801/745-0051. 8 units. $60–$100 double. Rates include breakfast. AE, DISC, MC, V.

This unique little inn used to be an old family barn, believed to have been constructed in the 1920s, and is now in its third location. Each unit has two stories, with a spiral staircase leading to an upstairs bedroom loft. Rooms are brightly painted and cheery, with one or two queen-size beds and full bath; four rooms have whirlpool tubs. Although there's no air-conditioning, each unit does have a ceiling fan. A restaurant (see "Where to Dine," below) serves continental dinners. Smoking is not allowed in the rooms. Pets are accepted for an additional fee. A "Jackson fork," incidentally, is a type of hay fork used to load hay into the loft area of a barn.

IN NEARBY EDEN

✪ Snowberry Inn Bed & Breakfast

1315 N. Utah Hwy. 158, Eden, UT 84310. ☎ **801/745-2634**. Fax 801/745-0585. 5 units. $85–$95 double. Rates include breakfast. AE, DISC, MC, V. From Ogden, follow Utah 39 east about 8 miles and turn north on Utah 158; the inn is about 2^1/2 miles up on the west side of the road.

The Snowberry, built in 1992, is a large log cabin–style inn within 15 minutes of three ski areas and accessible to all the outdoor activities of the surrounding national forest. Each room is individually decorated with antiques and collectibles according to its name: The Indian and Pioneer rooms (both handicapped accessible) are downstairs, and the Alaskan, Mountain Man, and Mexican rooms are upstairs. Each has its own bath, some with showers only; the Alaskan has a claw-foot tub but no shower. In-room massage and baby-sitting can be arranged. The inn has an open, friendly atmosphere; the dining room is right off the living room, and guests are welcome to gather around the tall kitchen counter for coffee while the morning meal is being prepared. A hearty vegetarian breakfast, made from scratch, might include breakfast burritos or blueberry French toast cobbler—and always freshly ground coffee. Pets are accepted with prior approval.

CAMPING

Century Park Mobile Home & RV Park

1399 W. 2100 South, Ogden, UT 84401. ☎ **801/731-3800**. Fax 801/731-0010. 142 sites. $17.25–$22.50. MC, V. Take exit 346 off I-15, head west on Utah 24 about a block, turn south at sign.

This campground, conveniently located just off the interstate and not far from downtown, has shade trees, pull-through and back-in gravel sites, and grass. Amenities include hot showers, a dump station, RV supplies, and a convenience store.

✪ Cherry Hill Family Campground

1325 S. Main St., Kaysville, UT 84037. ☎ **801/451-5379**. 240 sites. $17–$22. MC, V.

Every inch of this campground is utilized, but the entire park is immaculately maintained, with manicured lawns, shade trees, and paved interior roads. You'll find a heated pool, horseshoes, a recreation hall and game room, plus planned activities. The campground also offers RV hookups, a dump station, limited RV supplies, and a convenience store.

WHERE TO DINE

The tax added to dining bills totals just over 7%.

ABC Mandarin

5260 S. 1900 West, Roy, UT 84067. ☎ **801/776-6361.** Reservations accepted. Main courses $5.50–$8.25 dinner, $3.75–$4.95 lunch. AE, DC, DISC, MC, V. Daily 11am–9:45pm. From I-15, take exit 342 for Riverdale Rd. west; follow it to 1900 West, and turn right. Bus: 10. SZECHUAN/MANDARIN/CHINESE.

With its large windows and booths along three walls, this looks like an American cafe or coffee shop, with just a few Asian accents: about a half dozen faux marble-top tables, Chinese dragons on one wall, and a large tank of tropical fish. But the food is thoroughly Chinese—the menu is even written in both Chinese and English. All the standards are here for lunch, from chicken chow mein and several kinds of fried rice to Mongolian beef and sweet-and-sour shrimp. The dinner menu is expanded to include three-course family dinners and a variety of other dishes. Imported and domestic beers are available.

Berconi's Pasta House

4850 Harrison Blvd. ☎ **801/479-4414.** Reservations for 6 or more only. Main courses $5.95–$15.95 dinner, $4.50–$6.50 lunch. AE, DC, DISC, MC, V. Mon–Fri 11am–10pm; Sat 4:30–10pm; Sun 4:30–9pm. From downtown Ogden, follow 24th or 25th St. east to Harrison Blvd. and turn right (south); it's about 3^1/2 miles to the restaurant. ITALIAN.

Decorated to feel like an Italian vineyard, this restaurant has an open yet cozy atmosphere, with an indoor-greenhouse seating area and an outdoor patio. The menu includes Sicilian-style pizza, Italian sandwiches, salads, and innumerable pasta dishes. Specialties include chicken Parmesan, *Scampi alla Venezia* (shrimp sautéed in garlic butter), and *Bistecca alla Berconi,* New York strip steak smothered with sautéed onions, bell peppers, and mushrooms. Full liquor service is available.

Cactus Red's Restaurant

In Comfort Suites, 1150 W. 2150 South. ☎ **801/621-1560.** Main courses $4.95–$12.95. AE, DC, DISC, JCB, MC, V. Mon–Sat 6am–10pm; Sun 6am–9pm. From I-15, take exit 346 and head east on 20th St.; it's about a half block to the access road for Comfort Suites. SOUTH-WESTERN.

This is a light and airy restaurant serving tasty Southwestern cuisine, where everything's made from scratch. Breakfast includes the usual egg dishes, lighter fare like fruit and yogurt, and a wide range of Southwestern specialties such as the Fajita Scramble: grilled, marinated chicken strips, bell peppers, onions, and fajita spices sautéed with whipped eggs and served with flour tortillas, guacamole, salsa, and sour cream. The lunch and dinner menu includes salads, pasta platters, steaks, prime rib, hamburgers, and sandwiches. Two popular items are the Aztec Chicken Salad, a grilled chicken breast on a bed of mixed greens with tomato wedges, cucumber slices, bell pepper rings, and cheddar cheese; and Pollo Casa Grande, which consists of chunks of grilled chicken sautéed with zucchini, mushrooms, and black olives, simmered in Alfredo sauce, and tossed with a mushroom pasta. For dessert, try a slice of Painted Desert Pie, a house specialty that includes chocolate and mocha ice creams in a macaroon cookie crust, topped with crushed butter toffee crunch, mocha sauce, and whipped cream. Full liquor service is available.

Delights of Ogden

258 Historic 25th St. ☎ **801/394-1111.** Main courses $4.50–$10.95 dinner, $4.50–$5.50 lunch. AE, DC, DISC, MC, V. Lunch Mon–Sat 11am–4pm; dinner Wed–Sat 5:30–10pm. From I-15, take exit 345, head east on 24th St., then south on Wall Ave. to Union Station, and turn left (east) on 25th St. AMERICAN.

True to its name, this is a delightful little restaurant in one of the oldest buildings in this part of Ogden, built in 1888 and restored in 1984. There's a narrow front dining room and a magnificent old wooden bar complete with mirrors behind the glassware, a large atrium dining room in back, and an outdoor patio. The menu includes freshly made sandwiches and homemade soups, breads, pastas, and desserts. Favorites include an authentic Philly cheese steak sandwich and the blackened-chicken sandwich served on a home-baked rosette roll. Particularly popular with locals are the beer-batter–dipped french fries. Sandwiches are served at both lunch and dinner, and for dinner you can get homemade lasagna and tortellini as well. This is also a good place for after-theater coffee and dessert: Sweet specialties include carrot cake, cream with fresh berries in a puff pastry, and tiramisu. Beer is served with meals.

Farr Better Ice Cream—Utah's Original Ice Cream Shoppe

286 21st St. ☎ **801/393-8629**. Cones start at 95¢. MC, V. Daily 9am–11pm in summer, 9am–10pm in winter. ICE CREAM.

Farr Better Ice Cream has been making great ice cream since 1920. Choose from among 75 flavors and a wide range of malts, shakes, and sundaes, as well as frozen yogurt and sherbets. You can "dine in" or take your tasty treat with you—and you can also purchase your favorite flavor, of course, by the pint, quart, or gallon.

Prairie Schooner Steak House

445 Park Blvd. ☎ **801/621-5511**. Main courses $10.95–$25.95 dinner, $3.95–$9.95 lunch. AE, DC, DISC, MC, V. Lunch Mon–Fri 11am–2pm; dinner Mon–Thurs 5–10pm, Fri–Sat until 11pm, Sun 4–9pm. Head north on Washington Blvd. past 20th St.; turn right (east) on Park Blvd. STEAK/SEAFOOD.

Dine in your own private "Conestoga wagon," circled around a fire, at this theme restaurant. As you would expect, the main menu item is steak in all shapes and sizes, cooked just the way you like it—T-bone, filet mignon, New York strip, porterhouse, and prime rib. On Monday and Wednesday evenings you can try Prairie Bones—baked, marinated spareribs. The dinner menu also offers chicken, shrimp, and lobster dishes. Lunches are served at more traditional tables and booths in a dining room decorated with western decor. The lunch menu includes sandwiches, soups, salads, and steaks. A children's menu and full liquor service are available.

Roosters 25th Street Brewing Co.

253 Historic 25th St. ☎ **801/627-6171**. Reservations not accepted. Main courses $6.95–$16.95, sandwiches $4.95–$6.50, pizza from $2.25 per slice. AE, CB, DC, DISC, MC, V. Mon–Thurs 11:30am–10pm; Fri–Sat 11:30am–midnight; Sun 10am–9pm. Parking $2. From I-15, take exit 345, head east on 24th St., then south on Wall Ave. to Union Station, and turn left (east) on 25th St. INTERNATIONAL.

This two-story red brick brewpub, with its prominently displayed brewing vats and tables that are an intriguing juxtaposition of metal and wood, offers both indoor and patio seating. For an appetizer, try the crunchy Onion Loops, hand-dipped in a homemade beer batter. Pizzas come in four varieties, including a vegetarian version with mushrooms, bell peppers, onions, mozzarella, roasted garlic, sun-dried tomatoes, and parsley. The spicy seafood jambalaya, with shrimp, bay scallops, and mussels, has become a house favorite. A pub standard, beer-battered fish-and-chips (made with white cod), is light and crisp. Also on the menu are several other fish plates, fresh seafood, chicken, pasta, lamb, beef, and about a half dozen sandwiches. Freshly brewed beer is served, as you might expect.

Timbermine

1701 Park Blvd. ☎ **801/393-2155**. Reservations for 10 or more only. Main courses $11.95–$26.95. AE, DC, DISC, MC, V. Mon–Thurs 5–10pm; Fri–Sat until 11pm; Sun until 9pm. Follow

12th St. (which becomes Canyon Rd.) east to the mouth of Ogden Canyon, turn right and then right again onto Park Blvd. STEAK/SEAFOOD/PRIME RIB.

Utah's mining days are the theme here—the rough timbered rooms resemble mine shafts, and collectibles and antiques from the mining era are scattered about. The menu offers steaks, prime rib, fish, and seafood, and barbecue is featured on Monday, Tuesday, and Wednesday nights. Special menus are available for both children and senior citizens. Timbermine provides full liquor service.

Union Grill

In Union Station, 2501 Wall Ave. ☎ **801/621-2830.** Reservations not accepted. Main courses $4.25–$12.95. AE, DC, DISC, MC, V. Mon–Thurs 11:30am–10pm; Fri–Sat till 10:30pm. From I-15, take exit 345, head east on 24th St., then south on Wall Ave. to Union Station. AMERICAN.

Historic railroad photos and memorabilia dot the walls of this cafe-style room in Ogden's historic train depot, which offers diners a view of the trains rumbling by. Daily specials are written on a blackboard, and the menu includes fresh fish, pasta, homemade soups, and sandwiches. A special vegetarian pasta sauce changes weekly. The restaurant offers full liquor service, and a second dining room is available for private parties.

IN HUNTSVILLE

Jackson Fork Inn

7345 E. 900 South (Utah Hwy. 39), Huntsville. ☎ **801/745-0051.** Reservations recommended. Main courses $9.75–$26.25. AE, DISC, MC, V. Mon–Sat 5–9:30pm; Sun brunch 10am–2pm. CONTINENTAL.

A charming country atmosphere pervades the Jackson Fork Inn, an old barn that has been converted to an inn (see "Where to Stay," above) and restaurant. The menu includes items such as filet mignon or T-bone steak; slow-roasted prime rib; chicken teriyaki; fish selections such as salmon, mahimahi, and lobster; and a vegetarian entree. Full liquor service is available.

OGDEN AFTER DARK

Weber State University's Department of Performing Arts presents live entertainment at **Dee Events Center,** 4450 Harrison Blvd. (☎ 801/626-8500); call for schedule.

For classical offerings, contact the **Ogden Symphony and Ballet,** 2580 Jefferson Ave. (☎ 801/399-9214).

The **Utah Musical Theater** (ticket office at 3750 Harrison Blvd.; ☎ 801/626-8500), offers presentations in the summer only at Peery's Egyptian Theater (see "Walking Tour—Historic Downtown Ogden," above).

The **Golden Spike Events Center,** 1000 N. 1200 West (☎ 801/399-8544 or 801/399-8011), hosts concerts, rodeos, horse races, cutter and chariot racing, and other special events. Call for current listings.

For after-hours entertainment, there's the **City Club,** 264 25th St. (☎ 801/392-4447), with good food and nonstop Beatles. If you want to relax with background piano music, stop at **Attractions** in the Historic Radisson, 2510 Washington Blvd. (☎ 801/627-1900). **Señor Frogs,** 455 25th St. (☎ 801/394-2323), has a private dance club downstairs, with temporary memberships available. The **Tamarack Private Club** at the Flying J, 1254 W. 2100 South (☎ 801/394-4741), has '50s music and dancing during the week and western music on weekends.

3 Where East Met West: Golden Spike National Historic Site

On May 10, 1869—after the laying of nearly 2,000 miles of track over desert, rivers, and mountains—the Central Pacific met the Union Pacific at Promontory Summit, and America's East and West coasts were finally joined by rail. The nation's second transcontinental telegraph had been strung along the track as it was laid, and as the final spike was driven home, the signal "Done" flashed across the country—and jubilation erupted from coast to coast. A ragged town of tents quickly sprang up along the track at Promontory Summit, but in 6 months the railroads moved their terminal operations to Ogden. In 1904, the Lucin Cutoff bypassed Promontory altogether, and in 1942 the rails were torn up for use in military depots.

Today, there are only about 1.7 miles of track here, re-laid on the original roadbed, where you can see exact replicas of the two engines, the Central Pacific's "Jupiter" and Union Pacific's "119," that met here in 1869. From the end of April into early October, the magnificent machines are on display and make short runs (inquire at visitor center for schedule). Presentations are given track-side, sometimes in period dress.

JUST THE FACTS

The park is open daily from 8am to 6pm from Memorial Day to Labor Day, and 8am to 4:30pm the remainder of the year. Admission is $7 per vehicle or $3.50 per adult, whichever is less, during the summer months, and $4 and $2 respectively the rest of the year. There are no camping facilities.

GETTING THERE   From Ogden, head north on I-15 to exit 368, turn west on Utah 83 for 29 miles to a sign for Golden Spike; then turn south and continue for $7^1/_2$ miles.

INFORMATION & VISITOR CENTERS   Contact ✪ **Golden Spike National Historic Site** at P.O. Box 897, Brigham City, UT 84302 (☎ **435/471-2209**). Rest rooms, picnic areas, vending machines with soft drinks and snacks, and a bookstore are located at the visitor center, which also offers slide programs, films, and museum exhibits detailing the linking of the nation. Ranger programs take place daily; check at the visitor center for the current schedule.

SPECIAL EVENTS   The park has several special events throughout the year, with free admission. On May 10, there's a reenactment of the original **Golden Spike Ceremony,** with hot food, souvenirs, and handicrafts. Reenactments are also held on weekends and holidays throughout the summer. In mid-August, the **Annual Railroader's Festival** features reenactments of the ceremony, a spike-driving contest, and handcar races and rides. Hot food, handicraft booths, and live music add to the festivities. The **Annual Railroader's Film Festival and Winter Steam Demonstration,** held during the Christmas season, includes classic Hollywood railroad films and a special winter appearance by one of the two resident steam locomotives.

EXPLORING THE HISTORIC SITE

Die-hard railroad buffs can drive the self-guiding **Promontory Trail** along 9 miles of the historic railroad grades. A booklet explaining the markers along the tour is available at the visitor center. You'll see the two parallel grades laid by the competing companies, clearings for sidings, original rock culverts, and many cuts and fills. Allow about $1^1/_4$ hours for the drive.

HIKING AT THE HISTORIC SITE

The **Big Fill Trail** is a 1¹/₂-mile loop hike along part of the original rail beds to the Big Trestle and the Big Fill. The Big Fill was created when some 250 dump-cart teams and over 500 workers—mostly Chinese immigrants—dumped load after load of rock and dirt into a ravine to create the 170-foot-deep, 500-foot span of fill required to lay the Central Pacific's track. The Union Pacific built their trestle just 150 feet away. It was never intended to be a permanent structure; speed was the goal, rather than strength. Constructed by hand by Irish and Mormon crews in 1869, the last spike went into the 85-foot-high, 400-foot-long trestle on May 5, just 36 days after it was begun.

The hike can be done on either the Central or Union Pacific rail bed, although the Central rail bed is an easier walk. There are markers along both grades pointing out cuts and fills, quarries, vistas, and caves.

This is the desert, so take water, wear a hat, and be prepared for mosquitoes and ticks. Remember that rattlesnakes, though rare on the trail, have the right-of-way. And be glad that you weren't one of the workers in that back-breaking labor effort of 1869.

4 Skiing Ogden Valley & the Northern Wasatch Front

Those looking for splendid powder skiing, low prices, few lift lines, and friendly people will find all this in abundance at the relatively undeveloped, uncommercial ski areas of northern Utah. Don't expect fancy lodges (at least not yet), but do be prepared for breathtaking scenery, a wide variety of fine terrain, and a relaxed family atmosphere.

THE OGDEN VALLEY RESORTS

These resorts are just northwest of Ogden; to reach any of them, exit I-15 at 12th Street in Ogden (exit 347) and follow Utah 39 east. **Nordic Valley** and **Powder Mountain** are just off Utah 158, and **Snowbasin** is just off Utah 226.

NORDIC VALLEY SKI MOUNTAIN

This family-oriented ski area, Utah's smallest and least expensive, has the best night-lighting system in the state. Refreshingly informal and casual, Nordic Valley is a favorite of Ogden-area families because it's a good place to learn, with enough variety in its terrain to keep everyone satisfied. Recently added snowmaking equipment has improved conditions, and several runs have been designed specifically for snowboarders.

Just the Facts

Nordic Valley Ski Mountain, P.O. Box 478, Eden, UT 84310 (☎ **801/745-3511**), has two double chairlifts serving 18 runs on 85 acres, and snowmaking on 50 acres. The vertical drop is 1,200 feet from the top elevation of 6,400 feet to the base of 5,200 feet. The ski season is generally mid-November to mid-March, with the lifts operating from 9am to 4pm, Thursday through Sunday and holidays; there's night skiing Monday through Saturday from 5:30 to 10pm. Annual snowfall averages 300 inches. The terrain is rated 30% beginner, 50% intermediate, and 20% advanced.

The ski shop has ski equipment for rent and accessories for sale. Sorry, no child-care facilities are available here.

GETTING THERE   From I-15, follow Utah 39 east about 11 miles, turn north (left) onto Utah 158 for about 3 miles, and turn west (left) onto North Fork Road to the ski area.

LIFT TICKETS   An all-day adult lift ticket costs $16; seniors over 65 pay $5. Night skiing is $12.

LESSONS & PROGRAMS   The **ski school** offers private lessons beginning at $30 for 1½ hours; 2-hour group classes are $15 per person, with a minimum of four people.

Where to Stay & Dine

There's no overnight lodging on the mountain; see "Where to Stay" in the Ogden section of this chapter for nearby accommodations.

Nordic Valley Lodge serves hot sandwiches, homemade soups and chile, pizza, and hot and cold beverages. You can relax around the fireplace or pot-bellied stove on a cold day, or outside on the deck when it's sunny and warm.

POWDER MOUNTAIN RESORT

This is a family ski area in two ways: It was begun in 1972 by the Cobabe family, who still own and run it, and it's aimed at providing a variety of skiing to suit everyone in the family—not just theirs, but yours, too. There are plenty of beginner runs, which, appropriately enough, seem to grade upwards in difficulty as you move from the Sundown to the Timberline to the Hidden Lake areas, so that by the time you're skiing Three Miles, you can consider yourself an intermediate and try cruising over the big, swooping blue fields. There's no dearth of expert and powder skiing in the wilds, either. Powder Mountain is very aptly named, and uses snow cats and shuttle buses to transport skiers to more than 2,400 acres of spectacular powder that are not served by its three lifts—it's an out-of-bounds, backcountry skier's dream come true. A bonus is the view: On a clear day, you can see across the Great Salt Lake or south all the way to Park City.

Powder Mountain is also a favorite among snowboarders; boarding is allowed everywhere on the mountain.

Just the Facts

Powder Mountain Resort, P.O. Box 450, Eden, UT 84310 (☎ **801/745-3772;** 801/745-3771 for snow conditions), has one triple and two double chairs, two surface lifts, and one platter lift, servicing 1,600 acres of packed runs and powder skiing. An additional 1,200 acres of backcountry powder skiing is accessible by snow cat, as well as another 1,200 acres on the back side of the mountain, with return to the lift via shuttle bus. The terrain is rated 10% beginner, 60% intermediate, and 30% advanced. With over 500 inches of snowfall annually, Powder Mountain doesn't have—or need—any snowmaking. The elevation at the summit is 8,900 feet, the vertical drop is 1,300 feet, and the base elevation is 7,600 feet. The season is generally mid-November through April, with day skiing from 9:30am to 4:30pm, and night skiing until 10pm.

Powder Mountain Lodge and Sundown Lodge both have ski shops. Skis and snowboards are available for rent, and accessories are for sale. No child-care facilities are available.

GETTING THERE   From I-15, follow Utah 39 east about 11 miles, turn north (left) onto Utah 158, and drive about 8 miles to the ski area.

LIFT TICKETS   An all-day adult lift ticket is $27, a half-day ticket is $22, and a children's all-day ticket is $16; night-skiing passes are $12.50. Seniors age 65 and over pay $21.

LESSONS & PROGRAMS   The **ski school** offers a full range of ski and snowboarding lessons and other activities, both group and private, from half day to multiday. These include children's lessons, a program designed especially for and taught by women, and guided Alpine tours. Private lessons start at $40. Call for other rates.

Where to Stay & Dine

Most skiers stay in Ogden (see "Where to Stay," in the Ogden section of this chapter), but for those who want to sleep slope-side, the **Columbine Inn,** P.O. Box 450, Eden, UT 84130 (☎ **801/745-1414**), has five rooms and two suites, all nonsmoking, with a pleasant ski-chalet atmosphere. It's located at the main parking lot next to the lodge. Rates are in the $80 to $90 range for double rooms, and $150 to $200 for suites. Room tax of a little over 9% is added to your bill.

Powder Mountain Lodge serves homemade soups and sandwiches. **Hidden Lake** provides food at the summit. The **Powder Keg** serves sandwiches and draft beer around a cozy fireplace.

SNOWBASIN

Begun in 1939, Snowbasin is among America's oldest ski areas, although the first real chairlift wasn't installed until 1946. Still, it has largely remained a locals' secret, particularly popular for its intermediate runs. It offers plenty of untracked powder, long, wide, well-groomed trails, and Utah's third-largest vertical drop. Beginners have plenty of terrain on which to develop their ski-legs, and some great transitional runs off the Wildcat lift will help them graduate from novice to intermediate status and start cruising.

Expert skiing at Snowbasin has been growing by leaps and bounds recently, beyond even its traditionally popular powder bowls and racing trails. This has always been a powder paradise of Alta status, and with the gearing up for the 2002 Olympics, many new black-diamond and racing runs are making their debuts.

Snowboarders are welcome at Snowbasin and all lifts are open to them, with retaining devices required.

Just the Facts

✪ **Snowbasin Resort,** P.O. Box 460, Huntsville, UT 84317 (☎ **801/399-1135** or 801/399-0198 for snow conditions; fax 801/399-1138), has 39 runs, rated 20% beginner, 50% intermediate, and 30% advanced. Included in its 1,800 acres are beautiful powder bowls and tree and glade skiing. There are one double and four triple chairlifts, and a vertical drop of 2,400 feet from a top elevation of 8,800 feet to the base of 6,400 feet. With over 400 inches of annual snowfall, Snowbasin has not really needed snowmaking facilities, although some are planned. The season generally runs from Thanksgiving to April, with lifts operating weekdays from 9:30am to 4pm and weekends and holidays from 9am to 4pm.

The base lodge offers ski and snowboard equipment rental and repairs, plus accessories for sale. No nursery or child-care facilities are available. Live entertainment and outdoor barbecues are usually offered on ski-season weekends.

GETTING THERE   From I-15, follow Utah 39 east about 15 miles, turn south (right) onto Utah 226; it's about 10 miles to the ski area.

From I-84, take exit 92 for Mountain Green and Huntsville, head east about 1½ miles and turn north (left) on Utah 167; go about 12 miles to Utah 39, turn west (left) and go about 2 miles to Utah 226, then turn south (left) to the ski area.

LIFT TICKETS   All-day adult lift tickets cost $28, half-day tickets are $23, a children's all-day ticket is $20, and seniors over 65 pay $20.

LESSONS & PROGRAMS   The **ski school** (☎ **801/399-4611**) offers both private and group skiing and snowboarding lessons 7 days a week for all ages and abilities. Learn-to-ski packages and half- or full-day children's programs—the Littlecat Kittens for ages 4 to 6, and Wildcat Kids for ages 7 to 11—are also available.

Where to Stay & Dine

No lodging is available at the ski area itself; most skiers stay in Ogden. **Snowbasin Day Lodge** serves both snacks and full meals and prepares outdoor barbecues on weekends.

NEAR THE IDAHO BORDER: BEAVER MOUNTAIN SKI AREA

Skiing at Beaver Mountain is like going home to see the family. Located at the top of beautiful Logan Canyon in the Wasatch-Cache National Forest, this small resort has been operated by the Seeholzer family since 1939. The emphasis is on friendliness, personal attention, and, as Ted Seeholzer puts it, "helping skiers find the right runs for them." You'll find plenty of snow, a good mix of terrain, extremely well-maintained slopes, and a northeast exposure that makes morning runs a warm, sunny experience. Snowboarders and bump skiers like the steep Lue's Run, named for Ted's mother Luella, while hotdoggers are directed to Harry's Hollow (named for Ted's father), which has plenty of bumps—and is located right under a lift so everyone can see them showing off.

Snowboarders are welcome at Beaver Mountain, but are restricted from Little Beaver run.

JUST THE FACTS

✪ **Beaver Mountain Ski Area,** 1045½ N. Main, Suite 4, P.O. Box 3455, Logan, UT 84323 (☎ **435/753-0921** or 435/753-4822 for ski reports; fax 435/753-0975), receives an average of 400 inches of snow annually and has a top elevation of 8,800 feet, a vertical drop of 1,600 feet, and a base elevation of 7,200 feet. Three double chairlifts service 16 runs on 464 acres. The terrain is rated 35% beginner, 40% intermediate, and 25% advanced. The season runs from early December through early April, with the lifts operating daily from 9am to 4pm. The mountain is closed on Christmas Day.

A ski shop in the day lodge has about 425 pairs of skis for rent, lockers, and a small retail shop that sells hats, gloves, and other accessories. No child-care facilities are available.

GETTING THERE   Take I-15 to exit 364, then go east on U.S. 89 about 50 miles through Logan and beautiful Logan Canyon, and take the turn-off (left) to the ski area.

LIFT TICKETS   All-day adult tickets are $22; half day, children's all-day, and tickets for seniors ages 65 to 69 are $17; those 70 and over ski free.

LESSONS & PROGRAMS   The **ski school** offers group and private lessons. Private lessons start at $23 for 1 hour; group classes start at $9.50 for a half day.

WHERE TO STAY & DINE

Most lodging and restaurants can be found 27 miles west in Logan (see section on Logan, below). A cafeteria at the day lodge sells hamburgers, sandwiches, and soft drinks.

Nearby places to stay include **Beaver Creek Lodge,** P.O. 277, Garden City, UT 84028 (☎ **435/946-3400;** fax 435/946-3620), located a half mile east of the ski area along U.S. 89. Open all year, this 10-room log lodge, which is completely nonsmoking, offers all the modern conveniences and then some, in a spectacular mountain setting surrounded by the national forest. Rooms have log furnishings and whirlpool tubs with showers. A large common room contains a stone fireplace and big-screen TV with VCR, and decks offer panoramic views. There's hiking, mountain biking, horseback riding, and snowmobiling on the property and in the surrounding national forest (see "Sports & Outdoor Activities," below). Rooms are $79 to $115 in winter and $69 to $85 in summer; breakfast and dinner are available at an additional charge. Room tax of about 9% is added to your bill.

WARM-WEATHER CAMPING

A small RV park, with 15 sites, is open at Beaver Mountain Ski Area in the summer. The charge is $12 for a site with hookups and $6 without.

5 Logan

At an elevation of 4,525 feet, Logan is nestled in the fertile Cache Valley, flanked by the Wasatch and Bear River Mountains. Once part of the prehistoric Lake Bonneville, then home to the Blackfoot, Paiute, Shoshone, and Ute Indians, the valley is now a rich farming area famous for its cheeses and high-tech businesses. Mountain men first came here in the 1820s to trap beaver in the Logan River, caching (hence the valley's and county's name) the pelts in holes they dug throughout the area. Brigham Young sent Mormons to the valley in 1855, and several villages soon sprang up.

Today, with a population of a little over 38,000, Logan is a small city, but with many of the attractions of its larger neighbors to the west. Particularly worthwhile are visits to the LDS Church's Tabernacle and Temple, both handsome 19th-century structures; and a drive out to the Ronald V. Jensen Living Historical Farm for a trip back to 1917.

Thanks in large part to Utah State University, Logan suffers from no lack of art exhibits, live music, or theater. Summer visitors can enjoy the Utah Festival Opera Company, Old Lyric Repertory Theatre, and Utah Music Festival.

But nobody who comes to Logan really wants to spend much time indoors. Beautiful Logan Canyon is a delightful escape for hikers, mountain bikers, anglers, and rock climbers—but our favorite activity is a horseback ride into the high mountains.

ESSENTIALS
GETTING THERE

BY CAR   Logan is 81 miles northeast of Salt Lake City. From Salt Lake City and Ogden, take I-15 north to exit 364, then follow U.S. 89/91 northeast about 24 miles to downtown Logan.

BY AIRPORT SHUTTLE   The **Cache Valley Limo Airport Shuttle,** 550 N. Main St., Logan (☎ **800/658-8526** or 435/563-6400), provides direct shuttle service to and from Salt Lake International Airport. Two-day notice is recommended. A round-trip fare costs about $65. **Classic Limousine and Airport Shuttle** (☎ **435/ 755-9299**) also provides service to Logan.

VISITOR INFORMATION

The **Cache Chamber of Commerce** maintains a visitor information center at 160 N. Main St., Logan, UT 84321-4541 (☎ **800/882-4433** or 435/752-2161).

GETTING AROUND

As with most Mormon cities, Logan is laid out on a grid, with ground zero at the intersection of Main (north to south) and Center (east to west). Tabernacle Square is the block to the northeast of the intersection. U.S. 89/91 enters town on a diagonal from the southwest, along the golf course at the south end of town. Utah State

University is located on the northeast side of town, north of U.S. 89 between 700 and 1400 East.

The **Logan Transit District Transportation System,** or LTD, is a free citywide bus service. A route map is available at the information center on Main Street, but one of the easiest ways to get bus information is to call ☎ **435/752-BUSS** (2877), Monday through Friday from 6am to 6:30pm and Saturday from 9am to 6:30pm. If you provide your location (street address or intersection) and desired destination, the staff can tell you where and when to catch your bus, along with its route number, letter, and destination sign. Hearing-impaired people can call ☎ **435/750-7118** for bus information, Monday through Friday from 8:30am to 5pm. LTD also offers service for people with disabilities; call ☎ **435/753-2255** for information.

Car-rental agencies with offices in Logan include **Dale's Car Rental,** 625 N. Main (☎ 435/752-8257), **Enterprise,** 1155 N. Main (☎ 800/325-8007 or 435/755-6111), **Hertz,** 447 N. Main (☎ 800/654-3131 or 435/752-9141), and **Palmers Freedom Car Rental,** 1220 N. Main (☎ 435/752-2075).

FAST FACTS: LOGAN

The **Logan Regional Hospital** is located at 1400 N. 500 East (☎ **435/752-2050**). The **main post office** is at 151 N. 100 West (☎ **435/752-7246**). The **state liquor store** is at 75 W. 400 North (☎ **435/752-4145**).

WHAT TO SEE & DO

Cache Valley Historical Museum
(Daughters of the Utah Pioneers Museum)
160 N. Main St., Logan, UT 84321. ☎ **435/752-5139.** Free admission. Memorial Day–Labor Day Tues–Sat 10am–4pm, otherwise by appointment.

Housed in the same building as the information center, this small museum displays pioneer artifacts from 1859 to 1899—basically the first 40 years of Mormon settlement in the area. You can see guns, musical instruments (including the first organ used in the LDS Tabernacle), handmade pioneer furniture, clothing, and kitchen items. On exhibit are several pieces of furniture made by Brigham Young for his daughter Luna Young Thatcher, who lived in Logan. Also on display are dresses made by Mary Ann Weston Maugham, the area's first white woman settler, who arrived in 1859.

LDS Tabernacle
50 N. Main St., Logan, UT 84321. ☎ **435/755-5555** for information. Free admission. June–Aug daily 9am–5pm.

The Tabernacle was built from locally quarried stone in a style that's an amalgam of Greek, Roman, Gothic, and Byzantine architectural styles. The main stone, quartzite, is from Green Canyon, 8 miles northeast of Logan, and the white limestone used for the corners and trimmings came from 20 miles north, in Idaho. The foundation was begun in 1864, but the building took 27 years to complete. The stained-glass windows were installed in the early 1900s, and the organ in 1908. The main hall and balcony can accommodate about 1,800 people. The ceiling decoration was originally painted on oil cloth and then attached, but during a 1989 renovation, the paintings were traced directly onto the ceiling. The pillars are made of wood that has been expertly painted to simulate marble, a technique widely used throughout pioneer Utah. The Tabernacle was again renovated in 1997.

LDS Temple

175 N. 300 East, Logan, UT 84321. ☎ **435/752-3611.** Not open to the public.

The site of the Temple was known to the Shoshone as "a most sacred place," where they held their healing ceremonies. It's on a slight rise, and can be seen from just about anywhere in the valley. Octagonal towers give the four-story limestone temple the appearance of a medieval castle. The site was chosen on May 17, 1877, by church president Brigham Young; the completed Temple was dedicated on May 17, 1884, by his successor. The building was extensively renovated in the late 1970s.

Ronald V. Jensen Living Historical Farm

4025 South U.S. 89/91 (6 miles southwest of Logan), Wellsville, UT 84339. ☎ **435/245-4064.** Admission $5 adults, $3 children, $4 seniors and students. June–Aug Tues–Sat 10am–4pm. Closed Sept–May except for special events.

This authentic 1917 dairy farm is a 120-acre interpretive center operated by Utah State University graduate students. Guides in period costume escort visitors around the property, discussing life on the farm and explaining the farm equipment and implements. Although not open on a regular basis from September through May, there are special events, which might include a turn-of-the-century wedding, apple-harvest festival, quilting bees, or an old-fashioned Christmas celebration, complete with horse-drawn sleigh and caroling. Call for schedule.

Utah State University

102 Old Main, Logan, UT 84322-1440. ☎ **435/797-1710.** The 400-acre campus lies north of U.S. 89 and mostly east of 800 East.

Founded in 1888, Utah State University (USU) is situated on a bench that was once the shore of the great Lake Bonneville. Established through the Federal Land Grant Program as the Agricultural College of Utah, USU has an international reputation for research and teaching.

Old Main was the first USU building, begun just 1 year after the college was established; it's the oldest building in continuous use on any Utah college campus. At various times it has housed nearly every office and department of the school. Its tall bell tower is a campus landmark.

The **Nora Eccles Harrison Museum of Art,** 650 N. 1100 East (☎ **435/ 797-0163**), has a fine collection of ceramics on display and offers changing exhibits in a variety of media. It's open Tuesday through Friday from 10:30am to 4:30pm, and Saturday and Sunday from 2 to 5pm. Admission is free.

If you'd like to grab a snack—like some of the famous Aggie's ice cream—stop at the **Taggart Student Center,** just a block north of Old Main (☎ **435/797-1710**). It also houses the campus bookstore, a ticket office, a post office, a movie theater, and a full restaurant on the fourth floor serving lunch during the week and dinner on weekends.

Willow Park Zoo

419 W. 700 South. ☎ **435/750-9893.** Admission 25¢. Daily 9am–dusk. From Main St., head west on 600 South for 3 blocks, turn south (left) onto 300 West for 1 block, then west (right) onto 700 South.

This small but intriguing zoo is home to cute capuchin monkeys, noisy macaws, ugly condors, a fun turtle pond, waddling raccoons, elegant swans, slinking coyotes, brightly colored Amazon parrots, and more. The grounds are quite attractive, with a lovely, grassy play and picnic area shaded by tall trees. Some of the animal enclosures are on the small side, and not as animal-friendly as many modern big-city zoos, but the personnel are making improvements when and where they can, money and space permitting.

NINETEENTH-CENTURY LOGAN COMES TO LIFE
Walking Tour of Historic Main Street

This tour will give you a glimpse into the city's colorful past, as well as a taste of life in late 19th-century Logan. Allow 45 minutes to 1 hour to browse the Victorian-lined street, plus additional time for browsing and window-shopping.

Start your walking tour at:

1. **The Chamber of Commerce,** at 160 N. Main St., in what was originally the Federal Building, built to house the post office and other government functions—hence the naming of the adjacent east–west street as Federal Avenue. Inside, in the old courtroom, you'll find the Daughters of Utah Pioneers Museum, with displays depicting the life of early settlers in the Cache Valley.

   Head south on Main Street to:

2. **Zion's Bank,** located on the corner of Tithing Square. Each Mormon settlement in the valley had a tithing house that constituted the economic center of the community. Residents were expected to contribute 10% of their income to the church. The tithing house or square was also the location for gathering and disbursing produce, livestock, and even, on occasion, cash. Above the door of the present bank is a sculptural depiction of the trappers and American Indians who were typical of the early inhabitants of Cache Valley.

   Turn east on 100 North and walk a block to:

3. **St. John's Episcopal Church.** The founders of St. John's were the first non-Mormon Christians to establish a congregation in Logan. They also set up a school in 1873. After that, Methodists, Congregationalists, and Presbyterians sent missionaries and school teachers.

   Cross the street and head over to the:

4. **Tabernacle,** in the center of Tabernacle Square facing Main Street. This imposing brick structure was begun before the Temple (3 blocks east), but finished after, taking more than 25 years to complete. Although the Temple is open only to Mormons, the Tabernacle is accessible to the general public and has been used over the years for both church and community meetings.

   Walk south to the corner of Main and Center, and cross over to the:

5. **First Security Bank,** on the site of the 1890 Thatcher Brothers Bank and Opera House. On April 17, 1912, the building was destroyed by fire; it was an event that overshadowed the sinking of the *Titanic* in the local paper. The opera house was on the second floor and could house an audience of about 800. Theater and opera productions by both local amateur and professional groups took place here, as did political and civic gatherings.

   Continue south along Main to the:

6. **Ellen Eccles Theatre.** Eleven years after the Thatcher Brothers Bank and Opera House fire, one of the brothers and some associates built a new theater, one of the finest of its day, with the only full-size stage and fly loft in the area. Since the 1950s, it's seen more movies than live productions, but it's being restored to its original splendor and has recently staged full productions of *Carousel, South Pacific,* and *The Mikado.*

   Continue to the corner of Main and turn west onto 100 South, looking across the street to the remains of the:

In case you want to see the world.

At American Express, we're here to make your journey a smooth one. So we have over 1,700 travel service locations in over 120 countries ready to help. What else would you expect from the world's largest travel agency?

do more ®

Travel

http://www.americanexpress.com/travel

In case you want to be welcomed there.

We're here to see that you're always welcomed at establishments everywhere. That's why millions of people carry the American Express® Card — for peace of mind, confidence, and security, around the world or just around the corner.

do more

Cards

In case you're
running low.

**We're here to help with more than 118,000 Express Cash
locations around the world. In order to enroll, just call
American Express before you start your vacation.**

do more

**Express
Cash**

And just in case.

We're here with American Express® Travelers Cheques and Cheques *for Two.*® They're the safest way to carry money on your vacation and the surest way to get a refund, practically anywhere, anytime.

Another way we help you...

do more

Travelers Cheques

7. Thatcher Milling and Elevator Co. In 1888, this now-crumbling facility had the capacity to mill 1,100 bushels of grain each day. After a half block, turn north on the drive into the mid-block parking lot; you'll walk past the back of the Ellen Eccles Theatre and through the drive-in for First Security Bank. At Center Street you'll reach the:

8. Lyric Theatre, also built by the Thatchers. Constructed in 1913, the theater was refurbished in 1962 and is operated by Utah State University and used by the Old Lyric Repertory Company during the summer months. It's reportedly the home of a friendly ghost, who appears on the edge of the balcony in Elizabethan costume wearing a fool's cap and has been heard laughing during rehearsals of *Hamlet.*

To the west of the theater, near the Bluebird Candy Company, is the location of the original stagecoach and livery stable for downtown Logan.

Now walk out to Main and turn north across Central to:

9. Larsen's Hallmark, in the old J.R. Edwards Saloon building; note the name carved in stone above the second-floor windows. This was Logan's finest saloon and billiard hall in the late 1800s. The president of the Agricultural College was incensed that his students were frequenting Edwards's establishment; when letters got him nowhere, President Paul strode into the saloon and was promptly struck on the back of the head by Edwards. After paying his $5 fine, Edwards finally posted notices excluding minors from his saloon, and Paul returned to his duties on College Hill. Next door to the Hallmark is the:

10. Bluebird Restaurant, in business since 1914, on this site since 1923. This has been a gathering place for generations of Loganites and is a place of nostalgia today, with its imported marble soda fountain and historic photos. It's a good place to stop for a snack from the soda fountain or for a more substantial meal.

Continue north along Main to the corner of 100 North to:

11. Zion's Bank, once the Cache Valley branch of Zion's Cooperative Mercantile Institution. ZCMI was begun by Brigham Young in the late 1860s to protect the local economy from the outside influences brought in by the newly completed transcontinental railroad. The plan included the establishment of a large wholesale store in Salt Lake City, with retail cooperatives in all outlying settlements. Mormons were to buy only from their local ZCMI, which in turn would deal only with the central Salt Lake wholesale store. This form of merchandising declined toward the end of the 1800s, and the Logan store was disbanded.

Cross the street and continue north on Main 1 block to the:

12. Cache County Courthouse, the oldest county building in Utah still in use as a county building. Before this structure was built in 1883, the old county office was on the site; in 1873, a lynching took place here—vigilantes, angered by the shooting of the sheriff's nephew, broke into the jail, took the prisoner out, and hung him from the courthouse signpost.

SPORTS & OUTDOOR ACTIVITIES

Many of the outdoor recreation opportunities are in the Wasatch-Cache National Forest, which covers almost 2 million acres of northern Utah. For maps and other information, contact the **Logan Ranger District** office, 1500 E. U.S. 89, Logan, UT 84321 (☎ 435/755-3620).

BIKING   Cache Valley's patchwork of farms, wetlands, and migratory-bird habitats offers excellent biking through the countryside on well-maintained roads. A booklet describing several bike trails in and around Logan is prepared jointly by the **Bridgerland Travel Region** (☎ 800/882-4433 or 435/752-2161) and the national forest's **Logan Ranger District** (☎ 435/755-3620). You can pick up a copy at the visitor center at 160 N. Main Street or at the ranger district office (address above).

If you'd like to rent either a mountain or road bike, stop at **Guido's Cycle and Sport,** 565 N. Main St., Logan (☎ 435/752-2770), open Monday through Saturday. Guido's also repairs bicycles and has a wide selection of clothing and accessories. Another rental shop is **Adventure Sports,** 51 S. Main St. (☎ 435/753-4044), open Monday through Saturday; Adventure Sports also offers guided bicycle tours.

FISHING   Logan Canyon is popular for rainbow and albino trout in impoundments. The Upper Canyon is great for natural cutthroat and brook trout. First, Second, and Third Dams are good for stocked fish, and Second Dam is handicapped accessible. For guide services and a full-service fly shop, stop at either the **Fly Cache,** 72 W. Center St. (☎ 435/750-6645), or **Rainy's Flies and Supplies**, 690 N. 100 East (☎ 435/753-6766).

GOLF   The **Logan River Golf Course,** 550 W. 1000 South (☎ **435/750-0123**), is an 18-hole, par-71 public course winding along the river among the trees. Greens fees are $8.50 for 9 holes and $16 for 18, with carts costing $10 and $17 respectively. About 12 miles southwest of Logan, on U.S. 89/91 on the way to Brigham City, is **Sherwood Hills** (☎ 435/245-6055), a 9-hole, par-36 public mountain course. The greens fee is $9, and carts rent for $9.

HIKING   For a brochure describing several hiking trails in the Wasatch-Cache National Forest east of Logan, stop at the visitor center on Main Street, the forest service office, or one of the sponsoring sporting-goods stores: **Al's Sporting Goods,** 99 W. Center (☎ 435/752-5151); **Trailhead Sports,** 117 N. Main (☎ 435/753-1541); or **Adventure Sports,** 51 S. Main (☎ 435/753-4044).

HORSEBACK RIDING   About 12 miles southwest of Logan, on U.S. 89/91 on the way to Brigham City, is **The Stables at Sherwood Hills** (☎ 435/245-5054), offering 1- and 2-hour rides, supper rides (with a minimum of 18 persons), and group hayrides. You'll ride into the surrounding forests, where you'll see breathtaking scenery and have a good chance of spotting wildlife.

Beaver Creek Lodge, in Logan Canyon (☎ **435/753-1076**), is about 25 miles northeast of Logan on U.S. 89 just east of Beaver Mountain Ski Resort. One-, 1¹/₂- and 3-hour guided rides are available for beginner through expert levels, costing from $15 to $35. Trails include a wide range of terrain, from rolling hills covered with aspens, pine trees, and wildflowers, to more challenging rides to the top of a mountain for panoramic views of the forest. Reservations are recommended; kids have to be at least 7 years old, although the little ones are often led around the stable area free of charge.

ROCK CLIMBING   The sheer rock walls of Logan Canyon make this one of the most challenging rock-climbing areas in the West. For detailed information and climbing-site recommendations, stop at the visitor center.

SNOWMOBILING & OTHER WINTER SPORTS   Snowmobiling opportunities can be found throughout the Wasatch-Cache National Forest. Rental snowmobiles are available at **Beaver Creek Lodge,** in Logan Canyon (☎ 435/753-1076), about 25 miles northeast of Logan on U.S. 89 just east of Beaver Mountain Ski Resort. The lodge offers access to more than 300 miles of groomed snowmobile trails. Rates for a 2-hour ride are $39 to $49, and a full day costs $95 to $120. Information on snowmobiling, snowshoeing, and cross-country skiing can be obtained from the Wasatch-Cache National Forest's **Logan Ranger District** (☎ 435/755-3620). Downhill skiing at **Beaver Mountain Ski Area** is discussed earlier in this chapter.

SPECTATOR SPORTS

A member of the Big West Athletic Conference, **Utah State University** takes part in intercollegiate athletics, plus a program of intramural sports. Call the school's ticket office (☎ **435/797-0305**) for information.

WHERE TO STAY

The sales and lodging taxes in Logan total just over 9%. Pets are not allowed unless otherwise noted.

Alta Manor Suites

45 E. 500 North, Logan, UT 84321. ☎ **435/752-0808.** Fax 435/752-2445. 8 suites. A/C TV TEL. $80–$100 double. Rates include continental breakfast. AE, CB, DC, DISC, MC, V.

A modern lodging, built in 1994 in the Old English Tudor style, these spacious suites are elegantly furnished with Queen Anne reproductions. All units have whirlpool baths and separate showers, natural-gas fireplaces, TVs with several premium movie channels, full kitchens, and one or two queen beds plus a sofa sleeper. The property is entirely smoke-free, and one wheelchair-accessible room is available.

Best Western Baugh Motel

153 S. Main, Logan, UT 84321. ☎ **800/462-4154** or 435/752-5220. Fax 435/752-3251. 77 rms, 5 suites. A/C TV TEL. $48–$66 double, $84–$88 suites. AE, CB, DC, DISC, MC, V.

This attractively landscaped property is great for those who prefer to relax outdoors rather than in: It has large shade and evergreen trees, an outdoor swimming pool and smaller children's pool, and a nice picnic area out back alongside a stream. The spacious standard rooms contain two extra-long double beds (or one king or queen bed) and comfortable lounge chairs. Some rooms have swivel rockers or recliners, and all have desks and plenty of storage. Suites are really just oversized rooms, but with a very nice sitting area and either one king or two queen beds. One suite has a whirlpool tub, the others have fireplaces, and some have a microwave and refrigerator.

Services include limited room service, video rentals, and free refreshments in the lobby. Baby-sitting can be arranged, and passes to a nearby recreation center are available. The Cottage Restaurant, featuring American cuisine, serves three meals Monday through Saturday plus Sunday brunch.

✪ Center Street Bed & Breakfast Inn

169 E. Center St., Logan, UT 84321. ☎ **435/752-3443.** 16 units. A/C TV. $57–$180 double. Rates include breakfast. AE, DISC, MC, V.

This three-story Victorian mansion, built in 1879, is Utah's own little Madonna Inn, for those of you familiar with that California coast landmark. Nothing is as you would expect it to be here, but everything is fun and comfortable. The living room features a Michelangelo-style fresco on the ceiling, and the theme rooms' names reflect their decor. Jesse James's Hide-Out and Waterhole Saloon, for instance, is huge, with a 60-inch TV, pool table, knotty pine walls, kitchenette, and gas fireplace. The decor is, of course, western, and includes wanted posters, a stuffed rattlesnake, and a pressed-brass ceiling; a private 900-gallon whirlpool tub sits just 20 yards away in the corner of the backyard. The Castle of the Purple Dragon feels like—you guessed it— a stone castle, and comes complete with a mounted purple dragon's head. The entire suite is medieval (except for the 45-inch TV, gas fireplace, and whirlpool tub), slightly decadent, and totally different. Other rooms include the Egyptian Suite, Amazon Rainforest, Arabian Nights Suite, Caribbean Sea Cave, Aphrodite's Court, and Space Odyssey. Smoking is strictly prohibited inside.

The Logan House Inn

168 N. 100 East, Logan, UT 84321. ☎ **800/478-7459** or 435/752-7727. Fax 435/752-0092. 6 rms, 3 suites. A/C TV TEL. $79–$150 double. Rates include breakfast. AE, DC, DISC, MC, V.

This 100-year-old Georgian manor house has a traditional American feel, relaxed and quiet, with solid wood furnishings. Each room has its own whirlpool tub and phones with computer modem hookups; all suites contain fireplaces. Smoking is permitted only on the verandah.

WHERE TO DINE

Angie's Restaurant

690 N. Main. ☎ **435/752-9252.** Main courses $5.69–$12.99 dinner, $4.99–$4.99 lunch, $1.65–$9.95 breakfast. AE, DISC, MC, V. Sun–Thurs 5:30am–10pm; Fri–Sat 5:30am–11pm. From Center St., head north about 7 blocks. AMERICAN.

This local favorite is a busy family restaurant, noisy and casual. It's particularly popular for breakfast, which is served all day. Scones and cinnamon rolls are baked fresh daily, and the omelets—all 11 varieties—are gigantic. In fact, all of Angie's portions are generous. The wide selection of breakfast goodies ranges from pancakes and waffles to skillet breakfasts, standard egg dishes, and Southwestern offerings. If it's after 11am and you're not in the mood for breakfast, the lunch menu offers about four dozen sandwiches and burgers, plus several salads and Southwestern platters. The dinner menu includes pasta, chicken, steak, and seafood. Seniors' and children's menus are available. No alcoholic beverages are served.

The Bluebird

19 N. Main St. ☎ **435/752-3155.** Main courses $5.50–$12.95. AE, DISC, MC, V. Mon–Thurs 11am–9pm; Fri–Sat 11am–10pm; Sun noon–6pm; slightly shorter hours in winter. Just north of Center St. AMERICAN.

The Bluebird opened in 1914 as a candy shop and soda fountain, and soon expanded to include a few lunch items. In 1921, it moved to its present location, expanding its menu yet again to include dinner. Today, the Bluebird continues to offer good food along with fountain treats. The decor, reminiscent of the 1920s, features the original marble behind the soda fountain and a mural depicting Logan from 1856 to modern times.

The menu offers the old-fashioned luncheon fare you'd expect, including a Monte Cristo and a minced ham sandwich. English-style chips can be ordered with any sandwich. There are also several full meal offerings for lunch, including a 6-ounce sirloin steak, chicken teriyaki, and a 5-ounce halibut steak. In addition to a few sandwiches, the dinner menu includes full dinners such as vegetarian pasta primavera, chicken-fried steak (not everything's like it was in the '20s—it's now grilled, not deep-fried), and the popular slow-roasted prime rib. A children's menu is available. No alcohol is served.

Copper Mill Restaurant

55 N. Main St., in the Emporium Building. ☎ **435/752-0647.** Main courses $7.95–$27.95 dinner, $4.25–$6.95 lunch. AE, CB, DC, DISC, MC, V. Mon–Thurs 11am–9:30pm; Fri–Sat 11am–10:30pm. A half block north of Center St. STEAK/SEAFOOD.

You'll feel right at home in this upscale family restaurant, with its wooden booths and tables, numerous plants, and copper-milling artifacts all around. Known for its unique beef seasonings, the restaurant's most popular items are the prime rib and a 6-ounce tenderloin steak. Also on the menu are several chicken entrees, including a version of Cordon Bleu, and seafood selections, such as halibut, scallops, and shrimp. A children's menu is available, and both beer and wine are served.

Grapevine
129 N. 100 East. ☎ **435/752-1977.** Reservations recommended. Main courses $13.95–$20.95. AE, DISC, MC, V. Wed–Sat 5:30–10pm. From Center and Main, head east on Center 1 block, turn left (north) onto 100 East; it's a little more than a block to the restaurant. CONTINENTAL.

The Grapevine offers informal elegance in a contemporary but comfortable dining room, with fresh flowers and white linen on the tables. In summer, diners can sit out on the patio. The menu changes about three times a year, as owner-chef Bill Oblock experiments with innovative cooking techniques and sauces from different countries. Dishes include game, fish, poultry, pasta, and beef. The Grapevine has a full liquor license and offers quality wines (mostly from California) and Utah beers.

Kate's Kitchen
71$^1/_2$ E. 1200 South. ☎ **435/753-5733** or 435/753-1223 for take-out. Reservations accepted for parties of 8 or more. Main courses $9.95–$11.95. MC, V. Tues–Sat 4–10pm. Closed Christmas, New Year's, and Fourth of July. Follow Main St. south and take Utah 165 towards Hyrum (the left fork when U.S. 89/91 heads right to Wellsville); turn east (left) onto 1200 South; Kate's is on the left. AMERICAN.

Kate was born in 1992, so it's her dad who is presently running the restaurant. You'll find home cookin' served family-style in the large, informal dining room; everything here is homemade, even the ice cream. Menu choices include Kate's pot roast, country-fried steak, country-style BBQ ribs, or home-roasted chicken. Dinners come with plenty of homemade muffins and honey butter, fresh garden salad with house dressing, mashed potatoes and gravy or seasoned rice, and corn on the cob or the veggie of the day. If you need more, just flag down a server; you can't miss them—they're the ones wearing hats. Once a month, Kate's offers an all-you-can-eat prime-rib dinner, by reservation only; call to see when it's on. An early-bird supper for $7.95 is available Tuesday through Thursday from 4 to 6pm. No alcohol is served.

Old Grist Mill Bread Co.
78 E. 400 North. ☎ **435/753-6463.** Sandwiches $3–$4; bagels 3/$1, with cream cheese $1. No credit cards. Mon–Sat 7am–8pm. From Center, head north on Main 4 blocks and turn right (east) on 400 North. BAKERY/DELI.

You can practically fill up just by breathing the bread-scented air here. On any given day, you can choose from five or six breads for your sandwich—standards like honey whole-wheat, multigrain, sourdough, and whole-wheat sourdough; and more unique breads such as sunflower whole-wheat, sourdough tomato-herb, onion-dill rye, cinnamon-raisin-walnut wheat, and apple-almond-cinnamon. A selection of bagels is also available, and both breads and bagels can be topped with a variety of cream-cheese spreads and top-quality meats and cheeses. All orders are take-out, and you're welcome to call in your order in advance. This is a great place to pick up a sandwich to take on a hike, a bike ride, or a picnic.

LOGAN AFTER DARK
A wide range of entertainment is presented at the historic **Ellen Eccles Theatre,** also known as the Capitol Theatre, at 43 S. Main (☎ 435/752-0026). The box office is open Monday through Saturday from noon to 6pm. Opera buffs will enjoy the **Utah Festival Opera Company's** (☎ 435/830-6088) performances of two or three operas each summer.

The **Utah Music Festival** offers fine chamber music at several locations in Logan, including the Tabernacle. Performances take place during July and most of August. Contact the Festival at P.O. Box 3381, Logan, UT 84323-3381 (☎ 800/816-UTAH).

Plays, concerts, and exhibitions featuring both students and faculty, plus a performing-arts series showcasing national and international artists, take place at **Utah State University.** Contact the University Relations Department (☎ 435/797-1158) for information on upcoming events.

The **Old Lyric Repertory Company** usually schedules four plays, running in rotation, for 8 weeks in summer. For information contact the Spectrum Ticket Office at USU (☎ 435/797-0305).

The Southern Wasatch Front: World-Class Skiing & More

9

Now we'll head to the area of the Wasatch Front south and east of Salt Lake City. This chapter is arranged geographically from north to south, from the Cottonwood Canyon and Park City resorts to Provo and nearby Timpanogos Cave National Monument, with a few stops in between, including pristine Strawberry Reservoir and Robert Redford's Sundance Resort and Institute.

1 The Cottonwood Canyon Resorts: Brighton, Solitude, Alta & Snowbird

You say you want snow? Here it is, some 500 inches of it piling up every year, just waiting for you powder-hungry skiers to make that short drive from Salt Lake City. You'll find Brighton and Solitude ski resorts in Big Cottonwood Canyon, and Alta and Snowbird in its sister canyon, known as Little Cottonwood.

If you're skiing on a budget, you might want to stay in Salt Lake City, where lodging is much cheaper, rather than at the resorts themselves. The resorts are so close—less than an hour's drive from Salt Lake—that city dwellers sometimes hit the slopes after a hard day at the office!

But this area is more than just a winter playground. Big Cottonwood Canyon, cut by ancient rivers over more centuries than we can imagine, is a spectacular setting for warm-weather picnicking, camping, mountain biking, and hiking. Rugged, glacier-carved Little Cottonwood Canyon, where you'll find Alta and Snowbird ski resorts, is filled with lush fields of wildflowers in the summer; that rainbow of color later takes a back seat to the brilliant hues of autumn.

GETTING THERE

BY CAR   From Salt Lake City, take I-215 to exit 7; follow Utah 210 south. Turn east onto Utah 190 to reach Solitude and Brighton in Big Cottonwood Canyon; continue on Utah 210 south and east to Snowbird and Alta in Little Cottonwood Canyon. From Salt Lake City International Airport, it'll take about an hour to reach any of the four ski areas.

BY BUS   The **Utah Transit Authority** (☎ **801/287-4636** or TDD 801/287-4657) provides bus service from downtown Salt Lake City hotels and various park-and-ride lots throughout the city into Big and Little Cottonwood Canyons during ski season.

BY SHUTTLE **Lewis Bros. Stages** (☎ **800/826-5844** or 801/359-8677; fax 801/359-5114) offers shuttles from the airport and downtown Salt Lake City, as well as between the ski resorts. **Park City Transportation Services** (☎ **800/637-3803** or 435/649-8567; fax 435/649-3549) offers airport service to all major Utah ski areas.

BIG COTTONWOOD CANYON

Utah 190 will take you through Big Cottonwood Canyon to Brighton and Solitude. Each turn along your drive to the summit of this 15-mile-long canyon brings you to yet another grand, dizzying vista. Rock climbers love these steep, rugged canyon walls—watch for them along your drive.

BRIGHTON SKI RESORT

Brighton has been hosting skiers since 1936. Located 25 miles from downtown Salt Lake City at the top of Big Cottonwood Canyon, this low-key, family-friendly resort is where many Utahns learn to ski. The ski school is highly regarded, children 10 and under stay and ski free with their parents, and teens particularly enjoy the bumps of Lost Maid Trail as it winds through the woods. But don't let its reputation as a beginner's mountain fool you: Brighton's slopes are graced with a full range of terrain, all the powder you can ski, and virtually no crowds. You'll find more Utahns than out-of-staters on the slopes here—visitors tend to stay away because of the paucity of lodgings in the area. So there's always plenty of elbow room on the intermediate and advanced slopes, even on weekends; you'll probably have them all to yourself on weekdays. Due to the relatively small number of skis crossing the mountain, the powder never gets skied out—you can ski all week without ever seeming to run out of deep virgin snow. And you can explore the slopes until late in the day: Brighton lights up 18 of its runs for night skiing until 9pm.

Brighton is also one of the best snowboarding destinations in the state; snowboarding is permitted everywhere on the mountain.

Just the Facts

Brighton Ski Resort, Star Route, Brighton, UT 84121 (☎ **800/873-5512** or 801/532-4731), has two high-speed quad lifts, two triples, and three double chairs servicing over 850 acres in the Wasatch-Cache National Forest. The vertical drop is 1,745 feet, with a base elevation of 8,755 feet and summit of 10,500 feet. There are 64 runs, 21% of which are rated beginner, 40% intermediate, and 39% advanced. Elk Park Ridge, at 3 miles, is the longest run.

Lifts are open daily from 9am to 4pm, mid-November to late April, with night skiing (18 runs on 200 acres) from mid-December to early April, Monday through Saturday, 4 to 9pm.

The resort can make snow on 170 acres, but with 500 inches average snowfall per year, the man-made stuff isn't usually necessary.

Brighton recently built a beautiful new 20,000-square-foot day lodge, the Brighton Center, which provides ticket windows, rest rooms, a common area, and a convenient depot for those using the bus. **Brighton Mountain Sports** is based here, too, providing retail and rental ski equipment plus repairs.

LIFT TICKETS An all-day ticket costs $31; a single ride is $10. Children ages 10 and under ski free with an adult (limit two children per adult); without an adult, children pay half price. Seniors 70 and over ski free.

LESSONS & PROGRAMS **Brighton Ski School,** located in the Alpine Rose building, offers both private and 2-hour group lessons for all levels. Group lessons range from $40 to $58 including equipment and lift ticket, or $20 for the lesson only (you'll get a discount on your lift ticket). The size of the class is limited to 10 people, and participants must be at least 7 years old. Private lessons start at $50. Night-ski lessons are available Thursday evenings from mid-December to late March and cost $20 (including lift ticket).

The Ski School also offers a variety of workshops and clinics, including a telemark series as well as adult parallel, senior, and women's workshops. Inquire at the school for details. Snowboarding lessons are $50, including equipment rental and lift ticket.

Kinderski, for ages 4 to 7 in classes no larger than six children, is $25; a lesson plus lunch is $37 to $57; equipment rental is $8 with class.

Where to Stay & Dine

Brighton Lodge, at the ski resort (☎ **800/873-5512** or 801/532-4731), is your only option. It has 20 rooms, with nightly rates of $60 to $110, plus special multinight packages. Its two whirlpools will help loosen those sore muscles for the next day's skiing. Room tax of about $9^1/_2$% is added to your bill.

Cafeteria-style dining is available daily 8am to 8:30pm at the **Alpine Rose** restaurant. **Molly Green's Pub,** a private club ($5 for 2-week membership), opens for lunch and stays open through aprés-ski and dinner.

Warm-Weather Activities

Mountain biking and hiking are popular summer activities. Although not available at this writing, mountain-bike rentals are a possibility in the future; check at the resort for information. Sorry, mountain bikers—lifts aren't open in the summer.

SOLITUDE SKI RESORT

Solitude is a friendly, family-oriented ski area that hasn't been "discovered" yet, so lift lines are virtually nonexistent. The snow is terrific, and it's easy to reach—just 28 miles from downtown Salt Lake City in Big Cottonwood Canyon.

Like its next-door neighbor Brighton—which is connected to Solitude via the Solbright Trail—Solitude enjoys excellent powder and no big crowds. Its 1,200-plus acres of skiable terrain range from well-groomed, sunny beginner and intermediate trails to gently pitched bowls and glades; advanced skiers who would rather avoid Alta at peak times will also find plenty to keep them happy. The mountain is well designed, with runs laid out so beginners won't suddenly find themselves in more difficult terrain. You can start at the bottom and work your way up through intermediate to expert runs. Intermediates have wide-open bowls in which to cruise and practice their powder skiing, several excellent forest runs, and some great bumpy stretches on which to hone their mogul skills. Advanced skiers have many long fall lines, open powder areas, and steeply graded chutes to choose from, and will often find themselves exploring the terrain surrounded only by the solitude of the mountain.

Solitude is the state's only downhill ski area with a world-class Nordic center out its back door: The University of Utah and U.S. Olympic teams train here.

Just the Facts

Solitude, 12000 Big Cottonwood Canyon, Solitude, UT 84121 (☎ **800/748-4754** or 801/534-1400; fax 435/649-5276), operates one high-speed quad lift, two triples, and four doubles to service 63 runs and three bowls. Runs are rated 20% beginner, 50% intermediate, and 30% advanced/expert. The resort is open from early November to late April, 9am to 4pm daily. With a summit elevation of 10,035 feet and a vertical drop of 2,047 feet, Solitude receives an average snowfall of 430 inches.

LIFT TICKETS   All-day lift tickets cost $36 for adults; those 10 and under or 70 and over ski free. Half-day lift tickets are $30.

LESSONS & PROGRAMS   Solitude's **ski school** has something for everyone. Adult classes are $40 for a half day and $55 for all day; customized private lessons are also available. The **Moonbeam Learning Center** is set up for kids ages 4 through 12; the children's all-day ski instruction program, including lunch, is $65, and the afternoon-only program is $40.

CROSS-COUNTRY SKIING   ✪ **Solitude Nordic Center** is Utah's oldest cross-country ski center. It has 20 kilometers of groomed trails, including a children's trail. The center is located between Solitude and Brighton at 8,700 feet and connects the two downhill areas. Trails pass through Alpine forests and meadows and around frozen Silver Lake. The **Silver Lake Day Lodge** offers rentals, retail sales, lessons, and light snacks. Trail passes for ages 11 to 69 cost $10 for a full day, $7 for a half day. Those 10 and under or 70 and over ski free.

Where to Stay & Dine

Room tax adds about 9¹/₂% to your bill.

Creekside at Solitude, a 36-unit condominium property, offers 1- to 3-bedroom units priced from $180 to $580. The restaurant serves Mediterranean and Italian cuisine; pizzas start at $7, and main courses are in the $9 to $15 range. Creekside is centrally located in the resort village, close to three of the lifts, and not far from the day lodge.

The **Inn at Solitude** is a full-service luxury hotel, with 46 rooms and nightly rates from $140 to $275. A favorite spot for après-ski fondue and refreshments is **St. Bernard's,** located in the Inn.

Adjacent to the Apex Chairlift and with terrific views of the mountain, the day lodge, **Last Chance Mining Camp,** offers heartier fare, breakfasts and lunches, plus après-ski refreshments.

The **Roundhouse Restaurant** and **Sunshine Grill** are partway up the mountain, at 9,000 feet elevation. The Roundhouse offers a special "one-cat open-sleigh" five-course gourmet dinner—accessible by snow cat, of course. Reservations are required (☎ 800/748-4754, ext. 5709). The **Sunshine Grill,** with an outside deck and terrific views of the slopes, serves lunch and snacks daily.

For an unusual experience, make reservations at the **Yurt** (☎ 800/748-4754, ext. 5709), in the forest above the main lodge. You can either cross-country ski or snowshoe through the evergreens to get to your elegant five-course gourmet meal, served at a table set with linen, silver, and crystal. Dress is casual, but the meal isn't.

Warm-Weather Activities

Solitude remains open on a limited basis in the summer, offering chairlift rides, mountain-bike rentals, and a place to hike or just kick back and watch the wildflowers grow. Call for exact open days and times.

LITTLE COTTONWOOD CANYON

With towering peaks rising 11,000 feet above the road on both sides, Utah 210 takes you on a lovely scenic drive through the canyon. At the mouth of the canyon, at the junction of Utah 209 and Utah 210, is the site where the first Mormons quarried the granite used to build the Salt Lake Temple.

ALTA SKI AREA

Alta may be famous for its snow—over 500 inches annually of some of the lightest powder in the world—but at just $28 for an all-day adult lift ticket, it's also one of the best skiing bargains anywhere.

Located about an hour's drive southeast of Salt Lake City at the end of Little Cottonwood Canyon, ✪ **Alta** is an excellent choice for serious skiers of all levels. Beginners have their share of runs; there's even a bit of easy-going tree skiing through the woods for the more adventurous novices. First-timers and slower skiers might want to steer clear of Sunnyside, though. The traffic can get heavy, and you'll often have to deal with the more advanced skiers who come swooshing through from off the higher runs.

Intermediates will find plenty of open cruising ground, forested areas, and long, arcing chutes to glide through, plus opportunities to work on their bumps technique (try Challenger for a moderately pitched set) or practice their turns in the powder. Experts will find an abundance of the Cottonwood Canyons' famous powder and spectacular runs, like steep, long Alf's High Rustler. Alta offers much for the expert and the extreme skier—far too much to cover here—but hard-core skiers should know that you'll have to step out of the bindings and do a bit of hiking to get to some of the longest drops and best powder-laden runs.

Alta's fans are many, and boy, are they loyal. That's because the emphasis here is on quality skiing. Alta has chosen to limit their uphill capacity by not installing high-speed quads. This is a classic ski resort, with both European-style terrain *and* sensibilities. This means that people are turned away on those occasions when the ski gods determine there are already enough skiers on the mountain. An announcement is made on 530 AM radio about a half hour before the closure. The slopes themselves are opened and closed throughout the day on a staggered schedule dictated by conditions, but they tend to follow a rough order. You may want to ferret out and follow some locals who know their way around the mountain and its timetable.

Snowboarders are not allowed on the slopes here.

Just the Facts

Although famous for its expert runs, **Alta,** P.O. Box 8007, Alta, UT 84092-8007 (☎ **801/359-1078**), also has fine beginner and intermediate trails. The breakdown is 25% beginner, 40% intermediate, and 35% advanced, with a base elevation of 8,550 feet rising to 10,650 feet at the top, yielding a vertical drop of 2,100 feet. Alta is generally open by mid-November and remains open until mid-April, with lifts operating daily from 9:15am to 4:30pm. There are six double and two triple lifts servicing 39 runs on 2,200 skiable acres, with snowmaking on 50 acres.

Alta Ski Lifts Company owns and operates only the ski area, while all other businesses and services are privately run. At the base of Albion and Sunnyside lifts, you'll find a day lodge with cafeteria, lift-ticket sales, day care, the ski school, and rentals. Two more cafeterias are located on the mountain.

A transfer tow connects the Albion and Wildcat lift areas; in this base area, there are four lodges with dining facilities, ski rentals, and kids' programs. See "Where to Stay & Dine," below, for contact information.

LIFT TICKETS   An all-day, all-lifts ticket costs $28—a real bargain in today's world—with half-day tickets at $21. Beginner lifts only are $20 for all day and $14 for half. In addition to the office at the day lodge, you can buy lift tickets at the base of the Wildcat and Collins lifts.

LESSONS & PROGRAMS   Founded in 1948 by Alf Engen, the highly-regarded **ski school** (☎ **801/359-1078**) is recognized for its contribution to the development of professional ski instruction. Morning and afternoon group lessons cost from $25 to $35; private instruction starts at $58. The **Children's Ski Adventures** program, for kids ages 4 to 12, offers fun, skill development, and lessons in ski etiquette. Choose either a 2-hour or all-day program.

Alta's **day-care program** (☎ **801/742-3042**) is open to children ages 2 months to 10 years old, and reservations are encouraged. The cost is $35 to $50 for a full day and $30 to $44 for a half day.

Where to Stay & Dine

You can check out the lodging possibilities in Alta by calling the **Alta Reservation Service** (☎ **801/942-0404**), which represents lodges and condominiums at Alta, books rooms in Snowbird and Salt Lake City, and arranges airline reservations and car rentals. Room tax of about 11% and restaurant tax of about 9% are added to bills.

Our favorite places to stay in Alta are slope-side. Both add a 15% service charge to your bill in lieu of tipping:

Alta Lodge (☎ **800/707-2582** or 801/742-3500) is perhaps the quintessential mountain ski lodge, simple and rustic, where you'll often find snowdrifts halfway up your windows as you look out toward the mountain. Rooms vary from small and basic to large and almost luxurious, with fireplace and private balcony. Rates, including an excellent breakfast and dinner, range from $240 to $350 for two people; or $95 to $103 per person for a dorm room with two bunk beds.

Rustler Lodge (☎ **800/451-5233** or 801/742-2200; fax 801/742-3832) is similar to Alta Lodge, with a great mountain-lodge ambiance and rooms that range from basic to deluxe; several two-room suites are also available. Rates, including full breakfast and dinner, range from $230 to $490 for two; a bed for one in a dorm room, with breakfast and dinner, costs $90 to $100.

SNOWBIRD SKI & SUMMER RESORT

A combination of super skiing and super facilities lures both hard-core skiers seeking spectacular powder as well as those who enjoy the pampering that accompanies a stay at a full-service resort. Consistently rated among America's top-ten ski resorts, Snowbird has been called classic Alta's "younger, slicker sister." You'll find the same wonderful snow here, but with a wider range of amenities with which to supplement your stay, including Snowbird's extremely popular spa and salon—worth the trip even if you don't ski. Some, however, find its dense, modern village and resort atmosphere cold compared to Alta's historic, European-style lodges and classic, ruggedly western attitude.

Snowbird gives over almost half of its skiable terrain to the expert skier, including plunging cliff runs like Great Scott, one of the steepest in the country. Mogulmeisters will want to take the Peruvian or Gad II lifts to find their happiness, popping off the bumps as they pick from among a great variety of fall lines on the steep and sinuous bump runs.

There's not a lot for beginners and intermediates, but enough to keep them happy—what is here is top-notch. There are even some "family-only" ski zones. Novices might want to head over to explore West Second South in its woodsy glade setting. Intermediates will enjoy the excellent runs coming off the Gad II lift, but if you decide to take the tram, wait around a bit at the top while your fellow riders take off; you'll then have these blue runs all to yourself—the next tramload won't get dumped off for another 5 minutes. Snowbird also has a particularly good program for skiers with disabilities.

Except for the Gad II chair, the entire mountain is open to snowboarders.

Just the Facts

Snowbird, P.O. Box 929000, Snowbird, UT 84092-9000 (☎ **800/453-3000** or 801/742-2222; fax 801/742-3300; 801/742-2222, ext. 4285, for snow conditions) has 66 runs on more than 2,500 acres, with 25% designated beginner, 30% intermediate, and 45% advanced. The ski season generally runs from mid-November to early May, although the record-breaking 600 inches—that's 50 feet—of snow received in 1994–95 allowed Snowbird to keep the lifts running through the Fourth of July—the latest lift-served skiing ever in Utah. From a base elevation of 7,760 feet, the vertical rise of 3,240 feet reaches Hidden Peak at 11,000 feet. The resort has snowmaking on about 25 acres, and about 50% of the mountain is groomed nightly—leaving the rest untouched for those who love to ski deep powder. With 2,500 skiable acres, you'll find plenty of quality skiing.

An aerial tram transports 125 skiers at a time up 2,900 vertical feet to Hidden Peak in about 8 minutes; it's quick, but can feel like a crowded New York City subway. With seven double chairlifts as well, Snowbird has a total uphill capacity of 9,200 skiers per hour. The tram and lifts operate between 9am and 3:45pm daily.

The **Cliff Spa and Salon** offers a lap pool and huge whirlpool, aerobic and weight-training rooms, plus individual treatment rooms for massages, body wraps, mud baths, and hydrotherapy. The **Snowbird Canyon Racquet Club,** 15 minutes from the slopes, has 23 tennis courts (10 indoor), racquetball, aerobic and cardiovascular facilities, and an indoor climbing wall. Snowbird provides a variety of facilities for children, including a state-licensed day-care center and a youth camp; call to inquire.

LIFT TICKETS Adult lift tickets are $39 for a full day and $32 for a half day; for both lifts and tram the cost is $47 and $39, respectively. Children 12 and under ski free with parents (two kids per paying parent). Seniors 65 and over are charged $27 for a full day ($34 including tram) and $24 per half day ($29 including tram).

LESSONS & PROGRAMS The **ski and snowboarding school's** 200 or so instructors provide lessons in either private or group format. Choose from among various options: an all-day class (which includes lunch), a package for first-timers, or specialized workshops for racers, women, and seniors. Adult rates for a full-day ski or snowboarding class start at about $62, while a 1-hour private ski lesson costs from $60 to $75.

Established in 1977, Snowbird's **Disabled Skier Program** is considered among the best in the country. Using state-of-the-art adaptive ski devices and a team of specially trained ski instructors, the program is available to both children and adults. Sit-skis, mono-skis, and outriggers are available at no cost.

HELI-SKIING Between December 15 and May 15, helicopter skiing is available on more than 80,000 acres in the Wasatch Mountains. Contact **Wasatch Powderbird Guides** (☎ 801/742-2800) for prices and information on both custom and scenic tours.

Where to Stay & Dine

The approximately 900 rooms at Snowbird range from standard lodge units to luxurious condominiums with kitchens and fireplaces. **Snowbird Central Reservations** (☎ 800/453-3000) books all lodging for the resort and can also arrange air and ground transportation. Room tax adds about 11%.

The Cliff Lodge, Spa, and Conference Center is in a ski-in, ski-out pedestrian mall. Practically every one of the 532 rooms, decorated in modern Southwest style, has splendid views of the mountain or canyon. Standard-size and extra-large rooms are available, as well as one- and two-bedroom suites and dorm rooms. You'll find a splendid spa, restaurants, shops, and practically anything else you could ask for. Dorm beds are in the $49 to $69 range; rooms for two people cost from $145 to $419; and suites for two range from $384 to $939.

The Lodge at Snowbird, The Inn, and **Iron Blosam Lodge** are condominium properties, offering individually decorated rooms, efficiencies, studios, and one-bedroom and one-bedroom-with-loft units. All have kitchens and fireplaces. Many are done in Southwest or western decor and have Murphy beds and/or sofa beds. Rates range from $135 to $727.

Dining facilities at the resorts include the luxurious **Aerie Restaurant** in the Cliff Lodge (see above), offering regional cuisine with French, Mediterranean, and northern Italian influences. Open for breakfast and dinner daily, the dining room boasts spectacular views of the ski slopes. Main courses range from $16 to $29 at dinner, with full liquor service available. For reservations, call ☎ **801/521-6040.** The **Keyhole Junction,** also at Cliff Lodge, serves Mexican dishes for breakfast and dinner daily, out on the patio if you so desire. Prices range from $10 to $21, and full liquor service is available. Reservations are not accepted. For steak and seafood, try the **Steak Pit** in Snowbird Center, open for dinner daily. Prices range from $12.50 to $39, and full liquor service is available. Reservations are not accepted. Basic Midwestern "homestyle" cooking can be found for breakfast and lunch daily at the **Forklift Restaurant** in Snowbird Center. Prices range from $4.75 to $12.50, and you can order beer or wine with your meal. Reservations are not accepted.

Warm-Weather Activities

After the skiers go home, Snowbird is still active with hikers and mountain bikers. Two lifts, the Aerial Tram and the Peruvian, haul mountain bikers up the slopes. And in the month of July, Snowbird's music program includes performances by the Utah Symphony; call for details.

2 Park City, Utah's Premier Resort Town

The cry of "Silver!" brought thousands to Park City in the 1870s, but today it's the thrill of skiing, biking, and other outdoor adventures that keeps the town bustling. Utah's most sophisticated resort community, Park City reminds us of Aspen, Colorado, and Taos, New Mexico—other historic western towns that have made the most of excellent ski terrain while evolving into popular year-round vacation destinations, offering a casual western atmosphere—plus a touch of elegance for those willing to pay for it.

Park City's 19th-century silver boom lasted for about 30 years, and saw a population of 10,000 at its height, with more than 30 saloons along Main Street and a flourishing red-light district. Once the minerals dwindled, Park City spent a half century dozing in the summer sun and under a blanket of winter snow. Then, in the late 1960s, the area's first ski lift was built (rates were $2.50 for a weekend of sledding and skiing), and Park City was on the road to becoming one of the West's most popular ski towns.

Today's visitors will find three separate ski areas, lodgings that range from basic to luxurious, some of the state's most innovative restaurants and best shopping opportunities, an abundance of fine performing-arts events, many of Utah's liveliest nightspots, and plenty of hiking, mountain biking, fishing, and other outdoor recreation possibilities.

As in many tourist towns, prices here can be a bit steep, so if you're watching your wallet, comparison shopping might be in order, and you may want to avoid visiting during the Christmas season and other peak periods. Those who are really pinching pennies might want to stay in Salt Lake City and drive to Park City in the morning for a day of skiing, exploring, or adventuring.

ESSENTIALS
GETTING THERE

Most visitors fly into Salt Lake City International Airport and drive or take a shuttle to Park City.

BY CAR   Park City is 31 miles east of Salt Lake City via I-80. At exit 145, take Utah 224 into Park City. Driving time from the airport is about 35 minutes.

BY SHUTTLE   Several companies offer shuttle service to and from Salt Lake International Airport. **Lewis Bros. Stages** (☎ **800/826-5844** or 435/649-2256) has been serving the Park City area since 1948.

Other companies offering shuttle service between Salt Lake City and Park City include **Park City Transportation Services, Inc.** (☎ 435/649-8567), **All Resort Express** (☎ 800/457-9457 or 435/649-3999), **Le Bus Motorcoaches** (☎ 800/ 366-0288 or 801/975-0202; fax 801/975-0289), and **Super Express Airport Shuttle** (☎ 800/321-5554 or 801/566-6400).

INFORMATION

The **Park City Chamber of Commerce/Convention and Visitors Bureau,** 1910 Prospector Ave. (P.O. Box 1630), Park City, UT 84060 (☎ **800/453-1360** or 435/649-6100), maintains an information center in the Park City Museum at 528 Main Street and at the Visitor Information Center at the junction of Utah highways 224 and 248 and Park Avenue as you enter town. Be sure to pick up a copy of the *Park City Main Street Historic Walking Tour* brochure, which will lead you to 45 buildings and historic sites that have somehow managed to survive fires, hard times, and progress through the decades. The historic walk, complete with engaging features and anecdotes, really brings the town's lively past to life.

GETTING AROUND

Parking in Park City is very limited, especially in the historic Main Street area, and just plain awful if you're driving a motor home or pulling a trailer. If you've arrived in a car, the best plan is to park it and ride the free city bus.

Park City's efficient transit system connects Deer Valley, Main Street, and the Park City Mountain Resort. The **Main Street Trolley** traverses Main Street daily from 1 to 5pm in the summer and from 10am to 11pm in the winter, connecting to the bus loops at the bottom of Main. In the winter, **public buses** run between 7:40am and 1am, every 10 minutes until 11pm, every 30 minutes thereafter. In the summer, buses start around 7:45am and run every 20 minutes until about 10:30pm. Routes are interconnecting, so you can get just about anywhere fairly easily. A good route map is printed in the weekly booklet *This Week Park City*, available at the visitor centers and most lodgings; it also contains several fine area maps, including one of Main Street.

If, however, you want to rent a car and brave the parking problem, several rental agencies in Park City can serve your needs: **All Resort,** 1821 Sidewinder Dr. (☎ 435/649-4909); **Budget,** at Shadow Ridge Condominiums (☎ 800/237-7251); and **Mountain,** 740 E. Kearns Blvd. (☎ 435/649-7626); in ski season, you can also call **Avis** (☎ 800/831-2847 or 435/649-7419).

FAST FACTS: PARK CITY

For medical services, call the **Park City Family Health and Emergency Center,** 1665 Bonanza Dr. (☎ **435/649-7640**), or the **Park City Chiropractic and Sports Medicine Clinic,** 1678 Bonanza Dr. (☎ **435/649-1017**).

The main **post office** is at 450 Main St. (☎ **435/649-9191**). The **local news-paper** is *The Park Record*, 1670 Bonanza Dr. (☎ **435/649-9014**), published every Wednesday and Saturday.

There are two state liquor stores in Park City. The outlet at 1901 Sidewinder Dr. offers a wide selection of liquor plus a good choice of wines; the one downstairs at 524 Main St. has a fine selection of wines, but a more limited liquor selection.

SKIING THE PARK CITY AREA RESORTS

The three area ski resorts, all within a few minutes' drive of Park City, are vastly different. There's something for everyone here: ✪ **Deer Valley** is Utah's version of Aspen; ✪ **Park City** is the party resort, big and lively; and **The Canyons** is casual and friendly. Many skiers make a point of trying all three. Snowboarders are welcome at Park City Mountain Resort and The Canyons.

DEER VALLEY RESORT

Unquestionably Utah's most elegant and sophisticated resort, Deer Valley offers perfectly manicured slopes, ski valet service, heated sidewalks, and some of the state's finest dining and lodging. Along with all this, you get great skiing—especially if you crave long, smooth, perfectly groomed cruising runs that let you enjoy the spectacular mountain scenery around you. Although half of the terrain is rated intermediate, beginners love Success, a long run that gives them the feeling they're actually getting somewhere; and much of the intermediate terrain is fit for advancing novices, as the entire mountain is kept very skiable. Experts will find some steep, scary-enough trails on top, through majestic aspen and evergreen glades, plus plenty of woodsy terrain to weave through. Deer Valley is primarily a pampering resort experience, meant for cruising the wide lanes of impeccably groomed snow all day, then hobnobbing all evening with the rich—and often famous—over gourmet meals in the plush lodges.

Just the Facts

Deer Valley, P.O. Box 1525, Park City, UT 84060 (☎ **800/424-3337** or 435/649-1000; 435/649-2000 for snow conditions), offers 68 runs and three bowls spread over Flagstaff, Bald, and Bald Eagle Mountains, served by a total of 14 chairlifts—three high-speed quad lifts, nine triple chairs, and two double chairs. The base is at 7,200 feet with the summit at 9,400 feet, yielding a 2,200-foot vertical drop. The ski season generally runs from early December to mid-April, with the lifts operating between 9am and 4:15pm daily. With 1,100 skiable acres, the terrain is rated 15% beginner, 50% intermediate, and 35% advanced. Deer Valley has snowmaking over 400 acres.

LIFT TICKETS   Adult lift tickets cost $54 ($57 during holidays) for a full day; $38 for half. Child all-day lift tickets are $29. Seniors 65 and older can buy an all-day lift ticket for $38.

LESSONS & PROGRAMS   There are several **ski school** options at Deer Valley, including private and group lessons, workshops, and clinics. Group lessons start at $65 for 4 hours for adults and $85 (including lift ticket) for 5 hours for children; private lessons start at $68 an hour.

The licensed **child-care center,** open 8:30am to 4:30pm daily, costs $55 per day for kids ages 2 to 12 years old, $68 for children ages 2 months to 24 months, and includes lunch. Half-day care is offered on a space-available policy and costs $45 and $55 respectively.

The Park City Area

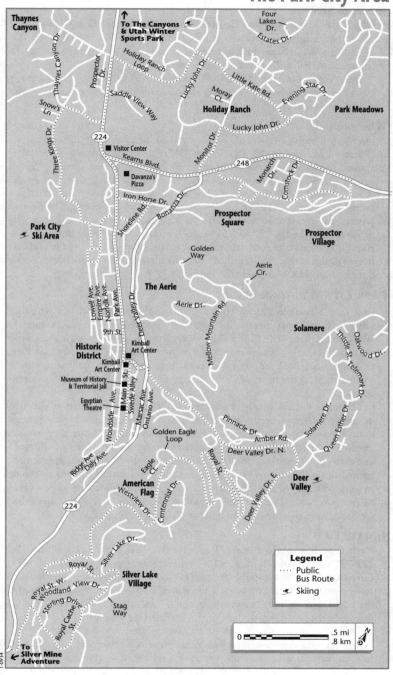

Thaynes Canyon

To The Canyons & Utah Winter Sports Park

Four Lakes Dr.

Estates Dr.

Thaynes Canyon Dr.

Prospector Dr.

Holiday Ranch Loop

Lucky John Dr.

Little Kate Rd.

Evening Star Dr.

Saddle View Way

Moray Ct.

Snow's Ln.

Holiday Ranch

Park Meadows

Three Kings Dr.

224

Lucky John Dr.

Monitor Dr.

248

Visitor Center

Kearns Blvd.

Monarch Dr.

Comstock Dr.

Davanza's Pizza

Iron Horse Dr.

Bonanza Dr.

Shoreline Rd.

Prospector Square

Park City Ski Area

Prospector Village

Golden Way

Aerie Cir.

The Aerie

Aerie Dr.

Lowell Ave.
Empire Ave.
Norfolk Ave.

Park Ave.

Deer Valley Dr.

Mellow Mountain Rd.

Solamere

Thistle St.
Telemark Dr.
Oakwood Dr.

9th St.

Historic District

Kimball Art Center

Kimball Art Center

Museum of History & Territorial Jail

Egyptian Theatre

Main St.

Swede Alley

Marsac Ave.

Ontario Ave.

Woodside Ave.

Pinnacle Dr.

Amber Rd.

Solamere Dr.

Queen Esther Dr.

Golden Eagle Loop

Deer Valley Dr. N.

Deer Valley

Ridge Ave.
Daly Ave.

Eagle Ct.

Royal St.

Deer Valley Dr. E.

224

American Flag

Westview Dr.

Centennial Dr.

Silver Lake Dr.

Royal St.

Silver Lake Village

Royal St. W.
Woodland

View Dr.

Sterling Drive

Royal Cachet St.

Stag Way

To Silver Mine Adventure

Legend

- ···· Public Bus Route
- Skiing

0   .5 mi / .8 km

N

1-0934

Where to Stay

Deer Valley Resort operates a **Central Reservation Service** (☎ 800/424-3337) that can reserve lodging for you at a nearby condo, at the **Goldener Hirsch Inn** (see p. 140), or at the **Stein Erikson Lodge** (see p. 140). The service can also make airline, car-rental, and lift-ticket reservations.

Deer Valley Lodging (☎ 800/453-3833 or 435/649-4040) offers a fine selection of upscale condos, each with daily housekeeping, bell, and concierge service; see p. 140 for details.

Where to Dine on the Mountain

Deer Valley boasts a variety of on-mountain dining options:

Snow Park Lodge (☎ 435/645-6603), at the base, houses a bakery, gourmet market, two restaurants, and a lounge. **Snow Park Restaurant,** serving breakfast and lunch daily, features a natural-foods buffet as well as the standard soup-and-sandwich fare. The **Seafood Buffet,** open Monday through Saturday evenings only, offers hearty hot dishes, a salad and seafood buffet, and fancy desserts. The **Snow Park Lounge** has hors d'oeuvres available after 3:30pm.

Silver Lake Lodge (☎ 435/645-6724), midway up the mountain, serves a variety of quick-and-easy food available all day, including continental breakfasts with fresh-baked pastries, salads, grilled fare, and pizzas. There's also a fine continental dining room, **The Mariposa** (☎ 435/645-6715), open evenings only.

PARK CITY MOUNTAIN RESORT

Park City Mountain Resort, Utah's largest and liveliest resort, is where the U.S. Olympic team comes to train. If it's good enough for them, it's good enough for us. What brings them here? Plenty of good, dependable, powdery snow and a variety of terrain and runs that offer something for everyone. Surveys continually rank Park City among the country's top resorts for both its terrain and its challenging runs. And, located right in the heart of Park City, what more could you ask for in terms of amenities?

Beginners will find plenty of great training ground, blessedly free of that frequent mountain problem—hordes of advanced skiers whizzing their way right through the green runs on their way down to the resort at the bottom. Once they have a good handle on the sport, beginners and novices can head up the lift to Summit House and then glide to the bottom of the hill on their own scenic 3 1/2-mile green run. Intermediates will find good cruising ground and powder runs, and experts can delight in some 650 acres of fun in the wide-open bowls and hair-raising narrow chutes up on top. After a good storm, the locals know to rise early, race to the top of the Jupiter Bowl, and carve their way back down through fresh powder.

Just the Facts

Park City Mountain Resort, P.O. Box 39, Park City, UT 84060 (☎ 800/222-7275 or 435/649-8111, 435/647-5449 for snow reports; fax 435/647-5374), has three six-passenger high-speed lifts, plus two quad, five triple, and four double chairs servicing 93 runs on 2,200 acres. There's even a triple-chair access lift directly from the Old Town onto the mountain, as well as two runs (Quit 'n' Time and Creole) that lead back into town, so those staying in Park City proper don't have to ride back and forth to the base resort every day. Trails are rated 16% beginner, 45% intermediate, and 39% expert. With a base elevation of 6,900 feet and summit of 10,000 feet, the vertical drop is 3,100 feet. Park City's season generally runs from mid-November to mid-April, with lifts operating between 9am and 4pm daily. Night operations usually run from Christmas through March from 4 to 9pm and include a snowboard park. Park City has snowmaking capabilities on 475 acres.

The **Resort Center,** at the base of the mountain, houses the ski school, equipment sales and rentals, a restaurant and bar, lockers, and ticket office.

LIFT TICKETS   An all-day adult lift ticket costs $52; a half-day ticket is $37. Seniors between 65 and 69 pay $25; those over 70 ski free. A child's all-day ticket costs $22.

LESSONS & PROGRAMS   The **Park City Ski and Snowboard School** (☎ 800/227-2754) offers a wide variety of choices for every level, including group and private lessons for adults and kids ages 7 to 13, plus a **kinderschule** for kids ages 3 to 6 that includes a snack, lunch, and lessons. Group lessons start at $41 for 2 hours; kinderschule starts at $79. Customized packages are also available. Reservations are highly recommended and are required for kinderschule during peak periods.

CROSS-COUNTRY SKIING   **White Pine** (☎ 435/649-8701 or 435/645-5158) is Park City's cross-country ski center, with 20 kilometers (12.4 miles) of groomed trails on the golf course on Utah 224. The center offers rentals, instruction (including telemark lessons), guided tours, and sales and service. The terrain is rated 60% beginner, 20% intermediate, and 20% advanced. Trail passes cost $6 for a full day and $3 for a half day. Seniors over 65 ski free. White Pine is open daily from 9am to 6pm.

ICE-SKATING   The ski area's Resort Center has an outdoor ice rink (☎ 435/649-8111), with skate rentals available.

SKI JUMPING   The **Utah Winter Sports Park,** 3000 Bear Hollow Drive, P.O. Box 682382, Park City, UT 84068-2328 (☎ 435/649-5447; fax 435/647-9650), already built for the 2002 Olympics, has four state-of-the-art ski jumps. The U.S. Ski Team regularly uses the facility. It's open for self-guided tours and public ski jumping, even for amateurs. A 2-hour ski-jumping session, with an introductory lesson, is $20 for adults, $12 for kids between the ages of 13 and 17, and $8 for kids under 13. Call for days and times.

Where to Stay

The town of Park City offers almost any kind of lodging you could want. See "Where to Stay" on p. 139 for details on what's available. Park City Mountain Resort operates a **Reservation Service** (☎ 800/222-7275) that books lodging in Park City, as well as airline reservations, ground transportation, and lift tickets.

Where to Dine on the Mountain

In addition to the wide variety of options in Park City (see "Where to Dine," p. 143), you'll find the following slope-side facilities. None require reservations.

Steeps Restaurant and Private Club, in the gondola building, offers homemade soups and stews, sandwiches, a salad and baked potato bar, and fresh roasted meats. A bar on the second floor also serves lunch and has live entertainment for aprés-ski from 4 to 6:30pm.

Mid-Mountain Lodge is at the base of Pioneer Lift on the Webster Ski Run, at 8,700 feet. Built around 1898, the lodge may be the oldest original mine building in Park City. Completely renovated in recent years, it's open daily, serving vegetarian dishes, homemade soups and stews, salads, burgers, sandwiches, and pizza.

Summit House Restaurant, located at 10,000 feet elevation, boasts an outdoor deck with magnificent panoramic views and a cozy fireplace inside.

The **Snow Hut,** at the bottom of the Silverlode six-passenger lift, serves breakfast and lunch daily.

THE CANYONS

The Canyons (formerly Wolf Mountain) has undergone a number of changes since the American Skiing Company took over in 1997, investing over $18 million in the resort before their first season. Five new lifts and an eight-passenger high-speed gondola were installed, and six state-of-the-art snow cats replaced the old grooming fleet. The new Red Pine day lodge and restaurant opened for the 1997–98 season.

Intermediate and expert terrains have been expanded on the new Tombstone lift, and the High Country Meadows Learning Area is a unique beginners area. Encompassing 25 acres in the middle of the resort, the learning area offers gentle slopes and a fixed-grip quad lift, plus grand views of the resort instead of the bottom-of-the-hill view beginners are usually limited to.

With increased pumping capability and additional water resources, The Canyons has doubled its snowmaking capacity. The six new Bombardier "Stealth" grooming vehicles, which replaced the existing fleet, have seriously improved the grooming of trails. Also on the agenda is reclamation of existing trails and old work roads to improve the overall look of the mountain.

Just the Facts

The Canyons Resort, 4000 Parkwest Dr., Park City, UT 84098 (☎ **888/ CANYONS** or 435/649-5400; fax 435/649-7374), has 74 runs on more than 2,000 skiable acres, serviced by two double chairlifts, three quads, three high-speed detachable quads, and the Flight of the Canyons, an eight-passenger high-speed gondola. It receives over 325 inches of snow a year, and has over 50 acres of snowmaking capabilities. The vertical drop serviced by lifts is 2,400 feet, from a base elevation of 6,800 feet. The summit elevation is 9,380 feet. Runs are rated 16% beginner, 38% intermediate, and 46% advanced. The scheduled season runs from mid-December to early April, with lifts operating from 9am to 4pm daily.

The Red Pine and lower-lot day lodges offer ski and snowboard rentals, and the base lodge houses a fully-licensed day-care center.

LIFT TICKETS   An all-day adult lift ticket is $47; half day is $36. A child's all-day ticket is $23; half day is $18.

LESSONS & PROGRAMS   The **ski school** offers lessons for both skiing and snowboarding. **Kids Central** provides top-notch instruction for children ages 4 to 12; it's also a fully licensed day-care center for children 18 months and older. The "skier in diapers" program offers private lessons for toddlers 3 and under.

TOURS   Complimentary mountain tours of the resort are offered daily, beginning at the base of the gondola. Contact the ticket office for information.

Where to Stay

Most skiers stay in Park City, Deer Valley, or Salt Lake City; however, on-mountain lodging is in the resort's expansion plans.

Where to Dine on the Mountain

Among the ski area's restaurants are the new **Red Pine Day Lodge and Restaurant;** the **Rockin' Mountain Grill**, which offers quick and inexpensive American lunch and dinner items, with beer available; and the upscale **Steakhouse at the Canyons,** which serves dinner only, with full liquor service available and reservations accepted (☎ **801/435-2086**).

OTHER WINTER ACTIVITIES

Sleigh rides and guided snowmobiling trips are available at the scenic mountain setting of Rockin' R Ranch, east of Park City, from **Rocky Mountain Recreation,** P.O. Box 680846, Park City, UT 84068 (☎ **800/303-7256** within Utah or 435/645-7256). Cost for a sleigh ride is $20, or $45 to $55 with dinner; rates are lower for children under 12 and seniors over 65. Snowmobile trips range from $44 to $114 for the driver ($20 to $40 for a passenger), depending on length and whether or not a meal is included.

WARM-WEATHER ACTIVITIES IN & AROUND PARK CITY

FLY-FISHING   Several professional guide services in Park City offer a variety of fishing trips. **Jans Mountain Outfitters,** 1600 Park Ave. (☎ 800/745-1020 or 435/649-4949), offers half- and full-day trips, ranging from $200 to $275 for one or two people. The rates include casting and fishing instruction as needed, plus lunch and transportation. Equipment rentals are available as well.

   The Park City Fly Shop, 2065 Sidewinder Dr., Prospector Square (☎ 800/324-6778 or 435/645-8382), offers guided trips, equipment sales and rentals, clinics, and general all-around information for the angler.

GOLF   **Park City Municipal Golf Course,** with a pro shop at 1541 Thaynes Canyon Dr. (☎ 435/649-8701), is an 18-hole, par-72 course near the bottom of the ski-resort area. Greens fees are $28 for 18 holes, $18 for 9.

HIKING   The mountains around Park City offer abundant opportunities for hiking and backpacking. For maps, equipment rentals, and tips on the best trails, contact **Jans Mountain Outfitters,** 1600 Park Ave. (☎ 800/745-1020 or 435/649-4949). For a good description of several trails in the area, pick up a copy of the *Park City Hiking & Biking Trail Guide* at the visitor center, or call ☎ 800/453-1360.

   Deer Valley Resort (☎ 800/424-3337 or 435/649-1000) offers more than 45 miles of panoramic trails for both hikers and bikers, with chairlift access Wednesday to Sunday in the summer. As you might expect, the terrain is steep but beautiful.

   For a short hike with a variety of terrain and good views of both the mountains and town, try the 1¹/₂-mile **Sweeny Switchbacks Trail,** on the west side of town above the Wasatch Brew Pub.

   The 30-mile **Historic Union Pacific Rail Trail State Park** path (see "Mountain Biking," below) is also popular with hikers.

HORSEBACK RIDING   Guided trail rides are available from several outfitters in the area. You can choose a 1- or 2-hour ride or a ride with a meal.

   Rocky Mountain Recreation, P.O. Box 680846, Park City, UT 84068 (☎ 800/303-7256 within Utah or 435/645-7256), operates stables at Park City Mountain Resort, Deer Valley Resort, and at 2,300-acre Rockin' R Ranch, located east of Park City in Weber Canyon. They operate daily between the end of May and the latter part of October. Rates range from $25 to $70 for adults, slightly less for children ages 6 to 12 and seniors over 65. Reservations are required for all meal rides and are recommended for others. The company also offers special getaway packages at their U Bar Wilderness Guest Ranch; call for details.

IN-LINE SKATING   You can rent in-line skates at **Cole Sport,** 1615 Park Ave. (☎ 800/345-2938 or 435/649-4806), and **Jans Mountain Outfitters,** 1600 Park Ave. (☎ 435/649-4949).

MOUNTAIN BIKING   Among local companies offering guided mountain-bike tours are **Sport Touring Ventures,** 4719 Silver Meadows Dr. (☎ **800/748-5009**

or 435/649-1551), and **White Pine Touring,** 201 Heber Ave., at the bottom of Main Street (☎ 435/649-8710). Rentals are available from these companies as well as **Cole Sport,** 1615 Park Ave. (☎ 800/345-2938 or 435/649-4806), and **Jans Mountain Outfitters,** 1600 Park Ave. (☎ 435/649-4949). Rates are about $18 for a half day and $26 for a full day.

The 30-mile **Historic Union Pacific Rail Trail State Park** bike path follows the old Union Pacific railroad bed from Park City to Echo Reservoir. The 135-foot-wide trail offers great views of meadows, the volcanic crags of Silver Creek Canyon, the Weber River, Echo Reservoir, and the steep walls of Echo Canyon. There's always the possibility of spotting deer, elk, moose, and bald eagles along the trail, too. An end-of-the-trail pick-up service is available from **Daytrips** (☎ 435/649-8294).

For a good description of several other area trails, pick up a copy of the *Park City Hiking & Biking Trail Guide* at the visitor center, or call ☎ 800/453-1360.

For information on ski lift–accessible trails, contact **Deer Valley Resort** (☎ 800/ 424-3337 or 435/649-1000).

TENNIS   Athletic clubs with tennis courts available to the public include **Park City Racquet Club,** 1200 E. Little Kate Rd. (☎ 435/645-5100), with four indoor and seven outdoor courts; and **Prospector Athletic Club,** in the Inn at Prospector Square, 2080 Gold Dust Lane (☎ 435/649-6670), with two outdoor courts. Tennis racquets can be rented from **Cole Sport,** 1615 Park Ave. (☎ 800/345-2938 or 435/ 649-4806).

MORE TO SEE & DO IN PARK CITY

Kimball Art Center

638 Park Ave., at the bottom of Main St. ☎ **435/649-8882.** Free admission. All bus loops will stop here.

This highly respected center for visual arts has two galleries, with changing exhibits that include regional traveling shows, as well as exhibits by local artists that are often surprisingly good. Art classes, workshops, and seminars are offered throughout the year, and the gift shop sells local and regional art.

Park City Museum of History & Territorial Jail

528 Main St. ☎ **435/649-6100.** Free admission. Nov–Mar and May–Sept Mon–Sat 10am–7pm, Sun noon–6pm; April and Oct daily noon–5pm. Bus: Main Street Trolley.

The original Territorial Jail downstairs is a must-see—the tiny cells were state-of-the-art in 1886! The upstairs is a bit more civilized, with an assay office, 19th-century mining equipment, historic photographs, early ski gear, and several beautifully tooled doorknobs and locks. You'll also see a variety of personal items that immigrants to Park City brought with them, ranging from a Dutch hymnal to a tin lunch bucket.

Park City Silver Mine Adventure

1¹/₂ miles south of Park City on Utah 224. ☎ **800/467-3828** or 435/655-7444. Admission $17.95 adults ($14 Utah residents), $12.50 seniors and children under 12 ($10.50 Utah residents). Daily 10am–7pm. Groups of 15 or more should call first ☎ 435/655-7456.

This mine offers not only interactive displays and exhibits demonstrating mining, but also a trip down into the Ontario, Park City's greatest silver mine. In operation from the 1870s to the 1980s, the Ontario produced enough silver to create some 22 millionaires.

You'll see actual core samples and mining equipment in the Geological Wall and Mineral Exhibit, visit Joseph and Ann McKreety's house and hear some of Joseph's tall tales, and sift for gemstones in a man-made drift containing deposits of pyrite and other treasures.

Next, don a hard hat and yellow slicker, and descend 1,500 feet into the No. 3 shaft of the Ontario Mine. There you'll board a train for a half-mile ride through tunnels into the heart of the mountain, and see for yourself the workings of a real silver mine. When you emerge from the shaft, you can refresh yourself at Tommy Knockers Sweet Shop, choosing from among 24 flavors of ice cream, candy bars, truffles, and hard candies.

SHOPPING

Historic Main Street is lined with galleries, boutiques, and a wide variety of shops, with transportation conveniently provided by the Main Street Trolley. Although you won't find many bargains here, prices aren't too far out of line for a tourist and ski town, especially when compared to places like Aspen and Santa Fe.

Start at **Main Street Marketplace,** 333 Main St., a mini-mall with about a dozen shops selling souvenirs, gifts, clothing, and snacks. Nearby, at **Rocky Mountain Christmas,** 355 Main St. (☎ 435/649-9169), it's Christmas year-round, with a good selection of ornaments, candles, holiday plates, antique quilts, and numerous other goodies. Animal lovers will enjoy browsing at **Images of Nature,** 556 Main St. (☎ 435/649-7579), where they'll find top-quality photographs of animals in their natural habitats—everything from the playful to the serene—in a variety of sizes, framed or unframed. **The Queen of Arts Gallery,** 515 Main St. (☎ 435/649-9370), features original oils and watercolors by international artists, including works on frontier women by gallery owner Bonnie Deffebach. The gallery also sells antique furniture.

If you have fond memories of old-time church bazaars or are simply looking for a unique gift, stop at **"Z" Treasure Trove,** 427 Main St. (☎ 435/645-7193). This delightful shop has gifts for all occasions, its numerous small booths stuffed with a variety of small, handcrafted, and imported items. At **A Woman's Place Bookstore,** Park City Plaza at Bonanza Drive and Prospector Avenue (☎ 435/649-2722), you'll discover a wide selection of books, including a number that are by, for, and about women, plus quality note papers, cards, and gifts.

Those looking for Southwest-style clothing and accessories should check out **Pleasures,** 513 Main St. (☎ 435/649-5733), which also carries Navajo rugs and Native American jewelry and paintings. **No Place Like Home,** Park City Plaza at Bonanza Drive and Prospector Avenue (☎ 435/649-9700), is the place to go for kitchen and home accessories. Choose from a wide variety of glassware, gadgets, gourmet coffee beans, bed and bath items, and lots more.

Bargain hunters will want to head for **The Factory Stores at Park City,** 6699 N. Landmark Dr. (☎ 435/645-7078), which is not in the historic downtown section, but nearby. To get there from downtown Park City, take Utah 224 north to I-80, but don't get on; instead, go west on the south frontage road to the mall. This center houses about 50 manufacturers' outlets, including American Tourister, Bass, Brooks Brothers, Carter's Childrenswear, Danskin, Eddie Bauer, Gap, Guess?, L'eggs, Leather Loft, Levi's, Maidenform, Mikasa, and Nike. There's plenty of parking, including room for RVs.

WHERE TO STAY

The Park City area offers a wide variety of places to stay, and it's probably home to the largest portion of the state's deluxe accommodations. Even some of the most luxurious properties, however, don't have air-conditioning; at this elevation—6,900 feet in Park City and higher in the mountains—it's seldom needed.

Rates are almost always higher—sometimes dramatically so—during ski season. Sales and lodging taxes in Park City total just over 10%. Pets are not allowed, unless otherwise noted.

PROPERTY MANAGEMENT COMPANIES

Although it's possible to book your reservations directly with the individual lodges, many people find it's more convenient to go the one-stop shopping route, calling one of Park City's major property management and reservation services.

Park City Reservations (☎ 800/453-5789 or 435/649-9598; fax 435/649-8063) is the largest reservations company in the area, representing 400 units, including dorm rooms, one- to five-bedroom condos, and private homes. Each property is individually decorated by the owner; all come with air-conditioning, TV, and telephone; and most have ski storage of some kind. Some units contain fireplaces, full kitchens with microwaves, and/or balconies. Those at the Park Meadows Racquet Club are near the golf course/cross-country ski center and have access to a year-round outdoor pool; units at Park City Village are slope-side, so you can ski in and out. Dorm rooms are very clean and modern, with two sets of bunk beds and two desks, much like a college dormitory.

Deer Valley Lodging (☎ 800/453-3833 or 435/649-4040; fax 435/645-8419) offers a fine selection of upscale condos—from one- to four-bedroom units, plus several luxury homes—each with cable TV and telephone, plus daily housekeeping, bell, and concierge service. Units come with a range of amenities, from stone fireplaces to full kitchens and outdoor whirlpool tubs with mountain views.

ACCOMMODATIONS IN DEER VALLEY

✪ Goldener Hirsch Inn

7570 Royal St. East, Silver Lake Village, Deer Valley (P.O. Box 859), Park City, UT 84060. ☎ **800/252-3373** or 435/649-7770. Fax 435/649-7901. 20 rms and suites. MINIBAR TV TEL. Winter (including continental breakfast) $200–$800 double; summer $100–$225 double. AE, MC, V. Closed mid-Apr–mid-June and Nov.

This chateau-style inn combines warm hospitality with European charm. Austrian antiques dot the common areas and decorate the walls, reminiscent of the inn's sister hotel in Salzburg, the Hotel Goldener Hirsch. Rooms are elegantly furnished with hand-painted and -carved furniture from Austria, king-size beds with down comforters, and minibars stocked with snacks and nonalcoholic beverages. Suites have wood-burning fireplaces and small private balconies. Some rooms face the ski slopes on Bald Mountain, offering a fascinating view of the "night monsters" grooming the runs. The restaurant, done in Austrian decor, features continental cuisine; the menu includes Austrian specialties, wild game, and fresh fish, as well as lighter dishes.

✪ Stein Eriksen Lodge

Deer Valley Resort (P.O. Box 3177), Park City, UT 84060. ☎ **800/453-1302** or 435/649-3700. Fax 435/649-5825. 131 rms, including 49 suites. TV TEL. Winter $450–$625 double, suites starting at $925; mid-Apr–late Nov $175–$225 double, suites starting at $250. Rates include buffet breakfast. AE, CB, DC, DISC, MC, V.

The Stein Eriksen is a luxurious, full-service lodge with a warm and friendly atmosphere. It opened in 1982 under the direction of Stein Eriksen, the Norwegian 1952 Olympic Gold Medalist, and retains the Scandinavian decor and charm of his original plan. The lobby is most impressive, with a magnificent three-story stone fireplace fronted by an elegant seating area.

There are 13 rooms in the main lodge, with the remaining units in nearby buildings. The connecting sidewalks are heated, and the grounds are beautifully landscaped with aspen trees, manicured lawns, and flowers cascading over rock gardens and retaining walls. The spacious deluxe rooms, each individually decorated, contain one king or two queen beds, lots of closet space, whirlpool tubs, vaulted ceilings, and tasteful, solid wood furniture. The one- to four-bedroom suites come with all the amenities, and three large mountain chalet–style townhouse suites each have a stone fireplace, full kitchen with service for eight, and private deck off the living room.

Dining: The lodge offers several dining venues, but only two are open year-round. The **Glitretind** (see "Where to Dine," below) serves three meals daily; **Troll Hallen Lounge** is open from 11:30am to midnight in the winter and from 4pm to midnight in the summer for beer and light meals, with hors d'oeuvres or fresh shellfish from the oyster bar available for aprés-ski. In the winter, the **Bald Mountain Deck Grill** offers light entrees and sandwiches outside, weather permitting, on a deck overlooking the ski slopes. The **Birkebeiner Café** serves American cafe favorites for lunch and dinner in winter.

Services: Concierge, room service, dry cleaning, newspaper delivered to room, turndown, in-room massage, twice-daily maid service in the winter, baby-sitting, secretarial service, valet parking, free refreshments in lobby.

Facilities: Video rentals, year-round outdoor heated pool, exercise room, whirlpool tub, sauna, sundeck, nature trails, business center, conference rooms, boutiques.

ACCOMMODATIONS IN PARK CITY

Among the franchise properties in Park City is the **Best Western Landmark Inn**, 6560 N. Landmark Dr., Park City, UT 84060 (☎ **800/548-8824** or 435/649-7300; fax 435/649-1760), with rates for two ranging from $69 to $164.

Chateau Apres-Ski

1299 Norfolk Ave., Park City, UT 84060. ☎ **800/357-3556** or 435/649-9372. Fax 435/ 649-5963. 32 rms. TV TEL. Winter (including breakfast) $72–$78 double; summer $40–$45 double; dorm rooms $25–$27 per bed. AE, DISC, MC, V.

This looks like a Swiss Alps–style lodge from the outside—simple but attractive. Rooms are basic and clean, with a queen bed or a double and a single, and private baths with showers only. The separate men's and women's dorms each have a shared bath. This is a good budget place close to the ski area.

The Old Miners' Lodge—A Bed & Breakfast Inn

615 Woodside Ave. (P.O. Box 2639), Park City, UT 84060. ☎ **800/648-8068** or 435/ 645-8068. Fax 435/645-7420. 9 rms, 3 suites. Winter $95–$250 double; summer $60–$125 double. Rates include breakfast. AE, DC, DISC, MC, V.

Established in 1889 as a boardinghouse for local miners, the lodge still exudes the spirited warmth and hospitality of that time. Rooms are comfortably decorated with antiques and country pieces, often of light knotty pine, and some historic photos. Each is named for an historic figure of the Old West and outfitted with touches suiting the individual's persona. Suites are spacious and come with mini-refrigerators; two have a queen hide-a-bed plus a king bed. Some rooms have terrific views of the valley and surrounding mountains.

The lodge is within easy walking distance of the triple-chair Town Lift—the only lift in historic downtown Park City—and historic Main Street. Evening refreshments are available in the large living room, where guests occasionally gather around the fireplace. There's no TV, but plenty of reading material and games, and you're welcome to play the electric organ. Breakfast is a hearty meal that often includes homemade omelets, waffles, French toast, or pancakes, plus cereal and granola.

Old Town Guest House

1011 Empire Ave. (P.O. Box 162), Park City, UT 84060. ☎ **800/290-6423,** ext. 3710 or 435/649-2642. Fax 435/649-3320. 4 units. Winter (including breakfast) $95–$190 double; summer $75–$90 double. MC, V.

This cozy little B&B caters to outdoor enthusiasts—the innkeeper is a backcountry ski guide in winter and avid hiker and biker in summer. Within easy walking distance of both the Park City Mountain Resort and Main Street, the delightfully homey living room retains its original 1910 fireplace. The decor is country, with lodge-pole pine furniture and hardwood floors throughout, but as with most bed-and-breakfasts, each guest room is unique. Treasure Hollow has its own entrance, a queen-size bed, TV, VCR, phone, lots of storage, and a private bath with shower. Two small rooms in back have private toilets and sinks, but share a shower. Each has a queen bed and a small table with chairs. McConky's Suite, upstairs, contains a queen bed in one room and bunk beds in another, a whirlpool tub and shower, TV, VCR, and phone.

Guests are welcome to use the outdoor deck and hot tub. You'll start your day off right here, with a hearty breakfast that will sustain your energy throughout a day of hiking, biking, or skiing.

Silver King Hotel

1485 Empire Ave. (P.O. Box 2818), Park City, UT 84060. ☎ **800/331-8652** or 435/649-5500. Fax 435/649-6647. 64 suites. A/C TV TEL. Winter $140–$540 double, higher on holidays; mid-Apr to mid-Nov $99–$330 double. AE, DISC, MC, V.

This five-story condominium hotel, located only about a hundred yards from the lifts, offers a variety of accommodations: studio suites, one- and two-bedroom suites, some spa suites, even a penthouse. Each unit is individually owned and decorated and comes with a fully equipped kitchen, a wood-burning fireplace, a jetted whirlpool tub, and washer and dryer. All but the studio suites have pull-out hide-a-bed sofas. Some units have a Southwest look, some are done in country style, and others are furnished with antiques. A large locker area holds your skis.

Washington School Inn

543 Park Ave. (P.O. Box 536), Park City, UT 84060. ☎ **800/824-1672** or 435/649-3808. Fax 435/649-3802. 12 rms, 3 suites. TEL. Winter (including breakfast) $145–$235 double, $225–$350 suite; summer $125–$175 double, $130–$165 suite. AE, DISC, MC, V.

Housed in an 1889 limestone schoolhouse nestled against the Wasatch Mountains, this lovely country inn has managed to preserve its original charm even though it's been completely modernized. The exterior has been faithfully restored to its late 19th-century appearance, while the interior has been reorganized to better meet the requirements of an inn—yet remain true to its historical roots. Rooms are individually decorated, many in country style, with antiques and reproductions of different periods. Two suites have wood-burning fireplaces. Most rooms have a king or queen bed; one has two twins. Although there's no air-conditioning, each room has a fan. All have private baths with shower/tub combos.

Downstairs facilities include a whirlpool spa and lounge area, sauna, shower rooms, and a bicycle storage area and ski lockers with outside access. The inn provides a full breakfast buffet each morning, afternoon tea in the summer, and some hearty après-ski refreshments in the winter.

The Yarrow Resort Hotel & Conference Center

1800 Park Ave. (P.O. Box 1840), Park City, UT 84060. ☎ **800/YARROWHOTEL** or 435/649-7000. Fax 435/649-4819. 181 units. A/C TV TEL. Winter $215–$235 double, $250–$260 efficiency, $280–$495 suite; off-season $115 double, $145 efficiency, $180–$275 suite. AE, CB, DC, DISC, MC, V.

This first-class mountain resort hotel offers choices ranging from one room with two double beds to a deluxe suite with a king bed and kitchenette. All rooms contain a refrigerator, coffeemaker, hair dryer, and irons and ironing boards. Second-floor rooms have small balconies; south-facing rooms look out over the parking lot to the ski runs and mountains. Five rooms meet ADA specifications, and two have roll-in showers. The Yarrow is located adjacent to the Holiday Village Mall, with several shops and restaurants, and Park City's complimentary shuttle service stops here every 20 minutes.

The guest services desk can arrange massage and baby-sitting; other services include dry cleaning/laundry and complimentary newspaper. Also available are an outdoor heated pool, exercise facilities, outdoor whirlpool tub, coin-operated laundry, and conference and banquet facilities.

The cafe serves American cuisine from 6:30am to 10pm daily; room service is available between 7am and 10pm; and a breakfast buffet is offered daily, 7:30 to 9:30am, December through March.

WHERE TO DINE

Burgie's
570 Main St. ☎ **435/649-0011.** Main courses $3.95–$7.95. AE, DISC, MC, V. Daily 11am–11pm. Bus: Main Street Trolley. AMERICAN.

At this 1950s-style cafe—complete with jukebox—you can sit at the wooden counter around the grill and watch your food being cooked. The menu includes—surprise!—a wide selection of burgers (even a vegetarian one), plus homemade soups, several chicken sandwiches, and killer Olympic onion rings, a local favorite. Pool tables, video games, and a big-screen TV add to the fun. Beer is served.

Cafe Terigo
424 Main St. ☎ **435/645-9555.** Main courses $10.95–$22.95 dinner, $6.95–$10.95 lunch. AE, DISC, MC, V. Daily 11:30am–2:30pm and 5:30–10pm. Bus: Main Street Trolley. EUROPEAN/CONTINENTAL.

In fine weather, you can dine outdoors under a large umbrella; otherwise, sit in the simple yet elegant European-style cafe with brocade upholstered booths, white tablecloths, fresh flowers, and wrought-iron chandeliers. Lunches include burgers, a roast turkey sandwich, a grilled pesto chicken breast, and our favorite: a grilled vegetable sandwich with sweet onions, zucchini, mushrooms, roasted red peppers, and provolone cheese on homemade foccacia. The dinner menu features such main courses as pan-seared duck breast, grilled flank steak, and fresh Atlantic salmon, plus a variety of pastas and unusual pizzas with toppings such as shrimp and artichoke hearts. They serve a mean lemonade, too, and offer espresso and full liquor service.

Chimayo
368 Main St. ☎ **435/649-6222.** Main courses $18–$28. AE, DISC, MC, V. Winter daily 5–10pm; summer Wed–Sun 5–9pm. Closed several weeks in Nov and May. Bus: Main Street Trolley. SOUTHWESTERN.

In this elegant restaurant, the hand-painted beams and corbels, hand-blown Mexican glass, and Spanish tile are set off by the gentle guitar music playing in the background. The Southwestern cuisine exhibits a European flair, in entrees such as Dungeness-crab-stuffed grouper, cooked in a banana leaf and served with jicama cucumber salsa; Ahi tuna taco rolled in Southwestern spices and pan-seared; and crown roast of ribs with chipotle marinade stuffed with garlic mashed potatoes. Choice appetizers include goat-cheese chile relleno rolled in crushed pumpkin seeds and served with green chile salsa.

The Claimjumper Steak House

573 Main St. ☎ **435/649-8051.** Main courses $10.95–$25.50. AE, DC, DISC, MC, V. Daily 5–10pm. Bus: Main Street Trolley. STEAK/RIBS/SEAFOOD.

This three-story brick-and-masonry building opened in 1913 as the New Park Hotel; all meals, including Sunday dinner, were 50¢. Prices are a bit higher now, but a meal at this renowned western-style restaurant is well worth the cost. The Claimjumper is known for its steaks—especially its thick buffalo steaks—as well as prime rib, seafood, and desserts. Full liquor service is available.

❑ Glitretind Restaurant

Stein Eriksen Lodge, Deer Valley. ☎ **435/649-3700.** Reservations requested. Main courses $21–$35 dinner, $7–$13 lunch, $4–$15 breakfast. AE, CB, DC, DISC, MC, V. Daily 7–10am, 11:30am–2:30pm, 6–9pm. Bus: Deer Valley Loop. CONTEMPORARY INTERNATIONAL.

Located in the elegant Stein Eriksen Lodge (see "Where to Stay," above), this equally elegant restaurant serves innovative, impeccably prepared cuisine. The modern, airy dining room looks out on the spectacular Wasatch Mountains.

Breakfast offerings include a super continental breakfast, French toast, pancakes, a fruit plate, and the Glitretind omelet, which is filled with grilled onions, bacon, cheddar, and potatoes. For lunch, choose from the salad, sandwich, and pasta selections. At dinner, you might start with a chilled seafood cocktail or Russian caviar. For the main course, go for the grilled Atlantic swordfish, dry-aged New York strip in red wine, or the chef's nightly special of a wild game duo. Full liquor service is available.

Grappa Italian Restaurant

151 Main St. ☎ **435/645-0636.** Reservations required. Main courses $6–$28. AE, DISC, MC, V. Daily 5:30–10pm in winter; closed Tues in summer; may close several weeks in Nov and Apr. Bus: Main Street Trolley. ITALIAN.

The chefs make everything from scratch at this elegant restaurant, using the freshest herbs and vegetables available—preparing the tomato sauce alone requires cases of Roma tomatoes each day. Located in a century-old building at the top of Main Street, its decor makes Grappa feel like a Tuscan farmhouse. The restaurant has three floors, with a small patio on the ground floor and a larger second-floor deck with a delightful view of historic Main Street and the surrounding mountains. Baskets of fresh fruits and vegetables decorate the dining areas.

Popular dishes include grilled chicken and spinach lasagna, pan-seared lamb chops stuffed with sausage and spinach, and open-spit-roasted guinea fowl. The meats and fowl are seasoned in the style of southern French and Italian cooking, then grilled or rotisseried over a wood-burning flame. Full liquor service is available.

Main Street Deli

525 Main St. ☎ **435/649-1110.** Reservations not accepted. Breakfast (till 11:30am) $1.35–$5.25, sandwiches $3.59–$5.99. No credit cards. Daily 7:30am–9pm. Bus: Main Street Trolley. DELI/CAFE.

At this busy, noisy little deli/cafe, you can make yourself at home for a while—there are plenty of newspapers scattered around to read. Breakfast offers omelets and other egg dishes, plus French toast, oatmeal, and the like. A wide range of sandwiches—two dozen in all—includes bratwurst, pastrami, and egg salad. Bagels are made fresh and the gourmet coffee is freshly ground. Homemade cakes, cookies, and pies are available for dessert, as well as ice cream and frozen yogurt. Beer is available.

Morning Ray

268 Main St. ☎ **435/649-5686.** Reservations not accepted. Main courses $3.95–$7.50. AE, MC, V. Daily 7am–3pm. Bus: Main Street Trolley. AMERICAN.

This bakery and cafe, with its solid wood furniture and Victorian-style decor, is a favorite breakfast stop among locals (breakfast is served until noon). Five kinds of omelets include the "Sweetheart," made with marinated artichoke hearts, scallions, and Havarti cheese, and the "Morning Ray," a large serving of house fries topped with sautéed vegetables, melted jack cheese, sour cream, and guacamole. Other eccentric breakfast dishes include organic buckwheat-cornmeal-buttermilk cakes (did they leave anything out?) and sourdough French toast. The croissants are phenomenal. There's also lots to choose from at lunch, from a standard Greek salad or Reuben to the Morning Ray's very own bean burger, a blend of black beans, lentils, and brown rice. The "Mandy Bagel"—a toasted open-face bagel with sautéed mushrooms, peppers, tomatoes, and scallions, topped with melted cheddar and sprouts—is either breakfast or lunch—you decide. Drinks include fruit smoothies, gourmet coffees, lattes, and mochas. Beer is available after 10am.

Texas Red's Pit Barbecue & Chili Parlor

440 Main St. ☎ **435/649-7337.** Reservations not accepted. Main courses $5.95–$16.95. AE, DISC, MC, V. Daily 11:30am–10pm. Bus: Main Street Trolley. BARBECUE/CHILE.

This is about as Texan as you can get in Utah—and you can get pretty Texan here. The walls are decorated with moose, deer, and buffalo heads, along with a picture of—who else?—John Wayne. Western music fills the air, and plenty of authentic Texas-style barbecue fills the paper plates. Barbecued beef is the specialty, but the barbecued pork ribs and homemade chile—made from a secret family recipe—are also popular. Beer, wine, and tequila drinks are offered.

Wasatch Brew Pub

250 Main St. ☎ **435/649-0900.** Reservations not accepted. Main courses $7.25–$15.25. AE, MC, V. Daily 11am–10pm (bar open until midnight). Bus: Main Street Trolley. AMERICAN.

The bar overlooks the brewing area in this popular, noisy brewpub. You can get the usual pub foods, including fish-and-chips, beer-battered shrimp, and cheese steaks. Dinner is a bit more adventuresome, with dishes such as fresh Utah trout with roasted garlic herb butter, rack of New Zealand lamb with fresh mint sauce, and an Oriental stir-fry of fresh vegetables cooked in seasoned sesame oil. You'll find a sports bar upstairs and an outside patio for warm-weather dining. In addition to the brewery's own award-winning beers, full liquor service is available with meals.

MUSIC & MORE IN THE MOUNTAINS: THE PERFORMING ARTS

In January, the **Sundance Film Festival** takes place, with numerous film showings in Park City (see the Sundance section later in this chapter).

Summer in Park City resounds with music. The annual **Music in the Mountains** series hosts different kinds of performances in several locales from mid-June through August. Free concerts take place every Wednesday evening from 6 to 8pm at the Jack Green Bandstand at City Park (☎ 800/453-1360 or 435/649-6100). One week you might hear bluegrass, the next, classical, and yet another it might be rock or jazz.

The **Saturday Afternoon Performing Arts Series** schedules free live entertainment Saturday afternoons in the summer on Main Street and at the Resort Center. The music simply wafts around the storefronts of the areas. Enjoy as you shop, eat, or rest.

The annual **Folk and Bluegrass Festival** (☎ 800/453-1360 or 435/649-6100) is probably one of the most popular events in the valley. Nationally-known bluegrass artists perform at the Deer Valley Resort outdoor amphitheater for a full day in mid-August. Tickets cost $18 to $22 single, $35 to $40 family.

The ✪ **Utah Symphony Summer Series** takes place during most of July at the outdoor amphitheater at Snow Park Lodge in Deer Valley. The music includes classical masterpieces like Tchaikovsky's *1812 Overture,* plus popular works by composers such as Rogers and Hammerstein and John Philip Sousa. The stage faces the mountainside, and listeners bring chairs or blankets and relax under the stars. Call the symphony box office (☎ 801/533-6683) or Deer Valley Resort (☎ 435/649-1000) for schedule and ticket information.

The **Canyons Concert Series** hosts nationally-known rock, country, and jazz performers. The Canyons recently added an indoor 3,000-seat arena and now showcases popular music all year long. For information, contact their events office (☎ 435/649-5400) or the concert hotline (☎ 801/536-1234).

The **Park City International Music Festival** (☎ 435/649-5309) has been presenting classical performances at locations throughout Park City since 1984. Classical musicians from around the world attend, and programs include soloists, small-ensemble and chamber music, and full orchestras. The festival runs from mid-July to mid-August.

The **Historic Egyptian Theatre,** 328 Main St. (☎ 435/649-9371), is the place to go for live theater. Built in 1926 in the popular Egyptian Revival style, the theater was originally used for vaudeville and silent films and was the first theater in Park City to offer the "new talking pictures." Today it's the home of the Park City Performers, who stage theatrical presentations throughout the year, including a children's play each spring. Recent productions have included the comedy *The Best Christmas Pageant Ever,* the musical comedy *Forever Plaid*, and Neil Simon's comedy *Rumors*. Tickets are $12 to $18 (subscription tickets are less).

PARK CITY AFTER DARK: THE CLUB SCENE

Park City is known as Utah's Party Town; it's got probably the best nightlife scene in the state.

If you're looking for drinking and dancing, join a private club. This isn't as difficult as you might think. Memberships are available on a short-term basis for a nominal fee, usually $5, and membership entitles you to bring several guests.

Adolph's (Park City Golf Course; ☎ 435/649-7177) is mainly a social bar with piano music on some nights. **The Alamo Saloon** (447 Main St.; ☎ 435/649-2380) offers live music and dancing most evenings, plus pool, darts, and pinball. **Cisero's** (downstairs at 306 Main St.; ☎ 435/649-5044), with a recently expanded dance floor, hosts good bands, including a jam band Wednesday nights, and has a big-screen TV for sports events. You'll find two bars at **The Club** (449 Main St.; ☎ 435/649-6693): The downstairs one serves food and drinks, and there's dancing to a DJ upstairs. **Cooters** (on the second floor of the Radisson Hotel, 2121 Park Ave.; ☎ 435/649-5000) offers terrific views of the surrounding mountains, plus a big-screen TV and a variety of live entertainment, from fashion shows to bands. **The Cozy** (438 Main St.; ☎ 435/649-6038) has a spacious dance area, live entertainment on weekends, a game room, and a number of TV monitors for sports enthusiasts. **Mileti's** (412 Main St.; ☎ 435/649-8230), a friendly, sociable place, is the oldest private club on Main Street.

3 Side Trips from Park City: Heber City, Strawberry Reservoir & Some Great State Parks

This region of the Wasatch Front isn't just about skiing. The great lakes and parks near Park City are some of Utah's best-kept secrets. To the northeast is Rockport State Park, a man-made lake that attracts water-sports enthusiasts, from swimmers to ice fishermen, year-round. Not far from Park City is Jordanelle State Park, Utah's newest state park and a great boating destination, and Wasatch Mountain State Park, Utah's second-largest state park and one of its major golf destinations. Heading southeast from Park City, you'll reach Heber City, whose main claim to fame is its historic steam train; it's also where you pick up U.S. 40 to northeastern Utah (see chapter 10). A bit farther afield along U.S. 40 is pristine Strawberry Reservoir, one of our favorite water playgrounds in Utah.

ROCKPORT STATE PARK

Rockport, one of the Utah State Park System's man-made lakes, is a great place to play. A full range of outdoor activities, from windsurfing to wildlife watching, all take place in, on, or around the lake in the summer. In the winter, add ice fishing and cross-country skiing.

JUST THE FACTS

At Rockport Lake, you'll find a marina, a concessionaire for rentals, a boat ramp and courtesy docks, a picnic area, and camping in a variety of settings.

The Wanship Dam, at the north end of the lake, is an important water-storage and flood-control dam on the Weber River, with headwaters high in the Uinta Mountains.

GETTING THERE   From Park City, head east on I-80 for about 10¹/₂ miles to exit 156, then go 4¹/₂ miles south on Utah 32 along the western bank of Rockport Lake to the access road. The park entrance is at the lake's southern tip. Turn east to the park entrance, and then follow the road around to the north along the eastern bank.

INFORMATION, FEES & REGULATIONS   Address inquiries to **Rockport State Park**, 9040 N. Utah 302, Peoa, UT 84061-9702 (☎ **435/336-2241**). The half-mile-wide, 3-mile-long lake is open year-round, with a day-use fee of $4 per vehicle. Pets are allowed, but must be confined or leashed. Unless otherwise posted, speed limit within the park is 15 mph, and off-highway vehicles are not permitted.

WARM-WEATHER SPORTS & ACTIVITIES

WATER ACTIVITIES   The day-use area, located about 3¹/₂ miles north of the park entrance, offers the lake's best swimming. The lake is also popular for boating, windsurfing, waterskiing, sailing, kayaking, and fishing. Both the lake and river are home to rainbow and brown trout, yellow perch, and smallmouth bass.

HIKING & WILDLIFE WATCHING   A 4-mile round-trip hike takes off from Juniper Campground. This easy, relatively flat walk among juniper and sagebrush offers an opportunity for a glimpse of mule deer, yellow-belly marmots, badgers, raccoons, weasels, skunks, and ground squirrels. Less visible are elk, moose, coyote, bobcat, and cougar. Birds also abound, and Western grebes, Canada geese, whistling swans, great blue herons, and golden and bald eagles can sometimes be spotted. More frequently seen are ducks, red-tailed hawks, magpies, scrub jays, and hummingbirds.

CROSS-COUNTRY SKIING

Groomed cross-country ski trails run through the open sagebrush areas, which offer a better chance of seeing wildlife than the more forested areas in the surrounding national forest. Ice fishing is popular on the lake in the winter.

CAMPING

Eighty-six campsites are located in six areas around the lake. The first campground is to the right of the access road, along the Weber River rather than the lake. Sites are shady and provide easy access to a trail along the river that's handy for fishermen. The remainder of the sites lie between the road and the lake, along its eastern bank, and most have vault toilets only. One campground, Juniper, has 34 sites with water and electric hookups, a dump station, and modern rest rooms. Primitive sites cost $9; developed sites are $4 more. The park generally fills on weekends, but reservations (with a $5 nonrefundable fee) can be made using Visa or MasterCard (☎ **800/ 322-3770**).

JORDANELLE STATE PARK

Utah's newest state park, completed in the spring of 1995, offers two recreation areas on ○ **Jordanelle Reservoir** in the beautiful Wasatch Mountains. Both sites are great for boating, fishing, picnicking, and camping.

JUST THE FACTS

The reservoir is shaped rather like a boomerang, with the dam at the elbow. The Perimeter Trail connects the highly developed **Hailstone Recreation Site** to the more primitive **Rock Cliff Recreation Site.** Hailstone is on the terraced peninsula poking into the upper arm just above the dam; Rock Cliff is at the southeastern tip of the lower arm of the reservoir. Hailstone's camping and picnicking areas face the widest part of the reservoir, which is perfect for speedboats, waterskiing, and jet skiing. Above Hailstone lies a wakeless water area, excellent for sailboats and quiet fishing. The narrow arm reaching down to Rock Cliff is designated for low-speed water use. Trails—27 miles of them—circle the reservoir and connect to other trails in the region, and are open to hikers, mountain bikers, horseback riders, and cross-country skiers.

GETTING THERE   From Park City, head east on Kearns Boulevard (Utah 248) for about 3³/₄ miles; at U.S. 40, go southeast 4 miles to exit 8 and follow the entrance road east into Hailstone. From Heber City, take U.S. 40 northwest about 6 miles. For Rock Cliff, follow U.S. 40 northwest from Heber City for about 4 miles, then head east onto Utah 32 for about 6 miles to the entrance. From Park City, continue southeast on U.S. 40 past Hailstone for about 2 miles to Utah 32, then east about 6 miles to the entrance.

INFORMATION, FEES & REGULATIONS   Address inquiries to **Jordanelle State Park,** P.O. Box 309, Heber City, UT 84032-0309 (☎ **435/649-9540**). Stop at the **visitor center** at Hailstone or the **Nature Center** at Rock Cliff, a nature-oriented visitor center for information and trail maps. The exhibit room in the visitor center at Hailstone presents an overview of human history in the area, from the early natives through the trappers, the Mormon settlers, and up to the present.

The park is open year-round at Hailstone, and from May through September at Rock Cliff. Day-use hours in the summer are 6am to 10pm; from October through March, 8am to 5pm. The visitor centers are open from 9am to 6pm April to September. The day-use fee is $5 per vehicle.

In order to protect the abundance of wildlife, particularly birds, pets are not allowed at Rock Cliff. They're welcome at Hailstone, but must be confined or leashed. Bicycling is permitted on established public roads, in parking areas, and on the Perimeter Trail; off-highway vehicles are prohibited.

HAILSTONE RECREATION SITE

At Hailstone, you'll find three camping areas and a group pavilion, along with a swimming beach and a picnic area available for day use. A 76-slip marina offers camping and picnicking supplies and rentals, a small restaurant, an amphitheater, boat ramps, a jet-ski ramp, a wheelchair-accessible fishing deck, and a fish-cleaning station.

Warm-Weather Sports & Activities

The Jordanelle Concession Rentals offers ski boats ($200 for 4 hours and $374 for all day), powerboats (two-seater for $50 per hour, or half-day rates of $100 from 8am to noon, and $125 from 1 to 5pm; three-seater for $60 per hour, or half-day rates of $125 from 8am to noon, and $150 from 1 to 5pm), and fishing boats (four-man for $15 per hour, $55 for half day, and $75 for all day; six-man for $15 per hour, $60 for half day, and $85 for all day). Waterskiing accessories are also available.

Camping

Hailstone's three camping areas offer a total of 100 sites, including walk-in tent sites, RV/tent sites without hookups, and RV sites with water and electric hookups. Facilities include modern rest rooms, showers, a small coin-operated laundry, and a playground. Cost is $11 for no hookups and $13 with hookups.

ROCK CLIFF RECREATION SITE

Rock Cliff contains three walk-in camping areas; three picnic tables; group pavilions; the **Nature Center,** offering maps, environmental programs, and exhibits on the various habitats of the area and how man's activities impact them; and the **Jordanelle Discovery Trail,** a boardwalk interpretive trail that winds through the Provo River riparian terrain.

Wildlife Watching

✪ **Rock Cliff** offers great opportunities for bird-watching, with more than 160 species either living here or passing through, and eagles and other raptors nesting in the area.

Situated as it is among numerous riparian wetlands, Rock Cliff is designed to protect these sensitive habitats. Trails and boardwalks traverse the area, and bridges cross the waterways at four points, enabling you to get quite close to a variety of wetland life without inadvertently doing any harm to the habitats.

Camping

You'll find three walk-in campgrounds with 50 sites and two modern rest rooms with showers. These sites are more nature-oriented than those at Hailstone and are scattered over 100 acres, providing great privacy. Cost is $11 per site.

WASATCH MOUNTAIN STATE PARK

The second-largest of Utah's State Parks (after Antelope Island) is also its most developed—and may be its most popular. This year-round destination is well maintained, well serviced, easy to enjoy, and just keeps getting better. It's a terrific golf and camping destination, and trails are continually being expanded to meet the demands of hikers and mountain bikers. In the winter, a network of groomed cross-country skiing and snowmobiling trails leads from the park into the surrounding forest, and both cross-country ski and snowmobile rentals are available. Wasatch Mountain also serves as a learning park—its rangers offer a variety of instructive and interpretive programs. For the photographer, fall is the best time to visit: The incomparable juxtaposition of rich reds, ochers, and deep evergreens defies the imagination.

JUST THE FACTS

A major draw is the scenic 27-hole golf course; another 9 holes will open in the spring of 1998. The course becomes a cross-country ski track in the winter. Both tent camping and RV sites with hookups are available here.

GETTING THERE   It's about 5^1/$_2$ miles from Heber City to the park: From downtown, turn west on Utah 113 (100 South) to Midway; following signs for the state park, jog north on 200 West, then west on 200 North, and finally north again on Homestead Drive. The visitor center is located on Homestead Drive (where it becomes Snake Creek Road), in the park.

INFORMATION & VISITOR CENTERS   Address inquiries to **Wasatch Mountain State Park,** P.O. Box 10, Midway, UT 84049-0010 (☎ **435/654-1791**).

The visitor center, which also serves as a lounge for golfers, is open daily from 8am to 5pm and includes a large mountain lodge–style room with comfortable seating. Rangers are on hand to discuss park activities and provide trail maps and other park information.

FEES & REGULATIONS   The day-use fee is $3 per vehicle; off-highway vehicles are permitted on designated roadways only; and pets are welcome in the park, but must be confined or leashed at all times.

RANGER PROGRAMS   Interpretive programs take place most Friday and Saturday summer nights at the amphitheater, and a junior ranger program is offered Saturday mornings. The stocked pond adjacent to the visitor center provides fishing fun for children under 16 in the summer. Call for details.

WINTER SPORTS & ACTIVITIES

CROSS-COUNTRY SKIING   A 12-kilometer (7.4 miles) Nordic ski track, with both diagonal stride and skating lanes, is laid out on the golf course. Neither dogs nor snowmobiles are allowed on the track, which is open from 8am to 5pm.

SNOWMOBILING   The park's 90 miles of groomed trails, very popular among snowmobilers, take you into Pine Creek, Snake Creek, and American Fork Canyons. Warming stations are located at the clubhouse and visitor center.

WARM-WEATHER SPORTS & ACTIVITIES

GOLF   With a USGA-sanctioned 27-hole, par-72 course, golfing is the most popular pastime at the park. Ten lakes are scattered throughout the tree-lined fairways, and the views of the lovely Heber Valley are grand. Facilities include a full-service pro shop, driving range, practice greens, and cafe. The course is open daily during daylight hours.

Greens fees on weekdays are $8.50 for 9 holes, $17 for 18 holes. Weekends and holidays, the fees are $9.50 and $19 respectively. Pull carts and riding carts are available.

Tee times should be reserved the preceding Monday for weekends, and the preceding Saturday for Tuesday to Friday play. Call ☎ 435/654-0532 for reservations.

HIKING & WILDLIFE WATCHING   The **Pine Creek Nature Trail** is just over a mile in length and encompasses three smaller loops. Many songbirds make their homes in the trees along the trail, so you might catch a glimpse of Steller jays, chickadees, wrens, robins, and Western tanagers. You might also see the tracks of mule deer along the creek, where they come to forage. From the large parking area in Pine Creek campground, follow the half-mile trail to the Pine Creek trailhead, which lies just north of the Oak Hollow loop. The trail begins at an elevation of 6,100 feet and climbs 220 feet, crossing Pine Creek four times and traversing several boulder ridges. The trail guide describes some of the plants you'll see on this hike. Don't attempt the trail after a rain, as it becomes quite muddy and slick. No bikes or motorized vehicles are allowed. Be sure to bring along water, a sun hat, and binoculars.

Literature describing the plant and animal life of the park is available at the camp manager's office near the entrance to the campground and at the visitor center.

MOUNTAIN BIKING & ATV TRAILS   An 18-mile loop affords great fun for mountain bikes and all-terrain vehicles. The road leaves the visitor center and heads west, winding through magnificent wooded country and offering occasional breath-taking views of the valley.

CAMPING

Three camping loops in the **Pine Creek Campground,** two of which do not allow tents, provide a total of 122 sites. All three loops have modern rest rooms with show-ers. Some sites are nestled among trees and are quite shady, while others are more open. All have a paved parking pad, water, electricity, a picnic table, and a barbecue grill; 66 sites have sewer hookups. Call for information about the group-use area. A dump station is located near the entrance to the campground. Camping fees are $15 for hookups, $9 for no hookups. Reservations (with a $5 nonrefundable reservation fee) are advised and can be made by calling ☎ **800/322-3770.** Both Visa and MasterCard are accepted.

HEBER CITY

Nestled in the lovely Heber Valley, Heber City has managed to retain its small-town atmosphere, despite its proximity to Salt Lake City and Park City. It's the point at which you pick up U.S. 40 if you're heading into the Northeast Corner, to Flam-ing Gorge Recreation Area or to Dinosaur National Monument.

ESSENTIALS

GETTING THERE   From Salt Lake City, head east on I-80 for 25 miles to exit 148, and follow U.S. 40 south about 25 miles. From Park City, Utah 248 east and U.S. 40 south take you the 20 miles to Heber City.

VISITOR INFORMATION   You'll find the visitor center at 475 N. Main St. (☎ 435/654-3666), in a delightful Bavarian chalet–style building with a split cedar roof.

WHAT TO SEE & DO

❂ Heber Valley Historic Railroad
450 S. 600 West. ☎ 435/654-5601; 801/581-9980 from Salt Lake City. Round-trip $8–$17 adults, $6–$10 children ages 3–12, $10–$15 seniors 65 and older. One-way $9–$10 adults, $5–$6 children ages 3–12, $8–$9 seniors 65 and older. DISC, MC, V. The railroad does not pro-vide transportation back for one-way trips. June–Sept one or two runs daily; reduced schedule remainder of year. Ticket office is open 8:30am–5pm.

"The Heber Creeper," as the train is affectionately known, is all that's left of the once busy branch connecting Heber City to Provo. For 70 years, the train carried people, livestock, and general freight up and down Provo Canyon. Sheep were frequent trav-elers as they were shipped to market from Heber City, one of the largest sheep-ship-ping centers in the nation. But in the late 1960s, the train stopped running; the automobile and truck had usurped its function.

Now it's an excursion train. The diversity of the landscape on this short trip is unparalleled. On its 1^1/$_2$-hour run, the train passes through a lush valley, along the shore of a fair-sized lake, and between towering canyon walls before reaching Vivian Park. During the half-hour stay there, the engine moves to the other end of the train via a passing track, and then starts the slow haul back up the 2% grade out of the canyon.

Fall is one of the prettiest times to ride the train, as the mountainsides are gradually decorated with the rich hues of changing leaves—the reds of oak and maple, golds of cottonwood and aspen, and the ever-present greens of piñon, juniper, spruce, and pine.

The train is powered by a turn-of-the-century steam engine on weekends, but more often by diesel. If steam power is critical to your enjoyment, call ahead to confirm locomotion. Special excursions, such as the Santa Claus Express, are scheduled periodically throughout the year; you might want to ask about them when planning your trip.

A NEARBY RESORT HOTEL & GOLF COURSE

The Homestead

700 N. Homestead Dr. (P.O. Box 99), Midway, UT 84049. ☎ **800/327-7220** or 435/654-1102. Fax 435/654-5087. 104 rms, 26 suites, 10 condos. TV TEL. $99–$130 double; $160–$249 suite; $249–$309 condo. AE, CB, DC, DISC, MC, V.

The historic Homestead is a small resort hotel with the atmosphere of a country inn. Swiss-born Simon Schneitter came here in 1886 to farm, but soon realized that the warm mineral springs, a bane to farming, offered a better opportunity for success. He built a board-enclosed pool and soon added his wife's chicken dinners to the attractions. The Schneitter family home (called the Virginia House) is now only one part of the Homestead, where you can enjoy old-fashioned charm with all the modern amenities.

The Homestead's facilities include both indoor and outdoor pools, a mineral bath, indoor and outdoor hot tubs, a fitness facility, sauna, two lighted tennis courts, lawn games, and even scuba diving and snorkling in the Homestead Crater. You can enjoy either a wagon ride ($5) or a horse-drawn buggy ride ($20) in the summer, and sleigh rides ($10 to $20 per person) in the winter. Also offered are horseback riding (cost ranges from $5 for a half hour around the barnyard to $45 for a picnic ride), mountain-bike rentals ($6 to $20), snowmobiling ($40 to $145), and cross-country skiing, with 19 kilometers (11.8 miles) of groomed trails (equipment rentals $7 to $12, lessons available).

The 18-hole, par-72 championship golf course meanders through the beautiful Snake Creek Valley, providing magnificent views of the surrounding mountains. Greens fees are $15 to $40. Private lessons cost $25 for a half hour and $40 for 1 hour. A 1-hour mini-clinic is $5 per person, with a minimum of six people.

In addition to lodge rooms and suites, the Homestead offers some condos for $249 to $309. A variety of packages are also available, which might include meals, golf, skiing, or other entertainment.

You can enjoy a romantic dinner at **Simon's Restaurant** (open 5:30 to 10pm daily, plus Sunday brunch from 10am to 3pm), where the dinner menu choices include grilled salmon, turkey scallopine, rack of lamb, and vegetable manicotti. **Simon's Pub** offers soups, salads, and finger food from 5:30 to 10pm daily. And **Fanny's Grill** serves hearty breakfasts and lunches daily, plus dinner in the summer.

STRAWBERRY RESERVOIR

Located along U.S. 40 in the eastern portion of the Uinta National Forest, the jewel-like Strawberry Reservoir is a terrific water playground offering amazing fishing—this is Utah's premier trout fishery—as well as boating, hiking, and mountain-biking opportunities. It's also great for cross-country skiing, ice fishing, and snowmobiling in the winter.

JUST THE FACTS

Strawberry Reservoir has four marinas, with the largest at **Strawberry Bay** (☎ **435/548-2261**). This is the only one that provides year-round services; the other three offer limited services, but all marinas provide rest rooms, convenience stores, boat and slip rentals, gas, and guide service. Strawberry Bay Marina also offers lodging (with prices for two in the $50 to $100 range), a cafe, dry boat storage, deep-moorage rental, public telephones, snowmobile rentals in the winter, propane and lantern fuel, firewood, charcoal, and ice.

The other marina on the main part of the reservoir is located at Renegade Point; and there are two in the Soldier Creek area at Aspen Grove and Soldier Creek.

GETTING THERE   From Heber City, drive 21^1/$_2$ miles southeast on U.S. 40 and turn south onto the access road. After about a half mile, you'll come to the USFS visitor center for Strawberry Reservoir.

INFORMATION & FEES   Address inquiries to **Heber Ranger District,** P.O. Box 190, Heber, UT 84032 (☎ **435/654-0470**), or stop by the **Strawberry Visitor Center,** open Thursday through Monday from 10am to 5pm, May through October (☎ **435/548-2321**). Day use is free, except for a $3 fee for boat-ramp parking.

WARM-WEATHER SPORTS & ACTIVITIES

FISHING & BOATING   ✪ **Strawberry Reservoir** is Utah's premier trout fishery—indeed, one of the premier trout fisheries in the West—with both huge cutthroat and rainbow, so it's no surprise that fishing is the number-one draw. Fishing boats with outboard motors are available at Strawberry Bay Marina for $55 to $125 per day; large pontoon boats start at $125 a day.

Powerboats are allowed everywhere on the main reservoir, while sailboats stay mostly in the smaller area below Haws Point; the Soldier Creek area to the east is best for canoes and kayaks. The water in Strawberry Reservoir is quite cold, so only the extremely hardy should try swimming.

HIKING   A number of hiking trails surround the reservoir. The easiest is **Telephone Hollow,** a 2^1/$_2$-mile loop hike rated easy to moderate, that takes off from the north side of U.S. 40 about 5 miles west of the entrance road to the reservoir.

For a much more strenuous hike, try the **25-mile loop** that follows forest roads 299 and 134 along Clyde Creek up to Strawberry Ridge, overlooking the reservoir from the west. Forest Road 135 heads south along the ridge to Squaw Creek; you'll follow it back to the main road around the reservoir, and finally back to your starting point.

Just outside the visitor center, you'll find a self-guided **nature trail** where you can learn about stream ecology and view fish, wildflowers, and a variety of birds.

MOUNTAIN BIKING   Several trails are available to mountain bikers, with maps available at the visitor center. The 7-mile **Willow Creek** trail is a short, easy trek. The two hiking trails discussed above under "Hiking" are also open to mountain bikers.

OFF-HIGHWAY VEHICLES   A number of dirt roads in the forests around Strawberry Reservoir are designated for OHVs, with signing on road number posts. If you have any questions, check with a forest ranger, campground host, or the Strawberry Visitor Center. The visitor center provides maps showing the roads plus a description of the post marker.

WILDLIFE WATCHING   Several places around the reservoir offer great birdwatching and wildlife viewing. Pick up the **Strawberry Valley Wildlife Viewing Guide** at the visitor center for a map and viewing site descriptions.

WINTER SPORTS & ACTIVITIES

You can explore the canyons, mountains, and meadows of the Strawberry Bay area on cross-country skis, snowmobiles, or snowshoes, or chop through the ice on the reservoir for some chilled trout. **Strawberry Bay Marina** (☎ 435/548-2261), open year-round, offers guide services, supplies, and snowmobile rentals.

CAMPING

Campgrounds are located at each of the four marinas on the reservoir. Sites in the Strawberry Bay and Soldier Creek campgrounds have hookups; Aspen Grove and Renegade do not. The camping fee is $11, $17 with hookups; the dump station fee is $2. Boat ramps and fish-cleaning facilities are located adjacent to each campground. Reservations can be made for a limited number of designated campsites at Strawberry Bay and Soldier Creek; contact the Strawberry Visitor Center (see above). The remainder of the sites are available on a first-come, first-served basis.

4 Sundance Resort & Institute

Situated in beautiful Provo Canyon at the base of 12,000-foot Mt. Timpanogos, Sundance is a year-round resort that emphasizes its arts programs as much as its skiing and other outdoor activities. That should come as no surprise, though—it's owned by actor/director Robert Redford, who bought the property in 1969 and named it after his character in the classic film *Butch Cassidy and the Sundance Kid.* You might recognize the area: Redford and director Sydney Pollack set their 1972 film *Jeremiah Johnson* here.

The goal for Sundance was to create a place where the outdoors and the arts could come together in a truly unique mountain community, and it seems to be a success. The rustic yet elegant, environmentally friendly retreat is a full-service ski resort in the winter. During the summer, you'll find great hiking trails and other outdoor activities, as well as the Sundance Institute, which Redford founded in 1980 to support and encourage independent American filmmaking and playwriting.

ESSENTIALS

GETTING THERE   Sundance is less than an hour's drive from Salt Lake City via I-15. From Park City, take U.S. 189 south to Sundance. From Provo, take I-15 to exit 275, go east on Utah 52 for 5¹/₂ miles, turn north on U.S. 189 up Provo Canyon for 7 miles, then turn north on Utah 92 for about 2 miles to Sundance, which is on the left. The road beyond Sundance is often closed by snow in winter.

A van shuttle service connects Sundance with both Salt Lake International Airport and Provo Airport. The charge is $50 per person, one-way; call **Sundance Guest Services** at ☎ **800/892-1600** or 801/225-4107 to arrange for pick-up.

VISITOR INFORMATION   For information, contact **Sundance Resort and Institute,** R.R. 3 Box A-1, Sundance, UT 84604 (☎ **800/892-1600** or 801/225-4107; fax 801/226-1937; 801/225-4100 for snow reports). The nearest hospital is in Provo, about 20 minutes away.

SKIING SUNDANCE

With a limit of 1,500 skiers per day, Sundance is known for its quiet, intimate setting and lack of lift lines. It offers runs for all levels—some quite challenging—including several delightfully long cruising trails for novices. The area is gaining a reputation as a good place to learn to ski, especially as the two levels of skiing are pretty well separated from one another: The beginner and some of the intermediate terrain are on the front mountain, while the prime blue runs and all of the expert slopes are on the back mountain. The expert crowd will be pleased with the steep glades, precipitous bump runs (due to the general lack of traffic, the mountain never really bumps up too high, though), and untracked snow on the back mountain, where you'll have to work at it to run into another skier.

Sorry, snowboarders—you're not welcome on the mountain here.

JUST THE FACTS

Sundance offers 20% beginner, 40% intermediate, and 40% advanced terrain, with a total of 41 runs over 450 acres. Seven double chairlifts serve the mountain, which has a vertical drop of 2,150 feet, from a base elevation of 6,100 feet to the top at 8,250 feet. Sundance is usually open from mid-December through April, although its relatively low elevation makes it susceptible to early closures due to fickle weather. Lifts operate daily from 9am to 4:30pm. A new quad lift was added in 1996.

Bearclaw's Cabin, the only mountaintop day lodge in Utah, offers snacks and hot drinks, as well as stupendous views. The newly renovated and enlarged **Creekside** day lodge, at the base of the ski area, serves excellent quick lunches during ski season.

Equipment rental and sales are available.

LIFT TICKETS   An adult all-day lift ticket costs $35; half-day is $27; children's lift tickets are $22 and $16 respectively; seniors over 65 ski free. If you're staying at the resort, the lift ticket is built into the price of your room.

LESSONS & PROGRAMS   The **ski school** (☎ 801/225-4100) at Sundance offers private and group lessons daily, as well as specialized ski workshops. One-hour private lessons start at $48, and group lessons start at $30 for a half day.

Sundance Kids ski school offers several programs, including group sessions for children ages 6 and older and all-day programs that include supervision, lunch, and instructions. You can enroll the younger kids in private lessons; however, there is no actual day-care facility.

CROSS-COUNTRY SKIING

Sundance's excellent ✪ **Nordic Center** (☎ 801/223-4170) is 1¹/₂ miles north of the main Sundance entrance. It has 15 kilometer (9.3 miles) of Nordic trails in the Elk Meadows Preserve, groomed for both classic and skate skiing. Classic, skating, and telemark rentals and lessons are available. Trails are rated 20% beginner, 40% intermediate, and 40% advanced. Trail passes for adults cost $8 for a full day and $5 after 2pm. Children 12 and under and seniors over 65 ski free. Night skiing is offered Wednesday to Saturday from 5 to 9pm.

WARM-WEATHER SPORTS & ACTIVITIES

An abundance of warm-weather activities and spectacular scenery make Sundance just as popular a destination in the summer as during the winter. The new quad ski lift operates in warm weather, carrying hikers and bikers to upper trails, and offering scenic rides to anyone.

HIKING   Sundance is home to a terrific network of close to a dozen hiking trails, some of which connect to trails farther afield in the Uinta National Forest (88 W. 100 North, Provo, UT 84601; ☎ 801/377-5780). The resort's trails range from hour-long nature walks to all-day affairs, and include three summit trails to the top of Mt. Timpanogos.

The **Sundance Nature Trail,** a 1- to 1¹/₂-hour hike, winds through groves of spruce, oak, and maple and across Alpine meadows before reaching a cascading waterfall. The **Great Western Trail,** one of the Wasatch Front's most spectacular trails, climbs nearly 4,000 feet to some amazing scenic vistas. It starts at the base of

So You Wanna Be in Pictures . . .

Forget Cannes; forget Hollywood. If you want to be (or at least be up on) the next art-house cinema sensation, go to Utah.

Tired of waiting for the next Great American Novel, many across the nation—maybe even you—have traded their reading glasses for tubs of popcorn. They're packing the movie houses to catch the latest work of the new creative hero: the American independent filmmaker. These next Tarantinos have to start somewhere—and that somewhere is, more often than not, the Sundance Film Festival.

For more than a decade now, the hottest independent films have been discovered at this week-long January event, hosted by Robert Redford's Sundance Institute. (The festival doesn't actually take place at Sundance, however; it's held 30 miles away, in Utah's premier resort town, Park City, covered earlier in this chapter.) The festival has seen the rise to glory of many pictures, from *sex, lies, and videotape* to *The Brothers McMullen*, with *Slacker, Gas Food Lodging, Paris Is Burning, Like Water for Chocolate, Hoop Dreams, Clerks,* and *Crumb* in between—and that's just the short list.

Hosting the nation's premier annual film festival is only part of the Sundance Institute's role in the world of American cinema. Think you might have what it takes to be the next Tarantino? Then it might be a good idea to take a summer trip to Sundance to take part in the Institute's Filmmakers Lab. Quentin did; afterwards, he released a little flick called *Reservoir Dogs*.

Since Robert Redford founded the Institute in 1981, it has brought some of the finest and most well-respected directors, actors, and producers to Utah for 3 weeks every June to serve as advisors while students rehearse, shoot, and edit scenes from their works. Denzel Washington and Glenn Close have lent their services; so have

Aspen Grove, winds to the crest of North Fork and American Fork Canyons, and ends at the top of Alta ski area. This is, as you might expect, an 8- to 10-hour hike.

And there's more to choose from: Contact the resort for a comprehensive trail guide. Guided hikes are also available.

HORSEBACK RIDING   The **Sundance Stables** offer guided mountain rides. Standard rides are an hour, but longer rides can be arranged. Rates are about $35 for an hour-long ride, about $55 for a 2-hour ride; call ☎ **800/892-1600** or 801/225-4107 for information and reservations.

FISHING   **Deer Creek Reservoir** provides great fishing just 10 minutes away. Sundance offers guided fishing trips that include equipment rentals and licenses. Rates range from $145 for a half-day fly-fishing trip; call ☎ **801/225-4107** for information and ☎ **800/892-1600** for reservations.

SHOPPING

The **General Store** at Sundance was the inspiration for the Sundance Catalog; it may have come to you in the mail at some time or another. If so, you'll recognize the Native American art and jewelry, local crafts, and high-end Southwest-style clothing and outdoor wear that line the shelves. Sundance's eco-sensitive bath-product line, Sundance Farms, is available here as well. You'll also find hiking and fishing apparel and gear in warm weather, ski accessories in the winter, and fresh-baked goodies year-round. The store is open daily from 8am to 10pm.

directors Terry Gilliam and Sydney Pollack, producer James L. Brooks, and actor Morgan Freeman. Redford himself even stops by occasionally to lend a hand. The Institute's success can be measured by the films it has helped develop: *El Norte, Impromptu, Reservoir Dogs, I Like It Like That, Mi Vida Loca,* and many others. Sundance also runs workshops to help writers polish their scripts, directors polish their actors, and producers polish their negotiating skills—in preparation for all the big-time studio distributors descending on them at the Festival, eager for the rights to the next *Devil in a Blue Dress* (another notable film developed through the Sundance Labs).

Unlike most staid film-industry institutions, Sundance—the Institute and the Festival—has grown and changed with the times. Since its inception, Sundance has supported American independent feature films and documentaries, and has slowly added workshops and scholarship programs for young, promising Latin American, French, and Japanese filmmakers, as well as development programs for children's plays and family entertainment. The festival also screens foreign films and film shorts. Although greater numbers of big names—from stars to studio executives—are showing up in little ol' Park City each year, Redford and the Institute's directors have made every effort to keep the festival uncompromised by Hollywood and a haven for American independent film.

Admission to the festival—as a filmmaker or as an audience member—is non-exclusive; that means you and I can rub shoulders with the rich and famous and the up-and-coming next January. To receive a free guide, or to reserve tickets, contact the **Sundance Institute,** P.O. Box 16450, Salt Lake City, UT 84116 (☎ **801/ 328-3456**).

—Reid Bramblett

ACCOMMODATIONS

Sundance offers one-, two-, and three-bedroom cottage suites that range from $295 to $425 per night, as well as several luxury mountain homes. The "Pines" are ten new cottages located in Sundance Village; the 20 "River Run" cottages are streamside, near the base area; and the original 62 "Mandan" cottages are nestled in the mountains and offer fabulous views. Each suite is outfitted with well-crafted handmade furnishings that suit the rustic luxury of the entire resort, as well as Native American crafts, stone fireplaces, and outdoor decks; most have fully equipped kitchens. All accommodations come complete with Sundance's own natural bath products—such as eco-sensitive oatmeal soap—and wildflower bouquets throughout. Summer theater packages and a complete range of ski packages are available; call ☎ **800/892-1600** or 801/225-4107 for information and reservations.

DINING

The Sundance restaurants' unique culinary approach stresses the use of natural, seasonal ingredients, prepared in a New American style that draws from a variety of traditions. Menus are designed around the seasonal availability of the vegetables, fruits, and herbs organically grown in the surrounding areas, and the meats—buffalo, venison, antelope, and elk—which are obtained from game farms. Dinner reservations are recommended, particularly in peak seasons. Full liquor service is available.

The **Tree Room,** the resort's most elegant dining room for over 25 years, is the place for relaxing and romantic dinners with wine and candlelight. Decorated with

Native American art and artifacts, the rustic room seats diners in cozy booths and at intimate tables. Chef Jean Louis Montecot draws from American, Southwestern, Mediterranean, and European cuisines, often combining two or more. The results include dishes such as the Tree Room pepper steak with mango chutney, mushroom-coated halibut with risotto and truffle oil, and grilled venison medaillons with shiitake hunter sauce.

The **Foundry Grill,** a less formal eatery combining Native American and Tex-Mex cuisines, serves all three meals daily. Wood is the predominant feature in both the decor and the preparation of food—a wood oven and wood-fired grill and rotisserie are the main cooking equipment here. Offerings include soups and salads, pizza and pasta, porterhouse and New York strip steaks, a homemade sausage platter, smoked prime rib, stuffed shrimp, salmon filet, and wood-roasted chicken.

The **Owl Bar** is just next door. This is the same 1890s bar frequented by Butch Cassidy's Hole-in-the-Wall Gang, moved here from Wyoming—but now locals and resort guests belly up to the Victorian rosewood bar to order their favorite tipple. Live music is often featured, and a limited grill menu is available.

SUNDANCE AFTER SUNDOWN

The excellent **Sundance Institute screening room** shows foreign films, movie classics, American independent films (see the box on the Sundance Institute), and documentaries year-round. Screenings are free to Sundance guests.

For 25 years, the **Sundance Summer Theatre** has been showcasing innovative productions in a beautiful outdoor setting, a natural amphitheater backed by firs. Generally, four productions are staged each season; call to find out what's planned during your visit.

5 Provo & Environs

Provo is the second-largest city in Utah, with a population of more than 90,000. Its largest draw is Brigham Young University, with its attendant museums, cultural events, and spectator sports. The Ute Indian tribe reigned here until Mormon leader Brigham Young sent 30 families south from Salt Lake City in March of 1849 to colonize the area. Today, the city remains primarily Mormon; most restaurants plus the museums on the BYU campus are closed on Sunday.

South of Provo lies **Springville,** a town of about 14,000 that likes to refer to itself as "Utah's Art City." Although not primarily a tourist destination, it boasts one of Utah's finest art museums.

Orem, which abuts Provo on the northwest, is the home of various computer-related businesses. Utah Lake State Park, just west of downtown Provo, is great for boating, and the surrounding Wasatch Mountains abound with natural beauty and recreational opportunities.

ESSENTIALS
Getting There

BY CAR   Provo is 45 miles south of Salt Lake City and 258 miles northeast of St. George. Provo and Orem are easily accessible from the north or south by I-15. If you're driving in from the east on I-70, take exit 156 at Green River and follow U.S. 6 northwest to I-15 north.

BY TRAIN   Amtrak (☎ 800/872-7245) offers intercity passenger service. The train station is located at 600 South and 300 West.

VISITOR INFORMATION

The **Utah Valley Convention and Visitors Bureau** runs a visitor center in the magnificent Historic Utah County Courthouse, 51 S. University Ave. (☎ **800/222-8824** or 801/370-8393), and an office at 100 E. Center St., Suite 3200 (☎ **801/370-8390**). Be sure to request a copy of their full-color visitor guide. For the visitor center, take I-15 to exit 268, follow Center Street east to University, turn south past the courthouse, and then turn east, where you'll find a visitors' parking lot behind the courthouse. Drivers of motor homes and vehicles with trailers should try to park along the street.

A *Parks and Recreation Map and Facilities Guide* is available at the information center. You can also obtain information from the **parks and recreation information hotline** at ☎ **801/379-6629.**

For information about the surrounding national forest, contact the **Uinta National Forest,** Supervisor's Office, 88 W. 100 North, Provo, UT 84601 (☎ **801/377-5780**).

GETTING AROUND

The easiest way to get around is by car. The streets are organized in a numbered grid pattern, beginning at the intersection of Center Street (exit 268 off I-15) and University Ave. (exit 266) in Provo. From there, the numbers increase by 100 in all four directions, such as 100 South, 200 West, 700 North, and so forth. University Parkway cuts diagonally northwest across the grid from Brigham Young University to connect with 1300 South (I-15 exit 272) in Orem. "Ground zero" in Orem is at the intersection of Center Street (I-15 exit 274) and Main Street. State Street (U.S. 89) crosses the city diagonally, right through "ground zero."

Car-rental agencies with offices in Provo include **Avis** (☎ 800/831-2847 or 801/359-2177), **Budget** (☎ 800/237-7251 or 800/527-0700), **Hertz** (☎ 800/654-3131 or 801/377-7495), **National** (☎ 800/227-7368 or 801/373-2114), and **Payless** (☎ 800/729-5377 or 801/374-9000).

The **Utah Transit Authority** has about a dozen routes in and around the Provo area, with connections to Salt Lake City, Lehi, and Springville. Call ☎ **801/375-4636** for schedules, between 6am and 7pm, Monday to Saturday. Route maps and schedules are also available at the visitor information center in the county courthouse.

FAST FACTS: PROVO

The main hospital is **Utah Valley Regional Medical Center,** 1034 N. 500 West (☎ 801/373-7850 or 801/371-7001 for emergencies). The main **post office** is at 95 W. 100 South (☎ 801/374-2000). The **local newspaper** is *The Daily Herald,* 1555 N. 200 West (☎ 801/373-6450). The sales tax is about 6%.

EXPLORING BRIGHAM YOUNG UNIVERSITY

Founded in 1875 by Brigham Young, Brigham Young University is the nation's largest church-owned private university, sponsored by the Church of Jesus Christ of Latter-day Saints. Home to more than 30,000 students, the beautiful 638-acre campus is located on the east side of Provo at the base of the Wasatch Mountains.

For advance information, contact Guest Relations, P.O. Box 23200, Provo, UT 84602; ☎ **801/378-4678.** To get to the university: From I-15 north, take exit 266, University Avenue, then U.S. 189 north to the campus; from I-15 south, take exit 272, 12th Street South (which becomes University Parkway), then Utah 265 east to the campus.

Free tours of the campus are offered through the **visitor center** (☎ 801/378-4678), Monday through Friday at 11am and 2pm, or at other times by appointment. Admission to campus museums is free unless otherwise noted.

The 112-foot-tall **Centennial Carillon Tower,** a campus landmark, houses 52 bells that toll at intervals throughout the day.

The **Monte L. Bean Life Science Museum,** 1430 North, just east of the Marriott Center (☎ 801/378-5051), houses extensive collections of insects, plants, reptiles, fish, shells, mammals, and birds from around the world, with an emphasis on Utah's wildlife. It's open Monday through Friday from 10am to 9pm and Saturday from 10am to 5pm.

The **Earth Science Museum,** 1683 N. Provo Canyon Rd., west of Cougar Stadium (☎ 801/378-3680), offers one of Utah's largest collections of dinosaur bones from the Jurassic period. Hours are Monday through Friday from 9am to 5pm and Saturday from noon to 4pm.

The **Harris Fine Arts Center,** Campus Drive (☎ 801/378-2881), houses galleries featuring American and European artists and shows student and faculty artwork. Hours are Monday through Friday from 8am to 11pm. The **B.F. Larsen Gallery** and **Gallery 303** house student and faculty exhibitions. The center also hosts theatrical and musical performances in its five theaters; call for the schedule and ticket prices.

The state-of-the-art **Museum of Art,** located north of the Fine Arts Center at 492 E. Campus Dr. (☎ 801/378-2787), is one of the largest museums in the West. Its 14,000-piece collection includes something for everyone, from ceramics to sculpture, paintings to pottery. You'll see etchings by Rembrandt and Monet and jade and ivory from Asia. The museum also contains a gift shop as well as a cafe that serves lunch. Hours are 10am to 6pm on Monday and Thursday; 10am to 9pm on Tuesday, Wednesday, and Friday; and noon to 5pm on Saturday. Admission is charged for special exhibitions only.

The **Museum of Peoples and Cultures,** in Allen Hall, 700 N. 100 East (☎ 801/378-6112), focuses on the cultures of the western hemisphere, but also looks at Colombian, Egyptian, Israeli, Polynesian, and Syrian societies. It is open Monday through Friday from 9am to 5pm.

The **Ernest L. Wilkinson Center,** located on East Campus Drive (☎ 801/378-3111), serves as the student union, housing the University Bookstore, barbershop, outdoor-equipment rental store, craft and floral shop, game center, post office, convenience store and movie theater. Most services are open Monday through Saturday from 10am to 6pm. For movie show times and prices call ☎ 801/378-3311. The box office opens at noon Monday through Saturday.

The **Harold B. Lee Library** (☎ 801/378-2926) is the largest library in Utah with over three million bound volumes. Library hours are 7am to midnight, Monday through Saturday. The fourth floor houses the second-largest **genealogical library** (☎ 801/378-6200) in the world, with free services to everyone. It is open Monday through Saturday from 8am to 9:30pm.

WALKING TOUR
Historic Downtown Provo

Here in Provo, home of Brigham Young University, it should be no surprise that you'll see a number of stately homes that once belonged to well-to-do church officials.

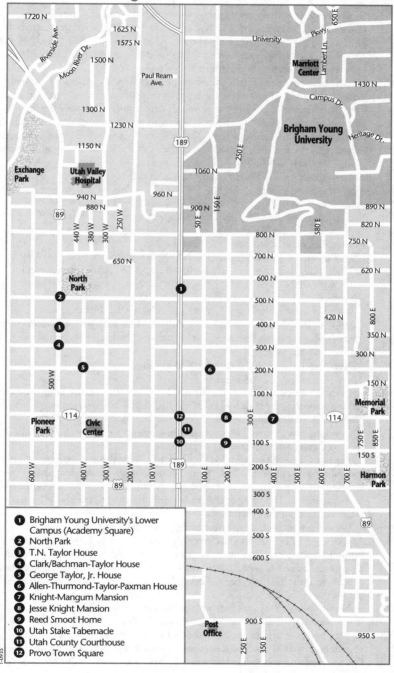

① Brigham Young University's Lower Campus (Academy Square)
② North Park
③ T.N. Taylor House
④ Clark/Bachman-Taylor House
⑤ George Taylor, Jr. House
⑥ Allen-Thurmond-Taylor-Paxman House
⑦ Knight-Mangum Mansion
⑧ Jesse Knight Mansion
⑨ Reed Smoot Home
⑩ Utah Stake Tabernacle
⑪ Utah County Courthouse
⑫ Provo Town Square

1. Begin the tour at Brigham Young University's "Lower Campus," officially known as Academy Square, 550 N. University Ave. The university started life in 1875 as Brigham Young Academy and moved to this site in 1892, almost 10 years after the first meeting place burned. The Provo Public Library is located here.

   Next, head west on 500 North to 500 West to:

2. North Park, where the Provo Daughters of Utah Pioneers Museum is located (for details, see below). Here's where the first Mormon settlers moved when the original Fort Utah became too swampy to support a community. The move began in 1850 and took about 2 years to complete. Several of the original cabins from this second fort are north of the museum. The museum is open Wednesday, Friday, and Saturday in the summer, from 2 to 5pm, and in the winter by appointment for groups (☎ 801/379-6609). Admission is free.

   Head south on 500 West a couple blocks to the:

3. T. N. Taylor House, 342 N. 500 West. "T.N.T.," as he was known, was manager of the Taylor Brothers Store and served as mayor of Provo and President of the Utah Stake of the LDS Church. His home, built in the first decade of the twentieth century, exemplifies the kind of house most second-generation Utahns aspired to have. Continue south a few buildings to the:

4. Clark/Bachman-Taylor House, 310 N. 500 West, thought to be the oldest home in Utah Valley still standing on its original site. The adobe structure was built in 1854, with later additions of the two-story front, trim around the windows, and the gables.

   Now turn east 1 block to 400 West and head south 2 blocks to the:

5. George Taylor, Jr. House, 187 N. 400 West. This blue-painted house is reminiscent of Gothic Revival architecture, as evidenced by its lace-decorated porch and high arched windows.

   Next, head east on 200 North for 5 blocks to the:

6. Allen-Thurmond-Taylor-Paxman House, 135 E. 200 North. Built in 1893, the house was later occupied by the wife of LDS Church president John W. Taylor. During antipolygamy raids by U.S. marshalls, Taylor hid in a cranny near the fireplace in the master bedroom.

   Continue east another 3 blocks and turn south onto 400 East for 2 blocks, then west on Center Street to the:

7. Knight-Mangum Mansion, 381 E. Center St. This three-story English Tudor–style home was completed in 1908 and cost $40,000. It was designed by one of Utah's most prominent architects of the time, Walter E. Ward, and is now divided into apartments. The color of the exterior was designed to match the bark on the sycamore trees on the grounds.

   Continue west on Center Street about 2 blocks to the:

8. Jesse Knight Mansion, 185 E. Center St. Built in 1905 by Knight, a financier and mining businessman, the home began a major trend in building, with similar designs and materials appearing throughout the county. The design is neo-classic, copied from the 1893 Chicago World's Fair, utilizing white pressed brick. Only the front sections are original.

   Now head south on 200 East a block to the:

9. Reed Smoot Home, 183 E. 100 South. Reed Smoot was a U.S. senator, advisor to five presidents, and an apostle in the Mormon Church. Presidents, senators, and church leaders alike assembled here for confidential conferences. Political and religious arguments were waged here, sometimes both at once—this house is a great candidate for the "Oh, if the walls could talk" award.

   Now head west on 100 South to the:

10. Utah Stake Tabernacle, 100 S. University Ave. This two-story brick edifice seats 2,000 and is still used for LDS Stake Conferences. Built in 1883, it was partly condemned when the roof started sagging under the weight of the central tower. Around 1916, the stained-glass windows were installed, the tower was removed, and the structure was again declared sound.

Turn north on University a short distance to the:

11. Utah County Courthouse, 51 S. University Ave. This magnificent structure was built of Manti limestone in the 1920s. The interior is well worth a visit: Notice the marble floors and detailing, the fine collection of artwork displayed on the walls, and the overall feeling of grandeur emanating from the classical balance of the design.

Continue along University north to the:

12. Provo Town Square, at the intersection of University Avenue and Center Street. Most of the commercial buildings date from the 1890s, when the core of the business community developed here. The **Knight Block,** a big red building with a large clock, was built in 1900. The **Gates & Snow Furniture Co.,** to the east of the Knight Block, has one of Utah's best pressed-tin fronts. The **Zion Bank,** at the northwest corner, is situated in what was originally the Bank of Commerce building. West along Center Street sits a row of period storefronts, with the newer businesses of today capitalizing on the original details still apparent on their second stories.

MORE TO SEE & DO IN & AROUND PROVO

Bridal Veil Falls

Provo Canyon, U.S. 189 about 4 miles north and east of Provo.

This double cataract waterfall drops 607 feet, affording awe-inspiring views from a turnout on the highway.

Daughters of Utah Pioneers Museum

175 S. Main St., Springville. ☎ **801/489-7525.** Free admission, donations accepted. Tues and Sat 2–5pm; Wed 1–5pm. From I-15, take exit 263 east to Springville; turn left, then north on Main St.; it's about 6 blocks to the museum.

This small museum houses memorabilia from the early settlers of Springville. You'll see clothing, furnishings (including an entire bedroom), musical instruments, children's furniture, weapons and tools, plus many photographs. You can research pioneers of the area here, too.

John Hutchings Museum of Natural History

55 N. Center St., Lehi. ☎ **801/768-7180.** Admission $2.50 adults, $2 seniors, $1.50 children. Mon–Sat 9:30am–5pm. Bus: 10 from Provo. From I-15, take exit 282, follow Main St. west to Center St., and turn right; it's a half block to the museum.

Born in 1889, John Hutchings had an insatiable curiosity about the world around him. Every facet intrigued him—the geological, historical, anthropological, and philosophical. He collected numerous things to study, discussing his observations with friends and family. In 1955, as his collections overflowed his home, he donated them to be held in trust for the people of the town of Lehi, and this museum was born.

Today, it houses mineral displays and rare specimens of varacite and crystal aluminum (and describes their links to mining districts of the region); fossils such as dinosaur bones, flamingo tracks from Spanish Fork Canyon, and a piece of tusk from a woolly mammoth; tools and pottery from early man; and artifacts from Mormon and other Utah pioneers.

McCurdy Historical Doll Museum

246 N. 100 East. ☎ **801/377-9935.** Admission $2 adults, $1 children under 12. Winter, Tues–Sat 1–5pm; summer, Tues–Sat noon–6pm. From I-15, take exit 268 and head east on Center St. to 100 East; turn left (north) and continue $2^1/2$ blocks to the museum.

Laura McCurdy Clark began collecting dolls from around the world in 1910, and in 1979, this museum was founded to exhibit her collection and others. Today, over 3,000 dolls are on display in this restored carriage house, including antique dolls crafted in Germany, France, and England; lovely wax dolls representing the work of such famous artists as Lewis Sorensen of Utah and California, and Tussaud's Eden Musee of London; rare dolls of yesteryear from the Laura Galbraith collection; 40 first ladies of America copied from their likenesses in the Smithsonian Institute; priceless antique dolls representing historical figures; and many dolls depicting fashions from the caveman to the present, plus dolls in national folk dress from around the world. In addition, the museum offers storytelling, lectures, craft classes, and a doll "hospital," which provides repair services. An Academy Award–winning documentary about dolls and toys is shown as part of the tour.

Peppermint Place

155 E. 200 North, Alpine. ☎ **435/756-7400.** Free admission. Mon–Sat 10am–6pm (optimum factory observation Mon–Fri 10am–2pm). Take I-15 to exit 287, head east on Utah 92, then north on Utah 74 to Alpine.

If you like candy, you'll love Peppermint Place. You'll find hand-dipped chocolates, crunchy nut brittles, 24 stick flavors, chocolate-covered potato chips(!), 15 kinds of licorice, and even sugar-free candies (there oughta be a law against such abominations). Also available are non-candy gift items, such as music boxes, porcelain dolls, and Bavarian cuckoo clocks. If you can't make the optimum observation time, a videotape is available.

Springville Museum of Art

126 E. 400 South, Springville. ☎ **801/489-2727.** Free admission, donations accepted. Tues–Sat 10am–5pm; Wed 5–9pm; Sun 3–6pm. Closed legal holidays. From I-15, take exit 263 east to Springville, entering town on 400 South.

The art of Utah is the cornerstone of this fine museum. The present Spanish colonial revival–style building was completed in 1937, with a two-story addition made in 1964. Today you can browse through nine galleries and see one of the finest displays of Utahn art available, arranged in chronological order to illustrate the development of art in the state. Four galleries are reserved for changing exhibits drawn from around the world. The museum also contains a research library and videos and offers lectures and guided tours on weekdays.

Thanksgiving Point

2095 N. West Frontage Rd., Lehi. ☎ **801/768-2300.** Free admission. Mon–Sat 8am–9pm. From I-15 exit 287, head west to the frontage road.

This garden paradise, which is undergoing development over a period of several years, was planned as a thank you from Alan Ashton, co-founder of WordPerfect software. The 550 acres display gardens, a tropical greenhouse, an animal farm, fishing pond, nurseries, an 18-hole golf course (see "Golf," below), and a restaurant featuring seasonal produce grown on-site.

Utah Lake State Park

4400 W. Center St. ☎ **801/375-0731.** $4 per vehicle day use; $10 camping. Take I-15 exit 268B, Center St. west; it's about 3 miles to the park.

Utah's largest freshwater lake, a favorite of local residents, is great for fishing, boating, and swimming. The 96,000-acre lake is particularly popular for those with speedboats, personal watercraft, and sailboats, although you will see the occasional canoe or kayak. The skyline is dominated by mountains in all directions, while at night the view to the east is illuminated by the lights of the city. Four boat-launching ramps and 78 boat slips are available, but no boat rentals. An Olympic-size ice rink is usually open from December through March. Although there are no hiking or biking trails in the park itself, the **Provo River Parkway Trail** leads from the edge of the park into Provo Canyon (see "Sports & Outdoor Activities," below). The 71-site campground—mostly just paved parking areas, although there are some grassy spots for tents—has no RV hookups, but you will find a dump station as well as modern rest rooms with showers in one bathhouse.

SPORTS & OUTDOOR ACTIVITIES

BIKING & HIKING   The 9-mile **Provo River Parkway Trail** winds through the city from Utah Lake to Provo Canyon, following the Provo River some of the way. A slag trail (slag is what's left over from mining out the metal desired), it's open to both bicyclists and hikers.

Hundreds of miles of trails wind through the **Uinta National Forest** (☎ 801/377-5780) in the mountains around Provo. The *Utah County Hiking and Bicycling Guide* describes over a dozen rides, including the one mentioned above. Bicyclists can pick up the guide at the visitor center (see "Visitor Information," above).

Pedersen's Ski & Sports, University Mall, Orem (☎ 801/225-3000), is a full-service bike shop, staffed by bikers who can direct you to some terrific area rides. **Gourmet Bicycles,** 1155 N. Canyon Rd., Provo (☎ 801/377-3969), rents and repairs mountain bikes. **The Bike Peddler,** 187 W. Center St., Provo (☎ 801/374-5322), and in Orem at 736 S. State St. (☎ 801/222-9577), is another full-service bicycle store.

BOATING   See Utah Lake State Park, above.

FISHING   Check with **Great Basin Fly & Outfitters,** 120 W. Center St. (☎ 801/375-2424), for all your supplies, as well as tips on where they're biting. One of the top fly-fishing streams in the nation is the Provo River.

GOLF   Four public golf courses are situated in the Provo/Orem area. **Ambush Course** at Thanksgiving Point (see "More to See & Do in & Around Provo," above), 2095 N. West Frontage Rd., Lehi (☎ 801/768-7400), is an 18-hole, par-72 championship course designed by golf pro Johnny Miller. Fees are $52 to $68 including mandatory golf cart. **Cascade Fairways Golf Course,** 1313 E. 800 North, Orem (☎ 801/225-6677), has a driving range and 9 holes, par-35. Reservations are required, and greens fees are about $7. The **East Bay Golf Course,** 1860 S. East Bay Blvd. (☎ 801/373-6262), on the south side of the city, requires reservations for its 18-hole, par-71 course as well; you'll also find a driving range, lodging, and RV facilities. Greens fees are about $15 weekdays, $17 weekends. The **Seven Peaks Resort** (☎ 801/375-5155) has a challenging mountainside 18-hole, par-59 course with spectacular views of the city to the west, and also offers a driving range, lodging, and RV facilities. Reservations are required. Fees are $6.50 to $7.50. The private **Riverside Country Club,** 2701 N. University Ave. (☎ 801/373-8262), is the site of the Nike Utah Classic and Brigham Young University's Cougar Classic. Reservations are required for the 18-hole, par-72 course.

ICE-SKATING   In the winter, **Utah Lake State Park** (see p. 164) opens its outdoor rink Monday through Friday from noon to 2pm and 4 to 6pm, plus on Tuesday, Wednesday, and Friday from 7 to 9pm; Saturday 2 to 4pm, 5 to 7pm, and 8 to 10pm; and Sunday from 1 to 3pm. Cost is $3 for adults, $2 for kids ages 6 to 11. Skate rentals are $1.

Seven Peaks (see below) has an ice-skating rink that opens for the season around Thanksgiving. It's open Monday to Thursday from 6 to 9pm, Friday from 6 to 11pm, and Saturday from 1 to 5pm and 6 to 11pm. Admission is $5 for adults, $3 for kids ages 4 to 11.

ROCK CLIMBING   The **Rock Garden Indoor Climbing Center,** 22 S. Freedom Blvd. (☎ 801/375-2388), offers classes for everyone from novice to advanced, and a place to practice your skills out of the elements. Beginner classes include an introduction to body, balance, and hand positions. Call for class schedules and costs. Equipment is available for rent, and a day pass is $5. Open Monday to Thursday from noon to 10pm, Friday from noon to midnight, and Saturday from 10am to midnight.

WATER PARKS & RECREATION CENTERS

Provo Recreation Center & Pool
1155 N. University Ave. ☎ **801/379-6610.** Mon–Sat; call for current rates and hours.

The center contains a large indoor swimming pool, 10 racquetball courts, 10 wallyball courts, two weight rooms, and one basketball court.

Seven Peaks Resort Water Park
1330 E. 300 North. ☎ **801/373-8777.** All-day admission is $14.50 adults, $11.50 children ages 3–11; half day (after 4pm) $7.50; free for seniors (63 and older) and toddlers (2 and under). Late May–mid-Sept Mon–Sat 11am–8pm, Sun noon–5pm. From I-15, take exit 268 and head east on Center St. Bus: 3.

This is the place for a wide variety of water fun—you'll encounter some 45 heated water attractions on 26 acres butting against the mountains. The facilities include a wave pool, winding slides, three children's pools, a 95-foot-high breaker, a lazy river, and a 550-foot-long, totally dark tube ride through foggers, lasers, and sound effects. For relaxing or picnicking, you'll find large pavilions, shaded cabanas, and plenty of lawn.

Trafalga Family Fun Center
168 S. 1200 West, Orem. ☎ **801/224-6000.** Admission to grounds free; miniature golf $4.50 adults, $2.50 children ages 7 and under, $20 family; basketball $2.75; arcade tokens 4 for $1, 25 for $5. Mon–Fri from 10am, Sat from 9am, closes late evening; closed Sun (hours may be shorter in the winter). From I-15 take exit 274, go east on Center St., and almost immediately turn right (south) onto 1200 West to the park.

This all-around family fun center has three 18-hole miniature golf courses, a huge arcade with more than 100 games, and "shoot-a-round" basketball with 17 baskets that move and talk, all open year-round. If weather permits, the slick-track raceway and batting cages are open. You say you like water fights? Try the bumper boats (open May through October). You'll also find a pavilion, picnic tables, and a snack bar.

Veterans Memorial Pool & Waterslide Park
450 W. 500 North. ☎ **801/379-6610.** Pool-only admission $1.50 adults, $1 seniors (65 and older) and children 12 and under. Pool and water slide passes $2.50–$5.50, depending on number of rides. Memorial Day–Labor Day Mon–Thurs 1–8pm, Fri–Sat 1–6pm.

Facilities include a large, heated outdoor swimming pool, two enclosed 100-yard-long water slides, sunbathing decks, and a snack bar.

SPECTATOR SPORTS

Brigham Young University is part of the Western Athletic Conference. The **Cougars football** team plays at the 65,000-seat Cougar Stadium; tickets are hard to come by, so call as far in advance as you can. The **basketball** team plays in the 23,000-seat Marriot Center, and you usually won't have too much trouble getting tickets. For general information on all BYU sports teams, call ☎ **801/378-4911;** for tickets call ☎ **800/322-2981** or 801/378-2981.

WHERE TO STAY

In addition to what's listed below, there are several chain and franchise motels in the Provo area: **Best Western Columbian,** 70 E. 300 South, Provo, UT 84606 (☎ 800/321-0055 or 801/373-8973), with rates of $43 to $68 double; **Best Western Cotton Tree Inn,** 2230 N. University Pkwy., Provo, UT 84604 (☎ 800/662-6886 or 801/373-7044), with rates of $70 to $75 double; **Motel 6,** 1600 S. University Ave. (I-15 exit 266), Provo, UT 84601 (☎ 801/375-5064), with rates of $38 to $40 double; **Provo Days Inn,** 1675 N. 200 West (I-15 exit 272, then east 3 miles), Provo, UT 84604 (☎ 800/DAYS-INN or 801/375-8600), with rates of $55 to $80 double; and **Super 8 Motel,** 1288 S. University Ave. (I-15 exit 266), Provo, UT 84601 (☎ 801/375-8766), with rates of $50 to $55 double.

Rates may be higher during Brigham Young University special events, and rooms can be very scarce at graduation time. Tax added to lodging bills is just over 9%. Pets are not allowed unless otherwise noted.

Fairfield Inn Marriott/Provo

East Bay Business Park, 1515 S. University Ave. (exit 266 off I-15), Provo, UT 84601. ☎ **800/228-2800** or 801/377-9500. Fax 801/377-9591. 72 rms, 6 suites. A/C TV TEL. Summer $55–$85 double, $99–$115 suite; higher for special events, but generally lower in the winter. Rates include continental breakfast. AE, DC, DISC, MC, V.

Every spacious room at the Fairfield Inn contains rich wood furnishings, comfortable upholstered chairs, and a well-lit desk; telephones have modem ports. Regular rooms have one queen, one king, or two double beds; extended king rooms offer a king bed plus a couch that pulls out into a bed, a microwave oven, and small refrigerator. The two-room suites have one king or two doubles in the bedroom, plus a hide-a-bed couch in the living area; they're equipped with a microwave, refrigerator, small sink, and two TVs.

Provo Park Hotel

101 W. 100 North, Provo, UT 84601. ☎ **800/777-7144** or 801/377-4700. Fax 801/377-4708. 333 units. A/C TV TEL. $99–$114 double. AE, CB, DC, DISC, MC, V.

This highly-rated high-rise hotel in downtown Provo provides comfortable—even luxurious—accommodations, with splendid views (especially from the upper floors) and all the amenities you might want. Both public areas and rooms are handsomely appointed, decorated primarily in light earth tones, with attractively upholstered seating. Some in-room refrigerators are available. Facilities include indoor and outdoor heated pools, a whirlpool, a sauna, and a fitness center. The hotel's two restaurants serve three meals daily, including room service; there's also a gift shop, coin-operated laundry, and free covered parking, with a height limit of 6'9".

Travelodge

124 S. University Ave. (I-15 exit 266), Provo, UT 84601. ☎ **800/578-7878** or 801/373-1974. Fax 801/373-1974 ext. 145. 60 rms. A/C TV TEL. $35–$65 double. AE, DISC, MC, V.

This basic, two-story motel offers rooms with queen or king beds, some with two doubles. Rooms may be a bit cramped, but are well appointed, with in-room coffee, walk-in closet, and a lighted dressing table. Some rooms have a tub/shower combination, some shower only. Five spacious three-bed family units sleep up to six persons each.

In Springville

Victorian Inn Bed & Breakfast

94 W. 200 South, Springville, UT 84663. ☎ **888/489-0737** or 801/489-0737. Fax 801/ 489-8875. 8 units, including 2 suites. A/C TV TEL. $75–$130 double. Rates include breakfast. AE, DISC, MC, V.

Located in the historic Kearns Hotel, this lovely B&B is a favorite of honeymooners and anniversary celebrants, but retirees and business travelers are also drawn by the mix of Victorian ambiance and modern amenities. One room boasts a double bed from the original hotel, built in 1910; the rest have queen beds. Suites have TVs in both the living room and bedroom; five rooms have whirlpool tubs; and all are decorated in grand Victorian style with a mixture of antiques and reproductions, such as marble-topped dressers and hand-carved beds. Breakfast is served in what used to be the parlor, which still has its original stained-glass windows.

WHERE TO DINE

Provo is a very conservative, family-oriented city, and many restaurants do not serve alcohol. The tax added to dining bills totals just over 7%.

La Dolce Vita

61 N. 100 East. ☎ **801/373-8482.** Reservations taken for large parties only. Main courses $6.50–$13 dinner, $4–$13 lunch. AE, DISC, MC, V. Mon–Thurs 11am–10pm; Fri 11am– 10:30pm; Sat 4–10:30pm. From I-15, take exit 268 and follow Center St. east to 100 East; turn left (north) to the restaurant. NEAPOLITAN/ITALIAN.

Giovanni Della Corte was born in Naples, where he began his restaurant career at the age of 12. In 1984, he moved his family to Utah and opened La Dolce Vita, where he continues to serve fine Italian dinners complete with salad and warm homemade breads. The outside is unprepossessing, but once you cross the threshold you'll feel as though you've just stepped into an Italian cafe.

You can choose from a variety of pastas, pizzas, and calzones. The homemade sauces are thick and subtly seasoned. Portions are large, but try to save room for one of the special desserts: spumoni, Amaretto or chocolate mousse cake, or tiramisu. Soft drinks, beer, wine, cappuccino, and espresso are served.

Magelby's

1675 N. 200 West, Village Green (behind Days Inn). ☎ **801/374-6249.** Reservations for 6 or more. Main courses $13–$21.95 dinner, $6.95–$10.95 lunch. AE, DISC, MC, V. Mon–Thurs 11am–10pm; Fri till 11pm (dinner service starts at 4pm); Sat 4–11pm. From I-15, take exit 272 and follow Utah 265 for 5 miles. STEAK/SEAFOOD.

This quietly elegant dining room has lace curtains at the windows, upholstered chairs at the tables, quiet booths, and decorative touches including antiques, collectibles, and original artwork. The house specialty is Black Angus rib eye smothered with sautéed mushrooms and onions. Also popular are Magelby's lightly breaded gourmet shrimp, blackened chicken, fresh fish, and prime rib. The most popular of the homemade desserts is Lenora's Famous Deep Dish Apple Pie. The locally popular all-you-can-eat buffet on Friday and Saturday evenings from 5:15 to 9:15pm features roast beef, roast ham, and all kinds of side dishes; the cost is $18.95. No alcohol is served.

Sensuous Sandwich

163 W. Center St. ☎ **801/377-9244.** Sandwiches "by the inch," $1.99 (4")–$8.79 (24"). No credit cards. Mon–Sat 10:30am–8pm. From I-15, take exit 268 and follow Center St. east. SANDWICHES.

You can eat at one of the few tables at this speedy sandwich shop, or take your selection with you. All sandwiches come with the usual condiments, including a spicy brown mustard and horseradish, as well as extras like olives, avocados, green peppers, sprouts, and cheese. Top-of-the-line is, of course, the Sensuous Sandwich, with ham, turkey, roast beef, and jack cheese. They also offer pastrami, crab, chicken breast, and tuna. No alcohol is served.

PROVO AFTER DARK
PERFORMING ARTS & MOVIE THEATERS

Brigham Young University Theatre, on the BYU campus, offers a variety of performances year-round (☎ 801/378-4322).

From summer through early fall you can see live musical productions under the stars at the **SCERA Shell Outdoor Theatre,** 699 S. State St., in SCERA Park, Orem (☎ 801/225-2560). The season usually includes five locally produced Broadway musicals, plus a variety of concerts, ranging from pop to country to classical, and a children's theater program.

The **SCERA Showhouse,** 745 S. State St., Orem (☎ 801/225-2560), is a family-oriented movie theater that shows first-run G- and PG-rated films.

NIGHTLIFE

Provo is not a drinker's town; virtually the entire nightlife scene is geared toward families. None of the following clubs serve alcohol.

Johnny B's Comedy Club, 177 W. 300 South (☎ 801/377-6910), is a popular place for stand-up comedy. Shows start at 9pm Thursday, and 8pm and 10pm on Friday and Saturday. Cover charge is $6.

For local musical entertainment, try **Mama's Cafe,** 840 N. 700 East (☎ 801/373-1525 or 801/371-8452 for the Hot Line). The entertainment starts around 9pm and goes to about 11:30pm.

For dancing, try **Club Omni,** 153 W. Center St. (☎ 801/375-0011), open Tuesday to Saturday from 9pm to 1am. Wednesday is ladies' night and Thursday is country night. Cover is $5.

6 Timpanogos Cave National Monument

This national monument is actually comprised of three caves—Hansen, Middle, and Timpanogos—linked together by man-made tunnels. Martin Hansen discovered the first cavern in 1887 while tracking a mountain lion. The other two were reported in the early 1920s, and the connecting tunnels were constructed in the 1930s. The caves are filled with 47 kinds of cave formations, from stalactites and stalagmites to draperies and helictites. They're not easy to reach, but the beauty and variety of the caves make them worth the climb.

JUST THE FACTS

The monument is open from mid-May to October, daily from 7am to 5:30pm. The caves close in the winter because snow and ice make the access trail too hazardous.

GETTING THERE/ACCESS POINTS Timpanogos Cave National Monument is 20 miles from Provo and 35 miles from Salt Lake City. From Salt Lake City, head south on I-15 to exit 287, and east on Utah 92 to the visitor center parking lots. From Provo, follow U.S. 89 north to Utah 146 north, and then east onto Utah 92 to the visitor center, which is on the south side of the road. The road through American Fork Canyon is narrow and winding, but quite lovely, so take your time.

INFORMATION & VISITOR CENTERS For information, contact **Timpanogos Cave National Monument** at R.R. 3, Box 200, American Fork, UT 84003-9800 (☎ **801/756-5239,** 801/756-1679 for reservations).

Parking at the visitor center is limited for large vehicles, such as motor homes over 20 feet. Although small, the visitor center offers a short film about the caves, plus a few explanatory displays, booklets, and postcards. You'll find a snack bar and gift shop next to the visitor center and two picnic areas located along the shady banks of the American Fork Creek. One is across from the visitor center; a larger one, with fire grills and rest rooms, is about a quarter mile west.

FEES & REGULATIONS   Cave tours are $6 for ages 16 to 61, $5 for ages 6 to 15, $3 for those 5 and under and for seniors over 61 with Golden Age Passports. Pets are not allowed on the trail or in the caves.

EXPLORING THE MONUMENT

The only way to see the caves is on a ranger-guided tour. You'll need to allow about 3 hours total: It's a 1 1/2-hour hike up to the cave, you'll spend an hour in the caves, and it's about a 30- to 45-minute hike back down. The tours are limited to 20 persons and often fill up early in the morning, so it's best to call ahead and reserve your space with a credit card. The temperature inside the caves is around 45° (about the same as a refrigerator), so bring a jacket or sweatshirt.

THE HIKE TO THE CAVES

The change in elevation between the visitor center and the cave entrance is 1,065 feet, and the steep trail is 1 1/2 miles long; it's a physically demanding walk, but quite rewarding. The trail is not navigable by either wheelchairs or strollers and should not be attempted by anyone with breathing, heart, or walking difficulties. You'll need good walking shoes, and it's wise to carry water and maybe even a snack.

This is a self-guided hike, so you can travel at your own pace, stopping at the benches along the way to rest and enjoy the views of the canyon, the Wasatch Range, and Utah Valley. A trail guide, available at the visitor center, will help you identify the wildflowers growing amid the Douglas fir, white fir, maple, and oak trees. You'll also spot chipmunks, ground squirrels, lizards, and a myriad of birds along the way. Rest rooms are available when you reach the cave entrance, so you can refresh yourself before your cave tour begins.

TOURING THE CAVES

The ranger-guided tour of the caves is along a surfaced, well-lit, and fairly level route. You'll enter at the natural entrance to Hansen Cave and continue through Hansen, Middle, and Timpanogos Caves. Nature decorated the limestone chambers with delicately colored stalactites, stalagmites, draperies, graceful flowstone, and the helictites for which the caves are famous, all in soft greens, reds, yellows, and white. The huge cave formation of linked stalactites in the Great Heart of Timpanogos is impressive, and the profusion of bizarre, brilliant white helictites in the Chimes Chamber of Timpanogos is stunning. Mirrorlike cave pools reflect the formations.

You'll need high-speed film or a flash if taking photos; tripods are not allowed. Remember that the formations are fragile and easily damaged by merely the touch of your hand; the oils from your skin will change their chemical makeup immediately.

Dinosaurs & Natural Wonders in Utah's Northeast Corner

10

Utah has more than its share of natural treasures, with Zion and Bryce Canyon national parks springing to mind first—and drawing ever-increasing crowds. But tucked away in the state's far northeastern corner, more rugged and less accessible, lies a playground of great scenic beauty, filled with fascinating historic (and prehistoric) sites. And you won't have to fight throngs of tourists here: This land where the dinosaurs once roamed is still relatively undiscovered and un-spoiled.

1 The Mirror Lake Highway & the Uinta Mountains

Just east of Park City lies the tiny town of Kamas. It's not much of a destination in itself, but here begins one of the loveliest drives in Utah, a route filled with gorgeous Alpine scenery.

Utah 150 (the **Mirror Lake Highway**) begins here and ascends into the pine-covered Uinta Mountains before heading into Wyoming. The road is open only from mid-June to mid-October, and the national forest campgrounds along the route are a popular destination for Utahns. Among the best-known scenic drives in the region, this route offers splendid views of towering peaks, virgin pine and spruce forests, and lush meadows carpeted with wildflowers as it climbs to Bald Mountain Pass (elevation 10,678 feet). Trailheads branch off from the road and head into the backcountry.

Along the way you'll pass a seemingly infinite string of blue-ribbon trout streams and crystal-clear Alpine lakes. Just bring a good supply of flies and try your luck—cutthroat and brook trout are fairly jumping out of the water.

Much of the route follows the Provo River; 24 miles from Kamas, you might want to stop to view the beautiful terraced cascades of **Upper Provo River Falls.**

The highway also passes a good number of developed campsites. The largest of these is the **Mirror Lake Campground,** with 85 sites in a lovely pine-forest setting on the lake. Located about 31 miles into the drive, it offers trout fishing, hiking trails, and picnicking. The campgrounds further along the drive tend to be less crowded.

Before starting out, check with the **Kamas Ranger District** office, 50 E. Center St. (☎ 435/783-4338), which provides detailed maps and information on hiking, camping, road conditions, and more.

East of the Mirror Lake Highway, the Uinta Mountains, the only major range in the continental United States that runs east to west, are the major feature of northeastern Utah's landscape. The **High Uintas Wilderness Area** remains wild and unspoiled, a refuge for bighorn sheep, elk, moose, mule deer, eagles, osprey, owls, and beaver. Tiny towns and lonely highways surround the preserve, making it accessible for the hikers, campers, and anglers who come to enjoy this region's summer beauty. The wilderness area itself is closed to wheeled vehicles (although horses are allowed on many trails); you do not need a permit to hike and explore the backcountry, but for safety's sake it's a good idea to register at the trailheads. A good reference for backpackers is *The Hiker's Guide to Utah* (Falcon Press), which describes several outings in greater detail.

2 Vernal: Gateway to the Region's Top Recreational Areas

A perfect base for exploring Dinosaur National Monument (which is only 20 miles from town) and Ashley National Forest, Vernal is the largest town in the region. You'll find all the outfitters and services you might need here, as well as a few attractions that serve as a good introduction to the compelling geologic and natural history of the surrounding region.

ESSENTIALS

GETTING THERE   From Heber City, U.S. 40 leads east, past Strawberry Reservoir (there's world-class fishing here if you have time to stop—see chapter 9) and through Duchesne and Roosevelt, each of which have a few motels, restaurants, and services, before leading to Vernal (158 miles from Heber City).

From I-70, take exit 156 west of Green River and follow U.S. 6/191 north 68 miles through Price and Helper (see chapter 16), branching northeast above Helper to follow U.S. 191 for 44 beautiful mountainous miles to Duchesne. Then take U.S. 40 east for 58 miles to Vernal.

Skywest/Delta (☎ 800/453-9417 or 435/789-7263) offers several flights daily from Salt Lake City to the Vernal airport (☎ 435/789-3400), located about 1¹/₂ miles southeast of the center of Vernal.

VISITOR INFORMATION   Information on area lodging, dining, and recreational facilities can be obtained from the **Dinosaurland Travel Board,** 25 E. Main St., Vernal, UT 84078 (☎ 800/477-5558 or 435/789-6932).

GETTING AROUND   Car rentals are available at the airport from **Avis** (☎ 800/331-1212 or 435/789-7264); and in town from **Utah Motor Co.** (☎ 435/789-0455) and **Allsave Car Rental** (☎ 435/789-4531). Travel trailers can be rented from **B&D RV Sales and Service** (☎ 435/789-1970).

Local transportation is available around the clock from **T-Rex Taxi** (☎ 435/790-7433); **Wilkins Bus Lines** (☎ 435/789-2476) provides shuttle services and tours.

SPECIAL EVENTS   The **Flaming Gorge Fishing Derby** takes place in May. The **Outlaw Trail Festival** runs from mid-June through July and features a historical outdoor musical, storytelling, trail rides, a western art show, and a parade. Call ☎ 800/477-5558 for details. Cowboys test their mettle in July at the **Dinosaur Roundup Rodeo;** call ☎ 800/421-9635 for details. August sees the **Uintah County Fair,** and in September there's the **Labor Day Celebration and Festival of Lights** at Flaming Gorge.

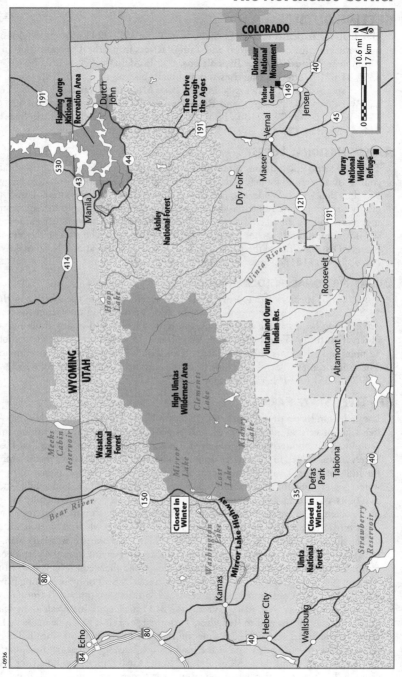

COLORADO

Dinosaur National Monument

Visitor Center

Flaming Gorge National Recreation Area

Dutch John

The Drive Through the Ages

Jensen

Vernal

Maeser

Ashley National Forest

Dry Fork

Ouray National Wildlife Refuge

Manila

Meeks Cabin Reservoir

Hoop Lake

WYOMING
UTAH

Uinta River

Roosevelt

High Uintas Wilderness Area

Clements Lake

Kidney Lake

Uintah and Ouray Indian Res.

Wasatch National Forest

Mirror Lake

Lost Lake

Altamont

Bear River

Mirror Lake Highway

Closed In Winter

Washington Lake

Defas Park

Closed In Winter

Tabiona

Strawberry Reservoir

Kamas

Uinta National Forest

Echo

Heber City

Wallsburg

10.6 mi
17 km

N

I-0936

GETTING OUTSIDE

Hatch River Expeditions, 55 E. Main St. (☎ 800/342-8243 or 435/789-4316), offers rafting trips on the Green and Yampa Rivers in nearby Dinosaur National Monument. **Dinosaur River Expeditions,** 550 E. Main St. (☎ 800/247-6197 or 435/781-0717), offers rafting trips and mountain-bike tours.

Raft and boat rentals are available from **Blue Mountain Marine,** 2217 N. Vernal Ave. (☎ 435/789-5661), and **River Runners' Transport & Rentals,** 126 S. 1500 West (☎ 435/781-1180). Fishing equipment is available from **Basin Sports,** 511 W. Main St. (☎ 435/789-2199).

ASHLEY NATIONAL FOREST

This vast forest encompasses more than a million acres of the beautiful mountain country near Vernal; in fact, Flaming Gorge National Recreation Area (see below) and the High Uintas Wilderness (see above) actually lie within the forest. Throughout the area you'll find numerous opportunities for backpacking, trout fishing, camping, cross-country skiing, and other activities. **Kings Peak,** Utah's tallest mountain, sits in the forest and reaches a height of over 13,000 feet. The staff at the **Vernal Ranger District** office of the Ashley National Forest, in town at 355 N. Vernal Ave. (☎ **435/789-1181;** open weekdays), can provide information.

OURAY NATIONAL WILDLIFE REFUGE

Hundreds of species of migratory birds and waterfowl make their home in this 11,827-acre wetlands refuge, which lies south of Vernal along the Green River. A driving loop begins at the information center; you'll also find hiking trails and an observation tower. To get there from Vernal, take U.S. 40 west out of town about 12 miles and turn left (south) onto Utah 88 for about 13 miles to the refuge entrance. The visitor center is less than a mile from the entrance. Call ☎ **435/545-2522** or 435/789-0351 for further information.

RED FLEET STATE PARK

Located 10 miles north of Vernal at 4335 North U.S. 191, this scenic park—it looks like a junior version of Lake Powell—offers good fishing, boating, swimming, and camping, plus about 200 well-preserved dinosaur tracks. The 650-acre Red Fleet Reservoir was named for three large deep-red sandstone rock formations that resemble the hulls of ships. You'll encounter sandy beaches, rock cliffs, and plenty of open water; good fishing for rainbow and brown trout, bluegill, and bass; and wildlife such as rabbits, ground squirrels, mule deer, and the occasional bobcat. On chilly mornings, golden eagles are sometimes spotted sunning themselves on rock outcroppings; other birds that frequent the park include hawks, vultures, owls, and bluebirds.

The dinosaur tracks, which are about 200 million years old, are on a large slab of rock that slants down into the water, located across the reservoir from the park's boat ramp. The greatest number of tracks can be seen when the water level is low, from late summer through winter. You can reach the tracks by boat or by swimming (wear a life jacket so you can return easily), or via a 1 1/2-mile hike (one-way) from a Bureau of Land Management road. To reach the BLM road, continue north along U.S. 191 1 mile past the turnoff to Red Fleet. Turn right (east) just past mile marker 212, cross a cattle guard, and drive 2.3 miles on the paved road to the trailhead. This is just a small turn-out with a sign at the trail; a stock tank sits across the road, partly hidden by bushes and trees. Allow about 2 hours for the moderate hike over low, sandy hills. During winter, when the reservoir is frozen, it's a quick walk from the boat ramp across the ice to the tracks.

Park facilities include the boat ramp, fish-cleaning stations, an RV dump station, and a 38-site campground. Although the campground is essentially a parking lot, it does offer splendid panoramic views across the lake. There are also grassy areas for tents, plus tables and fire pits. You'll find modern rest rooms, but no showers or RV hookups. Call ☎ **435/789-4432** for further information, or 800/322-3770 for reservations. Camping costs $10; the day-use fee is $3 per vehicle. Gates are open daily from 6am to 10pm in summer, from 8am to 5pm in winter.

STEINAKER STATE PARK

Steinaker offers a sandy swimming beach, good fishing for rainbow trout and largemouth bass, and an attractive campground, just 7 miles north of Vernal at 4335 North U.S. 191. This reservoir, which covers 780 acres when full, is also popular with water-skiers and boating enthusiasts.

Those interested in seeing wildlife should watch for mule deer, jackrabbits, cottontails, ground squirrels, porcupines, and an occasional elk or bobcat. Migratory waterfowl are often seen in spring and fall, and the park also attracts American robins, pheasants, and golden eagles. The landscape is composed primarily of juniper and sagebrush, with cottonwoods and aspen trees near the lake. Spring usually brings out an abundance of wildflowers, such as Indian paintbrush, larkspur, and sego lily. There are several unmarked hiking trails—ask a ranger for directions—and additional hiking opportunities on property managed by the Bureau of Land Management nearby.

Facilities include a boat ramp, fish-cleaning station, and RV dump station. The tree-shaded campground contains 31 sites and modern rest rooms, but no showers or RV hookups. Picnic tables, barbecue grills, and fire pits are available. Call ☎ **435/ 789-4432** for further information, or 800/322-3770 for reservations. Camping costs $10; the day-use fee is $3 per vehicle. Gates are open daily from 7am to 10pm in summer, from 8am to 5pm in winter.

SEEING THE SIGHTS IN TOWN

Daughters of Utah Pioneers Museum

2nd South St. at 5th West St. Free admission. Memorial Day–Labor Day Mon–Sat 1–7pm. Closed rest of year.

This small museum offers a fine display of pioneer relics and a history of the settling of the area.

Utah Field House of Natural History State Park

235 E. Main St. ☎ **435/789-3799.** Daily Memorial Day–Labor Day 9am–9pm; Labor Day–Memorial Day 9am–5pm. Admission $1.50 for those 16 and older, $1 for kids from 6 to 15, free for children under 6; maximum charge of $6 for families.

This park gives visitors a close-up look at a huge dinosaur skeleton, plus exhibits on paleontology, geology, and Fremont and Ute culture. Kids will love its ✪ **Dinosaur Garden,** with 17 life-size models of dinosaurs and other prehistoric creatures in a delightful garden that simulates the dinosaurs' actual habitat. You'll also find a picnic area (but no camping) and an attached gift shop that carries dinosaur-related souvenirs and books.

Western Heritage Museum

Western Park, 300 E. 200 South. ☎ **435/789-7399.** Fax 435/789-9210. Free admission, donations accepted. Memorial Day–Labor Day Mon–Sat 9am–6pm; rest of year Mon–Fri 9am–5pm.

There are NO dinosaurs here. Rather, this is one of the country's best collections of Fremont Indian artifacts plus some from the Anasazi and Ute. The museum also features changing art exhibits and historic photos, wagons from the late 1800s and early

1900s, a barber shop, country store, and other items from some of the early white pioneers in the area. A permanent exhibit on gilsonite—you'll have to visit to find out what that mineral is—was opened in 1997. The only commercial deposits of gilsonite are found in the Uintah Basin of Utah and Colorado.

THE DRIVE THROUGH THE AGES

One of the most scenic drives in the state is the Flaming Gorge–Uintas Scenic Byway—U.S. 191 from Vernal up to Manila and Flaming Gorge (see later this chapter); it was one of America's first designated national scenic byways. The 67-mile route climbs through foothills covered with pine and juniper trees and passes through the national forest and into the Uinta Mountains; signs along the way explain the evolution of the intriguing geologic formations you'll see. Near Flaming Gorge, you'll pass the billion-year-old exposed core of the Uintas. Stop at some of the many turnouts for scenic views, short walks, and wildlife viewing (you might spot bighorn sheep, elk, mule deer, and moose, especially in the spring).

ACCOMMODATIONS

There are about a dozen motels in town. Chain and franchise operations include the **Best Western Dinosaur Inn,** 251 E. Main St., Vernal, UT 84078 (☎ 800/528-1234 or 435/789-2660; fax 435/789-2467), with rates from $72 to $100 double in the summer and $45 to $65 double in the winter; **Weston Days Inn,** 260 W. Main St. (☎ 800/382-1011 or 435/789-1011; fax 435/789-0172), charging $48 to $62 double; and the **Econo Lodge,** 311 E. Main St. (☎ 800/424-4777 or 435/789-2000; fax 435/789-0947), charging $45 to $58 double. Room tax adds about 9%.

Split Mountain Motel

1015 East U.S. 40, Vernal, UT 84078. ☎ **435/789-9020.** Fax 435/789-9023. 40 rms. A/C TV TEL. $45–$54 double. AE, CB, DC, DISC, MC, V. Small pets allowed with prior approval.

This small, mom-and-pop operation is comfortable, attractively furnished, and exceptionally well maintained. Rooms are light colored with wood-grain furnishings; many are decorated with photos of the area. Most have tub-shower combos, although some have showers only. There's cable TV and free morning coffee, but no swimming pool. A restaurant and lounge are within a half block.

CAMPING

Among area campgrounds with full RV hookups and hot showers is **Campground Dina & RV Park,** 930 N. Vernal Ave. (☎ **435/789-2148**), with 95 sites, including grassy tent sites, with rates in the $18 to $20 range.

Both **Red Fleet** and **Steinaker State Parks** (see above) have camping, but no RV hookups.

DINING

Bakeries and delicatessens can be found at **IGA,** 575 W. Main St. (☎ 435/789-2001), and **Smith's,** 1080 W. Main St. (☎ 435/789-7135).

Betty's Cafe

416 W. Main St. ☎ **435/781-2728.** Main courses $7.97–$9.95 dinner, $3.50–$5.25 lunch, $3–$6.25 breakfast. No credit cards. Mon–Sat 6am–10pm; Sun 6am–noon. AMERICAN.

This simple, down-home cafe serves well-prepared homemade food. Breakfast, which includes all the usual offerings, is served until 2pm; lunch includes sandwiches, burgers, and specials; and dinner offers such choices as chicken-fried steak, liver and onions, roast beef, and hamburger steak. No alcoholic beverages are served.

Crack'd Pot Restaurant & Lounge

1089 E. Main St. ☎ **435/781-0133.** Reservations required for large parties. Main courses $8.34–$26.04 dinner, $3.59–$9.74 lunch. AE, DISC, MC, V. Mon–Sat 11am–10pm, later in summer. ECLECTIC.

This popular restaurant, with its mood lighting and solid wood tables and booths, claims to be the only place in Utah where you can get an ostrich fillet or ostrich fajitas. The most popular plate is the chicken-fried steak; the BBQ pork ribs are very good; and the Mexican food is the spiciest in the state—the owner is from New Mexico, so she knows what spicy is. Other offerings include sandwiches, burgers, steak, fish, seafood, and pasta, plus daily specials and a children's menu. Full liquor service is available.

3 Dinosaur National Monument

In some ways this park is two separate experiences: a look at the lost world of dinosaurs on one side, and a scenic wonderland of colorful rock, deep river canyons, and a forest of Douglas fir on the other.

About 150 million years ago, this region was a lush land of ferns, conifers, grasses, ponds, and rivers. This made it a suitable habitat for dinosaurs, including vegetarians such as Diplodocus, Apatosaurus, and Stegosaurus; and the sharp-toothed carnivores, such as Allosaurus, that hunted down their vegetarian cousins. When these huge creatures died, most of their skeletons decayed and disappeared, but in at least one spot floodwaters washed dinosaur carcasses into the bottom of a river. Here they were preserved in sand and covered with sediment, creating a sort of time capsule for today's visitor—the largest quarry of Jurassic-period dinosaur bones ever discovered.

But visitors who limit their trip to the Dinosaur Quarry, fascinating as it is, miss quite a bit. Encompassing 325 square miles of stark canyons at the confluence of two rivers, the monument also offers hiking trails, pioneer homesteads, thousand-year-old rock art, spectacular panoramic vistas, great wildlife-watching opportunities, and the thrill of white-water rafting.

The Yampa, Green, and other smaller rivers bring life-giving water into the area, creating micro-climates that support hanging gardens of mosses and ferns, cottonwoods, and even an occasional Douglas fir—all just yards from the predominant landscape of sagebrush, cactus, and dwarfed piñon and juniper trees. Wildlife includes species that can survive the harsh extremes of the high desert climate—bighorn sheep, coyote, rabbits, and snakes—but you'll also find mule deer, beaver, and porcupine along the river banks. Birds occasionally spotted in the area include the peregrine falcon, sage grouse, and Canada goose.

JUST THE FACTS

GETTING THERE/ACCESS POINTS   Situated partly in Utah and partly in Colorado, Dinosaur National Monument is accessible via two main roads—one from each state—that don't connect inside the monument.

The main **visitor center** and the Dinosaur Quarry are in Utah, 34 miles northwest of monument headquarters and the entrance to the Colorado side of the park. The visitor center and quarry are 20 miles east of Vernal (195 miles east of Salt Lake City). To get there, take U.S. 40 from either the east or west to Jensen, Utah (where you can gas up your car or pick up something to eat), and drive 7 miles north on Utah 149 into the park.

To get to the Colorado entrance to the park, take U.S. 40 to the visitor center and monument headquarters, 2 miles east of the community of Dinosaur.

Several other monument entrances exist, all without visitor centers: At the far eastern edge of the monument off U.S. 40, an entry road leads to Deerlodge Park (open in the summer only); at the northern tip, off Colo. 318, a road goes to the Gates of Ledore; just inside the Utah border at Jones Hole Fish Hatchery, a road leads into the park via the Jones Hole Road from Vernal; and at the Rainbow Park section, you'll find a park entry road off Island Park Road (impassable when wet) from the monument's western edge.

INFORMATION & VISITOR CENTERS   To receive a copy of the national monument's color brochure and other information, contact **Dinosaur National Monument,** 4545 East U.S. 40, Dinosaur, CO 81610 (☎ **970/374-3000**). In addition, the nonprofit **Dinosaur Nature Association,** 1291 East U.S. 40, Vernal, UT 84078 (☎ **800/845-3466** or 435/789-8807; fax 435/781-1304), offers numerous publications, maps, posters, and videos on the park and its geology, wildlife, history, and especially its dinosaurs. Information on area lodging, dining, and recreational facilities can be obtained from the **Dinosaurland Travel Board,** 25 E. Main St., Vernal, UT 84078 (☎ **800/477-5558** or 435/789-6932).

As noted above and discussed below, a visitor center with exhibits is located at the quarry (☎ **435/789-2115**). Attached is a shop where you can buy books, hiking and driving guides, maps, and, of course, model dinosaurs. Administrative offices and a small visitor center with a short slide program (☎ **970/374-2216**) are located about 2 miles east of the town of Dinosaur, Colorado, at the intersection of U.S. 40 and Harpers Corner Drive.

The visitor centers are open daily year-round, except on Thanksgiving, Christmas, and New Year's Day.

FEES, BACKCOUNTRY PERMITS, REGULATIONS & SAFETY   The admission fee, charged only at the Utah entrance as of this writing, is $10 per vehicle, and $5 per person for those on foot, motorcycles, bicycles, or in buses. If you want to camp in the backcountry, you must obtain a permit, available free from park rangers.

Regulations here forbid damaging or taking anything, particularly fossils and other natural, historical, or archaeological items. Off-road driving is not permitted. Dogs must be leashed at all times; pets are not allowed in buildings, on trails, more than 100 feet from developed roads, or on river trips.

Rangers warn that the rivers are not safe for swimming or wading; the water is cold and the current is stronger than it appears.

SEASONS & AVOIDING THE CROWDS   Summers are both the busiest and hottest time of the year at Dinosaur National Monument, with daytime temperatures often soaring into the upper 90s. Winters are a lot quieter but can be cold, with fog, snow, and temperatures below zero. The best times to visit are spring (although you should be prepared for rain showers) and fall (perhaps the very best time, when the cottonwood trees turn a brilliant gold).

RANGER PROGRAMS   Rangers present a variety of activities in the summer, including evening campfire programs; check the schedules posted at either visitor center.

SEEING THE HIGHLIGHTS

Those with only a short amount of time should make their first stop the **Dinosaur Quarry.** It's accessible only from the Utah side and is the only place in the monument where you can see dinosaur bones. It contains the remains of many long-vanished species, including fossils of sea creatures two to three times older than any land dinosaurs. This is believed to be one of the world's most concentrated and accessible deposits of the fossilized remains of dinosaurs, crocodiles, turtles, and clams. The quarry—which looks like a long slab of frozen pudding with bones sticking out of it—is enclosed in the visitor center, along with exhibits that help make sense of this prehistoric zoo. There's one section of bones you can actually reach out and touch, and models show what paleontologists believe these dinosaurs looked like when they still had their skin. Park naturalists are on hand to discuss what is known about dinosaurs, and workers can sometimes be seen carefully cleaning and examining fossils in the laboratory.

After spending about an hour in the quarry, drive the scenic **Tour of the Tilted Rocks,** which takes an hour or two. Then, if time remains, or if you're heading east into Colorado anyway, take another few hours to drive the very beautiful **Harpers Corner Drive.** See below for details.

EXPLORING DINOSAUR NATIONAL MONUMENT BY CAR

Scenic drives in both the Utah and Colorado sections of the park allow motorists to see spectacular scenery in relative solitude. Brochures for each of the following drives are available (50¢ each) at the visitor centers.

From the Quarry Visitor Center on the Utah side of the park, the **Tour of the Tilted Rocks** along Cub Creek Road is a 24-mile round-trip drive that's suitable for most passenger cars. This route takes you to 1,000-year-old rock art left by the Fremont people, a pioneer homestead, and views of nearby mountains and the Green River. Watch for prairie dogs both alongside and on the road. Although mostly paved, the last 2 miles of the road are dirt, narrow, and may be dusty or muddy. Allow 1 to 2 hours.

For the best scenic views you'll have to drive to Colorado and take the **Harpers Corner Drive.** This paved, 62-mile round-trip drive has several overlooks offering panoramic views into the gorges carved by the Yampa and Green rivers, a look at the derby-shaped Plug Hat Butte, and close-ups of a variety of other colorful rock formations. The drive also provides access to the easy half-mile round-trip Plug Hat Nature Trail, and the moderately difficult 2-mile round-trip Harpers Corner Trail (see "Hiking," below), at the end of the road. Allow about 2 hours for the drive, more if you also plan to do some hiking.

SPORTS & ACTIVITIES

BOATING   To many, the best way to see this beautiful, rugged country is from the river, where you can admire the scenery while crashing through thrilling white water and floating over smooth, silent stretches. About a dozen outfitters are authorized to run the ✪ **Yampa and Green rivers** through the monument, offering trips ranging from 1 to 5 days, usually from mid-May through mid-September. Among companies providing river trips is **Hatch River Expeditions** in Vernal (☎ **800/342-8243** or 435/789-4316), with prices starting at $60 to $70 for a 1-day trip. Reservations are recommended. A complete list of authorized river-running companies is available from monument headquarters (see "Information & Visitor Centers," above).

FISHING   You'll catch mostly catfish in the Green and Yampa rivers, although there are also some trout. Several endangered species of fish—including the Colorado squawfish and humpback chub—must be returned unharmed to the water if caught. You'll need either Utah or Colorado fishing licenses (or both), depending on which side of the state line you're fishing.

HIKING   Because most visitors spend their time at the quarry and along the scenic drives, hikers willing to exert a bit of effort can discover spectacular and dramatic views of the colorful canyons and enjoy an isolated and quiet wilderness experience.

The best times for hiking are spring and fall, but even then, hikers should carry at least a gallon of water per person, per day.

In addition to several developed trails, experienced backcountry hikers with the appropriate maps can explore miles of unspoiled canyons and rock benches. Ask rangers about the numerous possibilities.

In the Utah section of the park, you'll find both solitude and colorful uplifted rocks along the **Sound of Silence Trail,** a difficult 2-mile hike that leaves Cub Creek Road about 2 miles east of the Dinosaur Quarry. Sweeping panoramic views can be had along the moderately difficult **Desert Voices Nature Trail,** a 2-mile round-trip self-guided nature trail in the Split Mountain area off Cub Creek Road.

Visitors to the Colorado side of the park enjoy the **Cold Desert Trail,** which begins at headquarters' visitor center. This quarter-mile easy nature trail offers a good introduction to the natural history of this arid environment.

Panoramic vistas await the hiker on the **Plug Hat Nature Trail,** a quarter-mile easy trail that introduces you to the interactions between plants and animals in the piñon juniper forest.

The very popular **Harpers Corner Trail** begins at the end of the Harpers Corner Scenic Drive. This 2-mile round-trip hike is moderately difficult and highly recommended for a magnificent view of the deep river canyons.

HORSEBACK RIDING   Half-hour guided trail rides are offered by **Cassidy Trail Rides,** based just outside the park's Utah entrance (☎ **435/789-9334**). Cost is about $8 per person.

CAMPING

The **Green River Campground,** 5 miles east of the Dinosaur Quarry within park boundaries, has 88 sites, modern rest rooms, drinking water, tables, and fireplaces, but no showers or RV hookups. Cost is $10 per night in the summer, and free in the winter when water is turned off and only pit toilets are available. Several smaller campgrounds with limited facilities are also available in the park; check with the visitor centers or superintendent's office.

4 Flaming Gorge National Recreation Area

Tucked away in the far northeast corner of Utah and stretching up into Wyoming, Flaming Gorge National Recreation Area was created entirely by man. A dam was built on the Green River for flood control, water storage, and the generation of electricity, but the wonderful by-product was the creation of a huge and gorgeous lake—some 91 miles long, with more than 350 miles of coastline—that has become one of the prime fishing and boating destinations of the region.

Here you'll find some of the best fishing in the West, well over 100 miles of hiking and mountain-biking trails, and hundreds of camp and picnic sites. It's a boater's paradise: Out on the water you'll see everything from kayaks and canoes to personal watercraft, ski and fishing boats, pontoons, and gigantic houseboats complete with everything (including the kitchen sink).

Named by Major John Wesley Powell during his exploration of the Green and Colorado Rivers in 1869, Flaming Gorge has a rugged, wild beauty that comes alive when the rising or setting sun paints the red rocks around the lake with a fiery, brilliant palette. It's a land of clear blue water, colorful rocks, tall cliffs, and dark forests, of hot summer sun and cold winter wind. It'll take more than a dam to tame Flaming Gorge.

JUST THE FACTS

Flaming Gorge National Recreation Area lies in the northeast corner of Utah, crossing into the southwest corner of Wyoming. The dam and main visitor center, in the southeast section of the national recreation area, are 41 miles north of Vernal (210 miles east of Salt Lake City via U.S. 40).

GETTING THERE   From Vernal and other points to the south, take U.S. 191 north to its intersection with Utah 44 at the southern edge of the reservoir. U.S. 191 goes up the east side of the reservoir, leading to the dam and the community of Dutch John; Utah 44 goes around the reservoir on the west side, eventually ending at the village of Manila. Both of these towns offer accommodations, restaurants, fuel, out-fitters, and other services.

From I-80 in Wyoming, follow U.S. 191 south around the reservoir's east side to the dam; or Wyo. 530 and Utah highways 43 and 44 to Manila and the west and south sides of the reservoir.

INFORMATION & VISITOR CENTERS   The recreation area is administered as part of the Ashley National Forest. For information, contact the **District Ranger,** Flaming Gorge National Recreation Area, USDA Forest Service, Box 279, Manila, UT 84046 (☎ **435/784-3445**). The **Flaming Gorge Natural History Association,** P.O. Box 188, Dutch John, UT 84023 (☎ **435/885-3305**), sells maps, books, and other publications.

The **Flaming Gorge Dam Visitor Center** (☎ **435/885-3135**), along U.S. 191 on the east side of the recreation area, is open daily year-round except Thanksgiving, Christmas, and New Year's Day. Here you'll find information on the geology, history, plants, and wildlife of the area; the construction of the dam; and facilities and recreation possibilities. You can talk with rangers about where to camp, hike, boat, and fish, and take a guided or self-guided tour of the dam and generating plant.

FEES & REGULATIONS   Admission to the recreation area is $2 for 1 day, $5 for up to 16 days, or $20 for an annual pass. Camping fees are additional (see "Camping," below). Administered by the U.S. Forest Service, regulations here are based mostly on common sense, aimed at preserving water quality and protecting the forest and historic sites. In addition, Utah and Wyoming fishing and boating regulations apply in those states' sections of the recreation area, and the appropriate fishing licenses are required. Dogs are not permitted in buildings and should be leashed at all times, but are allowed on hiking trails.

SEASONS & AVOIDING THE CROWDS   As one would expect, summer is the busy season at this major boating destination, when both the air and water are at their warmest. This is the best time to come for water sports, and with elevations from 5,600 feet to over 8,000 feet, it never gets as hot here as in many other parts of Utah. Although the summer is the busiest time of year, this remains a relatively undiscovered destination, and you will likely have no trouble finding campsites, lodging, or boat rentals. Hikers will enjoy the area in fall, and during the cold, snowy winter, it's popular with cross-country skiers and ice fishermen.

Impressions

The river enters the range by a flaring, brilliant red gorge, that may be seen from the north a score of miles away . . . . We name it Flaming Gorge.

—Explorer Major John Wesley Powell, May 26, 1869

EXPLORING FLAMING GORGE NATIONAL RECREATION AREA BY CAR

Numerous viewpoints are situated along U.S. 191 and Utah 44 in the Utah section of Flaming Gorge; especially dramatic is the **Red Canyon Overlook** on the southern edge, where a rainbow of colors adorns 1,000-foot-tall cliffs. In Wyoming, highways are further from the lake, offering few opportunities to see the river and its canyons.

Sheep Creek Canyon, south of Manila on the western side, has been designated a special geological area by the Forest Service because of its dramatically twisted and upturned rocks. A mostly paved 11-mile loop road cuts off from Utah 44, offering a half-hour tour of this beautiful, narrow canyon, with its lavish display of rocks that have eroded into intricate patterns, a process that began with the uplifting of the Uinta Mountains millions of years ago. This loop may be closed in the winter; check at the visitor center before heading out.

SPORTS & ACTIVITIES

BIKING   A number of mountain-biking trails provide splendid views of the recreation area's scenery, especially in the Utah section. Bikes are permitted in most of Flaming Gorge and adjacent Ashley National Forest, except in the High Uintas Wilderness, where all wheeled vehicles are prohibited. Bikes are also outlawed on a section of the Little Hole National Recreation Trail along the Green River below the dam, because of very heavy use by fishermen and hikers. Keep in mind that mountain bikers here often share trails with hikers and four-wheelers. A free mountain-biking brochure is available at visitor centers and at area businesses.

For an easy 3-mile round-trip ride to a scenic overlook offering a terrific view of the lake, try the **Bear Canyon–Bootleg Trail,** which starts just off U.S. 191 opposite Firefighters Memorial Campground, 3 miles south of the dam. **Death Valley Trail,** a moderately difficult 15-mile round-trip ride, offers good views of the Uinta Mountains and ends with a fine view of the lake from the top of Sheep Creek Hill. The trailhead is located along Utah 44, south of Manila, at milepost 16.5.

Mountain-bike rentals are available at Red Canyon Lodge (☎ **435/889-3759**), with rates of $8 for 1 hour, $15 for a half day, and $25 for a full day.

BOATING & HOUSEBOATING   Boaters get to enjoy a unique perspective of some memorable scenery, with magnificent fiery red canyons surrounding the lake in the Utah section, and the wide-open Wyoming badlands farther north.

Three marinas on ✪ **Lake Flaming Gorge** provide boat rentals, fuel, launching ramps, and boating and fishing supplies. **Cedar Springs Marina** (☎ 435/889-3795) is located 2 miles west of Flaming Gorge Dam; **Lucerne Valley Marina** (☎ 435/784-3483) is on the west side of the lake, 7 miles east of Manila; and **Buckboard Marina** (☎ 307/875-6927) is also on the west side of the lake, off Wyo. 530, 25 miles south of the town of Green River, Wyoming.

Nine boat ramps serve those who bring their own craft, while boat and water-ski rentals are available at the three marinas. Although types of boats and costs vary, a 14-foot fishing boat with a small outboard motor will cost from about $60 to $75 per day, a 19-foot ski boat with a powerful outboard motor will cost about $160 to $190 per day, and a 24-foot pontoon boat with a 50-horsepower outboard motor will cost from about $120 to $160 per day. Hourly rentals are also available. At Lucerne Valley Marina, three-person personal watercraft run about $175 per day, while a 36-foot houseboat costs about $625 for 3 nights during the summer, with discounts in spring and fall. Fuel is extra and damage deposits are required.

Boating is permitted on a 20-acre private lake at Red Canyon Lodge (just north of Utah 44 via Red Canyon Road; ☎ 435/889-3759), where you can rent canoes, rowboats, and paddleboats. Rates are $8 for 1 hour, $15 for a half day, and $25 for a full day.

FISHING   You might want to bring along a muscular friend if you plan to fish Lake Flaming Gorge, which is becoming famous as the place to catch record-breaking trout, such as the 51-pound, 8-ounce lake (Mackinaw) trout caught in 1988, the 26-pound, 2-ounce rainbow caught in 1979, or the 33-pound, 10-ounce brown caught in 1977. You'll also catch other cold-water species such as smallmouth bass and kokanee salmon. Fishing is popular year-round, although ice fishermen are warned to make sure the ice is strong enough to hold them. Utah and/or Wyoming fishing licenses are required and can be purchased at the three marinas (see "Boating & Houseboating," above) and local sporting-goods stores.

Cedar Springs and Lucerne Valley Marinas (see above) offer a variety of fishing guide services. Call for current rates. Also providing guided fishing trips on the lake, in a 28-foot sport fishing boat, is Bruce Parker of **Conquest Expeditions,** P.O. Box 487, Manila, UT 84046 (☎ 435/784-3370). His rates for a 4-hour fishing trip, with all equipment but not fishing licenses, are $225 for one or two people and $325 for three or four people. Rates for an 8-hour fishing trip are $400 for one or two people; $500 for three or four.

Trout fishing on the Green River below the dam is also outstanding. **Flaming Gorge Recreation Services,** based in Dutch John (☎ 435/885-3191), offers guided fishing trips for one or two people. A full-day float trip costs about $300; a half day costs $175. A guided walk-and-wade trip costs $225 for a full day or $150 for a half day. Rafts can be rented for about $35 per day, and camping gear, fishing supplies, groceries, and souvenirs are available. The company also provides transportation for anglers, their boats, and vehicles.

You'll also find two stocked lakes at Red Canyon Lodge (just north of Utah 44 via Red Canyon Road; ☎ 435/889-3759). The 20-acre lake is open to nonmotorized boats; the 17-acre lake is not open for boating. During the summer, Red Canyon Lodge offers on-site fly-fishing instruction (private lessons start at $25), as well as a multiday fly-fishing school (call for details).

HIKING   Many of the trails here offer spectacular, scenic views of the reservoir and its colorful canyons. Remember, though, that in most cases you'll be sharing the trail with mountain bikers, and in some cases horses and four-wheel-drive vehicles as well. Dogs are permitted on the trails, but must be leashed.

The **Canyon Rim Trail** runs 5 miles (one-way) from the Red Canyon Visitor Center to the Greendale Rest Area, which is located along Utah 44 1 mile northwest of the highway's intersection with U.S. 191. You can access the trail at either of those points or at Green's Lake or Canyon Rim Campgrounds. The trail wanders through a forest of Douglas fir and pine, with stops along the canyon rim providing outstanding views of the lake far below.

One trail popular with hikers is the **Little Hole National Recreation Trail,** which runs about 7 miles from the dam spillway downstream to Little Hole, where you'll find fishing platforms and picnic areas. The trail is easy to moderate and offers splendid vistas of the Green River, which appears to be a mere ribbon of emerald when seen from the cliffs above. It's also a good trail for bird-watchers, who may spot osprey in the summer and bald eagles in the winter.

Hikers can also use the mountain-biking trails listed above. A free hiking-trails brochure is available at the visitor centers.

HORSEBACK RIDING   Many of the more than 100 miles of trails in Flaming Gorge are open to riders. Guided rides are available from **Red Canyon Stables** at Red Canyon Lodge (just north of Utah 44 via Red Canyon Road; ☎ 435/889-3759), with prices starting at $12 for a 1-hour ride and $75 for a full day. Rates for children under 12 and seniors over 65 are slightly less. Overnight backcountry trips are also offered.

SWIMMING   Sometimes you've just got to dive right in, even though the water is pretty cold. Lake Flaming Gorge has two designated swimming beaches: Sunny Cove, just north of the dam, and Lucerne Beach, a mile west of Lucerne Campground. Neither has a lifeguard.

WILDLIFE VIEWING & BIRD WATCHING   This is one of the best places in Utah for ✪ **seeing a wide variety of wildlife.** Boaters out on the lake should watch for osprey, peregrine falcons, swifts, and swallows along the cliffs. Bighorn sheep are sometimes spotted clambering on the rocky cliffs on the north side of the lake in the spring and early summer. On land, watch for pronghorn antelope year-round along the west side of the lake, particularly in Lucerne Valley and even in the campground there. Hikers on the Little Hole National Recreation Trail should watch for a variety of birds, including bald eagles in the winter.

WINTER SPORTS   Ice fishing is popular, but check with rangers first on the ice conditions. Also popular from mid-January until the snow melts are cross-country skiing on groomed trails (an excellent way to see wildlife), snowshoeing, and snowmobiling. At Red Canyon Lodge (☎ 435/889-3759), you can rent cross-country skis for $10 per day.

MAN-MADE ATTRACTIONS
FLAMING GORGE DAM & POWER PLANT

Completed in 1963 at a cost of $50 million for the dam and another $65 million for the power plant, Flaming Gorge is part of the Colorado River Storage Project, which also includes Glen Canyon Dam on the Colorado River along the Arizona-Utah border, Navajo Dam on the San Juan River in New Mexico, and a series of three dams on the Gunnison River in Colorado. At full capacity the lake is 91 miles long and holds almost 4 million acre-feet of water. The dam, constructed in an arch shape for strength, is 1,285 feet long and stands some 450 feet tall; its three turbine generators can produce 152,000 kilowatts of electricity, enough to take care of the needs of 210,000 people.

The dam and power plant are open for free guided tours most of the year and self-guided tours daily year-round, except Thanksgiving, Christmas, and New Year's Day. Allow about 30 minutes; total round-trip walking distance is just under half a mile. Check at the visitor center for hours and times of guided tours. You'll walk along the crest of the dam, then take an elevator ride to the power plant below, where you'll see the inner workings of the hydroelectric plant, with its huge transformers, generators, and turbines.

SWETT RANCH HISTORIC SITE

This homestead, listed on the National Register of Historic Sites, was constructed by Oscar Swett starting in 1909, and contains two cabins, a five-room house, a meat house, a root cellar, sheds, a granary, and a barn, built and improved upon over the next 58 years. Swett and his wife, Emma, raised nine children here, running the 397-acre ranch using only horse and human muscle power, before selling the property in 1968. To get to the ranch, from Utah 44 take U.S. 191 north for a half mile and turn west (left) onto Forest Road 158, which you follow 1.5 miles to the ranch. The unpaved Forest Road is muddy when wet, and not recommended for large RVs or trailers at any time. The ranch is open Thursday through Monday from Memorial Day to Labor Day only. Admission is free.

UTE MOUNTAIN FIRE LOOKOUT TOWER

Built by the Civilian Conservation Corps in the mid-1930s, this was the first fire lookout tower in Utah, and the last one in operation in the state before being replaced by aircraft reconnaissance in the late 1960s. It offers a panoramic view of the Flaming Gorge area and Uinta Mountains.

The lookout tower is located off Utah 44 on the western side of the lake. Take the Sheep Creek Geologic Loop to Forest Road 221 (signs say Browne and Spirit Lakes), and go west 1 mile to Forest Road 5, which you follow south 1.5 miles to the tower. Forest Road 5 is not recommended for low-clearance vehicles. The historic tower is usually open weekends from Memorial Day to Labor Day.

CAMPING

U.S. Forest Service campgrounds are located throughout Flaming Gorge Recreation Area, and they range from primitive boat-in-only sites to modern facilities with showers (open in summer only) and flush toilets, but no RV hookups. Some are open year-round, and others in the summer only. Rates range from free for some of the primitive sites to $17 for the more developed campgrounds. Most sites cost $10 to $14. Dispersed forest camping (with no facilities) is free; check with park rangers for suggested locations. All campers, as well as other recreation-area users, must also pay the recreation-area use fee of $2 for 1 day, $5 for up to 16 days, or $20 for an annual pass.

Commercial campgrounds with full RV hookups are located in Vernal (see earlier this chapter). In Manila, you'll find a KOA campground (☎ **435/784-3184**), open from mid-April through October, that charges from $17 to $22 per night.

ACCOMMODATIONS

In addition to the lodging suggestions below, see the "Camping" and "Accommodations" sections in Vernal, above.

Flaming Gorge Lodge
155 Greendale, U.S. 191 (4 miles south of Flaming Gorge Dam), Dutch John, UT 84023. ☎ **435/889-3773.** Fax 435/889-3788. 45 units. A/C TV TEL. Mar–Oct $58–$110 double; Nov–Feb $45–$91 double. AE, DISC, MC, V.

Units here are either standard modern motel rooms or one-bedroom condominiums. Motel rooms have two double beds and an optional roll-away. Condominium units contain one queen-size bed, a single, and a hide-a-bed, plus a fully equipped kitchen. Facilities include a restaurant that serves three meals daily, a gas station, raft rentals, a liquor and convenience store, and a fly and tackle shop.

✪ Red Canyon Lodge
Just north of Utah 44 via Red Canyon Rd. within Flaming Gorge National Recreation Area (mailing address: P.O. Box 211145, Salt Lake City, UT 84121-8145). ☎ **435/889-3759.** 24 units. $45–$110 double. AE, DISC, MC, V. Closed Nov–Mar, except luxury cabins, which are available Sun–Thurs mid-Jan–Mar at reduced rates.

A variety of delightful cabins, some dating from the 1930s and remodeled in the 1990s, plus eight new ones built in 1996 and '97, offer a range of possibilities from rustic to luxurious. The most basic contain one queen-size bed and share a central bathhouse; simple cabins with private bath are also available. The top-of-the-line luxury units are beautifully appointed cabins with two queen beds in a separate bedroom, a hide-a-bed in the living room, full bath, vaulted ceilings, kitchenettes, and a covered porch. All cabins have free-standing wood stoves. The lodge offers two private lakes plus a free kids' fishing pond, tackle shop and fly-fishing instruction, mountain-bike rentals, hiking and mountain-biking trails, horseback rides (see "Sports & Activities," above), a restaurant (see below), and a convenience store. Pets are not permitted in the luxury units, but are allowed in the rustic cabins.

DINING

Red Canyon Lodge Dining Room

In Red Canyon Lodge, just north of Utah 44 via Red Canyon Rd. within Flaming Gorge National Recreation Area. ☎ **435/889-3759.** Reservations not accepted. Main courses $8–$18 dinner, $3–$9 breakfast and lunch items. AE, DISC, MC, V. Apr–Oct daily 7am–10pm; mid-Jan–Mar Fri noon–9pm, Sat 8am–9pm, Sun 8am–noon. Closed Nov–mid-Jan. AMERICAN.

You'll find a classic mountain-lodge atmosphere here, along with views of tall pines and a small lake. Popular among locals as well as visitors, the menu features steaks, chicken, pasta, fish, and prime rib. You'll also find standard American breakfasts, and burgers and sandwiches at lunch. Full liquor service is available.

Utah's Dixie & the Colorful Southwest Corner

11

Small lakes and big rocks, golf courses and ski areas, Shakespeare and the latest special effects—you'll find it all in the southwest corner of Utah, dubbed "Color Country" by the locals for its numerous and colorful rock formations. Another plus is the warm winter weather. The region's largest city, St. George, and its immediate surroundings are known as "Utah's Dixie" for its mild climate as well as its Civil War–era cotton growing. Although the cotton-growing days are long gone, hot summers and delightfully mild winters remain, making this region a terrific winter playground. Snow-weary Salt Lake City residents come here every year, seeking an escape from frigid temperatures and the cold-and-flu season. There's no need to ever put away the golf clubs or swimsuits in this neighborhood.

There's lots to see and do in this colorful corner of Utah. You can step back more than a hundred years in history at Mormon leader Brigham Young's winter home in St. George, or cheer on the Dixie College Rebels football team. Our favorite stops are outdoors: the rugged red rock cliffs at Snow Canyon State Park; the ruddy sands of Coral Pink Sand Dunes State Park; the panoramic views from Cedar Breaks National Monument.

This region isn't only a warm-weather destination, though. Its extremes of elevation mean you can often lounge around the pool in the morning and build a snowman that same afternoon. From the scorching desert at St. George, it's only 74 miles—and 7,500 feet up—to the cool mountain forest at Cedar Breaks National Monument. Home to a variety of scenic and recreation areas (you'll even find ski resorts here), a surprising number of historic attractions, and some excellent performing-arts events (such as the Utah Shakespearean Festival), this area also serves as the gateway to most of Utah's spectacular national parks—probably the main reason you're here.

Despite the number of attractions, don't expect a lot of super-fancy amenities. Many of the motels and restaurants here are somewhat basic—perfectly adequate and quite nice, but not overly exciting. Keep in mind that distances are long—"nearby" can mean 100 miles away—and services may be far apart. But this is a starkly beautiful part of the American West—still very much like it was more than 100 years ago, and well worth a visit.

1 Getting Outside in Utah's Color Country

This is Utah's playground, a year-round mecca for hikers, mountain bikers, golfers, boaters, anglers, and anybody else who just wants to get outdoors. Among the top spots for experiencing nature at its best are Cedar Breaks National Monument, a high-mountain oasis of towering pines and firs, and wildflowers galore; and state parks such as Snow Canyon, Coral Pink Sand Dunes, and Quail Creek.

The best seasons for outdoor activities here are based on elevation: In St. George and other lowlands, the spring and fall are best, the winter's okay, and the summer is awful, with temperatures soaring well over 100°. But not everyone says no to St. George in the summer: Its desert climate makes it the **golfing** capital of Utah. The Sunbrook is considered the state's best course, with a challenging layout and spectacular views of the White Hills, but you can also stay a week in St. George and play a different course each day. On the other side of the seasonal coin, don't try to drive to Cedar Breaks until June at the earliest; the roads will be closed by snow.

A good way to see this part of Utah is on foot. **Hiking** trails abound throughout the Dixie and Fishlake National Forests north of St. George. But you'll discover several of the best trails in state parks, particularly Snow Canyon State Park near St. George.

Biking here generally means **mountain biking.** This is true even for those who confine most of their riding to city streets, because you never know when you're going to discover that great little trail turning off into the red rock desert or through Alpine meadows. Also, some of the roads—especially secondary roads—can be a bit rough, with only minimal shoulders; a sturdy mountain bike will survive better than a road bike. The best mountain biking is at Brian Head Ski Resort near Cedar Breaks National Monument. Both road and mountain bikes can take you to beautiful areas in and around Snow Canyon State Park near St. George.

For an area with so much desert, there's certainly a lot of **boating** here: Utahns have had to create reservoirs to provide the desert and its residents drinking and irrigation water. The best boating is at Quail Creek State Park near St. George, but those who would like a bit more solitude might prefer the relatively undeveloped Gunlock State Park nearby, or try Minersville State Park west of Beaver. The top fishing hole in these parts is at Quail Creek State Park, but plenty of smaller lakes and hidden streams are located in the Dixie and Fishlake National Forests.

Off-road vehicles can simply be a means to get to an isolated fishing stream or hiking trail, or part of the adventure itself. The old mining and logging roads in the national forests are great for four-wheel exploring. Visitors with their own dune buggies will want to challenge the shifting dunes at Coral Pink Sand Dunes State Park, just outside Kanab.

An abundance of **wildlife** makes their home in this part of the state. Sure, you'll see deer, squirrels, chipmunks, and other furry creatures at Cedar Breaks National Monument, but there's also animal life in the desert, including our favorites: the luminescent scorpions at Coral Pink Sand Dunes State Park and the Gila monster at Snow Canyon State Park, also home to numerous songbirds.

It may be hot down in the desert, but there's plenty of snow up on those mountaintops, and the **skiing** is great at Brian Head and Elk Meadows ski areas. Cross-country skiers and snowmobilers will want to head to nearby Cedar Breaks National Monument after the winter snows have closed the roads to cars.

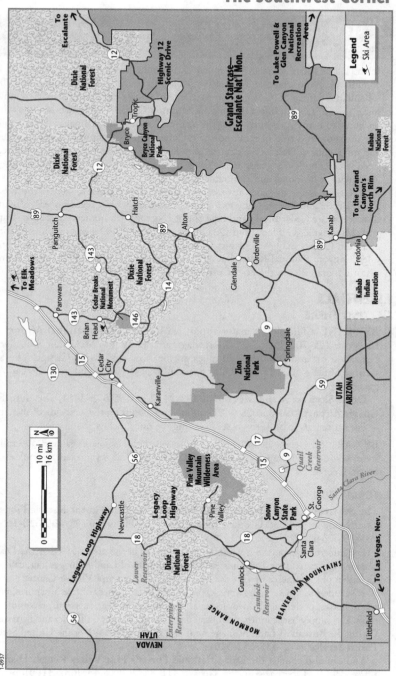

Legend

↗ Ski Area

1-0937

2 St. George, Gateway to Southern Utah's Natural Wonders

In the fall of 1861, Brigham Young sent 309 families to establish a cotton-growing community in the semi-arid Virgin River Valley; today, St. George has almost 40,000 inhabitants. Life in St. George, known as one of Utah's more conservative communities, is still strongly influenced by the Mormon Church. The town is also a winter home to many snowbirds—not the feathered variety, but humans who annually flee the snow and cold of more northern climes for this region's hot, dry summers and mild winters. Despite the climate, this desert city appears quite green, with tree-lined streets and lovely grassy areas. You'll find more than a half-dozen golf courses, along with recreational and cultural facilities to suit every taste.

St. George is also the gateway to some of the most spectacular scenery in the West. Zion, Bryce, and Grand Canyon National Parks are within relatively easy driving distance, as are Cedar Breaks and Pipe Springs National Monuments and Snow Canyon, Minersville, Gunlock, and Quail Creek State Parks. Depending on your itinerary, St. George may be your biggest stopping point en route to Lake Powell and Glen Canyon National Recreation Area, Capitol Reef National Park, and the prehistoric Indian sites in the Four Corners area.

ESSENTIALS

GETTING THERE

BY PLANE   The closest major airport is **McCarran International Airport** in Las Vegas (☎ 702/261-5743). Most major airlines fly into McCarran, where you can rent a car and drive the 120 miles northeast on I-15 to St. George. The **St. George Shuttle** (☎ 435/628-8320) provides daily service to and from the Las Vegas airport.

Delta/Skywest Airlines (☎ 800/453-9417 or 435/673-3451) flies into **St. George Airport** (☎ 435/628-0481), located on a bluff on the west side of the city. For car rentals in St. George, see "Getting Around," below.

BY CAR   St. George is on I-15, 120 miles northeast of Las Vegas and 305 miles southwest of Salt Lake City. Take exit 6 (Bluff Street) or 8 (St. George Boulevard) for St. George.

INFORMATION

The **St. George Area Chamber of Commerce** is located in the historic Pioneer Courthouse at 97 E. St. George Blvd., St. George, UT 84770 (☎ **435/628-1658;** fax 435/673-1587).

For information on the state and national parks in the area, as well as the Dixie National Forest and land administered by the Bureau of Land Management, call the Chamber of Commerce or visit the **Interagency Offices and Visitor Center** at 345 E. Riverside Dr. Open 7 days a week, the office offers a variety of free brochures, plus maps, books, posters, and videos for sale. Rangers can answer questions, recommend trails, and supply backcountry permits. To get there, take exit 6 off I-15 and turn east. Or call the **Bureau of Land Management** at ☎ **435/628-4491** or the **United States Forest Service** at ☎ **435/652-3100.**

You can also contact the **Dixie National Forest's Pine Valley Ranger District** office, 198 E. Tabernacle St., St. George, UT 84770 (☎ **435/652-3100**), or the **BLM's Dixie Resource Area office,** 225 N. Bluff St., St. George, UT 84770 (☎ **435/673-4654**).

St. George & Environs

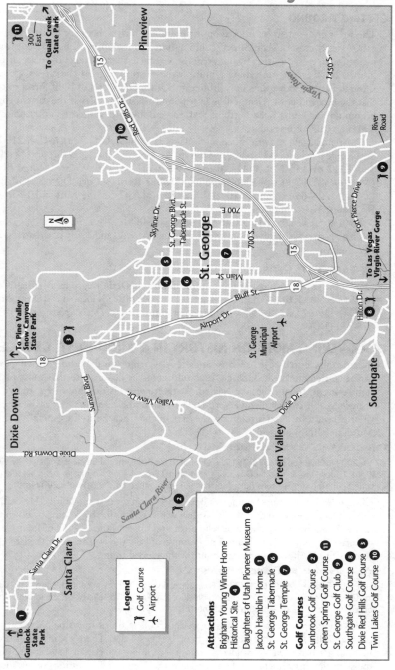

Legend
- 🏌 Golf Course
- ✈ Airport

Attractions
- Brigham Young Winter Home Historical Site ④
- Daughters of Utah Pioneer Museum ⑤
- Jacob Hamblin Home ①
- St. George Tabernacle ⑥
- St. George Temple ⑦

Golf Courses
- Sunbrook Golf Course ②
- Green Spring Golf Course ⑪
- St. George Golf Club ⑨
- Southgate Golf Course ⑧
- Dixie Red Hills Golf Course ③
- Twin Lakes Golf Course ⑩

GETTING AROUND

The street grid system is centered on the point at which Tabernacle Street (running east to west) crosses Main Street (running north to south), with numbered streets increasing in each direction by hundreds. St. George Boulevard takes the place of 100 North, Bluff Street runs along a bluff at the western edge of the city, I-15 cuts through in a northeast direction (from exit 6 at the south end of Bluff Street to exit 8 at the east end of St. George Boulevard), and River Road lies at the eastern edge, becoming Red Cliffs Road north of St. George Boulevard. Other than that, the system stays true to the grid.

Car-rental agencies with offices in St. George include **ABC Rent-A-Car,** 219 W. St. George Blvd. (☎ 435/628-7355); **Avis,** St. George Municipal Airport (☎ 800/331-1212 or 435/674-3941); **Budget Rent-A-Car,** 116 W. St. George Blvd. (☎ 800/527-0700 or 435/673-6825); **Dollar Rent-A-Car,** 1175 S. 150 East (☎ 435/628-6549); and **National Car Rental,** St. George Municipal Airport (☎ 800/CAR-RENT or 435/673-5098).

For a taxi, call **Dixie Taxi Cab** (☎ 435/673-4068).

Free on-street parking is available in much of the city, and many of the streets are tree-lined and shady.

FAST FACTS: ST. GEORGE

One of the larger hospitals in this part of the state is **Dixie Regional Medical Center,** 544 S. 400 East (☎ 435/634-4000). The **post office** is located at 180 N. Main St. (☎ 435/673-3312). The regional **newspaper** is the *Daily Spectrum* (☎ 435/673-3511).

DISCOVERING MORMON HISTORY IN & AROUND ST. GEORGE

Because the Church of Jesus Christ of Latter-day Saints was the primary driving force in the settlement of St. George, it should come as no surprise that most of the sightseeing in town is church related. At the town's historic buildings, staffed by knowledgeable church members, you'll learn about the church as well as the specific sites; expect a little sales pitch on the benefits of Christianity in general, and the Mormon faith in particular.

Brigham Young Winter Home Historical Site

67 W. 200 North. ☎ **435/673-2517.** Free guided tours. Memorial Day–Labor Day daily 9am–8:30pm; Labor Day–Memorial Day daily 9am–6pm. From I-15, take exit 8, head west on St. George Blvd. to Main St., turn right (north) for 1 block, then left (west) onto 200 North.

Church leader Brigham Young was one of St. George's first snowbirds. He escaped the Salt Lake City cold during the last few winters of his life by coming south to this house. In addition to its obvious religious importance to the Church of Jesus Christ of Latter-day Saints, it's a handsome example of how the well-to-do of the late 19th century lived. Allow about a half hour for the guided tour.

Daughters of Utah Pioneer Museum

145 N. 100 East. ☎ **435/628-7274.** Free admission, donations accepted. Mon–Sat 10am–5pm. Closed second Mon of Dec–second week of Jan. From I-15 take exit 8, head west on St. George Blvd. to 100 East, and turn right (north).

This "Grandma's attic" contains an eclectic collection of items belonging to the pioneers who settled this area more than 100 years ago. There's some furniture—including a bed used by Brigham Young—spinning wheels, an 1894 loom, guns, tools, musical instruments, and other relics from bygone days. Historic photos, mostly of pioneer families, are on display; copies are available for purchase. Guided tours are given by volunteers from the Daughters of Utah Pioneers.

○ Jacob Hamblin Home

Main St., Santa Clara. ☎ **435/673-2161.** Free guided tours. Memorial Day–Labor Day daily 9am–8pm; Labor Day–Memorial Day daily 9am–5pm. From St. George, go 3 miles west on U.S. 91 to the community of Santa Clara, then watch for sign.

This stone and pine house, built in 1862, is typical of pioneer homes throughout the West—and closer to what you'd think of as a pioneer home than the refined houses of St. George—except for one aspect that is definitively Mormon: It has two identical bedrooms, one for each of Hamblin's wives. You'll also notice that the dining table is set in typical Mormon fashion, with plates upside down and chairs facing away from the table to facilitate kneeling for before-meal prayers. The guided tour lasts about a half hour.

○ St. George Tabernacle

Main and Tabernacle sts. ☎ **435/628-4072.** Free guided tours. Daily 9am–6pm. From I-15 take exit 8, head west on St. George Blvd. to Main St., turn left (south) for a block to the Tabernacle.

This is the most beautiful building in St. George. It's an excellent example of fine old-world craftsmanship, from the hand-quarried red stone walls to the intricate interior woodwork; its craftsmen finished pine, which was all they had, to look like exotic hardwoods and even marble. Completed in 1876 after 13 years of work, the Tabernacle served as a house of worship and town meeting hall. During the 1880s, when a nearby silver strike brought many Catholics to the area, the Tabernacle was used for a Roman Catholic high mass led by a Roman Catholic priest, but with music from the liturgy sung by the local Mormon choir—in Latin. Today, the Tabernacle functions as a community center, presenting free weekly concerts and other cultural events. The guided tour takes about a half hour.

St. George Temple

440 S. 300 East. ☎ **435/673-5181.** Temple not open to the public; free guided tours of visitor center exhibits. Daily 9am–9pm. From I-15 take exit 8, head west on St. George Blvd. to 200 East, turn left (south) and go about 6 blocks to the large parking lot on your left.

Completed in 1877, the St. George Temple was the first Mormon temple in Utah and remains the oldest still in use in the world today. The majestic white temple is not open to the general public, but you can walk among the beautiful gardens and stop at the visitor center south of the Temple for a multimedia program on the beliefs of the Church of Jesus Christ of Latter-day Saints. At the conclusion of the tour/program, which takes just under an hour, you'll be asked if you would like a member of the Church to call on you to further discuss Mormon beliefs.

EXPLORING SNOW CANYON STATE PARK

○ **Snow Canyon** is among Utah's most scenic state parks, offering an abundance of opportunities for photography, hiking, and horseback riding. The park is surrounded by rock cliffs and walls of Navajo sandstone in every shade of red imaginable, layered with white and black from ancient lava flows. Hike the trails and discover shifting sand dunes, mysterious lava caves, colorful desert plants, and a variety of rock formations. You'll also encounter an attractive cactus garden, whose plants are described in a brochure, and several ancient petroglyphs (ask park rangers for directions).

Because the summers here are hot—well over 100°F—the best time to visit is any other time. Winters are mild, but nights can be chilly. Spring and fall are usually perfect weather-wise, and therefore the busiest. By the way, don't come looking for snow—Snow Canyon was named for pioneers Lorenzo and Erastus Snow, who found it.

JUST THE FACTS

GETTING THERE   The park is located 11 miles northwest of St. George, off Utah 18.

INFORMATION, FEES & REGULATIONS   For a copy of the park's brochure, contact **Snow Canyon State Park Headquarters,** P.O. Box 140, Santa Clara, UT 84765-0140 (☎ **435/628-2255**). Day-use fee is $4 per vehicle, or $1.50 per person on foot, bike, or motorcycle. Like most state parks, dogs are welcome, including on the trails, but must be leashed.

SPORTS & ACTIVITIES

HIKING   The best way to see Snow Canyon is on foot or horseback (see below). Several short trails make for easy full- or half-day hikes. The **Hidden Piñon Trail** is a 1¹/₂-mile round-trip self-guided nature trail that wanders among lava rocks, through several canyons, and onto rocky flatlands, offering panoramic views of the surrounding mountains. The trail begins across the highway from the campground; you can pick up a brochure at the park office/entrance station. The walk is fairly easy, but allow at least an hour, especially if you're planning to keep an eye out for Mormon tea, cliffrose, prickly pear cactus, and banana yucca.

An easy three-quarters-mile one-way trail leads to **Johnson Arch.** It begins just south of the campground, passes by the popular rock-climbing wall (see below), some low sand dunes, and then a small canyon with a view of Johnson Arch (named after pioneer wife Maude Johnson) high above.

Also popular is the **Lava Caves Trail,** a 1¹/₂-mile round-trip that starts just north of the campground. The caves are about a half mile along the trail, but watch carefully—it's easy to miss them. The caves were formed from liquid lava, and the large rooms have at times been occupied by Native American tribes. Another quarter mile past the caves is the West Canyon Overlook, with a breathtaking view into West Canyon.

Several longer and steeper trails lead to spectacular views of the canyons and distant vistas; check with park rangers for details.

HORSEBACK RIDING   **Snow Canyon Stables,** P.O. Box 577, Santa Clara, UT 84765 (☎ **435/628-6677**), offers horseback rides of various lengths into some of the more inaccessible and beautiful parts of the park, year-round. Prices start at $15 for a 1-hour ride; an overnight camping trip, including dinner and breakfast, is $125.

MOUNTAIN BIKING   Although bicycling is not allowed on the park trails, West Canyon Road is open to mountain biking. It lies just west of the park and is 7 miles round-trip. Ask park rangers for directions.

ROCK CLIMBING   Climbers love the tall wall of rock on the east side of the road just south of the campground, but it has become so popular that the park has issued a moratorium on bolting. Check with the park office for information.

WILDLIFE WATCHING   You're likely to see cottontail rabbits, ground squirrels, and songbirds; luckier visitors may also spot desert mule deer, bobcats, coyote, kit foxes, eagles, and owls. Although it's unlikely you'll see one, desert tortoises (a federally listed threatened species) and Gila monsters also live in the park. The park is also home to some rattlesnakes, which you'll want to avoid.

CAMPING

The 36-site campground is one of the best in the state. One section has rather closely spaced sites with electric hookups; those not needing electricity can set up camp in delightful little side canyons, surrounded by colorful red rocks and Utah juniper. The views are spectacular no matter where you choose to set up. Facilities include hot showers, modern rest rooms, and an RV sewage dump station. Campsites with electricity cost $13, and those without are $11. Reservations (with a $5 nonrefundable reservation fee) are recommended from February to May and September to November; call ☎ **800/322-3770.**

MORE OUTDOOR ACTIVITIES IN THE ST. GEORGE AREA

In addition to what's available in Snow Canyon State Park, there's great hiking, biking, and fishing in the Dixie National Forest and on nearby lands administered by the Bureau of Land Management. For contact information, see "Information" under "Essentials," above.

ROAD BIKING & MOUNTAIN BIKING   For bike repairs and accessories, stop at **Bicycles Unlimited,** 90 S. 100 East (☎ 435/673-4492). You can get repairs or rentals at **Swen's Cyclery,** 1060 E. Tabernacle (☎ 435/673-0878), where mountain-bike rental prices run from $5 per hour to $25 per day.

A popular road trip is the scenic **24-mile loop** from St. George through Santa Clara, Ivins, and Snow Canyon State Park. The route follows paved roads with narrow shoulders but generally little traffic. Allow 2 to 3 hours. Head north out of St. George on Bluff Street (Utah 18), and follow it to its intersection with U.S. 91. Turn west (left) and go about 6 miles to the village of Santa Clara, where you can visit the Jacob Hamblin Home (see "Discovering Mormon History in & Around St. George," above). From Santa Clara, continue west about a mile before turning north (right); follow the signs to Ivins and the Tuacahn Amphitheater. At Ivins, turn east (right) onto the Snow Canyon Road, following signs for Snow Canyon State Park, where you can easily spend from several hours to several days exploring the red rock formations, lava pools, and sand dunes. From the park, continue east to Utah 18, turn south (right), and pedal back into St. George.

Mountain-biking opportunities abound on land administered by the **U.S. Forest Service** (☎ 435/652-3100) and the **Bureau of Land Management** (☎ 435/628-4491); call for details.

FISHING   Quail Creek and Gunlock State Parks (see below) are the local fishing holes. For equipment, licenses, and tips on where they're biting, visit **Hurst Sports Center,** 160 N. 500 West (☎ 435/673-6141).

GOLF   Utah's golf capital attracts golfers from around the country to more than a half-dozen public courses (and more on the way), known for their challenging designs, well-maintained fairways and greens, and spectacularly scenic settings. The best is the 18-hole, par-72 **Sunbrook Golf Course,** 2240 W. Sunbrook Dr. (☎ 435/634-5866), rated tops in the state for 1997 by *Golf Digest,* for both its design and its spectacular scenery. Greens fees in the winter are $16 for 9 holes and $26 for 18 holes; in the summer they're $10 and $17, respectively. Also highly rated by *Golf Digest*—and considered by many to be the state's second-best course—is **Green Spring Golf Course,** 588 N. Green Spring Dr., Washington (☎ 435/673-7888), several miles northeast of St. George. Challenging Green Spring is an 18-hole, par-71 course, with winter greens fees of $16 for 9 holes and $30 for 18 holes ($11 and $20, respectively, in the summer).

Other 18-hole courses include the par-73 **St. George Golf Club,** 2190 S. 1400 East (☎ 435/634-5854), and the par-70 **Southgate Golf Course,** 1975 S. Tonaquint Dr. (☎ 435/628-0000). Greens fees at both of these city-owned courses are $15 for 9 holes and $29 for 18 holes in the winter, and $10 and $17 respectively in the summer. Southgate also has a **Family Golf Center** (☎ 435/674-7728), with an outdoor driving range and putting and chipping greens, plus state-of-the-art indoor facilities that include computerized golf-swing analysis. The par-72 **Entrada,** 2511 W. Entrada Trail (☎ 435/674-7500), is St. George's newest 18-hole golf course, with fees in winter of $50 for county residents and $60 for guests, and $35 and $40 respectively in summer. Twilight playing fees are $35 in winter and $20 in summer. Fees include cart.

Nine-hole courses in St. George include the par-34 **Dixie Red Hills Golf Course,** 100 N. 700 West (☎ 435/634-5852), with winter greens fees of $15 for 9 holes and $25 for 18 holes and summer fees of $10 and $17 respectively; and the par-27 **Twin Lakes Golf Course,** 660 N. Twin Lakes Dr. (☎ 435/673-4441), with year-round fees of $6.50 for 9 holes and $10.50 for 18 holes.

Golfers can often save money by checking with local motels on various lodging/golf packages; see "Where to Stay," below.

HIKING   Some of the best hiking in the area is at Snow Canyon State Park (see above). The Dixie National Forest to the north also offers vast opportunities, with some 200 miles of trails. Check with forest rangers on current trail conditions, and be sure to carry detailed maps on any long hikes, especially if you're venturing into the Pine Valley Wilderness Area. Stop in at the **Interagency Offices and Visitor Center** at 345 E. Riverside Dr. for maps and details.

TWO STATE PARKS FOR WATER-SPORTS ENTHUSIASTS

Year-round warm weather makes the southwest corner home to several large reservoirs, a mecca for water-sports enthusiasts. ✪ **Quail Creek State Park** (P.O. Box 1943, St. George, UT 84770-1943; ☎ **435/879-2378**), 14 miles northeast of St. George off I-15 and Utah 9, has the warmest water in the state in the summer, making it extremely popular with boaters, water-skiers, windsurfers, scuba divers, and swimmers. Here you'll find docks, sandy beaches, and two boat ramps that can accommodate practically all types of watercraft. Quail Creek Reservoir is considered one of the state's best fishing holes for largemouth bass; anglers also catch rainbow trout, bluegill, and crappie. Facilities include a fish-cleaning station, modern rest rooms, a campground with 23 sites (but no showers or RV hookups), and a picnic area with barbecue grills. The park is open year-round; day-use costs are $5 per vehicle or $2 per individual on foot, bike, or motorcycle; camping is $8.

Gunlock State Park (P.O. Box 140, Santa Clara, UT 84765-0140; ☎ **435/628-2255**), 15 miles northwest of St. George via U.S. 91, is also a great place to enjoy water sports year-round. Activities at the 240-acre Gunlock Reservoir include boating (there's a boat ramp), waterskiing, swimming, and excellent fishing for bass and catfish. There's no day-use fee. The park offers free primitive camping, although with pit toilets and no security; you'll probably be happier camping (and paying) at Snow Canyon State Park (see above), about 20 miles away.

Neither Quail Creek nor Gunlock State Parks offer on-site boat rentals, but rentals are available from several dealers in St. George. **RV Rental Express,** 875 E. St. George Blvd. (☎ **435/680-7447**), offers 14-foot aluminum fishing boats with 10-horsepower outboard motors starting at about $50 per day and ski boats from about $150 per day; both include trailers and life jackets.

SPECTATOR SPORTS

TEAM SPORTS   The **Dixie College Rebels** are the ones to root for in St. George. The football, women's volleyball, women's soccer, men's and women's basketball, men's baseball, and women's softball teams at this community college are often nationally ranked. You're not likely to have any trouble getting tickets to join the school's 3,000 students in the 5,000-seat Hansen Stadium or Burns Arena. Tickets cost from $3 to $7 and are available at the Athletic Department offices (☎ **435/ 652-7525**).

DRAG RACING   Fans of drag racing head to **High Country Raceway** (☎ **435/ 652-9066**), which runs an outlaw super-street class with a dozen races from January through November. Admission costs $5, and is free for children 12 and under. To get to the raceway, take I-15 to exit 8 and head south on River Road for about 4¹/₂ miles, then watch for signs to the track.

SHOPPING

You probably wouldn't travel across the country to shop in St. George; the stores are similar to what you'd find almost anywhere in Middle America. Some of the town's more interesting shops (and one of our favorite local restaurants—see "Where to Dine," below) are located at **Ancestor Square,** at the corner of St. George Boulevard and Main Street. Among the shops is **Cassidy's Casuals,** 2 W. St. George Blvd. (☎ 435/628-6665), specializing in all-cotton fashions.

You'll find WalMart, ZCMI department store, and the standard mall fare at **Red Cliffs Mall,** 1770 E. Red Cliffs Dr. (☎ 435/673-0099). It's located on the east side of I-15, between exits 8 (St. George Boulevard) and 10 (Green Springs Drive), and is open Monday through Saturday from 10am to 9pm and Sunday from noon to 5pm.

If you can't resist a bargain, head for **Zion Factory Stores,** 250 N. Red Cliffs Dr. (☎ 435/674-9800), where you'll find more than three dozen outlet shops, including Corning-Revere, Down East Outfitters, Book Warehouse, Kay-Bee Toy Liquidators, Bass, Etienne Aigner, Carter's Childrenswear, J. Crew, Westport Ltd., Clothestime, and Van Heusen. Located on the east side of I-15 just north of exit 8, the mall is open Monday through Saturday from 10am to 8pm and Sunday from 11am to 5pm.

Those in the market for alcoholic beverages will find them at the **Utah State Liquor Store,** 929 W. Sunset Blvd. (☎ 435/673-9454).

WHERE TO STAY

You'll find a good selection of lodgings in St. George, with a range of facilities and prices. Most are on St. George Boulevard and Bluff Street, within easy walking distance of restaurants and attractions. Summer is the slow season here—people tend to head to the mountains when the temperature hits 115°F—so prices are lowest then. High seasons are spring and fall. Golfers will want to ask about special golf packages offered by many hotels and motels in St. George.

In addition to the accommodations described below, you'll find branches of the following reliable chain and franchise motels: **Comfort Inn**, 999 E. Skyline Dr., St. George, UT 84770 (☎ 800/228-5150 or 435/628-4271; fax 435/628-5196), with rates for two of $48 to $62; **Days Inn**, 150 N. 1000 East St. (exit 8 off I-15), St. George, UT 84770 (☎ 800/527-6543, 800/DAYSINN, or 435/673-6123; fax 435/ 673-7030), with rates for two from $54 to $69; **Econo Lodge**, 460 E. St. George Blvd., St. George, UT 84770 (☎ 800/553-2666 or 435/673-4861), which charges $38 to $68 for two people; **Hampton Inn**, 53 N. River Rd. (exit 8 off I-15), St. George, UT 84770 (☎ 800/HAMPTON or 435/652-1200; fax 435/652-1500), with a rate of $61 for two; **Motel 6**, 205 N. 1000 East St. (exit 8 off I-15), St. George, UT 84770 (☎ 800/466-8356 or 435/628-7979), with a rate for two of $38;

and **Super 8 Motel,** 915 S. Bluff St., St. George, UT 84770 (☎ 800/800-8000 or 435/628-4251; fax 435/628-6534), which charges $43 to $49 for two people.

Room tax adds about 9% to your lodging bill. Pets are generally not accepted at the properties below unless otherwise noted.

MODERATE

Best Western Abbey Inn

1129 S. Bluff St., St. George, UT 84470. ☎ **888/222-3946** or 435/652-1234. Fax 435/652-5950. 130 rms. A/C TV TEL. $59–$89 double. Rates include deluxe continental breakfast. AE, CB, DC, DISC, MC, V.

This lovely property has a small but elegant lobby. The rooms, on the other hand, are spacious and very attractively furnished with graceful solid wood furniture, plush seating, and old master–style paintings. Facilities include a pool in an outside courtyard, spa, exercise room, guest laundry, and video game room. Six restaurants are located within 1 block.

Best Western Coral Hills

125 E. St. George Blvd., St. George, UT 84770. ☎ **800/542-7733** or 435/673-4844. Fax 435/673-5352. 98 rms, including 5 suites. A/C TV TEL. $45–$75 double. Rates include deluxe continental breakfast. AE, CB, DC, DISC, MC, V.

A bit more homey than your average Best Western, the Coral Hills has king- or queen-size beds and polished-wood furnishings that include an armoire or dresser. Swimmers can choose between good-sized indoor and outdoor heated pools, both with whirlpools, plus a kiddie pool. You'll also find an exercise room, a putting green, and, if you're here to work, fax and photocopy services.

Greene Gate Village Historic Bed & Breakfast

76 W. Tabernacle St., St. George, UT 84770. ☎ **800/350-6999** or 435/628-6999. Fax 435/628-6989. 19 rms. A/C TV TEL. $50–$125 double. Rates include full breakfast. AE, DISC, MC, V.

One of the most delightful places to stay in southwest Utah, this bed-and-breakfast inn is actually 10 separate buildings, all restored pioneer homes from the late 1800s, sitting in their own flower-filled little "village" in downtown St. George. You'll find lots of genuine antiques—mostly Victorian—plus modern "necessities" such as TVs and VCRs. Most rooms have shower/tub combos, but some have showers only. Breakfasts are generous, and the Bentley House Restaurant (see "Where to Dine," below) also serves dinner Thursday, Friday, and Saturday evenings, by reservation only. Facilities include a small outdoor heated pool and hot tub. Unlike many other B&Bs, this one welcomes children, even babies. Tobacco use of any kind is prohibited inside.

Hilton Inn of St. George

1450 S. Hilton Dr., St. George, UT 84770. ☎ **800/662-2525** in Utah or 435/628-0463. Fax 435/628-1501. 100 rms, including 2 suites. A/C TV TEL. $70–$105 double (rates are highest in spring and fall, lowest in the summer). AE, CB, DC, DISC, EU, JCB, MC, V.

One of the few full-service hotels in southwest Utah, this Hilton is everything you'd expect from such a respected chain. What makes the hotel particularly interesting is the individuality of all the rooms: Some have two sinks, some one; some are decorated with dark wood, others light; and a variety of color themes and wallpaper designs are used. All, however, have Southwest decor. Each room comes with a coffeemaker, computer data ports, and voice mail, plus HBO and the Disney channel; some have desks. A full range of services is provided, and facilities include an outdoor heated pool in a tropical setting, hot tub, two saunas, three lighted tennis courts, gift shop, and conference rooms for up to 200 people. Tony Roma's restaurant serves three meals daily and offers complete liquor service.

Holiday Inn Resort Hotel & Convention Center

850 S. Bluff St., St. George, UT 84770. ☎ **800/457-9800** or 435/628-4235. Fax 435/628-8157. 164 rms, including 7 suites. A/C TV TEL. Winter, $69–$99 double; summer, $69–$89 double. AE, CB, DC, DISC, JCB, MC, V.

With its Holidome recreation center, this is an excellent choice for travelers with kids or for anyone who wants easy access to a large indoor-outdoor heated pool, whirlpool, lighted tennis court, putting green, weight room, pool table, Ping-Pong table, video arcade, and separate children's play area. That should keep you busy, but if you find time to get to your room, you'll find it attractively decorated, with king- or queen-size beds and solid wood furniture. Family rooms are slightly larger and come with hide-a-beds; king rooms have hair dryers and hot beverage makers in addition to the standard furnishings; and the luxury suites have individual whirlpool spas. The hotel offers a full range of services, and just off the beautiful cathedral-ceilinged lobby you'll find a gift shop selling local crafts in addition to the standard magazines, T-shirts, and souvenirs. The restaurant is open daily from 6am to 10pm (11pm on Friday and Saturday nights) and offers an extensive soup and salad bar, homemade breads, steaks, and seafood. Full liquor service is available. Small pets may be accepted with management approval.

✪ Seven Wives Inn Bed & Breakfast

217 N. 100 West, St. George, UT 84770. ☎ **800/600-3737** or 435/628-3737. Fax 435/673-0165. 13 units, including 2 suites. A/C TV TEL. $55–$125. Rates include full breakfast. AE, CB, DC, DISC, JCB, MC, V.

There are no polygamists hiding in the attic of Seven Wives Inn anymore—as there were in the 1880s after polygamy was outlawed—but it's still fun to imagine what things must have been like in those days. Innkeepers Jay and Donna Curtis will be happy to chat with you about the property's history. This bed-and-breakfast is decorated with antiques, mostly Victorian and Eastlake, and consists of two historic homes: the main house, built in 1873, where the polygamists hid; and the President's house next door, a four-square Victorian built 10 years later that played host to many of the Mormon Church's early presidents. All of the rooms have private baths, two with shower only; the honeymoon suite contains a whirlpool tub for two. Many rooms have functioning fireplaces or wood-burning stoves, as well as decks or balconies. The inn is completely nonsmoking.

Singletree Inn

260 E. St. George Blvd., St. George, UT 84770. ☎ **800/528-8890** or 435/673-6161. Fax 435/674-2406. 48 units, including 2 family suites. A/C TV TEL. $50–$55 double; $60–$70 family suite. Rates include continental breakfast. AE, CB, DC, DISC, MC, V.

A few personal touches, such as dried-flower wall decorations and prints depicting area attractions, give this family-owned and -operated motel a homey feel. You'll also find an outdoor heated pool and whirlpool, one king- or two queen-size beds in every room, and a golf package better than most other deals in the area. Small pets are accepted.

INEXPENSIVE

Claridge Inn

1187 S. Bluff St., St. George, UT 84770. ☎ **800/367-3790** or 435/673-7222. Fax 435/634-0773. 50 rms. A/C TV TEL. Sun–Thurs $34 for 1–4 people; Fri–Sat $44 for 1–4 people; higher for special events. Rates include continental breakfast at a nearby restaurant. AE, DISC, MC, V.

This motel is popular with families because of its outdoor heated pool and low rates. The rooms—each with two queen-size beds—are well kept but rather plain, with stucco walls and no artwork. All have a small dining table with two comfortable chairs. The Claridge Inn is entirely nonsmoking.

Dixie Palms Motel

185 E. St. George Blvd., St. George, UT 84770. ☎ **435/673-3531.** 15 rms. A/C TV TEL. $26–$30 double. MC, V.

Travelers on tight budgets should head to the Dixie Palms for basic lodging at bargain-basement rates. Located right in the center of town, within walking distance of several restaurants and attractions, this older, red brick property doesn't have a swimming pool, and some units have showers only, but the rooms are clean and well maintained, and the price is right.

Rococo Inn

511 S. Airport Rd., St. George, UT 84770. ☎ **888/628-3671** or 435/628-3671. Fax 435/673-6370. 27 rms, 3 suites. A/C TV TEL. $35–$50 double. AE, DISC, MC, V.

Perched on a bluff on the west side of St. George, this white stucco motel affords great views of the city spread out below. The basic motel rooms are very clean, simply decorated, and quite attractive; each contains one king or two queen beds, plus a tub/shower combo. Facilities include an outdoor pool and an excellent restaurant (see "Dining," below).

RV PARKS

Redlands Park Inc.

2 miles north of St. George on Frontage Rd., take I-15 exit 10. (P.O. Box 2000, Washington, UT 84780.) ☎ **800/553-8269** or 435/673-9700. 204 sites. $19.95 full hookups; $14.95 electric only and tents. DISC, MC, V.

This huge RV park has two or three trees at every site—it looks almost like a bunch of campers hiding in a forest. Facilities include a coin-operated laundry, a convenience store with RV supplies and propane, as well as a large sauna, heated pool, playground, game room, horseshoes, shuffleboard, and volleyball. Discount tickets for the golf course across the street are also available.

Settler's RV Park

1333 E. 100 South, St. George, UT 84770. ☎ **435/628-1624.** 155 sites. $16.90 full hookups. MC, V. From I-15, take exit 8 (St. George Blvd.), go east 1 block, turn right onto River Rd., then left onto 100 South.

Situated below a bluff just off I-15, this RV park is convenient for those seeing the area's attractions. The paved sites are fairly well spaced, and once the trees grow a bit, they'll be at least partly shaded. In addition to the large, well-kept bathhouse, facilities include a coin-operated laundry, heated pool and spa, playground, game room, barbecues, shuffleboard, and horseshoes.

WHERE TO DINE

Andelin's Gable House Restaurant

290 E. St. George Blvd. ☎ **435/673-6796.** Reservations required spring and fall for prix fixe only. Main courses $4.50–$15.95; lunch $4.50–$9.95. Prix fixe dinner $25.95 for 5 courses, $21.95 for 3 courses. AE, DISC, MC, V. Mon–Sat 11:30am–10pm. From I-15, take exit 8 and head west on St. George Blvd. for about 8 blocks. AMERICAN.

The Old English–garden decor, with lots of plants, flowered wallpaper, an eclectic display of antiques and collectibles, and a somewhat casually elegant atmosphere, makes the Gable House a popular special-occasion spot. At lunch you'll find

croissant sandwiches, a good selection of salads, and chicken potpi
flaky crust. This very popular potpie is offered again at dinner,
such as slow-cooked beef brisket and pink mountain trout, whi
and sautéed in butter. Among the dinner entree salads, we part
the Oriental salad, with grilled chicken breast, Chinese noodles, mandarin
and almonds. The prix fixe dinners give you a choice of prime rib, roast rack of pork,
or the fish of the day. No alcohol is served.

The Bentley House Restaurant

Greene Gate Village Bed & Breakfast, 76 W. Tabernacle St. ☎ **435/656-3333**. Reservations
required. 5-course prix fixe $21. AE, DC, DISC, MC, V. Thurs–Sat 5–9pm. Closed major holi-
days. From I-15, take exit 8, head west on St. George Blvd. to Main St., turn left (south) on Main
for 1 block to Tabernacle St., then right (west) to the restaurant. AMERICAN.

Come to this handsome Victorian home for a romantic, elegant evening. A pianist
plays quietly in the background as you dine, surrounded by antiques from the 1870s.
Although the menu varies, you might have broiled filet mignon with sautéed mushrooms, chicken Cordon Bleu, or salmon poached in white wine. Desserts are always
homemade and include a variety of pies and cheesecakes. No alcoholic beverages are
served.

⭐ Cafe Basila's—Mediterranean

Ancestor Square No. 38, 2 W. St. George Blvd. ☎ **435/673-7671**. Reservations for 6 or more
only. Main courses $7.95–$16.95; lunch $4.25–$6.95. AE, DISC, MC, V. Tues–Sat 11am–10pm.
From I-15, take exit 8, head west on St. George Blvd. to Main St.; Ancestor Square is on the
northwest corner. MEDITERRANEAN/EUROPEAN.

Tucked away toward the back of Ancestor Square, Basila's is worth finding. You'll
start off with crusty homemade bread and "Greek butter," a delightfully light mixture of olive oil and Balsamic vinegar. Highly recommended choices include the four-
cheese (ricotta, parmesan, romano, and feta) ravioli in marinara sauce; a gyro with
layers of seasoned lamb and beef on a bed of parsley and tomato with Tzatziki cucumber yogurt sauce; and spanakopita, baked on the premises with thin layers of
phyllo dough rolled with fresh spinach, ricotta, and parmesan cheese and served with
a lemon sauce. For dessert, try the house favorite: Greek custard bread pudding. The
tables are closely spaced in the fairly narrow, L-shaped dining room, and there's also
an outdoor patio. Plants sit in the windows, an eclectic collection of Mediterranean
artwork is arranged on high shelves around the exposed adobe walls, and slow-moving
fans hang from the open-beamed ceiling. Complete liquor service is available.

Dick's Cafe

114 E. St. George Blvd. ☎ **435/673-3841**. Reservations required for groups and on holidays.
Main courses $4.50–$10.95; lunch $3.25–$5.95; breakfast $2.50–$7. AE, DISC, MC, V. Daily
6am–9:30pm. From I-15 take exit 8, head west on St. George Blvd. for about 11 blocks and
the cafe will be on your left. SOUTHWESTERN/AMERICAN.

Dick's, which claims to be the oldest restaurant in St. George, opened in 1935. It's
the sort of place you would expect to find in the Old West: a funky hometown cafe,
with a long counter plus booths and tables, frequented by regulars who specialize in
drinking pots of coffee and swapping lies. Dick's offers good home cooking, with
breakfast items served at any time of day; all the American standards are available,
as well as a few spicy Mexican dishes that will really open your eyes. Lunches include
sandwiches and burgers, salads and some other healthy stuff, and luncheon plates such
as fresh roast turkey or liver and onions. At dinner, you'll find more of the roast turkey and liver and onions, plus steaks, roast beef, grilled halibut, and fish-and-chips.
Fans of chicken-fried steak say Dick's is about the best around. Pies are fresh baked
on the premises. Children's and seniors' menus are available. No alcohol is served.

...n's Rococo Steakhouse

Airport Rd. ☎ **435/628-3671.** Reservations accepted. Main courses $8.95–$35.95; ...ch $3.50–$7.95. AE, DISC, MC, V. Mon–Fri 11am–10pm; Sat–Sun 5–10pm. From I-15, take exit 8, head west on St. George Blvd. to Bluff St., cross over onto Airport Rd., which immediately turns to the left and climbs the bluff; follow Airport Rd. to the restaurant. STEAK/SEAFOOD.

Excellent beef and the best views from any restaurant in the area make this a great spot for special occasions. Perched upon a bluff overlooking St. George, Sullivan's large glass windows take full advantage of a spectacular panorama of the city and its surrounding red rock formations, especially as the sun begins to set and the city lights twinkle below. Generous portions of prime rib and a variety of steaks are king here; the Rococo is also considered to be one of the best spots in southwest Utah for lobster. All baking is done in-house, so save room for a piece of pie—the shredded apple with caramel sauce and ice cream is spectacular. Those dropping by for lunch can choose from several sandwiches, including an extra-special prime-rib sandwich, burgers, and salads. The restaurant offers full liquor service.

Tom's Delicatessen

175 West 900 S. Bluff, in Holiday Square. ☎ **435/628-1822.** Sandwiches $3.85–$6.35. MC, V. Tues–Sat 11am–6pm. DELI.

Tucked away in a narrow storefront in a small shopping center beside the Holiday Inn, Tom's quietly goes about its business of creating tasty, filling sandwiches. A St. George institution since 1978, Tom's offers 14 hot and 21 cold selections—just about all the basics, including roast beef, turkey, and pastrami. You can eat yours at one of the Formica tables along the wall, or carry it out for a picnic. No alcohol is served.

ST. GEORGE AFTER DARK

St. George, with its large nondrinking Mormon population, isn't one of the West's hot spots as far as bar scenes go. Locals going out on the town will often attend a performing-arts event (see below), and maybe stop in for a nightcap at one of the local restaurants that serve alcohol, such as Sullivan's Rococo Steakhouse or Cafe Basila's (see "Where to Dine," above). Keep in mind that these are not private clubs, so you'll need to buy something to eat in order to purchase a drink.

The Dixie Center, 425 S. 700 East (☎ 435/628-7003), is St. George's primary performing-arts venue. The four-building complex hosts a wide range of events, from country and rock music to the symphony, ballet, opera, and even sports.

Dixie College, 225 S. 700 East (☎ 435/652-7994), offers a variety of events throughout the school year. The Celebrity Concert Series, running from October through April, has developed a strong following for its programs of music, ballet, modern dance, and other disciplines by national and international performers. Not to be outdone, the college's drama department offers its own series of five productions each year. There's usually a major musical in December; other productions will likely include dramas, comedies, a children's show, maybe even a Greek tragedy. Admission to college productions usually costs between $5 and $8 per person, and performances are presented at one of two theaters at the college's **Graff Fine Arts Center.** Call the box office (☎ 435/652-7800) to find out what's scheduled during your visit.

Music lovers will enjoy St. George's own **Southwest Symphonic Chorale and Southwest Symphony** (☎ 435/652-7994), the only full symphony orchestra between Provo and Las Vegas. Their repertoire includes classical, opera, and popular music. You'll want to get tickets early for the annual Christmas production of Handel's *Messiah,* performed with the Dixie College Concert Choir, which usually sells out. Concerts are scheduled from October through early June, and tickets are in the $5 to $10 range.

The **St. George Tabernacle** (☎ 435/628-4072) presents free weekly concerts in a beautiful setting; see "Discovering Mormon History in & Around St. George," above, for further details.

For a spectacular outdoor musical drama that blends history, song, drama, and dynamite special effects, take the short trip from St. George to the **Tuacahn Amphitheater and Center for the Arts,** 1100 Tuacahn Dr., Ivins (☎ 800/746-9882 box office or 435/674-0012; fax 435/674-0013). Presented Monday through Saturday at 8:30pm from mid-June through early September, *Utah!* depicts the settling of southern Utah by Mormon pioneers, particularly the life of Jacob Hamblin, known for his peacekeeping efforts with the Native Americans of the area. The musical, with live vocals and recorded instrumental accompaniment, comes to life with its state-of-the-art sound system and special effects, including lightning, a gigantic flood, and dazzling fireworks for the finale. Reservations are recommended. Tickets cost $14.50 to $24.50 for adults, $9 to $16 for children under 12. Free pre-show entertainment and backstage tours are offered, and Dutch-oven dinners are served at $10.50 for adults and $7.50 for children under 12; call for details.

3 Enjoying the Outdoors Around Cedar City: Cedar Breaks National Monument & the Southern Ski Resorts

This great little area is home to some unheralded—and uncrowded—natural gems. Cedar Breaks National Monument is like a miniature Bryce Canyon—a stunning multicolored amphitheater of stone, with great hiking trails, camping, and a plateau ablaze with wildflowers in the summer. Brian Head is Utah's southernmost ski resort, but because it has the highest base elevation of any of the state's ski areas, it gets about 400 inches of powder each winter. Where else but southern Utah can you be on the links in the morning and on the slopes by the afternoon? And because Brian Head—and Elk Meadows Ski Resort, a bit farther afield—are off the average skier's beaten track, lift lines are usually nonexistent.

But this area is more than an outdoor playland—with Iron Mission State Park and the nationally renowned Utah Shakespearean Festival, Cedar City happens to be a great place to step back in time. Even if the past isn't your thing, you'll probably end up in Cedar City anyway—it's where you'll find almost all of the area's accommodations and restaurants.

BASING YOURSELF IN CEDAR CITY

Since there are no lodging or dining facilities at Cedar Breaks National Monument, you may want to stay in Cedar City. If you're here to ski and you'd like to save money on accommodations, Cedar City also offers an economical alternative to Brian Head's more expensive condos. You can head to the slopes in the morning—it's only 28 miles to Brian Head (but beware: it can be a mean 28 miles when the weather's bad). In addition to what we've mentioned below, you'll find a good selection of motels, restaurants, campgrounds, gas stations, grocery stores, and other services on I-15 at exits 57, 59, and 62.

ESSENTIALS

GETTING THERE   Cedar City is just off I-15, 53 miles northeast of St. George and 251 miles southwest of Salt Lake City.

Delta/Skywest Airlines (☎ 800/453-9417) flies into Cedar City Airport (☎ 435/586-3033).

INFORMATION   Contact the **Iron County Tourism and Convention Bureau,** 286 N. Main St. (P.O. Box 1007), Cedar City, UT 84720 (☎ 800/354-4849 or 435/586-5124).

CAR RENTALS   Car-rental agencies at the Cedar City Airport include **Avis** (☎ 800/831-2847) and **National** (☎ 800/227-7368 or 435/586-7059).

FAST FACTS   The hospital serving this area is Cedar City's **Valley View Medical Center,** 595 S. 75 East, Cedar City (☎ 435/586-6587).

WHERE TO STAY & DINE

Lodging possibilities here include the **Abbey Inn,** 940 W. 200 North, Cedar City, UT 84720 (☎ 435/586-9966; fax 435/586-6522), with rates for two of $64 to $79 in the summer and $57 to $71 in the winter; **Best Western El Rey Inn,** 80 S. Main St., Cedar City, UT 84720 (☎ 800/528-1234 or 435/586-6518; fax 435/586-7257), with rates for two of $59 to $89 in the summer and $49 to $69 in the winter; **Best Western Town & Country,** 200 N. Main St., Cedar City, UT 84720 (☎ 800/528-1234 or 435/586-9900; fax 435/586-1664), with rates for two of $78 to $91 in the summer and $71 to $73 in the winter; **Comfort Inn,** 250 N. 1100 West, Cedar City, UT 84720 (☎ 800/627-0374, 800/228-5150 or 435/586-2082; fax 435/586-3193), with rates for two of $65 to $80 in the summer and $49 to $73 in the winter; and **Quality Inn,** 18 S. Main St., Cedar City, UT 84720 (☎ 800/228-5151 or 435/586-2433; fax 435/586-4425), with rates for two of $66 to $86 in the summer and $49 to $74 in the winter. Room tax adds about 9% to lodging bills.

The **Cedar City KOA Campground,** 1121 N. Main St., Cedar City, UT 84720 (☎ 435/586-9872), is open year-round and charges $16 to $20 per site.

Cedar City eateries include **Brad's Food Hut,** 546 N. Main St. (☎ 435/586-6358), an attractive, independent fast-food restaurant offering sandwiches, burgers, and ice cream in the $1 to $5 range for lunch and dinner; **Rusty's Ranch House,** 2 miles east of town on Utah 14 (☎ 435/586-3839), serving dinners of steak and seafood for $15 to $35; **Adriana's,** 161 S. 100 West (☎ 453/865-1234), serving health-conscious meals for lunch (about $6) and dinner ($10 to $18); and the locally recommended **Milt's Stage Stop,** 5 miles east of Cedar City on Utah 14 (☎ 435/586-9344), serving steak and seafood for dinner only, from $12 to $35, with complete liquor service.

A Brief Look at Cedar City's Pioneer Past: Iron Mission State Park

If you're into the horse-drawn wagons of the past, this is the place to go. Essentially a local museum, Iron Mission has several dozen wagons and horse-drawn sleighs on display. In addition to all the usual buckboards, a bullet-scarred Old West stagecoach, and elaborate, for-the-very-very-rich-only coaches, you'll see an original Studebaker White Top Wagon (predecessor of the present-day station wagon) and several hearses. (You might be interested to learn—we were—that black hearses drawn by black horses were used only for deceased adults—white hearses pulled by white horses were reserved for children.) Also on exhibit are Native American and pioneer artifacts from the region and a diorama depicting the 1850s iron furnace and equipment for which the park is named. Demonstrations of pioneer crafts, such as weaving, spinning, candle making, cooking, and toy making, are held periodically.

Renaissance Pleasures on the Colorado Plateau: The Utah Shakespearean Festival

As you would expect, Southern Utah is no hotbed of cultural activity—most of the year, that is. But when summer rolls around, all that changes: Humble Cedar City becomes home to Utah's premier theater event, the ✪ **Utah Shakespearean Festival.** The Bard's plays have been professionally staged in this unlikely setting since 1962, and the festival has been going strong and getting better ever since.

If you're going to be anywhere near Cedar City between mid-June and early September, it's well worth working one of the season's productions into your travel plans—four plays by Shakespeare are staged every year, plus two by other playwrights. They're presented by top actors in true Elizabethan style, in an open-air replica of the original Globe Theatre, with musicians trained in the music of the Renaissance. (If it rains, productions are moved into the adjacent enclosed theater.) At press time, productions scheduled for the 1998 season were *Romeo and Juliet, The Taming of the Shrew, All's Well That Ends Well,* and *King John,* plus *Relative Values* by Noël Coward and the musical *Joseph and the Amazing Technicolor Dreamcoat* by Tim Rice and Andrew Lloyd Webber.

The festival is held on the Southern Utah University campus at 351 W. Center St., Cedar City, UT 84720. Ticket prices for the 1998 season range from $15 to $38 for evening performances, $10 to $38 for matinees. For tickets and information, call ☎ **800/PLAYTIX** or 435/586-7878.

The plays are only part of the fun. "Royal Feastes," complete with medieval entertainment and winsome serving wenches, are held several evenings each week in festival season; the Elizabethan-style prix fixe dinner is $29 per person. Backstage tours are offered Tuesdays through Saturdays for $7 per person. A variety of other programs, including literary seminars and special workshops, are held during the season; call for further details.

Iron Mission State Park (☎ **435/586-9290**) is located in downtown Cedar City at 585 N. Main St. Admission is $1.50 for adults, $1 for kids 6 to 16, and free for children under 6; the whole family can get in for $6. It's open daily from 9am to 7pm from Memorial Day through Labor Day and until 5pm at other times of the year; the park is closed Thanksgiving, Christmas, and New Year's Day.

CEDAR BREAKS NATIONAL MONUMENT

This delightful little park is a wonderful place to spend a few hours, or even several days, gazing down from the rim into the spectacular natural amphitheater, hiking the trails, and camping among the spruce, fir, and wildflowers that blanket the plateau in the summer.

This natural coliseum, which reminds us of Bryce Canyon, is more than 2,000 feet deep and over 3 miles across; it's filled with stone spires, arches, and columns shaped by the forces of erosion and painted in ever-changing reds, purples, oranges, and ochers. But why "Cedar Breaks"? Well, the pioneers who came here called such badlands "breaks," and they mistook the juniper trees along the cliff bases for cedars.

JUST THE FACTS

At over 10,000 feet elevation, it's always pleasantly cool at Cedar Breaks. It actually gets downright cold at night, so bring a jacket or sweater, even if the temperature is

g just down the road in St. George. The monument opens for its short sum-
eason only after the snow melts, usually in late May, and closes in October—
ess you happen to have a pair of cross-country skis or a snowmobile, in which case
you can visit year-round.

GETTING THERE   Cedar Breaks National Monument is 21 miles east of Cedar
City, 56 miles west of Bryce Canyon National Park, and 247 miles south of Salt Lake
City.

From I-15, drive east of Cedar City on Utah 14 to Utah 148, turn north (left),
and follow Utah 148 into the monument. If you're coming from Bryce Canyon or
other points east, the park is accessible from the town of Panguitch via Utah 143.
If you're coming from the north, take the Parowan exit off I-15 and head south on
Utah 143. It's a steep climb from whichever direction you choose, and vehicles prone
to vapor lock or loss of power on hills (such as motor homes) may have some problems.

INFORMATION & VISITOR CENTERS   One mile from the south entrance
gate, you'll find the visitor center, open daily from June to late September, with exhibits on the geology, flora, and fauna of Cedar Breaks. You can purchase books and
maps here, and rangers can help plan your visit. For advance information, contact
the Superintendent, **Cedar Breaks National Monument,** P.O. Box 749, Cedar City,
UT 84720 (☎ **435/586-9451**).

FEES & REGULATIONS   Admission is $4 per vehicle or $2 per person on foot,
bike, or motorcycle; there is no charge for those passing through the park on Utah
143. Regulations are similar to those at most national parks: Leave everything as you
found it. Mountain bikes are not allowed on hiking trails. Dogs, which must be
leashed at all times, are prohibited on all trails, in the backcountry, and in public
buildings.

HEALTH & SAFETY CONCERNS   The high elevation—10,350 feet at the visitor center—is likely to cause shortness of breath and tiredness, and those with heart
or respiratory conditions should probably consult their doctors before making the trip
to Cedar Breaks. Avoid overlooks and other high, exposed areas during thunderstorms; they're often targets for lightning.

RANGER PROGRAMS   During the monument's short summer season, rangers
offer nightly campfire talks at the campground; talks on the area's geology at Point
Supreme, a viewpoint near the visitor center, daily on the hour from 10am to 5pm;
and guided hikes on Saturday and Sunday mornings. A complete schedule is posted
at the visitor center and the campground.

EXPLORING CEDAR BREAKS BY CAR

The 5-mile road through Cedar Breaks National Monument offers easy access to the
monument's scenic overlooks and trailheads. Allow 30 to 45 minutes to make the
drive. Start at the visitor center and nearby **Point Supreme** for a panoramic view of
the amphitheater. Then drive north, past the campground and picnic ground turnoff, to **Sunset View** for a closer view of the amphitheater and its colorful canyons.
From each of these overlooks you'll be able to see out across Cedar Valley, over the
Antelope and Black Mountains, into the Escalante Desert.

Continue north to **Chessman Ridge Overlook,** so named because the hoodoos
directly below the overlook look like massive stone chess pieces. Watch for swallows
and swifts soaring among the rock formations. Get back into your car and head north
to **Alpine Pond,** a trailhead for a self-guided nature trail (see "Hiking," below) with

an abundance of wildflowers. Finally, you'll reach **North View,** which offers perhaps your best look into the amphitheater. The view here is reminiscent of Bryce Canyon Queen's Garden, with its stately statues frozen in time.

A LATE SUMMER BONANZA: THE WILDFLOWERS OF CEDAR BREAKS

During its brief summer season, Cedar Breaks makes the most of the warmth and moisture in the air with a spectacular wildflower show. The rim comes alive in a blaze of color—truly a sight to behold. The dazzling display begins practically as soon as the snow melts and reaches its peak during late July and August. It's as though the flowers are trying to outshine the colorful rocks below. Watch for mountain bluebells, spring beauty, beard tongue, and fleabane early in the season; those beauties then make way for columbine, larkspur, Indian paintbrush, wild roses, and other varieties.

WARM-WEATHER SPORTS & ACTIVITIES

HIKING   There are no trails from the rim to the bottom of the amphitheater, but the monument does have two high-country trails. The fairly easy 2-mile **Alpine Pond Trail** loop leads to a picturesque forest glade and pond surrounded by wildflowers and through a woodlands of bristlecone pines, offering panoramic views of the amphitheater along the way. A trail guide is available at the trailhead.

A somewhat more challenging hike, the 4-mile **Spectra Point Trail** (also called the Ramparts Trail) follows the rim more closely than the Alpine Pond Trail, offering changing views of the colorful rock formations. It also takes you through fields of wildflowers and by bristlecone pines more than 1,500 years old. You'll need to be especially careful of your footing along the exposed cliff edges, and allow yourself some time to rest—there are lots of ups and downs along the way.

WILDLIFE WATCHING   Because of its relative remoteness, Cedar Breaks is a good place for spotting wildlife. You're likely to see mule deer grazing in the meadows along the road early and late in the day. Marmots make their dens near the rim and are often seen along the Spectra Point Trail. You'll spot ground squirrels, red squirrels, and chipmunks everywhere. Pikas, which are related to rabbits, are here too, but it's unlikely you'll see one. They're small, with short ears and stubby tails, and prefer the high, rocky slopes.

Birders should have no trouble spotting the Clark's nutcracker in the campground, with its gray torso and black-and-white wings and tail. The monument is also home to swallows, swifts, blue grouse, and golden eagles.

CAMPING

The 30-site campground, **Point Supreme,** just north of the visitor center, is open from June through mid-September, with sites available on a first-come, first-served basis. It's a beautiful high-mountain setting, among tall spruce and fir. Facilities include rest rooms, drinking water, picnic tables, grills, and an amphitheater for the ranger's evening campfire programs. No showers or RV hookups are available. Camping fee is $9 per night. Keep in mind that even in mid-summer, temperatures can drop into the 30s at night at this elevation, so bring cool-weather gear.

WINTER SPORTS & ACTIVITIES

The monument is essentially shut down from late October to mid-May because of the blanket of deep snow that covers it. The snow-blocked roads will keep cars out, but they're perfect for snowmobilers and cross-country skiers, who usually come over from nearby Brian Head ski area (see below). Keep in mind, though, that all

~e closed; the only people you're likely to see will be an occasional park
patrolling on a snowmobile.

~ING THE SLOPES

Like the ski areas in the Ogden and Logan areas, Southwest Utah's ski resorts—Brian Head and Elk Meadows—keep their energies focused on terrain and snow; they don't have the wide range of amenities you'll find in Park City, Deer Valley, and Snowbird. In the summer, mountain bikers and hikers converge on both Brian Head and Elk Meadows.

BRIAN HEAD RESORT

Brian Head has the distinction of being Utah's southernmost ski resort, just a short drive from the year-round shirtsleeve warmth of St. George. But with the highest base elevation of any of the state's ski areas, it gets an average of 400 inches of powdery snow each winter. Its location makes it particularly popular with skiers from the Las Vegas area and Southern California.

Brian Head is known for its variety of terrain, especially with snow-cat service to the top of Brian Head Peak (elevation 11,307 feet) offering spectacular advanced terrain for the adventurous. Intermediates will enjoy fine cruising runs a little farther down the mountain, and beginners can ski Navajo Peak, a good learning hill. Another plus at Brian Head is the scenery: The only ski resort in Utah's famed red rock country, it offers stunning views, especially from the tops of the lifts.

Snowboarders are welcome here—there are two snowboarding parks just for them.

For the 1997–98 season, Brian Head opened a Snow Tubing Park with a special surface lift for those looking for a "water slide park" kind of adventure. Cost is about $7 for 2 hours.

Just the Facts

Brian Head Resort (Brian Head, UT 84719; ☎ **435/677-2035** or 800/272-7426 for lodging and snow conditions) has one double and five triple chairlifts servicing 53 trails on 500 acres. The vertical drop is 1,707 feet, from a top elevation of 11,307 feet to a base of 9,600 feet. The highest elevations are serviced by snow cat. Terrain is rated 30% beginner, 40% intermediate, and 30% advanced. Brian Head has snowmaking capabilities on 150 acres. The ski season generally runs from early November to late spring, with lifts operating daily from 9am to 4:30pm. On weekends and holidays, night skiing is available from 4:30 to 10pm.

Giant Steps Lodge, at the base of Brian Head Peak, and **Navajo Lodge,** at the base of Navajo Peak, offer ski shops with sales and rentals, ski school, and information services. Navajo Lodge also has arcade games. The closest hospital is in Cedar City (see "Basing Yourself in Cedar City," above).

GETTING THERE   From Cedar City, it's 28 miles to Brian Head; take I-15 to exit 75 and head south on the very steep Utah 143 about 12 miles.

LIFT TICKETS   An adult all-day lift ticket is $35; a half-day ticket is $28. An all-day child's or senior's (65 and over) ticket is $40. Night skiing costs $10.

LESSONS & PROGRAMS   The **ski school** at Brian Head offers private and group lessons, as well as clinics, snowboard classes, and children's ski instruction. Adult group ski and snowboard lessons start at $59 for a full day. Private lessons start at $46 for an hour; lessons for children ages 5 and up start at $23. The adult learn-to-ski program, for ages 11 and up, offers several options, with prices starting at $30.

Day care is available at an hourly rate of $5 for kids 2 1/2 and older, $6.50 for infants and toddlers. Also available are packages combining day care and ski lessons.

CROSS-COUNTRY SKIING   Brian Head has 42 kilometers (26 miles) of trails, 10 kilometers (6.2 miles) of them groomed—rated 50% beginner, 30% intermediate, and 20% advanced. Lessons and rentals are available, and there's no charge for trail use.

ICE-SKATING   From mid-December to early March, weather permitting, ice-skating is available at no charge at Navajo Lodge. Rentals are available.

Where to Dine

Quick breakfasts and lunches are served at several places at Brian Head, including the Navajo and Giant Steps Base Lodge Grilles, with meals around $5. The Summit Dining Room at Brian Head Hotel offers fine dining nightly from 5 to 10pm, with steaks, seafood, and pasta dishes in the $12 to $22 price range.

Where to Stay

The Brian Head area offers a variety of lodging possibilities, with rates ranging from just under $100 to about $400 per night. Contact **Brian Head Resort Central Reservations** (☎ **435/677-2035**). Room tax here is about 10%. You can also stay in Cedar City, 28 miles away (see "Basing Yourself in Cedar City," above).

   Cedar Breaks Lodge (P.O. Box 190248, Brian Head, UT 84719; ☎ **888/ 282-3327**), near the base of Navajo Peak, recently underwent an extensive multi-million dollar renovation. It offers studio, parlor, and master suites ranging from $95 to $175 in summer and $150 to $250 in winter. Facilities include three restaurants, a spa, indoor pool, two hot tubs, fitness center, game room, laundry, and gift and sports shops. Both ski and summer packages are available.

Warm-Weather Activities

Once the snow melts, mountain bikers, hikers, and horseback riders claim the mountain. With elevations ranging from 9,700 feet to 11,307 feet, Brian Head is always cool, crisp, and just perfect for working up a sweat. Evenings are busy, too, with live musical entertainment ranging from jazz and country to bluegrass and classical; there's even an occasional bagpipe performance.

MOUNTAIN BIKING   This ski resort isn't just for skiers anymore. It's fast becoming a major destination for serious—and we do mean serious—mountain bikers. This is a wonderful place for ✪ **mountain-biking**, with endless trails, superb scenery, and about the freshest air you're going to find. What's more, mountain biking here can be oh-so-very easy: a mountain bike chairlift hauls you and your bike up the mountain; it's about $12 for a full-day pass. Or, for about $10, you can take a shuttle to and from several locations. That way, you can pedal the fun parts, but travel under someone else's power for the steeper sections.

   If you didn't bring your own, mountain-bike rentals are available for about $25 per day for adults, $20 for kids ages 12 and younger. Contact **Bike Brian Head** (☎ **435/677-2035**) for details.

HORSEBACK RIDING   If newfangled bikes with all those gears are too much for you, make your saddle the western kind, and do your traveling on the back of a sure-footed horse. **High Adventure Trail Rides** (☎ **435/559-2362**) offers guided trail rides starting at $15 for an hour, $70 for a full day.

ELK MEADOWS RESORT

An excellent ski area for families, Elk Meadows offers a well-respected program for beginners, who even get their own mountain. Of course, they won't stay beginners long, which is good—Elk Meadows rates over 60% of its terrain intermediate, more than any other Utah ski area. Its high base elevation, second only to Brian Head,

...tee plenty of powder snow, and its location—somewhat off the beaten ...eans that lift lines are practically nonexistent. In addition to its designated ...ill runs, there's off-trail skiing, Nordic skiing, and snowshoeing. Snowboarders ...welcome. In summer, the resort becomes a haven for hikers, mountain bikers, and ...nglers.

Just the Facts

Elk Meadows Resort (P.O. Box 511, Beaver, UT 84713; ☎ **888/881-SNOW** (7669) or 435/438-5433) has a vertical drop of 1,300 feet from a top elevation of 10,400 feet to a base of 9,100 feet. Five lifts—three doubles, one triple, and a new quad—service 35 runs on 220 skiable acres. The terrain is rated 14% beginner, 62% intermediate, and 24% advanced. Elk Meadows receives about 400 inches of snow each year and has no snowmaking capabilities. The season generally runs from late November to mid-April, with lifts operating from 9am to 4pm daily.

A recently renovated and expanded day lodge contains a ski shop with rental equipment, a general store, and meeting space for small groups. The resort also provides child-care services. The closest medical facility is **Beaver Valley Hospital,** at 85 N. 400 East, in Beaver (☎ **435/438-2531**).

GETTING THERE   The ski area is about 230 miles from Salt Lake City and about 70 miles from Cedar City. From I-15, take exit 109 or 112 into Beaver, and head east on Utah 153 (200 North Street in Beaver) about 18 miles. Utah 153 is paved and well maintained but has grades from 4% to 10% and sharp curves.

LIFT TICKETS   An all-day adult lift ticket is $30; a half-day ticket costs $22. An all-day student's ticket (ages 12 to 17 and college students) costs $25; half day costs $22. All-day tickets for seniors (ages 60 to 70) and children (ages 7 to 12) cost $15; half day costs $12. Children 6 and younger and seniors over 70 ski free. Multiday discounts are also available.

LESSONS & RENTALS   The **ski school** offers an excellent learn-to-ski program, as well as downhill, Nordic, and snowboarding lessons. Private lessons start at $42 per hour, and group lessons start at $25 for a half day. Downhill rental equipment costs $20 for adults and $12 for children for full-day packages; half-day rates are $15 and $10, respectively. Full-day snowboard rentals are $25 for adults and $15 for children.

CROSS-COUNTRY SKIING & SNOWSHOEING   Some fine Nordic trails head off from the resort into the national forest. Cross-country skiers who use the lifts buy a regular pass; those who don't use the lifts ski free. There are also trails for snowshoers. Both Nordic equipment and snowshoes are available for rent (call for rates).

Where to Stay & Dine

A variety of condominiums are available, from studios to one-, two-, and three-bedroom units, all with full kitchen and either a fireplace or wood-burning stove. Studios cost $97 to $128 nightly, a one-bedroom unit runs $135 to $182, a unit with one bedroom plus a loft costs $156 to $199, a two-bedroom unit runs from $200 to $250, and a three-bedroom condo costs $220 to $260. Rates are lower mid-week and higher during the Christmas holiday period; check on lower off-season rates. Minimum stays are usually required during holiday periods. Call ☎ **888/881-SNOW** (7669) or 435/438-5433 for particulars. The resort also contains a restaurant, cafeteria, and lounge. Room tax of about 9% is added to your bill.

Warm-Weather Activities

The beautiful mountain scenery here is just as pretty without the snow. Lifts at the 2,000-acre resort run in summer to take hikers, mountain bikers (with their bikes), and anglers to numerous trails and streams on the resort's property, with easy access to the adjacent Fishlake National Forest (see below). Fly-fishing is considered world-class, and this is one of the best spots in Utah to see mule deer. You are also likely to spot elk, golden eagles, hawks, and numerous other birds.

Activities in the Fishlake National Forest

Elk Meadows Resort is surrounded by the 1.4-million acre Fishlake National Forest, which offers an abundance of opportunities for both winter and summer activities, from snowmobiling, snowshoeing, and cross-country skiing to hiking, mountain biking, horseback riding, fishing, all-terrain-vehicle use, and camping. Several forest service campgrounds and picnic areas are located along the road to Elk Meadows, with parking areas for fishermen as well. For information, contact the Fishlake National Forest's **Beaver Ranger District office,** 190 N. 100 East (P.O. Box E), Beaver, UT 84713 (☎ **435/438-2436**). The office is located just off I-15 exit 109 on the I-15 Business Loop.

A Nearby State Park

Minersville State Park, about 35 miles west of Elk Meadows on Utah 21, has a lovely lake set among rolling hills sprinkled with sagebrush, piñon, and juniper. Naturally, water sports dominate the activities here, but you'll also find a volleyball court, as well as opportunities for picnicking, camping, bird-watching, and waterfowl hunting in season. Fishermen come for rainbow and cutthroat trout and smallmouth bass. The 29-site campground has picnic tables under shelters with built-in supply cabinets and modern rest rooms with showers. Eight sites have water and electric hookups. Fees are $3 for day use and $11 to $13 for camping. For information contact **Minersville State Park,** P.O. Box 1531, Beaver, UT 84713-0051 (☎ **435/438-5472**).

4 Kanab: Movies, Sand Dunes & Gateway to the Grand Canyon

Another southern Utah town founded by Mormon pioneers sent by Brigham Young in the 1870s, Kanab is best known for its starring role in the movies and on TV. This is the Wild West many of us grew up with, on TV shows like *Gunsmoke, The Lone Ranger, Death Valley Days,* and *F Troop;* and on the big screen in *She Wore a Yellow Ribbon, Sergeants Three, Bandolero,* and *The Outlaw Josie Wales.*

But Kanab lives on more than just memories of the Old West; it also serves as a stopping point for travelers on their way to southern Utah's major sights. Visitors coming from Arizona are likely to pass through on their way to Zion and Bryce Canyon National Parks. If you're starting your Lake Powell trip in Page, Arizona, you'll probably come through Kanab. And the Grand Canyon is directly to the south, so if you're heading to the north rim, Kanab is a good choice for a home base. None of these natural wonders are all that close to Kanab, but in Utah terms, they're "just around the corner."

ESSENTIALS

GETTING THERE   Kanab is 82 miles east of St. George, 80 miles south of Bryce Canyon National Park, 42 miles east of Zion National Park, 68 miles west of Lake

Powell and Glen Canyon Recreation Area, 79 miles north of the Grand Canyon, and 303 miles south of Salt Lake City.

By Car   Kanab is located on U.S. 89 at the junction of U.S. 89A, which crosses into Arizona just 7 miles south of town.

VISITOR INFORMATION   Contact the **Kane County Visitors Center,** 78 S. 100 East, Kanab, UT 84741 (☎ **800/733-5263** or 435/644-5033).

GETTING AROUND   Kanab is pretty easy to get a handle on. It's laid out on a grid, with ground zero at the intersection of Center and Main streets. U.S. 89 comes in from the north on 300 West Street, turns east onto Center Street, south again on 100 East Street, and finally east again on 300 South. U.S. 89A follows 100 East Street south to the airport and, after about 7 miles, Arizona.

Fast Facts

The **Kane County Hospital and Skilled Nursing Facility** is at 220 W. 300 North St. (☎ 435/644-5811). The **post office** is at 39 S. Main St. (☎ 435/644-2760). In an **emergency,** call ☎ 435/644-2667 if you're outside of town; otherwise use ☎ 911.

CORAL PINK SAND DUNES STATE PARK

Long a favorite of dune-buggy enthusiasts (off-road vehicle users lobbied hard to have this designated a state park), Coral Pink Sand Dunes has recently been attracting an increasing number of campers, hikers, photographers, and all-around nature lovers as well. While big boys—and occasionally big girls—play with their expensive motorized toys, others hike; hunt for wildflowers, scorpions, and lizards; or just sit and wiggle their toes in the smooth, cool sand. The colors are especially rich at sunrise and sunset. Early-morning visitors to the dunes will find the tracks of yesterday's dune buggies gone, replaced by the tracks of lizards, kangaroo rats, snakes, and the rest of the park's animal kingdom, who venture out in the coolness of night once all the people have departed.

Just the Facts

GETTING THERE   From downtown Kanab, go about 8 miles north on U.S. 89, then southwest (left) on Hancock Road for about 12 miles to the park.

INFORMATION & VISITOR CENTERS   For copies of the park brochure and off-highway-vehicle regulations, contact the **park office** at P.O. Box 95, Kanab, UT 84741-0095 (☎ **435/648-2800**). At the **park entry station,** you'll see a small display area with sand from around the world, fossils of the area, and live scorpions, lizards, and tadpoles.

FEES & REGULATIONS   The day-use fee is $3 per vehicle for up to eight people. The standard state park regulations apply, with the addition of a few extra rules due to the park's popularity with off-road-vehicle users: Quiet hours last from 10pm to 9am, a bit later in the morning than in most parks. The dunes are open to motor vehicles between 9am and 10pm and to hikers at any time. Vehicles going onto the dunes must have safety flags, available at the entry station; while on the dunes, they must stay at least 10 feet from vegetation and at least 100 feet from hikers. Dogs are permitted on the dunes but must be leashed.

RANGER PROGRAMS   Regularly scheduled ranger talks explain the geology, plants, and animals of the dunes. For a real thrill, take a guided evening **Scorpion Walk,** using a black light to find luminescent scorpions that make the park their home. You'll definitely want to wear shoes for this activity! Call to find out if there's one scheduled during your visit.

SPORTS & ACTIVITIES

FOUR-WHEELING This giant 1,000-acre sandbox offers plenty of space for ✪ **off-road-vehicle enthusiasts,** who can race up and down the dunes, stopping to perch on a crest to watch the setting sun. Because the sand here is quite fine, extra-wide flotation tires are needed, and lightweight dune buggies are usually the vehicle of choice. Adjacent to the park on Bureau of Land Management property, you'll find hundreds of miles of trails and roads for off-highway vehicles.

HIKING The best time for ✪ **hiking the dunes** is early morning, for several reasons: it's cooler, the lighting at and just after sunrise produces beautiful shadows and colors, and there are no noisy dune buggies until after 9am. Sunset is also very pretty, but you'll be sharing the dunes with off-road vehicles. Keep in mind that hiking through fine sand can be very tiring, especially for those of us who insist on hiking barefoot. A self-guided half-mile loop nature trail has numbered signs through some of the dunes; allow a half hour for it.

Several other good hikes of various lengths are possible within and just outside the park, but because there are few signs and landmarks change with the shifting sands, it's best to check with park rangers before setting out. Those spending more than a few hours in the dunes will discover that even their own tracks disappear in the wind, leaving few clues to the route back to park headquarters.

CAMPING

The spacious and mostly shady 22-site campground, open year-round, offers hot showers, modern rest rooms, and an RV dump station, but no hookups. Camping costs $11. Call ☎ **800/322-3770** for reservations, with an additional $5 reservation fee per site.

MORE TO SEE & DO IN & AROUND KANAB

Heritage House

At 100 South and Main sts., Kanab. ☎ **435/644-2381.** Fax 435/644-3506. Adults $3, children 12 and under $1. Apr–Oct Tues–Sat 10am–5pm. Nov–Mar special events Saturdays only. From the intersection of Center and Main sts., head south 1 block.

Although there are 16 historic houses in the downtown area of Kanab, this is the only one open to the public. Built in 1894, this Victorian was purchased by Thomas H. Chamberlain in 1896. (Chamberlain's sixth wife, Mary, was elected mayor of Kanab in 1912.) Purchased by the city in 1974, the house has been restored to its original appearance. A self-guided tour brochure describes what you see now and discusses planned reconstructions.

A booklet describing all of Kanab's historic houses, with a map showing their locations, is available for $4.

Moqui Cave

On the east side of U.S. 89, about 5.5 miles north of Kanab. ☎ **435/644-2987.** Admission $3.50 adults, $3 seniors, $2.50 youths 13–17, $1.50 children 6–12. Memorial Day–Labor Day Mon–Sat 9am–7pm; spring and fall Mon–Sat 9:30am–6pm. Closed mid-Nov–Mar.

Native Americans known as the Moqui are believed to have spent time in this cave 800 to 900 years ago. Times have changed since then, and so has the cave; the Moqui would be amazed at what they'd find here today. The Chamberlain family, descendants of Thomas and Mary Chamberlain (see Heritage House, above), bought the cave in 1951, and the following year opened a tavern and dance hall in it. Although you can't order a drink today, the unique bar is still here, along with a huge collection that ranges from authentic dinosaur tracks more than 140 million years old to a beautiful fluorescent mineral display. You'll also see Native American pottery, spear points, and other art and artifacts. A large gift shop specializes in Native American arts and crafts.

WHERE TO STAY

Kanab offers a range of lodging choices. In addition to the properties described below, Kanab has a **Super 8 Motel,** 70 S. 200 West, Kanab, UT 84741 (☎ 800/ 800-8000 or 435/644-5500; fax 435/644-5576), with rates for two of $50 to $70.

Room tax adds about 10% to lodging bills. Pets are not accepted unless otherwise noted.

Best Western Red Hills

125 W. Center St., Kanab, UT 84741. ☎ **800/830-2675** or 435/644-2625. Fax 435/644-5915. 72 units. A/C TV TEL. Mid-Apr–May $60–$80 double, $85–$100 suite; June–Oct $75–$90 double, $100–$135 suite; Nov–mid-Apr $45–$60 double, $65–$85 suite. AE, CB, DC, DISC, MC, V.

The spacious rooms in this well-kept Best Western each contain two queen-size beds or one king, and all king rooms have refrigerators. Framed photos highlight the area's scenery. VCRs are available, as well as an outdoor heated swimming pool, whirlpool, and sundeck. Free coffee and tea are served in the lobby.

Holiday Inn Express

815 East U.S. 89, Kanab, UT 84741. ☎ **800/574-4061** or 435/644-8888. Fax 435/644-8880. 67 rms. A/C TV TEL. May–mid-Nov $69–$85 double; mid-Nov–Apr $49–$64 double (including breakfast bar). AE, DC, DISC, MC, V.

This is the place for golfers. Adjacent to the 9-hole Coral Cliffs Golf Course, this comfortable three-story motel, built in mid-1994, has a relaxed western atmosphere. One golf pass per day is included in the price of the rooms, all of which have good views. Most contain two queen-size beds, although a few have a king and a comfortable recliner. The rooms and lobby are decorated with photos of southern Utah attractions. Facilities include a heated outdoor pool, whirlpool, self-service laundry, and gift shop.

Nine Gables Inn Bed & Breakfast

106 W. 100 North, Kanab, UT 84741. ☎ **435/644-5079.** 3 rms. A/C. $70–$80. Rates include full breakfast. MC, V. Closed mid-Oct–mid-May.

This stately white brick home, built in 1872, is considered Kanab's first permanent residence. Today, its three guest rooms offer not only an attractive alternative to the standard motel, but also a glimpse into southern Utah's past. All rooms have private baths with showers only (which is somewhat ironic, since this house was the first in town to have a bathtub). The house is furnished with owners Frank and Jeanne Bantlin's family antiques, an eclectic collection from the late 1800s and early 1900s, including a marvelous horsehair rocking chair and a variety of bed sizes.

The homemade full breakfasts include innovative selections such as fresh asparagus quiche. The Bantlins grow many of their own vegetables and serve whatever fresh fruits are in season. Guests share a parlor with TV and VCR, and parking is off-street. If by chance you get a creative urge here, you won't be alone: Western writer Zane Grey reportedly stayed at the Nine Gables while researching his novel *Riders of the Purple Sage.*

Parry Lodge

$57.⁰⁰

89 E. Center St. (U.S. 89), Kanab, UT 84741. ☎ **800/748-4104** or 435/644-2601. Fax 435/644-2605. 89 units. A/C TV TEL. Summer $46–$65 double, $73 family unit; winter $30–$46 double, $54 family unit. AE, DISC, MC, V.

This is where the stars stayed—Frank Sinatra, Dean Martin, John Wayne, Roddy McDowell, James Garner, and Ronald Reagan, to name just a few—while filming in Kanab. In 1931, Chauncey Parry decided to open a motel for the film people who were regularly coming to town. Two chandeliers from Paris hang in the lobby, and photos of movie stars scattered about the public areas accent the lodge's colonial atmosphere. Doors to the original rooms, which make up about one-third of the total number, are each adorned with the name of a movie star who stayed there. The newer rooms date from the 1970s, and are smaller than the original ones (although none are huge); a few of the units come with shower only. Facilities include an outdoor heated pool, coin-operated laundry, one unit with kitchenette, and a gift shop open in the summer. Room service is available when the restaurant is open (see "Where to Dine," below). Both smoking and nonsmoking rooms are available, and pets are accepted with a $5 fee.

Shilo Inn

296 W. 100 North, Kanab, UT, 84741-3228. ☎ **800/222-2244** or 435/644-2562. Fax 435/644-5333. 68 units. A/C TV TEL. Summer $65–$85; winter $35–$55. Rates include continental breakfast. AE, DC, DISC, JCB, MC, V.

This attractive modern motel with a Southwestern flair offers all mini-suites, each with three phones, built-in hair dryers, microwave ovens, small refrigerators, and an above-average amount of storage space. The king rooms contain a king-size bed and a small hide-a-bed; other rooms have either one or two queen beds. Rooms adjacent to the small outdoor pool can be a bit noisy, but the rest are very quiet. The motel also offers a whirlpool, self-service laundry, and conference rooms for up to 130. VCRs and videos are available for rent. Pets are permitted with a $7 fee.

CAMPING

Kanab RV Corral

483 S. 100 East, U.S. 89A, Kanab, UT 84741. ☎ **435/644-5330.** Fax 435/644-5464. 40 sites with hookups; 10–15 tent sites. $18–$20 hookups; $12–$18 tent. MC, V.

Open year-round, this campground and RV park makes a good base camp for exploring this part of Utah. The sites are a bit close together and you do get some highway noise; on the flip side, the bathhouses are exceptionally nice (with extra-large shower stalls), the coin-operated laundry is kept spotless, and the small kidney-shaped pool is a lot of fun.

WHERE TO DINE

Houston's Trail's End Restaurant & Mobile Catering

32 E. Center St. ☎ **435/644-2488.** Main courses $7.90–$16.75; lunch $4.90–$7.25; breakfast $3.25–$6.50. AE, DISC, MC, V. Memorial Day–Labor Day daily 6am–10pm; slightly shorter hours in winter. Closed Christmas–mid-Feb. From the intersection of Center and Main sts., head east on Center a short distance; the restaurant will be on your right. STEAK/SEAFOOD/MEXICAN.

Houston's offers a fun western atmosphere, with historic photos and memorabilia displayed on wood-plank walls and waitresses with "guns on their hips and smiles on their lips." Family-owned since 1975, the Houstons age their own beef and make their famous gravy fresh daily. For breakfast, choose from among all the usual egg dishes, plus biscuits and gravy and an especially hearty western omelet. Lunch entrees include sandwiches and burgers, pork spareribs, fish-and-chips, roast beef, and salads. For dinner, the rather darker steakhouse in the back is opened. Its computerized player piano, flocked red wallpaper, and neon designs of cowboy hats, boots, and brands add to the Old West atmosphere. Houston's is best known for its chicken-fried steak, but the rib eye is also popular. A children's menu is available. No alcohol is served.

Parry Lodge

89 E. Center St. ☎ **435/644-2601**. Reservations recommended for dinner. Main courses $7.50–$17.75; breakfast and lunch $2.95–$6.95. AE, DISC, MC, V. Summer daily 7am–10pm; spring and fall daily 7am–noon and 6–10pm. Closed Nov–Easter. From the intersection of Center and Main sts., head east about a block; the lodge will be on your left. AMERICAN.

The restaurant at the Parry Lodge (see "Where to Stay," above) is Victorian in style, with photos of the many movie stars who have stayed and dined here covering the walls. The small but elegant main restaurant contains only 14 tables, a bit close together, but plenty more seating and the same menu are available in the coffee shop. Most of the American standards are offered for breakfast; lunches (served only in the summer) include burgers, sandwiches, and salads, plus chicken-fried steak and the house specialty, chicken and dumplings, for those looking for something more substantial.

For dinner, we highly recommend the boneless chicken with gravy, cranberry sauce, and the fresh, homemade, soft dumplings. Beef eaters should thoroughly enjoy the slow-cooked roast prime rib. Other dinner selections include poached salmon, grilled baby beef liver, deep-fried chicken, and several broiled steaks. Portions are large, and half portions of some dinner items are available at 20% off the menu price. All desserts are made daily in-house. Full liquor service is available.

The Wok Inn

86 S. 200 West. ☎ **435/644-5400**. Main courses $5.95–$15.95, combo lunch plate special $3.95. AE, DISC, MC, V. Mon–Fri 11:30am–10pm; Sat–Sun 3–10pm. From the intersection of Center and Main sts., head west on Center for 2 blocks and turn left (south) onto 200 West for about a block. HUNAN/SZECHUAN/CHINESE.

The decor here is western steakhouse overlaid with Chinese lanterns, parasols, screens, and artwork, plus a Chinese garden and pagoda. But you won't find any western influence in the food: It's strictly Chinese, prepared by Chinese chefs. The Moo Goo Gai Pan and Szechuan Pork (the special during our visit) were both good; the pork was spicy, but not too hot. Several items on the menu are marked hot, and reliable locals informed us they are to be believed! The chicken curry could have been spicier, but was tasty nonetheless. Full liquor service and children's portions are available.

SOUTH TO ARIZONA

This section of Arizona, called the Arizona Strip, actually belongs in Utah. Isolated from the rest of Arizona by the Grand Canyon, it was settled mainly by Mormon

Impressions

Ours has been the first and will undoubtedly be the last party to visit this profitless locality. It seems intended by nature that the Colorado River, along the greater portion of its lonely, majestic way, shall be forever unvisited and undisturbed.

—Lieut. Joseph Ives, 1858.

pioneers sent by church leader Brigham Young in the mid- to late 1800s, when northern Arizona was part of the Mormon state of Deseret. Even today, this area is more often claimed by Utah's town of Kanab than anywhere in Arizona. It's certainly easier to reach from Utah than from cities in Arizona. The major draws here are the north rim of the Grand Canyon and Pipe Spring National Monument.

GRAND CANYON NATIONAL PARK—NORTH RIM

If we're going to visit the Grand Canyon, this is the side we choose. It's not that the north rim is any more scenic than the South Rim—in some ways the South Rim is more colorful and awe-inspiring—but the North Rim is more pristine, wilder, more of what we expect from our national parks. It's a pain in the neck to get to, and for that reason the North Rim receives considerably fewer visitors than the South Rim.

Just the Facts

The North Rim of the Grand Canyon is 78 miles south of Kanab, and 216 road miles (21 foot or mule miles, and 10 as-the-crow-flies miles) north of Grand Canyon Village at the South Rim. From Kanab, take U.S. 89A south through Fredonia, Arizona, to the town of Jacob Lake, Arizona, and follow Ariz. 67 through the Kaibab National Forest into the park.

There is no visitor center at the Grand Canyon's north rim, but an information desk is located in the lobby of Grand Canyon Lodge, and you can also get information at the entrance station. Be sure to ask for a copy of *The Guide,* a newspaper-style visitor guide that describes park activities. Before your trip, you can write to **Grand Canyon National Park,** P.O. Box 129, Grand Canyon, AZ 86023 (☎ **520/638-7888**), for a copy of the Grand Canyon Trip Planner. Those who want more in-depth information can buy books, maps, and videos from the Grand Canyon Association, P.O. Box 399, Grand Canyon, AZ 86023 (☎ **520/638-2481;** fax 520/638-2484). Call ☎ **520/638-7888** for recorded weather information.

Admission to the park, good for 1 week, costs $20 per vehicle, or $10 per individual on foot, bike, or motorcycle.

Backcountry permits ($20 plus $4 nightly impact fee) are required for all overnight hikes in the park.

North Rim facilities are open only from late spring to early fall, usually from mid-May to late October, although the lodge and campground may close a bit earlier. Day use may be permitted through November, but check before making the trip.

Ranger Programs

A variety of ranger programs and guided hikes and walks are offered, with schedules posted on bulletin boards at Grand Canyon Lodge and at the campground.

Kids under 15 can join the Junior Rangers and earn certificates, badges, and patches. Information packets are available at the information desk at Grand Canyon Lodge.

Exploring Grand Canyon by Air

Several companies offer a bird's-eye view of the canyon; **Lake Mead Air** at Kanab Airport (☎ 435/644-2299) offers a 40-minute flight for $79 per person and a 75-minute flight at $119 per person.

Sports & Outdoor Activities

EDUCATIONAL FIELD TRIPS   Grand Canyon Field Institute, P.O. Box 399, Grand Canyon, AZ 86023 (☎ 520/638-2485), offers a series of hikes, walks, river trips, and other excursions. Small groups study geology, wildlife, wilderness skills, history, photography, or art on multiday treks, and college credits can be arranged.

HIKING   Foot-power is our preferred mode of transportation at Grand Canyon's north rim. The paved half-mile ✪ **Bright Angel Point Trail** is an easy walk to a viewpoint that offers a spectacular view of the canyon and serves as an excellent introduction to the park. Allow about half an hour. Another easy walk, especially good for those in wheelchairs, is the Cape Royal Trail. This 0.6-mile flat, paved trail also offers spectacular views of the canyon, plus it's the only viewpoint from which you can see the Colorado River. Trail markers discuss the area's natural history. Allow half an hour.

The only maintained trail down into the canyon from the North Rim is ✪ **North Kaibab Trail,** and no matter how much time you spend looking down from the rim, the canyon just doesn't become real until you've hiked at least partway in. North Kaibab Trail will take you all the way to the bottom—28 miles round-trip—which is certainly not a one-day jaunt for any normal person, but even a relatively short hike partway down and back can be enormously fulfilling. You'll see the changing vegetation, geology, and light, and get a sense of the canyon's immense size. Keep in mind that temperatures rise as you descend into the canyon, and carry plenty of water—at least 1 gallon per person per day in summer. Rangers recommend that day hikers determine beforehand how long they want to be on the trail, and then turn around when one-third of that time has passed.

A shuttle from Grand Canyon Lodge to the North Kaibab Trailhead operates daily, and shuttles between the rims can be arranged. Check at the lodge transportation desk (☎ **520/638-2820**). By the way, mules have right-of-way on all trails.

MULE RIDES   To see the canyon from atop a mule, stop at the Trail Rides desk in Grand Canyon Lodge, or contact Grand Canyon Trail Rides (☎ **520/638-2292** or 435/679-8665). Operating from mid-May to mid-October, weather permitting, 1-hour rim rides cost $12 per person, half-day rim or canyon trips cost $35 per person, and full-day canyon rides, including lunch, cost $85 per person.

RAFTING   Seeing the Grand Canyon from the water, as explorer John Wesley Powell did over 100 years ago, can be thrilling, but with close to 20 companies offering raft trips into the Grand Canyon, it certainly isn't a wilderness experience anymore. Trips through the canyon last from 3 days to several weeks, with prices starting at $300 to $400 per person. You can request a complete list of licensed raft companies from Grand Canyon National Park headquarters (see above).

Camping

The **North Rim Campground,** just north of Grand Canyon Lodge, offers 82 sites, rest rooms, and water, but no RV hookups. Nearby showers are available for a fee. A typically attractive and shady national park campground, it offers the best possible location. Cost is $15.

A good alternative to camping in the national park is the **Kaibab National Forest,** with both dispersed camping (free) and several developed campgrounds ($10 per night). Camping is on a first-come, first-served basis. For information, contact the North Kaibab Ranger District, Kaibab National Forest, P.O. Box 248, Fredonia, AZ 86022 (☎ **520/643-7395**).

Accommodations & Dining

The center of activity at Grand Canyon's North Rim is **Grand Canyon Lodge** (☎ **520/638-2611;** information and reservations: AmFac Parks & Resorts, 14001 E. Iliff Ave., Suite 600, Aurora, CO 80014 (☎ **303/29-PARKS;** fax 303/338-2045). Listed on the National Register of Historic Places, this handsome—almost majestic— stone lodge offers a spectacular view of the canyon. Its 201 units include standard motel rooms and cabins that range from rustic to nearly luxurious. Motel rooms cost $68 to $72 double, and cabins range from $57 to $90.

The lodge's restaurant offers a good selection of American cuisine, such as red mountain trout, the house specialty. The menu also includes several chicken dishes, such as a skinless chicken breast basted with a spicy Caribbean sauce, and several vegetarian items as well. Breakfast items cost $3.50 to $6; lunch selections cost $4.50 to $7; and main courses at dinner range from $7 to $17. Dinner reservations are required.

Other lodge facilities include a gift shop, bookstore, and national park information desk. The lodge is open from mid-May to late October.

PIPE SPRING NATIONAL MONUMENT

Located in the Kaibab-Paiute Indian Reservation in northwestern Arizona, this national monument preserves the stone headquarters of a large 19th-century cattle ranch that was operated by the Church of Jesus Christ of Latter-day Saints.

Just the Facts

Pipe Spring National Monument is located about 20 miles southwest of Kanab, via U.S. 89A and Ariz. 389.

A visitor center and museum, at the entrance to the monument, has exhibits depicting the lives of both the Native Americans of the area and Mormon settlers. Nearby, you'll find a bookstore, gift shop, and snack bar. There are no other dining, lodging, or camping facilities at the monument.

The monument is open daily from 8am to 4:30pm mountain standard time. Admission costs $2 per person. For information, write **Pipe Spring National Monument,** Moccasin, AZ 86022 (☎ **520/643-7105**).

This well-preserved 19th-century combination fort and cattle ranch was another of the many settlements established at the direction of Mormon leader Brigham Young. Nicknamed "Winsor Castle" for early ranch superintendent Anson Perry Winsor, it was built in 1870 as a fort because Mormon settlers had been killed by Navajo raiders just 4 years earlier. Fortunately, the thick rock walls, made from stone quarried from the red sandstone cliffs just west of the fort, never had to withstand an attack. Its real purpose was as a ranch for the church's southern Utah tithing herd, the cattle contributed by Mormon families as one-tenth of their incomes. Some of the beef, cheese, and butter produced here were sent to St. George for the workers building the St. George LDS Temple.

Today we can see not only what the Mormon Church created here, but also an excellent example of a 19th-century ranch—crafted from materials at hand, located as close as possible to a reliable water source, and fortified to protect the settlers from attack.

From the visitor center, follow the walkway by the orchards, gardens, and irrigation ponds to the massive fort—actually two stone houses sharing a spring and joined by high walls with sturdy wooden gates. During summer you can take a guided tour, which lasts about 45 minutes; or you can explore the fort and grounds on your own at any time of year, using a map and descriptive brochure provided free at the visitor center.

Inside the fort you'll see the bedrooms, furnished as they would have been in the late 1800s; the meeting room; the relatively fancy parlor; the cheese-making room; and the all-important kitchen, with the table set in Mormon fashion (with plates upside down and chairs facing away from the table to facilitate kneeling for before-meal prayers). You'll also step inside the telegraph room, with the original telegraph stand and a photograph of the first telegraph operator, Luella Stewart; this served as the Arizona Territory's first telegraph office. Outside the fort you'll find the blacksmith shop, with a display of pioneer tools; a bunkhouse used by explorer John Wesley Powell's survey crew in 1871; a harness room with ranch equipment; corrals and pens; and a half-mile loop trail that leads up the sandstone cliffs behind the house.

During the summer you're likely to see demonstrations of pioneer life, such as weaving, cheese making, and cooking.

Zion National Park 12

Early Mormon settler Isaac Behunin is credited with naming his homestead "Little Zion," because it seemed to be a bit of heaven on earth. Today, 150 years later, Zion National Park will cast a spell over you as you gaze upon its sheer multicolored walls of sandstone, explore its narrow canyons, hunt for hanging gardens of wildflowers, or listen to the roar of the churning, tumbling Virgin River.

It's easy to conjure up a single defining image of the Grand Canyon or of the delicately sculpted rock hoodoos of Bryce, but Zion, a collage of images and secrets, is more difficult to pin down. It's not simply the towering Great White Throne, deep Narrows Canyon, or cascading waterfalls and emerald green pools. There's an entire smorgasbord of experiences, sights, and even smells here, from massive stone sculptures and monuments to lush forests and rushing rivers. Take time to walk its trails, visiting viewpoints at different times of the day to see the changing light, and let the park work its magic on you.

Because of its extremes of elevation (from 3,700 feet to almost 9,000 feet) and climate (with temperatures soaring over 100°F in the summer and a landscape carpeted in snow in the winter), Zion harbors a vast array of plants and animals. About 800 native species of plants have been found: cactus, yucca, and mesquite in the hot, dry desert areas; ponderosa pine trees on the high plateaus; and cottonwoods and box elders along the rivers and streams. Of the 14 varieties of cactus that grow in the park, watch for the red claret cup, which has spectacular blooms in the spring. Wildflowers common in the park include the manzanita, with its tiny pink blossoms; buttercups; and the bright red hummingbird trumpet. You'll also see the sacred datura—dubbed the "Zion Lily" because of its abundance in the park—with its large funnel-shaped white flowers that open in the cool of night and often close by noon.

While exploring Zion, be sure to watch for "spring lines" and their hanging gardens, which you'll see clinging to the sides of cliffs. Because sandstone is porous, water can percolate down through it until it is stopped by a layer of harder rock. Then the water simply changes direction, moving horizontally to the rock face, where it oozes out, forming the "spring line" that provides life-giving nutrients to whatever seeds the wind delivers.

Zion National Park

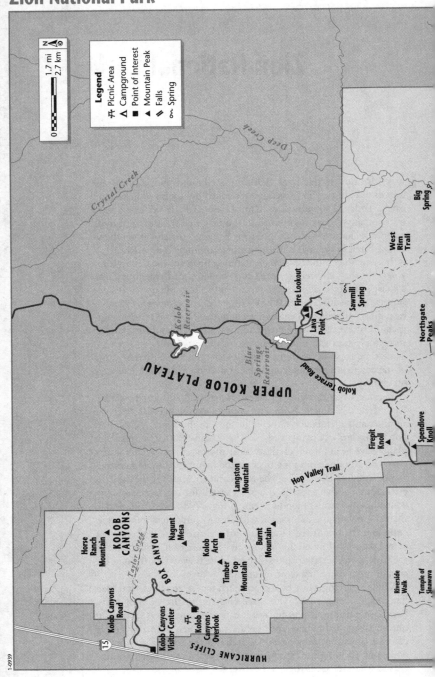

1-0939

Legend
⅄ Picnic Area
▲ Campground
■ Point of Interest
▲ Mountain Peak
✦ Falls
∿ Spring

N

1.7 mi
2.7 km
0

Deep Creek

Crystal Creek

Big Spring

West Rim Trail

Fire Lookout

Sawmill Spring

Kolob Reservoir

Lava Point

Northgate Peaks

Blue Springs Reservoir

UPPER KOLOB PLATEAU

Kolob Terrace Road

Spendlove Knoll

Firepit Knoll

Hop Valley Trail

Langston Mountain

Horse Ranch Mountain

KOLOB CANYONS

Nagunt Mesa

Kolob Arch

Burnt Mountain

Taylor Creek

BOX CANYON

Timber Top Mountain

Riverside Walk

Temple of Sinawava

Kolob Canyons Road

Kolob Canyons Visitor Center

Kolob Canyons Overlook

15

HURRICANE CLIFFS

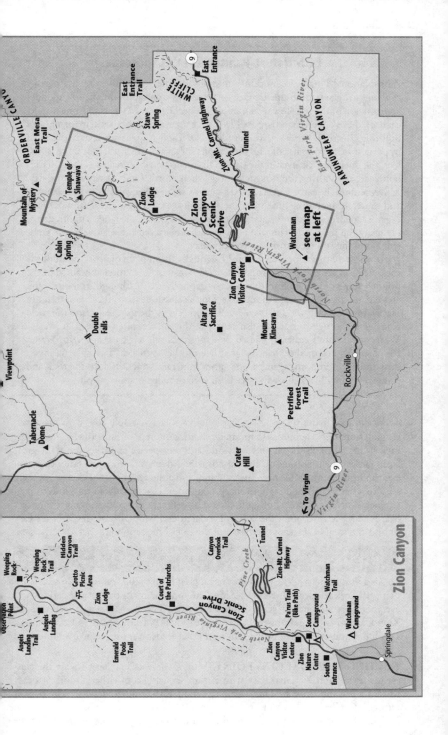

ORDERVILLE CANYON

East Mesa Trail

East Entrance Trail

WHITE CLIFFS

Stave Spring

East Entrance

9

East Fork Virgin River

Zion-Mt. Carmel Highway

Tunnel

PARUNUWEAP CANYON

Mountain of Mystery ▲

Temple of Sinawava

Zion Lodge

Zion Canyon Scenic Drive

Tunnel

Tunnel

see map at left

Cabin Spring

Watchman ▲

North Fork Virgin River

Viewpoint ■

Double Falls

Zion Canyon Visitor Center

Altar of Sacrifice ■

Mount Kinesava ▲

Tabernacle Dome ▲

Petrified Forest Trail

Rockville ○

Crater Hill ▲

9

◄ To Virgin

Virgin River

Observation Point ■

Weeping Rock

Weeping Rock Trail

Hidden Canyon Trail

Angels Landing Trail

Angels Landing ■

Grotto Picnic Area

Zion Lodge ■

Canyon Overlook Trail

Tunnel

Emerald Pools Trail

Court of the Patriarchs ■

Pine Creek

Zion-Mt. Carmel Highway

Zion Canyon Scenic Drive

North Fork Virgin River

Pa'rus Trail (Bike Path)

Watchman Trail

Zion Canyon Visitor Center

Zion Nature Center

South Campground

Watchman Campground ▲

South Entrance

Springdale ○

Zion Canyon

223

How Nature Painted Zion's Landscape

Zion National Park is many things to many people: a day hike down a narrow canyon, a rugged climb up the face of a massive stone monument, or the quiet appreciation of the red glow of sunset over majestic peaks. At least to some degree, each of these experiences is possible only because of rocks—their formation, uplifting, shifting, breaking, and eroding. Of Zion's nine rock layers, the most important in creating its colorful formations is Navajo sandstone—at up to 2,200 feet, the thickest rock layer in the park. This formation was created some 200 million years ago, during the Jurassic period, when North America was hot and dry. Movements in the earth's crust caused a shallow sea to cover windblown sand dunes, and minerals, including lime from the shells of sea creatures, glued sand particles together to form sandstone. Later crust movements caused the land to uplift, draining away the sea but leaving rivers that gradually carved the relatively soft sandstone into the spectacular shapes we see today.

So where do the colors come from? Essentially, from plain old rust. Most of the rocks at Zion are colored by iron or hematite (iron oxide), either contained in the original stone or carried into the rocks by groundwater. Although iron often creates red and pink hues, seen in much of Zion's sandstone faces, it can also result in blacks, browns, yellows, and even greens. Sometimes the iron seeps into the rock, coloring it through, but it can also stain just the surface, often in vertical streaks. White streaks are frequently caused by deposits of salt left by evaporating water. Rocks are also colored by bacteria that live on their surfaces. The bacteria ingest dust and expel iron, manganese, and other minerals, which stick to the rock and produce a shiny black, brown, or reddish surface called desert varnish.

Speaking of living things, Zion National Park is a veritable zoo, with mammals ranging from pocket gophers to mountain lions, hundreds of birds (including golden eagles), lizards of all shapes and sizes, and a dozen species of snakes (only the great basin rattlesnake is poisonous, and they usually slither away from you faster than you can run from them). Mule deer are common, and although they're seldom seen, there are also a few shy elk and bighorn sheep, plus foxes, coyote, ringtail cats, beaver, porcupines, skunks, and plenty of squirrels and bats. Practically every summer visitor sees lizards of some sort, often the colorful collared and whiptail varieties, and it's easy to hear the song of the canyon wren and the call of the piñon jay.

1 Just the Facts

Located in southwest Utah, at elevations ranging from 3,700 feet to 8,726 feet, Zion National Park has several sections: **Zion Canyon,** the main part of the park, where everyone goes, and the less-visited **Kolob Canyons.** The main east–west road through Zion Canyon is the park-owned extension of Utah 9, from which you can access a 14-mile round-trip scenic drive/tram route that leads to most scenic overlooks and trailheads.

GETTING THERE/ACCESS POINTS   St. George and Cedar City are the closest towns to Zion National Park with airport service. From either airport, it's easy to rent a car and drive to Zion (see chapter 11 for complete details). The park is located 46 miles northeast of St. George and 60 miles south of Cedar City. From I-15 on the park's western side, the drive into Zion Canyon, the main part of the park—following Utah 9 or Utah 17 and Utah 9 to the south entrance—is easier but less scenic than the approach on the eastern side. Though the western approach is less scenic, it's the best route into the park; it's more direct, avoids possible delays at the Zion–Mt. Carmel Tunnel, and delivers you to Springdale, just outside the park's southern entrance, where most of the area's lodging and restaurants are located. Outside Zion Canyon, you'll find additional viewpoints and trailheads along Kolob Terrace Road, which heads north off Utah 9 from the village of Virgin, about 15 miles west of the park's southern entrance. This road is closed in the winter.

The Kolob Canyons section, in the park's northwest corner, can be reached via the short Kolob Canyons Road off I-15 exit 40.

From the east, it's a spectacularly scenic 24-mile drive from Mt. Carmel on Utah 9, reached from either the north or south via U.S. 89. The park is 41 miles northwest of Kanab. However, be aware that this route into the park drops over 2,500 feet in elevation, passes through the mile-long Zion–Mt. Carmel Tunnel, and winds down six steep switchbacks. The tunnel is too small for two-way traffic that includes vehicles larger than standard passenger cars and pickup trucks. Buses, trucks, and most recreational vehicles must be driven down the center of the tunnel, and therefore all oncoming traffic must be stopped. This applies to all vehicles over 7'10" wide (including mirrors) or 11'4" tall (including luggage racks, etc.). From March through October, large vehicles are permitted in the tunnel only from 8am to 8pm daily; during other months, arrangements can be made at park entrances or by calling park headquarters (☎ 435/772-3256). Affected vehicles must pay a $10 fee, good for two trips through the tunnel during a 7-day period. All vehicles over 13'1" tall and certain other particularly large vehicles are prohibited from driving anywhere on the park road between the east entrance and Zion Canyon.

From March to October, all vehicles over 21 feet long are prohibited from stopping at two parking areas: Weeping Rock (these vehicles may not enter the area) and the Temple of Sinawava (vehicles may be driven through but cannot park between 9am and 5pm).

You might also want to know that the park is 86 miles southwest of Bryce Canyon National Park; 120 miles northwest of the north rim of Grand Canyon National Park in northern Arizona; 309 miles south of Salt Lake City; and 158 miles northeast of Las Vegas, Nevada.

INFORMATION & VISITOR CENTERS   For advance information on what to see in the park, hiking trails, camping, and lodging, contact Superintendent, **Zion National Park,** Springdale, UT 84767-1099 (☎ **435/772-3256**). It's best to write at least a month before your planned visit and to specify what type of information you need. Officials request that those seeking trip-planning information write rather than call, leaving the phone lines open for those needing current and changeable information such as hiking trail conditions and closures.

If you'd like even more details to help plan your trip, you can order books, maps, and videos from the nonprofit **Zion Natural History Association**, Zion National Park, Springdale, UT 84767 (☎ **800/635-3959** or 435/772-3264). The association publishes several excellent books, including the colorful and informative 55-page *Zion National Park, Towers of Stone,* by J. L. Crawford, and the easy-to-understand 22-page booklet *An Introduction to the Geology of Zion National Park,* by Al Warneke. Some publications are available in foreign languages, and several videos can be purchased in either VHS or PAL formats. Major credit cards are accepted. Those interested in supporting the nonprofit association can join ($15 single or $25 family annually) and get a 20% discount on purchases.

The park has two visitor centers. The more comprehensive **Zion Canyon Visitor Center** (☎ 435/772-3256), near the south entrance to the park, has a museum with exhibits on the geology and history of the area and presents an orientation video program on the park. Rangers are on hand to answer questions and provide backcountry permits. Several free brochures are available, and books, maps, videos, postcards, and posters can be purchased. The smaller **Kolob Canyons Visitor Center** (☎ 435/586-9548), in the northwest corner of the park off I-15, can provide information, permits, books, and maps.

The Zion Park Guide, a small free newspaper-format guide available at both visitor centers, is packed with extremely helpful information about the park.

FEES, BACKCOUNTRY PERMITS & REGULATIONS   Entry into the park (for up to 7 days) costs $10 per private vehicle or $5 per motorcycle, bicycle, or pedestrian. A $20 annual pass is also available.

Oversized vehicles (see "Getting There/Access Points," above) are charged $10 for use of the Zion–Mt. Carmel Tunnel on the east side of the park.

Permits, available at either visitor center, are required for all overnight trips into the backcountry. Cost is $5 per person per night.

Backcountry hikers should practice minimum-impact techniques, are prohibited from building fires, and cannot travel in groups of 12 or more. A free booklet on backcountry travel, available at the visitor centers, lists all regulations plus descriptions of close to 20 backcountry trails.

Bicycles are prohibited in the Zion–Mt. Carmel Tunnel, the backcountry, and on all trails except the Pa'rus Trail. Feeding or otherwise disturbing wildlife is forbidden, as is vandalizing or upsetting any natural feature of the park. Dogs, which must be leashed at all times, are prohibited on all trails, in the backcountry, and in public buildings.

SEASONS & AVOIDING THE CROWDS   The park is open year-round (visitor centers are closed Christmas Day), 24 hours a day, although weather conditions may limit some activities at certain times. For instance, you'll want to avoid long hikes in midsummer, when the park bakes under temperatures that can exceed an unbearable 110°F, or during and immediately after winter storms, when ice and snow at higher elevations can make trails dangerous.

If possible, try to avoid the peak summer months of June, July, and August, when Zion receives almost half of its annual visitors. The quietest months are December, January, and February, but of course it's cold then, and you may have to contend with some snow and ice.

A good compromise, if your schedule permits, is to visit in April, May, September, or October, when the weather is usually good but the park is less crowded than in the summer.

The best way to avoid crowds is to simply walk away from them, either on the longer and more strenuous hiking trails or into the backcountry. It's sad but true—most visitors never bother to venture far from their cars, and their loss can be your gain. You can enjoy a wonderful solitary experience if you're willing to expend a little energy to get it. You can also avoid hordes of tourists by spending time in Kolob Canyons, in the far northwest section of the park; it's spectacular and receives surprisingly little use, at least in comparison to Zion Canyon.

RANGER PROGRAMS   Park rangers present a variety of free programs and activities. Evening programs, which sometimes include a slide show, take place most nights at campground amphitheaters. Topics vary, but could include the animals or plants of the park, geology, man's role in the park, or perhaps some unique feature such as Zion's slot canyons. Rangers also give short talks on similar subjects several times daily at the Zion Canyon Visitor Center and other locations. Ranger-guided hikes and walks, which may require reservations, might take you to little-visited areas of the park, on a trek to see wildflowers, or out at night for a hike under a full moon. Schedules of the various activities are posted on bulletin boards at the visitor centers, campgrounds, and other locations.

Kids from 6 to 12 years old can join the ✪ **Junior Rangers,** participate in a variety of programs, and earn certificates, badges, and patches. Morning and afternoon sessions, each lasting $2^{1}/_{2}$ hours, are scheduled daily from Memorial Day through Labor Day, with children meeting at the Nature Center in the South Campground. There's a one-time fee of $2 per child, and the age range is strictly enforced.

GETTING A BIRD'S-EYE VIEW OF THE PARK   Scenic Airlines (☎ 800/ 634-6801) offers combination air tours over Bryce Canyon and Zion national parks, plus the north rim of Grand Canyon National Park. Tours are given year-round, with prices starting at $275 for adults and $225 for children.

2 Seeing the Highlights

The best way to see Zion is to spend a week there, starting with the visitor center displays and programs, taking a driving or guided tram tour, and gradually working from short hikes and walks to full-day and overnight treks into the backcountry. That's the ideal, but for most visitors, time and finances dictate a shorter visit.

If you have only a day or two at the park, we recommend thoroughly reviewing the free Zion Park Guide, which describes the available options, then heading to the Zion Canyon Visitor Center for the orientation video and exhibits, and finally talking with a ranger about the amount of time you have, your abilities, and interests. Because Zion offers such a variety of landscapes and activities, each visitor can easily create his or her own itinerary. If your goal is to see as much of the park as possible in one full day, we suggest the following:

After a quick stop at the visitor center, drive to **Zion Lodge** and take a **tram tour,** which hits the major roadside viewpoints and leaves the driving to someone else so you can enjoy what you're seeing. The 1-hour ride goes from the lodge to the Temple of Sinawava and back, with an informative and entertaining commentary by the tram driver, who points out prominent formations, historic sites, and things you might have missed on your own, such as daring climbers scaling the seemingly sheer rock walls. Passengers can get off at several stops for better views or to connect with trailheads, with the option of returning to the lodge on a later tram. Cost is about $3 for adults and $2 for children under 12, with tickets available at a window inside Zion Lodge. The tram operates daily from April to October, on the hour from 10am to 4pm.

Instead of staying on the same tram all the way back to the lodge, we suggest you get off at the **Temple of Sinawava** and take the easy 2-mile round-trip **Riverside Walk,** which follows the Virgin River through a narrow canyon past hanging gardens. Then take the next tram back to the lodge (total time: 2 to 4 hours), where you might stop at the gift shop and possibly have lunch in the lodge restaurant. Near the lodge, you'll find the trailhead for the **Emerald Pools.** Especially pleasant on hot days, this easy walk through a forest of oak, maple, fir, and cottonwood trees leads to a waterfall, hanging garden, and the shimmering lower pool. This part of the walk should take about an hour round-trip, but those with a bit more ambition may want to add another hour and another mile to the loop by taking the moderately strenuous hike on a rocky, steeper trail to the upper pool. If time and energy remain, drive back toward the south park entrance and stop at **Watchman** (east of Watchman Campground), for the 2-mile, 2-hour round-trip, moderately strenuous hike to a plateau with beautiful views of several rock formations and the town of Springdale. That evening, try to take in the campground amphitheater program.

3 Exploring Zion by Car

If you enter the park from the east, along the steep **Zion–Mt. Carmel Highway,** you'll travel 13 miles to the **Zion Canyon Visitor Center,** passing Checkerboard Mesa, a massive sandstone rock formation covered with horizontal and vertical lines that make it look like a huge fishing net. Continuing on, you'll view a fairyland of fantastically shaped rocks of red, orange, tan, and white, as well as the Great Arch of Zion, carved high in a stone cliff.

Historically, almost all Zion National Park visitors have aimed their cars toward the 14-mile round-trip **Zion Canyon Scenic Drive,** which starts at the Zion Canyon Visitor Center. At this writing, visitors have the option of driving their own vehicles into the canyon, stopping at viewpoints and trailheads, and setting their own pace.

But that's expected to change. Traffic congestion, damage to roadside vegetation, noise, pollution, and a lack of parking are making the experience less and less pleasant, especially during the busy summer months, and park officials expect to have a mandatory shuttle bus service operating in Zion Canyon by 2000. In the meantime, motorists can still drive themselves, but be forewarned: Traffic is awful, particularly in the summer. Parking is hard to find, and you'll feel more like a Los Angeles or New York commuter than a national park visitor. We strongly recommend that you leave your car at the Zion Lodge parking lot and take the open-air tram.

You can also take a much less crowded scenic drive in the northwest corner of the park. The **Kolob Canyons Road** (about 45 minutes from Zion Canyon Visitor Center at I-15 exit 40) runs 5 miles among spectacular red and orange rocks, ending at a high vista. Allow about 45 minutes round-trip, stopping at numbered viewpoints. Be sure to get a copy of the "Kolob Canyons Road Guide" at the Kolob Visitor Center. Here's what you'll pass along the way:

Leaving **Kolob Canyons Visitor Center,** you'll drive along the Hurricane Fault to **Hurricane Cliffs,** a series of tall, gray cliffs composed of limestone, and onward to **Taylor Creek,** where a piñon-juniper forest clings to life on the rocky hillside, providing a home to the bright blue scrub jay. Your next stop is **Horse Ranch Mountain,** which, at 8,726 feet, is the national park's highest point. Passing a series of colorful rock layers, where you might be lucky enough to spot a golden eagle, your next stop is **Box Canyon,** along the south fork of Taylor Creek, with sheer rock walls soaring over 1,500 feet high. Next you'll see a multicolored layer of rock, pushed upward by tremendous forces from within the earth. Continue to a canyon, which exposes a rock wall that likely began as a sand dune before being covered by an early sea and cemented into stone. Next stop is a side canyon, with large, arched alcoves boasting delicate curved ceilings. Head on to a view of **Timber Top Mountain,**

Impressions

Nothing can exceed the wondrous beauty of Zion . . . in the nobility and beauty of the sculptures there is no comparison.

—Geologist Clarence Dutton, 1880

which is a sagebrush-blanketed desert at its base, but is covered with stately fir and ponderosa pine at its peak. Watch for mule deer on the brushy hillsides, especially between October and March, when they might be spotted just after sunrise or before sunset. From here, continue to **Rockfall Overlook;** a large scar on the mountainside marks the spot where a 1,000-foot chunk of stone crashed to the earth in July 1983, the victim of erosion. And finally, stop to see the canyon walls themselves, colored orange-red by iron oxide and striped black by mineral-laden water running down the cliff faces.

4 Sports & Activities

BIKING & MOUNTAIN BIKING

With one notable exception, bikes are prohibited on all trails and forbidden to travel cross-country within the national park boundaries. This leaves only the park's established roads (except for the Zion–Mt. Carmel tunnel, where bikes are also prohibited), which are often clogged with motor vehicles.

But there's hope. The **Pa'rus Trail,** open since late 1994, is the first phase of a new transportation plan for Zion National Park. It runs 2 miles along the Virgin River from the entrance of South Campground to the beginning of the Zion Canyon Scenic Drive, crossing the river and several creeks and providing good views of Watchman, West Temple, the Sentinel, and other lower canyon formations. The paved trail is open to bicyclists, pedestrians, and those with strollers or wheelchairs, but closed to cars. Future plans call for allowing only shuttle buses, bicyclists, and hikers on the scenic drive, making the park truly bike-friendly.

Although mountain bikers will find they are generally not welcome in Zion National Park, just outside the park, mostly on Bureau of Land Management and state-owned property, are numerous rugged jeep trails that are great for mountain biking, plus more than 70 miles of slickrock cross-country trails and single-track trails. Gooseberry Mesa, above the community of Springdale, is generally considered the best mountain-biking destination in the area, but you'll also find good trails on nearby Wire and Grafton Mesas. Talk with the knowledgeable staff at **Bike Zion,** 1458 Zion Park Blvd., Springdale (☎ **800/4SLIKROK** or 435/772-3929), about the best trails for your interests and abilities. This full-service bike shop also offers maps, a full range of bikes and accessories, repairs, shuttle service for you and your bike, and rentals ($23 per day for a 21-speed mountain bike). Bike Zion offers guided mountain-bike trips, starting at $35 for a $2^{1}/_{2}$-hour tour, and a variety of multiday excursions, including some with catered gourmet meals or educational themes.

A Mountain Bike Festival, held annually in mid-October and organized by Bike Zion, includes trail rides, races and other contests, and an all-you-can-eat pasta dinner.

HIKING

Zion offers a wide variety of hiking trails, ranging from easy half-hour walks on paved paths to grueling overnight hikes over rocky terrain along steep drop-offs. Several free brochures on hiking trails are available at the visitor centers, and the **Zion Natural History Association** publishes a good 48-page booklet describing 18 trails (see "Information & Visitor Centers," earlier in this chapter). Hikers with a fear of heights should be especially careful when choosing trails; many include steep, dizzying drop-offs. What follows are our hiking suggestions:

The **Weeping Rock Trail,** among the park's shortest and easiest rambles, is a half-mile round-trip walk from the Zion Canyon Scenic Drive to a rock alcove with a spring and hanging gardens of ferns and wildflowers. Although paved, the trail is steep and not suitable for wheelchairs.

Another short hike is the ◊ **Lower Emerald Pools Trail,** which can be an easy 1-hour walk or a moderately strenuous 2-hour hike, depending on how much of the loop you choose to do. A 0.6-mile paved path from the Emerald Pools Parking Area, through a forest of oak, maple, fir, and cottonwood, leads to a waterfall, hanging garden, and the Lower Emerald Pool, and is suitable for those in wheelchairs, with assistance. From here, a steeper, rocky trail (not appropriate for wheelchairs) continues past cactus, yucca, and juniper another half mile to Upper Emerald Pool, with another waterfall. A third pool, just above Lower Emerald Pool, offers impressive reflections of the cliffs. The pools are named for the green color of the water, which is caused by algae.

A particularly scenic hike is the **Hidden Canyon Trail,** a 2-mile moderately strenuous hike that takes about 3 hours. Starting at the Weeping Rock parking area, the trail climbs 800 feet through a narrow water-carved canyon, ending at the canyon's mouth. Those wanting to extend the hike can go another 0.6 mile to a small natural arch. Hidden Canyon Trail includes long drop-offs and is not recommended for anyone with a fear of heights.

Another moderately strenuous but relatively short hike is the **Watchman Trail,** which starts by the service road east of Watchman Campground. This 2-mile round-trip hike, which takes about 2 hours, gets surprisingly light use, possibly because it can be very hot in the middle of the day. Climbing to a plateau near the base of the formation called The Watchman, it offers splendid views of lower Zion Canyon, the Towers of the Virgin, and West Temple formations.

For a strenuous 4-hour, 5-mile hike—one that is most certainly not for anyone with even a mild fear of heights—take the **Angel's Landing Trail** to a summit that offers spectacular views into Zion Canyon. But be prepared: The final half mile follows a narrow, knife-edge trail along a steep ridge, where footing can be slippery even under the best of circumstances. Support chains have been set along parts of the trail.

◊ **Hiking the Narrows** is not hiking a trail at all, but walking or wading along the bottom of the Virgin River, through a spectacular 1,000-foot-deep chasm that, at a mere 20 feet wide, definitely lives up to its name. Passing fancifully sculptured sandstone arches, hanging gardens, and waterfalls, this moderately strenuous hike can be completed in less than a day or in several days, depending on how much you want to do. However, the Narrows are subject to flash flooding and can be very treacherous. Park service officials remind hikers that they are responsible for their own safety and should check on current water conditions and weather forecasts. This hike is NOT recommended when rain is forecast or threatening. Permits are required for full-day and overnight hikes (check with park rangers for details). Permits are not required for easy, short day hikes, which you can access from just beyond the end of the Riverside Walk, a 2-mile trail that starts at the Temple of Sinawava parking area.

Guided hikes in the park and nearby areas are offered by **Bike Zion,** 1458 Zion Park Blvd., Springdale (☎ **800/4SLIKROK** or 435/772-3929), starting at $35 for a 2¹/₂-hour hike; also available are multiday backpacking trips, including rugged excursions through slot canyons with a qualified rappelling instructor. The company also offers a shuttle service for hikers and backpackers.

HORSEBACK RIDING

Guided rides in the park are available March through October from **Canyon Trail Rides,** P.O. Box 128, Tropic, UT 84776 (☎ **435/679-8665**), with ticket sales and information at Zion Lodge. A 1-hour ride along the Virgin River costs $12 and a half-day ride on the Sand Beach Trail costs $35. Riders must weigh no more than 220 pounds, and children must be at least 5 years old for the 1-hour ride and 8 years old for the half-day ride. Reservations are advised.

ROCK CLIMBING

Technical rock climbers like the sandstone cliffs in Zion Canyon, although rangers warn that much of the rock is loose, or "rotten," and climbing equipment and techniques suitable for granite are often less effective on sandstone. Free permits are required for overnight climbs, and because some routes may be closed at times, climbers should check at the visitor center before setting out.

WILDLIFE VIEWING & BIRD WATCHING

It's a rare visitor to Zion who doesn't spot a critter of some sort, from mule deer—often seen along roadways and in campgrounds—to the numerous varieties of lizards, including the park's largest, the chuckwalla, which can grow to 20 inches. The ringtail cat, a relative of the raccoon, prowls Zion Canyon at night and is not above helping itself to your camping supplies. Along the Virgin River, you'll see bank beaver, so named because they live in burrows instead of building dams. The park is also home to several types of squirrels, gophers, and pack rats. If you're interested in spotting birds, you're in luck at Zion. The rare peregrine falcon, among the world's fastest birds, sometimes nests in the Weeping Rock area, where you're likely to see the dipper, winter wren, and white-throated swift. Also in the park are golden eagles, several species of hummingbirds, ravens, piñon jays, and possibly a roadrunner or two.

Snakes include the poisonous great basin rattler, found below 8,000 feet elevation, as well as nonpoisonous kingsnakes and gopher snakes. Tarantulas, those large, hairy, usually slow-moving spiders, are often seen in the late summer and fall. Contrary to popular belief, the tarantula's bite is not deadly, although it may be somewhat painful.

Remember, it's illegal to feed the wildlife. No matter how much you may want to befriend an animal by offering food, please remember that it's not healthy for the wildlife to eat human food or to get used to being fed this way.

5 Camping

The absolutely best places to camp are at one of the ✪ **national park campgrounds,** if you can find a site. Reservations are not accepted, and the campgrounds often fill by noon in the summer, so get there early in the day to claim a site. Some campers stay at nearby commercial campgrounds their first night in the area, then hurry into the park the next morning, circling like vultures until a site becomes available.

Both of Zion's main campgrounds, just inside the park's south entrance, have paved roads, well-spaced sites, lots of trees, and that national park atmosphere you came here to enjoy. Facilities include rest rooms with flush toilets but no showers, a dump station, public telephone, and sites for those with disabilities. The fee is $10 per night. **South Campground** has 126 sites and is usually open from mid-March to mid-October only; **Watchman Campground** has 231 sites, with at least 50 electric hookups on Loop D (additional fee) and is open year-round.

Lava Point, with only six sites, is located on the Kolob Terrace. It has fire grates, tables, and toilets, but no water, and there is no fee. It is usually open from May through October.

If you can't get a site in the park, or if you prefer hot showers or complete RV hookups, there are several campgrounds in the surrounding area. The closest, **Zion Canyon Campground,** on Zion Park Boulevard a half mile south of the park entrance (P.O. Box 99), Springdale, UT 84767 (☎ **435/772-3237;** fax 435/ 772-3844), is open year-round and offers 180 sites, of which many are shaded. Although it's quite crowded in the summer, the campground is clean and well maintained, and in addition to the usual showers and RV hookups, you'll find a self-service laundry; dump station; store with groceries, souvenirs, and RV supplies; and restaurant. Tenters are welcome; rates are from $15 to $20 for two people.

6 Accommodations

The only lodging actually in Zion National Park is at Zion Lodge (see below). The other properties listed here are all in Springdale, a village of some 350 people at the park's south entrance that has literally become the park's bedroom. Room tax is about 10% in Springdale and 9% in the park. Pets are not accepted unless otherwise noted.

You can also base yourself in St. George, which is 42 miles away; Kanab, which is 40 miles away; or Cedar City, 56 miles away. See chapter 11 for listings.

Bumbleberry Inn

97 Bumbleberry Lane, Springdale, UT 84767. ☎ **800/828-1534** or 435/772-3224. Fax 435/ 772-3947. 23 rms. A/C TV TEL. Apr–Oct $54–$59 double; Nov–Mar $49–$54 double. DISC, MC, V.

Set back from the main highway, the Bumbleberry offers large, quiet rooms at a good price. Furnishings are simple but more than adequate, with a desk in addition to a table and two chairs, and prints depicting the area's scenery. Most rooms contain two queen-size beds and tub/shower combinations, although five rooms have one queen bed and shower only. Facilities include indoor racquetball, an arcade, indoor Jacuzzi, heated outdoor pool, and an adjacent restaurant that serves three meals daily. Pets are accepted at the discretion of the management.

Canyon Ranch Motel

668 Zion Park Blvd. (P.O. Box 175), Springdale, UT 84767. ☎ **435/772-3357.** Fax 435/ 772-3057. 21 units. A/C TV. Mar–Oct $58–$68 double; Nov–Feb $44–$54 double. AE, DISC, MC, V.

Consisting of a series of two- and four-unit cottages set back from the highway, this motel has the look of an old-fashioned auto camp on the outside while providing modern motel rooms inside. Rooms are either new or newly remodeled, and options include one queen- or king-size bed, two queens, or one queen and one double. Some rooms have showers only, while some have shower/tub combos. Kitchen units are also available. Room 13, with two queen-size beds, offers spectacular views of the Zion National Park rock formations through its several large picture windows; views from most other rooms are almost as good. The units surround a lawn with trees and picnic tables; an outdoor heated swimming pool and Jacuzzi are also available. Pets are accepted at the discretion of the management.

Cliffrose Lodge & Gardens

281 Zion Park Blvd. (P.O. Box 510), Springdale, UT 84767. ☎ **800/243-UTAH** or 435/ 772-3234. Fax 435/772-3900. 36 units, including 6 suites. A/C TV TEL. Summer $88–$145 double. Lower rates in the winter. AE, DISC, MC, V.

With river frontage and 5 acres of lawns, shade trees, and flower gardens, the Cliffrose offers a beautiful setting just outside the entrance to Zion National Park. The modern, well-kept rooms have all the standard motel appointments, with unusually large bathrooms with shower/tub combinations. On the lawns, you'll find comfortable seating, including a lawn swing, plus a playground and large outdoor heated pool. Guests have use of a self-service laundry.

Desert Pearl Inn

707 Zion Park Blvd., Springdale, UT 84767. ☎ **888/828-0898** or 435/772-8888. Fax 435/772-8889. 61 units. A/C TV TEL. $70–$150 double. AE, DISC, MC, V.

This handsome, brand-new property, which opened late in 1997, offers luxurious and comfortable accommodations with beautiful views of the area's scenery. Spacious rooms are furnished with either two queen-size beds and a queen sleeper or one king and a queen sleeper. Units also have comfortable seating, refrigerators, microwave ovens, wet bars, and bidets. The grounds are nicely landscaped, and facilities include a huge outdoor heated pool and whirlpool. Plans call for construction of a restaurant and additional units.

Flanigan's Inn

428 Zion Park Blvd. (P.O. Box 100), Springdale, UT 84767. ☎ **800/765-RSVP** or 435/772-3244. Fax 435/772-3396. 39 units. A/C TV TEL. Mid-Mar–Nov $79–$89 double; Dec to mid-Mar $49–$69 double. Rates include continental breakfast buffet. AE, DISC, MC, V.

A mountain-lodge atmosphere pervades this very attractive complex of natural wood and rock, set among trees, lawns, and flowers just outside the entrance to Zion National Park. Parts of the inn date to 1947, but all rooms were completely renovated in the early 1990s, with Southwest decor, wood furnishings, and local art. One room has a fireplace; other units have whirlpool tubs and bidets; and kitchenettes are available. You might actually want to spend some time here, unlike other options in the area, which are simply good places to sleep at the end of long days spent exploring Zion. Flanigan's has a heated outdoor swimming pool and its own nature trail leading to a hilltop vista. An on-site restaurant serves dinner, in addition to a continental breakfast for guests only (see "Dining," below). Summer reservations are often booked 3 to 4 months in advance.

Harvest House Bed & Breakfast at Zion

29 Canyon View Dr. (P.O. Box 125), Springdale, UT 84767. ☎ **435/772-3880**. Fax 435/772-3327. 4 rms. A/C. $80–$100 double. Rates include full breakfast. DISC, MC, V.

This Utah territorial–style house was built in 1989 and has a cactus garden out front and a garden sitting area in back with a koi (Japanese carp) pond and spectacular views of the national park rock formations. Rooms are charming, comfortable and quiet, with private baths; they're furnished with an eclectic mixture of contemporary and wicker items, and original art and photography dot the walls. One upstairs room faces west and has grand sunset views, while the other two have private decks facing the impressive formations of Zion. The downstairs suite can accommodate up to five adults.

The gourmet breakfasts are sumptuous yet low fat, and include fresh-baked breads, fresh-squeezed orange juice, granola, fruit, yogurt, and a hot main course that changes daily. Facilities include an outdoor whirlpool. Children over 6 years old are welcome.

Zion Lodge

In Zion National Park. ☎ **435/772-3213**. Fax 435/772-2001. Information and reservations: AmFac Parks & Resorts, 14001 E. Iliff Ave., Suite 600, Aurora, CO 80014. ☎ 303/29-PARKS. Fax 303/338-2045. 121 units. A/C TEL. Motel rms $80–$90 double; suites $113–$120 double; cabins $85–$95 double. AE, DISC, MC, V.

The motel units and cabins are nice enough, but then again, you don't come to Zion National Park to stay indoors—you come for the scenery, and there's a pretty incredible view from the lobby's large picture windows. Situated in a forest, with spectacular views of the park's rock cliffs, the charming cabins each have a private porch, stone (gas-burning) fireplace, two double beds, pine-board walls, and log beams. The comfortable motel units are basically just that—motel units—with two queen-size beds and all the usual amenities except televisions. Motel suites each have one king-size bed, a separate sitting room, and refrigerator. A gift shop offers everything from postcards to expensive silver and turquoise Native American jewelry.

Zion Park Inn and Conference Centre

1215 Zion Park Blvd., Springdale, UT 84767. ☎ **800/934-7275** or 435/772-3200. Fax 435/772-2449. 120 units. A/C TV TEL. Mid-Mar to mid-Oct $80–$95 double, $110–$160 suites and family units; mid-Oct to mid-Mar $58–$68 double, $85–$125 suites and family units. AE, DC, DISC, MC, V.

This new, casually elegant two-story complex is located 1 1/2 miles from the south entrance of Zion National Park. Rooms are tastefully appointed in Southwest style, with two double beds, two queens, or one king-size bed. The grounds are beautifully landscaped, with phenomenal views of the area's red rock formations. Facilities include a heated outdoor swimming pool and hot tub, restaurant (see "Dining," below), gift shop, country market store, guest laundry, liquor store, and conference and meeting rooms. The grounds are available for weddings and receptions. Pets are accepted for an extra fee at management discretion.

Zion Park Motel

855 Zion Park Blvd. (P.O. Box 365), Springdale, UT 84767. ☎ **435/772-3251.** 21 rms, 2 family suites. A/C TV TEL. $55–$66 double, $79–$99 suite. AE, DISC, MC, V.

This economical motel offers comfortable, attractively furnished rooms. All units have either showers or tub/shower combos, and two of the suites have full kitchens. Facilities include a seasonal outdoor heated pool, picnic area, and playground. A self-service laundry, market with camping supplies, and restaurant are adjacent.

7 Dining

With the exception of Zion Lodge, which is in the park, these restaurants are all located on the main road to the park through Springdale.

Bit & Spur Restaurant & Saloon

1212 Zion Park Blvd., Springdale. ☎ **435/772-3498.** Reservations recommended. Main courses $7–$15. MC, V. Mar–Oct 5–10pm (full bar open until 1am); Nov–Feb Thurs–Mon 5–10pm. Closed Christmas holidays. MEXICAN/SOUTHWESTERN.

This may look like an Old West saloon, with its rough wood-and-stone walls and exposed beam ceiling, but it's an unusually clean saloon that also has a family dining room, patio dining, and walls decorated with original oil paintings that are for sale. The food here is a notch or two above what we expected, a bit closer to what you'd find in a good Santa Fe restaurant. The menu includes Mexican standards such as burritos, flautas, chile rellenos, and a traditional chile stew with pork; but you'll also find more exotic creations including the pollo relleno—a grilled breast of chicken stuffed with cilantro pesto and goat cheese, served with smoked pineapple chutney. Also good are the smoky chicken—a smoked, charbroiled game hen with sourdough stuffing and chipotle sauce—and the deep-dish chicken enchilada, with scallions, green chiles, and cheese. The Bit & Spur has a full liquor license and an extensive wine list.

Flanigan's Inn

428 Zion Park Blvd., Springdale. ☎ **435/772-3244.** Reservations recommended. Main course grills $5.50–$14.95. AE, DISC, MC, V. Mon–Thurs 3–9:30pm; Fri–Sun until 10pm. Shorter hrs. in the winter. AMERICAN/REGIONAL.

With a greenhouse/garden atmosphere, this restaurant makes the most of the area's spectacular scenery with large windows for inside diners plus an outdoor patio. Flanigan's uses fresh local ingredients and herbs from the inn's garden whenever possible. The menu includes items such as burgers, grilled vegetable burrito, chicken breast sandwich, mesquite-smoked chicken marinated in herbs, broiled beef tenderloin, and broiled fresh Atlantic salmon with melted dill butter. Microbrewery draft beers are available.

Switchback Grille

1149 Zion Park Blvd., Springdale. ☎ **435/772-3777** or 435/772-3888. Reservations recommended. Main courses $7.95–$21.95. AE, DC, DISC, MC, V. Daily 7am–10pm year-round. CONTINENTAL.

The well-designed 150-seat dining room at Zion Park Inn and Conference Centre offers spectacular views of Zion National Park's famed red rock formations from every table. Diners also get to see the restaurant's open-oven rotisserie, where the house specialty, flame-broiled chicken, is prepared. The menu includes steaks, a variety of pastas, and pizzas, which are wood-fired in a kiln. Patio dining is available, and outdoor barbecues are held for special occasions. The Switchback also offers a children's menu and prepares box lunches to go. It provides full liquor service, including imported beers and an international wine list.

Zion Lodge

Zion National Park. ☎ **435/772-3213.** Dinner reservations required in the summer. Main courses $8.95–$16.25 dinner; lunch items $4.75–$8.95; breakfast items $2.95–$5.95. AE, DC, DISC, MC, V. Daily 6:30–10am, 11:30am–3pm, and 5:30–9pm. AMERICAN.

A mountain-lodge atmosphere prevails here, complete with large windows that look out toward the park's magnificent rock formations. House specialties at dinner include an excellent slow-roasted prime rib au jus and the very popular Utah red mountain trout. The menu also includes several chicken dishes, such as a skinless chicken breast basted with a spicy Caribbean sauce and served with a red onion relish. Several vegetarian items are on the menu, such as pasta marissa and black bean ragout. Ask about the lodge's specialty ice creams and other exotic desserts. At lunch, you'll find the trout and barbecued pork ribs, plus burgers, sandwiches, and salads; breakfasts offer all the usual American selections. The restaurant will pack lunches to go for hikers and offers a children's menu and full liquor service.

Zion Pizza & Noodle

868 Zion Park Blvd., Springdale. ☎ **435/772-3815.** Reservations not accepted. Main courses $7.95–$11.95 dinner; $3.95–$11.95 lunch. No credit cards. President's Day–Thanksgiving noon–10pm daily; shorter hrs. in the winter. Closed Jan–Feb. PIZZA/PASTA.

Located in a former LDS church with a turquoise steeple, this cafe has small, closely spaced tables and is decorated with black-and-white photos. Patrons order at the counter and help themselves at the beverage bar while waiting for their food to be delivered. The 12-inch pizzas, baked in a slate stone oven, are good, but New York–style pizza purists might be put off by oddly topped specialty pies such as the Southwestern burrito pizza or barbecue chicken pizza. But have no fear—you can also get a basic cheese pizza, or add any of some 15 extra toppings from pepperoni to green chiles to pineapple. The noodle side of the menu offers a variety of pastas, such as fettuccine with roma tomatoes, fresh mushrooms, pesto sauce, cream, and grated parmesan; stromboli; and very often a locally popular nightly special of manicotti marinara. The restaurant serves no alcohol. Take out and delivery are available.

8 Virtual Nature at Two Nearby Theaters

Just outside the south entrance to Zion National Park, in Springdale, are two worthwhile attractions.

   "The Grand Circle: A National Park Odyssey," a multimedia production presented on a 24-by-40–foot screen in the outdoor Obert C. Tanner Amphitheater, is an excellent introduction to the national parks and monuments of southern Utah and northern Arizona. Using a state-of-the-art sound and projection system, and with the cliffs of Zion National Park in the background, the 1-hour program gives a brief look at the geology of the area, but devotes most of its time, sounds, and sights to the awe-inspiring scenery. Showings are scheduled at dusk nightly from late May to early September. Tickets cost $4 for adults, $3 for students and children under 12, or $10 per family.

The amphitheater, located just off Zion Park Boulevard, is also the venue for about 18 **concerts** each summer, ranging from the annual Utah Symphony pops concert in late June or early July, to bluegrass, country, and acoustic. Tickets cost $5 to $9, depending on the performer (most are $7). For information on the multimedia production or concert series, contact **Dixie College** in St. George (☎ **435/652-7994**).

You'll find an even bigger screen—some six stories high by 80 feet wide—at **Zion Canyon Cinemax Theatre,** just outside the south entrance to Zion National Park at 145 Zion Park Blvd. (☎ **435/772-2400**). Here you can see the dramatic film "Treasure of the Gods" with thrilling scenes of the Zion National Park area, including a hair-raising flash flood through Zion Canyon's Narrows and some dizzying bird's-eye views. Also shown is "The Great American West," in which the Old West comes alive through the words of pioneers, Indian chiefs, and explorers. Admission costs $7 for adults and $4.50 for children 3 to 11. Shows begin hourly, 365 days a year: March through October from 9am to 9pm, and November through February from 11am to 7pm. The theater complex also contains a tourist information center, ATM, picnic area, gift and souvenir shops, food emporium, 30-minute photo processor, bookstore, and art gallery.

Bryce Canyon National Park 13

If you could visit only one national park in your lifetime, we'd send you to Bryce Canyon. Here you'll find magic, inspiration, and spectacular beauty among thousands of intricately shaped hoodoos: those silent sentinels and congregations gathered in these colorful cathedrals, in formations that let your imagination run wild.

Hoodoos, geologists tell us, are simply pinnacles of rock, often oddly shaped, left standing by the forces of millions of years of water and wind erosion. But perhaps the truth really lies in a Paiute legend. These American Indians, who lived in the area for several hundred years before being forced out by Anglo pioneers, told of a "Legend People" who lived here in the old days; because of their evil ways, they were turned to stone by the powerful Coyote, and even today they remain frozen in time.

Whatever the cause, Bryce Canyon is certainly unique. Its intricate and often whimsical formations are smaller and on a more human scale than the impressive rocks seen at Zion, Capitol Reef, and Canyonlands National Parks. And Bryce is far easier to explore than the huge and sometimes intimidating Grand Canyon. Bryce is comfortable and inviting in its beauty; we feel we know it simply by gazing over the rim, and we're on intimate terms after just one morning on the trail.

Although the colorful hoodoos are the first things to grab your attention, it isn't long before you notice the deep amphitheaters that enfold them, with their cliffs, windows, and arches—all colored in shades of red, brown, orange, yellow, and white—that change and glow with the rising and setting sun. Beyond the rocks and light are the other faces of the park: three separate life zones, each with its own unique vegetation that changes with the elevation; and a kingdom of animals, from the busy chipmunks and ground squirrels to the stately mule deer and their archenemy, the mountain lion.

Human exploration of the Bryce area likely began with the Paiutes, and it's possible that trappers, prospectors, and early Mormon scouts may have visited here in the early to mid-1800s, before Major John Wesley Powell conducted the first thorough survey of the region in the early 1870s. Shortly after Powell's exploration, Mormon pioneer Ebenezer Bryce and his wife Mary moved to the area and tried raising cattle. Although they stayed only a few years before moving on to Arizona, Bryce left behind his name and his oft-quoted description of the canyon as "a helluva place to lose a cow."

1 Just the Facts

GETTING THERE/ACCESS POINTS **Bryce Canyon Airport** (☎ 435/834-5239) is located several miles from the park entrance on Utah 12 and has a 7,400-foot lighted runway. Direct flights from Las Vegas, Nevada, are provided by **Scenic Airlines** (☎ 702/739-1900), **Air Vegas** (☎ 702/795-7144), and **Air Nevada** (☎ 702/736-2702). Car rentals at Bryce Canyon Airport are available from **Bryce Air Service** (☎ 435/834-5208) and **Bryce Canyon Car Rental** (☎ 800/432-5383 or 435/834-5200), which also has a desk in the lobby of Ruby's Inn.

You can also fly into St. George (126 miles southwest of the park on I-15) or Cedar City (also on I-15, about 80 miles west of the park), and rent a car at either of these airports. See chapter 11 for details on airlines and rental companies.

From St. George, travel north on I-15 10 miles to exit 16, then head east on Utah 9 for 63 miles to U.S. 89, north 43 miles to Utah 12, and east 17 miles to the park entrance road. The entrance station and visitor center are just 3 miles south of Utah 12. From Cedar City (I-15 exits 57, 59, and 62), take Utah 14 west 41 miles to its intersection with U.S. 89 and follow that north 21 miles to Utah 12, then east 17 miles to the park entrance road.

Situated in the mountains of southern Utah, the park is traversed east–west by Utah 12, with the bulk of the park, including the visitor center, accessible via Utah 63, which branches off from Utah 12 and goes south into the main portions of the park. Utah 89 runs north to south, west of the park, and Utah 12 heads east to Tropic and eventually Escalante.

From Salt Lake City, it's 260 miles to the park. Take I-15 south about 200 miles to exit 95, head east 13 miles on Utah 20, south on U.S. 89 for 17 miles to Utah 12, and east 17 miles to the park entrance road.

From Capitol Reef National Park, take Utah 24 west 10 miles to Torrey, turn southwest onto Scenic Highway Utah 12 (through Boulder and Escalante) for about 110 miles to the park entrance road.

A couple of other handy driving distances: Bryce is 83 miles east of Zion National Park and 245 miles northwest of Las Vegas, Nevada.

GETTING AROUND Most visitors to Bryce Canyon National Park have cars or RVs, and the park has a good road and parking system. Those without vehicles can see many of the viewpoints on a tour (see "Guided Tours" below) and transportation can be arranged from **Bryce Canyon Scenic Tours & Shuttles** (☎ 800/432-5383 or 435/834-5200).

INFORMATION & VISITOR CENTERS For advance information on what to see in the park, hiking trails, camping, and lodging, write: Superintendent, **Bryce Canyon National Park**, P.O. Box 170001, Bryce Canyon, UT 84717, or call weekdays between 8am and 4:30pm mountain time (☎ **435/834-5322**). It's best to write at least a month before your planned visit, and ask for a copy of the national park newspaper, *Hoodoo,* which contains a map of the park, plus information on hiking trails, services, weather, ranger-conducted activities, and current issues such as road construction in the park. The website for the park is www.nps.gov/brca.

If you want even more details to help plan your trip, you can order books, maps, posters, and videos from the nonprofit **Bryce Canyon Natural History Association,** Bryce Canyon, UT 84717 (☎ 435/834-4602; fax orders 888/362-2642 or 435/834-4102). The association publishes a number of excellent books and offers a special trip-planning packet that includes a driving and hiking guide, natural history guide, and a descriptive and photographic guide to both Bryce and Zion National

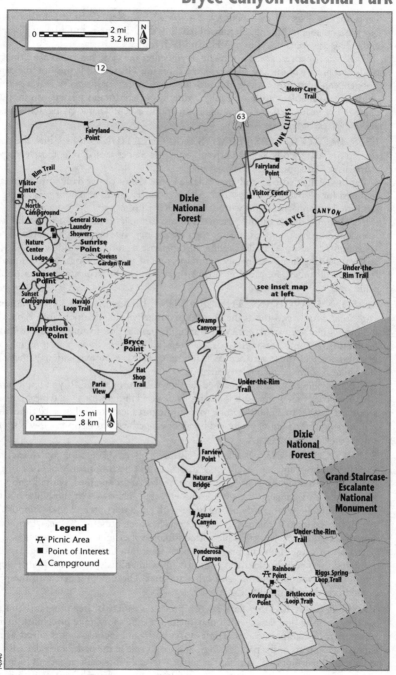

Bryce Canyon National Park

0 — 2 mi / 3.2 km

N

12

63

Mossy Cave Trail

PINK CLIFFS

Fairyland Point

Visitor Center

BRYCE CANYON

Dixie National Forest

Under-the-Rim Trail

see inset map at left

Swamp Canyon

Under-the-Rim Trail

Dixie National Forest

Grand Staircase-Escalante National Monument

Farview Point

Natural Bridge

Agua Canyon

Under-the-Rim Trail

Ponderosa Canyon

Rainbow Point

Riggs Spring Loop Trail

Yovimpa Point

Bristlecone Loop Trail

Inset map

Fairyland Point

Rim Trail

Visitor Center

North Campground

General Store Laundry Showers

Nature Center Lodge

Sunrise Point

Queens Garden Trail

Sunset Point

Sunset Campground

Navajo Loop Trail

Inspiration Point

Bryce Point

Hat Shop Trail

Paria View

0 — .5 mi / .8 km

N

Legend

- ⅄ Picnic Area
- ■ Point of Interest
- △ Campground

1-0940

Parks, for a package price of about $9. A 48-page book, *Bryce Canyon: The Continuing Story,* is available in English, German, French, Italian, Japanese, or Chinese; and several videos are available, both in VHS and PAL formats.

The **visitor center,** at the north end as you enter the park, has exhibits on the geology and history of the area and presents a short introductory slide show on the park. Rangers can answer questions and provide backcountry permits. Several free brochures are available, and books, maps, videos, postcards, and posters can be purchased. The visitor center is open daily year-round except Thanksgiving, Christmas, and New Year's days.

FEES, BACKCOUNTRY PERMITS & REGULATIONS   Entry into the park (for up to 7 days) costs $10 per private vehicle or $5 per motorcycle, bicycle, or pedestrian. A $20 annual pass is also available.

Permits, which cost $5 and are available at the visitor center daily until 8pm, are required for all overnight trips into the backcountry, and backcountry camping is permitted on only two trails, with details at the visitor center.

Backcountry hikers should practice minimum-impact techniques, are prohibited from building fires, and must carry their own water. Bicycles are prohibited in the backcountry and on all trails. Feeding or otherwise disturbing wildlife is forbidden, as is vandalizing or upsetting any natural feature of the park. Dogs, which must be leashed at all times, are prohibited on all trails, in the backcountry, and in public buildings.

SEASONS & AVOIDING THE CROWDS   Although Bryce Canyon National Park receives only two-thirds the number of annual visitors that pour into Zion, the park can still be crowded, especially during its peak season from mid-June to mid-September, when the campgrounds are often full by 2pm. If you have to visit then, head for some of the lesser-used trails (ask rangers for recommendations), and start your hike as soon after sunrise as possible.

A better time to visit, if your schedule allows, is spring or fall. If you don't mind a bit of cold and snow, the park is practically deserted in the winter—a typical January sees some 22,000 to 25,000 visitors, while in August there are well over 10 times that number—and the sight of bright red hoodoos capped with fresh white snow is something you won't soon forget.

SAFETY CONCERNS   While most visitors to Bryce Canyon enjoy an exciting vacation without mishap, accidents can occur, and here—possibly because of the nature of the trails—the most common injuries by far are sprained, twisted, and broken ankles. Park rangers strongly recommend that hikers—even those just out for short day hikes—wear sturdy hiking boots with good traction and ankle support.

Another concern in the park in recent years has been bubonic plague, which, contrary to popular belief, is treatable with antibiotics if caught in its early stages. The bacteria that causes bubonic plague has been found on fleas in prairie dog colonies in the park, so you should avoid contact with wild animals, especially prairie dogs, chipmunks, ground squirrels, and other rodents. Those taking pets into the park should first dust them with flea powder.

RANGER PROGRAMS   Park rangers present a variety of free programs and activities. Evening programs, which may include a slide show, take place most nights at campground amphitheaters. Topics vary, but could include such subjects as the animals and plants of the park, geology, and man's role in the park's early days. Rangers also give half-hour talks on similar subjects several times daily at various locations in the park, and lead hikes and walks, including a moonlight hike (reservations required) and a wheelchair-accessible 1-hour canyon rim walk. Schedules are posted on bulletin boards at the visitor center, general store, campgrounds, and Bryce Canyon Lodge.

During the summer, children 12 and younger can join the **Junior Rangers**, participate in a variety of programs, and earn certificates and patches. Junior Ranger booklets are available at the visitor center.

GETTING A BIRD'S-EYE VIEW OF THE PARK   For an unforgettable view of the canyon and its numerous formations, contact **Bryce Canyon Helicopter Scenic Flights** (ask for the flight desk at Ruby's Inn, ☎ 435/834-5341). Tours last from 17 minutes to more than an hour, and the longer trips include the entire park plus the surrounding attractions of Kodachrome Basin State Park and a nearby ghost town. Air is clearest and lighting is best in the morning, and reservations should be made a day ahead, if possible. Prices start at $55 for a 17-minute flight over the northern section of the park, and range up to $225. Passengers weighing less than 100 pounds are charged half.

Scenic Airlines (☎ 800/634-6801) offers combination air tours over Bryce Canyon and Zion National Parks plus the north rim of Grand Canyon National Park. Tours are given year-round, with prices starting at $275 for adults and $225 for children.

2 Seeing the Highlights

Because Bryce Canyon is our absolute favorite national park, we would be happy to spend our entire vacation here. But, if you insist on being unreasonable and saving time and energy for the many other fascinating and extremely beautiful parts of Utah, there are ways to see a good deal of Bryce in a short amount of time.

Start at the **visitor center**, of course, and watch the short slide show that explains some of the area geology—the why of Bryce. Then either drive the 18-mile (each way) dead-end **park road**, stopping at viewpoints to gaze down into the canyon (see "Exploring Bryce Canyon by Car," below), or hop on the **Bryce Tours van** for a 2-hour guided tour, complete with lively commentary (see "Guided Tours," below).

Whichever way you choose to get around, make sure you spend at least a little time at **Inspiration Point**, which offers a splendid (and yes, inspirational) view into **Bryce Amphitheater** and its hundreds of statuesque pink, red, orange, and brown hoodoo stone sculptures. After seeing the canyon from the top down, it's time to get some exercise, so walk at least partway down the Queen's Garden Trail. If you can spare 3 hours, hike down the Navajo Loop and return to the rim via Queen's Garden Trail (see "Sports & Activities," below). Those not willing or physically able to hike into the canyon can enjoy a leisurely walk along the **Rim Trail**, which provides spectacular views down into the canyon, especially about an hour before sunset. That evening, try to take in the campground amphitheater program.

GUIDED TOURS

Bryce Canyon Scenic Tours & Shuttles (☎ 800/432-5383 or 435/834-5200) offers 2-hour tours year-round, leaving from Ruby's Inn just outside the park entrance several times daily. Cost is $18 for adults and $9 for youths 14 and younger. Specialized sunrise, sunset, and wildlife tours are also offered; call for details.

3 Exploring Bryce Canyon by Car

The park's **18-mile scenic drive** (one-way) follows the rim of Bryce Canyon, offering easy access to a variety of views into the fanciful fairyland of stone sculptures below. Trailers are not permitted on the road, but can be left at several parking lots. Also, because all overlooks are on your left as you begin your drive, it's best to avoid crossing traffic by driving all the way to the end of the road and stopping at the overlooks on your way back. Allow from 1 to 2 hours.

After leaving the visitor center, drive 18 miles to **Yovimpa and Rainbow Point overlooks**, which offer expansive views of southern Utah, Arizona, and sometimes even New Mexico. From these pink cliffs, you can look down on a colorful platoon of stone soldiers, standing at eternal attention. A short loop trail from Rainbow Point leads to an **1,800-year-old bristlecone pine**, believed to be the oldest living thing at Bryce Canyon.

From here, drive back north to **Ponderosa Canyon Overlook**, where you can gaze down from a dense forest of spruce and fir at multicolored hoodoos, before continuing to **Agua Canyon Overlook**, with some of the best color contrasts you'll find in the park. Looking almost straight down, watch for a hoodoo known as **The Hunter**, wearing a hat of green trees.

Now continue on to **Natural Bridge**, actually an arch carved by rain and wind and spanning 85 feet. From here, continue to **Fairview Point**, where there's a panoramic view to the distant horizon and the Kaibab Plateau at the Grand Canyon's north rim. Passing through **Swamp Canyon**, you'll turn right off the main road to three viewpoints, the first of which is **Paria View**, with views to the south of the White Cliffs, carved into light-colored sandstone by the Paria River. To the north of Paria View, you'll find **Bryce Point**, a splendid stop for seeing the awesome **Bryce Amphitheater**, the largest natural amphitheater in the park, as well as distant views of the Black Mountains to the northeast and Navajo Mountain to the south. From here, it's just a short drive to **Inspiration Point**, offering views similar to those at Bryce Point plus the best view in the park of the **Silent City**, a sleeping city cast in stone.

Now return to the main road and head north to **Sunset Point**, where you can see practically all of Bryce Amphitheater, including the aptly named **Thor's Hammer** and the 200-foot-tall cliffs of **Wall Street**.

Continue north to a turnoff for your final stop at **Sunrise Point**, where there's an inspiring view into Bryce Amphitheater. This is the beginning of the ✪ **Queen's Garden Trail**, an excellent choice for even a quick walk below the canyon's rim.

4 Sports & Activities

BIKING & MOUNTAIN BIKING

Bikes are prohibited on all trails and forbidden from traveling cross-country within the national park boundaries. This leaves the park's established scenic drive, which is open to cyclists, although you should be aware that the 18-mile road through the park is narrow and winding and can be crowded with motor vehicles during the summer.

Because mountain bikers are not welcome on national park hiking trails, you'll have to leave Bryce in search of trails. Fortunately, you won't have to go far. The ✪ **Dave's Hollow Trail** starts at the Bryce Canyon National Park boundary sign on Utah 63, (the park entrance road), about a mile south of Ruby's Inn. The double-track trail goes west for about a half mile before connecting with Forest Road 090, where you turn south and ride for about three-quarters of a mile before turning right onto an easy ride through Dave's Hollow to the Dave's Hollow Forest Service Station on Forest Road 087. From here, you can retrace your route for an 8-mile round-trip ride; for a longer 12-mile trip, turn right on Forest Road 087 to Utah 12 and then right again back to Utah 63 and the starting point. A third option is to turn left on Forest Road 087 and follow it to Tropic Reservoir (see "Fishing," below). For further information, contact the **Dixie National Forest**, 82 N. 100 East, Cedar City, UT 84720 (☎ **435/865-3700**).

Mountain bikes can be rented across the street from Ruby's Inn (☎ **435/ 834-5341**) for $5 an hour or $15 for up to 4 hours. Repairs are also available.

FISHING

The closest fishing hole to the park is at **Tropic Reservoir**, a large lake in a ponderosa pine forest. From the intersection of Utah 63 (the park entrance road) and Utah 12, drive west about 3 miles to a gravel road, and then drive about 7 miles south. You'll find a forest service campground open in the summer, two boat ramps, and fishing for rainbow, brook, and cutthroat trout. Locals say fishing is sometimes better in streams above the lake than in the reservoir itself. For further information, contact the **Dixie National Forest,** 82 N. 100 East, Cedar City, UT 84720 (☎ **435/865-3700**).

HIKING

One of the things we like best about Bryce Canyon is that you don't have to be an advanced backpacker to really get to know the park.

The park's twice-yearly free newspaper, *Hoodoo*, contains short information and a map on nine day hikes, and *The Bryce Canyon Auto and Hiking Guide* ($2.95), published by the Bryce Canyon Natural History Association, describes them in greater detail (see "Information & Visitor Centers," earlier this chapter).

All trails below the rim have at least some steep grades, so you should wear hiking boots with a traction tread and good ankle support to avoid ankle injuries, the most common accidents in the park. During the hot summer months you'll want to hike either early or late in the day, and keep in mind that it gets hotter the deeper you go into the canyon.

The **Rim Trail**, which does not drop into the canyon but offers splendid views from above, meanders along the rim for over 5 miles. An easy to moderate walk, it includes a half-mile section between two overlooks—Sunrise and Sunset—that is suitable for wheelchairs. Overlooking Bryce Amphitheater, the trail offers excellent views almost everywhere and is a good choice for an after-dinner walk, when you can watch the changing evening light on the rosy rocks below.

Your best bet for getting down into the canyon and seeing the most with the least amount of sweat is to combine two popular trails—✪ **Navajo Loop** and **Queen's Garden**. The total distance is just under 3 miles, with a 521-foot elevation change, and it takes most hikers from 2 to 3 hours. It's best to start at the Navajo Loop trailhead at Sunset Point and leave the canyon on the less-steep Queen's Garden Trail, returning to the rim at Sunrise Point, half a mile to the north. The Navajo Loop section is considered fairly strenuous, while Queen's Garden is rated moderate. Along the Navajo Loop section, you'll pass Thor's Hammer, wonder why it hasn't fallen, and ponder the towering skyscrapers of Wall Street. Turning onto the Queen's Garden Trail, you'll see some of the park's most fanciful formations, including majestic Queen Victoria herself, for whom the trail was named, plus the Queen's Castle and Gulliver's Castle.

Those looking for more of a challenge might consider the **Hat Shop Trail**, a strenuous 3.8-mile hike (round-trip) with a 900-foot elevation change. Leaving from the Bryce Point Overlook, you'll drop quickly to the Hat Shop, so-named because it consists of hard gray "hats" perched on narrow reddish-brown pedestals. Allow 4 hours.

For die-hard hikers who don't mind rough terrain, Bryce has two backcountry trails, usually open in the summer only. The **Under-the-Rim Trail** runs for some 22.6 miles, providing an excellent opportunity to see the park's spectacular scenery on its own terms. **Riggs Spring Loop Trail**, 8.8 miles long, offers splendid views of the pink cliffs in the southern part of the park. The really ambitious can combine the two trails for a week-long excursion. Permits, which cost $5 and are available at the visitor center, are required for all overnight trips into the backcountry.

HORSEBACK RIDING

To see Bryce Canyon the way the early pioneers did, you need the view from a horse. **Canyon Trail Rides** (☎ **435/679-8665**), with a desk inside Bryce Lodge, offers a close-up view of Bryce's spectacular rock formations from the relative comfort of a saddle, and welcomes first-time riders. A 2-hour ride to the canyon floor and back costs $26.50, including tax, per person (no one under 5 years old), and a half-day trip farther into the canyon costs $40 per person (no one under 8 years old). Riders for both trips must weigh 220 pounds or less, and rides are offered, weather permitting, from April through October.

Guided rides are also provided by **Ruby's Scenic Rim and Outlaw Trail Rides** (☎ **800/679-5859** or 435/679-8761), at Ruby's Inn, at similar rates; in addition, Ruby's offers a full-day ride with lunch for $75. There may be age and weight limits, and reservations are recommended for both companies. Ruby's will also board your horse.

CHUCK WAGON DINNER RIDE

Another Old West experience is a wagon ride through the rugged and beautiful country around Bryce to a covered-wagon camp where the chuck wagon is all ready to serve a barbecued chicken dinner followed by western music and dancing. Available from May 27 to October 1, with departures Monday through Saturday at 6:30pm. Wagons leave from Old Bryce Town, across from Ruby's Inn. Cost is $28 for adults, $24.50 for ages 9 through 15, and $16.50 for ages 4 through 8; tickets are available at Ruby's Inn. For advance information, contact **B-Bar-D Covered Wagon Co.,** P.O. Box 49, Bryce, UT 84764 (☎ **435/834-5202**).

WILDLIFE WATCHING

The park is home to a variety of wildlife, ranging from mule deer—which really seem to get around—to the commonly seen mountain short-horned lizard, often spotted while hiking down into the canyon. Occasionally you'll catch a glimpse of a mountain lion, most likely on the prowl in search of a mule-deer dinner; elk and pronghorn may also be seen at higher elevations.

The Utah prairie dog, listed as a threatened species, is actually a rodent. It inhabits park meadows, but should be avoided, as its fleas may carry disease (see "Safety Concerns," earlier this chapter).

Of the many birds in the park, you're bound to hear the rather obnoxious call of the Steller's jay. Watch for swifts and swallows as they perform their exotic acrobatics along cliff faces; binoculars will come in handy.

The Great Basin rattlesnake, although pretty, should be given a wide berth. Sometimes more than 5 feet long, this rattler is the park's only poisonous reptile. However, like most rattlesnakes, it is just as anxious as you are to avoid confrontation.

WINTER ACTIVITIES

Bryce is beautiful in the winter, with the white snow creating a perfect frosting on the red, pink, orange, and brown statues standing proudly against the cold winds. A limited number of **snowshoes** are loaned free of charge at the visitor center and may be used anywhere in the park except on cross-country ski tracks. ✪ **Cross-country skiers**, meanwhile, will find several marked, ungroomed trails (all above the rim), including The Fairyland Trail, which leads 1 mile through a pine and juniper forest to the Fairyland Point Overlook. From here, you can take the 1-mile Forest Trail back to the road, or continue north along the rim for another 1.2 miles to the park boundary. Although the entire park is open to cross-country skiers, rangers warn that it's extremely dangerous to try to ski on the steep trails leading down into the canyon. Stop at the visitor center for additional trail information, and go to Best Western Ruby's Inn, just north of the park entrance (☎ **435/834-5341**), for information on cross-country ski trails and **snowmobiling** opportunities outside the park. Ruby's grooms over 50 kilometers of ski trails and also rents cross-country ski equipment starting at $7 for a half day.

5 Camping

IN THE PARK

Typical of the West's national park campgrounds, the two at Bryce offer plenty of trees with a genuine "forest camping" experience, easy access to trails, and limited facilities. **North Campground** has 105 sites and **Sunset Campground** has 111 sites. A section of North Campground is open year-round, but Sunset Campground is open May through September only. We prefer North Campground because it's closer to the Rim Trail—making it easier to rush over to catch those amazing sunrise and sunset colors—but we would gladly take any site in either campground. Neither has RV hookups or showers, but you will find modern rest rooms with running water. Reservations are not accepted, so get to the park early to claim a site (usually by 2pm in the summer). Cost is $10 per night, with a 14-day limit. Private showers ($2 in quarters) are located at a general store in the park, although it's a healthy walk from either campground. The park service also operates an RV dump station ($2 fee) in the summer.

The store provides a coin-operated laundry and snack bar, plus bundles of firewood, food and camping supplies, and souvenirs. Tables on a covered porch run along one side of the building.

NEARBY

Bryce Pioneer Village

80 S. Main St. (Utah 12) (P.O. Box 119), Tropic, UT 84776. ☎ **800/222-0381** or 435/679-8546. Fax 435/679-8607. 10–15 sites. $15 hookups, $10 tent. $3 dump station. $2 showers for noncampers. DISC, MC, V.

This small motel/cabins/campground combination in nearby Tropic offers an adequate campground at a reasonable price, with RV hookups, hot showers, and easy access to several restaurants. It's usually open mid-April through October.

King's Creek Campground

Dixie National Forest, 82 N. 100 East, Cedar City, UT 84720. ☎ **435/865-3700**. 34 sites. $8. No credit cards.

Located above Tropic Reservoir, this forest service campground is open from Memorial Day to Labor Day, with graded gravel roads and sites nestled among tall ponderosa pines. Facilities include flush toilets, drinking water, and an RV dump station, but no showers or RV hookups. The reservoir has two boat ramps; see "Fishing," earlier in this chapter. To get to the campground from the Bryce Canyon National Park entrance, go north 3 miles on Utah 63 to Utah 12, turn west (left), and go 2.5 miles to the King's Creek Campground Road; turn south (left) and follow signs to Tropic Reservoir for about 7 miles to the campground.

Ruby's Inn RV Park & Campground

Utah 63 (P.O. Box 22), Bryce, UT 84764. ☎ **435/834-5301** or 435/834-5341. Fax 435/834-5481. 227 total sites: 127 with RV hookups, 100 tent. Full hookups $21.50, electric/water only $20, tent space $13.50. AE, DC, DISC, MC, V.

The closest campground to Bryce Canyon National Park that offers complete RV hookups, Ruby's even has shuttle bus service into the park during July and August. Many sites are shaded, including an attractive tent area; a lake and horse pasture are adjacent to the campground. Campers have free use of the swimming pools at Ruby's Best Western motel next door, and the campground facilities include two coin-operated laundries, a game room, horseshoes, barbecue grills, and a store with groceries and RV supplies. It's open April through October.

6 Accommodations

IN THE PARK
FRI-SAT

Room taxes add about 9% to the total cost. Pets are not accepted unless otherwise noted.
435

○ Bryce Canyon Lodge

Bryce Canyon National Park, UT. ☎ **435/834-5361.** Information and reservations: AmFac Parks & Resorts, 14001 E. Iliff Ave., Suite 600, Aurora, CO 80014. ☎ 303/29-PARKS. Fax 303/338-2045. 114 units in motel rooms and cabins; 3 suites and 1 studio in lodge. TEL. $83–$90 motel double; $93–$105 cabin; $115–$120 lodge unit. AE, DISC, MC, V. Closed Nov–Mar.

Location is what you're paying for here, and there's no denying that this is the perfect place to stay while seeing Bryce Canyon National Park, allowing you to watch the play of changing light on the rock formations at various times of the day. The handsome sandstone and ponderosa pine lodge, which opened in 1924, contains a busy lobby, with information desks for horseback riding and other activities, and a gift shop that offers everything from postcards and souvenirs to top-quality silver-and-turquoise jewelry and Navajo rugs. The staff are very knowledgeable, and there is a good selection of fine Indian pawn jewelry. The luxurious lodge suites are wonderful, with white wicker furniture, ceiling fans, and separate sitting rooms. The motel rooms are just that. Although the outside looks like a hunting lodge, the guest units are pleasant, modern motel rooms, quite spacious, with two queen-size beds and either a balcony or patio. There's nothing at all wrong with them, except that the surroundings and exterior lead you to expect something more interesting. Our choice would be the "rustic luxury" of one of the cabins, which are being restored to their 1924 decor. They're fairly small, although the tall ceilings give a feeling of spaciousness, with stone (gas-burning) fireplaces, two queen beds, and log beams. It seems just the right place to stay in a beautiful national park setting like Bryce Canyon. Reserve 4 to 6 months in advance.

NEARBY
39 miles W (435) 477 3391

Best Western Ruby's Inn

Utah 63 at the entrance to Bryce Canyon (P.O. Box 1), Bryce, UT 84764. ☎ **800/528-1234** or 435/834-5341. Fax 435/834-5265. 369 units, including 60 suites. A/C TV TEL. June–Sept

$85–$110 double, $120–$125 suite; Apr–May and Oct $60–$92 double, $100–$115 suite; Nov–Mar $44–$70 double, $80 suite. AE, CB, DC, DISC, EU, JCB, MC, V.

This large Best Western provides most of the beds for tired hikers and canyon-rim gazers visiting Bryce Canyon National Park. The lobby, with a stone fireplace and a western motif of animal-head trophies and Indian blankets, is among the busiest places in the area, with an ATM, small liquor store, car rentals, beauty salon, 1-hour film processor, and tour desks where you can arrange excursions of all sorts, from horseback and all-terrain-vehicle rides to helicopter tours. Just off the lobby, you'll find a restaurant; a western art gallery; a huge general store that carries souvenirs, cowboy hats and western clothing, camping supplies, and groceries; and a U.S. post office. Outside are two gas stations.

Spread among nine separate buildings, the modern motel rooms feature wood furnishings, art depicting scenes of the area, and shower/tub combos. Some have whirlpool tubs, including a few with two-person whirlpool tubs. Rooms at the back of the complex will be a bit quieter, but you'll have to walk farther to all the lobby activities. Services include a concierge and courtesy transportation from the Bryce Airport; and facilities include two indoor pools, one indoor and one outdoor whirlpool, a sundeck, bicycle rental, nature and cross-country ski trails, a game room, a business center, conference rooms for up to 300, and two coin-operated laundries. Also see "Activities & More Beautiful Scenery Just Outside Bryce Canyon," below. The motel accepts pets.

Bryce Pioneer Village

80 S. Main St. (Utah 12) (P.O. Box 119), Tropic, UT 84776. ☎ **800/222-0381** or 435/679-8546. Fax 435/679-8607. 47 motel rms, 20 cabins. A/C TV TEL. Rooms $60–$85 double; cabins $39–$85. DISC, MC, V.

The small, no-frills motel rooms in this modular building have showers only (no tubs), but they're clean, have fairly large walk-in closets, and are completely adequate for those seeking a night's rest at a reasonable rate. The cabins, which were relocated from inside the national park, are more interesting. Most are small but cute, and each one is unique. Furnishings may include one queen bed plus a twin bed, one chair, and a small bathroom with a corner shower but no tub. Several others, which have been renovated within the past few years, are much larger, with two queen beds, attractive floral-print wallpaper, and average-size bathrooms with shower/tub combinations. There are also two rooms with three queen beds. The motel has no pool, but does offer a whirlpool, two hot tubs, a picnic area, and a small curio shop. Just outside the motel office, you can see the cabin in which Ebenezer and Mary Bryce, for whom the national park is named, lived in the late 1870s. The motel accepts pets. Check on possible winter closure.

Bryce Point Bed & Breakfast

61 N. 400 West (P.O. Box 96), Tropic, UT 84776-0096. ☎ **435/679-8629.** 5 rms, 1 honeymoon cottage. TV. $70 double, $90–$120 honeymoon cottage. Rates include full breakfast. MC, V.

Each room in Lamar and Ethel LeFevre's bed-and-breakfast is named for and decorated in the style of one of the couple's children. For instance, son Les is a firefighter, so the Les and Dela room contains firefighting memorabilia and photos; and because son Lynn is in the airline industry, you'll find airplane-related mementos in Lynn and Karen's room. The decor is tasteful and not overdone, and most rooms offer beautiful views of Bryce Point through large picture windows. All rooms contain queen beds and private baths (showers only), and all have TV/VCR combos, with free use of the LeFevre's video collection. The full breakfasts are homemade and satisfying, with selections such as bacon and eggs with pancakes and apple cider syrup. The honeymoon cottage is beautifully furnished in country style, with a gas fireplace in the living room, full kitchen, washer and dryer, and king bed in the spacious bedroom. The B&B is entirely nonsmoking.

Foster's
Utah 12 (mailing address: Star Route, Panguitch, UT 84759), Bryce, UT. ☎ **800/475-4318** or 435/834-5227. Fax 435/834-5304. 52 units. A/C TV TEL. Winter $49.95 double; summer $59.95 double. AE, DISC, MC, V.

You'll find clean, quiet, and economical lodging at Foster's, located 1 1/2 miles west of the Bryce Canyon National Park access road turnoff. Also on the grounds are a restaurant (see "Dining," below) and a grocery store (open 7am to 8pm, closed December and January) with a rather nice bakery. A modular unit contains small rooms, each with either one queen-size or two double beds and decorated with posters showing scenery of the area; bathrooms have showers only.

World Host Bryce Valley Inn
200 N. Main St., Tropic, UT 84776. ☎ **800/442-1890** or 435/679-8811. Fax 435/679-8846. 65 rms. A/C TV TEL. Apr–Oct $60–$75 double; Nov–Mar $30–$45 double. AE, DISC, MC, V.

Located 8 miles east of the park entrance road, these simply-decorated, basic motel rooms offer a clean, economical choice for park visitors. Rooms, all with shower/tub combos, are furnished with either one or two queen beds. There's one suite with two queens and a hide-a-bed, and one handicapped-accessible room. The motel has an outdoor whirlpool tub (but no pool) and a 24-hour coin-operated laundry. The Hungry Coyote Restaurant & Saloon (see "Dining," below) serves American and Mexican cuisine and has a separate ice cream parlor. A gift shop on the premises offers a large selection of American Indian arts and crafts, handmade gifts, rocks, and fossils. Pets are accepted with a fee.

7 Dining

IN THE PARK

Bryce Canyon Lodge
Bryce Canyon National Park. ☎ **435/834-5361.** Reservations required for dinner. Main courses $10.50–$15.95 dinner; $4.95–$6.95 lunch; $3.75–$6.25 Breakfast. AE, DC, DISC, MC, V. Daily 6:30am–4:30pm and 5:30–9:30pm. Closed Nov–Mar. AMERICAN.

It's worth coming here just for the mountain-lodge atmosphere, two large stone fireplaces, American Indian weavings and baskets, huge 45-star 1897 American flag, and large windows looking out on the park. But the food's pretty good, too—and reasonably priced considering that this is the only real restaurant actually located in the park. House specialties at dinner include an excellent slow-roasted prime rib au jus and broiled chicken breast; we also recommend the fresh mountain trout. The menu offers several vegetarian items, such as grilled polenta and vegetarian lasagna. Ask about the lodge's specialty ice creams and desserts, such as the exotic and very tasty wild "Bryceberry" crumb cake. At lunch you'll find the trout, plus burgers, sandwiches, and salads; breakfasts offer all the usual American selections. Service is attentive and friendly, but a bit too speedy at dinner. The restaurant will pack lunches to go for hikers and offers a children's menu and full liquor service.

NEARBY

Foster's Family Steak House
Utah 12 about 1 1/2 miles west of the park entrance road. ☎ **435/834-5227.** Reservations not accepted. Main courses $8.99–$18.99 dinner; breakfast and lunch items $1.75–$5.99. AE, DISC, MC, V. Mar–Nov daily 7am–10pm; Dec–Feb daily 5–10pm. STEAK/SEAFOOD.

The simple western decor here provides the appropriate atmosphere for a family steakhouse, popular among locals for its slow-roasted prime rib and steamed Utah trout. Foster's also offers several steaks, including a 14-ounce T-bone, sandwiches, a soup of the day, and homemade western-style chile with beans. All the pastries, pies, and breads are baked on the premises. Foster's has a children's menu, and all menu items can be ordered to go. Bottled beer is available with meals.

Hungry Coyote Restaurant & Saloon

200 N. Main St. (Utah 12; 8 miles east of the park entrance road), at the World Host Bryce Valley Inn, Tropic. ☎ **435/679-8822.** Main courses $4.95–$20.75 dinner; $3.95–$6.95 breakfast. AE, DISC, MC, V. Daily 6–11am and 5–11pm; shorter hours in winter. AMERICAN/MEXICAN.

The Old West is king here, evident in the rough wood walls, old ranch tools, kerosene lanterns, and warnings that patrons must "check your gun with the waitress." Beef eaters will savor the thick 20-ounce T-bone, the most expensive item on the menu, while fans of Mexican food might opt for the fajitas. You can also get pork chops, grilled chicken breast, or trout. The restaurant has a full liquor license.

Ruby's Inn Cowboy's Buffet and Steak Room

Just north of the park entrance on Utah 63, in the Ruby's Inn complex, Bryce. ☎ **435/834-5341.** Breakfast buffet $7 adults, $6 children 3–12; lunch buffet $9 adults, $7 children 3–12; dinner buffet $14.50; main courses $3–$13.50 breakfast and lunch; main courses $5.50–$19.50 dinner. AE, CB, DC, DISC, EU, JCB, MC, V. Summer daily 6:30am–9:30pm; winter daily 6:30am–8:30pm. STEAK/SEAFOOD.

The busiest restaurant in the Bryce Canyon area, Ruby's moves 'em through with buffets at every meal plus a well-rounded menu and friendly service. The breakfast buffet offers the usual family-restaurant staples of scrambled eggs, fresh fruit, several breakfast meats, potatoes, and cereals; you can also get omelets and eggs cooked to order. At the lunch buffet, you'll find country-style ribs, fresh fruit, salads, soups, vegetables, and breads; the dinner buffet features slow-roasted beef and other meats, pastas, potatoes, and salads. Regular menu dinner entrees include prime rib, huge ribs, breaded-and-grilled southern Utah rainbow trout, broiled chicken breast, burgers, and salads. Full liquor service is available.

8 Activities & More Beautiful Scenery Just Outside Bryce Canyon

The **Best Western Ruby's Inn** (☎ 435/834-5341), on Utah 63 just north of the Bryce Canyon National Park entrance (see "Accommodations," above), is practically a one-stop entertainment center for those looking for a bit of variety in their Bryce Canyon National Park vacation.

Directly across Utah 63 from the motel are **Old Bryce Town Shops,** open from mid-May through September, where you'll encounter a rock shop, a Christmas store, souvenirs, and an opportunity to buy that genuine cowboy hat you've always wanted. Next to the shops is a children's petting farm (free admission), with performing horses and a cowboy poet; you can also try your hand at panning for gold ($4 pan rental).

In Ruby's vast complex, you'll find a U.S. post office, Utah state liquor store (closed Sundays and holidays), two coin-operated laundries (one of which is open 24 hours), seasonal game room, 1-hour photo lab, foreign currency exchange (front desk), ATM, and fax and photocopy machines.

Nearby, **Bryce Canyon Country Rodeo** has bucking broncos, bull riding, calf roping, and all sorts of rodeo fun in a 1-hour program from Memorial Day through August, Monday through Saturday evenings at 7:30pm. Admission is $7 for adults and $4 for children under 12.

RED CANYON

About 9 miles west of Bryce Canyon National Park in the Dixie National Forest is **Red Canyon**, named for its vermilion-colored rock formations, accented by stands of rich green ponderosa pine. The canyon is a favorite of hikers and mountain bikers in the summer and cross-country skiers and snowshoers in the winter.

There are about a dozen trails in Red Canyon, and a free map is available at Forest Services offices. Some are open to hikers only, others to mountain bikers, horseback riders, and those with all-terrain vehicles. One especially scenic multi-use trail is the 5.3-mile (one-way) **Casto Canyon Trail,** which runs along the bottom of Casto Canyon. It connects with the 8.7-mile (one-way) **Cassidy Trail** and 3-mile (one-way) **Losee Canyon Trail** to produce a 17-mile loop that is ideal for a backpacking trip of several days. Watch for elk in the winter, and pronghorn antelope and raptors year-round. The Casto Canyon and Losee Canyon Trails are considered moderate, while Cassidy Trail ranges from easy to strenuous.

For maps, specific directions to trailheads, current trail conditions, and additional information, contact **Dixie National Forest,** 82 N. 100 East, Cedar City, UT 84720 (☎ 435/865-3700), or the Dixie's **Powell Ranger District,** 225 E. Center St., Panguitch, UT 84759 (☎ 435/676-8815). There's also a **Dixie National Forest Visitor Center** (open Memorial Day to Labor Day) about 10$^{1}/_{2}$ miles west of the intersection of Utah 12 and Utah 63 (the Bryce Canyon National Park entrance road).

9 A Nearby State Park: Kodachrome Basin State Park

Located about 22 miles from the entrance to Bryce Canyon National Park, Kodachrome Basin lives up to its name, its wonderful scenery begging to be captured on film (regardless of brand or type). Named by the National Geographic Society in 1949, the park is filled with tall stone towers—called chimneys—and pink-and-white sandstone cliffs, all set among the contrasting greens of sagebrush and piñon and juniper trees. It also abuts and makes a good base for exploring the new Grand Staircase-Escalante National Monument, which is discussed later in this chapter.

JUST THE FACTS

Because temperatures get a bit warm here during the summer—the park is at 5,800 feet elevation—the best times to visit, especially for hikers, are the months of May, September, and October, when there are also fewer people.

GETTING THERE From Bryce Canyon National Park, go 3 miles north to the junction of Utah 63 and Utah 12, go east (right) on Utah 12 for about 12 miles to Cannonville, turn south onto the park's access road (there's a sign), and go about 7 miles to the park entrance.

INFORMATION, FEES & REGULATIONS Contact the **park office** at P.O. Box 238, Cannonville, UT 84718 (☎ **435/679-8562**) for a color brochure and answers to questions about park facilities and services.

The day-use fee is $3 per vehicle or $1 each for those entering the park by foot, bicycle, or motorcycle.

Dogs are permitted in the park and on trails, but must be kept on leashes no more than 6 feet long.

SPORTS & ACTIVITIES

HIKING Kodachrome Basin offers several hiking possibilities. Starting just south of the campground, the **Panorama Trail** is only moderately difficult, with no steep climbs. At first, it follows an old, relatively flat wagon route, then climbs to offer views of the park's rock formations before reaching the well-named Panorama Point. Along the way are several possible side trips, including a short walk to the **Hat Shop,** so named because the formations resemble broad-brimmed hats, and **White Buffalo Loop,** where you'll try to find a formation that looks like—guess what?—a white buffalo. The optional **Big Bear Geyser Trail** is a bit more difficult, winding past Big Bear and Mama Bear before returning to Panorama Trail. Allow 2 to 3 hours for the Panorama Trail and an extra hour for Big Bear Geyser Trail.

Fans of arches will want to drive the dirt road to the trailhead for the half-mile round-trip hike to **Shakespeare Arch,** discovered by park manager Tom Shakespeare. This trail also provides views of a large chimney-rock formation.

HORSEBACK RIDING & STAGECOACH RIDES   Located in the park, **Trail Head Station** (☎ **435/679-8536**) offers guided horseback or horse-drawn stagecoach rides. Call for rates and seasons.

WILDLIFE WATCHING   Jackrabbits and chukar partridges are probably the most commonly seen wildlife in the park, although you'll also hear the piñon jay and might see an occasional coyote or rattlesnake.

CAMPING

The park's attractive 24-site **campground** has flush toilets, showers, drinking water, picnic tables, barbecue grills, and an RV dump station, but no RV hookups. Camping costs $10. Contact the park office (see "Information, Fees & Regulations," above) for more information.

10 From Bryce Canyon to Capitol Reef: Grand Staircase-Escalante National Monument & the Highway 12 Scenic Drive

Even if it didn't have a beautiful national park at each end—Bryce Canyon and Capitol Reef—the Highway 12 Scenic Byway and the Grand Staircase-Escalante National Monument that it passes by and through would be well worth the drive. Here, you'll find richly varied scenery: red rock spires and canyons, dense forests of tall evergreens, pastoral meadows, colorful slickrock, and plunging waterfalls. Whether you're just passing through, pausing briefly at scenic viewpoints along the way, or stopping to explore America's huge new national monument, you'll have plenty to see. Those driving between Bryce Canyon and Capitol Reef National Parks should allow at least 4 hours for the trip, but we suggest you stop in the small community of Escalante, visit its fine state park, and investigate the wild areas in the Grand Staircase-Escalante National Monument and other nearby public lands.

BASING YOURSELF IN ESCALANTE

Originally called Potato Valley, this community's name was changed in the 19th century to honor Spanish explorer and missionary Father Silvestre Velez de Escalante. However, it's believed Escalante never actually visited this particular part of southern Utah on his trek from Santa Fe, New Mexico, to California a hundred years earlier. Home to nearly 100 historic buildings (a free walking tour map is available at the information booth and local businesses), Escalante is your best bet for lodging, food, and supplies as you travel Utah 12. It's also a good base for exploring the nearby mountains and the new Grand Staircase-Escalante National Monument, or for finally taking a hot shower after a week of backpacking. Be aware, though, that services in this town of 800 are somewhat limited in the winter.

ESSENTIALS

GETTING THERE   Escalante is 50 miles east of Bryce Canyon National Park and 63 miles south of Capitol Reef National Park on the Highway 12 Scenic Byway. Utah 12 becomes Main Street as it goes through Escalante.

INFORMATION   An information booth is open during the summer months on Main Street (Utah 12), just east of Center Street, and many local businesses have racks of brochures on area attractions.

The **National Park Service, Dixie National Forest**, and the **Bureau of Land Management** operate an interagency office that provides recreation and other tourist information year-round. It's located on the west side of town at 755 W. Main St. (Utah 12), P.O. Box 246, Escalante, UT 84726 (☎ **435/826-5499**). From mid-March to October, the office is open daily from 7:30am to 5:30pm; the rest of the year, it's open Monday through Friday from 8am to 4:30pm.

Information is available by mail from the **Escalante Chamber of Commerce,** P.O. Box 326, Escalante, UT 84726 (☎ **435/826-4810**).

FAST FACTS   The only medical facility in town is the **Ivan Kazan Memorial Clinic** at 65 N. Center St. (☎ **435/826-4374**), which is open Mondays, Wednesdays, and Fridays only. The **post office** is at 230 W. Main St. (☎ **435/826-4314**).

WHERE TO STAY

A room tax of about 9% is added to all bills. Pets are not accepted unless otherwise noted.

Circle D Motel

475 W. Main St. (Utah 12) (P.O. Box 305), Escalante, UT 84726. ☎ **435/826-4297.** Fax 435/826-4402. 29 units. A/C TV TEL. $30–$45 double; $50–$75 family units. AE, MC, V.

You'll find clean, well-maintained basic lodging at this family-owned and -operated motel, one of the few in Escalante that's open year-round. Rooms are simply decorated and furnished, with two double beds, one or two queen beds, or a king. Family units sleep from five to eight, and some units have small refrigerators. There's no swimming pool, but at these rates, who can complain? Pets are accepted for a $5 fee.

Escalante Outfitters, Inc.

310 W. Main St. (Utah 12) (P.O. Box 570), Escalante, UT 84726. ☎ **435/826-4266.** Fax 435/826-4388. 7 cabins. $24.95 double. DISC, MC, V. Check on possible closure Nov–Feb.

These cute little log cabins are a favorite of backpackers who want a break from sleeping on the ground. Think of this place as a cross between a motel and a campground; actually, it's closer to the auto camps of the 1930s. Built in 1994–95, the cabins have either one double bed or a pair of bunk beds, a chair, a small table with a lamp, and two small windows. There's heat in cool weather and fans for warm weather. That's it. No private baths are available; guests share a simple but adequate and well-maintained bathhouse. On the grounds are a duck pond, barbecue pits, picnic tables, horseshoe pits, and a volleyball court. A pay phone is nearby. A gourmet coffee shop and pizza parlor were added in 1997.

Prospector Inn

380 W. Main St. (Utah 12) (P.O. Box 296), Escalante, UT 84726. ☎ **435/826-4653.** Fax 435/826-4285. 50 rms. A/C TV TEL. $50 double. AE, MC, V.

You can't miss this distinctive two-story motel (built in 1994), with its vertically set red brick exterior. Rooms are particularly quiet and spacious, furnished with two double beds and decorated with framed photos of the area's scenery. There's a small gift shop, but no swimming pool. Free morning coffee is available in the lobby. The adjacent Ponderosa Restaurant serves three meals daily.

WHERE TO DINE

Circle D Restaurant

475 W. Main St. (Utah 12), Escalante. ☎ **435/826-4550.** Main courses $6.50–$13.75; sand-wiches $2–$5.50. AE, MC, V. Apr–Sept or Oct Mon–Sat 11am–9pm. Closed the rest of the year. MEXICAN/AMERICAN.

This Southwestern cafe-style restaurant, with three separate dining rooms, offers a good variety of food, from burgers and sandwiches to the popular rib-eye steak, pot roast with red cabbage and apples, and a vegetarian shepherd's pie. The Mexican side includes hard or soft tacos, enchiladas, burritos, and baked quesadillas. You can also get a sack lunch or a take-out breakfast (by prior arrangement). No alcohol is served.

Cowboy Blues Diner

530 W. Main St. (Utah 12), Escalante. ☎ **435/826-4251.** Main courses $4.75–$13.95; break-fast $2.25–$8.75; sandwiches $3.50–$5.75. DISC, MC, V. Daily 7am–9:30pm; shorter hours in the winter. SOUTHWESTERN/AMERICAN.

This western diner—the wood plank walls are even decorated with steer skulls—offers steak, hot and cold sandwiches, and specialty Southwestern dishes such as chicken quesadillas, Navajo tacos, and the combo: a beef enchilada, a cheese enchi-lada, soft taco, rice, beans, chips, and salsa. The tasty but not overly spicy chile is served on the side to let you add just the right amount. Breakfasts include all the usual selections. Alcohol is not served.

GRAND STAIRCASE-ESCALANTE NATIONAL MONUMENT

Covering some 1.7 million acres, this vast area of red-orange canyons, mesas, plateaus, and river valleys became a national monument by presidential proclamation on Sep-tember 18, 1996. Known for its stark, rugged beauty, it contains a unique combi-nation of geological, biological, paleontological, archaeological, and historical resources. In announcing the creation of the monument, President Bill Clinton pro-claimed, "This high, rugged, and remote region was the last place in the continen-tal United States to be mapped; even today, this unspoiled natural area remains a frontier, a quality that greatly enhances the monument's value for scientific study."

Under the jurisdiction of the Bureau of Land Management, the monument is ex-pected to remain open for grazing and possible oil and gas drilling under existing leases (although no new leases would be issued), as well as hunting, fishing, hiking, camping, and other forms of recreation. A 3-year study was begun, and a manage-ment plan is expected to be completed by late 1999.

Unlike most other national monuments, almost all of this vast area is undevel-oped—there are few all-weather roads, only one maintained hiking trail, and two developed campgrounds. But the adventurous will find miles upon miles of dirt roads and practically unlimited opportunities for hiking, horseback riding, mountain bik-ing on existing dirt roads, and camping.

The national monument can be divided into three distinct sections: the Grand Staircase of sandstone cliffs, which includes five life zones from Sonoran Desert to coniferous forests, in the southwest; the Kaiparowits Plateau, a vast, wild region of rugged mesas and steep canyons in the center; and the Escalante River Canyons sec-tion, along the northern edge of the monument, a delightfully scenic area contain-ing miles of interconnecting river canyons.

JUST THE FACTS

GETTING THERE   The national monument takes in a large section of southern Utah—covering an area almost as big as the states of Delaware and Rhode Island combined—with Bryce Canyon National Park to the west, Capitol Reef National

Park on its northwest edge, and Glen Canyon National Recreation Area along the east and part of the south sides.

Access is via Utah 12 along the monument's northwest edge, from Kodachrome Basin State Park and the communities of Escalante and Boulder; and via U.S. 89 to the southern section of the monument, east of the town of Kanab.

INFORMATION & VISITOR CENTERS   Contact the **Escalante Interagency Office** on the west side of Escalante at 755 W. Main St. (Utah 12), P.O. Box 246, Escalante, UT 84726 (☎ 435/826-5499); or the **Bureau of Land Management** office at 318 N. First East St., Kanab, UT 84741 (☎ 435/644-2672). These offices offer maps, a handsome color brochure, and handouts on a variety of activities.

FEES, REGULATIONS & SAFETY   There is no charge to enter the monument; those planning overnight trips into the backcountry should obtain permits (free at this writing) at either of the offices listed above. Regulations are similar to those on other public lands; damaging or disturbing archaeological and historic sites in any way is particularly forbidden. Water is the main safety concern here, either too little or too much. This is generally very dry country, so those going into the monument should carry plenty of drinking water. However, thunderstorms can turn the monument's dirt roads into impassable mud bogs in minutes, stranding motorists, and potentially fatal flash floods through narrow canyons can catch hikers by surprise. Anyone planning trips into the monument should check first with one of the offices listed above on current and anticipated weather and travel conditions.

SPORTS & ACTIVITIES

HIKING, MOUNTAIN BIKING & HORSEBACK RIDING   At this writing, the national monument has only one maintained hiking trail. Located about 15 miles northeast of Escalante via Utah 12, the **Calf Creek Recreation Area** has a campground (see "Camping," below), a picnic area with fire grates and tables, trees, drinking water, and flush toilets. The tree-shaded picnic and camping area lies along the creek at the bottom of a high-walled, rather narrow rock canyon. The best part of the recreation area, though, is the moderately strenuous 5¹/₂-mile round-trip hike to **Lower Calf Creek Falls.** A sandy trail leads along **Calf Creek,** past beaver ponds and wetlands, to a beautiful waterfall, cascading 126 feet down a rock wall into a tree-shaded pool. You can pick up an interpretive brochure at the trailhead.

Even though the Calf Creek Trail is the monument's only officially marked and maintained trail, numerous unmarked cross-country routes are ideal for hiking, mountain biking (on existing dirt roads only), and horseback riding. We strongly recommend that hikers stop at the Interagency Office in Escalante or the BLM office in Kanab to get recommendations on hiking routes and to purchase topographic maps. Hikers need to remember that this is wild country and can be hazardous. Rangers recommend carrying at least 1 gallon of water per person per day, and say that all water from streams should be treated before drinking. The potential for flooding is high, and hikers should check with the BLM before attempting to hike through the monument's narrow slot canyons, which offer no escape during flash floods. Other hazards include poisonous snakes and scorpions and, in the wetter areas, poison ivy. Slickrock, as the name suggests, is slippery, so hikers should wear sturdy hiking boots with good soles.

Among popular and relatively easy-to-follow hiking routes is the footpath to **Escalante Natural Bridge**, which repeatedly crosses the river, so be prepared to get wet up to your knees. The easy 2-mile (one-way) hike begins at a parking area at the bridge that crosses the Escalante River near Calf Creek Recreation Area, 15 miles northeast of the town of Escalante. From the parking area, hike upstream to Escalante

Grand Staircase–Escalante National Monument

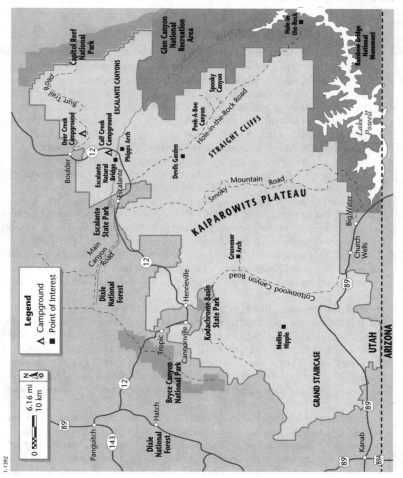

Natural Bridge, on the south side of the river. The bridge is 130 feet high and spans 100 feet.

Also starting at the Utah 12 bridge parking area is a hike downstream to **Phipps Wash.** Mostly moderate, this hike goes about 1½ miles to the mouth of Phipps Wash, which enters the river from the west. You'll find Maverick Natural Bridge in a north side drainage of Phipps Wash, and climbing up the drainage on the south side leads to Phipps Arch.

Hiking the national monument's **slot canyons** is very popular, but we can't over-emphasize the importance of checking on flood potentials before starting out. A sudden rainstorm can cause a flash flood through a narrow canyon miles away, trapping hikers.

One challenging and very strenuous slot-canyon hike is through **Peek-a-boo** and **Spooky Canyons,** which are accessible from the Hole-in-the-Rock Road (see "Sightseeing & Four-wheeling," below). Stop at the Escalante Interagency Office for precise directions.

A National Monument Is Born in Controversy

On September 18, 1996, in a move that was hailed by environmentalists but condemned by developers, President Bill Clinton took the country—and especially the state of Utah—by surprise when he announced that by presidential proclamation, he was creating a new national monument. At 1.7 million acres, the Grand Staircase-Escalante National Monument covers almost 2,700 square miles in southern Utah, a huge tract that includes some of the West's most rugged and scenic terrain, but also an area that is rich in coal, oil, and gas.

Using the 1906 Antiquities Act, Clinton bypassed Congress and avoided public hearings by creating the new national monument through presidential proclamation. This law was last used in 1978, when President Jimmy Carter created 15 monuments covering some 56 million acres in Alaska.

Clinton took action during his 1996 re-election campaign, and there is little argument that one of its chief purposes was political—Clinton wanted, and received, the support of environmentalists and conservationists. And while it was an unpopular move in Utah, this didn't matter to the President's political campaign. As far as most Utah voters were concerned, they would have voted for anybody other than Clinton, anyway. In fact, Clinton kept his planned proclamation a secret from Utah's governor and congressional delegation until the very last minute.

While the President's timing may have been political, few doubt that he was convinced that this vast chunk of real estate needed to be protected. In his proclamation, Clinton said, "The Grand Staircase-Escalante National Monument's vast and austere landscape embraces a spectacular array of scientific and historic resources." A Question and Answer brochure prepared by the Bureau of Land Management states: "The President created the Grand Staircase-Escalante National Monument to preserve extraordinary scientific resources and landscapes in a unique part of America."

However, Utah's political leaders and many of the state's citizens did not take kindly to the President's "protection," with Utah Senator Orrin Hatch denouncing Clinton's action as "the mother of all land-grabs." Newspaper reports said that residents of the town of Escalante hanged Clinton and Interior Secretary Bruce Babbitt in effigy. In mid-1997, a Utah government agency and its association of counties filed lawsuits against the federal government, seeking to overturn the President's proclamation by claiming that Clinton exceeded his authority.

Although part of the controversy has to do with states' rights—Utah has traditionally been opposed to federal government intervention in what it considers its own business—the main reason people in Utah are upset is most likely money. The monument contains more than 60 billion tons of coal, believed to be the state's largest deposit, and a planned mine has now been scrapped, in large part because of the national monument designation, according to its developers. Opponents of the national monument designation claimed that this cost the area up to 900 jobs, plus royalties amounting to $1 billion over the next 50 years that would have been used for Utah's public schools. Supporters, however, said that this was all federal land to begin with—no state or private land was affected—and the only real change is that no new mining claims can be made. The President's proclamation specifically states that existing permits and leases are not affected.

SIGHTSEEING & FOUR-WHEELING   Since this is one of America's least-developed large sections of public land, it offers a wonderful opportunity for exploration by the adventurous. Be aware, though, that the dirt roads inside the monument turn muddy—and impassable—when it rains.

One particularly popular road is the **Hole-in-the-Rock Scenic Backway,** which is partly in the national monument and partly in the adjacent Glen Canyon National Recreation Area. Like most roads in the monument, this should be attempted in dry weather only. Starting about 5 miles northeast of Escalante off Utah 12, this clearly marked dirt road travels 57 miles (one-way) to the Hole-in-the-Rock, where Mormon settlers, in 1880, cut a passage through solid rock and used ropes to lower their wagons down a 1,200-foot cliff to the canyon floor and Colorado River below. About 12 miles in, the road passes by the sign to **Devil's Rock Garden,** an area of classic red rock formations and arches, where you'll also find a picnic area (about 1 mile off the main road). The road continues across a plateau of typical desert terrain, ending at a spectacular scenic overlook of Lake Powell. The first 35 miles of the scenic byway are relatively easy (in dry weather) in a standard passenger car, then it gets a bit steeper and sandier, and the last 6 miles of the road require a high clearance 4X4 vehicle. Allow about 6 hours round-trip, and make sure you have plenty of fuel and water.

Another recommended drive in the national monument is the **Cottonwood Canyon Road,** which runs from Kodachrome State Park south to U.S. 89, along the monument's southern edge, a distance of about 46 miles. The road is sandy and narrow, and washboard in places, but usually passable for passenger cars in dry weather. It mostly follows Cottonwood Wash, with good views of red rock formations and distant panoramas from hilltops. About 10 miles east of Kodachrome Basin State Park, you'll find a short side road to **Grosvenor Arch.** This magnificent stone arch, with an opening 99 feet wide, was named for National Geographic Society founder and editor Gilbert H. Grosvenor, and is well worth the trip.

WILDLIFE VIEWING & BIRD WATCHING   This isolated and rugged terrain offers good habitat for a number of species, including desert bighorn sheep and mountain lions. Over 200 species of birds have been seen, including bald eagles, golden eagles, Swainson's hawks, and peregrine falcons. The best areas for seeing wildlife are along the Escalante and Paria Rivers and Johnson Creek.

CAMPING

Backcountry camping is permitted in most areas of the monument with a permit (free at this writing), available at the Interagency office in Escalante and BLM office in Kanab. There are also two designated campgrounds. **Calf Creek Recreation Area,** about 15 miles northeast of the town of Escalante via Utah 12, has about a dozen sites and a picnic area. Open year-round, the tree-shaded campground is situated in a scenic, steep canyon along Calf Creek, surrounded by high rock walls. Facilities include a volleyball court, an interpretative hiking trail (see "Hiking, Mountain Biking & Horseback Riding" above), modern rest rooms, and drinking water, but no showers, RV hookups, RV dump station, or garbage removal. From November through March, water is turned off and only vault toilets are available. Vehicles must ford a shallow creek, and the campground is not recommended for vehicles over 25 feet long. Campsites cost $7 per night; day use costs $2 per vehicle. The national monument's other designated campground is **Deer Creek,** located 6 miles east of the town of Boulder along the scenic Burr Trail Road. Camping at one of the four primitive sites here is free, but no drinking water or other facilities are available.

ESCALANTE STATE PARK

Large chunks of colorful petrified wood decorate this unique park, which offers hiking, fishing, boating, camping, and panoramic vistas of the surrounding countryside. There's wildlife to watch, trails to hike, and a 30-acre reservoir for boating, fishing, and somewhat chilly swimming. It's open all year, but spring through fall are the best times to visit. Hikers should be prepared for hot summer temperatures and carry plenty of water.

JUST THE FACTS

GETTING THERE   The park is 48 miles from Bryce Canyon. It's located about 2 miles southwest of Escalante on Utah 12 at Wide Hollow Road.

INFORMATION & VISITOR CENTERS   For a copy of the park brochure, contact **Escalante State Park,** P.O. Box 350, Escalante, UT 84726-0350 (☎ **435/ 826-4466**). The **visitor center** has displays of petrified wood, dinosaur bones, and fossils, plus an exhibit explaining how petrified wood is formed.

FEES & REGULATIONS   Admission costs $3 per vehicle for day use. As at most state parks, regulations are generally based on common sense and courtesy: Don't damage anything, drive slowly on park roads, and observe quiet hours between 10pm and 7am. In addition, you're asked to resist the temptation to carry off samples of petrified wood. Pets are welcome, even on trails, but must be restrained on leashes no more than 6 feet long.

SPORTS & ACTIVITIES

FISHING & BOATING   **Wide Hollow Reservoir**, located partially inside the park, has a boat ramp (sorry, no rentals are available) and is a popular fishing hole for rainbow trout and bluegill, and ice fishing in the winter.

HIKING   The 1-mile self-guided ✪ **Petrified Forest Trail** is a moderately strenuous hike among colorful rocks, through a forest of stunted juniper and piñon pine, past a painted desert, to a field of colorful petrified wood. The hike also offers panoramic vistas of the town of Escalante and surrounding stair-step plateaus. A free brochure is available at the visitor center. Allow about 45 minutes for the walk.

An optional three-quarter-mile loop off the main trail leads through lots more petrified wood, but is considerably steeper than the main trail.

WILDLIFE WATCHING   This is one of the best spots in the region ✪ **to see wildlife.** The reservoir is home to ducks, geese, and coots. Chukar partridges wander throughout the park, and you're also likely to see eagles, hawks, lizards, ground squirrels, and both cottontails and jackrabbits. Binoculars are helpful.

CAMPING

The 22-unit **campground**, within easy walking distance of the park's hiking trails and reservoir, is open all year. Facilities include hot showers, modern rest rooms, and drinking water, but no RV hookups. Camping is $10. Reservations (☎ **800/ 322-3770**) are available for a $5 nonrefundable fee using MasterCard or Visa.

Impressions

On this remarkable site, God's handiwork is everywhere.

—President Bill Clinton, September 18, 1996

Rock or Wood—What Is This Stuff?

It looks like a weathered, multicolored tree limb, shining and sparkling in the light—but it's heavy, hard, and solid as a rock. Just what is this stuff? Why, it's petrified wood.

Back in the old days—some 135 to 155 million years ago—southern Utah was not at all like we see it today. It was closer to the equator than it is now, which made it a wet and hot land, with lots of ferns, palm trees, and conifers providing lunch for the neighborhood dinosaurs.

Occasionally, floods would uproot the trees, dumping them in flood plains and along sandbars, then burying them with mud and silt. If this happened quickly, the layers of mud and silt would cut off the oxygen supply, halting the process of decomposition—and effectively preserving the tree trunks intact.

Later, volcanic ash covered the area, and groundwater rich in silicon dioxide and other chemicals and minerals made its way down to the ancient trees. With the silicon dioxide acting as a glue, the cells of the wood mineralized. Other waterborne minerals produced the colors: Iron painted the tree trunks in reds, browns, and yellows; manganese produced purples and blues in the preserved wood.

Later, uplifts from within the earth, along with various forms of erosion, brought the now-petrified wood to the surface in places like Utah's Escalante State Park and the Grand Staircase-Escalante National Monument, breaking it into the shapes we see today in the process—one that's taken only a hundred million years or so to complete.

NORTH FROM ESCALANTE ALONG SCENIC UTAH 12

Heading toward Capitol Reef National Park from the town of Escalante, you'll see rugged mountain scenery, with forests of pine and fir producing a deep green contrast to the rosy red, orange, and brown hues of the region's rock formations. Along the way are several opportunities to stop.

Picturesque Posy Lake (sometimes spelled Posey), under the jurisdiction of the **U.S. Forest Service** (☎ 435/826-5499), is located in a mixed conifer forest at 8,600 feet elevation some 16 miles northwest of Escalante via Utah 12 and Forest Road 154 (gravel). The lake is open to nonmotorized boats only. The fishing's good—the lake is stocked with rainbow trout—and you'll also find a picnic area, two floating docks, and a boat ramp. The numerous dirt roads are popular with mountain bikers and hikers in the summer and with cross-country skiers and snowmobilers in the winter. The **Posy Lake Campground,** open in the summer only, has 22 sites, drinking water, and rest rooms, but no showers or RV hookups. Camping costs $8 per night.

Visitors to **Anasazi Indian Village State Park,** in the village of Boulder (about 27 miles northeast of Escalante along Utah 12), step back to the 12th century A.D., when the Kayenta Anasazi (also known as ancestral Puebloans) lived here in one of the largest Anasazi communities west of the Colorado River. The 6-acre park includes the ruins of the village, a full-size six-room replica of an Anasazi home, gift shop, picnic area, 30-seat auditorium, and museum. From mid-May to mid-September, the park is open daily from 8am to 6pm; the rest of the year, it's open daily from 9am to 5pm. Admission is $1.50 for those 16 and older, $1 for those ages 6 to 15, and free for children under 6; there's a family rate of $6. The park has no campground. For further information, contact **Anasazi Indian Village State Park**, P.O. Box 1329, Boulder, UT 84716-1329 (☎ 435/335-7308).

For some of the most dramatic views along Utah 12, you'll be practically in the clouds, at an elevation of 9,670 feet, atop ✪ **Boulder Mountain**, some 45 miles northeast of Escalante. From viewpoints such as **Point Lookout**, you'll gaze out over the colorful sandstone rock cliffs of Capitol Reef National Park to the imposing Henry Mountains, Navajo Mountain, and sights more than 100 miles away.

Those venturing into the backcountry by foot, four-wheel-drive, mountain bike, or horse will discover rugged, remote beauty; the area is also a trout fisherman's paradise, with dozens of secluded mountain lakes and streams hidden among the tall pines and firs. Don't be surprised to see mule deer, elk, and wild turkey in the open meadows.

Several beautiful and quiet campgrounds are operated by the **U.S. Forest Service** (☎ 435/826-5499), with both RV and tent sites. One of them, Singletree Campground, is about 16 miles south of Torrey (see "Nearby" under "Camping," in chapter 14). The **Wildcat Ranger Station** of the Dixie National Forest has an information center about 18 miles south of Torrey, open from Memorial Day to Labor Day.

After Boulder, it's not too much farther to Capitol Reef National Park, but first you'll reach the community of Torrey, where Utah 12 intersects with Utah 24. Turn right and proceed to the park. See chapter 14 for complete coverage of Capitol Reef.

Capitol Reef National Park 14

We don't want to write this chapter. Capitol Reef National Park is one of those little-known gems, drawing far fewer visitors than its more famous neighbors, Bryce Canyon and Zion. To be honest, we'd like to be selfish, and keep this jewel of a park to ourselves.

Alas, we can't. For one thing, Capitol Reef is a place you really should know about. For another, the secret's already getting out. Not long ago, *Outside* magazine sang the praises of Capitol Reef as one of America's eight under-visited national parks—"parks as they were meant to be."

Capitol Reef offers more of that spectacular southern Utah scenery, but with a unique twist and a personality all its own. The area's geologic formations are downright peculiar. This is a place to let your imagination run wild. You'll see the appropriately named Hamburger Rocks, sitting atop a white sandstone table; the tall, bright red Chimney Rock; the silent and eerie Temple of the Moon; and the commanding Castle. The colors of Capitol Reef's canyon walls draw from a spectacular palette, which is why the Navajos called the area "The Land of the Sleeping Rainbow."

But unlike some of southern Utah's other parks, Capitol Reef is more than just brilliant rocks and barren desert. Here the Fremont River has helped create a lush oasis in an otherwise unforgiving land, with cottonwood, willow, ash, and other trees along its banks. In fact, 19th-century pioneers found the land so inviting and the soil so fertile that they established the community of Fruita, planting orchards that have been preserved by the Park Service.

Because of differences in elevation and availability of water in various sections of the park, you'll find an assortment of ecosystems and terrain, as well as a variety of possible activities. There are hiking, mountain-biking, and four-wheeling trails; the lush fruit orchard; rich, green forests and desert wildflowers; an abundance of songbirds; and a surprising amount of wildlife—from lizards and snakes to the bashful ringtail cat (which isn't a cat at all, but a member of the raccoon family). You'll see thousand-year-old petroglyphs, left behind by the ancient Fremont and Anasazi peoples, and other traces of the past left by the relatively modern Southern Paiutes, Wild West outlaws, and industrious Mormon pioneers (in the Fruita Schoolhouse, their children learned the three Rs and studied the Bible and Book of Mormon).

The name Capitol Reef, which conjures up an image of a tropical shoreline, seems odd for a park composed of cliffs and canyons and situated in landlocked Utah. But many of the pioneers who settled the West were former seafaring men, and they extended the traditional meaning of the word "reef" to include these seemingly impassable rock barriers. The huge round white domes of sandstone reminded them of the domes of capitol buildings, and so this area became known as Capitol Reef.

Actually, to be accurate, the park should probably be called The Big Fold. When the earth's crust uplifted some 65 million years ago, creating the Rocky Mountains and Colorado Plateau, most of this uplifting was relatively even. But here, through one of those fascinating quirks of nature, the crust wrinkled into a huge fold. Running for 100 miles, almost all within the national park, it's known as the Waterpocket Fold.

1 Just the Facts

GETTING THERE   Capitol Reef National Park is 121 miles northeast of Bryce Canyon National Park, 204 miles northeast of Zion National Park, 224 miles south of Salt Lake City, and 366 miles northeast of Las Vegas, Nevada. The park straddles Utah 24, which connects with I-70 both to the northeast and northwest. Those coming from Bryce Canyon National Park can follow Utah 12 northeast (see chapter 13) to its intersection with Utah 24, and follow that east into Capitol Reef. If you're approaching the park from Glen Canyon National Recreation Area and the Four Corners region, follow Utah 276 and/or Utah 95 north to the intersection with Utah 24, where you'll then go west into the park.

INFORMATION & VISITOR CENTERS   For advance information on what to see in the park, hiking trails, and camping, write: Superintendent, **Capitol Reef National Park,** Torrey, UT 84775 (☎ **435/425-3791**).

The **visitor center** is located on the park access road at its intersection with Utah 24. A path alongside the access road connects the visitor center and campground, passing the historic blacksmith shop of Fruita, orchards, and a lovely shaded picnic ground. The visitor center has exhibits on the geology and history of the area and presents a short introductory slide show on the park. Rangers can answer questions and provide backcountry permits. Several free brochures are available, and books, maps, videos, postcards, and posters can be purchased. The visitor center is open daily year-round.

FEES, REGULATIONS & BACKCOUNTRY PERMITS   Entry into the park (for up to 7 days) costs $4 per vehicle or $2 per motorcycle, bicycle, or pedestrian.

Free permits, available at the visitor center, are required for all overnight trips into the backcountry.

As for regulations, bicycles are prohibited in the backcountry and on all hiking trails. Feeding or otherwise disturbing wildlife is forbidden, as is vandalizing or upsetting any natural feature of the park. Because skunks refuse to follow park rules regarding wildlife diet, campers should be especially careful of where they store food, and dispose of garbage promptly. Dogs, which must be leashed at all times, are prohibited on all trails, more than 100 feet from any road, and in public buildings.

SEASONS & AVOIDING THE CROWDS   Although Capitol Reef National Park receives only about 700,000 visitors annually—making it among the least-visited national parks in the West—it can still be busy, especially during its peak summer season. For this reason, the best time to visit is fall, particularly in October and

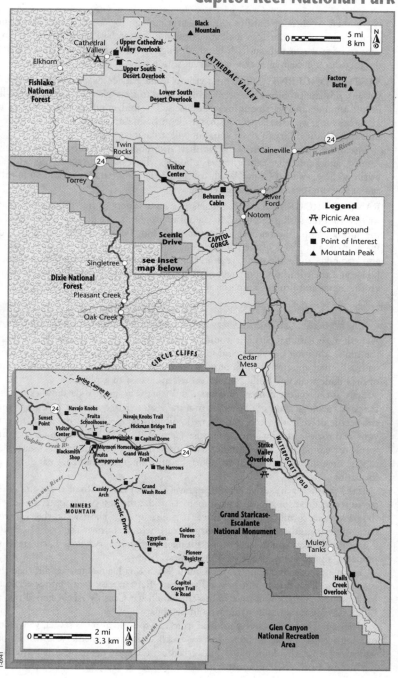

Capitol Reef National Park

Legend
- ⚘ Picnic Area
- △ Campground
- ■ Point of Interest
- ▲ Mountain Peak

0   5 mi
0   8 km
N

Black Mountain

Cathedral Valley

Upper Cathedral Valley Overlook

Elkhorn

Upper South Desert Overlook

Fishlake National Forest

Lower South Desert Overlook

CATHEDRAL VALLEY

Factory Butte

Twin Rocks

Caineville

Fremont River

24

Torrey

Visitor Center

Behunin Cabin

River Ford

Notom

Scenic Drive

CAPITOL GORGE

Singletree

see inset map below

Dixie National Forest

Pleasant Creek

Oak Creek

CIRCLE CLIFFS

Cedar Mesa

WATERPOCKET FOLD

Spring Canyon Rd

Navajo Knobs

Fruita Schoolhouse

Navajo Knobs Trail

Hickman Bridge Trail

Sunset Point

24

Visitor Center

Sulphur Creek Rv

Petroglyphs

Capitol Dome

Blacksmith Shop

Mormon Homestead

Fruita Campground

Grand Wash Trail

24

Strike Valley Overlook

Freemont River

The Narrows

Cassidy Arch

Grand Wash Road

MINERS MOUNTAIN

Scenic Drive

Egyptian Temple

Golden Throne

Grand Staircase-Escalante National Monument

Muley Tanks

Pioneer Register

Capitol Gorge Trail & Road

Halls Creek Overlook

Pleasant Creek

Glen Canyon National Recreation Area

0   2 mi
0   3.3 km
N

1-0941

263

November, when temperatures remain warm enough for comfortable hiking and camping, but not so hot as to send you constantly in search of shade. You also don't have to be as worried about flash floods through narrow canyons as you do during the July-through-September thunderstorm season.

SAFETY CONCERNS While most visitors to the park enjoy a wonderful vacation without mishap, problems can occur. Hikers need to carry plenty of water, especially in midsummer, and watch out for rattlesnakes. The midget rattlesnake is only 12 to 18 inches long, while its larger cousin, the Great Basin rattlesnake, can grow to 2 feet in length. Both will try to avoid you, but will strike if cornered.

The other major concern is the weather: Afternoon thunderstorms during July, August, and September can bring flash floods, which fill narrow canyons without warning. Steep-walled Grand Wash can be particularly hazardous, and should be avoided whenever storms are threatening.

RANGER PROGRAMS Park rangers present a variety of free programs and activities from the spring through fall. Campfire programs take place most evenings at the outdoor amphitheater near Fruita Campground. Topics vary, but could include the animals and plants of the park, geology, and man's history in the area. Rangers also lead hikes and walks and give short talks on history at the pioneer Fruita Schoolhouse and the Mormon homestead. Schedules are posted on bulletin boards at the visitor center and Fruita Campground.

2 Exploring the Highlights by Car

As with most national parks, it would be easy to spend a week or more here, hiking the trails, admiring the views, and loafing about the campground. However, those with a limited amount of time, or who prefer the comfort of a car to the demands of the hiking trail, will find Capitol Reef relatively easy to explore.

Start at the **visitor center,** of course, and watch the short slide show explaining the park's geology and early history. From the visitor center, a paved 25-mile round-trip **scenic drive** leads south into the park, offering good views of the dramatic canyons and rock formations that comprise Capitol Reef. Pick up a copy of the free scenic drive brochure at the entrance fee station, then set out, stopping at viewpoints to gaze up and out at the array of colorful cliffs, monoliths, and commanding rock formations.

If the weather is dry, drive down the gravel **Capitol Gorge Road** at the end of the paved scenic drive for a look at what many consider the best backcountry scenery in the park. It's a 5-mile round-trip drive. If you're up for a short walk, the relatively flat 2-mile (round-trip) **Capitol Gorge Trail**, which starts at the end of Capitol Gorge Road, takes you to the historic **Pioneer Register**, a rock wall where traveling pioneers "signed in" (see "Sports & Activities," below).

Another dry-weather option is the **Grand Wash Road**, a maintained dirt road that is subject to flash floods, but in good weather offers an easy route into spectacular backcountry. Along the 2-mile round-trip you'll see **Cassidy Arch**; famed outlaw Butch Cassidy is said to have hidden out nearby.

Utah 24, which crosses Capitol Reef from east to west, also has several viewpoints offering a good look at the park's features, such as the monumental **Capitol Dome**, which resembles the dome of a capitol building; the aptly named Castle formation; the historic **Fruita Schoolhouse**; and some roadside **petroglyphs** left by the prehistoric Fremont people (see below).

Butch Cassidy, Utah's Most Infamous Son

Robert LeRoy Parker wasn't a bad kid. He was born into a hard-working Mormon family in a little southwestern Utah town called Beaver on April 13, 1866. Robert was the oldest of 13 children; he was a great help to his mother, working on the small ranch his parents bought near Circleville.

Circleville was where the problems began. Teenaged Robert fell in with some rather unsavory characters, including one Mike Cassidy, the ne'er-do-well role model who gave the youth his first gun. The boy made his way to Telluride, Colorado, worked for one of the mines there for a while, and then wandered up to Wyoming. A little more wandering took him back to Telluride—and, strangely enough, the Telluride bank was robbed. Butch Cassidy had officially begun his life of crime.

In the following years, Butch—who gained the nickname after a short stint working in a butcher shop—became an expert at rustling cattle, robbing banks, and, his ultimate glory, robbing trains. Butch wanted to call his gang the Train Robbers Syndicate, but they raised such hell in celebration of their economic successes that saloon keepers in Vernal and other Utah towns began calling them "that wild bunch," and the name stuck. The Wild Bunch would travel through Utah, hiding out in the desolate badlands that were to become Bryce Canyon, Capitol Reef, and Canyonlands National Parks. Capitol Reef's Cassidy Arch was named after Butch; this area was supposedly one of his favorite hiding places.

If you've seen the 1969 movie *Butch Cassidy and the Sundance Kid,* with Paul Newman as Butch and Robert Redford as his partner-in-crime Sundance, you can't forget that spectacular scene in which Butch and his cohorts blow the door off a railroad car; they then use too much dynamite to open the safe, sending bills flying into the air. Apparently, the story is basically true, having taken place on June 2, 1899, near Wilcox, Wyoming. According to reports of the day, they got away with $30,000.

The Union Pacific Railroad took exception to Butch's antics. When the posses started getting a bit too close, Butch, Sundance, and Sundance's lady friend, Etta Place (Katharine Ross in the film), took off for South America, where it's said they continued a life of crime for a half dozen or so years. There are also some stories—unconfirmed—that it was in South America that Butch first killed anyone, that up until that time he had avoided bloodshed whenever possible.

According to some historians (as well as the movie version of Butch's life), Butch and Sundance were shot dead in a gun battle with army troops in Bolivia. But others say it's not so—that Butch returned to the United States, visited friends and family in Utah and Wyoming, and eventually settled in Spokane, Washington, where he lived a peaceful and respectable life under the name William T. Phillips, until he died of natural causes in 1937.

3 From Petroglyphs to a Pioneer Schoolhouse: Capitol Reef's Historic Sites

In the park, you'll find evidence of man's presence here through the centuries.

THE FREMONT PEOPLE   The Fremont people lived along the river as early as A.D. 700, staying until about A.D. 1250. Primarily hunters and gatherers, the Fremont also grew corn, beans, and squash to supplement their diet, and when they abandoned the area, they left little behind. They lived in pit houses, which were dug into the ground and surrounded by boulders that supported the roof. The remains of one can be seen from the **Hickman Bridge Trail**. Many of the Fremont's petroglyphs (images carved into rock) and some pictographs (images painted on rock) are still visible on the canyon walls. If we could read them, they might even tell us why these early Americans left the area, a puzzle that continues to baffle historians and archaeologists.

NINETEENTH-CENTURY PIONEERS Prospectors and other travelers passed through the **Capitol Gorge** section of the park in the late 1800s, leaving their names on the Pioneer Register. You can reach the **Pioneer Register** via a 2-mile loop; see "Hiking," below.

Mormon pioneers established the appropriately named community of **Fruita** when it was discovered that this was a good locale for growing fruit. The tiny Fruita School-house, built in 1896, served as a church, social hall, and community-meeting hall in addition to a one-room schoolhouse. The school closed in 1941, but was carefully restored by the National Park Service in 1984 and is authentically furnished with old wood and wrought-iron desks, a wood stove, chalkboard, and textbooks. The handbell used to call students to class still rests on the corner of the teacher's desk. The orchards planted by the Mormon settlers continue to flourish, tended by park workers who invite you to sample the "fruits" of their labors. The historic **Gifford Farmhouse,** built in 1908, is typical of early-20th-century Utah farms. Located about a mile south of the visitor center, the farmhouse has been authentically renovated and furnished and is open from April through September. In addition to the displays, it contains a gift shop that sells reproductions of household items used by Mormon pioneers.

4 Sports & Activities

Among the last areas in the continental United States to be explored, many parts of Capitol Reef National Park are still practically unknown, perfect for those who want to see this rugged country in its natural state. Several local companies offer guide and shuttle services, including **Wild Hare Expeditions,** P.O. Box 750194, Torrey, UT 84775 (☎ **888/304-HARE** (4273) or 435/425-3999). In addition to the treks discussed below, Wild Hare offers photo tours, cross-country ski tours, and snowshoe tours, and also rents snowshoes ($7 per day).

FOUR-WHEELING & MOUNTAIN BIKING

As in most national parks, bikes and four-wheel-drive vehicles are restricted to established roads, but Capitol Reef has several so-called roads—actually little more than dirt trails—that provide exciting opportunities for those using 4X4s or pedal-power.

The only route appropriate for road bikes is the 25-mile round-trip scenic drive, described above, but both the Grand Wash and Capitol Gorge roads (see "Exploring the Highlights by Car," above), plus three much longer dirt roads, are open to mountain bikes as well as four-wheel-drive vehicles. Be aware that rain can make the roads impassable, so it's best to check on current conditions with park rangers before setting out.

One recommended trip, the **Cathedral Valley Loop**, covers more than 60 miles on a variety of road surfaces, including dirt, sand, and rock, and requires the fording of the Fremont River, where water is usually 1 to 1¹/₂ feet deep. But you'll be rewarded with beautiful, unspoiled scenery, including bizarre sandstone monoliths and majestic cliffs, in one of the park's most remote areas. A small, primitive campground is located in Cathedral Valley (see "Camping," below). Access to this loop is from Utah 24, just outside the park, 11.7 miles east of the visitor center via the River Ford Road, or 18.6 miles east of the visitor center on the Caineville Wash Road.

Mountain-bike and four-wheel-drive tours into the national park and surrounding areas are provided by **Wild Hare Expeditions** (see address and phone above). Full-day tours, including lunch, cost $60 to $75; a variety of other guided trips, including multiday excursions, are offered as well. The company rents mountain bikes at $20 for a half day and $30 for a full day, with discounts for those taking guided tours and for multiday rentals. **Four-wheel-drive tours** are also available from **Hondoo Rivers and Trails** in Torrey (☎ **800/332-2696** or 435/425-3519), with similar rates.

HIKING

Trails through Capitol Reef National Park offer sweeping panoramas of colorful cliffs and soaring spires, eerie journeys through desolate, steep-walled canyons, and cool oases along the tree-shaded Fremont River. Watch carefully for petroglyphs and other reminders of this area's first inhabitants. This is also the real Wild West, little changed from the way cowboys, bank robbers, settlers, and gold miners found it in the late 1800s; one of the best things about hiking here is the unique combination of scenic beauty, Native American art, and western history you'll discover.

Park rangers can help you choose trails best suited to the time of year, weather conditions, and your personal physical condition; those planning serious backpacking will want to buy topographic maps, available at the visitor center. The summer sun is intense, so hats and sunscreen are mandatory, and a gallon of water per person is recommended. Also see the "Safety Concerns" section above.

Among our favorite short hikes at Capitol Reef is the 2-mile round-trip **Capitol Gorge Trail**. It's easy, mostly level walking along the bottom of a narrow canyon, but looking up at the tall, smooth walls of rock conveys a strong sense of what the pioneers must have seen and felt 100 years ago when they moved rocks and debris to haul their wagons up this canyon. Starting at the end of the dirt Capitol Gorge Road, the hiking trail leads past the **Pioneer Register,** where prospectors and other early travelers carved their names. The earliest legible signatures were made in 1871 by J. A. Call and "Wal" Bateman.

Another short hike, but quite a bit more strenuous, is the 3.5-mile round-trip **Cassidy Arch Trail**. This offers spectacular views as it climbs steeply from the floor of Grand Wash to high cliffs overlooking the park. From the trail, you'll also get several perspectives of Cassidy Arch, a natural stone arch named for outlaw Butch Cassidy, who is believed to have occasionally used the Grand Wash as a hideout. The trail is off the Grand Wash dirt road, which branches off the east side of the highway about halfway down the park's scenic drive.

Those seeking a longer outing might enjoy the strenuous **Navajo Knobs** hike, a 9-mile round-trip hike that starts with a look at **Hickman Natural Bridge,** then climbs up 1,000-foot cliffs for a view of the **Fruita Orchard and campground.** It then continues several miles to Navajo Knobs for a spectacular 360-degree panoramic view of the park. The trail starts at Utah 24 at the Hickman Bridge trailhead, east of the visitor center, and follows that trail until it branches off to the north.

Guided hikes and backpacking trips into the national park and surrounding areas are offered by **Wild Hare Expeditions** (see address and phone above), ranging from 2-hour hikes starting at $20 per person to multiday backpacking trips, with meals and equipment provided, starting at about $150 per person. Most groups are small, although large groups can be accommodated. Rates are lower for children.

HORSEBACK RIDING

Horses are welcome on some park trails but prohibited on others; check at the visitor center. **Pleasant Creek Trail Rides,** P.O. Box 102, Bicknell, UT 84715 (☎ **800/ 892-4597** or 435/425-3315; fax 435/425-3806), offers a variety of rides in the area, ranging from 1 hour to 6 days. A 1-hour ride costs $15; a full-day ride through Capitol Reef National Park, including lunch, costs about $90. Horseback trips are also provided by **Hondoo Rivers and Trails** (☎ **800/332-2696** or 435/425-3519).

WILDLIFE VIEWING

Although summer temperatures are hot and there's always the threat of a thunderstorm, it's a good season for wildlife viewing. Many species of lizards reside in the park, and you will probably catch a glimpse of one warming itself on a rock. The western whiptail, eastern fence, and side-blotched lizards are the most common, but the loveliest is the collared lizard, dark in color but with light speckles that allow it to blend easily with lava rocks and become almost invisible to its foes. Watch for deer throughout the park, especially along the path between the visitor center and Fruita Campground. This area is also where you're likely to see chipmunks and antelope ground squirrels. If you keep your eyes to the sky, you may spot a golden eagle, and numerous songbirds pass through each year. Although they're somewhat shy and only emerge from their dens at night, the ringtail cat, a member of the raccoon family, also makes the park his home, as do the seldom-seen bobcat, cougar, fox, marmot, and coyote.

5 Camping

IN THE PARK

The 71-site **Fruita Campground**, open year-round, offers modern rest rooms, drinking water, picnic tables, fire grills, and an RV dump station, but no showers or RV hookups. It's located along the main park road, 1 mile south of the visitor center. Reservations are not accepted. Camping costs $8 year-round, and water may be turned off in the winter, leaving only pit toilets.

The park also has two primitive campgrounds, free and open year-round on a first-come, first-served basis. **Cedar Mesa Campground** is located in the southern part of the park, about 8 miles down unpaved Notom-Bullfrog Road, which heads south off Utah 24 just outside the eastern entrance to the park. It has five sites, tables, fire grills, and pit toilets, but no water. Check road conditions before going, as it may be impassable in wet weather. **Cathedral Valley Campground** is located in the northern part of the park. From Utah 24 (about 5 miles east of the park), turn north on unpaved Cathedral Valley Road and go about 30 miles. Here you'll find five sites, tables, fire grills, and pit toilets, but no water. A high-clearance or four-wheel-drive vehicle is necessary, and the road may be impassable in wet weather.

Impressions

The colors are such as no pigments can portray. They are deep, rich, and variegated; and so luminous are they, that light seems to flow or shine out of the rock.

—Geologist C. E. Dutton, 1880

Backcountry camping is permitted in much of the park with a free permit, available at the visitor center.

NEARBY

In addition to the campgrounds listed here, see Austin's Chuck Wagon Lodge and General Store in the "Accommodations, Etc." section below.

Sandcreek RV Park & Hostel

540 Utah 24 (P.O. Box 750276), Torrey, UT 84775. ☎ **435/425-3577.** 12 sites with full hook-ups (30 and 50 amps), 12 grassy tent sites. $15–$18 with hookups for 2 people, $9 tents and no hookups for 2 people; each extra person $2.50. DISC, MC, V. Closed mid-Oct to mid-Mar. Located 5 miles west of the park entrance in Torrey.

The open, grassy area in this new park affords great views in all directions. Trees have been planted and will provide shade as they grow, and a swimming pool is planned. Facilities include a large, clean bathhouse; gift shop; espresso bar; and laundry. There is a $5 fee for the dump station if you are not camping here.

The hostel is a new building with one large room in which everyone—both men and women—sleeps, bunkhouse-style. Facilities include sleeping space for eight, a TV, microwave, high ceilings, and a porch with tables and chairs. The walls, high ceiling, and beams are of Ponderosa pine.

Singletree Campground

Utah 12 about 16 miles south of Torrey. Teasdale Ranger District of the Dixie National Forest, Box 99, Teasdale, UT 84773. ☎ **435/425-3702.** 31 sites, 5 multiple-family units. $8; $16–$24 multiple-family units for up to 4 vehicles. Closed mid-Sept to Memorial Day.

Located in a forest of tall pines at an elevation of 8,200 feet, this campground features paved sites, nicely spaced. Some sites are situated in the more open center area, while others are set among trees along the edge of the campground. Sites offering distant panoramic views of the national park are the most popular. Facilities include a picnic table and grill at each site; rest rooms with flush toilets but no sinks; water hydrants scattered about; and a horseshoe pit and volleyball court near two large multifamily sites.

Sleepy Hollow Campground

Utah 24, 15 miles east of the park. HC 70 Box 40, Caineville, UT 84775. ☎ **435/456-9130.** 36 sites, 1 apartment. $15 with electric (10 and 30 amps), $12 no hookups; apartment $60 double. Closed Oct–Mar.

Although the terrain is generally desert, the tent sites are nicely shaded, with a few trees in the RV area as well. A convenience store carries beverages, snack items, film, ice, and souvenirs. The rest rooms are clean, and even if you aren't camping, you can take a shower for $4. After visiting the national park, you can hike and go rock hounding in the BLM lands around here. The attractive one-bedroom apartment sleeps four and contains a kitchen.

Thousand Lakes RV Park & Campground

Utah 24, 6 miles west of Capitol Reef National Park (P.O. Box 750070), Torrey, UT 84775. ☎ **800/355-8995** for reservations or 435/425-3500. 58 RV sites with hookups, 9 tent sites, group tenting area, 4 cabins. $13.50–$16.50 RV site, $9–$10.50 tent site, $26–$29 cabin. DISC, MC, V. Closed Nov–Mar.

Good views of surrounding rock formations are a plus for this campground, which also has some shade trees. RV sites are gravel; tent sites are grass. Facilities include hot showers, a convenience store, coin-operated laundry, dump station, heated swimming pool, horseshoes, and barbecues. In addition, western dinners are offered Tuesday through Saturday, and 4X4 rentals are available at $75 per day.

6 Accommodations

There are no lodging or dining facilities in the park itself, but the town of Torrey, just west of the park entrance, can take care of most needs. The attractive **Days Inn,** 675 E. Utah 24 (at its intersection with Utah 12), Torrey, UT 84775 (☎ 800/ DAYSINN or 435/425-3111; fax 435/425-3112), charges $59 to $79 for two in summer, with lower rates the rest of the year. Room tax adds about 9% to lodging bills. Also see the Sleepy Hollow Campground listing in the "Camping" section above.

While in Torrey, art lovers might want to stop at the **Entrada Institute,** 85 W. Main St. (☎ 435/425-3265), which displays works by Utah artists and sponsors a variety of workshops, lectures, and other programs. Recent projects have included 3-day workshops for photographers and watercolorists, with excursions into the national park and surrounding scenic areas. Costs for workshops range from $110 to $200 per person.

Austin's Chuck Wagon Lodge and General Store

12 W. Main St. (P.O. Box 750180), Torrey, UT 84775. ☎ **800/863-3288** or 435/425-3335. Fax 435/425-3434. 20 rms, 1 family suite. A/C TV. New units $58 double, older units $39 double, family suite $80 double plus $5 for each additional person. AE, MC, V. Closed Dec–Feb.

There are two sections to this attractive motel—the newer, modern motel rooms, with Southwest decor, telephones, satellite TV, free in-room movies, and two queen-size beds; and the older, slightly rustic units, which have knotty pine walls, one queen bed, and no phones. Also available is a family suite, which includes a large living room, fully-equipped kitchen, and three bedrooms that sleep six. The grounds are nicely landscaped, with a lawn and large trees, and facilities include an outdoor pool and whirlpool. Located on the property are a grocery store/bakery, coin-operated laundry, and hair salon. An attached RV park has six sites with full hookups, at $15 per night including tax.

Best Western Capitol Reef Resort

2600 E. Utah 24 (P.O. Box 750160), Torrey, UT 84775. ☎ **800/528-1234** or 435/425-3761. Fax 435/425-3300. 50 units. A/C TV TEL. June–Sept $75–$85 double; Oct–May $47–$75 double; suites $90–$125. AE, CB, DC, DISC, MC, V.

Located a mile west of the national park entrance, this attractive Best Western provides an excellent location for park visitors. Try to get a room on the back side of the motel; you'll be rewarded with fantastic views of the area's red rock formations. Standard rooms have two queen-size beds, white stucco walls, and Southwestern-style scenic prints. A restaurant serves three meals daily year-round. The outdoor heated pool, whirlpool, and sundeck are a plus; all are situated out back, away from road noise, with glass wind barriers and spectacular views.

Boulder View Inn

385 W. Main St. (Utah 24), Torrey, UT 84775. ☎ **800/444-3980** or 435/425-3800. 12 rms. A/C TV TEL. $52 double. Rates include continental breakfast. AE, DISC, MC, V.

Located just 1 mile west of the junction of Utah highways 12 and 24, and within walking distance of several restaurants, this is an attractive modern motel with a Southwestern motif. Rooms are large and comfortable, with tub/shower combos, queen or king beds, and a table with two chairs. There is no swimming pool. All rooms are nonsmoking; pets are not accepted.

Capitol Reef Inn & Cafe

360 W. Main St. (Utah 24), Torrey, UT 84775. ☎ **435/425-3270**. 10 rms. A/C TV TEL. $42 double. DISC, MC, V. Closed Nov–Mar.

This is a small, beautifully landscaped, western-style motel, set back from the road. Rooms are large, homey, and comfortable, with either two queen beds or one queen and a double. Only one room has a tub/shower combo; the others have showers only. Furniture is handmade solid wood. Facilities include a playground, trampoline, and 10-person Jacuzzi. Adjacent, under the same ownership, are an excellent restaurant (see "Dining," below) and a gift shop with Native American crafts, guide books, and maps.

Sandcreek RV Park & Hostel

540 Utah 24 (P.O. Box 750276), Torrey, UT 84775. ☎ **435/425-3577.** Hostel $10–$12 per person. DISC, MC, V. Closed mid-Oct–mid-Mar. Located 5 miles west of the park entrance in Torrey.

This hostel is a new log building with one large room in which everyone—both men and women—sleeps, bunkhouse-style. The hostel offers sleeping space for eight, a TV, microwave oven, high ceilings, and a porch with tables and chairs. The walls, high ceiling, and beams are of Ponderosa pine, and the bunk beds are made of logs. Hostelers use the same bathhouse as the campers (see above), and linens are available. You'll also find a gift shop, espresso bar, and coin-operated laundry here.

Skyridge Bed & Breakfast Inn

On Utah 24, just east of its intersection with Utah 12 (P.O. Box 750220), Torrey, UT 84775. ☎ **435/425-3222.** 6 rms. TV TEL. $82–$120 double. Rates include breakfast and evening hors d'oeuvres. MC, V.

This combination bed-and-breakfast and art gallery offers a delightful alternative to the standard motel. The three-story contemporary inn, with territorial-style appearance, has six distinctive rooms, each with private bath and VCR. Each is decorated with an eclectic mix of antiques, collectibles, folk sculpture, and contemporary art, including at least one piece by innkeeper/artist Karen Kesler. One room has a private deck with hot tub, while another features a two-person whirlpool tub. An impressive fireplace, decorated with over 30 pounds of roofing nails, sits in the shared gallery/living room, which also contains books, games, and a collection of classic and contemporary movies available for guest use. A new, outdoor hot tub has been added. The inn is located on 75 acres, with its own hiking and biking trails and spectacular views of the national park and Boulder Mountain. Full breakfasts include homemade granola, fresh-baked muffins or scones, and a hot entree such as green chile cheese frittata or an omelet made from fresh vegetables or smoked trout. Smoking is not permitted inside.

Wonderland Inn

At the junction of Utah 24 and 12 (P.O. Box 67), Torrey, UT 84775. ☎ **800/458-0216** or 435/425-3775. 50 rms, 2 suites. A/C TV TEL. Summer $58–$80 double; winter $40–$60 double. AE, CB, DC, DISC, EU, JCB, MC, V.

This modern motel, built in 1990, is perched on a hill set back from the highway, making it very quiet and peaceful. Built, owned, and managed by Ray and Diane Potter and family, the property is especially well kept. Standard motel rooms have two queen-size beds or one king, and typical modern motel decor with some genuine wood touches. Facilities include a combination indoor/outdoor heated swimming pool with tanning room, whirlpool, sauna, beauty salon, and gift shop. A restaurant serves three meals daily year-round, with a popular breakfast buffet in the summer.

7 Dining

Brink's Burgers Drive-In

165 E. Main St., Torrey. ☎ **435/425-3710**. Most items $1–$4.50. MC, V. Daily 11am–8pm. Closed in winter. BURGERS/SANDWICHES.

This nonfranchise fast-food restaurant serves great burgers and English-style chips in a cafelike setting, or you can take your food outside to the picnic tables. Like most fast-food restaurants, you order at the counter and pick up your food when your number's called. But in addition to much-better-than-average burgers, choices include chicken and fish selections, cheese sticks, onion rings, zucchini sticks, and spicy potato wedges. Brink's also offers wagon rides complete with Dutch-oven dinners ($15 for adults, $7.50 for children 10 and under). Milk shakes and ice cream cones are also available; no alcohol is served.

Cafe Diablo

599 S. Main St., Torrey. ☎ **435/425-3070**. Main courses $12.95–$16.95. MC, V. May–Oct 15, daily 4–10pm. Closed Oct 16–Apr. SOUTHWESTERN.

Looks can be deceiving. What appears to be a simple small-town cafe in a converted home is actually a very fine restaurant, offering innovative beef, pork, chicken, and seafood selections, many created with a Southwestern flair. The menu varies, but could include pumpkinseed-crusted local trout, served with cilantro-lime sauce and rice pancakes; polenta lasagna, composed of layers of polenta, ricotta, and grilled vegetables, with salsa and mozzarella cheese; or a simple charbroiled New York steak. Pastries, all made on the premises, are spectacular, and beer—both microbrewed and regular—is available.

Capitol Reef Inn & Cafe

360 W. Main St. ☎ **435/425-3271**. Main courses $5–$16; breakfast $4.25–$7.50. DISC, MC, V. Daily 7–11am, 5–9pm. Closed Nov–Mar.

A local's favorite, this restaurant offers fine, fresh, and healthy dining that is among the best you'll find in Utah. Famous for its locally raised trout, it is equally well known for its 10-vegetable salad served with all dinner entrees. Vegetables are grown locally, and several dishes, such as spaghetti, fettuccine primavera, and shish kabobs, can be ordered vegetarian or with various meats or fish. Steaks and chicken are also served. Portions are large and prices reasonable, and there's live music most evenings. The atmosphere is casual with comfortable seating, Native American rugs and crafts, and large windows that take advantage of the great scenery. The restaurant offers an extensive wine list, and both domestic and imported beers are served. A children's menu is available.

Lake Powell & Glen Canyon National Recreation Area

This huge canyon is a spectacular wonderland of stark contrasts—parched desert, deep blue water, startlingly red rocks, rich green hanging gardens. A joint effort by man and nature, Lake Powell and Glen Canyon National Recreation Area is a huge water park, with more shoreline than the West Coast of the continental United States. It's also a place of almost unbelievable beauty, where millions of visitors each year take to the water to explore, fish, water-ski, swim, or simply lounge in the sun.

Named for Major John Wesley Powell, a one-armed Civil War veteran who led a group of nine explorers on a scientific expedition down the Green and Colorado Rivers in 1869, the lake is 186 miles long and has almost 100 major side canyons that give it 1,960 miles of shoreline. And with more than 160,000 surface acres of water, it's the second-largest man-made lake in the United States (after Lake Mead).

Glen Canyon National Recreation Area, with Lake Powell as its heart, is three parks in one: a major destination for boaters and fishermen, a treasury of scenic wonders, and an important historic archive. Lake Powell is, in fact, best enjoyed by boat, gliding through the numerous side canyons among delicately sculpted sandstone forms—intricate, sensuous, and sometimes bizarre—formed by millions of years of erosion. One rock formation that's considered a must-see for every Lake Powell visitor is Rainbow Bridge National Monument, a huge natural stone bridge sacred to the Navajo and other area tribes. But there's much more to see: the 1870s stone fort and trading post at Lees Ferry, the ancient Anasazi ruins of Defiance House, and the dam itself, which supplies water and electric power to much of the West.

1 Just the Facts

ACCESS POINTS: THE MARINAS

Located in southern Utah and northern Arizona, Lake Powell and Glen Canyon National Recreation Area have four major access points: **Wahweap Lodge & Marina** (☎ 520/645-2433), on the lake's south end, is the most developed, with the largest number of facilities, plus lodging, dining, and services in nearby Page, Arizona; **Bullfrog Marina** (☎ 435/684-3000) and **Halls Crossing Marina**

(☎ 435/684-7000) are mid-lake, and are also fairly well developed. **Hite Marina** (☎ 435/684-2278), the lake's northernmost access point, is the smallest and least developed.

All four marinas, operated by Lake Powell Resorts and Marinas, are accessible by car, operate year-round, and provide boat rentals, docks, fuel, service, fishing and other supplies, and accommodations. A fifth marina, **Dangling Rope,** is accessible by boat only, and offers fuel, repairs, drinking water, ice, and limited supplies. **Lees Ferry,** about 15 miles downriver from Glen Canyon Dam, is a historic river crossing popular with hikers and campers, but does not offer direct access to Lake Powell.

GETTING THERE

Wahweap Lodge and Marina and **Glen Canyon Dam** are just off U.S. 89, about 6 miles north of Page, Arizona. Wahweap is 150 miles southeast of Bryce Canyon National Park; 130 miles northeast of the north rim of Grand Canyon National Park; about 65 miles east of Kanab; 267 miles east of Las Vegas, Nevada; and 381 miles south of Salt Lake City. **Halls Crossing** is 280 miles northeast of Wahweap, and **Bullfrog** is 283 miles northeast; both are reachable via Utah 276. **Hite,** about 40 miles uplake from Halls Crossing and Bullfrog, is off Utah 95.

BY PLANE   Flights between Page and both Phoenix and Las Vegas are provided year-round by **Scenic Airlines** (☎ 800/245-8668 or 520/645-2494), which also offers a variety of scenic flights in northern Arizona and southern Utah. Rental cars are available at the Page Airport from **Avis** (☎ 520/645-2024), which rents standard passenger cars as well as four-wheel-drive vehicles.

BY CAR   Motorists can reach the dam and **Wahweap Marina** via U.S. 89 from Kanab or Grand Canyon National Park, and via Ariz. 98 from the east.

To get to the **Lees Ferry** section of the recreation area, south of Wahweap, drive south on U.S. 89 and then north on U.S. 89A to Marble Canyon, where you pick up the Lees Ferry access road.

Bullfrog and **Halls Crossing** marinas, which are connected by a toll ferry midlake, are accessible via Utah 276, which loops southwest from Utah 95. The cost for the 25-minute, 3.1-mile crossing is about $10 for cars and trucks less than 20 feet long, with higher rates for longer vehicles and vehicles with trailers. Bicyclists and adult foot passengers are charged $2 (children $1), and motorcyclists $3. Ferries run six times daily each direction in the summer, and less frequently at other times. The service is often shut down for several weeks in December for maintenance. **Hite Marina,** the northernmost section of the recreation area, is just south of Utah 95.

INFORMATION & VISITOR CENTERS

For advance information, contact Superintendent, **Glen Canyon National Recreation Area,** P.O. Box 1507, Page, AZ 86040, or call the **Carl Hayden Visitor Center** (☎ 520/608-6404). For lodging, tour, and boat-rental information, contact the licensed park concessionaire, **Lake Powell Resorts and Marinas,** Box 56909, Phoenix, AZ 85079 (☎ 800/528-6154 or 602/278-8888; fax 602/331-5258), which also sells books and videos on the lake and the national recreation area.

Numerous services, including lodging and dining, are available in nearby Page, Arizona. For information, contact the **Page/Lake Powell Chamber of Commerce,** P.O. Box 727, Page, AZ 86040 (☎ 520/645-2741). The **John Wesley Powell Memorial Museum** in Page (☎ 520/645-9496; fax 520/945-3412), which is discussed in more detail below, also provides area lodging, dining, and attraction information.

The **Carl Hayden Visitor Center** at Glen Canyon Dam, 2 miles north of Page, Arizona, via U.S. 89, has exhibits on the construction of the dam and serves as the

Glen Canyon National Recreation Area

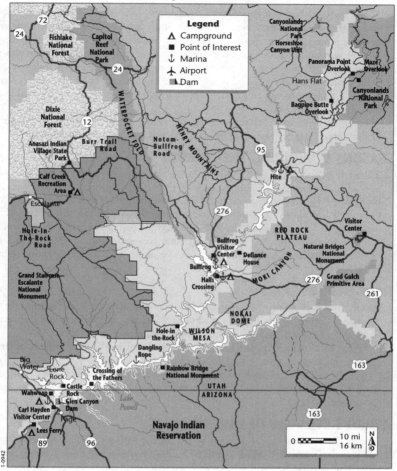

starting point for year-round self-guided and summer-only guided tours of the dam, which usually take from 30 to 45 minutes. Audiovisual programs, free brochures, and books, maps, and videos are available.

At the **Bullfrog Visitor Center,** at mid-lake off Utah 276, you'll find a variety of exhibits and information. Ranger stations at Lees Ferry, Dangling Rope, Halls Crossing, and Hite also offer park information, but these stations are only open when rangers aren't busy doing other things.

The latest addition, the **Navajo Bridge Interpretive Center,** is located at Marble Canyon on the Colorado River south of Page via U.S. 89A. Here you'll find outdoor exhibits, a pedestrian bridge over the river, and a bookstore, open seasonally.

FEES, BACKCOUNTRY PERMITS & REGULATIONS

Entry into the park costs $5 per vehicle or $3 per person for up to 7 days, or $15 for an annual pass. Backcountry permits, which are free, are required for overnight trips into the Escalante River section of the national recreation area.

The standard National Park Service regulations—such as not damaging anything and driving only on established roadways—apply here; additional regulations are aimed at protecting water quality of the lake by prohibiting any dumping of garbage into the water plus requiring the containment and proper disposal of human wastes within a quarter-mile of the lake. Safe-boating requirements include mandatory use of life jackets by children 12 and younger. Keep in mind that boating regulations are slightly different in Utah and Arizona; brochures listing regulations are available at recreation area marinas.

Pets must be leashed at all times, except on houseboats, and are prohibited in public buildings. Dogs are permitted on standard, but not carpeted, houseboats.

SEASONS & AVOIDING THE CROWDS

The park is open year-round and is busiest in the summer—when it's also the hottest, with temperatures sometimes reaching over 100°F. Spring is pleasant, but can be a bit windy. We recommend October, when the water's still warm enough for swimming but most of the crowds have gone home. Winter can also be beautiful, with snow only rarely dusting the rock, and daytime temperatures usually in the 40s and 50s. Discounts on lodging and tours from November through March, and on boat rentals between October and May, offer yet another advantage to visiting in the off-season.

RANGER PROGRAMS

Amphitheater programs take place several evenings each week in the summer at Wahweap Campground. Topics vary, but may include such subjects as the animals or plants of the park, geology, or the canyon's human history.

Free guided tours of the dam leave from the Carl Hayden Visitor Center daily, and rangers give periodic talks at Rainbow Bridge.

Kids 12 and younger can become **Junior Rangers** and receive badges by completing projects in an activity book available free at the Carl Hayden and Bullfrog visitor centers.

A BIRD'S-EYE VIEW OF LAKE POWELL

The quickest way to see the sights is by air. **Scenic Airlines,** P.O. Box 1385, Page, AZ 86040 (☎ **800/245-8668** or 520/645-2494), provides half-hour flights over the dam, Rainbow Bridge, and other scenic attractions, at about $75 per person; and 1-hour flights over the lake to the Escalante River and Hole-in-the-Rock, a favorite hideout of outlaw Butch Cassidy, for about $120 per person. They also offer longer flights that take in the Grand Canyon, Canyonlands, Monument Valley, and even Bryce Canyon, with rates ranging from $149 to $235 and taking anywhere from 1 1/2 to 5 hours.

2 Exploring Lake Powell by Boat

The best way to see Lake Powell and Glen Canyon National Recreation Area is by boat, either your own or a rental, or on a boat tour. Our favorite way to explore is ✪ **to rent a houseboat** for at least a week and wander among the numerous side canyons.

However, if your time is limited, try to spend a few hours touring the dam and seeing the exhibits in the Carl Hayden Visitor Center, particularly the excellent relief map that helps you see the big picture. Then take one of the boat tours, such as the half-day trip to Rainbow Bridge. Adventurous types might want to buy some good maps, rent a boat for the day, and explore the canyons on their own. But whatever you do, try to get to Rainbow Bridge.

BRINGING YOUR OWN BOAT

If you happened to bring your own boat with you, whether it's a one-person kayak or family-size cabin cruiser, you'll have a wonderful time. Boat-launching ramps are located at Wahweap, Lees Ferry, Bullfrog, Halls Crossing, and Hite; and fuel, supplies, sewage pump-out stations, drinking water, and boat repairs are available at all of these except Lees Ferry. Services and supplies are also available at Dangling Rope Marina, about 40 miles uplake from Wahweap Marina and accessible only by boat. Pick up maps and charts at one of the marinas (see above).

As part of the Lake Powell Pure campaign, new facilities are being added for the disposal of human waste. Two floating rest rooms/dump/pump-out stations are in place: at Padre Bay near Dominguez Butte and at the mouth of Rock Creek. Six more are planned lakewide, so check at a marina for further information.

BOAT RENTALS

Lake Powell Resorts and Marinas, Box 56909, Phoenix, AZ 85079 (☎ **800/ 528-6154** or 602/278-8888; fax 602/331-5258), rents powerboats of all sizes, from two-passenger personal watercraft to luxurious 50-foot houseboats for 10 or more.

Generally, anybody who can drive a car can pilot a boat. The only tricks are learning to compensate for wind and currents. Be sure to spend a few minutes practicing turning and stopping; boats don't have brakes! No lessons or licenses are required; the marinas supply all the equipment you'll need and offer some training as well.

Summer is the most expensive time to rent a boat; spring and fall rates are about 25% lower, and winter rates are the lowest—about 40% less than in summer. Summer rates for houseboats that sleep from 6 to 12 people range from $825 to $2,100 for 3 days, and $1,450 to $4,200 for 7 days. Rates for smaller runabouts, ski boats, and personal watercraft range from $110 to $275 per day in summer. These rates are approximate, and there are also a variety of packages that include boat rentals plus lodging, houseboats with smaller powerboats, and powerboats with water-skiing equipment. A variety of nonmotorized water toys is also available for rent. Damage deposits are required. Most types of boats, although not necessarily all sizes, are available at Wahweap, Bullfrog, Halls Crossing, and Hite marinas. We strongly recommend making reservations well in advance.

BOAT TOURS

Year-round boat tours will take you to those hidden areas of the lake that you might never find on your own. Tours range from a 1-hour trip aboard the paddle wheeler *Canyon King,* for $10 per person, to the all-day tour to Rainbow Bridge that costs about $85 per person, including lunch. Rates for children from 3 to 11 years old are about two-thirds of the price for adults. Other options include sunset cruises, dinner cruises, half-day trips to Rainbow Bridge, Colorado River float trips, and numerous packages that combine tours with lodging and/or RV spaces. For information and reservations, contact **Lake Powell Resorts and Marinas,** Box 56909, Phoenix, AZ 85079 (☎ **800/528-6154** or 602/278-8888; fax 602/331-5258).

3 Seeing the Sights

Among the many attractions here, several deserve special mention as must-sees. They're arranged here geographically, from the south end of the lake to the north.

LEES FERRY

Downriver from Glen Canyon Dam, Lees Ferry is a historic river crossing and the site of a stone fort built by Mormon pioneers in 1874 for protection from the Navajo, used later as a trading post. You can see remains of the fort and a post office, built in 1913. Nearby at Lonely Dell, you'll find 19th- and early–20th-century ranch buildings, an orchard, and a cemetery containing graves dating from 1874 to 1928. Upriver, during low water, you can spot the remains of a steamboat, the *Charles H. Spencer*, a 92-foot-long paddle wheeler that was used briefly in the early part of this century to haul coal for a gold-dredging operation.

Lees Ferry is also the starting point for white-water river trips through the Grand Canyon.

GLEN CANYON DAM

Construction began on this U.S. Bureau of Reclamation project in October 1956; by the time the $155-million dam was completed in September 1963, almost 10 million tons of concrete had been poured, creating a wall 587 feet high and 3,700 feet long. It took until 1980 for the lake to reach its "full pool," covering much of the area that had been explored over 100 years earlier by Major John Wesley Powell. Today the dam provides water storage, mostly for agriculture and hydroelectric power. Its eight generators, which cost an additional $70 million, produce more than 1 million kilowatts of electrical energy per day.

RAINBOW BRIDGE NATIONAL MONUMENT

This huge natural bridge is considered sacred by the Navajo, who called it a "rainbow turned to stone"; in the summer of 1995, they briefly blocked the route to the bridge to conduct a blessing ceremony and to protest what they considered the bridge's commercialization. Located about 50 miles by boat from Wahweap, Bullfrog, or Halls Crossing marinas, the bridge is so spectacular that it was named a national monument in 1910, long before the lake was created by the construction of Glen Canyon Dam. Believed to be the largest natural bridge in the world, Rainbow Bridge is almost perfectly symmetrical and parabolic in shape, measuring 275 feet wide and 290 feet tall. The top is 42 feet thick and 33 feet wide. Get here if you can manage it—you won't be disappointed.

DEFIANCE HOUSE

This archaeological site 3 miles up the middle fork of Forgotten Canyon, uplake from Halls Crossing, is believed to have been occupied by a small clan of Anasazi (also known as ancestral Puebloans) between A.D. 1250 and 1275. The cliffside site includes ruins of several impressive stone rooms, food storage areas, and a kiva where religious ceremonies would have taken place. The rock art panel, high along a cliff wall, includes a pictograph for which the ruin is named—an image of three warriors carrying clubs and shields. The panel also contains paintings of sheep and men.

Impressions

So we have a curious ensemble of wonderful features—carved walls, royal arches, glens, alcove gulches, mounds, and monuments. From which of these features shall we select a name? We decide to call it Glen Canyon.
                                    —Explorer Major John Wesley Powell, August 3, 1869

Lake Powell: Natural Wonder or Man-Made Curse?

If preservationists had had their way in 1937, Lake Powell would not exist. There would be no dam, no electric generators—only the free-flowing Colorado River. If their proposal had been adopted, that which is Glen Canyon National Recreation Area and Canyonlands National Park would instead be one 6,000-square-mile protected area called Escalante National Park. Ironically, some of the lands covered by the 1937 proposal are situated in the new, also controversial Grand Staircase-Escalante National Monument, which is discussed in chapter 13.

The story actually dates back to the early part of the 20th century, when a major flood of the Colorado River brought to everyone's attention the need for agreement among western states on flood control and water rights. In 1922, a federal commission created the Colorado Compact to allocate water, and in 1935, Hoover Dam was built to help control water supplies in the lower part of the Colorado River Basin. States in the upper basin couldn't agree on what to do. Then everyone became distracted by World War II, and the issue was put aside for a few years.

Finally, in 1953, the U.S. Bureau of Reclamation proposed a series of dams. These would be on the Colorado River in Glen Canyon, on the San Juan River in northwestern New Mexico, on the Green River in northwestern Colorado through Dinosaur National Monument, and on the Gunnison River in western Colorado.

The inevitable war between development and preservation factions began, with the needs for water storage and electric power pitted against the value of preserving the unspoiled wilderness. Some argued that building Glen Canyon Dam would drown a magnificent system of canyons, but this battle was overshadowed by an even louder battle to save Dinosaur National Monument. Eventually a compromise was reached: the Dinosaur National Monument project was dropped, and a dam over the Green River in northeastern Utah, at Flaming Gorge, was added. Despite increasing protests, it was decided that Glen Canyon Dam would also be built, but preservationists did put an end to a proposal to build two additional dams on the Colorado River in the Grand Canyon.

Today, close to 4 million people visit Glen Canyon National Recreation Area each year, and the boats that cruise Lake Powell allow almost all of them to see spectacular Rainbow Bridge and the wondrous canyons and formations that would be practically inaccessible without the dam. And although most people wouldn't deny the beauty of Lake Powell and the Glen Canyon Recreation Area today, many conservationists remain bitter, believing the dam flooded what could have been one of our country's most magnificent national parks. In fact, in May 1997, the Sierra Club went so far as to formally propose that the lake be drained.

4 Sports & Activities

FISHING

Although March through November is the most popular season, the fishing is good year-round, especially for the huge rainbow trout sometimes caught in the Colorado River between the dam and Lees Ferry. Lake fishermen also catch largemouth, smallmouth, and striped bass; catfish; crappie; and walleye. Because Glen Canyon National Recreation Area lies within two states, you'll need Utah and/or Arizona fishing licenses, depending on where you want to fish. The marinas sell licenses as well as fishing supplies.

HIKING, MOUNTAIN BIKING & FOUR-WHEELING

Although boating and related water sports are the main activities here, most of this recreation area is solid ground—actually hard rock. Lake Powell makes up only 13% of the area, so hikers and other land-based recreationists will find plenty to do. There are few marked trails, however, and changing water levels create a constantly shifting shoreline.

HIKING   Several short hikes lead to panoramic vistas of Lake Powell. For a view of the lake, Wahweap Bay, the Colorado River channel, and the sandstone cliffs of Antelope Island, drive $^1/_2$ mile east from the Carl Hayden Visitor Center, cross a bridge, and turn left onto an unmarked gravel road; follow it for about a mile to its end and a parking lot in an area locally known as **The Chains.** Heading north from the parking lot, follow the unmarked but obvious trail across sand, up slickrock, and across a level gravel section to an overlook that provides a magnificent view of the lake. This is usually a 10-minute walk one-way. To extend the hike, you can find a way down to the water's edge, but be aware that the steep sandstone can be slick. The Chains is a day-use area only.

Several hikes originate in the Lees Ferry area, including a moderate 2-mile round-trip hike through narrow **Cathedral Canyon** to the Colorado River. The trailhead is at the second turnout from U.S. 89A along Lees Ferry Road. This hike isn't along a marked trail, but rather down a wash, past intriguing rock formations. During wet weather, be alert for flash floods and deep pools. Allow 1 to $1^1/_2$ hours.

Another relatively easy hike, the **River Trail,** starts just upriver from the Lees Ferry fort and follows an old wagon road to a ferry-crossing site, passing the historic but submerged steamboat, the *Charles H. Spencer.* Allow about an hour for this 2-mile round-trip walk. A self-guiding booklet is available at Lees Ferry.

A heavy-duty 34-mile hike through the **Paria Canyon Primitive Area,** which departs from Lonely Dell Ranch at Lees Ferry, takes you through beautiful but narrow canyons. Beware: Flash flooding can be hazardous. This hike requires a permit from the Bureau of Land Management office in Kanab (☎ 435/644-2672).

Although most visitors take an easy half- or full-day boat trip to see beautiful Rainbow Bridge National Monument, it is possible to hike to it, although the 14-mile one-way trail is difficult and not maintained. It crosses the Navajo Reservation and requires a permit. Contact the Navajo Parks and Recreation Department, P.O. Box 9000, Window Rock, AZ 86515 (☎ 520/871-6647).

Serious backcountry hikers should obtain current maps of the area and discuss their plans with rangers before setting out. Hikers should carry at least 1 gallon of water per person, per day.

MOUNTAIN BIKING & FOUR-WHEELING   Mountain bikers and four-wheel-drive enthusiasts must stay on established roadways within the recreation area, but quite a few challenging dirt roads can be found both in the recreation area and on adjacent federal land. Get information from the national recreation area office (see above) and Canyonlands National Park office (☎ 435/259-4351).

In the Hite area, the **Orange Cliffs** are particularly popular among mountain bikers. The 53-mile one-way **Flint Trail** connects Hite with Hans Flat in the far-northern section of the national recreation area. It's rocky, with some sandy stretches and steep grades. For a shorter ride, the **Panorama Point/Cleopatra's Chair Trail** follows recreation area routes 744, 774, and 775 for 10 miles (one-way) from Hans Flat to Cleopatra's Chair, providing a spectacular view into Canyonlands National

Park. Camping in the Orange Cliffs area requires a permit, and strict regulations apply; contact the Hans Flat Ranger Station (☎ 435/259-2652).

The Escalante River canyons of the national recreation area are accessible by four-wheel-drive vehicle via the 57-mile one-way **Hole-in-the-Rock Road,** which leaves Utah 12 5 miles east of Escalante, traversing part of the Grand Staircase-Escalante National Monument (see chapter 13). Managed by the Bureau of Land Management (☎ 435/826-5499), the dirt and sometimes rocky road passes through **Devil's Rock Garden,** an area of unique rock formations, and offers a spectacular overlook of Lake Powell. Although four-wheel-drive is not always needed, the last 6 miles of the road require a high clearance vehicle. Regardless of what you're driving, you'll want to avoid the road in wet weather. Allow about 6 hours round-trip.

5 Camping

National recreation area concessionaire **Lake Powell Resorts and Marinas** (☎ 800/528-6154 or 602/278-8888; fax 602/331-5258) operates year-round full-service RV parks at Wahweap, Bullfrog, and Halls Crossing, with complete RV hookups, showers, modern rest rooms, coin-operated laundries, RV dump stations, drinking water, groceries, and LP gas. Rates are about $23 per site in summer, $16 in winter, and reservations are accepted. Package deals that include RV sites and boat tours are offered. The concessionaire also has several campgrounds without hookups, but with showers and flush toilets, at $12 per night. Reservations are not accepted for the nonhookup campgrounds.

The National Park Service operates a campground year-round at Lees Ferry, with 51 sites, flush toilets, and drinking water, but no showers or RV hookups. Reservations are not accepted; rates are $10 per site. There's also camping at Lone Rock, above Wahweap, for $6.

The only camping at Hite is a primitive campground with no amenities. It's open year-round and camping is free.

You'll also find several free primitive campgrounds in the recreation area's backcountry. Free dispersed camping is permitted throughout the recreation area, except within 1 mile of marinas and Lees Ferry, and at Rainbow Bridge National Monument.

6 Accommodations & Dining

Lake Powell Resorts and Marinas (☎ 800/528-6154 or 602/278-8888; fax 602/331-5258) operates all of the recreation area's lodging and dining facilities, as well as the houseboat rentals; call them to make reservations and to obtain additional information.

Although plenty of hotels, motels, and condominium-type units are available, our choice for lodging is that wonderful floating vacation home, the **houseboat.** Powered by two outboard motors and complete with full kitchens, bathrooms with hot showers, and sleeping for up to 12, houseboats serve not only as your home-away-from-home, but also as your means of exploring the fascinating red rock canyons that make Lake Powell the unique paradise it is. Hungry? There's the refrigerator, along with the kitchen stove with oven and the gas barbecue grill. For prices and additional information, see "Exploring Lake Powell by Boat," above.

In addition to the facilities described below, which are operated by Lake Powell Resorts and Marinas (address above), a variety of motels are located in Page, Arizona. For information, contact the **Page/Lake Powell Chamber of Commerce,** P.O. Box 727, Page, AZ 86040 (☎ 520/645-2741).

WHERE TO STAY & DINE AT WAHWEAP If you prefer a bedroom that can't float away in the night, consider the **Wahweap Lodge,** the largest (350 units) and fanciest hotel in the area. Right at the Wahweap Marina, it offers good access for boat tours and rentals, has two swimming pools and a whirlpool, and provides shuttle service into Page. Rooms on the west side have spectacular views of Lake Powell. Rates for two range from $139 to $149 in the summer, with discounts of up to 30% in other seasons. Nearby, the **Lake Powell Motel** offers 24 standard motel rooms, each with two queen-size beds and views of the lake. Rates for two are $75 to $80, and it's closed from November through March.

Restaurants at Wahweap Marina include the **Rainbow Room** at Wahweap Lodge (☎ 520/645-2433), serving good American and Southwestern dishes along with a panoramic view of Lake Powell. Breakfast, lunch, and dinner are served daily, with dinner main course prices in the $14 to $20 range. You'll also find a fast-food restaurant at the marina, open from April through mid-September.

WHERE TO STAY & DINE AT BULLFROG & THE OTHER MARINAS
The concessionaire also operates **Defiance House Lodge** at Bullfrog Marina, an attractive 50-room lodge with beautiful views of the lake; prices for two range from $99 to $109 in the summer, with rates up to 25% less at other times. The fine-dining restaurant here is open year-round; a fast-food restaurant is open in the summer only.

Three-bedroom mobile-home family units are available at Bullfrog, Halls Crossing, and Hite marinas. Prices for up to six people are about $150 during the summer, with lower rates at other times.

7 In Memory of John Wesley Powell: A Nearby Museum

John Wesley Powell Memorial Museum
6 N. Lake Powell Blvd., Page, AZ 86040. ☎ **520/645-9496.** Fax 520/945-3412. Free admission, donations welcome. May–Sept daily 8am–6pm; mid-Feb–Apr and Oct–mid-Dec slightly shorter hours and closed Sundays. Closed mid-Dec–mid-Feb.

The boat on the front lawn immediately tells you that this small museum has something to do with water. Actually, it's dedicated to the memory of Major John Wesley Powell, who in 1869 led a small group of men on a courageous—some said foolhardy—expedition down the Green and Colorado Rivers, traveling almost 1,000 miles through largely uncharted territory. The museum documents Powell's expedition with photographs, etchings, and artifacts. It also contains exhibits of Native American arts and crafts, from ancient Anasazi pottery to modern Navajo and Hopi weavings, pottery, and jewelry. Highlights of the museum include the collection of fluorescent minerals and a new addition of dinosaur tracks with explanatory signage. Changing exhibits of works by local artists are also featured.

16

From Moab to Arches & Canyonlands National Parks

Canyonlands country they call this—a seemingly infinite high desert of rock, with spectacular formations and rugged gorges that have been carved out over the centuries by the forces of the Colorado and Green rivers. Massive sandstone spires and arches that seem to defy gravity define the national parks of southeastern Utah. This is a land that begs to be explored—if you've come to Utah for mountain biking, hiking, four-wheeling, or rafting, this is the place. And the region holds a few surprises, too, from ancient Anasazi dwellings and rock art to dinosaur bones.

1 Moab: Gateway to the National Parks

Named for a biblical kingdom at the edge of Zion, the promised land, Moab has evolved into a popular base camp for mountain bikers, four-wheel-drive enthusiasts, hikers, and rafters eager to explore the red rock canyon country that dominates southeastern Utah. A drive down Main Street confirms that yes, this is a tourist town, with scores of businesses catering to visitors.

Not far from the Colorado River, Moab sits in a green valley among striking red sandstone cliffs, amid a scenic beauty that has lured Hollywood filmmakers for hits that include John Wayne's *The Comancheros,* the biblical epic *The Greatest Story Ever Told, Indiana Jones and the Last Crusade, Thelma and Louise,* and *City Slickers II.* It's also become a favorite location for Madison Avenue. Remember those great Chevy commercials in which the car sits perched atop a huge red tower of stone? That's Castle Rock, one of the Moab area's landmarks—and the only way to get to the top is by rock climbing or helicopter. According to Bette Stanton, local author and film historian, when the first commercial in the series was being made in 1963, Chevrolet successfully hauled a car and a negligee-clad model to the top of the 1,000-foot tower, but by the time filming was done for the day, gusty winds made it impossible for the helicopter to land to pick up the model. However, a crew member, carrying extra clothes, was dropped to keep her company, and after a chilly night they were both airlifted down.

Like most Utah towns, Moab was established by Mormon pioneers sent by church leader Brigham Young. But Moab was actually founded twice. The first time, in 1855, missionaries set up Elk Mountain Mission to see to the spiritual needs of the local Utes.

Apparently unimpressed with the suggestion that they abandon their own religion for the ways of the LDS Church, the Utes killed several missionaries, sending the rest back to Salt Lake City in a hurry. It wasn't until 20 years later that the settlers tried again, bringing cattle and sheep, and this time they successfully established a small farming and ranching community.

Today Moab remains a relatively small town, with only 4,000 or so permanent residents, but that still makes it the biggest town in southeastern Utah, offering the best services for the traveler. Practically within walking distance of Arches National Park, Moab is also close to Canyonlands National Park and is surrounded by the Manti-La Sal National Forest and vast open spaces under the jurisdiction of the Bureau of Land Management.

ESSENTIALS
GETTING THERE

BY PLANE   **Alpine Air** (☎ 801/575-2839) provides daily commuter service between Salt Lake City and Moab's Canyonlands Field Airport (☎ 435/259-7421).

The closest major airport is Walker Field in Grand Junction, Colorado (☎ 970/244-9100), which has direct flights or connections from most major cities on **America West Express** (☎ 800/235-9292), **Delta/Skywest** (☎ 800/453-9417), **Mesa Airlines** (☎ 800/637-2247), and **United Express** (☎ 800/241-6522). From Grand Junction it's easy to rent a car and drive the 125 miles west to Moab.

BY CAR   Situated on U.S. 191, Moab is about 30 miles south of I-70 (take exit 180 at Crescent Junction) and 53 miles north of Monticello. Moab is 238 miles southeast of Salt Lake City and 399 miles northeast of the north rim of Grand Canyon National Park. From Salt Lake City, follow I-15 south to Spanish Fork; then take U.S. 6 southeast to I-70; follow that east to Crescent Junction, where you'll pick up U.S. 191 south to Moab.

BY TRAIN   The closest train transportation is via **Amtrak**'s (☎ 800/872-7245) *Desert Wind,* which stops in Green River, about 52 miles north, and provides service to Salt Lake City and Grand Junction, Colorado, several times weekly. If you plan to go from Green River to Moab, you'll need to make arrangements, in advance, with **West Tracks Taxi and Shuttle** (☎ 435/259-2294).

VISITOR INFORMATION

For advance information, contact the **Grand County Travel Council,** P.O. Box 550, Moab, UT 84532 (☎ 800/635-6622 or 435/259-8825; fax 435/259-1376). The website for Moab is www.canyonlands-utah.com.

Once you've arrived, stop by the **Moab Information Center,** located in the middle of town at the corner of Main and Center streets, open from 8am to 9pm in the summer, with slightly shorter winter hours. This multi-agency visitor center is staffed by the Park Service, Bureau of Land Management, U.S. Forest Service, Grand County Travel Council, and Canyonlands Natural History Association. You can get advice; request free showings of a number of videos on Southwest attractions; pick up brochures describing numerous local motels, restaurants, and outfitters; and purchase books, videos, and other materials. A board displays current weather and campground conditions.

GETTING AROUND

Rentals, either standard passenger cars, vans, or four-wheel-drive jeeps, are available from **Thrifty** (☎ 800/367-2277 or 435/259-7317), which offers a shuttle service to

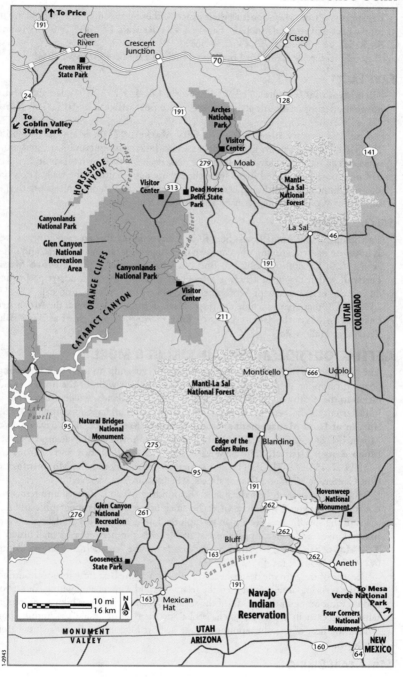

transport you from the airport to their office. Other local companies specializing in four-wheel-drive rentals include **Farabee 4X4 Rentals** (☎ 435/259-7494) and **Slickrock 4X4 Rentals** (☎ 435/259-5678).

Local taxi service is provided by **West Tracks Taxi** (☎ **435/259-2294**).

FAST FACTS

Allen Memorial Hospital, 719 W. 400 North (☎ 435/259-7191), is a full-service hospital offering 24-hour emergency care. The **post office** is at 50 E. 100 North (☎ 435/259-7427).

The best grocery store in town is **City Market,** 425 S. Main St. (☎ 435/259-5181), open 24 hours a day, 7 days a week. Hikers, mountain bikers, and four-wheelers can pick up sandwiches from the deli, assemble their own salads at the salad bar, or choose fresh-baked items from the bakery before hitting the trail. The store also sells hunting and fishing licenses, money orders, and stamps; offers photo finishing and Western Union services; and contains a pharmacy.

SPECIAL EVENTS

The Spanish Trail Arena hosts the **PRCA Canyonlands Rodeo** each June, as well as horse racing, team roping, the county fair in August, occasional concerts, and other events. Call ☎ 800/635-6622 to find out what's happening. The **Moab Music Festival,** which began in 1993, is a series of chamber music concerts performed during the first 2 weeks of September. For tickets and information call ☎ 435/259-7003. Other events include the **Jeep Safari,** over Easter weekend; the **Moab Arts Festival** in May; the **Grant County Fair** in August; and the **Fat Tire Bike Festival** at Halloween.

GETTING OUTSIDE: MOUNTAIN BIKING & MORE

The Moab area is one of Utah's main outdoor playgrounds, an ideal spot for hiking, boating, camping, or just plain horsing around (with or without the horse). In addition to the nearby national parks, Arches and Canyonlands, which are covered in full later in this chapter, there's plenty of room to roam on land administered by the **Bureau of Land Management's Grand Resource Area** office, 82 Dogwood Ave., Moab, UT 84532 (☎ 435/259-6111), and the **Manti-La Sal National Forest's Moab Ranger District,** 2290 S. West Resource Blvd. (P.O. Box 386), Moab, UT 84532 (☎ 435/259-7155). The best source for information is the **Moab Information Center,** at Main and Center streets, which is discussed above.

Much of the best of the federal land surrounding Moab is isolated and remote—not somewhere you'd want to get lost. So stock up on detailed topographic and trail maps of the specific areas you plan to explore. These, along with guidebooks, compasses, knives, and other supplies, are available, either in person or by mail order, at **T.I. Maps, Etc.,** 29 E. Center St., across from the Moab Information Center (☎ 435/259-5529; fax 435/259-7741).

Because of the extreme desert heat in the summer, the best time for most outdoor activities is spring or fall—and even the relatively mild winters are inviting. But if you end up vacationing in the middle of the summer, plan your serious hiking and mountain biking early in the day, enjoy a siesta along the river or beside a swimming pool during the heat of the afternoon, and take a short hike in the evening, just before sundown.

MOUNTAIN BIKING

With hundreds and hundreds of miles of trails, a wide variety of terrain, and spectacular scenery, Moab is easily the mountain-bike capital of Utah, and possibly the

United States (although the folks in Crested Butte, Colorado, might disagree). In addition to the mountain-biking possibilities on four-wheel-drive roads (described in this chapter's sections on Arches and Canyonlands National Parks), there are abundant trails on Bureau of Land Management and National Forest lands that are much less trafficked than national-park trails. Your first stop when you get into town should be the Moab Information Center (see above) to pick up free copies of the pamphlets *Moab Area Mountain Bike Trails* and *Moab Slickrock Bike Trail.* Be sure to discuss your plans with the rangers there; they're very knowledgeable and will be able to help you find the trails that are most suitable to your interests, ability, and equipment.

You can also get information, as well as rent or repair bikes, at **Rim Cyclery,** 94 W. 100 North (☎ 435/259-5333); **Poison Spider Bicycle Shop,** 497 N. Main St. (☎ 800/635-1792 or 435/259-7882); **Chile Pepper Bike Shop,** 702 S. Main St. (☎ 435/259-4688); and **Moab's Bike Service Station,** 478 Miller Creek Dr. (☎ 435/259-8732). **Kaibab Mountain/Desert Bike Tours,** 391 S. Main St. (☎ 435/259-7423), not only rents and repairs bikes, but also offers a wide range of guide services plus camping-equipment rentals. Bike rentals cost about $30 per day, including helmet. Bike shuttle services are available from **West Tracks Taxi and Shuttle** (☎ 435/259-2294) and **Coyote Shuttle** (☎ 435/259-8656), among others. Several local companies (see "Outfitters," below) also offer multiday mountain-bike/camping tours.

The area's most famous trail is undoubtedly the ✪ **Moab Slickrock Bike Trail,** a scenic but challenging 9.6-mile loop that crosses a mesa of heavily eroded pale orange Navajo sandstone just a few minutes from downtown Moab. Along the way it offers views far and wide that take in the towering La Sal Mountains, the red rock formations of Arches National Park, a panorama of Canyonlands National Park, and the Colorado River. The trail, open to both mountain bikes and motorcycles, is physically demanding and technically difficult, and not recommended for children, novices, or those who are out of shape or have any medical problems. Allow 4 to 5 hours, and expect to have to walk your bike in some areas. If you're not sure you're ready for the Slickrock Trail, a 1.7-mile practice loop will give you an idea of what lies ahead. To get to the trailhead from the visitor information center, take Center Street east to 400 East. Turn south (right) and follow 400 East to Mill Creek Drive. Turn east (left) and follow Mill Creek Drive to Sand Flats Road, which you take 2.3 miles east to the Bureau of Land Management's Sand Flats Recreation Area and the trailhead.

Those looking for a somewhat less challenging experience might try the **Gemini Bridges Trail,** a 13.5-mile one-way trip that shows off the area's colorful rock formations, including the trails' namesakes—two natural rock bridges. Considered relatively easy, this trail follows a dirt road mostly downhill, ending at U.S. 191, so it's best to arrange a shuttle. To get to the trailhead from the Moab Information Center, drive north along U.S. 191 to Utah 313, turn west (left), and go about 13 miles to the trailhead. Allow a full day for this ride, including getting to and from the trail, and be sure to watch for the magnificent view of Arches National Park from a hilltop as you approach U.S. 191 near the end of the ride. The trail ends at U.S. 191 just under 10 miles from the center of Moab.

Although there are dozens of fabulous trails to explore in the immediate area, mountain bikers who really want to go somewhere—perhaps all the way to Colorado to get some full-strength beer—will want to check out Kokopelli's Trail and the San Juan Hut System.

Winding for 128 miles across sandstone and shale canyons, deserts, and mountains, **Kokopelli's Trail** connects Moab and Grand Junction, Colorado. It combines all types of mountain biking, from demanding single track to well-maintained dirt roads, and passes primitive campsites along the way. The west end of the trail is near Sand Flats Road in Moab; the east end is at the Loma Boat Launch, 15 miles west of Grand Junction. The project was organized by the Colorado Plateau Mountain-Bike Trail Association, P.O. Box 4602, Grand Junction, CO 81502 (send a self-addressed, stamped envelope for a free trail map).

The **San Juan Hut System** links Moab with Telluride, Colorado, via a 206-mile-long network of backcountry dirt roads. Every 35 miles you'll find primitive cabins, each with bunks, a wood stove, a propane cooking stove, and cooking gear. The route is appropriate for intermediate-level mountain-bike riders in good physical condition; an advanced technical single track is found near the huts for more experienced cyclists. The cost for riders who plan to make the whole trip is $395, which includes use of the six huts, three meals daily, sleeping bags at each hut, and maps and trail descriptions. Shorter trips, guide services, and vehicle shuttles are also available. **Trail system offices** are located in Telluride at 117 N. Willow St. (☎ **970/728-6935**). For a brochure, write to P.O. Box 1663, Telluride, CO 81435.

FOUR-WHEELING

There are thousands of miles of four-wheel-drive roads in the Moab area, most left over from mining days, that offer a popular way to explore this scenic country without exerting too much personal energy.

A number of local companies (see "Outfitters," below) provide guided trips, starting at about $50 per person for a half day and $80 for a full day. Photographers especially enjoy the Lin Ottinger tours, designed especially for catching the right light and the best angles. You also can rent a 4X4 of your own, usually from about $80 per day, and fill it up with your kids and even the family dog (see "Getting Around," above).

Those who want to hit the trail themselves, either with a rental or their personal 4X4, will find a number of possibilities, from fairly easy dirt roads to "You-don't-really-expect-me-to-take-this-$30,000-truck-up-there-do-you?" piles of rocks. Several four-wheel-drive trips are described in the Canyonlands section of this chapter, and a free brochure, available at the Moab Information Center (see above), covers several others.

Our favorite is ✪ **Poison Spider Mesa Trail,** which covers 16 miles of 4X4 road, providing stupendous views down to the Colorado River and Moab Valley. It's considered moderately difficult; a short-wheelbase high-clearance vehicle is best. Allow at least 4 hours. To reach the trail from the Moab Information Center, drive north on U.S. 191 for about 6 miles and turn west (left) onto Utah 279. Continue another 6 miles to the DINOSAUR TRACKS sign, where the trail leaves the pavement to the right, passing over a cattle guard. From here you'll simply follow the main trail, which is usually obvious, up switchbacks, through a sandy canyon, and over some steep, rocky stretches. From a slickrock parking area on top you can take a short walk to Little Arch, which isn't really so little.

One easy 4X4 road is the **Gemini Bridges Trail,** which four-wheelers share with mountain bikers, described above in the mountain-biking section. Those with 4X4s often drive the route in the opposite direction of the mountain bikers, though, starting at a dirt road departing from the west side of U.S. 191, about 10 miles north of the Moab Information Center. This involves more uphill driving, which is safer for motor vehicles—mountain bikers usually prefer going downhill, for some reason.

The self-guiding **Mill Canyon Dinosaur Trail** provides a close-up view of dinosaur bones and fossils from the Jurassic period, 150 million years ago, that include a sauropod leg bone, vertebrae, ribs, and toe bones. You'll also see the fossil remains of a large tree trunk. To reach the trailhead, drive about 15 miles north of Moab on U.S. 191, then turn left at an intersection just north of highway mile marker 141. Cross the railroad tracks and follow a dirt road for about 2 miles to the trailhead. Allow about 1 hour. On the south side of the canyon you'll see the remnants of an old copper mill that operated in the late 1800s. Also nearby are the ruins of the Halfway Stage Station, a lunch stop in the late 1800s for stagecoach travelers making the 35-mile trip between Moab and Thompson, the nearest train station at that time. From the dinosaur trailhead, go north as though you were returning to U.S. 191, but at the first intersection turn right and drive to a dry wash, where you turn right again onto a jeep road that takes you a short distance to the stage station. The trail is managed by the **Bureau of Land Management's Grand Resource Area office**, 82 Dogwood Ave., Moab, UT 84532 (☎ **435/259-6111**).

HIKING

The Moab area offers hundreds of hiking possibilities, many of them just a few miles from town. Talk to the BLM and National Forest rangers at the Moab Information Center (see above), and pick up their free brochure that describes seven local trails. Hikes in nearby Arches and Canyonlands National Parks are described later in this chapter, in those parks' sections. Particularly in the summer, carry at least a gallon of water per person; wearing a broad-brimmed hat is also recommended.

A favorite hike of the locals is the **Negro Bill Canyon Trail,** named for William Granstaff, who lived in the area in the late 1800s. Allow about 4 hours for this hike, which is 4 miles round-trip and is considered easy to moderate. Be prepared to get your feet wet, depending on the level of the stream you follow up the canyon. To get to the trailhead, go north from Moab on U.S. 191 to Utah 128, turn east (right), and go about 3 miles to a dirt parking area. About 2 miles up the trail, in a side canyon to the right, you'll find Morning Glory Bridge, a natural rock span of 243 feet. Avoid touching the poison ivy that grows by a pool under the bridge (in case you don't remember from your scouting manual, poison ivy has shiny leaves with serrated edges, and grows in clusters of three).

The Hidden Valley Trail is a bit more challenging, taking you up a series of steep switchbacks to views of rock formations and a panorama of the Moab Valley. Allow about 3 hours for the 4-mile round-trip hike. To get to the trailhead, drive about 3 miles south of the Moab Information Center on U.S. 191, turn west (right) onto Angel Rock Road, and go 2 blocks to Rimrock Road. Turn north (right), and follow it to the parking area. The trail is named for a broad shelf, located about halfway up the Moab Rim. Many hikers turn around and head back down after reaching a low pass with great views of huge sandstone fins (the 2-mile point), but you can extend the hike by continuing all the way to the Colorado River on a four-wheel-drive road.

The highly recommended **Corona Arch Trail** offers views of three impressive arches, a colorful slickrock canyon, and the Colorado River. Allow 2 hours for this 3-mile round-trip hike, which involves a lot of fairly easy walking plus some rather steep spots with handrails and a short ladder. From Moab, go north on U.S. 191 to Utah 279, turn west (left), and go about 10 miles to a parking area on the north side of the road. You'll find a registration box and trailhead near the railroad; after crossing the tracks, follow an old roadbed onto the trail, which is marked with cairns (piles of stones).

WATER SPORTS: BOATING, CANOEING, RAFTING & MORE

After spending hours in the blazing sun looking at mile-upon-mile of huge red sandstone rock formations, it's easy to get the idea that the Moab area is a baking, dry, rock-hard desert. Well, it is. But Moab is also the only town in Utah that sits along the ✪ **Colorado River,** and it's rapidly becoming a major boating center.

You can travel down the river in a canoe, kayak, large or small rubber raft (with or without motor), or speedy, solid jet boats (see "Outfitters," below). Do-it-yourselfers can rent kayaks or canoes for $25 to $40 for a half day and $30 to $50 for a full day, or rafts from $50 to $60 per half day and $65 to $90 for a full day. Half-day guided river trips cost from $25 to $35 per person, and full-day trips are usually in the $35 to $60 range. Multiday rafting expeditions, which include meals and camping equipment, start at about $300 per person. Jet-boat trips, which can cover a lot more river in a given amount of time, start at about $30 for a 1 1/2-hour trip, with full-day trips about $75 per person. Children's rates are usually about 20% less. Some companies also offer sunset or dinner trips. Sheri Griffith Expeditions even offers a 4-day, 3-night "Expedition in Luxury," at about $900 per person, offering gourmet food served with white tablecloths, wine glasses, and candles, and your every need anticipated. See "Outfitters," below.

Public boat-launching ramps are opposite Lion's Park, near the intersection of U.S. 191 and Utah 128; at Take-Out Beach, along Utah 128 about 10 miles east of its intersection with U.S. 191; and at Hittle Bottom, also along Utah 128, about 23.5 miles east of its intersection with U.S. 191. Recorded information on river flows and reservoir conditions statewide can be obtained from the Colorado Basin River Forecast Center (☎ **801/539-1311**).

GOLF

It might be hard to keep your eye on the ball at the 18-hole, par-72 **Moab Golf Club** course, 2750 S. East Bench Rd. (☎ **435/259-6488**). Located 5 miles south of downtown Moab in Spanish Valley (take Spanish Trail Road off U.S. 191), the challenging course, nestled among red sandstone cliffs, offers spectacular views in every direction. Open daily year-round (weather permitting), the course has a driving range, pro shop and lessons, cart rentals, and a snack bar serving breakfast and lunch.

HORSEBACK RIDING

Those who want to see the canyons and rock formations from the top of a horse can choose from several companies that lead guided rides (see "Outfitters," below). A 1-hour ride starts at about $15; half-day rides are in the $40 to $50 range; and full-day trips cost $80 to $90. Sunset and dinner rides are also available.

WINTER SPORTS

Although the immediate Moab area does get some snow, for the best winter sports conditions you'll want to head into the mountains of the Manti-La Sal National Forest to the southeast. Snow turns many forest roads into perfect snowmobile and cross-country ski trails, and you'll also find good telemarking terrain. However, the mountains are also subject to avalanches, so it's a good idea to check on conditions first with the rangers at the **Manti-La Sal National Forest's Moab Ranger District office,** 2290 S. West Resource Blvd. (P.O. Box 386), Moab, UT 84532 (☎ **435/259-7155**). The Forest Service also maintains a recorded **avalanche and winter weather–condition hotline,** updated daily (☎ **435/259-SNOW**).

OUTFITTERS

Although Moab offers plenty for the do-it-yourselfer, some 50 local outfitters offer excursions of all kinds, from lazy canoe rides to hair-raising jet-boat and four-wheel-drive adventures. The chart below lists some of the major companies that want to help you fully enjoy this beautiful country. They are all located right in Moab; the zip code is 84532. Advance reservations are often required for outings, and it's best to check with several outfitters before deciding on one. In addition to asking about what you'll see and do and what it will cost, it doesn't hurt to make sure the company is insured and has the proper permits with the various federal agencies. Also ask about its cancellation policy, just in case.

Outfitter	4X4	Bike	Boat	Horse	Rent	Shuttle
Adrift Adventures 378 Main, Box 577 ☎ 800/874-4483, 435/259-8594	•	•	•	•	•	•
Canyon Voyages River Trips 352 N. Main, Box 416 ☎ 800/733-6007, 435/259-6007			•		•	
Kaibab Mountain Bike Tours 391 S. Main ☎ 800/451-1133, 435/259-7423		•			•	
Lin Ottinger Tours 600 N. Main ☎ 435/259-7312	•					
Moab Rafting Co. 4725 S. Zimmerman Lane Box 801 ☎ 800/RIO-MOAB, 435/259-RAFT			•			
Navtec Expeditions 321 N. Main, Box 1267 ☎ 800/833-1278, 435/259-7983	•	•	•			
Nichols Expeditions 497 N. Main ☎ 800/648-8488, 435/259-3999		•	•	•		
North American River Expeditions/ O.A.R.S. 543 N. Main ☎ 800/346-6277, 435/259-5865		•		•		
Pack Creek Ranch U.S. 191, S. of Moab P.O. Box 1270 ☎ 435/259-5505				•		
Red River Canoe Co. 497 N. Main ☎ 435/259-7722			•		•	•
Rim Tours 1233 South U.S. 191 ☎ 800/626-7335, 435/259-5223	•			•		

Outfitter	4X4	Bike	Boat	Horse	Rent	Shuttle
Sheri Griffith Expeditions 2231 South U.S. 191 Box 1324 ☎ 800/332-2439, 435/259-8229			•			
Tag-A-Long Expeditions 452 N. Main ☎ 800/453-3292, 435/259-8946	•		•		•	•
Tex's Riverways 691 N. 500 West Box 67 ☎ 435/259-5101			•		•	•
Western River Expeditions 1371 North U.S. 191 ☎ 800/453-7450, 435/259-7019			•		•	
Western Spirit Cycling 38 S. 100 West Box 411 ☎ 800/845-BIKE, 435/259-8732		•			•	

SEEING THE SIGHTS

Arches Vineyards
420 Kane Creek Blvd. ☎ **800/723-8609** or 435/259-5397. Free admission. Mon–Thurs 11am–7pm; Fri–Sat 11am–9pm; slightly shorter hrs. in the winter. Closed legal holidays by state law. From U.S. 191 on the south side of town, turn west at McDonald's; the winery is about a half mile ahead on the right.

One of Utah's few commercial wineries, Arches offers free personalized tours, lasting from 15 to 30 minutes, during which you can learn how wine is made and see much of the process for yourself, from the pressing equipment to the French oak barrels to bottling. Free tastings of the winery's dozen or so varieties are offered, and wine can be purchased at the winery or from state-run liquor stores. Bottles cost $5 to $20. Arches Vineyards' wines are also served at several local restaurants. The wine-bottle labels, depicting scenes of Arches National Park, were designed by a Salt Lake City artist.

The Dan O'Laurie Museum
118 E. Center St. (2 blocks east of Main St.). ☎ **435/259-7985.** Free admission, donations welcome. Summer Mon–Sat 1–8pm; winter Mon–Thurs 3–7pm and Fri–Sat 1–7pm.

This small museum has numerous displays depicting the history of Moab from pre-historic times to the present. It starts with exhibits on the geology of the area and the resultant uranium and radium mining. Early home medical remedies are on display, as is the first incubator, which used only a 25-watt bulb and was invented by a local doctor. You'll see primers from the early 1900s and a 1920 high school annual called "The Whizzer," as well as the expected ranching and farming exhibits—even a hand-made quilt depicting cattle brands. Upstairs is a gallery with changing art exhibits featuring local artists. There is also a small gift shop.

Hole 'n the Rock
La Sal Route. ☎ **435/686-2250.** Admission $2.50 adults, $1.50 children ages 6–12. Daily 9am–5pm; open until 6pm in the summer. Take U.S. 191 south out of Moab 15 miles.

This 5,000-square-foot cave-home was excavated from solid stone by Albert and Gladys Christensen, who removed some 50,000 cubic feet of sandstone over a 12-year period to create their 14-room living space. Visitors can take tours, which are given every 10 minutes; see the fireplace—with a 65-foot chimney drilled through solid rock—and other rock-solid furnishings; and browse through the gift shop.

Moab to Monument Valley Film Commission and Museum

50 E. Center no. 1 (a half block east of Main St.). ☎ **435/259-6388.** Free admission. Mon–Fri 8am–noon and 1–5pm.

Southeastern Utah has been in so many Hollywood movies that some directors, actors, and crew members are starting to call it home. Since 1925, when *The Vanishing American* was filmed in Monument Valley, numerous films have been shot here, including countless westerns—John Wayne was a regular. More recent westerns have included *City Slickers II,* starring Billy Crystal, and *Riders of the Purple Sage,* featuring Ed Harris and Amy Madigan. Plenty of nonwesterns have used this area as a backdrop, too, such as *Thelma and Louise* and *Indiana Jones and the Last Crusade.* Various movie leftovers, photos, posters, and related memorabilia have been collected and are on display at the film commission office and museum, located behind the Moab Visitor Center.

WHEN YOU NEED TO COOL OFF

A good way to beat the summer heat is with a day or even a few hours at **Butch Cassidy's King World Waterpark,** 1500 North U.S. 191 (☎ **435/259-2837**). Hidden from the highway on 17 acres on the north side of town, this family-oriented water park has three large water slides, two kiddie slides, three pools, sand volleyball, a refreshment stand, and picnic areas. You'll find paddleboats in a pond once used by outlaw Butch Cassidy as a watering hole for stolen horses and cattle. The water park is open from mid-April to mid-September, weather permitting, usually daily from 10am to 10pm, although Sunday hours may be slightly shorter. An all-day pass costs $8.50 for adults, $6.50 for children ages 3 to 12, and is free for those over 65 or under 3. Lower fees are charged for shorter periods of time.

Those looking for a regular swimming pool, open year-round, can head to the **Moab Swim Center,** 181 W. 400 North (☎ **435/259-8226**). Admission costs $5 for adults, $2.50 for youth under 18 and seniors. Call for hours.

SHOPPING

Moab may not be a shopper's mecca, but you'll find enough interesting stores to keep you busy for an afternoon, and possibly some unique items to take home.

For handcrafted Navajo, Hopi, and Zuni jewelry, as well as pottery, weavings, and carvings, try **Lema Indian Trading Company,** 60 N. Main (☎ 435/259-5055), or **Hogan Trading Company,** 100 S. Main (☎ 435/259-8118). If it's Native American music you're after, **Music of Moab,** at 82 S. Main (☎ 435/259-4405), is the place to go, with a huge selection on tape and compact disc.

The **Moab Rock Shop,** 600 N. Main (☎ 435/259-7312), carries all sorts of rocks, minerals, gems, dinosaur bones, and fossils. **The Western Image,** 79 N. Main (☎ 435/259-3006), sells western art and collectibles, cowboy boots, and genuine Stetson hats. In the beverage category, there's the local wine, at **Arches Vineyards** (see above), and the local beers, at **Eddie McStiff's** and **Moab Brewery** (see "Where to Dine," below). The **Utah State Liquor Store** is at 260 S. Main (☎ 435/259-5314).

WHERE TO STAY

The highest room rates in Moab are generally charged from mid-March through October, and sometimes drop by up to half in the winter. Rates may also be higher during special events. Room tax of about $11^1/_2$% is added to all bills. Pets are not accepted unless otherwise noted.

Most visitors are here for the outdoors, and since they don't plan to spend much time in their rooms, they book into one of the very adequate chain and franchise motels. The town's largest lodging property is the **Super 8 Motel,** on the north edge of town at 889 N. Main St. (☎ 800/800-8000 or 435/259-8868; fax 435/259-8968), with 146 rooms, charging $59.88 to $78.88 double during the high season. The **Days Inn,** 426 N. Main St. (☎ 800/DAYS-INN or 435/259-4468; fax 435/259-4018), charges $50 to $90 double in the high season. Moab has two Best Westerns: the **Best Western Canyonlands Inn,** 16 S. Main St. (☎ 800/528-1234 or 435/259-2300; fax 435/259-2301), charges $89 to $141 double, including breakfast, in the high season; and the **Best Western Greenwell Inn,** 105 S. Main St. (☎ 800/528-1234 or 435/259-6151; fax 435/259-4397), has rates of $59 to $115 double in the high season.

Aarchway Inn

1551 North U.S. 191, Moab, UT 84532. ☎ **800/341-9359** or 435/259-2599. Fax 435/259-2270. 90 rms, 7 suites. A/C TV TEL. May–Oct $79–$97 double, $140–$150 suites; lower rates Nov–Apr. Rates include continental breakfast. AE, DISC, MC, V.

This brand-new two-story motel, just 2 miles from the entrance to Arches National Park on the north edge of Moab, has large rooms with great views, decorated in Southwestern style and with photos depicting the scenic attractions of the area. Most rooms contain two queen-size beds; eight family units have two queen beds plus a queen hide-a-bed. There are also several whirlpool suites, executive suites, meeting-room suites, and a honeymoon suite. All units have refrigerators and microwave ovens. Facilities include a large outdoor heated pool, a courtyard with barbecue grills, an indoor hot tub, exercise room, bike storage room, coin-operated laundry, conference rooms, and gift shop. Plans are underway for a restaurant (serving three meals daily) and a convenience store with a gas station. The entire motel is nonsmoking.

Bowen Motel

169 N. Main St., Moab, UT 84532. ☎ **800/874-5439** or 435/259-7132. 40 rms. A/C TV TEL. $65–$75 double; off-season 40% less. AE, DC, DISC, MC, V.

This family-owned and -operated motel offers fairly large, comfortable, clean, basic rooms with one or two queen-size beds and shower/tub combos. Most rooms have attractive murals that add interest to the plain white walls, and two family rooms sleep up to six each. The original structure was built in the 1940s, with additions made in the 1980s; a major renovation was completed in 1993–94. Facilities include an outdoor heated swimming pool and locked bike storage ($2 per night extra). Several restaurants are within easy walking distance.

The Lazy Lizard International Hostel

1213 South U.S. 191, Moab, UT 84532. ☎ **435/259-6057.** 30 dorm beds, 5 private rms, 8 cabins, 1 teepee; total capacity 65 persons. $7 dorm bed; $20 private rm.; $25 and up cabin; $5 per person teepee and camp space. Showers $2 for nonguests. Hostel membership not necessary. No credit cards.

Located on the south side of town, behind a bowling alley and self-storage units, this hostel offers exceptionally clean, comfortable lodging at bargain rates for those willing to share. The main house, which is air-conditioned, has basic dorm rooms plus one private room. A separate building contains four additional private rooms, which look much like older motel units (with fans but no air-conditioning). The best facilities are the cabins, constructed of real logs and with beds for up to six. The teepee is, well, a teepee. Everyone shares the bathhouses, and there's a telephone in the main house. Guests also have use of a fully equipped kitchen; living room with television, VCR, and a collection of movies; whirlpool; self-service laundry; gas barbecue grill; and picnic tables. Groups should inquire about the two nearby houses that can be rented by the night ($120 for the one that sleeps 20; $90 for the one that sleeps 10).

Red Stone Inn

535 S. Main St., Moab, UT 84532. ☎ **800/772-1972** or 435/259-3500. Fax 435/259-2717. 50 rms. A/C TV TEL. Winter $29.95–$34.95 double; summer $49.95–$54.95 double; slightly higher in Sept and during special events. AE, DISC, MC, V.

This centrally located motel, built in 1993, is among Moab's best deals for travelers who want a clean, quiet place to sleep at a bargain rate. The exterior gives the impression that these are cabins, and the theme continues inside with attractive light-colored knotty pine walls, decorated with colorful posters and maps showing off the area's attractions. Rooms are a bit on the small side, although perfectly adequate and spotlessly maintained, and contain either one queen-size bed or two doubles. All but three rooms have kitchenettes with microwave ovens, refrigerators, sinks, and coffeemakers complete with coffee and other supplies. Roll-away beds are available at $5 extra. Three handicapped-accessible rooms have shower/tub combos, while the rest have showers only. There is no swimming pool, but a picnic area has gas barbecue grills for guests' use. Pets are permitted at an extra charge of $5.

✪ Sunflower Hill Bed & Breakfast Inn

185 N. 300 East, Moab, UT 84532. ☎ **435/259-2974.** Fax 435/259-3065. 11 units. A/C TV. Mar–mid-Nov and holidays $75–$150 double; mid-Nov to Feb $45–$120 double. Rates include breakfast. DISC, MC, V.

This country-style B&B is located 3 blocks off Main Street on a quiet dead-end road, and offers elegant rooms and lovely outdoor areas for relaxing. The grounds are grassy and shady, with fruit trees and flowers in abundance. There's an outdoor hot tub (usable year-round), a swing, a picnic table, and a barbecue for guests' use.

Each guest room features a different motif, but all have handmade quilts with matching sham pillows and coordinated sheets on the beds, as well as private baths. The Rose Room has roses stenciled on the walls, an old picture of a mother and daughter with roses in the lower left corner, and a rose-design wallpaper. The Sun Porch has a flowered rock-wall mural in the bedroom, and sunflowers stenciled along the bottom of the walls in a separate sitting area, which overlooks the shady side yard. The Garret, an upstairs suite, is decorated in an apple motif, and its bath has a wonderful old claw-foot tub, painted red outside, with a surround shower curtain.

Breakfasts are substantial, with homemade breads and granola, fruit juices, fresh fruits, freshly ground Colombian coffee, and a hot entree, which might be Belgian waffles, baked French toast, or individual casseroles.

CAMPING

Canyonlands Campark

555 S. Main St., Moab, UT 84532. ☎ **800/522-6848** outside Utah, or 435/259-6848. 113 total sites, 70 with full hookup, 43 with water and electric only. $19.50 full hookup, $17 with water/electric. AE, DISC, MC, V.

This campground is surprisingly shady and quiet, given its in-town Main Street location. Open year-round, it's a good choice for those with RVs or for anyone who wants a hot shower after hiking or mountain biking all day. Facilities include a dump station, self-service laundry, playground, and outdoor unheated swimming pool. A convenience store carries food and some RV supplies, and a City Market grocery store is just a block away.

Moab Valley RV & Campark

1773 North U.S. 191, Moab, UT 84532. ☎ **435/259-4469.** 130 total sites (68 pull-throughs with full hookup, 24 back-ins with water and electric only, 38 tent); 6 cabins. For 2 people: $20–$22 hookup, $15 tent, $32 cabin; $3 each additional person. DISC, MC, V. Closed Nov–Jan.

Situated on the north side of Moab near the intersection of U.S. 191 and Utah 128, this campground is just 2 miles from Arches National Park. Practically any size RV can be accommodated in the park's extra-large pull-through sites, and all sites have great views of the surrounding rock formations. Both tenters and RVers will enjoy the trees and patches of grass, and full RV hookups include cable television connections. The park facilities include an RV dump station, coin-operated laundry, propane sales, and a convenience store with groceries and RV and camping supplies. The park does not have a swimming pool or playground. Dogs are permitted in RV sites, but not in tent sites. Those who neglected to bring a tent or RV can rent one of the six comfortable cabins, which provide shelter but still require a walk to the bathhouse.

WHERE TO DINE

Buck's Grill House

1393 North U.S. 191. ☎ **435/259-5201.** Reservations for 6 or more. Main courses $5.75–$19. DC, DISC, MC, V. Daily 5:30pm–closing. Closed Dec–Jan. About 1¹/₂ miles north of town. AMERICAN WESTERN.

This popular restaurant, which many locals consider the area's best steak place, offers a number of choices to suit a variety of palates. The decor might be described as subdued western, with white walls, carpeting, white linen tablecloths, and dark wood beams. On display are western and scenic paintings by local artist Pete Plastow. There is also patio dining when the weather cooperates. The menu includes steaks, of course, plus the extremely popular prime rib—prepared fresh daily—and fresh fish. Those looking for a light (or inexpensive) meal will also find several salads and sandwiches, including a grilled buffalo meatloaf sandwich for under $6. The buffalo meatloaf can also be ordered as a full dinner, with black onion gravy and mashed potatoes; another especially popular dish is Buck's zucchini pie, made from polenta stuffed with a zucchini filling and topped with a tomato and garlic sauce. All meats are chemical-free, the vegetables are fresh, and breads and other baked items are made in-house. A children's menu is available. Buck's offers full liquor service and serves a variety of Utah microbrews.

Center Cafe

92 E. Center St. ☎ **435/259-4295.** Reservations recommended. Main courses $9–$28. DISC, MC, V. Daily 5:30–10pm. Closed Dec–Feb. About 1 block east of Main St. CONTEMPORARY AMERICAN.

Not really a cafe at all, this fine small restaurant, with white tablecloths, black chairs, and a bright, contemporary look, is the place to come for innovative game, vegetarian, and pasta selections. The menu changes seasonally, but might include roast pork loin with balsamic–port wine glaze; roasted eggplant lasagna layered with feta cheese and cured Moroccan olive marinara; or grilled Black Angus beef tenderloin. The restaurant offers full liquor service.

Eddie McStiff's

57 S. Main St. (in Western Plaza, just south of the information center). ☎ **435/259-2337.** Reservations not accepted. Main courses $5.50–$16.50; pizza $5–$20. MC, V. Daily 3–10pm. Closed Dec–Jan. ECLECTIC.

This bustling, somewhat noisy brewpub is half family restaurant and half tavern. In the restaurant dining room, you'll find Southwest decor and paintings by local artists, while the tavern looks just like a tavern should, with a long bar, low light, and lots of wood. The menu changes seasonally to accommodate sports enthusiasts in spring and fall, Europeans and families in summer. There's always a wide range of appetizers, salads, and burgers, plus grilled steaks, pasta, and Southwestern items. At least a dozen fresh-brewed beers are on tap at any given time and can also be purchased to go in 22-ounce bottles and half-gallon refillable growlers. Mixed drinks, wine, and beer are sold in the dining room with food only, and beer can be purchased with or without food in the tavern. (You must be at least 21 to eat in the tavern.)

Fat City Smokehouse

36 S. 100 West (1 block west of Main St. just south of Center St.). ☎ **435/259-4302.** Main courses $5.50–$16.50. AE, MC, V. Daily 11am–10pm. Closed Sun in the winter. BARBECUE/VEGETARIAN.

Genuine Texas-style pit barbecue has made this a favorite of locals, who pile into the plain, cafe-style dining room for pork ribs, beef tips, chicken, and homemade sausage, all rubbed with a variety of seasonings, slow-smoked from 12 to 14 hours, and served with the restaurant's own sauce. Flame-grilled dinners, cooked over apple and cherry hardwoods, include fresh catfish with sweet pepper seasoning; a popular summer special is the 24-ounce T-bone. For the nonbarbecue-lover, there are several vegetarian sandwiches, such as the veggie club, with grilled eggplant, zucchini, onion, and green pepper on three layers of toasted nut bread, with fresh tomato pesto and a choice of cheese. Service at this casual restaurant is fast and friendly, and beer is available with meals.

Honest Ozzie's Cafe & Desert Oasis

60 N. 100 West (1 block west of Main St. and just north of Center St.). ☎ **435/259-8442.** Breakfast items $1.50–$6.50; lunch $3.50–$6.50. MC, V. Daily 7am–3pm. Closed Nov–Feb. INTERNATIONAL/HEALTH FOOD.

This cheery little cafe recently added a waterfall and shade cloth to their garden patio—still a favorite with hummingbirds. Inside, you'll find a cafe-style atmosphere with white walls, light-colored woods, and local artwork. The food is all homemade, with lots of baked items plus deli salads, daily specials, and wraps—a full meal all wrapped up in a large tortilla. Popular breakfasts include whole-grain waffles with real maple syrup and fruit, bagels with flavored cream cheese, and breakfast burritos. For lunch, try the all-American wrap, which contains chicken-fried steak, fried potatoes, corn, cranberry sauce, and gravy. Other wraps include the Thai veggie with tofu and the Cajun catfish. The restaurant serves beer from a local microbrewery.

Moab Brewery

686 S. Main St. ☎ **435/259-6333.** Main courses $6.45–$14.99 dinner; $5.45–$7.95 lunch. AE, DISC, MC, V. Daily 11:30am–10pm summer; 11:30am–9pm winter. Closed first 2 weeks in Jan. ECLECTIC.

Fresh handcrafted ales brewed on-site, along with a wide variety of burgers, sandwiches, salads, soups, vegetarian dishes, and assorted house specialties, are served at this open, spacious microbrewery/restaurant on the south side of town. You can sample the brews—from a German-style unfiltered wheat ale to a light-bodied easy-drinking American lager—at the separate bar. In all, the brewery produces some 16 different ales and about half a dozen are available on tap at any given time. The restaurant is popular with families, who gobble down basic American fare like burgers, steaks, and fresh fish. The adventuresome can choose from the more exotic selections, such as curried shrimp pasta, the mixed sausage grill plate, and the spicy chicken burrito. Especially popular is the vegetarian lasagna, composed of layers of four cheeses, spinach, sunflower seeds, pasta, and topped with garlic tomato-basil sauce and parmesan cheese. The large dining room, which seats 250, is decorated with light-colored woods, outdoor sports equipment—including a hang glider on the ceiling—and local artwork. Patio dining and a children's menu are also available. Beer is sold in the bar; in the restaurant, diners can purchase beer, wine, or several tropical-type mixed drinks.

Moab Diner

189 S. Main St. (2 blocks south of Center St.). ☎ **435/259-4006.** Main courses $5–$15 dinner; $4.25–$5.50 lunch; $3.25–$5 breakfast. MC, V. Daily 6am–10:30pm. Closes earlier in the winter. AMERICAN/SOUTHWESTERN.

Late risers can get breakfast—among the best in town—all day here, with all the usual egg dishes, biscuits and gravy, six kinds of omelets, and a spicy breakfast burrito. The decor tells you that this is definitely a diner, but it does have lots of green plants (real, not plastic). Hamburgers, sandwiches, and salads are the offerings at lunch, of course, and for dinner there's steak, shrimp, and chicken, plus liver and onions. Dinners include roll, potato, and soup or salad. In addition to ice cream, you can get sherbet, frozen yogurt, malts, and shakes, plus sundaes with seven different toppings. No alcoholic beverages are served.

Poplar Place Restaurant & Pub

11 E. 100 North (just east of Main St., 1 block north of Center St.). ☎ **435/259-6018.** Pizza $7–$16.75; main courses $4.95–$9.95. MC, V. Daily 11:30am–11pm. Shorter hrs. in the winter. MEXICAN/ITALIAN.

This two-story corner pub has been a busy lunch stop for locals since it opened in 1972, serving several microbrewed beers plus lots of pizzas, pasta, sandwiches, and Mexican dishes. The pizzas, with homemade crust and sauces, are probably the most popular items on the menu. They come with either a tomato or Alfredo sauce and your choice of toppings. For the indecisive, several specialty pizzas are also listed. Mexican selections include crab or vegetable enchiladas, chicken burrito with green chile sauce, and what the Poplar Place calls a "faco," a cross between a fajita and taco. Dine inside or in the fresh air on their new patio. Full liquor service is available.

MOAB AFTER DARK

For a small town in conservative, nondrinking Utah, this is a pretty wild place. After a day on the river or in the back of a jeep, don't be surprised to see your outfitter letting his or her hair down at the **Rio Colorado Restaurant and Bar,** 1 block west of Main on Center Street (☎ 435/259-6666). Locals just call it The Rio. There's live regional music—usually rock, reggae, or jazz—most weekend evenings in the summer.

Another local hangout is the **Sportsman's Lounge,** 1991 South U.S. 191 (☎ 435/259-9972), which claims to have the biggest dance floor in town. There's live country music on summer weekends and dart tournaments and other fun activities during the week.

Popular with beer drinkers is **Eddie McStiff's,** 57 S. Main St. (☎ 435/259-2337), a microbrewery that's part family restaurant (see "Where to Dine," above), part busy tavern, with several TVs plus a game room with pool tables, foosball, and shuffleboard. There are a dozen fresh-brewed beers on tap, and for those who order food of some kind, a full bar. Another option for the beer-lover is the **Moab Brewery** (see "Where to Dine," above).

Those looking for a foot-stompin' good time and a western-style dinner will want to make their way to the **Bar M Chuckwagon Live Western Show and Cowboy**

Supper, 8 miles north of Moab on U.S. 191 (☎ 435/259-2276), which is similar to chuckwagon suppers in other parts of the West. Diners go through a supper line to pick up barbecued beef or chicken, potatoes, beans, applesauce, biscuits, dessert, and nonalcoholic beverages. Vegetarian meals can be prepared with advance notice, and beer and wine coolers are also available. After dinner, a stage show entertains with western-style music, jokes, and down-home silliness from the Bar M Wranglers. The grounds, which include a small western village and gift shop, open at 6pm, with gunfights starting at 7pm, dinner at 7:30pm, and the show at 8:30pm. The Bar M is open Fridays and Saturdays in April and May, and Monday through Saturday from June through September. Supper and show cost about $16 for adults, $8 for children ages 4 to 10, and free for children under 4. Call for reservations and directions.

Canyonlands by Night (☎ 435/259-5261) is an evening river trip, operating May through October, that combines a sunset boat ride with stories of outlaws, rock formations, and a show of colored lights on the canyon walls. The office and dock are just north of Moab at the Colorado River Bridge. Cost is $20 for adults, $10 for children ages 6 to 12, and free for children under 6. Reservations are recommended.

The **Fallen Arches Square Dance Club** (☎ 435/259-5637) invites visitors to join them Thursday evenings year-round at the Moab Community Civic Center, at 100 N. 400 East. Line-dancing lessons start at 6:30pm and square-dancing lessons begin at 7pm; square dancing starts at 8pm. Admission costs $5 per couple.

2 Arches National Park

Natural stone arches and fantastic rock formations, sculpted as if by an artist's hand, are the defining feature of this park, and they exist in remarkable numbers and variety. Just as soon as you've seen the most beautiful, most colorful, most gigantic stone arch you can imagine, walk around the next bend and there's another—bigger, better, and more brilliant than the last. It would take forever to see them all, with more than 1,700 officially listed and more being discovered or "born" every day.

Just down the road from Canyonlands National Park in eastern Utah, Arches is much more visitor friendly, with relatively short, well-maintained trails leading to most of the park's major attractions. It's also a place to let your imagination run wild. Is Delicate Arch really so delicate? Or would its other monikers (Old Maid's Bloomers or Cowboy Chaps) really be more appropriate? And what about those tall spires? You might imagine they're castles, giant stone sailing ships, or perhaps petrified skyscrapers of some ancient city. Exploring the park is a great family adventure. The arches seem more accessible and less forbidding than the spires and pinnacles at Canyonlands and other southern Utah parks. Some think of arches as bridges, imagining the power of water that literally cuts a hole through a solid rock. Actually, to geologists there's a big difference between arches and bridges. Bridges are formed when a river cuts a channel, while the often bizarre and beautiful contours of arches result from the erosive force of rain and snow, freezing and thawing, as it dissolves the "glue" that holds sand grains together and chips away at the stone.

Although arches usually grow slowly—*very* slowly—something dramatic happens every once in a while: like that quiet day in 1940 when a sudden crash instantly doubled the size of the opening of Skyline Arch, leaving a huge boulder lying at its feet. Luckily, no one (at least no one we know of) was standing underneath at the time. The same thing happened to the magnificently delicate Landscape Arch in 1991, when a slab of rock about 60 feet long, 11 feet wide, and $4^1/_2$ feet thick fell from the underside of the arch. Now there's such a thin ribbon of stone that it's hard to believe it can continue hanging on at all.

Spend a day or a week here, exploring the terrain, watching the rainbow of colors deepen and explode with the long rays of the setting sun, or the moonlight glistening on ribbons of desert varnish on tall sandstone cliffs. Watch for mule deer, cottontail rabbits, and the bright green collared lizard as they go about the difficult task of desert living. And let your own imagination run wild among the Three Gossips, the Spectacles, the Eye of the Whale, the Penguins, the Tower of Babel, and the thousands of other statues, towers, arches, and bridges that await your discovery in this magical playground.

JUST THE FACTS

See the Moab section of this chapter for camping options outside the park, plus lodging, restaurants, and other nearby services.

GETTING THERE   From Moab, drive 5 miles north on U.S. 191. Arches National Park is located 27 miles east of Canyonlands National Park's Island in the Sky Visitor Center, and 233 miles southeast of Salt Lake City. The park is 404 miles northeast of the north rim of Grand Canyon National Park in Arizona, and 371 miles west of Denver, Colorado.

INFORMATION & VISITOR CENTERS   For advance information on what to see in the park, plus hiking and camping, contact Superintendent, **Arches National Park,** P.O. Box 907, Moab, UT 84532-0907 (☎ **435/259-8161** or 435/259-5279 for TTY). It's best to write early and to specify what type of information you need. The website for the park is http://www.nps.gov/arch.

Books, maps, and videos on Arches as well as Canyonlands National Park and other southern Utah attractions can be purchased from the nonprofit **Canyonlands Natural History Association** (C.N.H.A.), 3031 South U.S. 191, Moab, UT 84532 (☎ **435/259-6003;** fax 435/259-8263). Some publications are available in foreign languages, and several videos can be purchased in either VHS or PAL formats. MasterCard and Visa are accepted. Those wanting to help the nonprofit association can join ($20 annually) and get a 20% discount on purchases.

Once you arrive in the area, you can get information at the **Moab Information Center,** located in the middle of town at the corner of Main and Center streets. Open from 8am to 9pm in the summer, with slightly shorter winter hours, the center is staffed by Park Service, Bureau of Land Management, Forest Service, and C.N.H.A. personnel.

The **Arches National Park Visitor Center,** located just inside the entrance gate, provides maps, brochures, and other information.

FEES, REGULATIONS & BACKCOUNTRY PERMITS   Entry into the park (for up to 7 days) costs $10 per private vehicle or $5 per motorcycle, bicycle, or pedestrian. A $25 annual pass is also available. Free permits, available at the visitor center, are required for all overnight trips into the backcountry.

Backcountry hikers should practice minimum-impact techniques, packing out all trash. Naturally, feeding or otherwise disturbing wildlife is prohibited, as is vandalizing or upsetting any natural feature of the park. Wood fires are not permitted. Dogs, which must be leashed at all times, are prohibited in public buildings, on all trails, and in the backcountry.

SEASONS & AVOIDING THE CROWDS   Summer days here are hot, often reaching 100°F, and winters can be cool or cold, dropping below freezing at night, with snow possible. The best time to visit, especially for hikers, is in the spring or fall, when daytime temperatures are usually between 60 and 80°F and nights are cool.

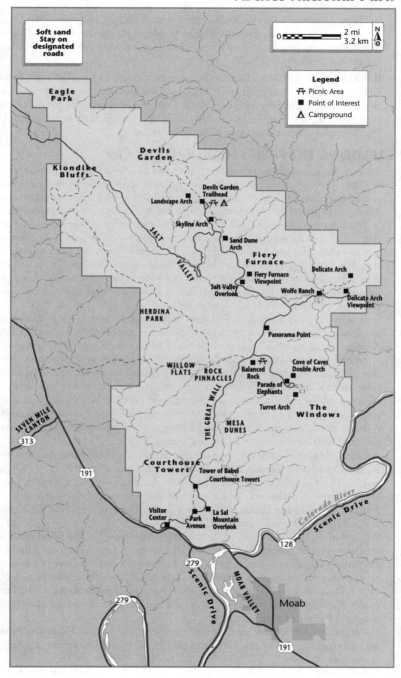

Arches National Park

Soft sand
Stay on
designated
roads

0 [_____] 2 mi
3.2 km

N

Legend
⛏ Picnic Area
■ Point of Interest
△ Campground

Eagle
Park

Devils
Garden

Klondike
Bluffs

Devils Garden
Trailhead
Landscape Arch ■ ⛏ △

Skyline Arch ■

Sand Dune
Arch ■

SALT

VALLEY

Fiery
Furnace
■ Fiery Furnace
Viewpoint
Salt Valley
Overlook ■
Wolfe Ranch ■

Delicate Arch ■

■ Delicate Arch
Viewpoint

HERDINA
PARK

■ Panorama Point

WILLOW
FLATS
ROCK
PINNACLES
■ ⛏
Balanced
Rock

Cove of Caves
Double Arch ■

Parade of
Elephants ■
Turret Arch ■

The
Windows

THE GREAT WALL

MESA
DUNES

SEVEN MILE
CANYON

313

191

Courthouse
Towers
■ Tower of Babel
■ Courthouse Towers

Visitor
Center ■
Park
Avenue
■ La Sal
Mountain
Overlook

Colorado River
Scenic Drive

128

279
Scenic
Drive

MOAB VALLEY

Moab

279

191

The peak months follow the temperatures, with June, July, and August being busiest, when you're likely to experience parking problems; the quietest times are December, January, and February. As with most popular parks, avoid visiting during school vacations if possible.

RANGER PROGRAMS During the summer, rangers lead guided hikes on the Fiery Furnace Trail twice daily (see "Sports & Outdoor Activities," below), as well as daily nature walks from various park locations. Evening campfire programs, also in the summer only, are on topics such as rock art, geological processes, and wildlife. A schedule of events is posted at the visitor center.

EXPLORING THE PARK'S HIGHLIGHTS BY CAR

Arches is the easiest of Utah's national parks to see in a day if that's all you can spare. An 18-mile (one-way) **scenic drive** offers splendid views of countless natural rock arches and other formations, and several easy hikes open up additional scenery. Allow 1½ hours for the 36-mile round-trip drive, adding time for the optional hikes.

You can see many of the park's most famous rock formations without even getting out of your car—although we strongly urge you to venture out and explore on foot. You have the option of walking short distances to a number of viewpoints, or stretching your legs on a variety of longer hikes along the way (see "Sports & Outdoor Activities," below). The main road is easy to navigate, even for RVs, but parking at some viewpoints is limited. Please be considerate and leave trailers at the visitor center parking lot or in a Moab campground.

Start out by viewing the short slide show at the **visitor center** to get a feel for what lies ahead. Then drive north past the Moab Fault to the overlook parking for **Park Avenue,** a solid rock "fin" that reminded early visitors of the New York skyline.

From here, your next stop is **La Sal Mountain Viewpoint,** where you look southeast to the La Sal Mountains, named by early Spanish explorers who thought the snow-covered mountains looked like huge piles of salt. In the overlook area is a "desert scrub" ecosystem, composed of sagebrush, saltbush, blackbrush, yucca, and prickly pear cactus, all plants that can survive in sandy soil with little moisture. Animals that inhabit the area include the kangaroo rat, black-tailed jackrabbit, rock squirrel, several species of lizards, and the coyote.

Continuing on the scenic drive, you begin to see some of the park's major formations at **Courthouse Towers,** where large monoliths such as Sheep Rock, the Organ, and the Three Gossips dominate the landscape. Leaving Courthouse Towers, watch for the **Tower of Babel** on the east (right) side of the road, then proceed past the petrified sand dunes to **Balanced Rock,** a huge boulder weighing about 3,600 tons, perched on a slowly eroding pedestal.

Continuing, you'll soon take a side road to the east (right) to **The Windows.** Created when erosion penetrated a sandstone fin, they can be seen via a short walk from the parking area. Also in this area you'll see **Turret Arch** and the **Cove of Caves.** As erosion continues in the back of the largest cave it will probably become an arch one day. A short walk from the parking lot takes you to **Double Arch,** which looks exactly like what the name implies. From the end of this trail you can also see the delightful **Parade of Elephants.**

Return to the main park road, turn north (right), and drive to **Panorama Point,** with an expansive view of Salt Valley and the Fiery Furnace, which can really live up to its name at sunset.

Next, turn east (right) off the main road onto the Wolfe Ranch Road and drive to the **Wolfe Ranch** parking area. A very short walk leads to what's left of this ranch.

John Wesley Wolfe and his son Fred moved here from Ohio in 1898, and in 1907 were joined by John's daughter Flora, her husband, and their two children. The cabin seen here was built for Flora's family (John's cabin was later destroyed by a flash flood). In 1910 the family decided this was not the greatest location for a ranch, and they packed up and returned to Ohio. If you follow the trail a bit farther, you'll see some Ute petroglyphs. More ambitious hikers can continue for a moderately difficult 3-mile round-trip excursion to **Delicate Arch,** with a spectacular view at trail's end. If you don't want to take the hike, you can still see this lovely arch, albeit from a distance, by getting back in your car, continuing down the road for 1 mile, and walking a short trail to the **Delicate Arch Viewpoint.**

Returning to the park's main road, turn north (right), and go to the next stop, the **Salt Valley Overlook.** The various shades and colors in this collapsed salt dome have been caused by varying amounts of iron in the rock, as well as other factors.

Continue now to the viewpoint for **Fiery Furnace,** which offers a dramatic view of colorful sandstone fins. This is also the starting point for 2-hour ranger-guided hikes in the summer.

From here, drive to a pull-out for **Sand Dune Arch,** located down a short path from the road, where you'll find shade and sand—a good place for kids to play—along with the arch. The trail also leads across a meadow to Broken Arch (which isn't broken at all—it just looks that way from a distance).

Back on the road, continue to **Skyline Arch,** which doubled in size in 1940 when a huge boulder tumbled out of it. The next and final stop is the often crowded parking area for the **Devils Garden Trailhead.** From here you can hike to some of the most unique arches in the park, including **Landscape Arch,** among the longest natural rock spans in the world. It's a pretty easy 1.6-mile round-trip hike.

From the trailhead parking lot, it's 18 miles back to the visitor center.

SPORTS & OUTDOOR ACTIVITIES

FOUR-WHEELING   Although there aren't nearly as many four-wheel-drive opportunities here as in nearby Canyonlands National Park, there are a few—but check first with rangers on possible road closures and conditions that make the routes impassable. One possibility is the 17-mile ✪ **Klondike Bluffs to Willow Flats Road,** which is best driven from north to south because of soft sand on steep grades. Turn west off the main park road 1 mile south of Devils Garden Trailhead, and follow the road up through the Salt Valley about 7.7 miles to the turnoff for Klondike Bluffs. The next 17 miles are strictly for four-wheelers, heading into high desert terrain, opening up panoramas of surrounding mountains and red rock formations. The route also passes Eye of the Whale Arch, views of Elephant Butte (the highest point in the park at 5,653 feet), and the imposing Courthouse Towers. Also seen along the route are drifting sand dunes and the red rock Marching Men formation. The road brings you out at Balanced Rock parking area.

Four-wheel-drive vehicles are available for rent, or you can travel in a jeep tour. See the "Moab" section earlier in this chapter.

Impressions
_____

Ten thousand strangely carved forms in every direction, and beyond them mountains blending with clouds.

—Major John Wesley Powell, 1869

BIKING Bikes are prohibited on all trails and are not allowed to travel cross-country within the national park boundaries. This leaves the park's established scenic drive, which is open to cyclists, although you need to be aware that the 18-mile dead-end road is narrow and winding in spots and can be a bit crowded with motor vehicles during the summer.

Mountain bikers also have the option of tackling one of several four-wheel-drive roads (see the "Four-Wheeling" section above). For guided mountain-bike trips outside the park, as well as rentals, repairs, and supplies, see the "Moab" section earlier in this chapter.

HIKING Most trails here are short and relatively easy, although because of the hot summer sun and lack of shade, it's wise to carry a good amount of water on any jaunt expected to last more than 1 hour.

One easy walk, and a good place to take kids who want to play in the sand, is to **Sand Dune Arch.** It's only 0.3 miles long (round-trip), but you can add an extra 1.2 miles by continuing on to Broken Arch. Sand Dune Arch is hidden among and shaded by rock walls, with a naturally created giant sandbox below the arch. By the way, please resist the temptation to climb onto the arch and jump down into the sand. Not only is it dangerous, but it can also damage the arch. Those who continue to Broken Arch should watch for mule deer and kit foxes, which inhabit the meadow you'll be crossing. Allow about 30 minutes to Sand Dune Arch and back; 1 hour to Broken Arch.

From the **Devils Garden Trail** you can see about 15 to 20 arches, on a fairly long, strenuous, and difficult hike, or view some exciting scenery by following only part of the route. We suggest taking at least the easy-to-moderate 1.6-mile round-trip hike to **Landscape Arch,** a long, thin ribbon of stone that is one of the most beautiful arches in the park. Allow about an hour. Past Landscape Arch the trail becomes more challenging, but offers numerous additional views, including the curious Double O Arch and a large, dark tower known as Dark Angel. You are now 2.5 miles from the trailhead. Allow about 3 hours round-trip.

Considered by many to be the park's best and most scenic hike, the 3-mile round-trip **Delicate Arch Trail** is a moderate-to-difficult hike, with slippery slickrock, no shade, and some steep drop-offs along a narrow cliff, but it rewards hikers with a dramatic and spectacular view of Delicate Arch. Along the way, you'll see the John Wesley Wolfe ranch and have an opportunity to take a side trip to a Ute petroglyph panel that includes drawings of horses and what may represent a bighorn sheep hunt. When you get back on the main trail, watch for collared lizards. Arches' largest lizard, up to a foot long, are usually bright green with stripes of yellow or rust, with a black collar. They feed primarily in the daytime, particularly enjoy insects and other lizards, and can stand and run on their large hind feet in pursuit of prey. (Didn't we see this in *Jurassic Park?*) Continuing along the trail, watch for Frame Arch, off to the right. Its main claim to fame is that numerous photographers have used it to "frame" a photo of Delicate Arch in the distance. Just past Frame Arch, the trail gets a little weird, having been blasted out from the cliff. Allow 2 to 3 hours. Those who opt out of this hike should consider driving to the Delicate Arch Viewpoint Trail, which provides an ideal location for a photo, preferably with the arch highlighted by a clear blue sky. From the parking area, it's about a 5-minute walk to the viewpoint.

The **Fiery Furnace Guided Hike** is a difficult and strenuous 2-mile round-trip naturalist-led hike to some of the most colorful formations in the park. Guided hikes are given into this restricted area twice daily in summer only, by reservation, and last from 2¹/₄ to 3 hours. Cost is $6 per adult and $3 per child over the age of 6. Permits to enter the Fiery Furnace on your own cost $2 per person, but there are no marked trails, and unless you are experienced in the Fiery Furnace, it is best to join a guided hike.

CAMPING IN THE PARK

Located at the north end of the park's scenic drive, **Devils Garden Campground** is Arches' only developed camping area. The 51 well-spaced sites are nestled among rocks, with plenty of piñon and juniper trees. Camping costs $10 per night, with no reservations; the campground fills early during the summer. No showers or RV hook-ups are available. There's water and flush toilets in the summer; chemical toilets and no water from November to mid-March.

3 Canyonlands National Park

Utah's largest national park is not for the sightseer out for a Sunday afternoon drive. It rewards those willing to spend time and energy—*lots* of energy—to explore the rugged backcountry. Sliced into districts by the Colorado and Green Rivers, the park's primary architects, this is a land of extremes: vast panoramas, dizzyingly deep canyons, dramatically steep cliffs, broad mesas, and towering red spires.

The most accessible part of Canyonlands is the Island in the Sky District, in the northern section of the park, where a paved road leads to sites such as Grand View Point, overlooking some 10,000 square miles of rugged wilderness. Island in the Sky also has several easy-to-moderate trails offering sweeping vistas of the park. A short walk provides views of Upheaval Dome, which resembles a large volcanic crater but may actually have been created by the crash of a meteorite. For the more adventurous, the 100-mile White Rim Road takes experienced mountain bikers and those with high-clearance four-wheel-drive vehicles on a winding loop tour through a vast array of scenery.

The Needles District, in the park's southeast corner, offers only a few viewpoints along the paved road, but numerous possibilities for hikers, backpackers, and those with high-clearance 4X4s. Named for its tall, red-and-white-striped rock pinnacles, this diverse district is home to impressive arches, including the 150-foot-tall Angel Arch, as well as grassy meadows and the confluence of the Green and Colorado Rivers. Backcountry visitors to the Needles District will also find ruins and rock art left by the ancestral Puebloans (also known as Anasazi) some 800 years ago.

Most park visitors don't get a close-up view of the Maze District, but instead see it off in the distance from Grand View Point at Island in the Sky or Confluence Overlook in the Needles District. That's because it's inhospitable and practically inaccessible. You'll need a lot of endurance and at least several days to see even a few of its sites, such as the appropriately named Lizard Rock and Beehive Arch. Hardy hikers can visit Horseshoe Canyon in one day, where they can see the Great Gallery, an 80-foot-long rock art panel.

The park is also accessible by boat, which is how explorer Major John Wesley Powell first saw the canyons in 1869, when he made his first trip down the Green to its confluence with the Colorado, and then even farther downstream, eventually reaching the Grand Canyon. River access is from the towns of Moab and Green River; several local companies there offer boat trips of various duration.

Among the cottonwoods and willows along the rivers, you'll find Canyonlands' greatest variety of wildlife. Watch for deer, beaver, an occasional bobcat, and various migratory birds. Elsewhere in the park, you're apt to see red-tailed hawks in search of a tasty rodent, as well as bighorn sheep, coyote, Colorado chipmunks, and white-tailed antelope squirrels.

JUST THE FACTS

No lodging facilities, restaurants, or even stores are located inside the national park. Most visitors use Moab as a base camp.

GETTING THERE/ACCESS POINTS   To reach the Island in the Sky Visitor Center, take U.S. 191 (which runs north to south through eastern Utah from Wyoming to Arizona) north to Utah 313, which you follow south into the park. It's 34 miles west of Moab. To reach the Needles Visitor Center, leave U.S. 191 at Utah 211, which you follow west into the park. It's 75 miles southwest of Moab. Getting to the Maze District is a bit more interesting. From I-70 west of Green River, take Utah 24 south. Watch for signs and follow two- and four-wheel-drive dirt roads east into the park.

INFORMATION & VISITOR CENTERS   For advance information on what to see in the park, plus hiking and four-wheel-drive trails and camping, contact Superintendent, **Canyonlands National Park,** 2282 SW Resource Blvd., Moab, UT 84532-8000 (☎ **435/259-7164**). It's best to write at least a month before your planned visit and to specify what type of information you need. The website for the park is www.nps.gov/cany.

Books, some very useful maps, and videos can be ordered from the nonprofit **Canyonlands Natural History Association,** 3031 South U.S. 191, Moab, UT 84532 (☎ **800/840-8978** or 435/259-6003; fax 435/259-8263). Some publications are available in foreign languages, and several videos can be purchased in either VHS or PAL formats. MasterCard and Visa are accepted. Those wanting to help the nonprofit association can join ($20 annually) and get a 20% discount on purchases.

Once you arrive in the area, you can get information at the **Moab Information Center,** located in the middle of town at the corner of Main and Center streets, and open from 8am to 9pm in the summer, with slightly shorter winter hours. The staff at this multi-agency visitor center includes representatives of the park service.

Canyonlands National Park operates two visitor centers—**Island in the Sky Visitor Center,** in the northern part of the park, and **Needles Visitor Center,** in the southern section—where you can get maps, free brochures on hiking trails, and most important, advice from rangers. We can't overemphasize how brutal the terrain at Canyonlands can be, and it's important that you not only know your own limitations, but also the limitations of your vehicle and other equipment.

FEES, REGULATIONS & BACKCOUNTRY PERMITS   Entry into the park (for up to 7 days) costs $10 per private vehicle or $5 per motorcycle, bicycle, or pedestrian. A $25 annual pass is also available.

Permits, available at either visitor center, are required for all overnight stays in the park except at the two established campgrounds. Permit reservations can be made in

Impressions

We glide along through a strange, weird, grand region. The landscape everywhere, away from the river, is of rock.

—Major John Wesley Powell, during his 1869
boat trip down the Green and Colorado Rivers

Canyonlands National Park

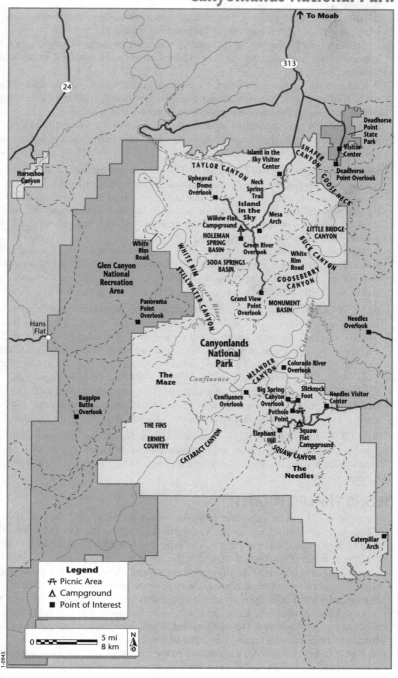

To Moab ↑

313

24

Horseshoe
Canyon

Deadhorse
Point State
Park

Visitor
Center

Island in the
Sky Visitor
Center

SHAFER CANYON

Deadhorse
Point Overlook

TAYLOR CANYON

GOOSE-NECK

Upheaval
Dome
Overlook

Neck
Spring
Trail

Island
in the
Sky

Mesa
Arch

LITTLE BRIDGE
CANYON

Willow Flat
Campground

HOLEMAN
SPRING
BASIN

Green River
Overlook

White
Rim
Road

BUCK CANYON

White
Rim
Road

GOOSEBERRY
CANYON

Glen Canyon
National
Recreation
Area

SODA SPRINGS
BASIN

WHITE RIM

STILLWATER CANYON

Green River

Grand View
Point
Overlook

MONUMENT
BASIN

Panorama
Point Overlook

Colorado River

Needles
Overlook

Hans
Flat

Canyonlands
National
Park

MEANDER CANYON

Confluence

The
Maze

Colorado River
Overlook

Bagpipe
Butte
Overlook

Confluence
Overlook

Big Spring
Canyon
Overlook

Slickrock
Foot

Needles Visitor
Center

Pothole
Point

THE FINS

ERNIES
COUNTRY

Elephant
Hill

Squaw
Flat
Campground

CATARACT CANYON

SQUAW CANYON

The
Needles

Caterpillar
Arch

Legend

⛺ Picnic Area

△ Campground

■ Point of Interest

0 ▭▭▭ 5 mi
8 km

N

1-0945

advance (☎ **435/259-4351**). For overnight four-wheel-drive and mountain-bike trips, permits cost $25; for overnight backpacking trips, $10.

There is also a $5 day-use fee for those visitors bringing motor vehicles, horses, or mountain bikes on roads into Salt Creek/Horse Canyon and Lavender Canyon in the Needles District.

Backcountry hikers should practice minimum-impact techniques, packing out all trash. Feeding or otherwise disturbing wildlife is prohibited, as is vandalizing or upsetting any natural feature of the park. Wood fires are also prohibited.

Dogs, which must be leashed at all times, are prohibited in public buildings, on all trails, and in the backcountry. This includes four-wheel-drive roads—dogs are not permitted even inside your vehicle.

SEASONS & AVOIDING THE CROWDS   Summers here are hot, and that's an understatement—temperatures occasionally reach 100°F. Winters can be cool or cold, dropping well below freezing at night, with light snow possible. The best time to visit, especially for hikers, is in the spring or fall, when daytime temperatures are usually from 60 to 80°F, and nights are cool. Late summer and early fall visitors should be prepared for afternoon thunderstorms.

Although Canyonlands does not get nearly as crowded as most other national parks in Utah, the summer is still the busiest time, and reservations for backcountry permits are recommended from spring through fall. As with most parks, if you want to escape humanity, pick the longest and most difficult trail you can handle.

SAFETY CONCERNS   Due to the extreme variety of terrain, the main safety problem at Canyonlands is that people underestimate the hazards. Rangers warn hikers to carry at least 1 gallon of water per person per day, be especially careful near cliff edges, avoid overexposure to the intense sun, and carry maps when going off into the backcountry. During lightning storms, avoid lone trees, high ridges, and cliff edges. Four-wheel-drive vehicle operators should be aware of their vehicles' limitations and carry extra food and emergency equipment. Also, anyone heading out into the backcountry should let someone know where they're going and when they plan to return. Traveling alone in Canyonlands is not the best idea.

RANGER PROGRAMS   On summer evenings at Squaw Flat campground in the Needles District, rangers offer campfire programs on various aspects of the park. Short morning talks are also presented during the summer at the Island in the Sky Visitor Center.

SEEING THE HIGHLIGHTS

Canyonlands is not an easy place to see in a short period of time. In fact, if your schedule permits only a day or less, we suggest skipping the Needles and Maze Districts entirely and driving directly to the **Island in the Sky Visitor Center.** After looking at the exhibits, drive to several of the overlooks, stopping along the way for a short hike or two. Make sure you stop at the **Grand View Point Overlook,** at the south end of the paved road. Among the trails we recommend for this quick trip is the **Grand View Trail,** especially scenic in late afternoon, when you literally get the "Grand View" of the park. Allow about 1¹/₂ hours for this easy 2-mile walk. We also recommend the **Upheaval Dome Overlook Trail,** which should take about a half hour, and brings you to a mile-wide crater of mysterious origins.

Perhaps a better choice for a quick visit to the park, especially for those with a bit of extra cash, is to take a guided tour—by four-wheel-drive vehicle, plane, or raft. See the "Moab" section of this chapter for a list of operators.

EXPLORING CANYONLANDS BY CAR

No driving tour has yet been designed to show off Canyonlands. The Island in the Sky District has about 20 miles of paved highway, some gravel roads accessible to two-wheel-drive vehicles, and several viewpoints. The Needles District has only 8 miles of paved roads and fewer viewpoints. Many (but not all) of Needles' viewpoints and trailheads are accessible only by high-clearance four-wheel-drive vehicles, mountain bikes, or plain old foot power. The Maze District has no paved roads. Essentially, both of the park's main roads lead to trailheads, and unless you plan to leave your car and hike for at least a half hour or so, it would be better to skip Canyonlands and spend your time instead at nearby Arches National Park, which is much more accessible by car.

Of course, if your "car" happens to be a serious 4X4, and you're equally serious about doing some hard-core four-wheeling, this is the park for you. See the "Sports & Outdoor Activities" section below. Due to constantly changing conditions of dirt roads, we strongly suggest that you discuss your plans with rangers before setting out.

A BIRD'S-EYE VIEW OF CANYONLANDS

Canyonlands is beautiful, but many of its most spectacular sections are difficult to get to, to say the least. One solution is to take to the air. **Redtail Aviation,** P.O. Box 515, Moab, UT 84532 (☎ **800/842-9251** or 435/259-7421), based at Moab's Canyonlands Field Airport, has been flying sightseeing tours over southeastern Utah since 1978, and offers several easy ways to see the most of Canyonlands and surrounding areas. A 1-hour flight covers all three of the park's districts, plus Dead Horse Point State Park (described later in this chapter), at about $60 per person. A 2-hour flight explores the same areas plus Capitol Reef National Park, Lake Powell, and Robber's Roost, where outlaw Butch Cassidy is said to have hidden out; cost is about $130 per person.

Slickrock Air Guides of Moab (☎ **800/332-2439** or 435/259-6216; fax 435/259-2226) offers a 1-hour scenic flight over Canyonlands National Park and Dead Horse State Park for about $70 per person. A 3-hour flight that takes in Canyonlands, Lake Powell (including Rainbow Bridge), Capitol Reef, and goes all the way to the edge of the Grand Canyon, costs about $200 per person.

SPORTS & OUTDOOR ACTIVITIES

FOUR-WHEELING   Unlike most national parks, where all motor vehicles and mountain bikes must stay on paved roads, Canyonlands has miles of rough four-wheel-drive roads where mechanized transport is king, and jacked-up jeeps with oversized tires rule the day. Four-wheelers must stay on designated 4X4 roads, but keep in mind that the term "road" can mean anything from a graded, well-marked, two-lane gravel byway to a pile of loose rocks with a sign that says "that-a-way." Many of the park's jeep roads are impassable during heavy rains and for a day or two after.

The best four-wheel-drive adventure in Canyonlands' Island in the Sky District is the ✪ **White Rim Road,** which runs some 100 miles, winding through the district and affording spectacular and ever-changing views, from broad panoramas of rock and canyon to close-ups of red and orange towers and buttes. A high-clearance 4X4 is necessary. Expect the journey to be slow, taking 2 to 3 days, although with the appropriate vehicle, it isn't really difficult. There are primitive campgrounds along the way, but reservations and backcountry permits are needed. (See "Fees,

Canyonlands' Creatures Great & Small

You'll find a fascinating mixture of mountain and desert animals in Canyonlands, depending on the time of year and particular location within the park. The best times to see most wildlife are early and late in the day, especially in the summer when the midday sun drives all Canyonlands residents in search of shade. Throughout the park you'll probably hear—if not see—coyotes, and it's likely you'll spot white-tailed antelope squirrels and other rodents scampering among the rocks as well. Watch for the elusive and rather antisocial bighorn sheep along isolated cliffs, where you might also see a golden eagle or turkey vulture soaring above the rocks in search of food. In the little pools of water in slickrock that appear after rainstorms, you're likely to see tadpole shrimp—1-inch-long crustaceans that look as though they would be more at home in an ocean. Your best chances of seeing deer, beaver, and other mammals are along riverbanks and the few natural springs in the park.

Regulations & Backcountry Permits," above.) Mountain bikers also enjoy this trail, especially when accompanying a four-wheel-drive vehicle that can carry supplies and equipment.

Four-wheeling in the Needles District can be an end in itself, with a variety of exciting routes, or simply a means to get to some of the more interesting and remote hiking trails and camping spots. Four-wheel-drive fans will find one of their ultimate challenges on the **Elephant Hill Jeep Road,** which begins at a well-marked turnoff near Squaw Flat Campground. Although most of the 10-mile trail is only moderately difficult, the stretch over Elephant Hill itself near the beginning can be a nightmare, with steep, rough slickrock, drifting sand, loose rock, and treacherous ledges. Coming down the hill, you'll reach one switchback that requires you to back to the edge of a steep cliff. This is also a favorite of mountain bikers, although bikes will have to be walked on some stretches because of an abundance of sand and rocks. The route offers views of numerous rock formations, from striped needles to balanced rocks, plus steep cliffs and rock "stairs," and side trips can add another 30 miles. Allow from 8 hours to 3 days. Backcountry permits are needed for overnight trips.

For a spectacular view of the Colorado River, the **Colorado River Overlook Road** can't be beat. This 14-mile round-trip is popular with four-wheelers, backpackers, and mountain bikers. Considered among the park's easiest 4X4 roads, the first part is very easy indeed, accessible by high-clearance two-wheel-drives, but the second half has a few rough and rocky sections that require four-wheel-drive. Starting at the Needles Visitor Center parking lot, the trail takes you past numerous panoramic vistas to a spectacular 360-degree view of the park and the Colorado River some 1,000 feet below.

BIKING   Bikes of any kind are prohibited on hiking trails or in the backcountry, except on designated two- and four-wheel-drive roads. Road bikes are of little use in Canyonlands, except for getting to and from trailheads, viewpoints, visitor centers, and campgrounds in the Island in the Sky and Needles Districts. See "Mountain Biking," below.

HIKING   With little shade, no reliable water sources, and temperatures soaring to 100°F in the summer, rangers strongly advise that hikers carry at least 1 gallon of water per person per day, along with sunscreen, a hat, and all the usual hiking and emergency equipment. If you expect to do some serious hiking, try to plan your trip for the spring or fall, when conditions are much more hospitable. Because some of the trails may be confusing, hikers attempting the longer ones should also carry good topographic maps, available at park visitor centers and at stores in Moab. While dozens of hiking possibilities exist throughout the park, we have chosen a select few of various ability requirements, listed by district.

Island in the Sky: The **Mesa Arch Trail** provides the casual visitor with an easy half-mile (round-trip) self-guided nature walk through an area forested with piñon and juniper trees, mountain mahogany, cactus, and a plant called Mormon tea, from which Mormon pioneers made a tealike beverage. The loop trail's main scenic attraction is an arch, made of Navajo sandstone, that hangs precariously on the edge of a cliff, framing a spectacular view of nearby mountains. Allow about a half hour.

Another half-hour hike, although a bit steeper and moderately strenuous, leads to the **Upheaval Dome Overlook.** Upheaval Dome doesn't fit with the rest of the Canyonlands' terrain—it's obviously not the result of gradual erosion like the rest of the park, but rather a dramatic deformity in which rocks have been pushed into a domelike structure. At one time it was theorized that the dome was formed by a hidden volcano, but a more recent theory suggests a meteorite may have struck the earth here some 60 million years ago. This hike is about 1 mile round-trip; a second overlook adds about a half mile and 15 minutes.

An easy 2-mile hike, especially scenic at sunset, is the **Grand View Trail.** Allow about 1¹/₂ hours. The trail follows the canyon rim from Grand View Point, showing off numerous canyons and rock formations, the Colorado River, and distant mountains.

A bit more strenuous is the 5-mile **Neck Spring Trail,** which starts about a half mile south of the Island in the Sky Visitor Center. Allow 3 to 4 hours for this hike, which follows the paths that animals and early ranchers created to reach water at two springs. You'll see water troughs, hitching posts, rusty cans, and the ruins of an old cabin. Plus, because of the water source, you'll encounter types of vegetation not usually seen in the park, such as maidenhair ferns and gamble oak. The water also draws wildlife, including mule deer, bighorn sheep, ground squirrels, and hummingbirds. If you climb to the top of the rim, you'll get a beautiful view of the canyons and even the Henry Mountains, some 60 miles away.

Those looking for more of a challenge can explore the **Lathrop Trail,** which meanders some 5 miles down into the canyon to the White Rim Road, affording beautiful views as you descend. Allow 5 to 7 hours for this strenuous hike over steep terrain and loose rock, remembering that it's another 5 miles back. It is possible to continue down to the Colorado River from here (another 4 miles each way), but check with rangers about the feasibility of this overnight trip before attempting it.

Needles: Hiking trails here are generally not too tough, but keep in mind that slickrock can live up to its name, and that little shade will be found along most of these trails. One relatively easy hike is the ¹/₃-mile **Roadside Ruin Trail,** a short, self-guided nature walk that takes about a half-hour round-trip and leads to a prehistoric granary, probably used by the ancestral Puebloans some 700 to 1,000 years ago to store corn, nuts, and other foods. Although easy, this trail can be muddy when wet.

For a bit more of a challenge, try the **Slickrock Foot Trail,** a 2.4-mile loop that leads to several viewpoints and takes 2 or 3 hours. Slickrock, a general term for any bare rock surface, can be slippery, especially when wet. Viewpoints show off the stair-step topography of the area, from its colorful canyons and cliffs to its flat mesas and striped needles.

From **Elephant Hill Trailhead** you can follow several interconnecting trails into the backcountry. The road to the trailhead is gravel, but is graded and driveable in most two-wheel-drive passenger cars; those in large vehicles such as motor homes, however, will want to avoid it. The 10.5-mile round-trip Elephant Hill–Druid Arch hike can be accomplished in 4 to 6 hours and is moderately difficult, with some steep drop-offs and quite a bit of slickrock. But the views are well worth it, as you hike through narrow rock canyons, past colorful spires and pinnacles, and on to the huge Druid Arch, its dark rock somewhat resembling the stone structures at Stonehenge, England.

Another worthwhile jaunt is on the **Confluence Overlook Trail,** an 11-mile round-trip day or overnight hike that leads to a spectacular view overlooking the confluence of the Green and Colorado Rivers and the 1,000-foot-deep gorges they've carved. The hike is moderately difficult, with steep drop-offs and little shade, but shows off splendidly the many colors of the Needles District, as well as views into the Maze District of the park. Allow 4 to 6 hours.

For those staying at Squaw Flat Campground, the **Big Spring–Squaw Canyon Loop** is a convenient, moderately difficult 7.5-mile loop over steep slickrock that can be hiked in 3 to 4 hours. The trail winds through woodlands of piñon and juniper, offering views of the needles for which the district is named, plus nearby cliffs and mesas as well as distant mountains. Watch for wildflowers from late spring through summer.

✪ **Horseshoe Canyon:** This detached section of the park was added to Canyon-lands in 1971 mainly because of its Great Gallery, an 80-foot-long rock art panel with larger-than-life human figures, believed to be at least several thousand years old. Only one road leads into the Horseshoe Canyon Unit, and you'll have to drive some 120 miles (one-way) from Moab and then hike 6.5 miles (round-trip) to see the rock art. To get to the area by two-wheel-drive vehicle, take I-70 west from Green River about 11 miles to U.S. 24, go south about 24 miles to the Horseshoe Canyon turnoff (near the WATCH FOR SAND DRIFTS sign), turn left, and follow this maintained dirt road for about 30 miles to the canyon's west rim, where you can park. From here it's a 1.5-mile hike down an 800-foot slope to the canyon floor, where you turn right and go 1.75 miles to the Great Gallery. There is no camping in Horseshoe Canyon, but primitive camping is available on Bureau of Land Management property on the rim just outside the park boundary.

MOUNTAIN BIKING Because bikes are not permitted on hiking trails, mountain bikers find themselves sharing four-wheel-drive roads with motor vehicles of every size, plus occasional hikers and horseback riders. Since some of the four-wheel-drive roads have deep sand in spots—which can turn into quicksand when wet—mountain biking may not be as much fun here as you'd expect, although it certainly is a challenge. It's wise to ask rangers about conditions on specific roads before setting out. Rides popular with mountain bikers include the Elephant Hill and Colorado River Overlook jeep roads, both in the Needles District. The 100-mile White Rim Road, in the Island in the Sky District, also makes a great mountain-bike trip, especially for bikers who can arrange for an accompanying 4X4 vehicle to carry water, food, and camping gear. See the "Four-Wheeling" section above.

CAMPING

There are two developed campgrounds in the park. In the Island in the Sky District, **Willow Flat Campground,** at an elevation of 6,200 feet, has 12 sites and virtually no facilities; camping is free here. In the Needles District, **Squaw Flat Campground,** at an elevation of 5,100 feet, has 26 sites, pit toilets, and trucked-in water in the summer; the fee is $8 per night. Neither campground accepts reservations. Primitive campsites are also available throughout the park for four-wheelers and backpackers (see "Fees, Regulations & Backcountry Permits," above).

Near Island in the Sky, the campground at **Dead Horse Point State Park** has electric hookups (see "Nearby Places of Interest," below). Additional camping facilities are available on nearby public lands administered by the Bureau of Land Management and U.S. Forest Service, and commercial campgrounds are located in Moab and Monticello. See the "Moab" section earlier in this chapter.

NEARBY PLACES OF INTEREST
DEAD HORSE POINT STATE PARK

One of Utah's most scenic state parks, this might be considered a junior Canyonlands. The Dead Horse Point Overlook offers a splendid view across the river to the nearby national park, as well as down past seven distinctive and colorful layers of rock to the Colorado River. A strip of land only 30 yards wide connects the point with the rest of the mesa, and in the late 1800s this natural corral was used by cowboys, who herded wild horses in, roped the ones they wanted, and left the rest to find their way out. According to one story, a herd of rejected horses couldn't find their way off the point and died of thirst within sight of the Colorado River, 2,000 feet below.

Just the Facts

From Canyonlands' Island in the Sky Visitor Center, drive north out of the park for 3$\frac{1}{2}$ miles to the intersection with Utah 313, and turn right. The state park's visitor center is about 7$\frac{1}{2}$ miles down the road. From Moab, head north on U.S. 191 for 16$\frac{1}{2}$ miles, and turn south on Utah 313 for about 20 miles to the park (passing the access road for Canyonlands National Park).

To receive a brochure on the park and/or answers to specific questions, contact **Dead Horse Point State Park,** P.O. Box 609, Moab, UT 84532-0609 (☎ **435/ 259-2614**).

The visitor center/museum is located near the entrance to the park, with exhibits on the park's geology, history, plants, and animals. Rangers are on hand to assign campsites and answer questions; books, posters, maps, and souvenirs are available for purchase. A video presentation on the human and geologic history of the area is shown by request in the visitor center, and during the summer, nightly campfire programs and short guided walks are scheduled.

Day-use fee is $4 per vehicle (up to 8 people), or $1.50 per person who enters the park on foot, by bike, or by motorcycle. In addition to the usual regulations requiring vehicles and bikes to stay on roads and pets to be leashed, visitors are asked to conserve water (which has to be trucked in) and to avoid stepping on cyanobacterial crusts—the fragile, bumpy, black mats composed of bacteria, algae, lichen, moss, and fungi that you'll often see along trails and roads.

Exploring the Park

Dead Horse Point Overlook is about 2 miles from the visitor center via a paved road. A short, wheelchair-accessible paved walkway leads from the parking area to a platform overlook that provides a magnificent panoramic view of the deep red canyons, the Colorado River, and distant mountains. The lighting is best either early or late in the day, but this is a worthwhile stop at any time.

Although you can easily drive to Dead Horse Point Overlook, it's a fun hike if you have the time. The main trail starts at the visitor center, follows the east rim of the mesa to the overlook, and returns on the west side. The loop is 4 miles long and fairly easy, and you can add another 3 miles in side trips out to overlook points. Along the way you'll see a variety of rock formations while scrambling over the slickrock.

Another 3.5-mile loop leads from the visitor center to a series of potholes (holes in the rock that catch rainwater and may contain tadpole shrimp and other aquatic life) and a canyon overlook.

Although it would seem at first that no animals could endure this barren, rocky terrain, you're likely to see ground squirrels, rabbits, lizards, and raptors. There are desert bighorn sheep in the area, but they're rarely seen in the park.

Camping

The park's attractive campground has 21 sites, all with electric hookups and covered picnic tables, plus flush toilets and an RV dump station. However, because water must be trucked in, there are no showers, and campers are asked to conserve the small amount of water available. Because the electric outlets are hidden on the underside of picnic tables, which may be 50 or 60 feet from the site parking area, those with recreational vehicles will likely need long extension cords. Camping costs $9, and reservations are accepted from mid-March through mid-October with a $5 processing fee (☎ **800/322-3770**). Those without reservations will find that the campground usually fills by mid-afternoon during the summer.

NEWSPAPER ROCK

This former state park, now administered by the Bureau of Land Management's **San Juan Resource Area office** (☎ **435/587-2141**), is famous for a large sandstone panel covered with petroglyphs that date from 1,500 to 200 years ago, from the Fremont people to the ancestral Puebloans, and finally the Utes and Navajo. The panel also includes initials and names left by early white settlers, including one J. P. Gonzales of Monticello, who herded sheep in the canyon in the early part of the 20th century. The site is located in Indian Creek Canyon, along the road to Canyonlands' Needles District, Utah 211, about 12 miles west of U.S. 191. Camping is free at a primitive campground located just across the road from Newspaper Rock, with dispersed camping for about 8 tents or small RVs, but no drinking water. Vault toilets are located at Newspaper Rock.

4 North & West of the Parks

GREEN RIVER

Travelers heading north to Salt Lake City or west toward Nevada will undoubtedly pass through the village of Green River, which sits on I-70 along the banks of the Green River about 54 miles northwest of Moab, and offers an interesting break.

The **John Wesley Powell River History Museum,** 885 E. Main St., Green River (☎ **435/564-3427**), details the phenomenal river expedition of explorer John Wesley Powell, a one-armed Civil War veteran who explored the Green and Colorado Rivers in the late 1800s. Museum exhibits also discuss the geology of the region and the history of river running, from a replica of Powell's heavy wooden boat, the *Emma Dean,* to examples of boats and rafts used on the river since then. A 20-minute multimedia program on Powell's adventures is shown throughout the day. Admission to the museum costs $2 for adults, $1 for students, and $5 for families. It's open daily from 8am to 8pm in the summer, and daily from 9am to 5pm in the winter.

Green River State Park, on Green River Road, P.O. Box 637, Green River, UT 84525-0093 (☎ **435/564-3633**), is a lush green oasis with big old Russian olive and cottonwood trees. Located right on the river, the park has a boat ramp for launching your raft or canoe, but be aware that once you start heading downstream you'll need a motor or mighty powerful arms to fight the current back to the park. The park also has a 9-hole championship golf course (☎ **435/564-8882**). Situated right along the river, it's open year-round (weather permitting), and has a pro shop, snacks, and carts ($4 per person for 9 holes). Fees are $8 for 9 holes and $15 for 18. Day-use admission costs $3 per vehicle or $1 for walk-ins, bicyclists, and motorcyclists. The shady 42-site campground, open year-round, has modern rest rooms and hot showers, but no RV hookups. Camping costs $10; reservations are accepted from mid-March through mid-October, using MasterCard or Visa, with a $5 nonrefundable fee (☎ **800/322-3770**).

Several river-running companies offer day and overnight trips on the Green. These include **Moki Mac River Expeditions, Inc.,** P.O. Box 71242, Salt Lake City, UT 84171-0242 (☎ **800/284-7280** for reservations). Cost for a day trip, including lunch, is about $50 per adult and $39 for children ages 15 and under.

For additional information on Green River, stop at the **Green River Information Center** in the John Wesley Powell River History Museum (see above), or contact the **Grand County Travel Council,** P.O. Box 550, Moab, UT 84532 (☎ **800/635-6622** or 435/259-8825; fax 435/259-1376).

A MAGICAL STATE PARK

Goblin Valley State Park, P.O. Box 637, Green River, UT 84525-0637 (☎ **435/564-3633**), is filled with fantasyland rock formations, hence its name. In the light of the full moon, the little munchkins almost come alive, with shadows giving them facelike features. Bikes and motor vehicles are restricted to paved areas, but visitors are welcome to hike among the goblins, and even to climb onto them with caution. Park residents include kit foxes, rabbits, and lizards.

The 29-site campground is laid out in a semicircle among tall multicolored rocks of varying heights. Facilities include showers and a dump station, but no RV hookups. Day-use fee is $3, camping is $10, and showering (if not camping) costs $2.

To get to the park from Green River, head west on I-70 for about 10 miles to exit 147, and turn south on Utah 24 for about 25 miles to the turnoff for the park. Go about 5 miles west on a paved road and then left on a dirt road for another 7 miles—this road is very rough, resembling an unending washboard, although plans to pave it are being made.

TO THE DINOSAURS OF PRICE & BEYOND

The town of Price, founded in 1879, began as a railroad and coal-mining center. A popular midway stopover for those traveling between southern Utah's national parks and the Salt Lake City area, Price is gaining in reputation as a destination, especially for those interested in dinosaurs.

Price is 119 miles from Moab and 63 miles from the town of Green River. From I-70 exit 156 follow U.S. 191/6 northwest 57 miles to Price. Take the business loop through the center of town and follow signs to the information center, located in the town's municipal building, to pick up maps and brochures on the area, including a walking tour brochure to the town's seven buildings listed on the National Register of Historic Sites. For advance information, contact **Carbon County Travel Bureau,** P.O. Box 1037, Price, UT 84501 (☎ **800/842-0789** or 435/637-3009; fax 435/637-7010).

Lodging possibilities in Price, both off U.S. 6 exit 240, include the **Holiday Inn,** 838 Westwood Blvd., Price, UT 84501 (☎ **800/HOLIDAY** or 435/435-8880;

fax 435/637-7707), with rates from $46 to $59 double; and the **Super 8,** 181 N. Hospital Dr. (☎ **800/800-8000** or 435/637-8088; fax 435/637-8483), with rates for two in the $50 to $54 range.

Located adjacent to the visitor center at 200 E. 100 North is one of the area's top attractions, the **CEU Prehistoric Museum** (☎ **435/637-5060**), operated by the College of Eastern Utah. Among the exhibits in this excellent museum are the huge skeletons of an allosaurus, a Utah raptor, and a strange-looking duck-billed dinosaur known as the prosaurolophus. Watch for the large Colombian mammoth, with its long tusks, that resembles a modern elephant and roamed this area over 10,000 years ago. You'll also see exhibits on the early Native American peoples of Utah, describing how they lived and adapted to changing environments. Included are displays of rare 1,000-year-old clay figures created by the Fremont Indians. Children will encounter a variety of interactive exhibits designed just for them, including a sandbox where they can do their own archaeological dig. Museum hours are from 9am to 6pm daily from April through September, and from 9am to 5pm Monday through Saturday from October through March. Admission is free but donations are welcome.

To see more dinosaurs, you'll have to drive about 30 miles out of town. Designated a National Natural Landmark in 1966, the **Cleveland-Lloyd Dinosaur Quarry** is a major world source of dinosaur fossils, where over 30 complete skeletons, 12,000 bones, and several dinosaur eggs have been discovered. The visitor center has a complete allosaurus skeletal reconstruction and a stegosaurus wall mount on display. At the quarry itself, you can watch scientists at work and see bones in place as they were found. The quarry is open from 10am to 5pm weekends, Easter to Memorial Day, and then daily through Labor Day. For advance information, contact the Bureau of Land Management office in Price at ☎ **435/637-4584.** To get there from Price, take Utah 10 southwest about 15 miles to Utah 155 south, following DINOSAUR signs another 15 miles to the quarry. The last 8 miles are on a gravel road; allow about 1 hour from Price.

For a look at somewhat more recent history of the area, go north of Price 11 miles on U.S. 191/6 to the town of Helper and follow signs to the **Western Mining and Railroad Museum,** 296 S. Main St. (☎ **435/472-3009**). Crammed into the four stories of the old Helper Hotel, built in 1913, are thousands of artifacts and exhibits from the area's mining and railroad days of the late 1800s and early 1900s. These include a complete jail cell, a simulated coal mine, mine models, wine- and whiskey-making equipment from Prohibition days (when bootlegging was a major business here), pictures of mine disasters, lots of railroad equipment and photos, and operating model trains. You can watch a 12-minute video on the area's history; wander the outdoor displays, which include mining equipment from the early 1900s; and browse the gift shop. The museum is open in summer from 10am to 6pm Monday through Saturday, and in winter from noon until 5pm Tuesday through Saturday. Admission is free, although suggested donations are $2 per person or $5 per family.

A NEARBY STATE PARK

Scofield State Park, P.O. Box 166, Price, UT 84501-0166 (☎ **435/448-9449** in summer, ☎ 435/637-8497 in winter), located about 35 miles northwest of Price, is Utah's highest state park at 7,600 feet. The park's picturesque lake, nestled among the hills, offers fishing and boating in the summer; in winter, the main draws are ice fishing, cross-country skiing, and snowmobiling. There are two developed campgrounds: One at the north end of the lake, with few trees, has modern rest rooms but no showers; the other, located a few miles south on the east side of the lake and over-looking it, has aspen trees at almost every site, as well as showers and a boat ramp. Both have dump stations but neither have RV hookups. It's a lovely place to camp in summer—nights are always comfortably cool at this elevation. Day-use fee is $3; camping costs $10. The park facilities are closed from December through April, but the lake is accessible.

To get to Scofield State Park from Price, head northwest on U.S. 6 for 25 miles, then turn left (west) onto Utah 6 for another 10 miles.

17 The Four Corners Area

The major archaeological center of the United States, the Four Corners area—where the borders of Colorado, New Mexico, Arizona, and Utah meet—is surrounded by a vast complex of ancient villages that dominated this entire region a thousand years ago. Here among the reddish-brown rocks, abandoned canyons, and flat mesas, you'll discover another world, once ruled by the ancestral Puebloans (also known as Anasazi), and today largely the domain of the Navajo.

Wander among the scenic splendors of Monument Valley, where the Navajo still tend their sheep and weave their rugs, and then step back in time to discover a civilization that vanished more than seven centuries ago, leaving behind more questions than answers. Those particularly interested in the ancient and modern Native American tribes of the Four Corners region will want to continue their travels into Arizona, New Mexico, and Colorado. Frommer's Travel Guides to those states can provide additional information.

The southeast corner of Utah is sparsely populated—downright desolate and deserted, some might say—and you're not going to find your favorite chain motel, fast-food restaurant, or brand of gasoline right around every corner. That's assuming you can even *find* a corner. So, many travelers discover a place they like, rent a room or campsite for a few days, and take day trips. We've laid out this chapter using the town of Bluff as a base; from there, we'll take you on a series of excursions that ring the town. First, we'll head southwest to Monument Valley, then northwest to Natural Bridges National Monument, then north to Edge of the Cedars State Historical Monument. (If you're driving to Bluff from the north on U.S. 191, you'll actually pass Edge of the Cedars on your way here, just north of Blanding.) Then we'll head east, to Hovenweep National Monument and Four Corners Monument. Finally, we'll venture beyond Utah's borders into Colorado, where we'll visit Mesa Verde National Park, site of the most impressive cliff dwellings in the United States.

1 A Base Camp in Bluff

We particularly enjoy the tiny village of Bluff, which sits near the intersection of U.S. 191 and U.S. 163 with roads leading off toward all the attractions of the Four Corners. With a population of almost 300, Bluff is one of those comfortable little places with most basic services, but not a lot more. Founded by Mormon pioneers in 1880, the town's site had already been home to both ancestral Puebloan and Navajo peoples. Local businesses distribute a free historic walking and biking tour guide that shows where ancient rock art and archaeological sites are located, as well as some of Bluff's handsome stone homes from the late 19th century.

WHITE-WATER RAFTING TRIPS & OTHER ORGANIZED TOURS OF THE AREA

Situated along the San Juan River, Bluff is a center for river rafting. ✪ **Wild Rivers Expeditions** (☎ **800/422-7654** or 435/672-2244; fax 435/672-2365) offers river trips on the San Juan that are not only fun, but also educational. Led by archaeology and geology professionals, boaters see dozens of Native American sites along the river plus spectacular rock formations. Trips, ranging from one full day to several weeks in length, are offered from March through October, starting at $75 for the full-day trip, which includes lunch.

Guided tours into Monument Valley Navajo Tribal Park and other scenic areas and archaeological sites surrounding the town are offered by **Far Out Expeditions** (P.O. Box 307, Bluff, UT 84512; ☎ **435/672-2294**). Prices start at $75 per person for a full-day Monument Valley tour in a four-wheel-drive vehicle, including lunch. Naturalist-led walking expeditions to Bluff-area canyons and archaeological sites are also available, at about $45 per person (no meal provided).

OTHER THINGS TO SEE & DO

About 2¹/₅ miles west of town is **Sand Island Recreation Site**, operated by the Bureau of Land Management. Located along the San Juan River among cottonwoods, Russian olives, and salt cedar, this area offers boating (there's a boat ramp) and fishing. Boaters must obtain river permits in advance from the Bureau of Land Management, P.O. Box 7, Monticello, UT 84535 (☎ **435/587-2144**). Nestled between the river and a high rock bluff, you'll find picnic tables, vault toilets, and graveled campsites; camping is free for river-permit holders, $6 per night for those without permits. There are no trash receptacles, so everything must be packed out. About a half mile west of the boat launch are petroglyphs.

Goosenecks State Park lies on a rim high above the San Juan River and received its name from the sharp curves in the river below. The park is about 23¹/₂ miles from Bluff, just off the route to Monument Valley Navajo Tribal Park. Head west on U.S. 163 for about 20 miles, turn north (right) on Utah 261 for about a mile, and then west (left) on Utah 316 for about 2¹/₂ miles to the park. You'll find picnic tables, trash cans, pit toilets, and two shelters in a gravelly open area at the end of the paved road, but no water. The main draw is the view out over the twisting, turning river below, which is quite spectacular. Primitive camping is permitted, at no charge.

WHERE TO STAY, CAMP & DINE

Facilities in this part of the state are few and far between, but you can find lodging, restaurants, vehicle fuel, and supplies in Bluff, Blanding, Monticello, and Monument Valley. For information, contact the **San Juan County Travel Council**, P.O. Box 490, Monticello, UT 84535 (☎ **800/574-4386** or 435/587-3235; fax 435/587-2425).

You'll find quiet, clean, and inexpensive rooms at **Recapture Lodge,** P.O. Box 309, Bluff, UT 84512 (☎ **435/672-2281;** fax 435/672-2284). This older, well-kept motel on the main street near the center of Bluff has an attractive western decor. A nature trail follows the San Juan River along the back of the motel property. Most of the 35 rooms contain two double beds or one queen, with shower/tub combos;

several budget rooms are available with shower only and one double bed. The motel has air-conditioning and televisions, but no room telephones. Rooms are also available in a nearby historic home for large families and groups. Rates for two range from $34 to $48. Local room tax adds almost 9%. Pets are welcome.

Campgrounds include **Cadillac Ranch RV Park,** U.S. 191 on the east side of town (☎ **800/538-6195** or 435/672-2262), a down-home sort of place with sites around a small fishing lake, where there's no license needed and no extra charge for fishing. There are 20 RV sites (17 with full hookups, 3 with water and electric only) and 15 tent sites, modern rest rooms with showers, coin-operated laundry, dishwashing area, and free firewood. Plans are underway to put in an RV dump station. The campground is open year-round, although water is turned off in the winter. Cost per site is $16; paddleboats can be rented at $4 for a half hour; and the park also offers boarding facilities for horses.

The **Cottonwood Steakhouse**, on U.S. 191 on the west side of town (☎ **435/672-2282**), is an Old West–style restaurant where the price of your meal includes a western melodrama complete with shoot-out. Solid western fare is served, including a 16-ounce T-bone steak, BBQ chicken or ribs, and 12-ounce rib-eye steak, plus specials such as rainbow trout. Dinners come with a large salad and western-grilled potatoes or baked beans. Diners sit at picnic tables, both inside the restaurant and outside under cottonwood trees. Portions are generous, with dinners priced from $12.95 to $19.95 and the child's plate at $5.95 (MC, V). The restaurant is open daily, March through mid-November, from 5pm in spring and fall, and from 6pm in summer. Beer is available.

For great basic food throughout the day, stop at the **Turquoise Restaurant**, in downtown Bluff (☎ **435/672-2279**). This is where locals hang out and solve the problems of the world. Breakfast includes all the usual items plus fresh-baked muffins—usually banana-nut or blueberry—while lunch offers sandwiches, soups, and salads. For dinner, there's roast beef, crispy fried chicken, country-fried steak, grilled pork chops, and fantail shrimp. Homemade cookies and pies are baked fresh daily. The children's menu is available to all ages. Breakfast and lunch cost from $3 to $6, and dinner from $6 to $9. American Express, Discover, MasterCard and Visa are accepted. Hours are 7:30am to 9pm daily.

2 Monument Valley Navajo Tribal Park

You've seen Monument Valley's majestic stone towers, delicately carved arches, lonely windswept buttes, forbidding cliffs, and mesas covered in sagebrush. You may have seen the proud Navajo gazing out across his land, herding sheep, or weaving a beautiful rug. Perhaps you didn't know you were in Monument Valley, instead believing this to be Tombstone, Arizona, or Dodge City, Kansas, or New Mexico, or Colorado. And possibly you couldn't fully appreciate the deep reddish brown colors of the rocks or incredible blue of the sky, which lost a bit of their brilliance in black and white.

For most of us, Monument Valley *is* the Old West. We've seen it dozens of times in movie theaters, on television, and in magazine and billboard advertisements. This all started in 1938, when Harry Goulding, who had been operating a trading post for local Navajo for about 15 years, convinced Hollywood director John Ford that Ford's current project, *Stagecoach,* should be shot in Monument Valley. Released the following year, *Stagecoach* not only put Monument Valley on the map, but also launched the career of a little-known actor by the name of John Wayne.

Ford and other Hollywood directors were attracted to Monument Valley then by the same elements that draw visitors today. This is the genuine, untamed American

West, with a simple, unspoiled beauty of carved stone, blowing sand, and rich colors, all compliments of Mother Nature. These same erosional forces of wind and water carved the surrounding scenic wonders of the Grand Canyon, Glen Canyon, and the rest of the spectacular red rock country of southern Utah and northern Arizona. But here the result is different: Colors seem deeper, natural rock bridges are almost perfect circles, and the vast emptiness of the land around them gives the towering stone monoliths an unequaled sense of drama.

JUST THE FACTS

Operated as a tribal park by the Navajo Nation (the country's largest tribe), Monument Valley straddles the border of southeast Utah and northeast Arizona. U.S. 163 goes through the valley from north to south, and a tribal park access road runs east to west.

GETTING THERE   Monument Valley is 50 miles southwest of Bluff; 150 miles south of Moab; 160 miles west of Cortez, Colorado; and 395 miles south of Salt Lake City.

From Moab, Monticello, and most points in eastern Utah, take U.S. 191 south to the village of Bluff, turn west (right), and follow U.S. 163 to Monument Valley. An alternative is to turn off Utah 95 south onto Utah 261 just east of Natural Bridges National Monument, follow Utah 261 to U.S. 163, turn southwest, and follow U.S. 163 to Monument Valley. This latter route is quite scenic, but because of switchbacks and steep grades is not recommended for motor homes or vehicles pulling trailers. Those coming from Arizona can take east–west U.S. 160 to U.S. 163, turn north, and follow it into Monument Valley.

INFORMATION & VISITOR CENTERS   For a brochure on Monument Valley and answers to questions, contact **Monument Valley Navajo Tribal Park,** P.O. Box 360289, Monument Valley, UT 84536 (☎ **435/727-3353** or 435/727-3287); or the **Navajo Parks and Recreation Department,** P.O. Box 9000, Window Rock, AZ 86515 (☎ **520/871-6647**).

The **visitor center/museum** is located about 4 miles east of U.S. 163 on the Monument Valley access road. Here you'll find a viewing deck, exhibits on the geology and human history of the valley, a gift shop, and a restaurant that serves three meals daily, featuring Navajo and American dishes.

HOURS, FEES & REGULATIONS   The tribal park is open daily from 7am to 7pm from May through September and from 8am to 5pm from October through April. It is closed Christmas and New Year's Day plus the afternoon of Thanksgiving Day.

Admission costs $2.50 for those from 8 to 59 years old, $1 for those 60 and older, and free for children under 8. National Park passes are not accepted. An extra fee is charged for tour busses.

Since this is part of the Navajo Nation, laws here differ somewhat from those in Utah, Arizona, or on public lands. All alcoholic beverages are prohibited within the boundaries of the Navajo reservation. Visitors must stay on the self-guided Valley Drive unless accompanied by an approved guide, and rock climbing and cross-country hiking are prohibited. Although photography for personal use is permitted, permission is required to photograph Navajo residents and their property, and you will usually need to pay them. All commercial photography requires a permit from the tribal government in Window Rock.

Both Utah and Arizona are on mountain time, and although the state of Arizona does not recognize daylight saving time, the Navajo Nation does.

A BIRD'S-EYE VIEW OF MONUMENT VALLEY

Slickrock Air Guides of Moab (☎ **800/332-2439** or 435/259-6216; fax 435/259-2226) offers a 2-hour scenic flight from Moab that includes Monument Valley, Canyonlands National Park, and Natural Bridges National Monument. Cost is about $140 per person.

EXPLORING MONUMENT VALLEY BY CAR

Driving the 17-mile self-guided loop lets you see most of the major scenic attractions of Monument Valley at your own pace, and at the lowest cost. The dirt road is a bit rough—not recommended for low-slung sports cars or vehicles longer than 24 feet, although it is passable for smaller motor homes. The road's first half mile is the worst, and you have to drive it both at the beginning and end of the loop. There are no rest rooms, drinking water, or other facilities along the route. Allow about 2 hours.

A free brochure and a more detailed booklet ($1) provide rough maps and information on 11 numbered sites, such as The Mittens—rock formations that resemble (you guessed it) a pair of mittens—and the aptly named Elephant and Camel Buttes, Totem Pole, and The Thumb. You'll also see Yei-Bi-Chei, a rock formation that resembles a Navajo holy man; and John Ford Point, a favorite filming location of famed Hollywood director John Ford, where he shot scenes from *Stagecoach, The Searchers,* and *Cheyenne Autumn,* among others. It's still popular with producers—watch for crews working on feature films, television shows, or commercials as you drive the loop.

GUIDED TOURS

Guided tours are the best way to see Monument Valley—without a guide, visitors are restricted to the 17-mile scenic drive, but ✪ **Navajo guides** can take you into lesser-visited areas of the tribal park, give you their personal perspectives on the landscape, and often arrange weaving demonstrations and other activities.

You'll find numerous guides waiting in the visitor center parking lot, offering trips in vehicles ranging from little four-passenger Jeeps to 10- and 12-passenger four-wheel-drive trucks. The fee is usually about $15 per person for a 1¹/₂-hour tour, which essentially covers the same route you can drive for yourself, and about $25 per person for a 2¹/₂-hour tour, which includes that, plus excursions into restricted areas. Some guides also offer longer tours. **Goulding's** (see "Where to Stay & Dine," below) offers a 2¹/₂-hour tour for $25 per adult and $15 for children 8 and under, a highly recommended ✪ **3¹/₂-hour sunset tour** for $30 and $18 respectively, and an all-day tour, with lunch, for $60 and $45 respectively. Also, refer earlier in this chapter for tour operators based in Bluff.

Horseback tours of Monument Valley are available from about a half-dozen companies, including **Ed Black Stables** (☎ **800/551-4039** or 435/739-4285; fax 435/739-4210), with rates from $25 for a 90-minute ride, plus very popular sunrise and sunset tours from $25 to $50 per person.

ADDITIONAL THINGS TO SEE & DO

Goulding's Trading Post Museum at Goulding's Lodge (see "Where to Stay & Dine," below) is the original Monument Valley trading post opened by Harry and Leona (Mike) Goulding in 1924; it served as their home as well as a trading post for many years. Furnished much as it was in the 1920s and 1930s, the museum contains exhibits that include Goulding family memorabilia, historic photos of the area, Navajo and Anasazi artifacts and crafts, and posters and other items from movies filmed at the trading post and in Monument Valley. The museum is open daily from April through October; call the lodge for hours. Admission is free but donations are welcome. Nearby, a more modern trading post sells souvenirs, books, videos, and top-quality Native American arts and crafts.

The **Earth Spirit Multi Media Show,** in Harry and Mike's Theater next to Goulding's Lodge (see listing below), is a 20-minute show describing the history and geology of the monoliths, utilizing magnificent photos of the area. It is shown several times nightly year-round and costs $3 per person.

CAMPING

Mittenview Campground (☎ 435/727-3287), operated by the tribal park administration, is across the access road from the tribal park's visitor center/museum and offers good views of Monument Valley's rock formations. It has about 100 sites with picnic tables and grills. You'll find an RV dump station but no hookups and modern rest rooms with hot showers available from spring through early fall. Campsites cost $10 per night; during the rest of the year, primitive camping is available at a reduced rate.

Goulding's Monument Valley Campground, on the Monument Valley access road about 3 miles west of its intersection with U.S. 163 (☎ **435/727-3231** or 435/727-3235; fax 435/727-3344), also offers splendid views of Monument Valley's scenery, plus full RV hookups including cable television, an indoor swimming pool, modern rest rooms with showers, a playground, and a large convenience store. The campground is open year-round, but with limited services from November to mid-March. Tent sites cost $14 to $17; RV sites are $22 to $25.

Goulding's also has a full grocery store, gas station, and propane sales.

WHERE TO STAY & DINE

Goulding's Lodge, P.O. Box 1, Monument Valley, UT 84536 (☎ **800/874-0902** or 435/727-3231; fax 435/727-3344), on the Monument Valley access road about 2 miles west of its intersection with U.S. 163, has 62 recently remodeled modern motel rooms, each with Southwestern decor, cable TV and VCR, refrigerator, hair dryer, iron and ironing board, and private patio or balcony. There's a small indoor heated swimming pool and a restaurant serving three meals daily—American cuisine including traditional Navajo dishes, with dinner prices in the $7 to $22 range. Room rates for two are $108 to $128 from mid-April to mid-October, and $62 to $92 the rest of the year. County room tax adds about 9%.

3 Natural Bridges National Monument

Utah's first National Park Service area, Natural Bridges was designated primarily to show off and protect its three outstanding natural rock bridges, carved by streams and other forms of erosion over millions of years. You can see the bridges from roadside viewpoints, take individual hikes to each bridge, or hike a loop trail that connects all three.

Giant **Sipapu Bridge** is considered a mature bridge. It's 220 feet high with a span of 268 feet and is the second-largest natural bridge in the world, after Rainbow Bridge in nearby Glen Canyon National Recreation Area (see chapter 15). **Owachomo Bridge,** the most advanced in age and possibly on the brink of collapse (then again, it could stand for centuries), is the smallest of the three at 106 feet high, with a span of 180 feet. And the youngest, **Kachina Bridge,** is 210 feet high with a span of 204 feet. At 93 feet wide, it's also the thickest of the monument's bridges. All three bridges were given Hopi names: Sipapu means the "gateway to the spirit world" in Hopi legend; Owachomo is Hopi for "rock mound," so called for a rounded sandstone formation atop one side of the bridge; and Kachina was named as such because rock art on the bridge resembles decorations found on traditional Hopi kachina dolls.

JUST THE FACTS

Natural Bridges National Monument is about 40 miles west of Blanding, 60 miles northwest of Bluff, 43 miles north of Mexican Hat, about 50 miles east of Glen Canyon National Recreation Area's Hite or Halls Crossing marinas, and about 360 miles south of Salt Lake City.

GETTING THERE   The national monument is located in southeast Utah, off scenic Utah 95, via Utah 275. To get there from Monument Valley, follow U.S. 163 north to Utah 261 (just past Mexican Hat); at Utah 95, go west to Utah 275 and the Monument. Beware, though—Utah 261 has numerous steep switchbacks; it's not recommended for motor homes, those towing trailers, or anyone with acrophobia. The less adventurous and RV-bound should stick to approaching from the east, via Utah 95.

Make sure you have enough fuel for the trip to Natural Bridges; the closest gas stations are at least 40 miles away in Mexican Hat or Blanding. In fact, there are no services of any kind within 40 miles of the Monument.

INFORMATION & VISITOR CENTERS   For a park brochure and other information, contact the Superintendent, **Natural Bridges National Monument,** Box 1, Lake Powell, UT 84533 (☎ **435/692-1234**).

A **visitor center** at the park entrance has exhibits and a video program on bridge formation, the human history of the area, and the monument's plants and wildlife. Rangers are available to advise you about hiking trails and scheduled activities. The visitor center is also the only place in the monument where you can get drinking water.

FEES & REGULATIONS   Admission to the monument is $6 per vehicle or $3 per person on foot, bicycle, or motorcycle. Regulations are similar to those in most areas administered by the National Park Service, which emphasize protecting the area. Be especially careful not to damage any of the fragile archaeological sites in the monument; climbing on the natural bridges is prohibited. Overnight backpacking is not permitted within the monument, and vehicles may not be left unattended overnight. Because parking at the overlooks and trailheads is limited, those towing trailers or extra vehicles are asked to leave them at the visitor center parking lot. Pets must be leashed and are not allowed on trails or in buildings.

SEASONS & AVOIDING THE CROWDS   Although the monument is open year-round, winters can be a bit harsh at its 6,500-foot elevation; the weather here is best between late April and October. Because trailhead parking is limited and most people visit during school vacation in June, July, and August, the best months to see the park, if your schedule permits, are May, September, and October.

RANGER PROGRAMS   A series of programs on geology, history, and other subjects are presented. Schedules are posted at the visitor center.

SEEING THE HIGHLIGHTS

Natural Bridges National Monument will not be your major vacation destination, but you can easily spend a half day or full day, even two days, here. For those who want to take a quick look and get on to the other, larger national park lands in southern Utah, stop at the visitor center for a brief introduction, and then take the 9-mile (one-way) loop drive to the various natural bridge overlooks. Those with the time and the inclination might also take an easy hike down to Owachomo Bridge; it's a half-hour walk.

GENERATING ELECTRICITY IN THE MIDDLE OF NOWHERE: MORE TO SEE AT THE MONUMENT

Isolated, virtually in the middle of nowhere, Natural Bridges National Monument has been forced to become self-sufficient. To provide power for the visitor center, offices, and employee housing, photovoltaic cells convert the sun's energy to electricity. Only about 10% of the sun's energy striking the cells is converted, but the small field of photovoltaic cells is able to produce about 50 kilowatts of power, sufficient for the daily needs of the monument with enough extra to store in batteries for use at night and during cloudy periods. You can see the photovoltaic cells, located across the main monument road from the visitor center, and read explanations of how they operate.

SPORTS & ACTIVITIES

Hiking is the number-one activity here. From the trailheads, you can hike separately to each of the bridges, or start at one and do a loop hike to all three. Hikers should be prepared for summer afternoon thunderstorms that can cause flash flooding. Although the possibility of encountering a rattlesnake is very small, you should still watch carefully. Also, summers are hot, and all hikers should wear hats and other protective clothing, use sunscreen, and carry a gallon of water per person for all but the shortest walks.

The easiest hike—more of a walk—is the four-tenths-of-a-mile trail (round-trip) to **Owachomo Bridge.** Look toward the eastern horizon to see the twin buttes named "Bear's Ears." Allow a half hour.

The Sipapu and Kachina Bridge trails are both considered moderately strenuous, and 1 hour should be allocated for each. To **Sipapu Bridge,** you'll have a 500-foot elevation change, climbing two flights of stairs with three ladders and handrails on a 1.2-mile round-trip trail. This is the steepest trail in the park, but you'll have a splendid view of the bridge about halfway down. The hike takes about 1 hour.

The 1.5-mile round-trip hike to massive **Kachina Bridge** has a 400-foot elevation change, descending steep slickrock with handrails. Under the bridge, you'll notice a pile of rocks that fell in June 1992, slightly enlarging the bridge opening. Allow about 1 hour.

Those planning to hike the **loop to all three bridges** can start at any of the trailheads, although rangers recommend starting at Owachomo. Round-trip, including your walk back across the mesa, is 8.6 miles. Although the trails from the rim to the canyon bottom can be steep, the walk along the bottom is easy.

CAMPING

A primitive **13-site campground** has pit toilets, tables, tent pads, and grills, but no drinking water, showers, or other facilities. It's limited to vehicles no more than 26 feet long, and only one vehicle is allowed per site. Cost is $6 per night, and sites are allotted on a first-come, first-served basis.

There's also an overflow campground—essentially a parking lot—where you can stay at no charge. It's about 6 miles from the visitor center, just off Utah 261 near its intersection with Utah 95.

4 Edge of the Cedars State Historical Monument

The site of an ancient Anasazi ruin, occupied from about A.D. 750 to 1220, the monument includes six complexes lying in a generally north–south alignment atop a ridge. Only one of the complexes has been excavated and is open for viewing. The other five sites are still underground, and they give the visitor an idea of what to watch for when hiking in the Southwest.

There's also a modern **museum** here, which functions as the regional repository for the long-term care and storage of archaeological collections excavated from public lands in southeastern Utah. There is a very fine collection of pottery on display and a gift shop with the usual tourist fare.

The monument is located at 660 West and 400 North, on the north side of Blanding, just off U.S. 191 (☎ **435/678-2238**). Hours are daily from 9am to 6pm in the summer, and 9am to 5pm the rest of the year; it's closed Thanksgiving, Christmas, and New Year's Day. Admission costs $1.50 for adults, $1 for ages 6 to 15, and is free for children under 6; there's a maximum charge of $6 per family.

5 Hovenweep National Monument

Located along the Colorado-Utah border, Hovenweep (the Ute word for "deserted valley") contains some of the ✪ **most striking and most isolated archaeological sites** in the Four Corners area.

JUST THE FACTS

No lodging, food, gasoline, supplies, or even phones are available in the national monument. The closest motels and restaurants are all in Bluff (see earlier this chapter).

GETTING THERE/ACCESS POINTS   Hovenweep National Monument is 35 miles northeast of Bluff; 47 miles west of Cortez, Colorado; 122 miles south of Moab; and 366 miles southeast of Salt Lake City.

Access is via some paved and some graded dirt roads that become muddy—sometimes impassably so—during and immediately after rainstorms. You can get to Hovenweep from either Colorado or Utah. From Utah, follow U.S. 191, southeastern Utah's major north–south route, to Utah 262, between the towns of Blanding and Bluff. Head east on Utah 262 to Hatch Trading Post; then, watching for signs, follow paved roads to the monument. One option is to take Utah 163 east from Bluff toward the village of Aneth, turn north (left) onto an unnamed paved road, and follow signs to the monument.

From Cortez, Colorado, follow U.S. 666 north to the community of Pleasant View and turn west (left) onto dirt and gravel roads, following signs to the monument.

VISITOR INFORMATION   For advance information or questions about current road conditions, contact **Hovenweep National Monument,** McElmo Route, Cortez, CO 81321 (☎ **970/749-0510**).

FEES, REGULATIONS & SAFETY CONCERNS   Admission to the national monument is $6 per private vehicle or $3 per person. Regulations are much the same here as at most National Park Service properties, with an emphasis on taking care not to damage archaeological sites. Summer temperatures can reach 100°F and water supplies here are limited; bring your own and carry a canteen, even on short walks. During late spring, gnats can be a nuisance. Dogs must be leashed, but are permitted on trails.

Kokopelli: Casanova or Traveling Salesman?

Of the many subjects of rock art found in the West, one claims both a name and a gender: He's Kokopelli, and he's been found in ruins dating as early as A.D. 200 and as late as the 16th century. The consistency of the depictions of him over a wide geographic area indicates Kokopelli was a well-traveled and universally recognized deity of considerable importance. The figure is generally hunchbacked and playing a flute. His image is still used by potters, weavers, and painters, as well as for decoration on jewelry and clothing. Kokopelli has never been an evil character, although he's frequently been a comic one.

Until quite recent times, legends of Kokopelli were still current in the Pueblo peoples of the Four Corners area. Although the many stories differ in detail, almost all are faithful to the fertility theme. Sometimes he is a wandering minstrel with a sack of songs on his back; other times he is greeted as a god of the harvest.

The Hopi of First Mesa seem to identify him with an unethical guide of Spanish friars searching for the Seven Cities of Cibola in 1539. This guide was more interested in making passes at Hopi maidens than in searching for the fabled cities, according to the legend, and Hopi men consequently shot him with arrows and buried him under a pile of rocks. Another Hopi village holds Kokopelli to be sort of a traveling salesman who traded deerskin shirts and moccasins for brides. Yet another Hopi legend has him seducing the daughters of a household and sewing shirts, while his wife, incidentally, chased the men.

The Hopi also make kachina dolls of Kokopelli, and one of his wife, Kokopelli-mana, which are sold to tourists. As with most kachina dolls, there was also a real-life kachina dancer, who used to make explicit gestures to female tourists and missionaries, until the visitors found out what the gestures meant. Many early peoples welcomed Kokopelli around corn-planting time, and married women, hoping to conceive, sought his blessing. Single maidens, however, fled from him in panic.

EXPLORING THE MONUMENT

Hovenweep is noted for its mysterious and impressive 20-foot-tall sandstone towers, some of them square, others oval, circular, or D-shaped. Built by the ancestral Puebloans (also known as Anasazi), the solid towers have small windows up and down their masonry sides. Archaeologists have suggested a myriad of possible uses for these structures, their guesses ranging from guard towers to celestial observatories, ceremonial structures to water towers or granaries.

In addition to the towers, you'll encounter the remains of cliff dwellings and a kiva, petroglyphs, stone rooms, walls, and a reconstructed dam. One of the first ruins you'll see is stately **Hovenweep Castle,** probably built around A.D. 1200. Once home to several families, this site contains two D-shaped towers plus additional rooms.

Your walk among the 700-year-old buildings will take you through yucca, cactus, saltbush, juniper, and even some cottonwood trees. Watch for lizards and snakes, rabbits, hawks and ravens, and an occasional deer or fox.

A **ranger station,** with exhibits, rest rooms, and drinking water, is located at the Square Tower Site. This should be your first stop. The other five sites are difficult to find, and you'll need to obtain detailed driving directions and check on current road conditions before setting out. The ranger station is open daily from 8am to 5pm year-round, but may be closed for short periods while the ranger is on patrol.

At the Square Tower Site, near the ranger station, the 2-mile **Square Tower self-guiding trail** includes two loops, which can be hiked individually or together. They wind past the remains of ancient Puebloan buildings, such as the appropriately named Hovenweep Castle, and both square and round towers. A trail guide, available at the ranger station, discusses the ruins and identifies desert plants used for food, clothing, and medicine. The two loops are not difficult, but can be rough in spots; allow about 2 hours for the entire trail.

This is but one of the six groups of archaeological sites in the monument; information on the others can be obtained at the ranger station.

CAMPING

The **Hovenweep Campground,** with 31 sites, is open year-round. It has rest rooms, drinking water, picnic tables, and fire pits, but no showers or RV hookups. Most sites will accommodate short trailers and motor homes under 25 feet in length. Cost is $10 per night and reservations are not accepted, although the campground rarely fills, even during the peak summer season.

6 Four Corners Monument

This is the only place in the United States where you can stand (or sit, if you prefer) in four states at once. Operated as a Navajo Tribal Park (with the Colorado section owned by the Ute Mountain Tribe), there's a flat monument marking the spot where Utah, Colorado, New Mexico, and Arizona meet, on which visitors can perch for photos. Official seals of the four states are displayed, along with the motto, "Four states here meet in freedom under God." Surrounding the monument are the flags of the four states, the Navajo Nation and Ute tribes, and the United States.

Rows of booths house vendors selling traditional Navajo food, such as fry bread, along with typical American snack food. There are often crafts demonstrations, and available for purchase are an abundance of jewelry, pottery, sand paintings, and other crafts, plus your basic T-shirts, postcards, and souvenirs.

Located a half mile northwest of U.S. 160, the monument is open year-round, daily from 7am to 8pm in the summer, with shorter hours in the winter; admission costs $1.50 per person.

7 Farther Afield in Colorado: Mesa Verde National Park

Mesa Verde is the ✪ **largest archaeological preserve** in the United States, with some 4,000 known sites dating from A.D. 600 to 1300, including the most impressive cliff dwellings in the Southwest.

The area was little known until ranchers Charles Mason and Richard Wetherill chanced upon it in 1888. More or less uncontrolled looting of the artifacts followed, until a Denver newspaper reporter's stories aroused national interest in protecting the site. The 52,000-acre area was declared a national park in 1906—the only U.S. national park devoted entirely to the works of man.

The earliest-known inhabitants of Mesa Verde (Spanish for "green table") built subterranean pit houses on the mesa tops. During the 13th century, they moved into shallow alcoves and constructed complex cliff dwellings. These homes were obviously a massive construction project, yet the residents occupied them for only about a century, leaving in about 1300 for reasons as yet undetermined.

Some of the archaeological sites at Mesa Verde can be seen up close only on ranger-led tours (see below).

JUST THE FACTS

GETTING THERE/ACCESS POINTS   The entrance to Mesa Verde National Park is about 10 miles east of Cortez, Colorado; 56 miles east of Hovenweep National Monument; 125 miles east of Bluff; and 390 miles southeast of Salt Lake City.

The park entrance is off U.S. 160, midway between Cortez and Mancos, Colorado. Daily air service and rental cars are available in Cortez (see "Information & Visitor Centers," below).

Morefield Village, site of Mesa Verde's 477-site campground (see "Camping," below), is 4 miles in from U.S. 160.

INFORMATION & VISITOR CENTERS   For a park brochure, contact Superintendent, P.O. Box 8, **Mesa Verde National Park,** CO 81330 (☎ **970/529-4461** or 970/529-4475). For information on camping, lodging, and dining, call park concessionaire **ARA** (☎ **970/533-7731**). Additional area information is available from the **Mesa Verde–Cortez Visitor Information Bureau,** P.O. Drawer HH, Cortez, CO 81321 (☎ **800/253-1616**).

Far View Visitor Center, 15 miles south of the park entrance, is open in the summer only, providing exhibits and general visitor information and selling tickets for cliff-dwelling tours.

FEES, HOURS & REGULATIONS   Admission is $10 per vehicle. The park is open 24 hours a day year-round; the cliff dwellings are open daily from 8am to 6:30pm in summer, with shorter hours in winter; the Chapin Mesa Museum is open daily from 8am to 6:30pm in the summer, daily from 8am to 5pm the rest of the year. Full interpretive services are available from mid-June to Labor Day. Dogs, which must be leashed at all times, are prohibited on all trails, in the backcountry, and in public buildings.

SEASONS & AVOIDING THE CROWDS   Summer is the best time to visit, mainly because that's when you'll get to see the most. Because of the elevation here—from 6,954 feet to 8,572 feet—winters can be quite cold and snowy, and although the park is open in the winter, activities are curtailed and even the Ruins Road drive may be temporarily closed by snow. However, a blanket of white snow can be beautiful, and the park won't be crowded.

RANGER PROGRAMS & TOURS   The only way to get a close-up view of several of the well-preserved Native American sites here is on a ranger-led tour. Tours of the Long House on Wetherill Mesa, Cliff Palace, and Balcony House are offered in summer only, at a charge of $1.35 each. In the winter, a free tour of Spruce Tree House is available. Check at the Chapin Mesa Museum or Far View Visitor Center for schedules and reservation information.

Park concessionaire ARA offers guided park tours, which cost about $17 for a half day and $22 for a full day.

SEEING THE HIGHLIGHTS

Open year-round, the **Chapin Mesa Museum,** 21 miles south of the park entrance, provides visitor information and houses artifacts and specimens related to the history of the area, including other nearby archaeological sites. It's open daily from 8am to 6:30pm in the summer and daily from 8am to 5pm the rest of the year.

The **Cliff Palace,** Mesa Verde's largest and most famous site, is a four-story apartment complex with stepped-back roofs forming porches for the dwellings above.

Its towers, walls, and kivas (large circular rooms used for spiritual ceremonies) are all set back beneath the rim of a cliff.

For those who want to avoid hiking and climbing, the two loops of the 12-mile **Ruins Road** provide easy access to overlooks with views of more than three dozen cliff dwellings and other archaeological sites. Snow may close the road in the winter. During the summer, you can drive to **Wetherill Mesa,** where rangers conduct tours of several cliff dwellings and villages.

But if you want to get out and walk (and we encourage you to do so), you'll find yourself hiking and climbing to get to the various sites. Several longer hikes into scenic **Spruce Canyon** let you stretch your legs and get away from the crowds. Hikers must register at the ranger's office before setting out.

If you'll be visiting in the winter, consider taking your cross-country skis or snowshoes; they will provide an excellent means of exploring the Ruins Road when it's closed by snow.

CAMPING

Open from early May to mid-October, **Morefield Campground** (☎ 970/533-7731), 4 miles south of the park entrance, has almost 500 sites, including 15 with full RV hookups. Facilities include modern rest rooms, showers, picnic tables, grills, and an RV dump station. Reservations are not accepted. Cost is about $10 for sites without hookups and about $17 for sites with hookups.

ACCOMMODATIONS & DINING

Contact the **Mesa Verde–Cortez Visitor Information Bureau,** P.O. Drawer HH, Cortez, CO 81321 (☎ 800/253-1616), or consult *Frommer's Colorado* for lodging and dining choices in the Cortez area.

For additional information on local camping, lodging, and dining, call park concessionaire **ARA** (☎ 970/533-7731).

Open from mid-April to mid-October, **Far View Lodge,** P.O. Box 277, Mancos, CO 81328 (☎ 970/529-4421; fax 970/533-7831), offers 150 rooms in 17 separate buildings right in the park, with spectacular views in all directions. Rates are in the range of $75 to $94 for two people. A lodge restaurant serves dinner nightly, specializing in steak, seafood, and game, with prices ranging from $7.95 to $16.95. Nearby, another lodge-operated restaurant serves three meals daily.

Index

Abbey of Our Lady of the Holy
    Trinity Trappist Monastery, 99
Accommodations
    best bed-&-breakfasts, 9
    best lodges, 9
    best luxury hotels & inns,
        8–9
Adventure travel, 46
Airlines and air travel, 31–32
    for foreign visitors, 39–40
Air tours
    Bryce Canyon National Park,
        241
    Canyonlands National Park,
        309
    Lake Powell, 276
    Monument Valley, 322
    Zion National Park, 227
Alta Ski Area, 6, 126–28
American Express, 25
American Indians. See Native
    Americans
America's Cup Ski Races, 28
America's Freedom Festival, 26
Anasazi. See Puebloans, ancestral
Anasazi Indian Village State Park,
    259
Annual Railroader's Festival, 108
Antelope Island State Park, 28,
    92–93
Arches National Park, 7,
    299–305
Arches Vineyards, 292
Area codes, 35
Arizona Strip, 216–20
Ashley National Forest, 174
ATMs (automatic teller
    machines), 25
ATVs (all-terrain vehicles).
    See also OHVs
    Wasatch Mountain State
        Park, 151
Auto clubs, 41
Automobile insurance, 30

Beaver Mountain Ski Area, 6,
    112–13
Bed-&-breakfasts, 9
Beehive House, 8, 78
Bicycling, 28
Big Cottonwood Canyon resorts,
    123, 124–26
Biking. See also Mountain biking
    Antelope Island, 92
    Arches National Park, 303

Bryce Canyon National Park,
    242–43
Canyonlands National Park,
    310
Flaming Gorge, 182
Logan, 117
Ogden, 100
Provo, 165
St. George Area, 195
Salt Lake City, 86
Bird watching. See Wildlife
    viewing & bird watching
Blanding, 28
Bluff, 318–20
Boating & sailing. See also
    Housebanting; Rafting; River
    trips; Water sports
    Dinosaur National
        Monument, 179
    Escalante State Park, 258
    Flaming Gorge, 1, 182–83
    Great Salt Lake State Park,
        93
    Lake Powell, 276–77
    Moab area, 290
    Parade of Lights, 28
    Salt Lake City, 86
    Strawberry Reservoir, 153
    Utah Lake State Park,
        164–65
    Wasatch Front, 58
Book of Mormon, 18, 21
Boulder Mountain, 2, 6
Brian Head Bash, 27
Brian Head Resort, 4, 28, 208–9
Bridal Veil Falls, 163
Brigham Young Monument and
    Meridian Marker, 78
Brigham Young University, 22,
    159–60, 162–63, 166
Brigham Young Winter Home
    Historical Site, 192
Brighton Ski Resort, 124–25
Bryce Canyon National Park, 1,
    13, 26, 237–60
    accommodations, 246–48
    air tours over, 241
    camping, 245–46
    cross-country skiing, 6
    fees, backcountry permits &
        regulations, 240
    information & visitor centers,
        238, 240
    Queen's Garden, 2
    ranger programs, 240–41

    restaurants, 248–49
    safety concerns, 240
    scenic drive, 241–42
    sights & activities, 241–45,
        249–50
    traveling to, 238
    when to go to, 240
Bryce Canyon Winter Festival, 26
Buffalo Roundup, 28
Bus travel, 40
Butch Cassidy and the Sundance
    Kid (movie), 23, 265
Butch Cassidy's King World
    Waterpark, 293

Cache Valley Historical Museum
    (Daughters of the Utah
    Pioneers Museum), 114
Camping, 48
    Antelope Island, 93
    Arches National Park, 305
    Beaver Mountain Ski Area,
        113
    Bryce Canyon National Park,
        245–46
    Canyonlands National Park,
        312–13
    Capitol Reef National Park,
        268–69
    Cedar Breaks, 207
    Coral Pink Sand Dunes State
        Park, 213
    Dead Horse Point State Park,
        314
    Dinosaur National
        Monument, 180
    Escalante State Park, 258
    Flaming Gorge, 185
    Glen Canyon National
        Recreation Area and Lake
        Powell, 281
    Grand Canyon National
        Park, 218
    Grand Staircase-Escalante
        National Monument, 257
    Great Salt Lake State Park,
        94
    Hovenweep National
        Monument, 328
    information on
        campgrounds, 51
    Kanab, 215
    Kodachrome Basin, 251
    Mesa Verde, 330
    Moab, 295–96

Camping *(cont.)*
  Monument Valley, 323
  Natural Bridges National
    Monument, 325
  Ogden, 104
  Rock Cliff Recreation Site,
    149
  Rockport State Park, 147–48
  RVs and tenting vacations,
    50–51
  Snow Canyon, 194–95
  Strawberry Reservoir, 154
  Vernal, 176
  Wasatch Mountain State
    Park, 151
  Zion National Park, 231–32
Canyon Cinemax Theatre, 236
Canyonlands Fat Tire Festival, 28
Canyonlands National Park,
  305–14
  four-wheeling, 7
  Great Gallery in Horseshoe
    Canyon, 7
Canyons, The (formerly Wolf
  Mountain), 136
Canyons Concert Series, 146
Capitol Building, 78–79
Capitol Reef National Park, 1–2,
  13, 260, 261–72
  accommodations, 270–72
  camping, 268–69
  exploring by car, 264
  fees, regulations &
    backcountry permits, 262
  historic sites, 265–66
  information & visitor centers,
    262
  ranger programs, 264
  restaurants, 272
  safety concerns, 264
  sights & activities, 266–68
  traveling to, 262
  when to go to, 262, 264
Cars and driving, 32. *See also*
  Scenic drives
    auto clubs, 41
    automobile insurance, 30
    best scenic drives, 3
    rentals, 32, 41
    road condition information,
      36
    roadside assistance, 34
    rules, 32, 34
    RVs, 50–51
    safety, 39
Casinos, 90
Cassidy, Butch, 265
Cattle drives, 48
Cedar Breaks National
  Monument, 203, 205–8
Cedar City, 27, 203–11
CEU Prehistoric Museum, 316
Chapin Mesa Museum, 329

Cherry Hill Family Campground,
  2
Children, 22
  Salt Lake City
    accommodations, 68
    restaurants, 75
    sights and attractions, 84
Children's Museum of Utah, 84
Christmas, special events, 28
Christmas Parade and Lighting of
  the Dinosaur Gardens, 28
Chuck wagon dinner ride, 244
Church of Jesus Christ of Latter-
  day Saints. *See* Mormons
Cleveland-Lloyd Dinosaur
  Quarry, 316
Cliff Palace, 329–30
Climate, 25
Clinton, Bill, 253, 256, 258
Colorado Plateau, 11, 13
Colorado River, 5, 52, 279, 290
Color Country, 187, 188
Consulates, 42
Coral Pink Sand Dunes State
  Park, 5, 212
  four-wheeling, 7
Cottonwood Canyon. *See* Big
  Cottonwood Canyon resorts;
  Little Cottonwood Canyon
  resorts
Council Hall, 79
Credit cards, 38
Cross-country skiing, 53. *See also*
  Winter sports & activities
    best places for, 6
    Bryce Canyon National Park,
      245
    Cedar Breaks, 209
    Elk Meadows Resort, 210
    Logan, 118–19
    Park City Mountain Resort,
      135
    Rockport State Park, 147
    Solitude Ski Resort, 126
    Sundance, 155
    Wasatch Mountain State
      Park, 150
Currency exchange, 41
Customs regulations, 38

Dan O'Laurie Museum, 292
Daughters of Utah Pioneers
  Museum, 163, 192
Dave's Hollow Trail, 4
Daylight saving time (DST), 44
Dead Horse Point State Park,
  313–14
Deer Valley, 6
  accommodations, 140–41
Deer Valley Resort, 132, 134
Defiance House, 278
Devil's Rock Garden, 281
Dinosaurland, 2–3

Dinosaur National Monument,
  12, 13, 177–80, 279
  Green River, 5
Dinosaur Quarry, 177, 178–79
Dinosaur Roundup Rodeo, 27
Dinosaurs, 28, 174, 289, 315–16
Disabilities, travelers with
  skiing, 129
  tips for, 30
Dixie College, 196–97, 202
Dixie region, 187
Downhill skiing. *See also* Skiing
  & ski resorts
    best places for, 6
    Solitude Ski Resort, 125
    special events, 28
    Sundance, 154–55
Drag racing, 197
Driving. *See* Cars and driving

Eagle Gate, 78
Eccles Community Art Center,
  95
Eden, accommodations, 104
Edge of the Cedars State
  Historical Monument, 326
Elk Meadows Resort, 209–11
Embassies, 41–42
Emergencies, 35, 42
  automobile, 34
Entry into the U.S., requirements
  for, 37–38
Escalante, 251–53. *See also* Grand
  Staircase-Escalante National
  Monument
Escalante State Park, 4, 5, 258

Fall Colors Fat Tire Festival, 28
Family History Library, 76
Farmington, 99
Festival of Lights, 29
Festival of the American West, 27
Festivals and special events,
  26–29
Fielding Garr Ranch House, 93
First Night Celebration, 29
First Night New Year's Eve
  Celebration, 29
Fishing, 49
  best destinations for, 4–5
  Bryce Canyon National Park,
    243
  Dinosaur National
    Monument, 179
  Escalante State Park, 258
  Flaming Gorge, 183
  Lake Powell, 279–80
  Logan, 118
  Ogden, 100
  Park City, 137
  Provo, 165
  St. George Area, 195
  Salt Lake City, 86

Strawberry Reservoir, 153
Sundance, 156
Wasatch Front, 58
Fishlake National Forest, 211
Flaming Gorge Dam and Power
    Plant, 184
Flaming Gorge National
    Recreation Area, 1, 5, 13,
    180–86
Folk and Bluegrass Festival, 145
Foreign visitors, 37–44
    entry requirements, 37–38
Fort Buenaventura State Park, 95
Four Corners Area, 13, 318
    accommodations and
        restaurants, 319–20
    Bluff, 318–20
    Four Corners Monument,
        328
    Hovenweep National
        Monument, 326
    Monument Valley Navajo
        Tribal Park, 320–23
    Natural Bridges National
        Monument, 323–25
    sights & activities, 319
Four Corners Monument, 12,
    328
Four-wheeling, 49
    Arches National Park, 303
    best places for, 7
    Canyonlands National Park,
        309
    Capitol Reef National Park,
        266, 267
    Coral Pink Sand Dunes State
        Park, 213
    Glen Canyon National
        Recreation Area, 280–81
    Grand Staircase-Escalante
        National Monument, 257
    Moab, 288–89
Fremont people, 265–66
Fruita, 266

Gardner Village, 85
Gasoline, 42
Gay and lesbian travelers, 30
Genealogical records and research,
    76
George S. Eccles Dinosaur Park,
    96
Gifford Farmhouse, 266
Glen Canyon Dam, 278, 279
Glen Canyon National
    Recreation Area, 13, 273
    accommodations & dining,
        281–82
    fees, backcountry permits &
        regulations, 275–76
    information & visitor centers,
        274–75
    ranger programs, 276

sights & activities, 279–81
    traveling to, 273–74
    when to go to, 276
Goblin Valley State Park, 315
Golden Access Passport, 30
Golden Spike Anniversary, 26
Golden Spike National Historic
    Site, 29, 108–9
Golden Spike Tour, 3
Golf, 49
    Color Country, 188
    Logan, 118
    Moab, 290
    Ogden, 100
    Park City, 137
    Provo/Orem area, 165
    St. George Area, 195–96
    Salt Lake City, 86
    Wasatch Front, 58
    Wasatch Mountain State
        Park, 150
Goosenecks State Park, 319
Goulding's Trading Post
    Museum, 322–23
Governor's Mansion, 79
Grand Canyon river trips, 52
Grand Canyon National Park
    (North Rim), 217–19
"Grand Circle, The: A National
    Park Odyssey," 235–36
Grand Staircase-Escalante
    National Monument, 49, 251,
    253–59
Great Basin Desert, 11, 13
Great Gallery (Horseshoe
    Canyon), 7
Great Salt Lake, 12, 58, 91–94
Great Salt Lake State Park,
    93–94
Greek Festival, 28
Green River, 5, 314–15
Green River State Park, 314–15
Gunlock State Park, 196

Hailstone Recreation Site,
    148–49
Hamblin, Jacob, Home, 8, 193
Hansen Planetarium, 79
Health concerns, 29, 47
Heber City, 151–52
Heber Valley Historic Railroad,
    2, 151
Helicopter skiing (heli-skiing),
    129
Heritage House, 213
Hidden Piñon Trail (Snow
    Canyon State Park), 3
Highway 12 Scenic Byway,
    251–52
Hiking, 49–50, 165
    Antelope Island, 92
    Arches National Park, 304–5
    best trails, 3–4

Bryce Canyon National Park,
    243–44
Canyonlands National Park,
    310–12
Capitol Reef National Park,
    267–68
Cedar Breaks, 207
Color Country, 188
Coral Pink Sand Dunes State
    Park, 213
Dinosaur National
    Monument, 179–80
Escalante State Park, 258
Flaming Gorge, 183
Glen Canyon National
    Recreation Area and Lake
    Powell, 280
Golden Spike National
    Historic Site, 109
Grand Canyon National
    Park, 218
Grand Staircase-Escalante
    National Monument,
    254–55
Kodachrome Basin, 250–51
Logan, 118
Moab area, 289–90
Natural Bridges National
    Monument, 325
Ogden, 100–101
Park City, 137
Rockport State Park, 147
St. George Area, 196
Salt Lake City, 86
Snow Canyon, 194
Strawberry Reservoir, 153
Sundance, 155
Timpanogos Cave National
    Monument, 170
tours and outfitters, 46–47
Wasatch Front, 58
Wasatch Mountain State
    Park, 150
Zion National Park, 229–30
Hill Aerospace Museum, 96
Historic Union Pacific Rail Trail
    State Park bike path, 138
History of Utah, 17–21
Hogle Zoo, 84
Hole-in-the-Rock Jeep Jamboree,
    28
Hole-in-the-Rock Road, 281
Hole-in-the-Rock Scenic
    Backway, 257
Hole 'n the Rock, 292–93
Holidays, 35, 42
Hopi, 282, 293, 323–24, 327
Horseback riding, 50–51, 58
    Antelope Island, 92
    Bryce Canyon National Park,
        244
    Capitol Reef National Park,
        268

Horseback riding *(cont.)*
Cedar Breaks, 209
Dinosaur National Monument, 180
Flaming Gorge, 184
Grand Staircase-Escalante National Monument, 254
Kodachrome Basin, 251
Logan, 118
Moab area, 290
Monument Valley, 322
Ogden, 101
Park City, 137–38
Snow Canyon, 194
Sundance, 156
Zion National Park, 230–31
Horseshoe Canyon, Great Gallery in, 7
Hostler Model Railroad Festival, 26
Houseboating, 51
Flaming Gorge, 182
Lake Powell, 276–77
Hovenweep National Monument, 7, 326–28
Huntsville, 99
accommodations, 104

Ice fishing, 147, 152, 184, 258
Ice-skating
Cedar Breaks, 209
Ogden, 101
Park City Mountain Resort, 135
Provo/Orem area, 165–66
Salt Lake City, 86
Utah Lake State Park, 165
Indian Trail (Ogden), 3
In-line skating
Ogden, 101
Park City, 137
Salt Lake City, 86
Insurance
automobile, 30
for foreign visitors, 38
medical, 29–30
travel, 29–30, 38
International Peace Gardens, 83
Iron Mission State Park, 204–5

Jacob Hamblin Home, 8, 193
John Hutchings Museum of Natural History, 163
John W. Gallivan Utah Center, 82
John Wesley Powell Memorial Museum, 282
John Wesley Powell River History Museum, 314
Jordanelle State Park, 4, 5, 146–49
Joseph Smith Memorial Building, 79

Kanab, 211–16
Kennecott's Bingham Canyon Mine, 85
Kodachrome Basin State Park, 250–51
Kokopelli, 327

Lagoon (Farmington), 99–100
Lake Powell. *See* Powell, Lake
Land Speed Opener, Bonneville Salt Flats, 27
Latter-day Saints (LDS). *See* Mormons
LDS Tabernacle (Logan), 114
LDS Temple (Logan), 115
Lees Ferry, 278
Legal aid, 42
Lion House, 78
Liquor laws, 35
Little Cottonwood Canyon resorts, 123, 126–30
Living Traditions Festival, 26
Logan, 12, 113–22
accommodations, 119–20
entertainment, 121–22
restaurants, 120–21
sights & activities, 114–17
sports & outdoor activities, 117–19
Lower Emerald Pools Trail (Zion National Park), 3

McCurdy Historical Doll Museum, 164
Maps, 34
Medical insurance, 29–30
Mesa Verde National Park, 7, 328–30
Minersville State Park, 211
Mirror Lake Highway, 171
Moab, 3, 283–99
accommodations, 294
camping, 295
festivals and special events, 28
four-wheeling, 288–89
golf, 290
hiking, 289–90
horseback riding, 290
mountain biking, 286–88
nightlife, 298–99
outfitters, 291–92
restaurants, 296–98
shopping, 293
sights & activities, 292–93
special events, 286
traveling to, 284
vehicle rentals and taxis, 284, 286
visitor information, 284
water sports & activities, 290, 293
winter sports & activities, 290

Moab Music Festival, 28, 286
Moab Slickrock Bike Trail, 4
Moab to Monument Valley Film Commission and Museum, 293
Money, 25, 38–39
currency exchange, 41
Monument Valley Navajo Tribal Park, 2, 3, 7–8, 319, 320–23
Moqui Cave, 213–14
Mormons (Church of Jesus Christ of Latter-day Saints), 266
beliefs of, 21–22
best history sites, 8
history of, 18–21
St. George, 192
modern, 21–23
Mormon Tabernacle, 12, 75
Mormon Tabernacle Choir, 10, 75
Moroni, 18
Mountain biking, 4, 51–52
Bryce Canyon National Park, 242–43
Canyonlands National Park, 312
Capitol Reef National Park, 266–67
Cedar Breaks, 209
Color Country, 188
festivals and special events, 28
Glen Canyon National Recreation Area, 280
Grand Staircase-Escalante National Monument, 254
Moab, 286–88
Park City, 137
St. George Area, 195
Snow Canyon, 194
Strawberry Reservoir, 153
tours and outfitters, 46–47
Vernal, 174
Wasatch Front, 58
Wasatch Mountain State Park, 151
Zion National Park, 229
Mountain Man Rendezvous, 26, 28
Mountain Man Rendezvous at Fort Buenaventura, 10
Movies
Butch Cassidy and the Sundance Kid, 23, 265
Moab to Monument Valley Film Commission and Museum, 293
Railroader's Film Festival and Winter Steam Demonstration, 29, 108
recommended, 23
Stagecoach, 23, 320
Sundance Film Festival, 26, 156–57

Mule rides, Grand Canyon National Park, 218
Museum of Church History and Art, 82
Music festivals and special events, 26, 27
Music in the Mountains series, 145

Narrows, The (Zion National Park), 2
National parks, 13, 47–48. *See also specific parks*
  passes, 48
  tour of, 3
Native Americans. *See also* Hopi; Navajos; Puebloans, ancestral
  best places to experience culture of, 7–8
Natural Bridges National Monument, 323–25
Navajo guides, Monument Valley, 322
Navajo Loop/Queen's Garden Trail (Bryce Canyon National Park), 4
Navajos
  Four Corners Monument, 328
  Monument Valley Navajo Tribal Park, 320–23
Newspaper Rock, 314
Newspapers, 35–36, 43
New Year's Eve, 29
Nordic Valley Ski Mountain, 109–10
Northern Wasatch Front, 12

Off-highway vehicles. *See* OHVs
Ogden, 12, 94–107
  accommodations, 102–4
  festivals and special events, 26, 28, 29
  nightlife and entertainment, 107
  restaurants, 104–7
  sights & activities, 95
  sports & outdoor activities, 100–102
  walking tour, 98
Ogden Christmas Parade and Christmas Village, 28
Ogden Nature Center, 96
Ogden Oktoberfest, 28
Ogden Valley, 109–12
OHVs (off-highway or off-road vehicles), 153. *See also* ATVs; Four-wheeling
Oktoberfest, 27
Old Deseret, 83–84
Orem, 158
Ouray National Wildlife Refuge, 174

Outdoor activities, 48–53. *See also specific activities and places*
  carrying or renting equipment, 45–46
  safety and health tips, 47
  tours and outfitters, 46–47
Outfitters, 46

Package tours, 34
Packing tips, 45–46
Parade of Lights, 28
Paria Canyon Primitive Area, 280
Park City, 6, 12–13, 130–46
  accommodations in and near, 139–43
  club scene, 146
  festivals and special events, 26
  performing arts, 145–46
  restaurants, 143–45
  shopping, 139
  side trips from, 146
  sights & activities, 138–39
  ski resorts near, 132–36
  sleigh rides and guided snowmobiling trips, 137
  warm-weather activities in & around, 137–38
Park City International Music Festival, 146
Park City Mountain Resort, 134–36
Park City Museum of History & Territorial Jail, 138
Park City Silver Mine Adventure, 138
Peppermint Place, 164
Performing arts, 10
Petrified Forest Trail, 4
Petrified wood, 259
Petrol, 42
Pets, travelers with, 31
Pioneer Day, 27
Pioneer Memorial Museum, 82
Pipe Spring National Monument, 219
Planetarium, Hansen, 79
Poison Spider Mesa Trail, 7, 288
Police, 36
Polygamy, 18, 20, 22
Powder Mountain Resort, 110–11
Powell, John Wesley, 180, 181, 237, 278, 303, 306
  Memorial Museum, 282
  River History Museum, 314
Powell, Lake, 5, 13, 273
  accommodations & dining, 281–82
  air tours, 276
  boating & houseboating, 276–77

  fees, backcountry permits & regulations, 275–76
  festivals and special events, 28, 29
  houseboating, 2
  information & visitor centers, 274–75
  sights & activities, 277–81
  traveling to, 273–74
Precipitation, average monthly high/low, 25
Price, 315–16
Provo, 13, 158–69. *See also* Brigham Young University
  accommodations, 167–68
  festivals and special events, 26
  nightlife and entertainment, 169
  restaurants, 168–69
  sights & activities, 163–65
  sports & outdoor activities, 165–66
  walking tour, 160, 162
Puebloans, ancestral (Anasazi), 7, 17, 259, 278
  Edge of the Cedars State Historical Monument, 326

Quail Creek State Park, 5, 196
Queen's Garden (Bryce Canyon National Park), 2

Radio, 43
Rafting, 52. *See also* River trips
  Four Corners region, 319
  Grand Canyon National Park, 218
  Moab area, 290
  Vernal, 174
Railroader's Festival, 27
Railroader's Film Festival and Winter Steam Demonstration, 29, 108
Rainbow Bridge National Monument, 278
Red Butte Garden and Arboretum, 82–83
Red Canyon, 250
Red Fleet State Park, 174–75
Redford, Robert, 154, 157
Red Rock Gem and Mineral Show, 28
Renting recreational equipment, 45–46
Reservations, 34
Restaurants, best, 10
River trips, 52, 174. *See also* Boating & sailing; Rafting
  Dinosaur National Monument, 179
  Moab area, 290
  near Bluff, 319

Robbers Roost, 12

Rock Cliff Recreation Site, 5, 149

Rock climbing, 52
    Logan, 118
    near Salt Lake City, 87
    Provo/Orem area, 166
    Snow Canyon, 194
    Zion National Park, 231

Rockport State Park, 147–48

Rocky Mountain region, 11

Rodeo
    Bryce Canyon Country, 249
    Dinosaur Roundup, 27
    PRCA Canyonlands, 286

Ronald V. Jensen Living
    Historical Farm, 115

RVs, 50–51. *See also* Camping;
    Four-wheeling

Safety, 39
    outdoors, 47

St. George, 13, 187, 188,
    190–93, 195–203
    accommodations, 197–200
    festivals and special events,
        26–28
    golf, 49, 195–96
    nightlife and entertainment,
        202–3
    outdoor activities, 195–97
    restaurants, 200–202
    shopping, 197

St. George Tabernacle, 8, 193,
    203

St. George Temple, 193

Saltair Resort & Pavilion, 94

Salt flats, near Salt Lake City, 90

Salt Lake Art Center, 82

Salt Lake City, 11–12, 59–90
    accommodations, 63–70
    arriving in, 59–60
    campgrounds, 69–70
    children
        accommodations, 68
        restaurants, 75
        sights and attractions, 84
    clubs, 89
    festivals and special events,
        26–29
    historic buildings &
        monuments, 78–79
    hospitals, 62
    hotlines, 63
    layout of, 60–61
    medical and dental referrals,
        62
    museums, 79, 82–83
    neighborhoods, 61
    newspapers and magazines,
        63
    nightlife and entertainment,
        88–89

organized tours, 85
outdoor activities, 85–87
parks & gardens, 83–84
post offices, 63
radio & TV stations, 63
restaurants, 70–75
shopping, 87–88
sights and attractions, 75–85
spectator sports, 87
Temple Square, 75–76
transportation, 61–62
visitor information, 60
Winter Olympic Games
    (2002), 56

Salt Lake City International, 31

Sand Island Recreation Site, 319

Scandinavian Festival, 26

Scenic drives
    Arches National Park, 302–3
    Bryce Canyon National Park,
        241–42
    Capitol Reef National Park,
        264
    Cedar Breaks, 206–7
    Dinosaur National
        Monument, 179
    Flaming Gorge-Uintas Scenic
        Byway-U. S. 191, 176
    Grand Staircase-Escalante
        National Monument, 257
    Highway 12 Scenic Byway,
        251–52
    Zion National Park, 228

Scenic flights. *See* Air tours

Scofield State Park, 316–17

Senecks State Park, 319

Senior citizens, 30–31

Seven Peaks Resort Water Park,
    166

Skating. *See* Ice-skating; In-line
    skating

Skiing & ski resorts, 52–53.
    See also Cross-country skiing;
    Downhill skiing; Winter sports
    & activities
    Beaver Mountain Ski Area,
        112–13
    Big Cottonwood Canyon,
        123–26
    Brian Head Resort, 208–9
    Color Country, 188
    Elk Meadows Resort, 209–11
    heli-, 129
    Ogden Valley, 109–12
    renting equipment, 45–46
    special events, 26, 28
    tours, 47

Ski jumping, Park City Mountain
    Resort, 135

Sleigh rides, 137

Smith, Joseph, 18, 21, 22

Smoking, 36

Snowbasin, 6, 111–12

Snowbird Ski & Summer Resort,
    128–30

Snowboarding
    Brighton Ski Resort, 124,
        125
    tours, 47

Snow Canyon State Park, 3,
    193–95

Snowmobiling, 53
    Bryce Canyon National Park,
        245
    Logan, 118–19
    Park City, 137
    Wasatch Mountain State
        Park, 150

SnowShine Festival, 26

Snowshoeing, 210

Solitude Nordic Center, 6

Solitude Ski Resort, 125–26

Southern Utah Folklife Festival,
    27

Southern Wasatch Front, 12

Southwest Utah. *See* Color
    Country; Dixie region

Special events, 26–29

Sports. *See also* Water sports &
    activities; Winter sports &
    activities; *and specific sports and*
    places
    special events, 28

Spring Salon, 26

Springville, 26, 27, 158

Springville Museum of Art, 164

Stagecoach (movie), 23, 320

Stagecoach rides, Kodachrome
    Basin, 251

State parks, 48. *See also individual*
    parks

Steinaker State Park, 175

Strawberry Reservoir, 4, 58,
    152–54

Sundance Film Festival, 26, 145,
    156–57

Sundance Nordic Center, 6

Sundance Resort & Institute,
    154–58

Swett Ranch Historic Site,
    184–85

Swimming. *See also* Water sports
    & activities
    Antelope Island, 92
    Flaming Gorge, 184
    Moab, 293
    Ogden, 101

Taxes, 36, 43

Telegraph, 44

Telephone, 43–44

Television, 43

Temperatures, average monthly,
    25

Temple Square (Salt Lake City), 8
  Christmas Lights, 28
  guided tours, 76
  shopping, 88
  sights and attractions, 75–76
Tennis, 87, 138
Thanksgiving Point, 164
Theater, special events, 26–27
This Is the Place State Park, 83–84
Thor's Hammer, 4, 242, 243
Time zones, 36, 44
Timpanogos Cave National Monument, 169–70
Tipping, 44
Tourist information, 24–25
Tour of the Tilted Rocks drive, 179
Tours
  air. *See* Air tours
  outfitters and adventure-travel operators, 46–47. *See also specific places*
  package, 34
Trails. *See* Hiking
Train travel, 32, 40
Traveler's checks, 25, 38
Traveling
  around the U. S., 40
  to the U. S., 39–40
  to Utah, 31–32
  within Utah, 32, 34
Travel insurance, 29–30, 38
Treehouse Children's Museum, 97
Twain, Mark, 60

Uinta Mountains, 172
Union Station (Ogden), 97
University of Utah
  Museums, 82–83
Utah! (show), 26–27
Utah Arts Festival, 27
Utah Belly Dance Festival, 27
Utah Field House of Natural History State Park, 175
Utah Fun Dome, 84
Utah Jazz and Blues Festival, 27
Utah Lake State Park, 164–65
Utah Museum of Fine Arts, 83
Utah Museum of Natural History, 83
Utah Music Festival, 89
Utah Music Festival (Logan), 122
Utah Shakespearean Festival, 10, 27, 205
Utah State Fair, 27
Utah State Historical Society Museum, 83

Utah State University (Logan), 115, 119, 122
Utah Symphony, 10, 27, 88–89
  Summer Series, 145–46
Utah Winter Games, 26
Ute Mountain Fire Lookout Tower, 185

Vernal, 27, 172
  accommodations, 176
  restaurants, 176–77
  sights & activities, 175–76
Videos, recommended, 23
Visas, 37
Visitor information, 24–25

Wagon Master (movie), 23
Wasatch Front, 11, 12, 57
  warm-weather activities, 58
  wildlife viewing & bird watching, 58
  winter activities, 57–58
Wasatch Mountain State Park, 149–51
Water sports & activities
  best destinations for, 4–5
  Great Salt Lake State Park, 93
  Gunlock State Park, 196
  Moab area, 290, 293
  Ogden, 101
  Quail Creek State Park, 196
  Rockport State Park, 147
Wayne, John, 13
Weather, 25, 36
Wendover, 13, 90
Western Heritage Museum, 175–76
Western Mining and Railroad Museum, 316
Wheeler Historic Farm, 84
White Rim Road, four-wheeling, 7
White-water rafting. *See* Rafting
Wildlife viewing & bird watching, 53
  Antelope Island, 92
  best places for, 5–6
  books on, 23
  Bryce Canyon National Park, 244
  Canyonlands National Park, 305–6, 310
  Capitol Reef National Park, 268
  Cedar Breaks, 207
  Color Country, 188
  Escalante State Park, 258
  Flaming Gorge, 184

Grand Staircase-Escalante National Monument, 257
Kodachrome Basin, 251
near Vernal, 174, 175
Rock Cliff Recreation Site, 149
Rockport State Park, 147
Snow Canyon, 194
Strawberry Reservoir, 153
Wasatch Front, 58
Wasatch Mountain State Park, 150–51
Zion National Park, 231
Willard Bay State Park, 102
Willow Park Zoo, 115–16
Winter Olympic Games (2002), 56
Winter sports & activities, 52–53. *See also* Ice fishing; Ice skating; Skiing; Snowboarding; Snowmobiling; *and other sports and activities*
  Bryce Canyon National Park, 245
  Cedar Breaks, 207–8
  Flaming Gorge, 184
  Logan, 118–19
  Moab area, 290
  special events, 26
  Wasatch Front, 57–58
Wolf Mountain. *See* Canyons, The
World Conference of the LDS Church, 26
World Folkfest, 27
World Senior Games, 28

Young, Brigham, 17, 19, 20, 190, 192

Zion National Park, 3, 13, 221–36
  accommodations, 232–34
  air tours over, 227
  camping, 231–32
  entertainment, 235–36
  fees, backcountry permits & regulations, 226
  information & visitor centers, 225–26
  The Narrows, 2
  ranger programs, 226–27
  scenic drives, 228
  sights, 227–29
  sports & activities, 229–31
  traveling to, 224–25
  when to go to, 226
Zoo
  Hogle, 84
  Willow Park, 115–16

FROMMER'S® COMPLETE TRAVEL GUIDES
(Comprehensive guides to destinations around the world, with selections in all price ranges—from deluxe to budget)

Acapulco, Ixtapa & Zihuatenejo
Alaska
Amsterdam
Arizona
Atlanta
Australia
Austria
Bahamas
Barcelona, Madrid & Seville
Belgium, Holland & Luxembourg
Bermuda
Boston
Budapest & the Best of Hungary
California
Canada
Cancún, Cozumel & the Yucatán
Cape Cod, Nantucket & Martha's Vineyard
Caribbean
Caribbean Cruises & Ports of Call
Caribbean Ports of Call
Carolinas & Georgia
Chicago
China
Colorado
Costa Rica
Denver, Boulder & Colorado Springs
England

Europe
Florida
France
Germany
Greece
Hawaii
Hong Kong
Honolulu, Waikiki & Oahu
Ireland
Israel
Italy
Jamaica & Barbados
Japan
Las Vegas
London
Los Angeles
Maryland & Delaware
Maui
Mexico
Miami & the Keys
Montana & Wyoming
Montréal & Québec City
Munich & the Bavarian Alps
Nashville & Memphis
Nepal
New England
New Mexico
New Orleans
New York City
Northern New England
Nova Scotia, New Brunswick & Prince Edward Island
Oregon
Paris

Philadelphia & the Amish Country
Portugal
Prague & the Best of the Czech Republic
Provence & the Riviera
Puerto Rico
Rome
San Antonio & Austin
San Diego
San Francisco
Santa Fe, Taos & Albuquerque
Scandinavia
Scotland
Seattle & Portland
Singapore & Malaysia
South Pacific
Spain
Switzerland
Thailand
Tokyo
Toronto
Tuscany & Umbria
USA
Utah
Vancouver & Victoria
Vienna & the Danube Valley
Virgin Islands
Virginia
Walt Disney World & Orlando
Washington, D.C.
Washington State

FROMMER'S® DOLLAR-A-DAY GUIDES
(The ultimate guides to comfortable low-cost travel)

Australia from $50 a Day
California from $60 a Day
Caribbean from $60 a Day
Costa Rica & Belize from $35 a Day
England from $60 a Day
Europe from $50 a Day
Florida from $50 a Day
Greece from $50 a Day
Hawaii from $60 a Day
India from $40 a Day

Ireland from $50 a Day
Israel from $45 a Day
Italy from $50 a Day
London from $60 a Day
Mexico from $35 a Day
New York from $75 a Day
New Zealand from $50 a Day
Paris from $70 a Day
San Francisco from $60 a Day
Washington, D.C., from $60 a Day

FROMMER'S® PORTABLE GUIDES

(Pocket-size guides for travelers who want everything in a nutshell)

Bahamas	Dublin	Puerto Vallarta, Manzanillo
California Wine Country	Las Vegas	& Guadalajara
Charleston & Savannah	London	San Francisco
Chicago	Maine Coast	Venice
	New Orleans	Washington, D.C.

FROMMER'S® NATIONAL PARK GUIDES

(Everything you need for the perfect park vacation)

Grand Canyon	Yosemite & Sequoia/
National Parks of the American West	Kings Canyon
Yellowstone & Grand Teton	Zion & Bryce Canyon

FROMMER'S® IRREVERENT GUIDES

(Wickedly honest guides for sophisticated travelers)

Amsterdam	Manhattan	San Francisco	Walt Disney World
Chicago	New Orleans	Santa Fe	Washington, D.C.
London	Paris		

FROMMER'S® BY NIGHT GUIDES

(The series for those who know that life begins after dark)

Amsterdam	Los Angeles	Miami	Prague
Chicago	Madrid	New Orleans	San Francisco
Las Vegas	& Barcelona	Paris	Washington, D.C.
London	Manhattan		

THE COMPLETE IDIOT'S TRAVEL GUIDES

(The ultimate user-friendly trip planners)

Cruise Vacations	New York City	San Francisco
Las Vegas	Planning Your Trip	Walt Disney World
New Orleans	to Europe	

SPECIAL-INTEREST TITLES

Arthur Fommer's New World of Travel
The Civil War Trust's Official Guide to
  the Civil War Discovery Trail
Frommer's Caribbean Hideaways
Frommer's Complete Hostel Vacation
  Guide to England, Scotland & Wales
Frommer's Europe's Greatest
  Driving Tours
Frommer's Food Lover's Companion
  to France
Frommer's Food Lover's Companion to
  Italy
Israel Past & Present
New York City with Kids
New York Times Weekends

Outside Magazine's Adventure Guide
  to New England
Outside Magazine's Adventure Guide
  to Northern California
Outside Magazine's Adventure Guide
  to the Pacific Northwest
Outside Magazine's Adventure Guide
  to Southern California & Baja
Outside Magazine's Guide to Family Vacations
Places Rated Almanac
Retirement Places Rated
Washington, D.C., with Kids
Wonderful Weekends from New York City
Wonderful Weekends from San Francisco
Wonderful Weekends from Los Angeles

WHEREVER YOU TRAVEL, *H*ELP IS NEVER FAR AWAY.

From planning your trip to providing travel assistance along the way, American Express® Travel Service Offices are always there to help you do more.

Utah

American International Travel (R)
655 E. Medical Drive
Bountiful
801-292-8687

American Express Travel Service
175 South West Temple
Salt Lake City
801-328-9733

do more **AMERICAN EXPRESS**

Travel